MW01627603

COMMUNISM VERSUS DEMOCRACY

Bulgaria 1944 to 1997

Introduction by
Prof. Mark Kramer

BULGARIA

American Research Center in Sofia

This book is published by the American Research Center in Sofia thanks to a generous subvention by the America for Bulgaria Foundation

Copyright © 2010 by Nassya Kralevska-Owens. All rights reserved.

This book, or parts thereof, may not be reproduced in any form without permission from the publisher. Exceptions are made for brief excerpts used in published reviews.
For information, contact American Research Center in Sofia - United States Office, Goldwin Smith 120, Department of Classics, Cornell University, Ithaca, NY 14853; or American Research Center in Sofia, 75 Vasil Petleshkov St., 1510 Sofia, Bulgaria.

This book is available at quantity discounts for bulk purchases.

Communism versus Democracy: Bulgaria 1944 to 1997 /
Nassya Kralevska-Owens
Introduction by Professor Mark Kramer
Includes abbreviations, bibliography and index of frequently used names.

ISBN 978-954-92571-1-3

Printed in 2010 in Sofia, Bulgaria, by Asi Print Ltd.
Jacket and covers designs © by Dimitar Kelbechev, 2010

To the memory of my mother, Atanassa Donkova-Kralevska, M.D.,
and my father, Atanas Kralevski, M.D.,
for whom freedom, democracy, people's dignity, and civil rights were paramount.

And to everyone for whom life under the
communist regime meant humiliation and pain.

CONTENTS

PART FOUR – CIVILIAN EMOTIONS

PART FIVE – PHILIP DIMITROV AND HIS TIME

About the book

Many people in the West are still unaware of the full extent of communist atrocities. Much of this history is largely unknown, and in intellectual circles communist ideology has often been mistakenly perceived as humane. *Communism versus Democracy* illustrates with brilliant clarity that communist rhetoric about the good of mankind only meant "the masses" as an impersonal abstraction, while in fact the communists preached and practiced profound disregard for the individual. The American Research Center in Sofia is very proud to have this work as the first monograph in its publication series. Those who wish to know about the Cold War, Eastern Europe, and Bulgaria in the second half of the 20th century will profit enormously from reading this book.
 - Professor **KEVIN CLINTON**, Cornell University; President and Co-founder, American Research Center in Sofia (ARCS)

Written in the best historiographical tradition, *Communism versus Democracy* is a passionate and honest account of Bulgaria's recent history (1944-1997). Balancing an amazingly rich array of sources - archival documents, history books, newspaper publications, eyewitness evidence, personal diaries, confessions and interviews - Nassya Kralevska-Owens' monograph offers the reader what no textbook can achieve: empathy with every event described. A goldmine for the historian of Eastern Europe, *Communism versus Democracy* will also be of substantial interest to anyone who wishes to learn what went on behind the Iron Curtain, both in its factual and human dimensions. On every page of the book one feels the author's pain for the immense physical and moral devastation caused by the communist regime, her happiness for the rebirth of freedom and human dignity, and her unfailing love for Bulgaria.
- Dr. **NORA DIMITROVA**, Co-founder and Trustee, ARCS

This is an original and compelling study of communism and especially the formative years of post-communism in Bulgaria. The author takes on important questions that most studies of democratic transition ignore - for example, why authoritarians welcomed, rather than resisted the transition and how they succeeded in controlling, even through pacting and privatization of the economy, much of what happened in the early years of post-communism. Perhaps the most original argument in the book is the similarly powerful impact

of external actors and precedents on the transitions to both communism and post-communism.
- Professor **VALERIE JANE BUNCE**, Cornell University, Department of Government

Communism versus Democracy is written with great vigor and sparkle, and the author's presentation is strongly convincing. Events, people, politicians, and eyewitnesses are vividly described. The book is an inspiring testimonial to the horrors of the Sovietization of Bulgaria and to the crucial stages of the democratization of the country in the 1990s. Nassya Kralevska-Owens concentrates on the leaders of both processes, as well as on the fate and emotions of the pro-democratic Bulgarians who struggled to give a new face to their homeland.

The author makes an impressive contribution to the search for historical truth. Her passionate and powerful writing grips the reader to the last page. I personally learned a lot, recalled many things, and was touched and affected by the book. As a Bulgarian-born journalist who lives in the U.S.A., Nassya Kralevska-Owens is uniquely suited to write on this topic. She knows her country from the inside, and living outside of it gives her the possibility to judge the events and people more objectively.
- Dr. **HEINZ BRAHM**, former Research Director of the Federal Institute of Eastern European and International Studies, Cologne, Germany

This book demonstrates that Bulgaria, a European country, which is generally ignored and frequently misunderstood, has finally found its masterful chronicler. Nassya Kralevska-Owens' greatest achievement is the skillful recreation of the drama of a nation's political awakening: the excitement which swept through every segment of society when communist dictator Todor Zhivkov was forced to step down; the massive mobilization of the anti-communist opposition and the emergence of democratic leaders and organizations; the inevitable clashes between the guardians of the communist past and the champions of a democratic future; the high hopes, Machiavellian intrigues, noble aspirations and hideous betrayals that marked the birth of Bulgarian democracy. The author has crafted a compelling narrative which will enthrall both readers fascinated by richly documented historical sagas and more analytically minded explorers interested in carefully constructed accounts of complex social contexts and dynamically unfolding political conflicts. Nassya Kralevska-Owens has undoubtedly set the standard against which future attempts to retell the story of Bulgaria's metamorphoses after 1989 will be measured.

- Professor **VENELIN I. GANEV**, Miami University, author of *Preying on the State: The Transformation of Bulgaria after 1989*

Communism versus Democracy: Bulgaria 1944 to 1997, by the renowned Bulgarian journalist Nassya Kralevska-Owens, is the most unique and authoritative documentary about two revolutionary decades in the country's history: the establishment of the communist regime in the 1940s and the struggling democratic movement of the 1990s. Well-reasoned and masterfully written, it is an important case study about communism, post-communism, and democratization in contemporary Bulgaria.

- **PETER STOYANOV**, President of the Republic of Bulgaria, 1997-2002

Introduction

Bulgaria has never been a country of great concern to most Americans, but in a remarkably short time since 1990 Bulgaria has ceased to be a Cold War enemy of the United States and has become a close ally. For nearly forty-five years after World War II, Bulgaria was ruled by Communist dictators, of whom the longest-serving by far was Todor Zhivkov, the General Secretary of the Bulgarian Communist Party from 1954 until his ouster in November 1989. Bulgaria was a founding member of both the Council for Mutual Economic Assistance and the Warsaw Pact, the economic and military organs of the Communist bloc that were strictly subordinated to Soviet control. Internal political life in Bulgaria during the Communist era was stifling and repressive, and the country's foreign policy was shaped largely by the Soviet Union. Although no Soviet troops were deployed on Bulgarian soil after 1947, that was mainly because Soviet leaders were highly confident about the Bulgarian regime's external loyalty and internal conformity.

Nowadays, Bulgaria is a member of both the North Atlantic Treaty Organization (NATO) and the European Union (EU), the chief multilateral institutions of the Western democratic community. National and local elections in Bulgaria are meaningful, free, and fair, and political debate is spirited. Political parties actively compete for power, knowing that even if they lose in one election, they stand a chance of winning in the next. Power has changed hands regularly and smoothly since 1997, and no party has felt the need to destroy its opponents, for fear of being permanently marginalized otherwise. Freedom of speech and respect for human rights are well entrenched. In many respects, then, liberal democracy has taken firm root in Bulgaria - something that seemed inconceivable during the decades of Communist rule.

Nassya Kralevska-Owens' wide-ranging book, which came out to much acclaim in Bulgaria in 2001 and is now finally available in English in an updated edition, helps readers to understand the difficult path Bulgaria has traversed since the Second World War. Kralevska-Owens underscores the great damage - physical, moral, psychological - that was done to Bulgaria by the imposition and prolonged existence of a Soviet-style Communist system. No sooner did Soviet troops enter Bulgaria in September 1944 than the cruel process of Sovietization began. The consequences were vividly conveyed in a Bulgarian film documentary produced in 1990, which featured a Bulgarian woman who recalled what happened to her family shortly after Soviet troops arrived:

> The day after my father was arrested, another policeman arrived around mid-day and instructed my mother to go to Police Station No. 10 at five o'clock that afternoon. My mother, a beautiful and kind woman, got dressed

> and left. We, her three children, all waited for her at home. She came back at half past one in the morning, white as a sheet, with her clothes tattered and torn. As soon as she came in, she went to the stove, opened the door, took off all her clothes, and burned them. Then she took a bath, and only then took us in her arms. We went to bed. The next day she made her first suicide attempt. She made three more attempts after that and tried twice to poison herself. She is still alive, I look after her, but she has severe mental illness. I never found out what they did to her.[1]

With the backing of Soviet troops, the Bulgarian Communists consolidated their hold over a society in which popular support for Communism was negligible. The destruction of the Agrarian Union Party in 1945-1946, the arrest and execution of the Agrarian Party leader Nikola Petkov in 1947, and the ruthless elimination of any other potential sources of organized opposition to Communist tyranny ensured that a Communist system was firmly entrenched in Bulgaria by the time Soviet troops left the country in late 1947.

Bulgaria, like several other Soviet-bloc countries, experienced violent repression and purges in the late 1940s and early 1950s as the mechanisms of Stalinist control were introduced and reinforced. After Josef Stalin's death in March 1953, the situation in Bulgaria gradually eased, but only by a relatively small amount. Zhivkov's assumption of supreme power in 1954 forestalled a more significant change that might have occurred along the lines of Hungary (after 1958) and Poland (after 1956), both of which, despite being under repressive Communist rule, were not as autocratic as Bulgaria. A few internal challenges to Zhivkov's hold on power emerged over the years, notably in 1965, but he fended off these threats and lasted in office longer than any other Communist ruler in Europe. Not until Mikhail Gorbachev, who became General Secretary of the Soviet Communist Party in March 1985, began proceeding with far-reaching political liberalization in the U.S.S.R. did Zhivkov's tenure begin to come into question.

Since 1990, several Bulgarian historians have done excellent work documenting the establishment and maintenance of Communist rule in Bulgaria, drawing on newly opened archives. Numerous anthologies of declassified documents and detailed academic analyses of Bulgarian political, economic, and social life under Communist rule have appeared over the past twenty years.[2]

---

[1] Cited in Tzvetan Todorov, *Au nom du peuple: Témoignages sur les camps communistes*, trans. by Marie Vrinat (La Tour d'Aigues, France: Éditions de l'Aube, 1992), pp. 52-53.

[2] See, for example, Mito Isusov, *Politicheskiyat zhivot v Bulgariya, 1944-1948* (Sofia: Universitetsko Izdatelstvo "Sv. Kliment Okhridski," 2000); Aleksandur Vezenkov, *Vlastovite strukturi na Bulgarskata komunicheskata partiya, 1944-1989* (Sofia: Institut za izuchavane na blizkoto minalo, 2008); Vesselin Dimitrov, *Stalin's Cold War: Soviet Foreign Policy, Democracy and Communism in Bulgaria, 1941-48* (New York: Palgrave Macmillan, 2008); Dimitur Ivanov, *Vuzkhod i padenie na sotsializma v Bulgariya, 1944-1989* (Sofia: Millennium, 2009); Lyubomir Ognyanov, *Politicheskata sistema v Bulgariya, 1949-1956* (Sofia:

Nassya Kralevska-Owens presents this history for a wider audience, allowing readers to understand how Communist rule was established in Bulgaria, how it was maintained, and how the country changed during the 35 years under Zhivkov. She brings to life the years of Communist rule for those who have no direct memory of them.

Kralevska-Owens then provides a riveting account of the downfall of Zhivkov's regime in November 1989 and the gradual shift, in fits and starts, to a more democratic polity. Because the Communist system took such an onerous toll on Bulgarian society, the transition from Communist autocracy to liberal democracy was bound to be difficult, and Nassya Kralevska-Owens shows just how hard it was. Even though the vestiges of Communist rule faded relatively soon (especially after 1990), the forces of inertia were strong, and many key individuals who favored retention of the status quo were still on the scene. Kralevska-Owens provides a detailed look at how this process unfolded, taking readers into the drama of a country undergoing sweeping, though often erratic, change. Until 1997 the fate of Bulgarian politics seemed in doubt. In the wake of the political and economic crisis in 1997, which marks the culmination of Kralevska-Owens' narrative, Bulgaria's place in the Western democratic community has seemed more assured. The country became a member of NATO in 2004 and a member of the EU in early 2007.

Even so, the democratic system in Bulgaria today still faces daunting challenges, above all the corruption that plagues almost every segment of Bulgarian society - corruption I have experienced firsthand during my frequent visits to Bulgaria. Petty corruption is so commonplace that most Bulgarians take it for granted. High-level corruption in Bulgaria reached new heights under the government headed by Sergey Stanishev that was in power until July 2009. The EU was so dismayed by the persistence of high-level corruption that it suspended funding to Bulgaria in July 2008. The government that emerged after Bulgaria's July 2009 elections, headed by Boyko Borisov, pledged to crack down on corruption, but the long-term success of these efforts remains to be seen.

A closely related problem is the tenaciousness of organized crime. Organized criminal gangs in Bulgaria, most of which have close ties to organized crime in Russia and Ukraine, have established networks in Sofia and other key cities, seeking to keep out potential rivals. Several leading political figures in Bulgaria, including a former prime minister, have been tied to organized crime. The strength of organized crime is a challenge not only for the Bulgarian economy but also for the future of democracy in Bulgaria. If other key officials in Bulgaria are suborned by the criminal underworld, the political system cannot

---

Standart, 2008); Mariya Radeva, ed., *Bulgarski durzhavnitsi 1944-1989* (Sofia: Skorpio, 2005); and Lyubomir Ognyanov, *Durzhavno-politicheskata sistema na Bulgariya, 1944-1948* (Sofia: Izdatelstvo na Bulgarskata akademiya na naukite, 1993).

help but be affected, and ordinary Bulgarians will continue to view politics with great cynicism.

One further challenge for Bulgaria is its heavy dependence on Russia for energy sources, especially natural gas. As of January 2010, Bulgaria was receiving 96 percent of its natural gas from Russia, leaving the country vulnerable to Moscow's pressure. The Russian government's prolonged termination of gas supplies flowing through Ukraine in January 2009 had a severe impact in Bulgaria, underscoring the country's dependence on *Gazprom*, the Russian state gas monopoly. The vested interests around Vladimir Putin and other Russian leaders who oversee *Gazprom* have attempted to perpetuate Bulgaria's dependence on Russian natural gas. Under Stanishev, the Bulgarian government sought to foster extremely close ties with Russia, a country that has become increasingly authoritarian at home and assertive in its foreign policy during the years that Putin has served as president and now prime minister. The Bulgarian government led by Borisov has sought to move away from Moscow, reversing the policy of the previous government. Even if these efforts prove fully successful, Bulgaria will remain highly dependent on Russian energy supplies over the long term unless alternative sources can be developed - something that appears unlikely for the time being. Even if Bulgaria sets out to rely more on nuclear power, that is only a longer-term option, and Bulgaria will still need to import large volumes of natural gas.

Formidable though all these challenges might be, they do not change the basic fact that Bulgaria is now a democratic country rooted in Western democratic organizations. Nassya Kralevska-Owens' book shows that this outcome was by no means preordained.

Anyone hoping to understand the broad political and economic changes that have transformed Central and Eastern Europe since 1989 will find this book immensely rewarding.

Mark Kramer
Harvard University
April 2010

Acknowledgments

This book would never have happened without the help of many Bulgarians who shared with me their memories, beliefs, experience, unpublished diaries, and private archives. It would never have been completed without several professionals in various institutions in Sofia who directed me to numerous sources and gave me access to legal documents, recently opened archives, parliamentary records, minutes of important meetings, vital publications, statistical data, tape recordings. I am deeply indebted to Stefka Dobreva, Elena Ilieva, Radka Grueva, Dr. Panayot Panayotov, Gocho Chakalov, Rudolph Schreiter, Dany Chakalova, Professor Dr. Georgi Markov, Dyanko Markov, Latchezar Toshev, Emilia Staneva, Professor Ivan E. Ivanov, Lyubomir Mladenov, Ivan Kurtev, Dr. Philip Dimitrov, Yossif Sarchadzhiev, Rayna Tomova, Anna Sarchadzhieva, Georgi G. Georgiev, Dr. Krum Savov, Ivan Tatarchev, Rosen Donkov, Andrey Radev, Christopher Owens, Maria Govedarova, Dr. Nina Marinova, Veselina Petkova, Dincho Dinchev, for their support and trust.

I owe special thanks to the publisher of the Bulgarian version of my work, *Untitled: Destroyers and Builders of Bulgaria*, Vasil Stanilov, who did a lot to popularize it among my compatriots. However, this book would never have crossed the frontier of my native land without Nedyalka Chakalova who masterfully completed the long and most arduous task of translating it from Bulgarian into English. My sincere gratitude goes to her.

Still it was necessary the English translation to be enriched, updated, modified, and re-targeted for the foreign reader. I needed help and I was lucky again: I met Marina Petrova. This young gifted and enthusiastic American-educated Bulgarian contributed enormously to achieving my goals. Marina was my best critic and most trusted advisor while she was editing the manuscript. My husband Dr. Aaron Owens also took a decisive part in the process.

When the final draft, entitled *Communism versus Democracy: Bulgaria 1944 to 1997,* was about to go to print, my niece, Petra Stanev, unexpectedly stepped in and carefully copyedited the whole text. I will never forget her help and desire to be useful.

All of this hard and long lasting work would have been fruitless were it nor for Professor Kevin Clinton, President, and Dr. Nora Dimitrova, Trustee, Co-

Founders of the American Research Center in Sofia, who offered to publish my work. Nora and Kevin dedicated to the project their energy and expertise and did everything necessary to complete it and to bring it into existence. I feel forever obliged to them not only for their invaluable assistance but also for their trust in the worthiness of my arguments.

I am especially grateful to the America for Bulgaria Foundation, which sponsored the publication of my work with a generous grant.

Last but not least, I thank my whole family for the love, understanding and patience with which it surrounded me during my work. Above all my gratitude goes to Aaron for his tireless help, counsel and encouragement.

Prologue

In the dusk of a winter afternoon in January 1990, about two thousand people were walking in the streets of Sofia, shouting and carrying signs with slogans, demanding a change in the political system. Such actions were a frequent occurrence in the capital city of Bulgaria in those days. People gathered for rallies and processions, thrilled at the possibility of stating their opinions out loud and feeling that they were free citizens at last. It seemed as though a gigantic iron grip had suddenly loosened, as if the floodgates of a powerful river had been released at once. The very sensation of having the right to express their own views in public was so unfamiliar and so exciting that many Bulgarians felt the need to experience it again and again. Their favorite slogans were "Democracy!", "Change!", "Elections!", and "Victory!" There were also cheers setting their protest in an international context, such as, "Sofia, Prague, Warsaw, Berlin!" Sometimes the demonstrators would stop their procession in front of the U.S. Embassy and would express their belief that "America is with us!"

How was all this possible?

The Berlin Wall, that ominous symbol of the division of Europe into democratic and communist parts, had been torn down on November 9, 1989. On the following day a peaceful intra-party coup forced the dictator Todor Zhivkov to step down. He had ruled the People's Republic of Bulgaria (PRB) for thirty-five years as the head of the Bulgarian Communist Party (BCP).

Holding their breath, people watched the televised plenary session of the leading body of the party, its Central Committee (CC). High-ranking communist state officials thanked Todor Zhivkov for his "warm care for the party and for the country", accepted his resignation, and relieved him of his high office. Zhivkov was taken aback. The 78-year-old despot had always ordered his subordinates around and had treated them as pawns. He was accustomed to their unconditional obedience. When he realized that there was no one to defend him, his morale crumbled, and he became a wretched, confused old man. Other members of the CC looked that way as well, especially those who had been his closest and most loyal associates. Several of them were also dismissed.

A group of younger, self-proclaimed "moderate" and "modern" leaders of the BCP took the reins of state. One of them was particularly eager to play the role of the reformer, namely, Andrey Lukanov, Zhivkov's Minister of External Economic Relations. He was personally acquainted with most Bulgarian dissidents, or "independents", as they were called then, and he had significant influence in their circles. For a while they even thought that he would join them and were always willing to heed his advice.

In contrast to the opposition in Czechoslovakia and Poland, the Bulgarian independents were not organized in a political party or a trade union and had no official links with the general population at first. They belonged to several informal societies and associations, which had been holding their meetings in private homes or offices since 1988. Only a few dissidents were known to the public as high-profile artists, writers or academics. Most of them were either current or former members of the communist party.

People had already heard about the writer and poet Blaga Dimitrova, her husband, the literary critic Yordan Vasilev, the poet Edwin Sugarev, and the philosopher Dr. Zhelyu Zhelev, author of the book *Fascism*, which suggested there were similarities between fascism and communism. These individuals had had the courage to speak on foreign radio about systematic violations of the human and intellectual rights of Bulgarian citizens, the persecution of the ethnic Turks in the mid 1980s, and the country's environmental problems.

During the second half of November 1989, a number of professionals little known outside their fields of expertise joined the associations of the independents. Among these new members were economists and lawyers supporting the idea of a free market. Other people who claimed to have been persecuted as opponents of the communist regime also drew close to the dissidents. Some of the latter subsequently proved to be agents of the secret services.

. . .

The citizens of Sofia knew little about the independents. Nevertheless, when a Steering Committee, founded by the dissident leaders, organized a public rally on November 18, 1989, tens of thousands gathered in front of the *St. Alexander Nevski* Cathedral, thrilled with excitement. They did the same on December 10th, after learning from posters glued to buildings that the Union of Democratic Forces (UDF) had been founded as a coalition of the independent societies and two leftist noncommunist parties, which were recently restored after having been banned by the red regime.

Soon people became familiar with the speakers at the UDF rallies: Zhelyu Zhelev, Peter Beron, Petko Simeonov, Rumen Vodenicharov and Konstantin Trenchev. The capital city's population also had a soft spot for the public vigils under open sky led by Father Christophor, a monk unknown to anyone just a year earlier. Huddled close together in the winter nights, holding lit candles, men and women shared a feeling of fraternity and understanding that bordered on magic. Hushed, absorbed in the sermon, and shivering with cold, they seemed to be seeking redemption for having endured totalitarian rule for so long.

Some pro-democratic citizens still had qualms about the nature of the Union of Democratic Forces. They noticed that the fervent dissident speeches of the

November 18th demonstration echoed the Soviet *perestroika* and did not seem to herald the removal of the communists from power. Still, with each day the three magic letters "U," "D," "F," chanted as a slogan at the rallies, attracted the Bulgarians more and more. They created a sense of belonging among those who felt disgusted with the red dictatorship. People started hoping that the leaders of the coalition would not betray their desire for a better future. The popular vision of that future was rather unclear, but what mattered more than that was the sense that freedom and human dignity would inevitably be restored to all.

In the early days of the Union of Democratic Forces, its anticommunist convictions were manifested mainly in symbolic ways. The change in the political climate could be detected primarily in the words that its leaders uttered in public. Yet, many things remained taboo even in that very choice of words. For example, no ambition for political power was openly declared by the UDF, and no political adversary of the coalition was named. At the meetings and rallies a man or a woman would often shout, "Down with the BCP!" only to be stopped by the leader of the demonstration or even by other participants. The communists were still numerous and strong and no one wanted clashes or bloodshed as there had been in neighboring Romania. Thus democratically minded Bulgarians initially pretended that they were not so much against the communist party, only against its "leading role" in the state.

...

That grim day in January 1990 was different. After so many rallies, processions, and demonstrations, after so many unspoken words, a deep male voice thundered, "Down with the BCP!"

A tense silence followed. The man shouted again, "Down with the BCP!"

Then somebody else repeated his words. Suddenly the slogan "Down with the BCP" erupted throughout the demonstration. People were frenzied with the joy of finally hearing the words they had kept hidden in their hearts for so long. "Down with the BCP," the whole street reverberated.

Andrey Lukanov sensed the imminent danger. An experienced member of the communist government, he knew perfectly well that an open anticommunist mood had to be prevented at all cost. His plan was clear and simple. Lukanov relied on his ability to keep the leaders of the UDF under control and to direct the actions of the opposition union through them. He was the father of the idea of a national political convention, called a Round Table, which was enthusiastically accepted by the dissidents. He was convinced that endless negotiations between the newly formed "blue" coalition, namely, the Union of Democratic Forces, and the "red" Bulgarian Communist Party were the best solution for his political organization. The BCP happily approved the scheme of its competent and prominent member. That plan would provide what the communist elite needed most at that moment: power, security and time.

...

Andrey Lukanov was quick to react to the rally in January of 1990. He summoned the UDF leadership and scolded Zhelyu Zhelev, who had become Chairman of the union on December 7, 1989. The opposition leaders felt ashamed. Zhelev and the UDF spokesperson Rumen Vodenicharov appeared on television that same evening and announced that their alliance distanced itself from the actions of the extremists who had shouted "Down with the BCP" in the streets of Sofia. This behaviour came as no particular surprise to anyone. To a greater or lesser extent, it was in the spirit of those times.

The real surprise came the next evening, when another declaration was read on national television. Its tone was composed, but passion could still be sensed between the lines. The key message was "we do not distance ourselves."

The man who had drafted this statement - originally using the first person singular - was hardly known to the general public. The future Prime Minister of Bulgaria and Chairman of the Union of Democratic Forces during its most stormy and fateful years did not have the charisma of a populist politician. Nor did he seek it. He had other qualifications to rely on.

Philip Dimitrov was an attorney dealing mostly with property claims. He also appeared in court as a defense lawyer for persecuted Bulgarian Turks in criminal and labor suits. One day after Todor Zhivkov was deposed, Dimitrov and a colleague of his pinned an appeal on the door of the lawyers' café in Sofia, insisting on the establishment of an Independent Lawyers' Union. The document also proposed amendments to some of the most severe pieces of communist criminal and civil legislation.

Having spent most of his time drafting the statutes for recently established political and professional organizations, participating in meetings, rallies, demonstrations and vigils, and writing letters, declarations and proclamations, Philip Dimitrov naturally became a member of one of the newly formed opposition parties and was elected its Deputy Chairman. A month later he sat at the National Round Table. Still, he failed to match the tone of the day, which was heavy with pathos. Instead, he aimed for specific political changes that would serve as the basis for rapid and reliable strides forward for his country.

One of the communist leaders once said that this man was dangerous for the BCP. No one paid any attention.

PART ONE

THE BEGINNING

1. Between Despair and Hope

The year 1989 started like dozens of other years in the People's Republic of Bulgaria. At midnight on January 1, the Secretary General of the communist party and Chairman of the State Council, Todor Zhivkov, appeared on television, smiling, and wished the nation a happy New Year in his paternalistic way, so familiar to all Bulgarians. The Head of State exuded self-satisfaction, vulgarity, and an excellent mood. Once again, he assured his subjects of the "upsurge of real socialism", their improved material welfare, and their higher standard of living.

The speech of the communist dictator sounded cynical against the backdrop of a country of eight and a half million residents with a foreign debt of almost eleven billion dollars, empty shops, closed state borders, irregular supply of electricity and gasoline, run-down hospitals, and low wages and pensions for the ordinary citizen. Still, no one was surprised at what Todor Zhivkov had to say. People were accustomed to the optimism of the 77-year-old party and state leader. Hence, in the first minutes of 1989, excited and animated by the New Year's champagne, most Bulgarians responded to Todor Zhivkov's televised toast as they always did, with mockery and curses. They expected to see his unchanged and joyful face the following year as well, even though they were not sure whether they would have something to put in their glasses on that festive occasion.

With the exception of the communist upper crust of society and a few privileged groups, the year 1989 began with scarcity for the population and no hope for positive economic and political changes. There was also something new and horrific.

The consequences of the disaster of April 26, 1986, which occurred at the nuclear power plant in Chernobyl, Soviet Ukraine, were painfully felt in the country. Many people suffered or died from cancer. The Chernobyl accident, which caused the most widespread radiation pollution in the history of mankind, had alerted the world to the low-quality technology and poor labor discipline in the industrial enterprises of the Soviet Union. For the Bulgarians, however, the accident meant much more than that. The nuclear catastrophe was further proof of the criminal obsequiousness of their communist rulers to their Moscow masters.

All the governments of Europe, starting with that of Sweden - the first to signal the fatal eruption in the Ukraine - warned their citizens of the potential radiation threat immediately and took the necessary steps to protect them against possible malignant diseases. The totalitarian leaders of Bulgaria chose a different course of action. They preferred to risk the life and health of their own nation rather than admit any failure in Soviet industry.

On April 29, three days after the Chernobyl tragedy, the daily newspaper of the communist party, *Rabotnichesko Delo,* deemed it acceptable to inform its readers of the disaster in the lower left-hand corner on p. 6.

> An accident occurred in the Chernobyl nuclear power plant. One of the units has been damaged. The necessary steps are being taken to eliminate the consequences of the accident. Assistance is being offered to the casualties. A government commission has been formed.[1]

On May 6, after heavy rain for several days - an occasion, later known as the "Chernobyl radioactive rain" - the same newspaper published the official press release of the Committee on the Use of Atomic Energy for Peaceful Purposes and of the Council of Ministers of the People's Republic of Bulgaria on page 3:

> A triple increase in radiation levels has been registered in some districts of the country. This increase poses no threat to the population. A reduction in the radiation level is already being noticed at the points where changes had previously been registered.
>
> All water sources in the country have been inspected. The water has proven to have normal parameters.
>
> The general radiation level shows that there is no danger to the health of the population. (Bulgarian Telegraph Agency)[2]

Communist journalism presented the fear of potential adverse consequences of the poisonous eruption, expressed by European heads of state, as a deliberate, malicious attack of the West against the Soviet Union. Throughout the month of May, *Rabotnichesko Delo* and the other leading newspaper, *Otechestven Front* [Fatherland Front], bent over backwards to write stories with titles like, "Some Agencies in the West Are Spreading False Rumors," "Provocation Campaign with Dirty Political Aims," "No Hand Can Eclipse the Sun," "The Truth *vs.* Hysteria," "The Poisonous Cloud of Anti-Sovietism," "The Gauge of Human Conscience Is Demonstrating a High Degree of Slanderous Activity," and

---

1 *Rabotnichesko Delo* [Worker's Cause] daily, April 29, 1986, in the column *News in Brief.*

2 *Ibid.*, May 6, 1986.

"Selfless Struggle Against the Invisible Enemy." Simulating concern for the people, the red press devoted pages to topics like "The Health of the Population is a Common Goal and a Shared Responsibility," "Ecology Is a Measure of Modern Technological Thinking," "In the Name of the People, in the Name of the Nation's Health," and "Everything for the Children, Everything for the Youth".

Scientists subservient to the dictatorial regime came to the rescue of the journalists and broadcasters. Through the TV screen and the pages of periodicals, the Professor of Medicine Dr. Chavdar Shindarov and other academics reassured Bulgarians with the following statements:

> Cow's milk is completely safe for consumption and we are not banning it for the time being.[3]

> There are no grounds for anxiety.
>
> The radiation background in districts where increased radiation levels had been registered is currently as follows: in Kardzhali - 0.007 milliroentgens per hour, in Gabrovo - 0.007 milliroentgens per hour, in Stara Zagora - 0.006 milliroentgens per hour, in Yambol - 0.007 milliroentgens per hour, in Sliven - 0.006 milliroentgens per hour. The normal radiation background for the country is 0.0015 to 0.0025 milliroentgens per hour.
>
> These findings are within normal limits.[4]

People in the cities and in the countryside happily ate lettuce, scallions and garlic, cherries and strawberries. They let their children drink milk and eat cheese, while the cattle and sheep grazed on the fresh May grass... In subsequent years, when the incidence of various forms of cancer - leukemia in particular - increased drastically and took the lives of many Bulgarians, their relatives remembered the poisonous fertility of 1986 with tears in their eyes.

The failure in the Soviet nuclear power unit demonstrated the sharp divide in Bulgarian society during communism. Neither the newspaper articles, nor the reassuring words of scientists on national television were relevant to the governing caste. The leaders of the totalitarian republic and their close circles had been warned about the real threat to their health posed by the nuclear accident. For a long time the communist party elite consumed only foods and beverages specifically tested for radioactivity. Much of their sustenance had been imported from distant parts of the world at great expense.

---

[3] *Ibid.*, May 8, 1986.

[4] *Ibid.*

...

The Chernobyl tragedy was not the only cause for people's growing concern about the state of the environment in Bulgaria. The air in Ruse, a city known for its rich history and beautiful architecture, became a health hazard for its citizens during the 1980s. Almost every day, the chimneys of a chemical plant in the Romanian town of Giurgiu, across the Danube, billowed poisonous gas clouds that drifted south, crossed the big river, and stayed over the Bulgarian city. The smell of chlorine was unbearable.

Although there were numerous protests by the citizens of Ruse, the government did nothing to stop the air pollution. Desperate and panic-stricken in the face of such indifference, many local residents tried to save themselves and their families from the high risk of lung diseases. They left their homes and resettled in other parts of the country, despite the fact that relocation was very difficult in communist times, as one needed a residence permit for any city or town in order to live there.

In 1987, a group of artists called attention to the environmental threat over Ruse with an exhibition on the subject. Some of the paintings were titled "Locked Horizons," "What Do We Gain, What Do We Lose," and "Sunset." The event was enthusiastically received by the public. However, its success incurred the wrath of the authorities, which soon closed down the show.

The people of Ruse expressed their support for the artists in the exhibit's visitors' book with comments such as these:

> We want to live, we want a breath of fresh air.
> *2nd year students at the Technical College of Design and Interior Architecture*
> Stop hiding reality behind misconceived economic interests!
> *Group of designers from Investmashproekt, Ruse*
> I don't want any more chlorine! When there is chlorine, I feel sick, I vomit, my head aches, I can't breathe and my eyes get irritated!
> *Boryana, 12 years old*
> Save our children!
> *Stoyanova, engineer*
> Let us not be silent, let us fight for our right to live!
> *Anonymous* [5]

In the beginning of 1988, mothers pushing babies in their strollers staged a peaceful rally to protest against the toxic air of Ruse. Militiamen [a communist

[5] *Zashtita na prirodata* [Nature Protection] magazine, 4/1990, p. 36.

term for "policemen" - *author's note*], sent by the mayor to disperse the crowd, joined them.

Similar actions followed in the cities of Kazanlak and Pirdop in the foothills of the Balkan Mountain Range, as well as in towns near the Rila and Pirin Mountains. These beautiful regions were also severely polluted. The fertile territory of the People's Republic of Bulgaria - a country with a marvelous climate and enormous potential for agriculture, light industry, and international tourism - was studded with factories, plants and industrial complexes that spewed clouds of poisonous smoke and lacked the equipment needed for environmental protection.

All this did not disturb the communist rulers in the least. It was common knowledge that the entire economy was subordinated to the needs of the U.S.S.R. and its satellites, and that production was tied to Soviet raw materials, markets, and obsolete technologies. During the last four decades, the industry of the state had been developed with total disregard for the interest of the Bulgarian nation.

...

In the spring of 1988, the newly established Committee for the Ecological Salvation of Ruse gained popularity by word of mouth. The organization had no official registration. It consisted of both active and expelled members of the Bulgarian Communist Party and some individuals with no party affiliation. The wife of the Speaker of the National Assembly [Parliament - *author's note*] at that time was also involved.

The general public reacted with satisfaction. There was a common discontent regarding environmental issues. In addition, the citizens with anticommunist convictions felt less threatened while discussing the country's ecological problems, instead of demanding political changes. For many, participation in the emerging movement for "clean air and a clean environment" gave vent to their carefully concealed disdain for the regime.

A number of similar dissident organizations with no legal status were formed in 1988. One of them was the Independent Society for Human Rights Protection in Bulgaria. Another was the Committee for the Protection of Religious Rights, Freedom of Conscience and Spiritual Values. The names of several authors and scientists - Blaga Dimitrova, Dr. Zhelyu Zhelev, Petko Simeonov, and Yordan Vasilev - came up often. They were associated with the Club in Support of *Glasnost* and *Perestroika* in Bulgaria.

People rejoiced but also wondered. The existence of such organizations was unthinkable in totalitarian Bulgaria. After all, it was a country in which printing a slogan with anti-government content or bringing an anticommunist book across the border could put one in prison, or at least make one lose one's job.

Yet, it appeared that these independent groups really existed. A large number of citizens regularly listened to the statements of their members, broadcast in Bulgarian on *Radio Free Europe*, the *Voice of America,* and other foreign radio stations. Further evidence of the presence of these organizations was provided by the fact that the Bulgarian Communist Party officially announced the expulsion of several dissidents from its ranks. Rumors spread that others had been placed under house arrest, or even that they had been taken into custody.

Still, the activities of the dissidents had no effect on the daily lives of the population. Undisturbed by the barely perceptible turmoil, the totalitarian government pursued its usual policies in every respect. A minor disturbance was caused only by the global outcry when the ruling communist party stripped the members of the Bulgarian Moslem minority of their names, language, traditions, and religious identity. These repressive measures affected one-tenth of the country's population.

...

The predominant mood in Bulgaria in the beginning of 1989 was one of insecurity, anxiety, and skepticism. People had already lost hope that *glasnost* and *perestroika* - with which Mikhail Gorbachev tweaked the communist system in the U.S.S.R. after 1985 - would ever reach them. Quite justifiably, they sensed that the reformation had skirted their national borders.

This was the first time since 1944 when a Soviet model policy was not received with enthusiasm and immediately implemented by the Bulgarian Communist Party. That may have been the case because *glasnost* and *perestroika* did not aim to buttress a totalitarian society, but to liberalize it partially. Hence, the politically engaged Bulgarians could only be consoled to read Soviet newspapers and magazines, which published shattering data about the colossal crimes of the Bolshevik regime. They watched dumbfounded as Russian television showed Members of Parliament openly attacking the leadership of the Communist Party of the Soviet Union during plenary sessions.

In contrast, everything in Bulgaria was "business as usual." Todor Zhivkov was in full control of the country's fate and everybody - from top-ranking officials to the grassroots party members - served him devoutly and obediently. Only from time to time, a chance phrase or a mere word in the official media hinted at criticism. Such memorable instances were excitedly discussed by people opposed to totalitarianism. Sometimes apocryphal writings by dissident authors found their way to the public. Quite audacious for that time, they were actually rather subdued. Nobody wrote or spoke openly about the numerous atrocities committed by the Bulgarian communists or their fatal mistakes in ruling the country.

In a feigned attempt not to lag too far behind the Soviet Union, the leaders of the People's Republic periodically informed the nation that reforms were forthcoming. However, they did not even try to conceal their apprehension that Gorbachev's tempo of *perestroika* was too fast and risky and that his *glasnost* was dangerous. As *The New York Times* put it, progress for the Bulgarian rulers meant discipline and measures against anarchy "so that the country would develop successfully and move forward step by step, rather than by leaps that could be devastating for society."[6]

Such a "step" was made in 1987 when the government declared that it would undertake extensive transformations in the administrative sphere, which would turn Bulgaria into the most renovated communist state in the world. The next supposed reform was announced personally by Todor Zhivkov at a meeting of the Central Committee of the BCP in December 1988. It was presented to the public as a revolution "from the bottom up," which would radically change the political system.

These promises remained on paper or were formally fulfilled. For the first time since the fall of 1946, in 1988 Bulgarians had a choice between two candidates in municipal elections. Nevertheless, it would have been ridiculous to speak of any independent opposition. The alternative candidates for mayors and other elected posts had been pre-approved by the district committees of the ruling party.

. . .

In the second half of the 1980s the economic program of the government changed virtually every year. Capitalist laws were passed even though they were blatantly incompatible with "real socialism" - a phrase that the BCP used to describe the current stage of Bulgaria's progress towards developing into a truly communist society.

In January 1989 the governing body of the totalitarian republic, the Council of Ministers, published Decree No. 56 on economic activities, which overturned the long-held doctrine of strict state ownership. It read as follows:

---

[6] *The New York Times*, October 7, 1989.

> Chapter One
> General Provisions
> Article 1. (1) The present Decree shall be enforced in the implementation of economic activities in all sectors and spheres of the people's economy.
> (2) Economic activities shall be conducted on the basis of all forms of ownership: state- and municipally-owned sites offered for management, property of cooperative and public organizations, of citizens, of foreign nationals, and of mixed ownership.
> Article 2. (1) Corporations shall be the principal form for conducting economic activities.
> (2) In the sphere of culture, it shall be possible to establish publishing, advertising, impresario, exhibition and other houses, which shall function as corporations.
> (3) Individual citizens and groups of citizens may engage in economic activities even without registering corporations.[7]

In fact, because of its other provisions discussed below, Decree 56, Article 2, (3) was relevant only for "individual citizens and groups of citizens" from the high-ranking *nomenklatura* [communist elite holding key positions in all spheres of activity - *author's note*]. During communist times, they were already transformed into big-time capitalists by this document.

The book *The Round Table of Politburo* by the prominent communist Zhivko Zhivkov explains the process:

> There was a grain of rationality in Decree 56. Yet, how were the corporations established? That was done following the old tradition, the Politburo, the Secretariat and the departments of the Central Committee [the top ruling bodies of the Bulgarian Communist Party - *author's note*] endorsed the structures, composition and management bodies of the corporations, once again following the well-trodden administrative way![8]

Bulgarian citizens of average means, with a monthly salary of about 200 levs or a pension of 110 levs, could not meet the requirements for establishing a shareholding corporation, as stipulated in Article 34 of Section Two of Decree No. 56:

---

[7] Decree No. 56/1988 of the Council of Ministers of the PRB, *State Gazette*, No. 4, January 13, 1989.

[8] Zhivkov 1991, p. 198.

> The statutory fund and the shares shall be determined according to their nominal value in levs. The minimum nominal value of the statutory fund shall be one million levs.[9]
>
> The minimum nominal value of one share shall be one thousand levs.[10]

The provisions of Section Three, Article 44, paragraph 3, concerning limited liability corporations, rendered that kind of enterprise just as inaccessible:

> The shares shall be indivisible. The statutory fund may not be below 50,000 levs [250 average monthly salaries or 455 average monthly pensions - *author's note*].[11]

Precisely because it concerned the privileged castes in the People's Republic of Bulgaria - communist leaders, their children and relatives, secret agents and their trusted associates - the Chapter "Corporations" in Section One of the General Provisions in the cited document granted the corporations the following liberties:

> Article 17. (3) The foreign economic activities of the corporations, including the formation of or the participation in foreign companies and other investments abroad, shall be performed freely, for which no permission from a state body shall be required, with the exception of the cases stipulated under the present Decree.[12]

> Article 30. (1) The corporations may form economic groups for the purpose of implementing the strategy in a certain sphere, developing fundamental investment solutions, marketing, managing innovations, etc.[13]

Decree No. 56 of the Council of Ministers also gave some rights to ordinary citizens. Section Five "Corporations of the Citizens" permitted the establishment of sole-proprietor corporations as well as collective corporations and associations. Due to this modest liberalization of the economic conditions some private cafés, launderettes, repair shops, and taxicab services appeared in 1989.

However, they were still few and far between. The laws and the government decrees changed quickly and unexpectedly. Individuals lacked a sense of stability

---

[9] Decree No. 56/1988 of the Council of Ministers of the PRB, *State Gazette*, No. 4, January 13, 1989.

[10] *Ibid.*

[11] *Ibid.*

[12] *Ibid.*

[13] *Ibid.*

and security, and they refrained from investing their modest savings in businesses. The more enterprising Bulgarians seemed to be biding their time, whereas the rest were growing more and more confused by the shifting economic regulations.

There was only one indisputable truth for the ordinary subjects of the regime: their living conditions were deteriorating each day. Some sort of explanation was necessary. At a plenary session of the BCP in the spring of 1989, its Secretary General Todor Zhivkov was forced to admit the unsatisfactory results of the implementation of the 1987 plan for transformation in the administrative sphere.

. . .

Yet, with every passing month of 1989, the tormented Bulgarians were seized by an unfamiliar emotion, an inexplicable excitement, an obsessive inner tension due to the vague premonition that something unusual was going to happen. It seemed as though a positive change was in store for them.

Once again by word of mouth, people discovered that Dr. Konstantin Trenchev, a member of the Independent Society for Human Rights Protection, had founded the *Podkrepa* Independent Trade Union for the defense of intellectual work in February of 1989. The new union had few members and was not recognized by the authorities. Still, it could turn into a Bulgarian version of the Polish *Solidarity*. In May it became well known that Dr. Trenchev and four other dissidents were arrested and taken into custody. The charge against them was that they had violated Article 273 of the Penal Code and were "spreading false information of a nature likely to generate discontent with the government and its actions."

In addition, at that time there were animated discussions about a recent law passed by the National Assembly, which gave the right to Bulgarian nationals to travel abroad with passports valid for 5 years. It was announced that the statute would be effective as of September 1, 1989.

This was a real miracle for the People's Republic. Following the establishment of the communist regime, the state frontier had been closed for decades. It was almost impossible for ordinary Bulgarians to receive permission to travel to the West. The authorities had gone so far as to stop certain individuals from visiting even the so-called "fraternal socialist" countries. Many of those who tried to cross the border illegally were killed by guards or captured and sentenced to death or long prison terms. Therefore, the euphoria about the new law ran so high that at first few people noticed that anyone wishing to travel to a capitalist country needed an exit visa issued by the militia in addition to a passport. In fact, a citizen could exchange Bulgarian currency for a maximum of 65 dollars of travel money per year, which made it virtually impossible to see the West.

The population grew more and more agitated. The "passport issue" proved to be directly related to the "Turkish" one. In the summer of 1989 the atmosphere in the countryside and in the smaller cities became practically explosive. After being compelled to change their names to Slavic ones, about 350,000 ethnic Turks left the territory of Bulgaria with their new passports, issued to them at the end of May. They took only a few of their personal belongings and moved to neighboring Turkey. This emigration was largely the result of coercion by the authorities. More often than not, members of the BCP from the same village or town quickly usurped the houses or the apartments of the refugees.

The general population was much more divided regarding the "Turkish issue" than it had been about the environmental problems. The members of the red party, with very few exceptions, supported the government's repressive measures against the Turkish minority and stood behind the slogan, "Bulgaria for the Bulgarians!" Most other citizens were ashamed and felt impotent and angry against the forced assimilation of the Bulgarian Moslems.

Simultaneously, another mass migration was taking place in Europe. Hungary had opened its borders and waves of East Germans went through its territory to settle in the Federal Republic of Germany. It became clear that the foundations of the sinister Berlin Wall had been undermined once and for all.

In September rumors started that the days of Todor Zhivkov as the head of the party and the state were numbered. Word also spread about the rise of a new dissident organization in Plovdiv, the Club of Individuals Repressed After 1945. The noncommunists followed these events with anticipation and growing hope. The members of the dictatorial party, on the other hand, were getting increasingly anxious. One could see them whispering nervously to each other in their offices, and even in the streets and squares.

2. The Awakening

Mass protests started in Sofia during the last days of October 1989. A rally at the Southern Park was convened by Rumen Vodenicharov, the new Chairman of the Independent Society for Human Rights Protection, who had ousted the organization's anticommunist founder, Iliya Minev. A memorial service for the victims of Chernobyl was conducted by Father Christophor Sabev. The *Ecoglasnost* Independent Society for Environmental Protection of the Population, founded in April 1989 as a successor to the Committee for the Ecological Salvation of Ruse, staged a march, followed by a campaign to collect signatures for the environmental preservation of the country in front of the *Crystal* Café.

An incident in the small park by the *Crystal* Café in downtown Sofia, which was later dubbed "the beating," provoked international interest in Bulgaria and great agitation in the country itself. At the end of October 1989, Sofia was the site designated for the convention of the International *Ecoforum*. Todor Zhivkov's government was pleased and proud that representatives and journalists from all over the world had come for the event. The fact that the People's Republic had been chosen to host the conference was perceived by the rulers as a token of approval for their ecological policies. Soon they would regret that choice.

The decision of the *Ecoforum* to convoke in Sofia served as a call to action for the Bulgarian citizens who knew perfectly well that they were living in one of the most polluted countries in the world, where no one in power cared about the quality of the food they ate, the water they drank, or the air they breathed. The *Ecoglasnost* Independent Society for Environmental Protection of the Population took the initiative. It organized a peaceful protest on October 26 and drafted a petition for its cause, which was to be signed in front of the *Crystal* Café. The Sofia City municipal leadership gave permission for the rally but changed its venue to the Southern Park. Nevertheless, after the march, the demonstrators gathered in front of the café to collect signatures from the chance passerby as well as the hundreds of people who had gone there specifically for that occasion.

More than a dozen militiamen were sitting in the café, disguised as athletes in jogging outfits. When the petition signing began, these ostensibly neutral customers jumped out of their seats and started shouting that those actions were against the state and that they should stop immediately. The members of *Ecoglasnost* refused to cease, insisting that they were not violating the law or public order.

During the altercation several minibuses stopped in front of the café. The "athletes" grabbed their opponents and started pushing them into the vehicles. The environmentalists kept protesting, but they soon filled the buses. One of them yelled to the militiamen that he would never surrender to them. "I would rather bash my head against the side of the bus so everyone can see and understand that Bulgarians have no right to collect even an innocent signature!" And then he added, pointing to several BBC reporters, "We are not that stupid. Look, we have invited foreign journalists to cover the event."

Four strong men took him by the arms and legs, thus keeping him from throwing himself against the vehicle. Another militiaman pretended to bump into a British journalist accidentally. The journalist fell and his camera broke.

At that moment the citizens who had been crammed into the minivans managed to break out and started fighting with the fake athletes. Other people with similar views joined them from the crowd that had gathered there. Even casual pedestrians, who happened to be walking along *Rakovski* Street, took part in the fierce exchange of blows. The initial street brawl had turned into something much larger and more threatening.

"Stop! Enough is enough! Let's not make a spectacle of ourselves in front of foreigners!" A group of men was trying to bring the "hooligans" fighting for a clean environment to their senses. Yet, nobody paid any attention to the words of what appeared to be secret service agents. People had run out of patience long ago. They were finally venting the anger that had accumulated over the years.

Soon there were about fifty victims in front of the café, including people with broken arms, legs or noses. Some of them were foreign journalists. The injured were taken to the *Pirogov* Emergency Hospital, where the doctors had received instructions from the authorities to treat the foreign nationals first. However, they ignored that order and started taking care of those most harmed. They even issued certificates to the members and supporters of *Ecoglasnost,* stating that their injuries were sustained as a result of the beatings.

There was no free press in Bulgaria at that time. The communist mass media gave a distorted account of the event, referring to the environmentalists as "hooligans" and "extremists." However, the incident became well known throughout the country, in Europe, and even in the United States, thanks to foreign broadcasts.

...

In that tense, unusual, and almost revolutionary situation about 4,000 residents of Sofia gathered in the square in front of the *St. Alexander Nevski* Cathedral in the late afternoon of November 3. After a brief rally, they formed a procession that slowly crossed the large square in the direction of the National Assembly.

Glowing with the thrill of an unfamiliarly solemn moment, the people were singing "How Beautiful You Are, My Forest." That song had almost been forgotten after having stirred many hearts and minds during the 19th century Bulgarian National Revival, leading to the liberation of the country from the Ottoman Empire. A multitude of voices repeatedly thundered the slogan "Democracy" after 43 years of collective silence.[1]

Several white-haired old men and women were leading the procession. They had volunteered to be there in case the militia began shooting.

The communist Parliament could not bear the appearance of a budding free nation. The "people's deputies" [a term used during communist time for "Members of Parliament" - *author's note*] shuddered, recognizing the sense of awakening among the demonstrators. As the procession neared the National Assembly, the windows of its huge beige building were suddenly closed and the curtains were rolled down.

Yet, the red deputies in the Assembly had no reason to be afraid. The citizens of the capital were not carrying arms. They were just bringing a petition, supported by the signatures of 12,000 peaceful individuals, asking for a safe environment in their homeland.

. . .

Elena Ilieva will never forget November 3, 1989:

> After the fight in front of the *Crystal* Café, we were all very agitated. Instead of feeling intimidated, we began shedding our fears. Everyone felt a sense of tension. We expected something to happen.
>
> My brother told me that there would be a rally of *Ecoglasnost* on November 3. We decided to go with a group of friends. Ecology was the last thing that made me join the protest. It is not that I was indifferent to the pollution; I didn't have enough information about it. My participation in the demonstration expressed my disagreement with the system, that is, with the communist system. This is how I was brought up at home, though not overtly.
>
> In comparison to other families, mine did not suffer that much from the communists. Only my grandfather, a lawyer, was arrested, and no one knew where he was for several months until he was released. As I was born in 1950, I have never experienced direct political harassment. It seems that the discontent in me grew and accumulated imperceptibly.

---

[1] *Sofia* monthly magazine, *This Happened in the Street*, August 1990.

I suppose that all who went to the rally felt some fear, to a greater or lesser extent. At least I was afraid. But this was a different kind of fear, somewhat sweet, more for my brother than for myself.

I went into the central building of the Bulgarian Academy of Sciences, where I used to work. From the window of my former office I saw crowds streaming towards the square in front of the *St. Alexander Nevski* Cathedral. Some of my former colleagues also wanted to go down and take part in the rally, but they finally decided against it, not knowing what would happen. It could have cost them their jobs at least. I was not working anyway.

I left the Academy building. It was about 5 p.m. People were gathering in the square from everywhere. Some had apparently come from work, others from home. Students had cut classes. There were mainly young and old people. The middle-aged were fewer.

I decided first to see what was happening in the streets nearby and then to join the demonstrators. I walked around the National Assembly Square, reached *Shishman* Street and then *Aksakov* Street, after which I went past the Italian Embassy and back to the *St. Alexander Nevski* Square.

The rally had already started. I tried to listen to the speeches, but I couldn't hear anything. There were no loudspeakers yet, as there were during the later demonstrations. The speakers shouted into megaphones and it was difficult to understand what they were saying.

I couldn't shake my premonitions after what I had seen during my brief round. I was shocked and kept repeating to myself, "Something terrible is going to happen!"

Ropes surrounded the two squares that I toured, and militiamen were standing close to one another along the ropes. Their uniforms had aroused fear in us our whole lives. I had never seen such a strong militia presence before! There were also militiamen at every street corner and in every entrance of the residential buildings close to the National Assembly. Grim individuals in plain clothes were hiding near the uniformed men. To be more precise, they were not really hiding; they were peeking out of the entrances of the houses and were spying on the people passing by.

I tried to find my brother in the crowd but failed. I had come late to the place where we were supposed to meet, so I remained alone to the end.

I was no longer afraid. A rather militant mood seized me. I had the feeling that if somebody dared even touch me or any of the people around me, trying to do something bad, I would fight back furiously. However, that feeling of inner savagery did not last long. It disappeared during the next rallies, giving way to endless joy.

That November day happened to be very pleasant, neither cold nor rainy. In spite of my expectations, everything went peacefully. No one impeded us. No one raised a hand against anyone. None of the militiamen and none of the plain-clothes cops showed any sign of aggression.

There was no provocation for that. People were not disturbing public order in any way. They were only singing and shouting ecstatically, "Ecoglasnost!" "Democracy!" There was nothing more. Nothing else. No criticism of Todor Zhivkov. No political slogans. The rally and the procession were under the aegis of *Ecoglasnost* Independent Society, and they ended after the petition had been submitted.

In the capacity of President of the ecological organization, the actor Peter Slabakov was at the heart of the action. I was happy to see one of my favorite actors, Yosif Sarchadzhiev, among the gathering. It was easy to recognize the actors; they were identifiable. I was not yet able to distinguish the other leaders, Vodenicharov, Beron, Karakachanov, the old social democrat Dertliev.

When I came home, I felt like a hero. I felt like a new person. But why? I hadn't really done anything! "No, that is not true," I thought, excited. "I have openly opposed the system at long last. I have voiced my protest against the authorities. It makes no difference that no one even mentioned anything about overthrowing Todor Zhivkov. Something is going to happen soon! Whatever that may be, I hope it will change things!"

These thoughts were not mine alone. Many people had gone to the rally and procession for the same reasons that had brought me there: they came out simply because something had ruined their lives. If it was not their own, the lives of their parents or grandparents had been ruined. Even those who had not suffered so much suddenly asked themselves, "What would my life have been like if there had been no communism in Bulgaria? And what about my brother's life? Or the life of the entire nation?"

This inner rebellion seeking external expression at all cost was incredible. You felt anger for everything your family had gone through, wrath at the heavy cross that your parents had had to bear. Actually, this is why I took part in the rally, not even knowing what would happen there or afterwards. Only a week later, the changes came from the top of the communist party.[2]

---

[2] Elena Ilieva in a conversation with the author, Sofia, Bulgaria, August 25, 1998.

3. "The King Is Dead! Long Live the King!"

Some people believe that the protests of the democratic-minded Bulgarians, the dissidents, and the communists who favored Mikhail Gorbachev's *perestroika* forced the red rulers of the country to allow pluralism and multiparty democracy. That conviction is too naive. The Bulgarian Communist Party had repressed the population for decades. It would have had no difficulty crushing the protests, bringing the supporters of Gorbachev to their senses, and coping with the dissidents. Many of the latter came from its ranks anyway or - as was to become clear later - collaborated with its secret services.

The simple truth is that, at that moment, the BCP did not need political assassinations, arrests, deportations and concentration camps. It had attained everything it wanted. The entire national capital and all convertible currency loans from Western banks were in the hands of its leaders and the State Security agents.

In addition, the autumn of 1989 was different. The Berlin Wall was expected to crumble any day. Overwhelmed by its own problems and the transfer of state funds into private accounts, the Soviet Union no longer manifested its earlier interest in Eastern Europe. Bulgaria remained isolated from the world. It appeared somewhere near the bottom of international rankings for political and civil rights protection in the 1980s.[1] Its population had the lowest *per capita* consumption in Europe in 1985.[2]

All this did not worry the top-ranking communists and the members of the security services. Many of them had other things to do. The Minister of Justice in 1991-1992, Svetoslav Luchnikov, explained their activities quite precisely in a historical novel. Its protagonist - a secret police agent - admits the following:

> They gave me tasks of ever increasing difficulty including the recruiting of foreign agents and opening of cover corporations for our work. I came up with a fabulous trick. We [the State Security services - *author's note*] established many business associations [abroad - *author's note*] with the participation of a local man who was our agent. We supplied machines from Bulgaria, absolute trash. Then we mortgaged the machines and took good credit from some bank, leaving the bank to worry about what to do with the mortgaged machines that no one wanted to buy. We played the stock exchanges as well. We were beginning to master the intricate mechanisms of the world market, of the commodity markets, and of the financial markets. We offered money-laundering services. We participated in arms and drugs smuggling. We counterfeited packaging and labels. Many of our corporations declared

---

[1] Melone 1998, p. 27.

[2] *Ibid.*

> bankruptcy, ripping the banks off with their bad credit. The local man who served as a cover quickly disappeared from the country with our assistance. However, many corporations accumulated a lot of money, especially companies in New Jersey, Liechtenstein and Singapore. The authorities hardly knew about them.
>
> A substantial part of the credit that the state received from major Western banks also went to such corporations, especially after 1985. "This is how capitalism is financing the struggle against itself," one of the biggest bosses explained. "It gives loans to lousy socialist states which can never pay them back, and half of that money comes to us."[3]

According to Albert Melone, an American professor of political science, far more than half of the loans extended to totalitarian Bulgaria went into private bank accounts:

> Besides these ideologically motivated crimes [of the Bulgarian Communist Party - *author's note*], there is evidence that approximately $10 billion in Western loans have disappeared, and forty-seven former officials are believed responsible.[4]

The Bulgarian investigative journalist and author Hristo Hristov was able to unveil more facts:

> The Prosecution made unsuccessful attempts to identify the exported financial capital through the overseas companies - an operation conducted by the intelligence services during the last years of Zhivkov's rule. The attempts of Philip Dimitrov's government in this regard were unsuccessful. According to prosecutors who participated in the investigation of the financial flows of the foreign trade companies, that capital amounted to nearly USD 20 billion, which is twice the foreign debt Bulgaria inherited from the communist regime. There were legal proceedings at the Sofia City Prosecutor's Office in the 1990s for various financial violations by several companies with foreign trade activities, including Expomed, Balkan Holidays - Rent-a-car, the Balkan Bulgarian Airlines, the Vinimpex representative office in Warsaw, Infosport, Paton, Inco, and others. Yet, no officials were tried in court.[5]

. . .

---

[3] Luchnikov 2000, p. 54.

[4] Melone 1998, p. 27.

[5] Hristov 2004, p. 76.

In the late 1980s, the time had come for the Bulgarian Communist Party to regroup, take care of its capital, and consolidate its economic supremacy. This would undoubtedly give it secure political power over Bulgaria, even though it would not always be official. The BCP had to overthrow the old dictator and his closest associates, accuse them of all its errors, extravagance and crimes, and declare to the world that it was taking Gorbachev's line of reforms.

The necessary steps to this end were made by several of Todor Zhivkov's trusted associates, namely Peter Mladenov, Member of the Politburo [the executive body - *author's note*] of the BCP Central Committee and Minister of Foreign Affairs for eighteen years, Andrey Lukanov, Candidate-Member of the Politburo, First Deputy Prime Minister until 1987 and subsequently Minister of External Economic Relations, and some other prominent communists.

In the first days of November 1989, Mladenov ostensibly left for an official visit to China. However, he made a stopover in Moscow unbeknown to the Head of State, Zhivkov. The Bulgarian Foreign Minister was received by Mikhail Gorbachev. During the meeting Mladenov informed the Soviet party and state leader of the intentions of a group of top-ranking BCP members to depose Todor Zhivkov and asked for his advice, i.e. permission. Gorbachev gave his consent.[6] According to another source, Peter Mladenov informed Gorbachev about the plan to remove Zhivkov in July, 1989, at a meeting of the leaders of the seven Warsaw Pact countries in Bucharest.[7] Despite these differences of place and time, the common message in these accounts is that the Act One of the political change in Bulgaria was staged with Soviet blessing.

It was followed by Act Two, which was much simpler. Zhivko Zhivkov - who had reached the top in the communist party and state hierarchy in the 1970s but was eliminated from the first echelons of power by his dictatorial namesake - gives the following description of the inner-party coup, or the "action for change", as he himself referred to it:

> The leading role in the action for change belonged to Peter Mladenov, Dobri Dzhurov, Andrey Lukanov, Nacho Papazov and Dimitar Stanishev. Alexander Lilov shared the ideas of this political nucleus, although in the last years he had been taken out of the Central Committee. After the first leader [Todor Zhivkov - *author's note*] was subjected to psychological preparation for several days, the main action took place in the afternoon of November 9, 1989, during a meeting of the Politburo. The main nucleus acted resolutely and convincingly. Other Politburo members assisted as well, including Georgi Atanasov, Yordan Yotov and Pencho Kubadinski. Milko Balev was disturbed.

---

[6] Konstantinov 1997, p. 329.

[7] Nedev 1999, pp. 31-33.

Grisha Philipov was abroad. Ivan Panev was in the hospital. Todor Zhivkov was compelled to step down from the two highest offices in the party and in the state.

...

On the surface, the action during the Politburo meeting in the afternoon of November 9 appeared to take place in a quiet and calm manner. Todor Zhivkov resigned, discussions followed, and his resignation was accepted. However, that was not the essence of the action undertaken. That was merely its final and external manifestation, the completion of the act and its legalization.

...

Todor Zhivkov was subjected to such great pressure that he could tell there was no way out. A number of meetings with other political figures suggested to him that there was no room for maneuvers. The most characteristic meeting he had was with three of his fellow-partisans and top-ranking political figures, Dobri Dzhurov, Yordan Yotov and Dimitar Stanishev, who made it clear that there was no other option for him but to resign.

It should be noted that those who executed the change knew who the next Secretary General was going to be. They rallied around Peter Mladenov.

If there was any concession at all, it would be the decision that everything had to be done legitimately, voluntarily and in accordance with the Party Statute.

...

The Central Committee plenary meeting on November 10, 1989, was convened to examine Todor Zhivkov's latest ideas on the country's development. The first item on the agenda was not changed, and he delivered a one hour speech with instructions for the future of the Bulgarian economy. There were even several vague comments.

Then a break was announced. The members of the Central Committee, clustered in the halls of the Boyana Residence, were busily exchanging views on the forthcoming replacement of the Secretary General. The majority of them were pleased with the news; hence, the certain success of the undertaking could be relied upon.

Item 2 on the agenda, a proposal for Todor Zhivkov's resignation from the post of Secretary General, was presented, along with another one to be submitted to the National Assembly for his resignation as State Council Chairman.

At first Todor Zhivkov was calm, a bit surprised not to be given the floor for his concluding speech on the first item of the agenda. The discussions started. One after another, the members of the Central Committee stood up and supported the proposal, stressing that it was high time for this change to be made so as to rejuvenate the party in the spirit of the new times.

This complete unanimity of the members of the Central Committee surprised Todor Zhivkov and he lapsed into a deep dejection. He sagged in his

> seat, looking around absent-mindedly with his head slightly inclined and his mouth half-open.
>
> ...
>
> After the break Georgi Atanasov chaired the plenary session with great energy and a sense of resolution. One of the members of the Central Committee said that he accepted Todor Zhivkov's resignation, but that he would remain his friend in the future as well. Another one unexpectedly suggested that the matter be postponed for a more comprehensive study and assessment. That was the entire defense. The proposal of the Politburo was put to the vote and was accepted almost unanimously.
>
> The next step was to elect a new Secretary General of the party's Central Committee. The Politburo nominated Peter Mladenov. The idea was received enthusiastically. Ivan Maslarov proposed Alexander Lilov to be elected to this post, supporting his choice with Lilov's unquestionable personal qualities.
>
> Peter Mladenov was elected Secretary General of the Central Committee by almost everyone. He delivered a brief speech, which revealed very concisely the reasons for the change and the need to restructure the entire command-administrative system, renovate the party and take a new course towards democratic socialism.[8]

Zhivko Zhivkov did not cite the sources he used to write his comments about the meeting of the Politburo of the BCP Central Committee on November 9. Ten years later, the Director of the Bulgarian State Archives declared before an Associated Press journalist that the minutes of the meeting of the Bulgarian Communist Party at which Todor Zhivkov was relieved of his office as Secretary General had disappeared.[9] Probably the events at that meeting had not been as neat and presentable as Zhivko Zhivkov made them out to be.

Conversely, the minutes of the 11th session of the Ninth National Assembly, which opened at 11 a.m. on November 17, 1989, still exist. When compared with the transcripts of previous sessions of the communist parliament, those minutes demonstrate amazing servility and lack of dignity on behalf of the Bulgarian totalitarian deputies. Stanko Todorov, Prime Minister of Bulgaria for ten years and Speaker of the National Assembly since 1981, read the proposal that Todor Zhivkov be relieved of the office of Chairman of the State Council of the People's Republic of Bulgaria. Sycophants and supporters of Zhivkov, who had welcomed every thought he expressed with standing ovations, and who had voted unanimously in favor of every idea he launched for thirty-five years, started hurling insults at him from the very moment that he was deposed as BCP Secretary General.

---

8 Zhivkov 1991, pp. 202-206.

9 *Radio Free Europe* Bulletin, November 11, 1999.

General Slavcho Transki, a former partisan and leading member of the BCP, stated the following in public for the first time:

> He [Todor Zhivkov - *author's note*] stood at the helm of the party and state, and tortured our economy with all kinds of concepts, reorganizations and various fabrications for 35 years. For 35 years he instilled his authoritative and bureaucratic methods consistently and persistently, announced the stages of socialism quite arbitrarily and unsuccessfully, qualifying it sometimes as mature, on other occasions as real, sometimes as being so developed that it gave birth to two Bulgarias. Now we see that there is not even one Bulgaria of the type that we wanted and dreamed about.
>
> Crude arbitrariness, infinite presumptuousness, high self-esteem and squandering characterized his long years of leadership. We are yet to understand how decisions were made to build colossal industrial plants for which billions were spent, this money being virtually buried in the ground. We are yet to hear about his leadership methods, about intolerable undertakings for a man of his rank: how he pitted his colleagues against one other, how he imposed his opinion, and how he eliminated those whom he considered to be inappropriate or others whom he suspected of ambitions to take his place. I myself have witnessed many of these things.[10]

Lyubomir Levchev, President of the Union of Bulgarian Writers and something of a Court Poet of Todor Zhivkov's, ardently supported the motion for his deposition. Before he had even heard the next item on the agenda, he promised his colleagues to vote in favor of whatever proposal was made, without making any additional comments.[11]

Academician Blagovest Sendov, President of the Bulgarian Academy of Sciences, who was not a member of the BCP, took advantage of the "hour of reckoning" to remind the communists of his total devotion to their organization:

> I am speaking as a non-party person, a non-member who has always believed in the leading Party, which is leading according to the Constitution. And when friends and enemies of mine have asked me why I am so obedient, I have told them that I want to work for my people. The Bulgarian Constitution says that the Bulgarian Communist Party is the leading party.
>
> ...

---

[10] Transcripts of the first meeting of the 11th Session of the Ninth National Assembly, November 17, 1989, p. 6.

[11] *Ibid.*, p. 12.

> I request a discontinuation of the debate. We believe in what the Bulgarian Communist Party is doing, and I for one, as a non-party member, will vote in favor of the proposal.[12]

Todor Zhivkov was relieved of the office Head of State with full unanimity.

Pencho Kubadinski, member of the Politburo of the BCP Central Committee and of the State Council, reported the proposal of the parliamentary groups to elect the new BCP Secretary General Peter Mladenov as Chairman of the State Council of the People's Republic of Bulgaria.

This triggered the flattery and praise for the new "First." No one proposed to stop the speeches. Everybody wanted to have a chance to appear in the best possible light in public. Among the speakers were the poet Leda Mileva, the poet Mladen Isaev, the lawyer Mihail Genovski, Academician Angel Balevski, the writer Mincho Semov, and others.

Angel Dimitrov, a member of the agrarian party, which was fully subordinated to the communist one, declared the following on behalf of the whole Bulgarian nation:

> I would say that if we had organized a referendum for the first leader of the Party and now for the first leader of the State, Comrade Peter Mladenov would have been elected with an enormous majority.[13]

Then Peter Vutov, an eminent communist and diplomat for many years, made a fool of himself when, after praising Mladenov euphorically, he blundered:

> I will vote with all my heart and soul for Comrade Todor..., I mean, for Comrade Peter Mladenov.[14]

Finally, it was time to vote. All Members of Parliament, with a single abstention, voted in favor of Peter Mladenov. That abstention was a historic phenomenon. It was the only abstention registered for nine successive communist-dominated National Assemblies and for 39 years of Bulgarian parliamentary life under red rule. Likewise, a vote "Against" was cast only once, on December 15, 1989.

Mladenov took the floor. Using the rhetoric of Mikhail Gorbachev, he outlined the course of restructuring, renovation and radical transformation of

---

[12] *Ibid.*, p. 14.

[13] *Ibid.*, p. 20.

[14] *Ibid.*, p. 23.

the state institutions with much inspiration. He urged the National Assembly to participate directly, competently and actively in drafting the laws that it passes.[15] According to the newly elected party and state leader, the ultimate aim was for Bulgaria to be built as a "contemporary, modern, humane and law-abiding democratic socialist state."[16]

At that moment it seemed as if it never crossed anybody's mind that one day the Bulgarian Communist Party might stop ruling the country. After prolonged applause at the new catch phrases "democratic socialism" and "socialist democracy", the parliamentarians were rubbing their hands with content.

The time for the Last Act in the drama of "the change" had come. It was necessary to select, legitimize and launch an opposition, which would be an essential part of "democratic socialism." There was hardly anyone who could do that job better than Andrey Lukanov. In fact, he had already started working at it.

. . .

On November 13, three days after Todor Zhivkov fell from power, the writer Nikolay Haytov and his wife Zheni Bozhilova telephoned representatives of the independent societies and some other individuals and invited them to their home at 15 *Latinka* Street in Sofia. Among those who accepted the invitation were the journalist Stefan Prodev, the biologist Peter Beron, the screenplay writer Anzhel Wagenstein, the philosopher Dr. Zhelyu Zhelev, the literary critic Yordan Vasilev, and the writer Toncho Zhechev.

Just before 8 p.m., Andrey Lukanov dropped by in his slippers at the apartment of the Haytovs, very informally, because he lived in the same building. The Candidate-Member of the Politburo of the BCP Central Committee and Minister of External Economic Relations suggested casually that they watch the 8 o'clock news together. The talking head announced that membership in the communist party had been restored for a number of individuals previously expelled for their participation in the Club in Support of *Glasnost* and *Perestroika* in Bulgaria and the Committee for the Ecological Salvation of Ruse. After the news broadcast was over, Lukanov briefly analyzed the latest political events and shared the intentions of the new party and state leadership.[17]

---

[15] *Ibid.*, p. 35.

[16] *Ibid.*, p. 37.

[17] Zhechev 1995, pp. 287-288.

Having taken the lead in the meeting of the dissidents, as if this was perfectly in order, Andrey Lukanov encouraged the people gathered there to express their opinions and recommendations freely.

> I remember well that the conversation was focused on the issue of the amnesty of political prisoners, an issue raised by Yordan Vasilev, which was met with understanding by all. The other focal point was the issue of the organization and actual execution of the rally of the budding opposition, already scheduled for Saturday, November 17 [Saturday was actually November 18 - *author's note*]. Stefan Prodev, Peter Beron and Anzhel Wagenstein were most active in discussing the many and varied problems connected with the rally: the proposed manifesto, communications and announcements, permission by the authorities, etc.
>
> ...
>
> Zhelyu Zhelev was rather grim throughout the evening; he was not active. I had the feeling that, like myself, he felt out of place. I didn't notice any whispering or any secret agreements. I can testify that there was not even a trace of the ominousness and demonism that were later attributed to that gathering. Quite on the contrary, everything seemed too ordinary.[18]

For Toncho Zhechev, the author of these lines, and a member of the BCP for many years, it was "too ordinary" for one of the highest ranking communists in Bulgaria - father of the country's bankruptcy and of its financial mafia - to take charge of the meeting of his political adversaries and to participate in the preparation of their first mass protest rally. Other Bulgarians would pass a different judgment on the meeting in Haytov's apartment on November 13, 1989. Some even would have left the gathering immediately at the appearance of the "well-intentioned" neighbor. Apparently the dissidents, also known as "the independents," did not think that way.

---

[18] *Ibid.*, pp. 288-289.

4. The Bulgarian Dissidents

Speaking from the improvised rostrum in front of the *St. Alexander Nevski* Cathedral on November 18, 1989, 29-year-old Alexander Karakachanov was right to declare that that was an unusual rally. More than fifty thousand citizens of Sofia had gone there of their own free will. Still, when the young man said that so many people had not gathered in the past twenty years, hundreds of voices corrected him, "Not twenty, forty-five!"

Karakachanov announced that permission for the rally had been received from the State leaders and that the People's Militia would guard it. Then he read the names of the twenty-eight members of the Steering Committee who had organized the event. The people responded with the exclamation "bravo," after hearing the names of Peter Beron, Peter Slabakov, Rumen Vodenicharov, Stefan Gaytandzhiev, Stefan Prodev, Christophor Sabev, Georgi Mishev, Chavdar Kyuranov, Yanko Yankov, Anzhel Wagenstein, and Svetlin Rusev. They were perfectly aware of the prevalence of present and former members of the Bulgarian Communist Party among the cited individuals. However, this was practically an advantage in the eyes of the euphoric citizenry gathered there. They perceived it as a sign of the totalitarian system disintegrating and Bulgaria embarking on the road to democratic development.

Tears of joy were glittering in the eyes of most of the men and women. Few of them had believed that they would ever live to experience this overwhelming moment of unfamiliar happiness, when they would inhale freedom along with the cold November air. It was not the time to recognize political adversaries or to recall former sins. People were anxious to see leaders and heroes, and they were ready to create them overnight, after listening to them and assessing their speeches.

Karakachanov listed the independent societies that had organized the rally, namely, the Club in Support of *Glasnost* and *Perestroika* in Bulgaria; the Committee for the Protection of Religious Rights, Freedom of Conscience and Spiritual Values; the Literary Circle 39; the Independent Society for Human Rights Protection; the *Podkrepa* Independent Trade Union; the Independent Students' Society; the *Ecoglasnost* Independent Society for Environmental Protection of the Population; and the Bulgarian Helsinki Committee.

"And the Bulgarian Communist Party too, or what," a man yelled, as if joking, after Karakachanov finished the list of the organizers. Laughter broke out, but applause and enthusiastic chanting drowned it out. People exclaimed from the bottom of their hearts, "Bravo!" "Hooray!" They were eager to show their support for those who had called them to the broad square on that Saturday morning to embrace the changes that took place after November 10.

"I do hope," Alexander Karakachanov went on, "that this rally will be one step, perhaps a small step towards ... I won't say towards *perestroika*, not for any other reason but because that word has been worn threadbare in the past two years..."

Again someone shouted, "Why not make a big step!" Yet another voice replied with the wisdom of the cautious, "Wait! It cannot happen overnight."

In the meantime the speaker was finishing his thought:

"I would say a step that would bring us back to a normal public life, in which everyone has the right to express his or her own opinion and to defend his or her rights. I would like to remind you of certain slogans that were put forward until only recently. 'Let us rule in the name of the people!' 'Let us rule through the people!' I am suggesting something else: let the people rule, not someone through them or in their name. Let the nation rule this country through the people it elects in that building there across the square!"

Karakachanov pointed to the National Assembly to the left of the rostrum. For four decades that building had housed the sessions of the Parliament, which were convened for two or three days two or three times a year. All of the members of the legislative body, referred to as "people's deputies," were selected by the ruling Bulgarian Communist Party and subsequently presented to the population for formal endorsement through the vote.

However improbable that might sound, this was not illegal. In December 1947, the Sixth Grand National Assembly, dominated by communists, adopted a new Constitution for Bulgaria. Following the Soviet model, it legitimized the unity of the legislative, executive and judiciary powers and merged the leadership of the state with that of the communist party. Ever since, Bulgarians whispered furtively that elections were actually a "one-horse race." Behind the curtains of the little cabin where they were supposed to cast their "secret" vote, they received ballot papers with all the names for all elected posts written on them already.

The citizens of the People's Republic of Bulgaria may not have had rights, but they had obligations. Each and every one of them had to appear at the polling stations on Election Day. Moreover, they had to appear happy, well dressed and content. Otherwise they risked being blacklisted.

The members of the communist party greeted each other even before lunchtime with the words "Happy victory!" Still, the official authorities were a little more tactful. It was not until the early evening hours that the election results were announced solemnly on the radio and on television, and they were invariably 99.98 to 99.99% turnout and 99.99% support for the Bulgarian Communist Party.

As a consequence of the way in which the elections were held, the legislators of Bulgaria unanimously endorsed everything proposed by what was then called the party-and-state apparatus. They considered debate in the plenary hall to be an anachronism of the non-democratic past, and they adopted a new practice. Deputies asked for the floor and went to the rostrum to read a statement prepared in advance, praising the bill that the dictatorial party was proposing.

The atmosphere in the lobby of the Parliament was also very amicable. The communists, the agrarians and the very few deputies ostensibly without any party affiliation never argued and never had differences of opinion. They never even discussed state matters. Instead, they shook hands warmly and patted each other on the shoulders, addressing each other as "Comrade" and arranging meetings and exchanges of favors among themselves.

Therefore, when Karakachanov suggested that Bulgaria should restore its normal parliamentary life, the multitude gathered in the square responded jubilantly, shouting, "Democracy!" "Free elections!" They quieted down only when Petko Simeonov started speaking on behalf of the Club in Support of *Glasnost* and *Perestroika* in Bulgaria.

"You must have realized a long time ago," he started, "that the society which we call 'developed socialism' is neither developed, nor socialist. It is a dictatorial and totalitarian society that ruined the life of several generations in the name of a proud and beautiful future. A new class of oppressors came to replace the bourgeoisie. That was the class of the *apparatchiks* [full-time professional functionary of the communist party or government - *author's note*]. That was the class of the *nomenklatura*."

"Listen, wasn't Petko Simeonov in the communist party?" someone asked his neighbor quietly. "Yes, he still is. I know it from my cousin. She works with him at the Institute of Sociology."

Simeonov continued:

"We were happy when Todor Zhivkov was deposed. A person who evoked deep fear among his subordinates has been overthrown, a person who evoked ridicule and laughter among the people. We are happy that there have been institutions and individuals who dethroned that dictator. But let us not rejoice too much. He has gone, leaving behind grave economic, political and moral problems. The country is in a crisis. We are left with empty shops; with omniscient bosses; with everyday life as if we are in the military barracks; with a ruined industry; with a polluted environment. He is gone, but the system remains and the ruling class of the *nomenklatura* remains practically intact."

The square exploded: "Away with them!" "Down with all of them!"

"The *nomenklatura* controls the mass media. The repressive apparatus is in its hands. Somewhere there, in its offices, in its mansions and residences, our everyday life and our fate are being decided behind the back of the nation. Of course, there are some decent and honest people among the *nomenklatura* - professionals - because running a country requires professional skills. The state cannot do without them. These people are our allies in the struggle for democracy. We are together. But now we are talking about the ruling class. It is not true that there was a leading role of the party. There was an aggressive personal dictatorship."

At that point people were divided. Some of them were shouting "bravo" enthusiastically, while others were rather confused and were asking, "What is this guy talking about? Why is he saying that there was no leading role of the communist party? This is even written in the Constitution!"

"When the dictator from Pravets [Todor Zhivkov's birthplace - *author's note*] was shown to be de*prave*d," Simeonov made the crowd laugh with his pun, "the *nomenklatura* was as if in a state of shock for five days. Indeed, it suffered a blow and started busily organizing its own rally. That happened yesterday. It is true that attendance was compulsory, but the rally was not so bad after all. The *nomenklatura* wants to preserve its privileges and its power, to live as it has lived until now. So when it learned that we, the independent associations, had organized a rally to hail the deposing of Todor Zhivkov, it ran quickly ahead of us and threw itself on the mat before the new leaders."

Bursts of laughter and shouts of "bravo" interrupted his speech for a moment. Pleased with his success, the orator continued:

"Let the *nomenklatura* lie down. We, all of us gathered here, remain standing firmly on our feet and we declare to Peter Mladenov, the BCP Secretary General and the Chairman of the State Council, 'Comrade Mladenov! We do not want privileges and power. We claim our rights. We claim them with peaceful and legitimate means only. Enough with dictatorship in our martyred land!'"

A wave of approval flooded the square again. The citizens were shouting at the top of their voices, "Yes!" "Hooray!" "Elections!" A solitary voice was barely heard to say, "There should be no State Council!"

A middle-aged woman asked anxiously, "What does he mean 'we don't want power?' Like hell we don't! We do! And what's so new about our "new" rulers anyway?" In the general commotion no one answered her questions. As a matter of fact, no one paid any attention to her. The people were hanging onto Petko Simeonov's words, and he was able to excite them with growing success.

"There should be a strict investigation of Todor Zhivkov's activities," he proposed. Applause and loud shouts of encouragement drowned out his words. A man carrying a small boy on his shoulders added in a booming voice, "And not only his! Of the entire communist apparatus!" Then the crowd took up the slogan and started chanting, "Of all of them!" "Of all!"

"And of his family, and of his circle," Simeonov added. "We don't want revenge. Revenge can never bring anything good. His biography should become transparent at long last and historical facts should no longer be distorted. There are rumors that Zhivkov committed crimes. Is it true?"

The square responded with an excited and resolute "Yes, it is."

"If it is true, then he should be brought to justice," the speaker insisted. "There is no doubt that the trial of Todor Zhivkov will serve as a lesson for all, big and small politicians, the politicians of today and of tomorrow. However, it is our duty to warn the corrupt members of the *nomenklatura*, who have a guilty conscience, that we do not want them to wash their hands with him!"

Again, he was interrupted by the spontaneous responses. "That's right!" "We don't want one to pay for all and everything to continue as it was before."

"Comrade Mladenov, we wish to live in a decent country," Petko Simeonov declared. "If you work to meet our demands, you will have the privilege of having our support and trust!"

"Did he say 'support and trust,'" a woman asked her husband. "Yes, yes," he replied irritably. "But isn't he asking a bit too much," the wife insisted. "After all, Mladenov was Todor Zhivkov's foreign minister for eighteen years. Moreover, he was at the very top of the communist party hierarchy. He was member of its Politburo, wasn't he?" "Won't you keep quiet! Let's hear what else he has to say," her spouse hushed her.

Simeonov ended his speech with the words of the national hero Vasil Levski - a perfect democrat and freedom-fighter who lived during the nineteenth century and whose name is holy to the Bulgarians. "The time has come to shout out loud that we want a pure and sacred republic! We want freedom and democracy!" Deeply moved, he added, "Long live Bulgaria!"

The rally gave him a long applause. Then the citizens of Sofia started chanting powerfully "Bulgaria!" Eventually, they were interrupted by the moderator Karakachanov, who announced the name of the next speaker. The latter needed no introduction.

Radoy Ralin was a bearded man with thinning white hair that fell unkempt on his forehead. He was a dissident poet and BCP member, who had been punished by the authorities on numerous occasions for his rather rebellious writing and for daring to criticize his own party. People liked him and met him with shouts of approval.

"Fellow-countrymen, fellow-sufferers," Ralin started in his slow drawling voice. "Three unrealized and deleted generations. We have all been crushed by the regime of the plutocracy. Over there I see a sign with the slogan, 'Down with the red bourgeoisie!' But that was not a red bourgeoisie because the bourgeoisie [property-owning class, declared by the communists as an enemy - *author's note*] became a class through hard work and production."

"And with morality," a man's voice added.

"The bourgeoisie made no money from power, but power made money from the bourgeoisie through the taxes it paid to the state," the poet explained. "And the red plutocracy was the power of those who became rich through power, a parasitic minority that wanted to rule for life."

"And take the life out of us," a young man commented.

"They wanted to rule over us to the end of their lives. Absolute power. Even billionaires do not live in such luxury! But the gravest of all were their crimes, which they tried to hide from the nation with the help of an enormous army of security guards. You know it all, you all know it," the dissident surmised.

"Sure we do. We are at the receiving end," several demonstrators confirmed noisily.

"This is why," Radoy Ralin expressed his hope, "may November 10 mark the second liberation of Bulgaria!"

Two men standing close to the rostrum, who probably recalled the speaker's affiliation with the Bulgarian Communist Party, called out half-jokingly, "Hey, surely you don't consider the seizing of power by the reds in 1944 as a liberation, do you?"

Behaving as if he did not hear their question, Ralin continued:

"Let us hope that this would not remain merely a romantic initiative or a heroic intention. We have been lied to as a nation many times. We have no more energy for empty hopes. This is why I want us to support the efforts of Comrade Peter Mladenov, to rally together all forces of the nation, to save our humanity, to save our Fatherland!"

The square seethed with passion. Only a few isolated sections of the crowd voiced their support for Ralin's last appeal. Most of the demonstrators were outraged by his suggestion. They angrily expressed their doubt that the new BCP Secretary General had the qualities necessary to save the Fatherland, and they denied him the top-level communist prerogative to lead the nation.

Radoy Ralin changed the subject. He started speaking about the meeting the independent associations had had with Peter Mladenov, in his capacity as Head of State, at the communist party headquarters. Peter Mladenov had delivered an encouraging speech about the future of Bulgaria.

This didn't calm the people down. They shouted indignantly: "Enough lies!" and "Down with all of them!"

"There we witnessed the obsequiousness of sunflowers," the poet remembered. "People with short memories. They forgot the crimes they were committing virtually until yesterday, their blind collaboration with the cult virtually until yesterday. The press, the radio and the television are still the same. The same cult institutions continue to exist, with their musty servile leaderships."

His last words won over the people. They started shouting enthusiastically, "Out! All of them out!"

"They are waiting for the storm to pass. But you, comrades, with your presence here, you are the living proof that the storm will not pass," the dissident encouraged his listeners.

With his keen sense of humor he went on to tell his audience what had happened to Nacho Papazov, a member of all communist governments, notorious for his low intellectual level. Having recently announced on television the expulsion from the communist party of several members of the independent groups, Papazov had been promoted both in the BCP hierarchy and in the state administration on the day before the rally.

"While overthrowing the cult we had so far, the National Assembly should have revoked the ban on Turkish names," Radoy Ralin suggested.

The people responded to this with applause. "Good!" "That's right!" Only a few booing voices and whistles were heard from one end of the square.

The poet added, "How dim-witted I am! Why do I forget that our National Assembly is not immune to the influences of Stalin's and Brezhnev's eras. That it follows an entirely authoritarian model. The first task of our nation is to hold free elections."

Thousands of voices exploded in unison, "Elections!" "Elections!"

Reassured by the general ovation, the orator continued his speech, calling for an independent Bulgarian Agrarian People's Union and for the restoration of the Liberal Party.

"Our great poet Atanas Dalchev," he went on in his slow, monotonous voice, "who saved with his poetry the few young people who were painfully aware of the evil, foresaw years ago - as a great spirit - the damage that totalitarian rule would inflict when he wrote his world-famous poem *Balcony*. About that ordinary balcony, like millions of other balconies all over the world, only walled in, so that the owners of the house never even suspected that they had a balcony. Just like our human rights that totalitarianism has walled in, so that we cannot even see them, and our country has turned into a prison."

"We knew it was a prison," an elderly man interjected. "Of course we knew our human rights were walled in."

This was followed by stormy and angry protests against totalitarian rule, long booing and whistling, which did not stop when Ralin started talking about Yordan Yotov, the Editor-in-Chief of the *Rabotnichesko Delo,* communist party daily newspaper, and Member of the Politburo of the BCP Central Committee.

"Comrade Yotov introduced the same obscurantist methods as Mitko Grigorov did. Pretending to introduce reforms, he actually banned magazines that had been published for half a century, merged totally incompatible publications, dismissed editors with clear thinking and forced a journalist like Stefan Prodev into retirement."

"Resignation!" "Down," the square shouted.

"And now Comrade Yordan Yotov plays the game 'see no evil, hear no evil' in his modification, 'see no cult, hear no cult,'" Radoy Ralin was saying indignantly. "He is to help Peter Mladenov. This makes no sense; this is ridiculous. This is not even a satire; it is an outrage. We need a reformation every day, every hour. We need a new Constitution."

The multitude greeted this with general approval and repeated many times the slogan "Constitution!" The poet had to wait long before he could finish his thought.

"We need to seek out the best in the spirit of the Tarnovo Constitution," he proposed.

The citizens of Sofia interrupted his speech again with a powerful "Hooray!" and long applause, which grew even stronger when Ralin started reciting Article 61 of the Tarnovo Constitution. That document was drafted and adopted by the Constituent Assembly of the Bulgarian Principality on April 16, 1879, just eleven months after the country's liberation from five centuries of Ottoman domination.

"No one shall either buy or sell human beings. Every slave, whatever his gender, faith or nationality may be, shall be free as soon as he steps onto Bulgarian soil."

Tears could be seen in the eyes of many people. The Tarnovo Constitution, one of the most liberal constitutions of its time, made every freethinking and freedom-loving Bulgarian justifiably proud. Replaced by a communist constitution in 1947, it was not forgotten. During the decades of totalitarian oppression older people often recalled it and that restored some of their self-esteem, their faith in the nation and in the intransient value of the democratic spirit.

However, the jubilant mood waned completely when Ralin brought up the Union of Active Fighters Against Fascism and Capitalism and the problems of its members. Indignant cries were heard. "Are there still such members? Didn't we run out of them at last?" "Do these terrorists want more privileges?" "We don't want to hear about them!"

Such anger was entirely justified. Immediately after the communists usurped power on September 9, 1944, the so-called "active fighters against fascism and capitalism" - most of them former partisans and members of terrorist groups - distributed to themselves the governmental, military and economic power. They received considerable material benefits, including additional wages and pensions, and had all kinds of privileges. For decades there were no laws for them, unlike those that were in force for ordinary Bulgarians. That was the case not only for the "active fighters", but also for their children. In order to make sure that the privileges reached even further, in the 1970s the "fighters" started adopting their grandchildren so that the latter would have the legal status of children. Thus, two or three generations gained access to elite high schools and universities even when they had low grades. Subsequently the graduates occupied high-ranking positions.

It is also worth noting that the majority of the people gathered in the square did not believe the lies of the communists about the existence of a fascist regime in Bulgaria. For most of the citizens who were not members of the ruling BCP, fascism came only after September 1944, and was labeled "communism."

Carried away in his thoughts and convictions, Radoy Ralin was coming to the end of his speech. "Finally, I would like to tell you that I have one request for the first citizen of our country, Peter Mladenov."

"There's no first citizen! He's not a part of our nation," a strong male voice boomed.

"First citizen," Radoy Ralin repeated, unperturbed. "Please don't raise the prices before you have abolished all privileges - all privileges, all special stores, starting with the *Rila* Hotel. Stop all special supplies and the special protection. They are an unbearable burden that will break the back of the state. If we have to guard you indeed - because the plutocrats will try to find some way to do something - anyway, if we have to guard you, this can be done by the honest soldiers in our People's Army. All of us who have gathered here are ready to take turns, day and night, to guard you. Don't rely on these overfed and callous goons! What did they do? Did they save the cult? Did they save it? As Machiavelli said - and he knew what he was talking about - no tyrant can ever predict who would take his place. Good luck!"

The demonstrators met the end of his speech chanting repeatedly, "Democracy!" A man shared with those near him, "Shame on him, I expected more from Radoy." Someone shouted "Radoy - Detour!" Then a woman's voice was heard saying, "I have no intention of guarding Mladenov!"

The well-known screenplay writer and movie director, Anzhel Wagenstein approached the microphone next. He addressed the multitude on behalf of the members of the Steering Committee who were not affiliated with any of the new independent organizations. "Citizens! Comrades!" These were his first words.

"Oh, no, not 'Comrades' again," people started complaining, unhappy to hear the form of address imposed by the communists. However, the speaker's fervor caught up with them and they listened to his words attentively.

"From the blood-drenched *Tiananmen* Square in Beijing to the square of the trodden Prague Spring, from the Great Chinese Wall via the ancient walls of the Kremlin and all the way to the collapsed wall of shame in Berlin ..."

This time cries of joy and excited applause interrupted Wagenstein.

"... there is a phenomenon much like a powerful ice-breaker, tracing its way across the ice-bound vistas of quasi-socialism," he went on when the square quieted down a little. "This process had swept Secretaries General, icebergs of partocracy, destroying the omnipotent command and repressive apparatus. Its road is marked by Gorbachev's three great milestones, *perestroika*, *glasnost* and democracy!"

Some people applauded; others chanted "Gorbachev!" However, there were also scathing comments like "one can see that he was educated in Moscow" or "a chip off the old Soviet bloc."

"I belong to the generation that walked on the partisan's paths," the screenplay writer proclaimed, "passed through the fascist camps and prisons in the name of the purest ideals of freedom and rule of the people, as well as for social justice among the people and nations."

"What fascist camps? Enough about these partisan's paths and pure ideals! We saw how pure they were! You didn't rule for a single day in the name of social justice," a man with graying hair burst out. "Let him talk! We are supposed to be democrats, aren't we," his friend snapped at him.

At that moment Anzhel Wagenstein was asking, "And how did it happen that we were building a bright temple out of this ideal, and when we looked around we saw that we had built military barracks instead, not a temple?!"

"What cynicism! It took you a half century to realize that," the man with the graying hair exploded again, shaking with indignation.

"And how did it happen that we were planting the seeds of goodness from which the weeds of heartlessness and cruelty sprouted," Wagenstein continued to wonder.

The people gathered in the square were agitated. The noise was increasing. Nevertheless, the speaker insisted on sharing his disappointment.

"We must have made some fatal mistake," he complained, "if today, we, former comrades-in-arms in the party and in destiny, are standing opposite each other as enemies, belligerent and speaking different languages. We must have done something wrong if the child of our rebellion, the shield and the sword of the revolution, started shielding the criminal and irresponsible rule of a party oligarchy with its shameless privileges, and the sword repressed the people in whose name we once uttered our oath."

The noise in the square continued, but the screenplay writer did not stop. "How did it happen that instead of light and truth, the dark shroud of secrets and silence descended upon society? Fear crept into our souls…"

A man's strong voice interrupted him, "Then get the hell out of here!" The general noise became long booing. The indignation with Wagenstein's speech grew, but he spoke even more loudly and with growing enthusiasm.

"… and white mansions grew over the bones of countless fighters for freedom and socialism. The forests owned by the royal family became nature reserves for the new aristocracy's leisure. The purest dreams for a just and humane system were raped and thrown out of the window as if they were air hostesses."

Wagenstein was referring to a hushed-up scandal involving Todor Zhivkov's son. Several years earlier there had been a rumor that Vladimir Zhivkov or someone from his drunken party had thrown a young TV newscaster and former stewardess out of a top-floor window. Zhivkov' son had not been brought to court and the case was not even investigated. Yet the people in the square had heard about the crime and started booing and demanding that all criminals be brought to court.

"The ability of faith to be reborn time and again is a gift from the gods. That is the faith about which the poet said that it has a steel armor." Wagenstein went on to mix up poetry with religion. "Isn't this the reason why for two thousand years people have been greeting each other with the words 'Christ has risen from the dead' on every Good Friday?"

"Not on Good Friday but on Easter," an elderly woman corrected him, embracing the shoulders of a little girl as if to keep her balance. But the crowd drowned out her words and repeated the Christian greeting which the communists had banned for decades, "Christ has risen from the dead!"

"But let me warn you," Wagenstein addressed the multitudes in the square, "not as an old man, but as someone who has seen it all and has experienced the distant April 1956 [when the Stalinist system was officially dismantled at a Politburo plenum of the BCP after the same happened in the Soviet Union - *author's note*]. Be vigilant, boys and girls! And you, comrade Peter Mladenov, be vigilant! The apparatus is still omnipotent, cunning and skilled! Act quickly and resolutely! Because if you slow down the tempo, if you look back and hesitate, if you don't purge it radically, it will surround you with gentleness and obedience.

It will give you the anesthesia of panegyric and will crush you in its iron embrace."

His last words were met with approval. Some people clapped; others spontaneously shouted, "True!" "That's right!" "Bravo!"

"And you, the people in this square," the speaker continued, encouraged, "be vigilant, because those who are personally responsible for the disgraceful ethnic crisis in our Fatherland and for its total isolation from the civilized world, and the others who completed the final transformation of the country's spiritual and intellectual life into a desert, these people are still in power."

The crowd interrupted him with a burst of applause and approval. A voice was heard saying, "Todor Zhivkov should be made the ambassador to Turkey!" This witty suggestion provoked an outburst of laughter, which subsided only when Wagenstein went on.

"They occupy the same offices as before and they are now watching us from their windows over there." For a long time the square booed and shouted indignantly, "Down!" "Out!" "There they are!"

"In the German Democratic Republic party activists commit suicide, stricken by repentance," the orator informed. "In Bulgaria the skies will open and God will give us His blessing if even one sinner hands in his resignation without coercion."

"I wonder if repentance or fear drove the communists in East Germany to commit suicide," a man with a threadbare grey coat asked ironically. "Who knows? But it seems to me that no one is more insolent than our communists," the woman next to him responded. At that time the people were chanting angrily, "Down!" "Resignation!" "Down with all of them!" "Without exception!" "All of them out!"

"Be vigilant! These are the lessons of April 1956," the screenplay writer insisted. "We must remember them so as to prevent the collapse of November 1989. I firmly believe in the new days to come. I wish to believe in a rejuvenated, humane and democratic form of socialism! I wish to believe in your resurrection, Bulgaria! This is why there should be a change now, democracy today, *glasnost* …"

At that point the square cut his speech short with the fervent slogans. "Bulgaria!" "Elections!" "Democracy!" "At once!" Wagenstein sensed that this was a good time to step down. Once he ceded his place to Karakachanov, lukewarm applause marked the end of his address.

"I need to make an announcement," Alexander Karakachanov was in charge again. "Two girls, Maria and Diana Dimitrova, aged 9 and 6, have been lost. If anyone has found them, please accompany them to the rostrum here. Maria and

Diana, 9 and 6. And now, after this announcement, I think the time has come to give the floor to a person with the pure soul and conscience of a poet, Blaga Dimitrova!"

Shouts "Blaga," "bravo," and applause drowned out his voice. The people were happy to welcome the famous poet and writer. In recent years she had earned their respect with her courage and valor as a citizen.

A group of men were still under the impression of Wagenstein's speech and were discussing it excitedly. "First and foremost it is important to elect decent people in Parliament so that they can draft the new Constitution, not the ones who were appointed yesterday. They are scoundrels," an angry young man insisted to an elderly gentleman next to him. "Yes, you are right. Above all, there should be a new Parliament. Just listen to the talk of the communist dissident and to his wishful thinking that their bloody party will be resurrected. Nothing good can come from them!" the white-haired man agreed. "Wagenstein would have felt more at home if he had spoken to the communists rally yesterday," a student added sarcastically.

The conversation stopped only after Blaga Dimitrova addressed the people in her stately way with a smile on her face.

"Sisters and brothers! Let us congratulate each other with the new Bulgarian Easter! Three decades of the life of our Fatherland passed in serfdom ..."

"Why three? Four and a half," a middle aged woman exclaimed in surprise. "Not only in Todor Zhivkov's time! Think about the others before him! Real murderers! Why doesn't she mention them as well?"

"... in serfdom under the feudal coat of arms of Pravets," Blaga added in her slow and clear voice. "In the past, Bulgaria was known to the world as the 'Land of Roses.'"

Someone interjected, "As a democratic land!"

"And then the monopoly of autocracy turned it into the 'Land of scleroses,'" Blaga Dimitrova evoked laughter and applause among her audience. "Even the children in this country are suffering from the ailments of the elderly, high blood pressure, diabetes, neuroses... What do these social diseases indicate?"

"Communist fringe benefits," a short, sturdy man responded.

"This is a symptom of a sclerotic society: amnesia, forgetting the past," insisted the poet. Someone shouted, "We never forget!" Others supported his lone cry with the resolute claim, "We remember!"

"Oblivion of the democratic traditions of our Fatherland established in the National Revival of the last century," the dissident continued. "What did the privileged vassals turn our life into? Grim boredom. Joyless labor. Silence. Fear and apathy. A good-for-nothing fellow is taking the job of someone intelligent and capable. The servile lackey chases the honest man down to his complete annihilation."

She was interrupted again by the shouts "True!" "Well said."

"A lazy person is wasting the time of his industrious colleagues with nonsense. A person without any gifts tends to stop any discovery. A fool organizes the likes of him to drown the voice of reason and of talent. No one is in his or her due place, with very few exceptions. The face of our Fatherland resembles a broken mirror, distorted, disfigured, unrecognizable, almost alien. However, I know that deep down, untarnished by the libel campaign against them and by discrimination, there are people who have preserved their character pure, hard and shining like diamonds, unsusceptible to corruption, lies and careerism," Blaga Dimitrova shared. "It is up to them to pull the spirit of the nation out of the mire. But will there be a real renaissance, or will inertia drag us back into a dead-end alley?"

"No, never," the crowd responded encouragingly.

"The top administration opened a deep abyss between the intellectuals and everyone else," Dimitrova reminded her audience. "Today we are extending arms to one another. Our arms were beaten with police batons and branded; we were stigmatized as apostates and traitors. We were thrown out of our jobs, arrested and persecuted. But now this bridge of hands firmly holding one another is like the rainbow after a storm, framing the horizon of the new day ahead. We are yet to fill the abyss with trust and understanding, with open and merciless mutual criticism. We need to find the solid foundation of truth, however harsh that truth may be. Our only pledge of allegiance to our Fatherland should be to roll up our sleeves and work hard, to work honestly, modestly..."

"Just not to work for *them*," a blond man exclaimed with justifiable concern.

Blaga Dimitrova did not hear his apprehensions. She was concluding her speech with a wish "for a new, free and civilized Bulgaria, a country of law and order, but above all, an independent Bulgaria!"

It seemed as though the word "independent" triggered the deepest emotion among the citizenry. They were tired of the humiliating truth that Bulgaria was the most obedient vassal of the Soviet Union among all countries of the so-called "socialist camp." The square exploded with the euphoric cries "We want an independent Bulgaria!" There were long applause and chanting, "Bravo, Blaga!" The jubilation went on for a long time.

"Now I would like to give the floor to a representative of a small trade union, as opposed to the official one. But I'm sure that this small organization will become very big soon," with these words Alexander Karakachanov's voice rose above the noise and excitement.

"This must be *Podkrepa*," a middle-aged man guessed. "His name is Trenchev, Doctor Konstantin Trenchev."

"It is my pleasure to give the floor to Konstantin Trenchev from the *Podkrepa* Independent Trade Union." Thus, Karakachanov completed his introduction of the next speaker.

The citizens of Sofia started applauding excitedly, impatient to hear Trenchev. His name had become known throughout the country in the early months of 1989, when the first independent trade union was established in Plovdiv. In May of that year Konstantin Trenchev, a physician by profession, was arrested and held in custody for three months in the building of the Central Investigation Office in Sofia. That made him a hero in the eyes of people and they were now anxious to see him.

Trenchev knew how to win his audience over. He started his speech with a series of rhetorical questions that touched upon painful social problems of vital importance to ordinary Bulgarians.

"Why are more than 50 percent of our fellow-Bulgarians living below the poverty line, while a mere one or two percent enjoy incomes that would make anyone in Switzerland livid with envy," the trade union leader asked. "Why does the foreign debt of Bulgaria exceed ten billion dollars, while the commodities with which we are known on the international market can be counted on the fingers of one hand? Why do we rank last but one in Europe in terms of average life expectancy, soon to become last, in spite of universal and free healthcare? Why did we fulfill and overfulfill one five-year plan after another under flying banners and huge slogans, only to find out that we have overfulfilled the plans for inflation and lowering of living standards? Why did those who were called upon to defend the rights of the working people from morning till night turn into paid collaborators and informers of the all-powerful communist party?"

Up to this point people had applauded Trenchev, but now they interrupted him with angry shouts of indignation against the communist-controlled official trade union. The square echoed with booing and chanting of slogans. "Down!" "Out!" "Liars!" "Go away!"

"Could it be that the reward for the thousands of ordeals that the suffering Bulgarian nation had to undergo amounted to corruption, lies, baseness and violence, while militant primitivism took the place of professional work and competence," the speaker continued fervently. "Hundreds and thousands of questions are burning in our souls after this long and painful awakening. Questions asked for months and years. Questions asked in private or among very close friends, behind curtains, shutters and locked doors. On behalf of the

Podkrepa Trade Union, I will take the liberty of asking one final question. Why were the new ideas of the Bulgarian Trade Unions, published a few days ago, not made public a month ago and why have four and a half million union members had no labor problems for forty-five years, but hundreds of such disputes have cropped up in the last few days?"

A man's voice stood out clearly against the noise. He said, "We are leaving the old trade union! At once! All of us!" Others kept repeating, "Good for Trenchev!" "Bravo!" "Podkrepa!" "Podkrepa!"

Someone asked someone else close by, "Is it true that Trenchev's father was an 'active fighter?'" But the answer could not be heard in the general commotion.

"We knew; we guessed; we feared; we were silent about or merely hinted at things," the physician recalled. "But was this a worthy stance and does it remove the burden of responsibility from our shoulders after decades of silence? Shall we have the courage to look into the eyes of our children and not despise ourselves for our cowardice? The *Podkrepa* Independent Trade Union believes that the crisis into which our society was plunged will only be exacerbated without radical changes. Social tension will grow invariably; it will be difficult and even impossible to prevent the destructive tendencies from gaining momentum. Today history is giving us our last chance to save ourselves and accept the final and irrevocable collapse of big illusions. Let the Bulgarian nation never be treated as an infantile and disoriented entity again and let it be given the right to elect its future freely."

"Elections!" "Freedom!" "We want freedom!" The square resounded with these slogans as if all were speaking in one voice.

"Freedom to choose between state, collective and private ownership, with constitutional guarantees for their equal rights," the leader of *Podkrepa* proposed. "Freedom of the ordinary Bulgarian citizens, not those with the many privileges, to choose where they want to work and where they want to live. Freedom to choose whom to vote for in free and fair elections."

"Elections, elections," all chanted in total inebriation.

Trenchev insisted, "There should be no pseudo-pluralism; there should be real pluralism! Let Bulgarian citizens receive real, not fictitious, constitutional guarantees for freedom of speech, freedom of the press, freedom of strikes, freedom of association and public gathering." He continued with his list of demands amidst the warm and boisterous approval of the public. "Let the honor, dignity and good reputation of the innocent victims of totalitarian rule be restored, so that we can learn our lesson from the tragic death of leaders like Nikola Petkov. Let us abolish entirely and radically the whole system of privileges for the *nomenklatura*, thus making the first step towards a civilized state governed by the rule of law and ensuring the total break with neo-feudalism. Let the place of each citizen in the social hierarchy be determined by his or her competence and personal contribution, not by his genealogy or caste. Let the army and the security organizations be depoliticized and stripped of all ideology by law. Let the honest and free-thinking citizens, individually or united in independent democratic associations, never be arrested, fired, deported, extradited or sentenced for having had the audacity to be the alert conscience of the nation!"

A deep voice boomed, "Parties! We want political parties!"

The speaker made a promise to the people gathered in front of the cathedral:

"The *Podkrepa* Independent Trade Union pledges its readiness to support and assist all honest democratic associations which have set before themselves the noble objective of saving our country from a third national catastrophe."

A storm of applause drowned out his last words, after which Konstantin Trenchev drew his speech to a close. "We have waited far too long for the birth of reconstruction. Now that it is born, we wish it to start walking and talking soon! Happy Birthday, Bulgarian reconstruction!"

Shouts of "bravo" and "Podkrepa" accompanied his retreat from the rostrum. A man's voice resounded, "Not *re*construction, *new* construction!" The people took up this appeal and started chanting it as the refrain of a song.

Karakachanov then asked the writer Georgi Mishev to come to the microphone. Most people had heard about him already and welcomed him warmly. "Mishev, Mishev!" "Bravo," they cried happily. As the co-founders of the Committee for the Ecological Salvation of Ruse, he and the actor Peter Slabakov had earned their empathy and recognition.

Mishev gently addressed the citizens of Sofia, "People, people, all of you who have gathered here in this enormous square, having trodden upon the thin ice of fear, today you deserve the highest public honor, to be addressed as 'citizens.' Dear citizens! Happy Day One of the Bulgarian democracy! Let us add that the worst is over. We lived to see the unexpected but actually long-awaited change. Today is the seventh day after a major surgery was performed. A malignant formation was excised from the body of our society."

He was interrupted by loud approval.

"We have gathered here to thank the surgeons," the speaker declared, "that everything went well and without dramatic consequences both for the individuals and for the country as a whole. This is an encouraging sign of a civilized approach."

At that point not everybody agreed with the speaker. Angry voices came from different directions. "It is not over yet!" "More is needed, a lot more!" Gradually the entire square started chanting, "More, more!"

"Three or four decades" was all that Georgi Mishev could say before a young tall man interrupted him energetically. "Stop beating about the bush! Stop these deliberate mistakes! Why don't you blurt it out at last. It has been four and a half decades since the communists usurped the power in the country!"

"... of running in circles or in one place," the dissident continued his thought, "but let us hope now that we are on the right track to a civilized Bulgaria - a modern, affluent, calm and stable state, where the only thing that would swing would be babies' cradles and the bronze bells of this great cathedral. This is the seventh day after Bulgaria threw the heavy millstone of totalitarianism off its shoulders. Apathy is disappearing. The appetite for life is coming back. Some unknown reserves of strength have been activated in our immune system, as if after a hypnotic session. The hypnosis in which we had drifted for decades gave way to reason, faith, and hope."

Then a woman's voice was heard to say, "We are still far from the right track! We are for socialism, but without the communists!"

Mishev was calmly listing the sins of totalitarian rule. "They taught the nation in study circles and educated it in a moronic school system. They informed it with pseudo-information. Let us leave the nation to live as it wishes."

The square was swept by the powerful slogan "Freedom!" There were also individual shouts of "that's right," "yes," and "good!"

"We must let Bulgarians marry whom they want," Georgi Mishev proposed. "They should be free to build their houses over as many square feet and with as many stories as they can afford, with as many garages as they want to have, to create as many children as they wish and to give to their children names of their own choice. Let them bring their kids up and educate them in the spirit of universal human values and virtues, above and beyond all class bias. This is the only way in which we can bring back the warmth and coziness of the home and the appeal and coziness of Bulgaria as well. It will not be easy, however!"

"No, it won't be," an elderly man agreed.

"The destructive forces of selfishness and avarice have been active for many years. The economy is ruined. The politicians are corrupt. The political activity of the population is paralyzed. The nation's spiritual life has been smothered. There needs to be a transfusion from the fresh blood of the independent movements into the veins of our civil society. In this way we shall restore the real meaning of concepts like Constitution, National Assembly, Member of Parliament, free elections," the writer was advising his audience.

Loud chanting of "free elections" drowned out the speaker's voice for a while.

A little later he managed to continue. "We must hurry. We are all impatient, but we must demonstrate wisdom as well. We can reach our goal not only by hurrying towards it, but also by not stopping. Let us move towards our goal with persistence! And with patience! Without illusions and with hopes! And may our path be illuminated only by sound reasoning and may our actions be guided by common sense! Hail, citizens!"

After the euphoric applause subsided, Karakachanov stood behind the microphone again. "And now I would like to give the floor to the oldest independent association among those present, and hence probably the one that had suffered the most. The President of the Independent Society for Human Rights Protection ..."

"Rumen, Rumen!" People interrupted him, eager to hear the words of Rumen Vodenicharov, who had already gained popularity through the open-air gatherings in the Southern Park in October.

He started talking, stressing every word he uttered. "The Independent Society for Human Rights Protection is a free association of democratically thinking Bulgarian citizens, whose activities are aimed at transforming Bulgaria into a state of law and order. It is open for membership to any individual who firmly rejects violence and believes in the principles of the International Charter of Human Rights. The Society has existed with no registration for almost two years. Its members are 400 intellectuals, peasants, workers, retired people, and political prisoners with unjust sentences issued to them in the past. More than thirty of its members were forced to emigrate to the West; more than a hundred others left to the East, in Turkey. Several dozen of its members are still in prison with no sentences."

He was interrupted by angry booing and shouts, "Freedom!"

"The activities of the Society consist of human rights protection and education in the sphere of human rights," Vodenicharov continued. "It publishes a newsletter. For the time being, its meetings take place in the open, at 11 a.m. every Saturday in the Southern Park of our capital. The logo of the Independent Society for Human Rights Protection is a wide-open hand, which symbolizes openness, non-violence and readiness to offer protection. The Society drafts reports, surveys, appeals, petitions and other documents relevant to human rights in Bulgaria. Dear compatriots, distinguished members of the independent democratic associations, ladies and gentlemen!"

"At last someone addressed us as 'ladies and gentlemen,'" several people cried, amused. "Yes, before we were only 'comrades,'" others added in support.

A small man with thick glasses asked with anger, "I don't get it. How did Vodenicharov remove the founder of the organization Iliya Minev from the leadership position?" His friend did not know.

"Two months ago, the Independent Society for Human Rights Protection completed its first report on human rights violations in Bulgaria," its new president announced. "The report ended as follows: 'More and more people realize that the so-called "real socialism" in its existing forms is a system that has exhausted its potential and has become a historical absurdity...'"

Spontaneous applause and shouts of approval drowned out the end of this sentence. Then the people of Sofia listened attentively to Vodenicharov's words once again.

"More and more states are beginning to amend their legislation in compliance with the International Charter of Human Rights. The process appears to be irreversible. This colossal process, which swept the countries of Eastern Europe like a warm wind, cannot fail to rejuvenate Bulgaria as well if its citizens wish to be members with equal dignity and equal rights with those in the European and global democratic community in the next century. Dear citizens! On Saturday, November 11, people in the streets were congratulating each other. However, they were doing it without particular enthusiasm. After the long years of stagnation in the highest echelons of power, there is not one single person whose name has not been tarnished!"

"True, there isn't," the crowd confirmed unanimously. "We want elections!"

"At this moment there is not one single person in the Politburo with outstanding credentials as a reformer. All potential reformers are at the lower levels of the communist party hierarchy, or - more commonly - entirely outside of it. The appointment of Mr. Peter Mladenov as the first - albeit belated - step towards democratic changes should be welcomed with moderate skepticism. The situation, which he inherited, is not enviable. The treasury is empty. There is an enormous state debt. There is an excessive, unproductive and repressive state apparatus. There are ethnic tensions and a consequent shortage in work force. Lawlessness is prevalent, in the sense that the law does not apply equally to all. The decades of moral ambivalence caused a deep decline of the nation's values. A number of national virtues were lost, and this - in our opinion - is a more disturbing heritage than the economic decline and the pollution of the environment. We, the members of the Independent Society for Human Rights Protection, see the changes in the communist party leadership as an absolutely necessary step towards the preservation of however little is left of the reputation of Bulgaria. We believe that the new Secretary General - a product of the existing totalitarian system, even though he has not taken part in its lawlessness and extravagance - should share the responsibility and guilt of Mr. Todor

Zhivkov for the country's foreign policy pursued in the past fifteen years and the bad reputation that Bulgaria has abroad."

The square burst into applause and exclamations again. "True!" "He is right!" "Yes!"

"Without the critical evaluation of his past," Rumen Vodenicharov admonished, "the new Secretary General, Mr. Mladenov, will find it very hard to earn the respect and support of the Bulgarian Moslems. Neither will he win the support of most of the Bulgarian intellectuals, whose approval he should seek in order to prevent a national catastrophe. He has to clean and recreate the reputation of Bulgaria as a democratic country. A particularly urgent task for Mr. Peter Mladenov's new team is dealing with a critical problem for this country, namely, the violation of the rights of the Bulgarian Moslems."

The people enthusiastically supported his speech, shouting at the top of their voices "that's right," "good," "yes," and "Give them their names back!" Once the square calmed down a little, Vodenicharov continued confidently:

"We are talking about a million and a half Bulgarian citizens, ethnic Turks and Pomaks [ethnically Bulgarian Moslems - *author's note*], who have been subjected to coercive assimilation for twenty years by crude repressive measures and even bloodshed. The flow of Bulgarian citizens to the East…"

"Bulgaria should be for the Bulgarians," a man's voice boomed suddenly, and from that moment on hell broke loose in the square. Most of the participants in the rally were outraged by this nationalist appeal and responded to it, shouting, "Stop that nonsense!" "Only Zhivkov's stooges talk like that!" "Down with the communist propaganda!" "What do you want from these people? They are right. Look, they have come carrying a sign with the slogan 'Give us back our names.'" And why shouldn't they have their names back?"

However, there were people who agreed with the nationalist slogan. They were booing the speaker, screaming, "There is only one Bulgaria!" "Let those who are earning one million levs go to Turkey, if they are not Bulgarians!" "There are no Pomaks, you idiot! There are Bulgarians islamized by force!" "They exported Bulgaria to Turkey!" Others reminded them angrily, "Shame on you! People like you, not the Turks, sold Bulgaria!" "Would you have been happy if someone forced you to change your name overnight? Come on, tell me!"

Unable to take part in the general shouting match, two elderly women, dressed in black, were trying to talk to each other. "Turks or Bulgarians, what difference does it make," the taller of the two women said indignantly. "We are one nation, aren't we? Before the communist rule everyone had whatever religion he or she chose, gave whatever names they wanted to their children and minded their own business. Turks and Bulgarians had a mutual respect for each other. My Dad even told me that our Turks fought against Turkey as volunteers in the Balkan War. And what is this nonsense now about 'Bulgaria for the Bulgarians?' This is ridiculous!"

"Why are you so astonished? Don't you know the communists? They succeeded in dividing the nation first into communists and noncommunists and now into Turks and Bulgarians. They only know how to oppose people to one another while they are stealing and committing all kinds of outrage. I hope we get rid of them at last," the smaller, bent-over old woman replied angrily. She added in her frail voice, "Pity our husbands didn't live to see this!"

"God rest their souls! But let me tell you, I'm sure that communists have also come to this rally," her friend commented.

Vodenicharov's voice was heard again. "We cannot fail to respect the rights of this enormous labor force." Thunderous booing and exclamations of "right you are" and "bravo" resounded in the square.

The speaker was trying to continue. "As to the economic damage…"

"Let them go, all of them! The further away from us they are, the better," a coarse male voice insisted. "If they had beaten you as they beat them, you would have left Bulgaria too," a student snapped back at him.

"We are convinced," Rumen Vodenicharov managed to interject, "that just as 20,000 citizens of the German Democratic Republic are about to return to their native places after emigrating to the Federal Republic and after the fall of the Berlin Wall, tens of thousands of ethnic Turks, these unpretentious and hard working people…"

Once again there was indignant booing, fierce whistling and a new wave of exclamations: "What ethnic Turks?" "If this is so, let them go to Turkey!" "These are Bulgarian Moslems, you fool, not Turks!" "Do you hear? They are Bulgarian Moslems!" "Get down from the rostrum! Go away!" "Down!"

Yet, Rumen Vodenicharov persisted, "The new Secretary General…"

"Let the man finish," a tall man was trying in vain to restore some semblance of order.

Karakachanov intervened. "I think we need to respect the speaker, even if we may not agree with everything that he is saying…" Shouts "out with him" still came from here and there. "I can wait a long time too," Karakachanov warned. "Let's continue, so that we can show that we are a democratic state. Let's learn how we should live in a democratic state."

Those who wanted to bring the speaker back started calling him by name, "Rumen! Rumen!"

Once again behind the microphone, Vodenicharov changed the subject. "The new Secretary General should realize as soon as possible that the State Security as a system is a sinister anachronism of Stalinism in terms of both sheer size and financial support. The State Security succeeded in only one thing, cultivating a sense of fear in most Bulgarians. Tens of thousands - no one knows the exact figure, but definitely no less than 100,000 - healthy men have not been producing anything for years. These strong men, who are still clenching their fists in their pockets, should learn to put their energy to better use than following democrats and dragging them down the streets..."

This reminder of the clash between citizens and the militia in front of the *Crystal* Café excited the demonstrators. The differences of opinion were left behind and everybody applauded the dissident.

"Their energy should be used in the struggle against all violators of the law and in the production of material wealth," Rumen Vodenicharov proposed. "I think that the Independent Society for Human Rights Protection will voice the sentiments of all people gathered here by insisting on cuts in the staff of the State Security Service, shrouded in mystery, and on its being placed under parliamentary control. It is already clear to all of us that half-hearted measures will not allow us to go down the road that the other European democracies have traveled a long time ago. We are clearly very far from it."

"That's right! That's true," the crowd responded in one voice.[1]

Even this disappointing statement did not take away the euphoria, the joy and optimism of the citizens of Sofia. On November 18, 1989, they listened to more speeches. They went through more emotions, and they went back to their homes as free people.

From that moment on everything would be different. During the following years thousands and thousands of Bulgarians would gather in various streets and squares to express their willingness to build a democratic Bulgaria. Once they awakened from the timelessness of communism, they responded to every event, injustice, and betrayal with countless processions, rallies, demonstrations, and protest actions.

Yet only one or two of the dissidents who spoke at that first mass rally were to preserve their reputation unblemished as Bulgaria embarked on its transition to democracy.

---

[1] This Chapter is based on a tape recording of the rally at the *St. Alexander Nevski* Square on November 18, 1989, in Sofia, Bulgaria.

PART TWO

THE COMMUNIZATION AND SOVIETIZATION OF BULGARIA

5. Building the Foundation of a Communist State

Shortly after 1989, foreign political observers and journalists disseminated information about the events in Bulgaria that often proved to be superficial or even incorrect. This was only natural. For decades, Bulgaria had been known to the world as a poor, backward, fascist state - before the communists came to power - and as the most loyal satellite of the Soviet Union thereafter. Likewise, the Bulgarian nation was believed to unreservedly support the one-party dictatorship of the Bulgarian Communist Party as well as the U.S.S.R..

These impressions of the international community were based on the official statements of the government of the People's Republic of Bulgaria and its diplomatic corps. Also, the Bulgarian media as well as all historical studies, textbooks, reference publications, manuals, tourist leaflets, statistical reports, newspapers and other periodicals published in the country after 1947 supported this view of Bulgaria and its people. Authors and editors of world almanacs, encyclopaedias, history books and textbooks drew from these sources and misinformation turned into universally accepted fact.

One should not blame the foreigners for being uninformed. Most Bulgarians themselves had been educated in orthodox communist schools, universities and ideological institutions for forty-five years, and they knew little about their own history and about the political past of their native land.

The misinformation of the generations that had grown up under totalitarian rule explains why the change in Bulgaria's public life in the fall of 1989 came so unexpectedly. It did not result from mass local protests, but rather from earlier events in some of the other socialist states, above all the Soviet Union, which lost the Cold War.

In other words, everything started suddenly and was "imported". Just as communism had been imported to the country in the first place.

. . .

On September 5, 1944, the Soviet Union severed its diplomatic relations with the Kingdom of Bulgaria and declared war. Three days later, the Third Ukrainian Front under the command of Marshal F. I. Tolbukhin crossed the northern Bulgarian border and entered the territory of a state that had just proclaimed complete neutrality in World War II. Only then did the small Bulgarian Workers' Party (communists), or BWP(c), succeed in carrying out the military coup that it had been planning for so long.

That happened in the early hours of September 9.

From that day on, the land of the Bulgarians was transformed into a killing field. The communist executioners and their supporters were backed by the 200,000-strong Soviet occupation force. Their model was the bloody Bolshevik revolution in Russia. Hours after usurping power, the new red Minister of the Interior, Anton Yugov, distributed to members of the communist party a "large quantity of arms from the State arsenals, under the unfounded pretext of defense against allegedly expected attempts at restoration by the overthrown Government. In fact, all this was done in order to create terror upon the population and to extend the Communist control."[1]

In just two months - September and October 1944 - the BWP(c) collaborators murdered 30,000 innocent people from all walks of life, without trial or sentence. They did not spare the life even of the captain of the national soccer team, Dimitar Zografov, who was killed on September 10. The same was the fate of Vera Danailova Yankova, 34-year-old, clerk, divorced, mother of a 13-year-old son:

> Fault: After September 9, 1944, a woman dared hang the national flag of Bulgaria from her window, among the mandatory red flags.
>
> Type of repression: Taken from her office on September 16, 1944, to the Directorate of the Militia from where she "disappeared without a trace" [the quaint communist phrase for being murdered - *author's note*] on October 3.
>
> Circumstances: On September 16, 1944, uniformed and plain-clothed men barged into the office of Vera Yankova at the State Property Directorate on the second floor at 4, *Slaveykov* Square, around 11 a.m., and took her with them "for inquiry" at the Directorate of the Militia. From the few words exchanged it became clear that the "comrades" were attracted by the white-green-and-red national flag hanging from the woman's office window. This is why she was taken "for inquiry".[2]

The physical liquidation of freethinking and patriotic Bulgarians was the main prerequisite for strengthening the red dictatorship. However, it was even more essential for the BWP(c) to break the backbone of the pre-communist state and to crush the political and spiritual elite of the country, as fast as possible, and as thoroughly as possible. This strategy required something in

---

[1] Dolapchiev 1971, pp. 41-42.

[2] *Istina* [*Truth*] newspaper, *Death for hanging the Bulgarian national flag*, July-August 1993.

addition to assassinations in the streets, basements, squares, ravines and militia stations, known as "spontaneous purge campaigns." It was necessary to devise a more efficient way of exterminating leading individuals, with grave consequences for their families.

Joseph Stalin suggested the recipe, the "judiciary purge campaign".

The annihilation of prominent figures in the executive and judiciary systems, Members of Parliament, army officers, activists of noncommunist political organizations, mayors, journalists, scientists, academics, writers, physicians, lawyers, clergymen and administrators was arranged "through the court" with the help of a special law that allowed death sentences to be dispensed generously, without the right of appeal, and with the confiscation of the property of the convicted individuals.

In the fall of 1944, approximately 28,000 eminent Bulgarians were arrested. Some of them were killed during the interrogations, others were released, and 11,122 were handed over the so-called "People's Courts". These institutions were established on the basis of an unconstitutional decree on "Sentencing by People's Court", which was adopted by the Council of Ministers on September 30, 1944.

The "courts" were constructed to attain the goals that the new rulers had set. They consisted of fanatical political activists who were often almost illiterate. The only official requirement was that their chairpersons have some legal background. As a matter of fact, none of the members of these farcical tribunals needed a law degree. The sentences were not determined by them, but by the executive body of the Bulgarian Workers' Party (communists), the Politburo of the Central Committee.

On January 20, 1945, the Politburo called a meeting with the following agenda: "An exchange of thoughts on the sentences in the two trials".

The First trial was against the Regents of the Kingdom of Bulgaria, the ministers in the governments between January 1, 1941 and September 9, 1944, as well as the tsar's advisers. The defendants in the Second trial were the Members of Parliament in the Twenty-Fifth Ordinary National Assembly, in spite of the fact that they preserved the country's independence from Nazi Germany in World War II and had saved the lives of its 50,000 person Jewish minority.

During the "exchange of thoughts" the floor was given to the Chief Prosecutor in the "People's Court", Georgi Petrov, who shared his opinion with the party leadership:

> There should be a certain ranking of the sentences. Not all defendants should be treated equally, because their guilt is not the same. Some of them may not be guilty at all.[3]

Facts, data and arguments followed. Nikola Gavrilov, another prosecutor, added further information supporting the report of his senior. This made the communist Minister of Justice, Mincho Neychev, lose patience. He protested:

> The comrades public prosecutors have adopted a totally incorrect approach. They are looking for the gravest crime from which to start the ranking downwards. They wish to punish with death only those who are most guilty, and for the less guilty ones - compared to them - they foresee lesser punishments. They are not seeking to determine whether a sufficient crime has been committed, deserving in itself the death penalty, but seek to find out whether there are others who have committed more serious crimes.[4]

Georgi Chankov, Politburo Member and Secretary of the CC of the BWP(c), proved to be even more outraged by what he heard.

> The train of thought of our prosecutors is not that of people who have a political interest in striking a blow to that camarilla; they act as though they want to stay away from the entire struggle of the people and prefer to weigh who is guilty and how much exactly, etc. Our public prosecutors do not behave as people from our movement for whom even the minutest proof of the guilt of those bandits suffices.[5]

The man on the top of the party hierarchy among those present, Traycho Kostov - Politburo member and First Secretary of the CC of the BWP(c) - deemed it his prerogative to announce the sentences against the defendants:

> We cannot agree in any way with the line of argument pursued by the comrades prosecutors. I propose the following: regarding the Regents, death for all three of them. Kiril's degeneracy is not a mitigating circumstance. As for the advisers, Sevov and the other four should be given the most severe sentence. We are talking about the remaining five; they may be punished with something other than death, but their punishment has to be severe. When it

[3] Ognyanov, Dimova, Lalkov 1992, p. 24.

[4] *Ibid.*, p. 27.

[5] *Ibid.*

comes to the first Government of Filov [February 15, 1940 - April 11, 1942 - *author's note*], the issue is clear, death.[6]

For Filov's second Government [April 11, 1942 - September 14, 1943 - *author's note*] the same resolution is in order.

For Bozhilov's Government [September 14, 1943 - June 1, 1944 - *author's note*] the decisive factor is Decree No. 30, with which orders are given to the army to exterminate the partisans. Again death for all who have signed it is in order.

As for Bagryanov's Government [June 1, 1944 - September 2, 1944 - *author's note*], Gavrilov's assessment is not right in the least. Bagryanov did not serve the tsar and the people simultaneously. He served the tsar and fooled the people. For Bagryanov, Staliyski, General Rusev, Stanishev and Draganov death. For Kolchev and Arnaoudov life imprisonment; for the rest, Rusi Rusev, Dimitar Savov and Hristo Vasilev, less.

No one from Muraviev's government [September 2, 1944 - September 9, 1944 - *author's note*] can be pardoned. The question is how to sentence them. Konstantin Muraviev and Vergil Dimov should be sentenced most severely, but not by death.[7]

None of the Members of Parliament (except those who had died before 1941) should be acquitted. A list of the sentences of the Members of Parliament is to be submitted, and it should be coordinated with us. The indictment speeches for the First trial should start on Wednesday or Thursday, and for the Second trial on Friday or Saturday around January 25.[8]

The prosecutors and their colleagues heeded the orders of the red party.

On February 1, 1945, after a hectic couple of weeks, the First Supreme People's Court conducted a brief session at 4 p.m. for only 30 minutes during which the sentence was read.[9]

On that same day, the Second Supreme People's Court also read its sentences.

Following the two "court" rulings, in the night of that very same February 1, three Regents, eight advisers to the royal court, all ministers from the governments of Professor Bogdan Filov and Dobri Bozhilov, half of the ministers in Ivan Bagryanov's government, and 67 Members of Parliament from

---

[6] *Ibid.*, pp. 27-28.

[7] *Ibid.*, p. 28.

[8] *Ibid.*, p. 29.

[9] Iliev 1988, p. 49.

the Twenty-Fifth Ordinary National Assembly were executed by criminals and formal partisans near the pits dug by the bomb explosions in the Central Cemetery in Sofia.[10]

With that act the party of the Bulgarian communists committed the most massive and cold-blooded murder of statesmen in modern history, including the unparalleled extermination of nearly half of the members of Parliament.

The death sentences of the leaders of pre-communist Bulgaria were put into action hours after they were pronounced. This sort of "efficiency" appears to have been baffling even to the judicial authorities. On February 2, during the day, the wife of the Member of Parliament from the Ivaylovgrad Electoral College, Lazar Popov, received a note from the Prosecutor's Office in Sofia that she was allowed to visit her husband in prison in the presence of the jailer.[11] Needless to say, the meeting between the spouses did not take place. The eminent lawyer and public figure had already been shot down and buried in the mass grave among the corpses of his colleagues.

The widows and orphans of the executed persons were deprived of their property. In the depth of winter they were driven out of their homes and banished without money, food or income to the frozen, almost empty northeastern part of Bulgaria.

...

The daughter of Pavel Gruev, who had been convicted by the First Supreme People's Court, Radka Joy Grueva, sadly recalled the following, 63 years after the execution of her father in the night of February 1:

> I never thought that anyone could make an attempt on my father's life, not only because he was an honest man, but also because he was the head of the Tzar's administrative office, not a politician. He had served Tsar Boris III, his father, Tsar Ferdinand, and the regents of Tsar Boris son. I couldn't imagine that anyone would accuse my father of a crime against the State. For Dad, Bulgaria was most sacred. He considered his duty to his homeland more important than his wife and children. He never spoke ill of anybody. His values could not be corrupted with money. It was most important for him that a man should be honest and do his civic duty.
>
> After my father's execution we learned that he had been acquitted at first. Then, Georgi Dimitrov [the leader of the Bulgarian communists - *author's note*]

---

[10] *Istina* newspaper, Georgi Markov, *The People's Tribunal – an Unsurmounted Tragedy of the Bulgarian Nation*, Sofia, February 1992.

[11] Notes and documents from prison of Lazar Popov, personal archive.

had transmitted Stalin's order from Moscow, demanding that more people be shot. The order did not even say "more people;" it said "a larger number," which was even more insipid. Not names but numbers!

After my father's arrest we were able to visit him in jail only once in 1944, on my twentieth birthday. That is a terrible memory! My mother, my brother Simeon and I went together. They did not let my aunt, my father's sister, come. We saw them drag my father down the hallway. They placed the prisoners side by side. We could not hold their hands through the bars. We were yelling at them from a distance, all at the same time. I remembered my father's last words before they took him away. He said, "I am sorry that I became the reason for you to suffer as well." Later we learned that all the detainees had been anxious about the fate of their families. They knew Stalin's policy of no mercy for the relatives, and they were right to be concerned.

Only a week later - once again on Soviet orders - my mother and I were taken away in a horse-box along with the families of the men tried by the First Supreme so-called People's Court. In the dead of winter we were traveling to an unknown destination. We thought they were sending us to Siberia, but they unloaded us in icy Dobrudzha at the edge of a small remote village. We survived only because we were really optimistic and we all believed that there was no reason for the authorities to kill our husbands and fathers.

It turned out we were wrong. In April 1945 the communist militia came and called us by our names. My mother and I were among the first ones to be called. We did not know Dad's fate. They addressed my mother and told her, "You are a widow." I could not hold myself back and I screamed, "Murderers!" Of course, I was tortured for that, but the physical pain was of no significance.[12]

...

The collective execution of the Regents, royal advisers, government ministers and Members of Parliament was just the beginning. It was followed by fifteen mega-trials consisting of 135 "People's Courts". In the spring of 1945, they issued 2,730 death sentences, with no right of appeal. The convicted were executed immediately, with extreme sadism and no judiciary control. The same "courts of justice" sentenced to solitary life imprisonment 1,305 Bulgarian nationals, and punished another 5,571 individuals with prison sentences ranging from one to twenty years.

The Sixth Supreme People's Court can serve as an example of terror and arbitrariness. The accused were 104 intellectuals, including journalists, publishers, editors, curators, writers, scholars and artists. Sixteen of them were

[12] An interview with Radka Joy Grueva by the author, *For Dad Bulgaria Was the Most Sacred*, *Pro&Anti* weekly, February 1, 2008.

sentenced to death, 12 were punished with life imprisonment, and 69 received prison sentences of one to fifteen years. The convicted persons had written and lectured against Bolshevik terror. Their love for Bulgaria and their beliefs were their only crime.

The Professor of Criminal Law Nicola Dolapchiev was for a while close to the circle *Zveno* that helped the communists in the military coup on September 9, 1944. A political emigrant in 1971, he wrote in his book *Bulgaria - the Making of a Satellite - Analysis of the historical developments 1944-1953* the following:

> To prepare the atmosphere for the 'people's courts', the communists made use of crowds of hooligans, gypsies and common criminals released for that purpose, and conducted them up and down the streets and led them intoning the imprecation, 'death-death-death'. Later the defendants were taken through the streets in chains, as well-drilled Communist fanatics shrieked 'traitors', 'people's enemies', 'monsters'. Bands of 'black widows' were hired and conducted through the streets, while intoning 'death-death-death'. They marched about the court rooms at the time of the trials, shrieking 'death'. Then the defendants were taken out and exposed to the imprecations, abuses, mockeries, spitting in the face, beatings and other kinds of maltreatment. The radio, hour after hour, screamed 'death'. A special newspaper called 'People's Court' was published with every sort of hideous, hate-inciting picture, and with articles calling for vengeance. The Bulgarian people were indignant and stupefied in front of these shameful demonstrations, which were quite improper and alien to the Bulgarian character.
>
> 'One must not believe', points out R.H. Markham 'that this method of dispensing justice is peculiar only to Balkan Communists or due to 'wild' Balkan traditions. It flows from the Moscow of Lenin.'[13]

...

Considering the relative sizes of the populations, Bulgaria condemned more than 2,500 times as many "war criminals" than those convicted in Nazi Germany after World War II, although the Balkan kingdom never fought in the war and saved its Jews from Hitler's death camps. The arithmetic is very simple.

The Nurnberg International War Tribunal started its work in August 1945, three months after the end of the war in Europe. It summoned 24 Germans, 21 of whom sat on the bench of the accused. The International Tribunal was in session for eleven months, from November 1945 until October 1946. It dropped the charges against three of the defendants. After proving beyond any doubt the crimes of the others against peace and humanity, the Tribunal

---

[13] Dolapchiev 1971, pp. 92-93.

sentenced eleven people to death, three to life imprisonment and the rest to twenty, fifteen and ten years in prison. The indicted individuals were given the right to appeal the sentences. The executions were not carried out immediately but sixteen days after the sentences were passed. Consider that the defendants were Goering, Ribbentrop, Rosenberg, Kaltenbrunner and the like.

Another eloquent comparison can be made with Hungary, the last country that fought on the side of Hitler's Germany. It paid a very high price for that choice in terms of meaningless casualties and destruction, the extermination of its Jewish minority, and the loss of Transylvania. For all these crimes, the extraordinary courts of justice of Hungary issued 476 death sentences, but only 189 people were actually executed.[14]

Comparisons of this nature never had any significance for the Bulgarian Communist Party. The lightning speed with which the "People's Court" tried and executed people, for which it earned the name of "Bulgarian guillotine"[15], remained its eternal pride.

In 1988, at the height of *glasnost's* denouncements of crimes committed by the red Soviet regime, one old man, Boris Iliev, Chairman of Bulgaria's Twelfth Supreme People's Court, remembered with satisfaction:

> Immediately [on March 17, 1945 - *author's note*] I started working on the enormous material of the investigation and on the preparations for the trial that I scheduled for March 26, 1945.
>
> ...
>
> According to the indictment, there were 176 defendants and 138 witnesses.
>
> ...
>
> In spite of the enormous amount of work for the court - hearing the explanations of the defendants who had appeared and collecting information about those absent, as well as examining 138 witnesses - the court completed its work on April 28, 1945, because of the competence and efficiency with which the trial was conducted.
>
> ...
>
> Out of the 176 defendants, 66 were acquitted completely. The remaining 110 defendants received the following sentences: the death penalty for twenty people, life imprisonment for six, 15 years of imprisonment for fifteen, 10 years in prison for three, 12 years of imprisonment for one. The remaining 65 defendants received various prison terms, ranging from one to five years in length.[16]

---

[14] *Demokratsiya* daily, Georgi Markov, *The Tragedy and the Disgrace, Called "People's Tribunal"*, October 6, 1993.

[15] Meshkova and Sharlanov 1994, *passim*.

[16] Iliev 1988, pp. 82-83, 85, 166.

The "people's courts" committed another outrage. They sentenced to death several hundred Bulgarians who had already been killed without trial during the first weeks after September 9, 1944. A provision in the decree on "Sentencing by People's Court" read as follows:

> The death of a person who has committed an act according to the present law, prior to or after charges have been brought against the said person, shall not constitute an obstacle to the initiation or completion of a prosecution and the pronouncement of a sentence in accordance with the previous paragraph.[17]

The aim was to "legitimize" the liquidation of the people who had been murdered and to allow for the confiscation of all of their property, leaving their heirs penniless and on the streets.

During the sinister fall of 1944 and the winter that followed, the families of those convicted as well as thousands of public figures, diplomats, army officers, clergymen, lawyers, physicians, journalists, writers, scientists, publishers, merchants, academics, and factory and land owners, who had miraculously been spared the wrath of the "courts", were sent to labor camps [a communist term for concentration camps - *author's note*] or were deported to some remote part of the country.

Many eminent Bulgarians were forced to remain abroad because the military coup on September 9, 1944, caught them on a journey away from their homeland. Other Bulgarians living in the country after this tragic date, who wanted to escape to freedom, found their death at the borders of Greece or Turkey. Just a few lucky ones managed to emigrate to the West.

. . .

The sudden Stalinist-type terror in Bulgaria was just the first stage of political repression. The population was yet to be deprived of its civil liberties, after which all forms of anticommunist activities would stop.

The overall plan of the Bulgarian Workers' Party (communists) could not be executed overnight. The political involvement of the United States and Great Britain was an obstacle. In February 1945, at the Yalta Conference, they proposed a Declaration on Liberated Europe to their ally, the U.S.S.R., and it was adopted. Among the provisions of that historic document was a promise that the democratic rights of the citizens of every European state would be

---

[17] *State Gazette* No. 219, October 6, 1944.

restored after the end of World War II. These states were to be ruled by the representatives of political organizations that had won the popular vote in free and fair elections. The Declaration also included the warning that no peace treaties would be signed with governments that had not been recognized by the Allied Forces.

It would appear that this Declaration was an insoluble problem for the BWP(c). Its party members were fewer than 6,000 people before September 9, 1944. Therefore, the party of the communists, which came to power with the support of the Soviet army, would have no chance to retain its ruling position after free elections.

The leaders of BWP(c) were well aware of that. They had already applied the established Leninist practice of attracting allies by cunningly concealing their real intentions in order to deal with the predicament at hand. After long efforts and innumerable intrigues - as well as the promise of a joint government of the country - in 1943 the Bulgarian Workers' Party (communists) succeeded in creating a pro-Soviet underground organization, called the Fatherland Front (FF). It incorporated the *Zveno* political circle of Kimon Georgiev, which had masterminded two military coups and was known for its semi-fascist ideology, the *Alexander Stamboliyski* Bulgarian Agrarian People's Union, better-known by its Bulgarian acronym BZNS *Pladne*, headed by Nikola Petkov, the left wing of the Bulgarian Workers' Social Democratic Party (BWSDP), represented by Grigor Cheshmedzhiev, several independent intellectuals, and, last but not least, the BWP(c), which was at the head of the Fatherland Front and conducted all communications with Moscow.

Most of the Bulgarian politicians, however, categorically refused to collaborate with the communists and participate in the Fatherland Front. Among them were Dimitar Gichev, the leader of the other wing of the Agrarian Union, known as BZNS *Vrabcha-1*, the former Prime Minister Nikola Mushanov, the leader of the Democratic Party, Krastyu Pastuhov, the leader of the right wing of the Bulgarian Workers' Social Democratic Party, and a number of other influential public figures.

The latter individuals were in legal opposition to the policy of the Bulgarian governments after 1940, which believed that Germany would win the war and revise the 1919 Treaty of Neuilly, perceived as cruel and unfair. The Treaty deprived the kingdom of seven territories with Bulgarian population and imposed on it indemnities and reparations at the rate of 2 billion, 250 million gold francs, the most severe economic punishment *per capita* among the countries that lost the First World War. Gichev, Mushanov and Pastuhov were convinced that the Allied Forces would prevail in World War II, and their political preferences were the U.S.A. and Great Britain. Although they did not agree with many of the decisions of the recent Bulgarian governments, these experienced politicians had distanced themselves from the BWP(c). They rejected the Bolshevik method of armed struggle to usurp power and were convinced that the party of the communists was extremely dangerous for the Bulgarian nation and for its democratic future.

On August 7, 1944, Dimitar Gichev, Krastyu Pastuhov, Nikola Mushanov, Konstantin Muraviev, Atanas Burov, Alexander Girginov, Vergil Dimov and five other politicians in opposition sent a declaration to the Regents and to the government of the Kingdom of Bulgaria. In that document they insisted on a radical and immediate change in the country's foreign policy; to leave the Tripartite Pact, and to form a new Council of Ministers. Less than a month later their wishes were granted. The Regency asked Konstantin Muraviev, one of the leaders of the agrarians, BZNS *Vrabcha-1*, to form a government. It included four other agrarians, namely Dimitar Gichev, Vergil Dimov, Hristo Popov and Stefan Daskalov, as well as the democrats Nikola Mushanov, Alexander Girginov and Boris Pavlov, one of the leading figures in the Bulgarian Conservative Party, Atanas Burov, and finally Major-General Ivan Marinov.

On September 2, 1944, the democratically minded opposition peacefully and legitimately took power in Bulgaria. The coalition government immediately proclaimed complete neutrality in World War II and worked to appease the tense political situation in the country.

Little did Konstantin Muraviev and his cabinet members know that they had only a few days at their disposal. Just a week later, a party with less than 6,000 members usurped power and held it for nearly half a century, choking off the democratic development of the state.

...

On December 11, 1941, Germany and Italy declared war on the U.S.A., which had been supporting the Soviet Union with supplies since June of that year. Hitler and Mussolini compelled the countries in the Tripartite Pact to declare war on the United States and Great Britain immediately.

The Bulgarian leadership met this instruction without enthusiasm, particularly because the U.S.A. was the only great power to intervene in support of the country's cause after the First World War. After certain deliberations, the government reached a "diplomatic" solution. The Kingdom of Bulgaria declared war on the two giants, but in order to alert them that it actually had no intention of fighting against them, it qualified that war as "symbolic". That definition proved to be rather naive. In the fall of 1943, the great democracies started their air raids against Bulgaria, claiming the lives of 1,828 civilians.

The Fuehrer's other wish - for Bulgaria to declare war on the U.S.S.R. - was never granted in practice. The Balkan kingdom preserved its diplomatic relations with the Soviet Union. It was the only one among all the European states, allied with or occupied by Germany, which did not send a single soldier to fight against the Soviet troops at the Eastern Front.

In 1984 the American professor Michael M. Boll and his coauthors published the book *Cold War in the Balkans: American Foreign Policy and the Emergence of Communist Bulgaria, 1943-1947*. This in-depth study was compiled on the basis of recently declassified documents and resolutions of international conferences, and meetings. It covers the events as follows:

> In February 1944, the director of the Civil Affairs Division [of the U.S. Department of Defense - *author's note*], General J. H. Hildring, presented his department's final recommendations for the Bulgarian surrender to the Joint Chiefs. This document, designated WS-58, received final JCS approval in early March. Predicated upon the principle of unconditional surrender, the terms allocated to America and Britain alone "the right to occupy with any forces at their disposal and in any way they deem necessary, and to utilize in any way they deem appropriate, any or all parts of Bulgarian territory" ... In the final draft sent to London under the symbol WS-58b, America and Britain were charged with sole control over Bulgaria's return to a peaceful postwar status.[18]

> Winant [John Winant, U.S. Ambassador to London - *author's note*] informed Hull [Cordell Hull, U.S. Secretary of State; in July 1944 - *author's note*] that a British proposal for surrender terms had been tabled and that the two documents could probably be merged. No difficulty was anticipated with the Soviet delegate because he already had expressed Moscow's willingness to allow America and Britain to handle terms for states with which the Soviet Union was not at war.[19]

> America's central goal in Bulgaria was defined as the creation of a democratic, representative government and the nation's reentry into the mainstream of postwar international life. Considerable understanding for future border rectifications was expressed, including the possibility that Bulgaria would receive access to the Aegean Sea via free port facilities in the Greek city of Salonica. To ensure that Bulgaria's past economic dependence upon Germany would not be repeated, "Bulgaria should be encouraged to expand its world trade on a non-discriminatory basis and within the framework of such international economic organizations as may be established." An independent if pro-Western posture would be furthered by American support for Bulgaria's

[18] Boll 1984, p. 24.

[19] *Ibid.*, p. 34.

> participation in regional groups designed to "promote economic welfare and political security." In the transition period following surrender, "opportunity should be afforded ... for the establishment of a provisional government representative of democratic groups in Bulgaria as the best means of insuring a permanent government of a representative character".[20]

The Soviet Union did not object to these plans. It was the only one of the three Great Powers that was not at war with Bulgaria. In a "gentlemanly" fashion it ceded the right to decide the future of the Balkan country to its allies. The official policy of the U.S.S.R. was one of non-interference in the internal affairs of post-war Bulgaria. On this topic Professor Boll writes:

> On August 29, 1944, the last potential obstruction between the American-British draft armistice and the Soviet Union disappeared. The Soviet representative in the EAC, Gusev, informed his colleagues that he would take no further part in the discussions. Now all that appeared required to wrap up the Bulgarian surrender was the arrival of Bulgarian negotiators in Cairo, a prospect that seemed likely because concerted and coordinated pressure had been exerted upon Sofia during the summer months.[21]

...

On September 5, 1944, only a week after the Soviet representative Gusev presented the position of his government *vis-à-vis* Bulgaria, the Soviet Union severed its diplomatic relations with the neutral Balkan state, declared war on it and entered its territory with its troops, without informing its allies Great Britain and the United States.

Surprised and confused, the legitimate coalition government of Konstantin Muraviev gave orders to the army not to resist the foreign troops, and started peace talks with the U.S.S.R.. On September 8, Bulgaria declared war on Germany.

As often happens in history, a traitor "from within" was found. The Minister of Defense in Muraviev's government, General Ivan Marinov, had conducted secret negotiations with the Fatherland Front and assisted the *coup d'état* in the early hours of September 9. That morning the Bulgarians awoke to a new Council of Ministers. And that was the next in a long series of tricks.

On September 9, 1944, a government of the Fatherland Front, headed by the *Zveno* leader Kimon Georgiev rather than the communists, took the reins of

[20] *Ibid.*, p. 35.

[21] *Ibid.*, p. 36.

state. Konstantin Muraviev and his cabinet members were taken into custody and handed over to the "People's Court."

These developments were baffling to the majority of the population. People associated the name of the new Prime Minister with the military coup of May 1934. After its success, Georgiev had run Bulgaria for eight months. As soon as he took power, he revoked the Tarnovo Constitution, eliminated the parliamentary system, banned political parties and imposed censorship. Could it be possible that the honor of leading postwar democratic Bulgaria was bestowed precisely on a man like Kimon Georgiev?

The truth soon proved to be quite different. The 22-member government, in which all political organizations included in the Fatherland Front took part, was led not by its Prime Minister, but by the four representatives of the Bulgarian Workers' Party (communists), headed by the Minister of the Interior Anton Yugov. Its actions were entirely subordinated to the local leadership of the red party and its Political Secretary Traycho Kostov. He in turn sought the advice of the emigrant leaders of the BWP(c) - Georgi Dimitrov and Vasil Kolarov - for everything. The latter two high-ranking functionaries of the Comintern had been living in Moscow for years, and they pursued policies in the interest of the U.S.S.R. *vis-à-vis* Bulgaria, unquestioningly fulfilling the orders of Joseph Stalin.

Georgi Dimitrov enthusiastically applied Bolshevik practices in his native Bulgaria. He sent Kostov radiograms and letters in Russian with the instruction to carry out "spontaneous purges", i.e. assassinations of civilians, and "legal purges," or political trials staged by pseudo-tribunals. Dimitrov also demanded the deportation of families on a mass scale and the confiscation of their property, the elimination of political adversaries by means of concentration camps, the adoption of unconstitutional laws and ordinances, the establishment of a network of secret agents and informers in circles unfavorably disposed to the Fatherland Front, and departments for repression within the Ministry of the Interior and within the Army's General Staff, among other measures of terror.[22]

Traycho Kostov regularly informed the supreme leader of the BWP(c) about the fulfillment of his orders and about the general situation in the country. At the end of his reports, he usually reassured Dimitrov, "We shall hold your line," or dutifully asked the Soviet citizen who had left Bulgaria in 1923, "What is your advice?"[23]

This busy correspondence did not keep the daily newspaper of the communists, *Rabotnichesko Delo,* from writing the following on September 20, 1944:

---

[22] Sharlanov 1997, pp. 7, 12-13, 15-16.

[23] *Ibid.*, p. 54.

> Today's government of the Fatherland Front neither is nor should be a communist-Soviet government in view of the present concrete international and domestic situation. It is not such a government either in its task (program), or in its composition and methods. It is not a communist government in terms of its tasks for the simple reason that the issue of replacing capitalism with socialism has not been placed on the agenda. It is a people's democratic government.[24]

In his book *First Day - Last Day,* the social democrat Dr. Peter Dertliev cites a concrete example of the actions of the "people's democratic government":

> On October 6, 1944, the errand-man at the mayor's office in the Staliyska Mahala village near Lom, Petko Stoyanov, nicknamed Kehayata, made a tour of the village to tell twelve individuals to appear immediately before the Mayor, Asen Borissov Pavlov. Here are the names of these people:
>
> Milan Valchev - teacher, 41-year-old;
> Fidos Mladenov Tsenov - teacher, 28-year-old;
> Trendafil Damyanov - merchant, 45-year-old;
> Georgi Ivanov - teacher, principal of the Junior High School;
> Stefan Zahariev - teacher;
> Emil Stefanov - son of Stefan Zahariev, 18-year-old;
> Kiril Dimitrov Bechev - teacher;
> Yordan Daskalov - postmaster;
> Avram Popov - tavern-keeper;
> Yankul Simeonov Petrov - farmer;
> Marin Nikolov - farmer;
> Georgi Damyanov Vachev - farmer.
>
> To this day [until 1996 - *author's note*] these people have not returned from the "inquiry" at the Mayor's office. The former Mayor, now Professor Asen Pavlov, is retired and lives in Sofia.[25]

Calling people to appear before the authorities for an "inquiry" was commonly followed by beating them to death with clubs or stones, slaughtering them with axes, shooting them, hanging them, burning them, throwing them off cliffs into precipices or some other barbaric method of killing. The victims of the communists and their supporters were buried dead or half-alive in hastily dug pits in the outskirts of the settlements in which they lived. Records show

---

[24] *Rabotnichesko Delo* daily, September 20, 1944.

[25] Dertliev 1996, p. 111.

that in two months, September and October, 1944, about 30,000 men and women were massacred without a court sentence.

The author, Hristo Troanski, provides the following account of the atrocities after September 9, 1944:

> In Targovishte [name of a town - *author's note*], for instance, about fifty people were detained in the school of the nearby village Vubel. The fact that their number decreased by about seven or eight was almost unnoticeable. The latter were called out by name and taken away at midnight. The lawyer Todor Efremov, the priest Father Christo, the doctor Stefan Stoychev, the colonel from the reserve Ivan Bonchev, the teacher Ivan Drinov, and others had heard their names. They were all intelligent people who could not suppose that they would be shot just like that, without any trial. They did realize what was about to happen when the truck stopped in the wilderness of the area called Chireite. The men were unloaded from the truck. In order to be able to take aim properly, the executioners attached a flashlight onto each of the victims.
>
> That vulgar ingenuity went on to be discussed with admiration in the hallways of Yugov's ministry [Ministry of the Interior - *author's note*], and it became a model technique, which was applied often.[26]

Wolfgang Bretholz, a German journalist and author who fled from the Nazis and continued to fight against them as a correspondent of the Swiss *Nationalzeitung* and the Swedish *Svenska Dagbladet,* traveled extensively in Bulgaria during the fall of 1944. In several articles and a book he reported his observations:

> What I saw and learned in the small towns and villages showed me that the atrocities and tyranny of the Bulgarian communists jointly with the Soviet occupation powers had spread all over the country. The violence was targeted predominantly against those people from whom something could be taken, against the owners of factories and enterprises, property and lands, houses, workshops and small businesses. Every slightly more affluent Bulgarian was branded as "collaborationist" or "fascist", and if he put up any resistance, he was taken away or shot on the spot.[27]

The Bulgarians who had been murdered by Georgi Dimitrov's order of "spontaneous purges" were classified as "missing" in the state archives. The communist administration had taken the trouble to register their names meticulously because under the red system, which claimed to defend the equality

---

[26] Troanski 2004(a), pp. 175-176.

[27] Troanski 2004(b), p. 22.

and fraternity among people, the families and the descendants of the illegally killed individuals were subjected to discrimination for life. This practice had not been adopted even by the fascist and national socialist authorities.

Among the "missing" were teachers, farmers, priests, policemen, clerks, attorneys, army officers, doctors, booksellers, veterinarians, agronomists, industrialists and other people without any political aspirations whatsoever, but with a name and influence among their fellow citizens. They were a threat to the communists, who hastened to decapitate the nation by the physical extermination of its free-thinking citizens. The easiest way to get rid of them was to brand them as "fascists." That word was a sinister accusation, and the Bulgarian Bolsheviks used it with criminal irresponsibility against every compatriot who did not bow before their regime. They used that qualification as a front for the systematic annihilation of the spiritual and intellectual elite of their own nation, a typical communist strategy.

This is how the lawyer and journalist Milcho Spasov describes the most salient characteristics of true fascism:

> An absolutely mandatory element of that [the fascist - *author's note*] dictatorship is that a single party, serving as a conductor for the will of the LEADER, has a dominant position in state structures and society. The leader is usually also the chief ideologue, whose theoretical "works" constitute the law of the party and state (*Mein Kampf*) and allow for no competing visions of any sphere of human activity, be it of political, social, cultural or even religious nature. Centralized control is imposed on all economic activity without destroying any private enterprises. The secret services have their eyes and ears everywhere. The existence of a press that is not directly subordinated to the party ideologists is unthinkable.[28]

If that is what fascism was like, what was the situation in Bulgaria on the eve of World War II and after it broke out, when dictatorial regimes had become firmly established in most other countries in Europe?

. . .

In the beginning of 1935, the Bulgarian Tsar Boris III substantially extended his prerogatives in the ruling of the country. He worked behind the scenes to force Kimon Georgiev's cabinet to resign, and from that moment on he appointed the next Prime Ministers himself. The tsar also personally identified the ministers, who were not political figures but rather experts in their fields.

---

[28] Spasov 1998, p. 7.

In 1937, parliamentary order in the country was restored. Municipal elections were held in the summer in accordance with the majority representation system. In March of 1938 the Members of Parliament in the Twenty-Fourth Ordinary National Assembly were also elected according to this system, that is, they competed under their own name rather than on behalf of political party. As a result, 93 pro-government and 67 opposition Members of Parliament were elected; 32 of the latter were Agrarians, 8 were Social Democrats, and 6 were Communists. The parliamentary elections for the Twenty-Fifth Ordinary National Assembly were held in December 1939 and January 1940, and the communists won a total of nine seats.

At that time, events in Europe developed at breakneck speed. National Socialist Germany and Bolshevik Soviet Russia signed a pact for non-aggression and division of Poland on August 23, 1939. A week later, on September 1, Germany invaded its eastern Slavic neighbor. Two days later, France and Britain declared war on Germany. By the summer of 1940, almost all of Central and Western Europe was occupied by the German troops.

Joseph Stalin did not lag behind his first ally Adolf Hitler. He occupied a part of Poland and in 1940 annexed Latvia, Lithuania, Estonia and Bessarabia. He did not hide his appetite for Bulgaria.

On October 15, 1939, the government of Prime Minister Georgi Kyoseivanov, an experienced lawyer and diplomat, declared Bulgaria's firm neutrality. The next Prime Minister, the Professor of Archaelogy Bogdan Filov, who replaced him on February 15, 1940, attempted to pursue the foreign policy of his predecessor.

Even *A Brief History of Bulgaria*, a book from the communist era, confirms this:

> Filov's government continued the policy of non-alignment and neutrality. Hope that the war may remain far from the Balkans was still strong and it defined his ambitions to maneuver among the nations at war, to seek support now with the one side, later with the other, and to iron out misunderstandings with the neighbors.[29]

Tsar Boris III and his governments made enormous efforts to keep Bulgaria away from World War II. They were trying to find peaceful solutions to the nation's most pressing problems after the country had lost territories with Bulgarian population as a result of the Neuilly Treaty of 1919.

---

[29] Fol, Dimitrov, Lalkov *et al.* 1981, pp. 381-382.

The policy of the tsar and his ministers *vis-à-vis* Southern Dobrudzha was crowned with success. In September 1940, Romania returned the region to Bulgaria, as a result of diplomatic negotiations and with the consent of Germany, Britain, the United States and the Soviet Union.

Boris III was a deeply convinced opponent of capital punishment and of anti-Semitism. He used every conceivable maneuver to postpone his country's involvement in the global military conflict. However, Bulgaria was forced to join the Tripartite Pact on March 1, 1941. Nearly 700,000 German soldiers were along its northern border, ready to conquer the Balkans. Here are some details:

> It is interesting to know that Bulgaria signed the Tripartite Pact on March 1, 1941, at 1:30 p.m., and the German army entered the country at noon on that same day, i.e. before the signing of the agreement. In a conversation with the Tsar's Secretary, Stanislav Balan, the generals Jodl and Bodenschatz shared that Germany had a second option for its entry into Bulgaria in the event of resistance on the part of the Bulgarians. The army that passed through our territory to attack Greece and Yugoslavia numbered 680,000. After the attack, the Serbian army capitulated on the 9th day, which left the Bulgarian statesmen with the sense that their decision had been correct.[30]

When signing the military treaty with the Axis powers, the Bulgarian government did not fail to impose several essential conditions, including non-involvement of the country in direct military operations, and gave permission for the German troops to use its territory only as a transit corridor while they remained self-sufficient.

In a monograph Dr. Panayot Panayotov, who worked at the Ministry of Foreign Affairs between 1942 and 1944, wrote:

> It was typical of the Bulgarian foreign policy during World War II not to digress from its main goals and strategies. There were deviations in tactics and temporary adaptation to the conditions of the ever changing international situation. However, Bulgaria basically preserved its freedom of action and succeeded in protecting itself from foreign political isolation. This fact was of particular importance in setting the trends in the relations of Bulgaria with the U.S.S.R. and Turkey. In spite of the presence of a nearly 700,000-strong German army on Bulgarian territory at the beginning of the German operations in the Balkans, Bulgaria was not occupied; the entire state and administrative apparatus remained unchanged, and the Bulgarian army was not subordinated

[30] *Pro&Anti* weekly, Latchezar Toshev, *Everything collapses without the Tsar*, September 1, 2000.

to German command. In the summer of 1944, the German troops in Bulgaria were reduced to 22,000 without turmoil or complications.[31]

On September 7, 1944, the last hundred or so German soldiers left the territory of Bulgaria, disarmed by the authorities.[32] This happened without military clashes or loss of human life.

...

Hindsight makes it easy to criticize what was done on March 1, 1941, by Tsar Boris III, Prime Minister Bogdan Filov - who signed the Tripartite Pact in Vienna on that date - and the Members of Parliament in the Twenty-Fifth Ordinary National Assembly, who voted to legitimize that act.

Outside the context of global events, it is similarly difficult to believe that the great democracies of the United States and Great Britain would join forces during World War II with Stalinist Russia, a totalitarian Bolshevik state that had committed innumerable proven crimes against humanity.[33] However, the democratic West had no choice. On June 22, 1941, Germany invaded the U.S.S.R.. On December 7, the Japanese air force almost destroyed the U.S. Pacific Fleet at the military base in Pearl Harbor. Four days later, Germany and Italy declared war on the United States.

Still, every compromise has consequences. Small Bulgaria avoided the tragic fate of states that were trampled under the boots of Hitler's army, but with its participation in the Tripartite Pact, it lost some of its international prestige. The U.S. and British armies suffered an enormous loss of human life in World War II. When they stopped their military operations in Europe, and the global community celebrated the liberation of the western part of the continent from German occupation, the eastern part of it was plunged into the darkness of misanthropic communism, which took 100 million innocent lives.[34]

...

Even as an ally of Germany, Boris III defended his country's national dignity and interests. In Europe he becomes famous for his insubordination to the Fuehrer's orders. Several times the tsar categorically refused to comply with the

---

31 Panayotov 1986, p. 89.

32 Rudolph Schreiter in a conversation with the author, Wiesbaden, Germany, August 29, 1999.

33 Courtois, Kramer *et al.* 1999, *passim.*

34 *Ibid.*, p. 9.

Nazi dictator's request that the Bulgarian army take part in military operations, and he probably paid for his courage with his life. One of the leading theories about his mysterious death at the age of 49 was that he was poisoned during his last visit with Hitler in the middle of August 1943.

A brave policy was put in practice in Bulgaria with the decisive help of Tsar Boris. The Balkan Kingdom became the only country in Europe whose democratic community managed to preserve from annihilation its entire Jewish minority of nearly 50,000 people.

In 1998, the Israeli History Professor Michael Bar-Zohar tells the unique story of the rescue of the Bulgarian Jews in a fascinating book. In its introduction he relates:

> On a glorious November day in 1948, a long freight train ground to a halt at the Bulgarian-Yugoslav border. More than a thousand Jewish passengers stepped out of the crowded boxcars, stretching their numb limbs. The night before, at Sofia station, they had set off on their long journey to a secluded harbor in neighboring Yugoslavia, to board a ship sailing for Israel. They were part of a massive wave of immigration that, in a short period of time, would carry to the newborn state of Israel more than 90 percent of Bulgaria's fifty thousand Jews.
>
> I was one of these thousands, a little boy immigrating to Israel with my parents and baby sister. I jumped out of the dark, foul-smelling boxcar and looked around. We were in a lush green valley, breathtakingly beautiful. Alongside the locomotive, Bulgarian and Yugoslav border guards examined stacks of papers. Beyond them lay Yugoslavia.
>
> Almost as one our fellow passengers turned back, casting a long last look at the land of their birth. One began to sing, another joined him, then a third, and a fourth. Soon, hundreds of voices, male and female, young and old, joined together and echoed down the valley. They sang a tuneful Bulgarian anthem, "Mila Rodino" ("Dear Homeland").
>
> "Dear homeland," the huge choir sang with deep emotion, "you're paradise on earth. Your beauty, your charm, are endless."
>
> I remember looking up at my parents. Both were crying. Many people, standing beside us, were singing with hoarse, choking voices, tears streaming down their faces.
>
> "Why do you cry?" I asked my parents.
>
> "Because we love this country," my father said softly. "It's been good to us.[35]

We remembered the friends we had left behind, our homes, schools, and neighborhoods.

---

[35] Bar-Zohar 1998, pp. vii-viii.

And most of all we remembered our rescue from the Holocaust.

Many recall, to this very day, that dreadful night in March 1943, when we were ordered to pack a few belongings into a bag and get ready to be taken away by the police. We remember the tragedy of the Thracian and Macedonian Jews who were deported, through Bulgarian territory, to the death factories of Treblinka. We can still describe the long trains of boxcars waiting for the Bulgarian Jews at the railway stations. We remember the crying, the despair, the terrible feeling of doom and impending death, and the ominous mention of "camps in Poland", which meant cruel annihilation.

But we were not taken away. The boxcars left the stations, empty. We didn't know exactly what had happened, but the Jews of Bulgaria were saved at the very last minute.

In May 1943 a second deportation attempt was made, and the orders were canceled once again. Not one Bulgarian Jew was deported from the kingdom. The entire Jewish community survived the war, beyond Hitler's grasp.[36]

Clearly the love Dr. Bar-Zohar had for the country of his birth and for its people did not fade over the years:

"In Bulgaria there was no anti-Semitism in the conventional sense of the word," German jurists noted after the war. "My impression of the Bulgarians," said the former Swedish commercial attaché Utgren, "is that anti-Semitism is foreign to them and they regard deportation or other measures against anybody because of religious reasons as something absolutely illegal".[37]

The Bulgarian intellectual and political elite was even more tolerant. Most of the intellectuals and statesmen embraced, with fervent devotion, the goal of making the Bulgarian society one of the most enlightened in the world. They were extremely proud of their Constitution, which guaranteed absolute equality of minorities. They regarded its humane principles with a very innocent, Bulgarian idealism, bordering on naiveté. [38]

The last lines of his profound inquiry summarize the unparalleled achievement of tiny Bulgaria's standing up to Hitler and saving its Jewish minority:

Boris' actions in March and in May of 1943 were triggered by Peshev [Deputy Speaker of the Twenty-Fifth Ordinary National Assembly - *author's note*], Stefan [Bishop of Sofia - *author's note*], and other brave Bulgarians.

[36] *Ibid.*, p. ix.

[37] *Ibid.*, p. 260.

[38] *Ibid.*, pp. 261-262.

> Without them, the Bulgarian Jews were doomed. However the final responsibility was the king's, and his decisions saved the Jews of Bulgaria.
>
> Not one Bulgarian Jew was sent to the death camps of Poland.
>
> The Bulgarian Jews became the only Jewish community in the Nazi sphere of influence whose number increased during World War II.[39]

It is ironic that most of the heroes of this drama were soon cruelly punished by the new rulers of the country, the communists.

...

The nationwide movement to defend the Bulgarian Jews, as well as the victorious struggle of the country's leaders, intellectuals and heads of the Bulgarian Orthodox Church to save them from Hitler's death camps, furnished additional proof that there was no fascist dictatorship in the Kingdom of Bulgaria, but a free and freedom-loving civil society.

The situation would be very different four decades later. During the communist regime only an insignificant number of Bulgarians would dare publicly to defend nearly a million Bulgarian Turks who were subjected to coercive assimilation. In order to avoid prison, or at least in order to preserve their jobs, in the 1980s the subjects of the People's Republic of Bulgaria had to pretend that they did not notice the persecution and humiliation of the Moslem minority.

For decades the communists deliberately kept silent about the fact that the Bulgarian Jews were saved by the three worst enemies of their regime: the church, the royal court, and pro-German politicians. Whenever the subject was raised, they invented all kinds of stories. One of the most ridiculous of them was that the Jews in Bulgaria were saved by the young communist Todor Zhivkov,[40] that very same Zhivkov who took it upon himself to change the names of the Turks in the country in his capacity of dictator.

The communists concealed another fact as well. Their party, BWP(c), guided and financed by the Soviet Union, received the news of the Stalin-Hitler pact in August 1939 enthusiastically, because this was what their Kremlin master wanted. It intensified domestic terrorist activities only after Nazi Germany attacked the Soviet Union on June 22, 1941.[41] Hence, the tragedy of Bulgaria's modern history consisted of the bitter truth that its communists were actually not Bulgarian but Soviet in their allegiances. They did not work for the welfare

---

[39] *Ibid.*, p. 268.

[40] *Ibid.*, pp. 255-256.

[41] Dany Chakalova, *Notes and Commentaries*, 2000, personal archive.

of their own countrymen but for the U.S.S.R. and its international interests. Radical communist ideas never had deep roots in the local social milieu.

...

In 1885, Dimitar Blagoev returned to Bulgaria after spending many years in retrograde Russia. He was the first to spread the theories of the Russian and European nihilists, communists and socialists in his native land that had just been liberated from Ottoman domination.

The famous freedom fighter, statesman, journalist, and writer of non-fiction, Zahari Stoyanov, published his well-known article "Socialism in Bulgaria" in the *Svoboda* [Freedom] newspaper in 1887. In that masterpiece he pointed out that while patriotic citizens were laying the foundations of the modern democratic Third Bulgarian Kingdom, a handful of their compatriots, led by his contemporary Blagoev, memorized even "the commas in the works of Karl Marx, Lassale, Bakunin, Chernishevskiy and other fathers of the new doctrine, and proved not to be in a position to get to know Bulgaria, its economic state, the distribution of land, etc."[42] "They could not even imagine that a country could exist that would make an exception from Lassale's theories and would not need their prescriptions". They only troubled the minds of Bulgarian people with foreign theories and ideas that would prove harmful to their future.[43]

Thus Zahari Stoyanov accused Blagoev of being completely unfamiliar with the true condition of his birth land. He reminded the socialist, whose ideology had been shaped in Tsarist Russia, that Bulgarian peasants - unlike those in Russia - had owned their land for centuries. Stoyanov stressed that in the newly liberated state there was no cruel exploitation of the working masses by big capitalists and authoritarian aristocrats:

> In Bulgaria, where there is everything sought by nihilists, communists and democrats, we are simply Bulgarians; we only wish to have political freedom, of which we had been deprived for a long time, to remain masters of our own land, to guard our laws and to make sure that they are always executed by our most honest patriots. This is our message to all socialists and nihilists who are wondering why we, the Bulgarians, will not be incited. For the time being, we don't need it. Let the instigators go back to their fatherland [the Russian socialists, who arrived in Bulgaria to preach their ideas - *author's note*], where they can indeed bring some benefit. Regarding those of their followers among the Bulgarians, namely D. Blagoev, Mavrov, Zaimov, Marko Markov-

42 Stoyanov 1983, p. 213.

43 *Ibid.*

> Sakantiyata, and others, we are simply sorry for them, sorry that they remained blind to reality and to the situation in their own fatherland, having been carried away by the chimeras in some booklets written for Petersburg and for the Russian slaves. These booklets, the doctrine that is alien to the Bulgarians, the confused concepts, etc., entangled these people in such a net, that they took Kaulbars [Russian reactionary Major-General, Defense Minister of Bulgaria from June 1882 to September 1883 - *author's note*] for a nihilist and for a second Bakunin in Bulgaria, while the spying and thievery of the Russian government vis-à-vis Bulgaria was perceived as socialism.[44]

In 1891, Dimitar Blagoev succeeded in creating a small Bulgarian Social Democratic Party, which was not at all threatening. Yet, things changed drastically when that same party adopted the Bolshevik doctrine in 1919 and was transformed into the Bulgarian Communist Party. From that moment on there was nothing innocuous about it because of the changes in the world order.

The October Revolution was victorious and the Soviet Union was created to replace Tsarist Russia. It became the all-powerful master of the BCP. In 1919 Moscow commanded the small red Bulgarian party to take power through armed struggle and establish a "dictatorship of the proletariat" in the form of Soviet rule. It is undeniable that for 25 years it unswervingly worked towards that goal.

On June 14, 1923, the Secretary General of the Executive Committee of the Communist International gave orders to the Bulgarian Communist Party to set in motion the second revolutionary wave in Europe by preparing an uprising in the country, which had been plunged into poverty and depression after the end of the First World War.[45] The BCP immediately responded to the command and busied itself with its organization. Ill-fated rebellions broke out in several regions in September. Nearly 2,500 enticed Bulgarian peasants and over 1,000 Bulgarian soldiers perished pointlessly in armed fratricidal clashes.[46]

On April 16, 1925, Europe shuddered from another ugly crime. The *St. Nedelya* Cathedral in the centre of Sofia was blown up during a memorial service. A total of 150 people perished under its debris, among them 20 women and 10 children. About 500 other civilians were injured or mutilated.[47] For decades that assault remained the largest terrorist act in the world.

The investigation of the bloody disturbances in Bulgaria led to Vienna and Moscow, where the supreme leaders of the Bulgarian Communist Party, Georgi Dimitrov and Vasil Kolarov, lived like kings on Soviet money. These two men

---

[44] *Ibid.*, pp. 222-223.

[45] Konstantinov 1997, p. 219.

[46] Sharlanov 1997, pp. 10-11.

[47] Radev 1994, pp. 23, 26.

were doing their best to serve the U.S.S.R. and entrench not only the alien lie/idea of communism but also its disgusting reality in their native land.

. . .

Bulgaria and Tsarist Russia - later Soviet - were as different in their historical development, state system and social order, as they were unlike in size. At the end of the nineteenth century, the Russian state organization was the most backward in Europe. At the same time, newly liberated from the Ottoman Empire, Bulgaria was ruled by one of the most democratic constitutions in the world, the Tarnovo Constitution of 1879. This document guaranteed the rights and freedoms of the Bulgarian citizens, including equality before the law and universal voting rights. It gave Parliament the right not just to enact laws, but also to control the actions of the government. The Tarnovo Constitution denounced slavery. It established equality with respect to gender, religion, and national origin. It prohibited an aristocracy, except the members of the Tsar's family.[48]

In the first half of the 20th century, Bulgaria was still an agrarian state with a strong middle class. More than 85% of its population were real estate and land owners.[49] The national industry was predominantly light, and the owners of the factories often worked side by side with their workers. The difference between the rich and the poor was not as great as was the case in advanced capitalist countries. In fact, it was often overcome by the sons or daughters of urban or rural families of more modest means who equaled or even outstripped the children of the rich in terms of education.

In 2005, the lawyer Dr. Panayot Panayotov described pre-communist Bulgaria in the following way:

> Prior to September 1944, the Bulgarian state was founded on the Tarnovo Constitution, one of the most democratic and liberal constitutions in all of Europe. The social safety net was very strong. The economy was based on private business initiatives, which were protected by the law along with private property. The judiciary was independent and uncorrupted. The Bulgarian people enjoyed well-trained teachers, who were not subservient to a totalitarian doctrine like fascism, Marxism, nationalism, or Leninism and bolshevism. The youth did well in foreign universities, where they often earned their higher degrees. Sofia University "St. Kliment Ohridski" was a reputable European university. I still hold dear to my heart the memory of the celebration of its

48 Raychevski 2009, p. 69.

49 Luchnikov 2000, p. 27.

fiftieth anniversary in the fall of 1938, which was attended by prominent European and American academics.

Up until World War II, Bulgaria was primarily an agrarian state. Its main export was agricultural produce. An economic structure of such nature could not be changed through a revolution forced upon us by a foreign country. Many of the economic developments in Bulgaria were unique, that is, strictly specific to Bulgaria. The way in which the issue of middle class home ownership was resolved could serve as an example. That was largely made possible through the 1935 Law for Storied Property; the mortgage banks, and the municipal banks. That law was a uniquely Bulgarian law, allowing the citizenry to purchase homes with modest mortgages.

In my doctoral thesis, entitled "Collective Employment Contracts in the New Bulgarian Legal System," which I defended at Université Paris - Sorbonne in 1940, I wanted to demonstrate that Bulgaria was on the right track in its moderate approach to state aid and intervention. The enterprises of the Bulgarian Agricultural and Cooperative Bank, the Directorate for Food Exports, the export of rose oil, the set-up of the Pernik mines, electric power stations, and other undertakings supplied the evidence for my thesis. While the American citizens are proud of the "New Deal" programs of President Roosevelt, through which they overcame the economic crisis, the Bulgarian people can be proud of all the initiatives mentioned above, all of which were supported by moderate state aid.

Prior to the establishment of the communist regime in Bulgaria, 90% of farmers owned up to ten hectares (approximately 25 acres) of land each. The artisans and tradesmen were protected by a carefully worded law. The state encouraged and provided credit for voluntary economic co-operation, and 268,356 people had joined the agricultural co-operative society. A mere 6.5% of the gainfully employed were workers and most of them were associated with their familial agricultural property.

There was hardly any socioeconomic differentiation in Bulgaria. The percentage of the population owning no property was negligible even though the income of the proprietors was often small. In other words, there was no place for communism in Bulgaria. It was necessary that the peaceful development of the country should continue. We should also remember that Bulgaria was spared from the devastation of World War II. If Bulgaria had not been under communism, the standard of living of its population today would be comparable to that of the Finnish."[50]

According to the international reference book on trade and industry, published in France in 1934, Bulgaria was one of the leading countries in Europe

---

[50] An interview with Dr. Panayot Panayotov by the author, *I regret that Soviet Bolshevism was not defeated along with Fascism and Nazism*, *Pro&Anti* weekly, September 30, 2005; Panayotov 2002, p. 68.

in high-quality agricultural production. It exported considerable quantities of attar of roses, tobacco, cereal foods, flour, cheeses, oleaginous seeds, animal feed, sugar beet, vegetables, fruits, silk cocoons, wool, furs and wines. There were 142 metallurgical companies in the country employing 4,084 workers, 198 textile factories with a staff of 1,640 people, 55 leather and fur factories with 16,700 workers, 188 enterprises of the tobacco industry with 16,700 workers. A total of 4,330 people were employed in the chemical industry. In 1932, the export of commodities from Bulgaria amounted to 3,383,105,000 Bulgarian levs, and the imports came to 3,471,294,000 levs. That very same year, the exports to France were estimated at 89,554,000 levs, the imports from that country - 226,208,000 levs. The currency unit of the Bulgarians, the lev, was pegged to the dollar, which was exchanged for 139 levs. The lev was freely convertible.[51]

A German reference book from 1914 indicates that the average annual population growth in Bulgaria was 1.2%, or 50,000 newborn babies, while in France it was 0.2%, or 58,000 people. There were 9,452,000 goats and sheep in Bulgaria, i.e., nearly 100 per square kilometer, while in Great Britain they numbered 92 per square kilometer.[52]

The *Statistical Yearbook of the Kingdom of Bulgaria*, printed in Sofia in 1942 in a volume of about 1,000 pages, attests to the economic and financial stability of the country during World War II. It also shows the high level of professional training in the state administration, the social orientation of the public institutions and the material wellbeing of the nation overall.[53]

According to data of the League of Nations for 1939, Bulgaria was in tenth place in standard of living in Europe and in seventh place in terms of gross national product *per capita.* If there had been no communist rule in the country, it is easy to believe Dr. Panayotov's words that Bulgaria would have become one of the most prosperous states in Europe. Instead of this, now it is dragging at the bottom of the 27 nations belonging to the European Union (EU).

. . .

In order to justify their illegal ascent to power, after September 9, 1944, the Bulgarian communists lied that their fatherland had been poor, backward and isolated from the world. They repeated incessantly only two historical facts: that the Kingdom was one of the allies of Nazi Germany in World War II, and that

---

51 *Annuaire*, pp. 632-655.

52 Hickmanns 1914, pp. 43, 47.

53 *Godishnik* 1942, *passim.*

the state authorities had punished the underground terrorist members of the BWP(c) and the "people's partisans."

Phrases like "Bulgarian fascism", "monarcho-fascism", "fascist government", "enemy of the people", "war criminal", "fascist and reactionary" permanently entered the lexicon used in laws, ordinances, decrees, government statements, official documents, articles, speeches, books, comments and reports of the informers.

The writer Hristo Troanski accurately explains who was labeled fascist by the communists:

> For the communist leaders the word "fascist" did not stand for party identification and affiliation. In their scanty vocabulary, the word was used as an appellation that had acquired universal applicability, mostly for pointing a finger at the enemy, because the Bulgarian Communist Party (BCP/BWP), which was a militant party, could not exist without an enemy. Even if there had been no enemy, it would have invented an enemy and would have branded it as "fascist".
>
> ...
>
> Once set in motion, this concentrated expression of hatred for people with different ideas began to self-proliferate and multiply, placing the BCP/BWP in the paradoxical position of a party fighting against all who do not share its ideology. Fascists are those who have power, affluence and prosperity. Fascists are police officers, clergymen, army officers who pledged allegiance to the King, outstanding individuals in the arts, science and culture, the owners of factories and farmland, and the members of bourgeois parties.[54]

The satirist, poet and journalist Trifon Kunev was also declared to be a "fascist", "frenzied enemy", and "vicious oppositionary" for having had the courage to publish his creed in 1946:

> In this book I have collected a part of my protests - published daily in the opposition press - against the insult to man and against the robbery of his most sacred achievement, liberty.
>
> My decision to publish them in a separate book was prompted by the wish to leave a document of the resistance movement of the Bulgarian nation, which has always cherished freedom deep in its heart and will never be reconciled to the fate of nations that have been enslaved and deprived of individuality by both outsiders and people from within.
>
> The force of the resistance of the Bulgarians against political enslaving, which is an insult to their human dignity, is enormous, albeit almost invisible.

[54] Troanski 2004(b), p. 15.

> The Bulgarian nation wishes to preserve its freedom of labor; it wishes to be a master of its property and of its own fate, material and spiritual. It has the right to be the master of its land and of its state. It is fully aware of that right, which it is bent on acquiring in spite of some adverse circumstances.
>
> One of the most salient features of the Bulgarian is his rather rough individualism. The Bulgarian is unfit for herd instincts; he contemplates; he is original and he possesses a vast intellectual potential.
>
> Precisely these specificities of the Bulgarian character are the foundation on which our resistance stands firm, as well as our resolute refusal to become pulp that can be conveniently poured into the mold of political and economic daydreamers wishing to change the historical image of our nation.[55]

The communist government did not remain indifferent to the writings of that eminent member of the agrarian party. After his book was published, Trifon Kunev was arrested and sent to the Central Prison in Sofia, where he was kept for five months without trial. He was arrested again in 1947. This time he was sentenced to five years in prison. When he was released at the age of 70, his life and health were ruined.

. . .

It was not easy for the Bulgarian Communist Party to change the "historical image" of the nation and to instill "herd instincts" in the souls of its people. There were many strong Bulgarians who refused to be transformed into "pulp." The first popular resistance against communism, Soviet occupation, and the Bolshevik dictatorships in Eastern Europe, called the *goryani* [from the Bulgarian word 'forest' - *author' note*] movement, occurred in Bulgaria.

Professor Dinyu Sharlanov wrote:

> From the beginning of 1945 until the summer of 1955, when the *goryani* movement gradually died down, there were 28 armed sections and about 160 armed individuals, regarded as "vagrants" by the secret services. Most of them initiated local illegal organizations, while some created their own armed groups. At the same time about 52 armed sections of Bulgarian political emigrants entered the country by illegally crossing the border with Turkey, Greece, and Yugoslavia. Upon their arrival a number of them initiated underground organizations and armed groups with the purpose of organizing a mass struggle against the communist government.[56]

---

[55] Kunev 1946, pp. 3-4.

[56] Sharlanov 1999, p. 12.

Nikolay Iliev published the following:

> A document reporting on a formal inquiry of the secret services from August 11, 1951, specifies that "1000 illegal persons and members of the *goryani* movement were captured and liquidated" by July 30th. It is also noted that a significant number of illegal armed groups were under investigation by the intelligence services. Those data were taken from the archive of the State Security services and cannot be disputed. According to a number of inquiries and reports of the State Security Directorate, the number of *goryani* operating in Bulgaria at the time was approximately 1800. Their age range was from 20 to 30 years.[57]

Originally, the *goryani* movement was a reaction to the repression of the population immediately after September 9, 1944. Subsequently, it became a form of resistance to the persecution of the political opposition - including the agrarians and the social democrats - and to the banning of the noncommunist parties. The other major reason for the appearance of the *goryani* was the forced collectivization of the private farmland.

It should be noted that by 1944 Bulgaria was the European country with the second most developed co-operative societies of property owners, after Denmark. The original co-operative farms were disbanded by the communist rulers and replaced with Soviet-type cooperations, which the peasants were forced to join by means of threats, murder, banishment to concentration camps and more. As a result, most of the *goryani* were peasants. A number of former officers also joined the movement along with other citizens who could not tolerate the red regime. *The goryani* did not engage in personal revange or terrorist activities. Their aim was to build a national network for a future anticommunist revolt.

By 1955, the authorities had managed to cope successfully with the rebels. Step by step they eliminated all obstacles along the road to dictatorship and soon attained their goal. Out of the 7-million population of Bulgaria, after September 9, 1944, more than 250,000 people with democratic convictions were subjected to repression.[58] Thus, the Bulgarian Communist Party ranked first in cruelty *per capita* among the red parties of Eastern Europe that seized power after World War II. Deprived of political and moral leadership, the anticommunist resistance was stifled. After being the first to fight for its democratic future, Bulgaria later found itself at the tail end of the Soviet bloc countries in that respect. Other

---

57 *Ibid.*, p.15; *Pro&Anti* weekly, Nikolay Iliev, *The Goryani: The Real Resistance*, September 7, 2007.

58 Sharlanov 1997, p. 28.

states opposed the Soviet-type totalitarian system in the 1960s, 1970s and 1980s. In contrast, the former members of the illegal terrorist groups and the "people's partisans" steered the wheel of the Bulgarian state undisturbed for decades.

Who were these people? And what were the crimes for which they had been prosecuted by the Bulgarian governments until September 2, 1944, when Konstantin Muraviev's cabinet had declared amnesty for political prisoners and the partisan groups?

...

The partisan movement in Bulgaria had nothing in common with those in France, Yugoslavia, Greece or the Soviet Union. The others fought against the German army and against Hitler's occupiers in the name of their national freedom. Unlike them, the Bulgarian partisans had not declared war on a foreign force. They were fighting against their own government and against their own people. With guns and bombs in their hands, they risked their lives to make their homeland part of a foreign empire - the U.S.S.R. - and to bring the small BWP(c) to power.[59]

The partisans sprouted in the beautiful Bulgarian mountains only after Hitler violated his pact with Stalin and attacked the Soviet Union. At first, they were organized in small groups of three or four persons who were hiding in the forests close to their native places.[60] These groups consisted of local communists, criminals, expelled students, embittered youngsters, individuals with sadistic inclinations and young men and women abducted by force.[61] The partisans issued death sentences "in the name of the people" against "enemies of the people". At night they attacked towns and villages and killed peaceful citizens for personal revenge or on the orders of the BWP(c). Petty theft, armed robberies, and burning of archives, public buildings and private houses constituted an essential part of their activities.

In his book *Murderously Red*, Hristo Troanski offers an account of the only communist partisan attack against Hitler's army in Bulgaria, which took place at the end of August, 1944:

---

[59] Prof. Dr. Georgi Markov in a conversation with the author, Sofia, Bulgaria, August 25, 1998.

[60] *Istina* newspaper, Georgi Markov, *On the Ascending Spiral of Hate and Evil Deeds – the Crimes of the Communist Terrorism in the Memoir Guerrilla Literature*, March, 1993.

[61] *Pro&Anti* weekly, series of issues, 1998.

> Still, the greatest achievement was that of the partisans of Boyko Izvorski, namely the so-called youth division. They attacked the dining room of the Kocherinovo resort, which was a branch of the German military hospital in Dupnitsa, with grenades. In that location 18 German soldiers and one officer were recovering with the help of one doctor and two nurses. Most of the patients were war veterans with serious wounds and amputated extremities. That was so according to the account of the nurse Elena Manolova, entitled "We Carried the Sick in Our Arms. There Were Not Enough Wheelchairs." The staff and patients were caught unawares and attacked at dinner time. None of them were armed except for the officer, who had his personal gun on him. Still, it is questionable whether he could have reacted in time. That day Manolova was in Dupnitsa. When she returned to the resort after having heard about the attack, she witnessed a withering sight: "They said that the patients had been shot, but many were disfigured from repeated blows. One man's scull was missing. Another's eyes had been gouged out. A third man's nose had been slashed off...The metal vault, where we kept the money, had been opened and emptied...I did not see a living soul among the patients or the staff."[62]

The "people's partisans" also assisted in the campaigns of the urban underground terrorist organizations of the red party, referred to as "combat groups." The latter assassinated many eminent Bulgarians.

A Brief History of Bulgaria has the following take on the issue:

> The principal form of armed struggle during that period [the summer of 1941 - *author's note*] was combat-sabotage. The party organized small combat groups consisting of legal and clandestine communists and *remsists* [the members of the youth communist organization in Bulgaria - *author's note*] and their task was to sabotage industry, transportation and agriculture.
>
> ...
>
> Already in the summer of 1941, the combat group of young communists in Varna, led by Georgi Grigorov, set fire to a train using gasoline. The Varna-Sofia and Ruse-Varna railway lines were blown up. At the end of October, Leon Tadzher set fire to Petrol Ltd. in Ruse.[63]

According to Moscow, this subversive activity was not sufficient. Communist fanatics with richer experience in the preparation for civil war were sent illegally to Bulgaria:

> The Party's bureau abroad recruited volunteers among the circles of the Bulgarian political emigration to offer assistance in the armed struggle. These

---

[62] Troanski 2004(a), p. 124.

[63] Fol, Dimitrov, Lalkov *et al.* 1981, p. 388.

> were military men who had served in the Red Army, had fought in the Civil War in Spain, and had acquired vast organizational and political experience. On August 11 and 28 [1941 - *author's note*], during the night, two groups were unloaded from Soviet submarines on the Bulgarian Black Sea coast. On September 14 and 19 other groups were parachuted into Dobrudzha and in the Aegean region.[64]

In the summer of 1943, under the guidance of Bolsheviks sent from the U.S.S.R., the partisan groups were combined to form detachments that were well supplied with arms and ammunition. Their attacks acquired threatening proportions. There were no more than 2,000 partisans in Bulgaria, but they manifested exceptional cruelty in "dealing with the enemy" and often among themselves.

However, sometimes the partisan greed for material benefits exceeded their wish to shed enemy's blood. The story of the German citizen Rudolf Schreiter amply illustrates this trend:

> I shall never forget this experience. It was in the summer of 1944. For about a year and a half, I was a military courier and I traveled with a pickup truck back and forth between Bucharest and Sofia. I used to stop in villages and towns and made friends with many Bulgarians. I often visited Gabrovo. There I had been introduced to the families of several factory owners, and I sometimes stayed in their homes overnight.
>
> At the time everybody was talking about the partisans, calling them by their slang name, *shumkari* [those hiding in the foliage - *author's note*]. They were wandering in the Balkan Range, harrassing the people in the small towns and villages. The citizens of Gabrovo, who felt protected in their bigger town, which was the industrial center of Bulgaria, did not take them sufficiently seriously. They were hard-working and enterprising and they preferred to take pride in their recently opened self-service store. I, too, was pleased with it because I hadn't seen anything of this kind either in Germany or anywhere else in Europe.
>
> Yet, here is what happened. The wife of the factory owner O. from Kazanlak died. My friends from Gabrovo had to go to the funeral. In order to cross the Balkan Range, they rented a bus for the entire group of 36 people. As they were affluent people, the women were wearing all sorts of rings, bracelets, earrings, necklaces, etc. Their excuse was that they were doing it out of respect for their deceased friend.
>
> I was young and curious about everything. I decided to go to Kazanlak to attend an Orthodox commemoration service. I invited my best friends, the R. and G. families, to come with me in my pickup. The two husbands hesitated at

[64] *Ibid.*, pp. 388-389.

first. They explained, "You are a German soldier and you are driving a German car. The *shumkari* have become more active recently. We are going to be driving back after dark. They might attack you. Why don't you come with us in the bus?" Then, they changed their minds, smiled and added, "Let's go!"

We got into the pickup and set off for Kazanlak. I saw whatever there was to see, and towards the end of the day we started on our journey back to Gabrovo. I was traveling together with the R. and G. families. The others were in the bus. It was rather dark and my friends were silent, apparently a little afraid. As a soldier, I had no right to be afraid. Anyway, we reached Gabrovo uneventfully and started waiting for the bus to arrive at the central square. There was no sign of the bus, however. More than an hour and a half passed. Our anxiety grew, but we tried to reassure each other that nothing bad could have happened. They probably had a flat tire somewhere. The argument was that if the partisans were around, they would have attacked the German military truck, not the bus.

At long last the bus arrived. The men and women from Gabrovo descended from it, the men shoeless and with their heads bent in shame, the women without a single piece of their jewelry. I had been lucky. The partisans had preferred the gold, the precious stones, and the shoes to Hitler's soldier.[65]

Still, not all assaults ended only with material losses for the victims. Cruelty bred cruelty. Especially after 1943, when there were real battles between the partisans and the regular army, reinforced by the police troops called gendarmerie. The fate of the partisans and the members of the clandestine combat groups was not enviable, if they were caught. They were brought before the courts of justice, which - after proving their guilt - passed sentences against them in accordance with the strict wartime laws. About 370 people received the death sentence for terrorist acts and proven armed campaigns aimed at toppling the state. A total of 199 executions were actually carried out.[66]

Things changed after September 2, 1944. Dany Chakalova remembers the events quite clearly:

Konstantin Muraviev's government declared total amnesty for the partisans. Soldiers on motorcycles went to their groups, whose hiding places were known, and brought them the relevant documents. A whole partisan battalion from the Plovdiv region came down from the mountain after its commander declared on the radio, "The demands for a change in the country's policy have been met. Our mission as partisans has been completed."

---

[65] Rudolph Schreiter in a conversation with the author, Wiesbaden, Germany, August 29, 1999.

[66] Dyanko Markov and Prof. Dr. Georgi Markov in a conversation with the author, Sofia, Bulgaria, September 1, 2000.

> All members of the group were given free railway tickets to get back to their homes. Later it was rumored that the communist authorities took the tickets and destroyed them so as to hide any evidence of the amnesty before the so-called People's Court.[67]

The commander of the partisans who had made his peace with his state was most probably very naive. The mission of the partisans was certainly not completed. It did not matter in the least that their demands were met, nor did it make a difference that their own government had pardoned their acts against the law. Was it possible that this person had not understood that the Bulgarian partisans were serving under a foreign military command preparing to declare war on their native land? Had he not sensed that the dream in the name of which they had risked their lives was about to come true at any minute?

Indeed, in the morning of September 8, 1944, when the very last German soldier had left Bulgaria, disarmed by its authorities, the Red Army of the Soviet Union started its victorious march as occupier of the Bulgarian kingdom under the pretence of "defeating the Hitlerite troops."[68] Less than 24 hours later, the *coup d'etat* in favor of the Bulgarian Workers' Party (communists) took place.

On September 9, 1944, the partisans came down from the mountains. Some of them proceeded to take positions at the very top of the country's government. Others joined the ranks of the Bulgarian army and were promoted to commanding officers amazingly quickly. A third group of them preferred to become inquisitors or heads of departments in the Directorate of the People's Militia or in the Intelligence Department of the Army Headquarters. A fourth group went for a diplomatic career and started persecuting the Bulgarians who had remained in West Europe.

The time for open terror and revenge had come for the partisans, and they made brilliant use of it.

---

[67] Dany Chakalova, *Notes and Commentaries*, 2000, personal archive.

[68] Fol, Dimitrov, Lalkov *et al.* 1981, p. 400.

6. Upheavals After September 9, 1944

The *State Gazette* of November 6, 1944, published a decree entitled "Amendments to the Regulations for Appointing, Transferring, Dismissing, Discharging and Subjecting to Competitive Examinations of Teachers in the High Schools and in Secondary School Classes." It shows how graduate level degrees hitherto mandatory for high school teachers, were replaced as a requirement by affiliation to the Bulgarian Workers' Party (communists):

> Teachers shall be appointed according to the following qualifications:
> 1. Partisans and their wives, if the latter are not fascists.
> 2. Wives and children of individuals killed by the fascist dictatorship, if they themselves are not fascists.
> 3. Political prisoners and their wives, if the latter are not fascists.[1]

On November 17, the Minister of the Interior Anton Yugov, who had only completed junior high school, signed an order abolishing the educational and professional requirements for the following administrative positions: regional directors and their deputies, secretaries and under-secretaries of regional directorates, district governors and their secretaries, the Director and all bodies of the People's Militia, mayors, deputy mayors, and mayor's representatives. With the same order, antedated to be applicable as of September 9, the communist Yugov reduced the educational requirements for tax collectors to having completed the 5th grade.[2]

Following a report by the same Anton Yugov, the Council of Ministers of Bulgaria adopted a decree on "Labor Rehabilitation Communities for Politically Dangerous Persons" on December 20. The members of the Fatherland Front government ignored the fact that it was in gross violation of Article 73 of the Tarnovo Constitution, according to which "no one can be punished without a sentence from the appropriate court of justice, which has entered into legal force." Article 2 of the document reads as follows:

> The accommodation in labor rehabilitation communities [in concentration camps - *author's note*] takes place after a preliminary inquiry, a report by the Director of the Militia and an order of the Minister of the Interior.[3]

In the first months after September 9, 1944, people opened their newspapers in the morning with fear. The press was full of recently issued

---

1 *State Gazette*, No 245/1944, November 6.

2 *Rabotnichesko Delo* daily, November 18, 1944.

3 Ognyanov, Dimova, Lalkov 1992, pp. 23-24.

decrees, laws, orders, amendments to earlier legislation, signed and endorsed by the Fatherland Front ministers, totally disregarding the Tarnovo Constitution, which was still officially in force.

Most of the new "legal documents" contained ridiculous provisions whose purpose was to lay a solid and lasting foundation for the red dictatorship. Through them, highly educated and independently thinking professionals would either be liquidated or replaced with pseudo-intelligentsia obedient to the communists. Administrators, lawyers, university professors, teachers, and prominent scientists were indiscriminately fired *en masse.* They were subsequently stripped of their diplomas and civil rights. Books and publications of historians were banned, and so were numerous literary classics. At the same time, leading positions in the state apparatus, in the management of the economy, in public organizations, and in the educational institutions were given to people with no high school education or professional experience, sometimes even lacking elementary literacy.

The "legislation" passed after September 9th in the absence of Parliament by the red Council of Ministers was quasi-legislative. Still it has grave and lasting consequences for Bulgaria, relevant even in the 21st century. It divided the nation into two antagonistic groups of privileged and persecuted, communists and anticommunists.

...

One of the most frequently appearing words in the communist press was the word "purge," in both Russian and Bulgarian. It denoted a previously unknown, purely totalitarian concept, namely the dismissal of politically harmful individuals from their positions, or, more precisely, people falsely claimed to be harmful.

"Purges" were ubiquitous, even in politically neutral institutions like the Medical School of the *St. Kliment Ohridski* University of Sofia.[4] The daily newspaper *Izgrev* published the names of 25 internationally recognized Bulgarian professors, associate professors and assistant processors, proclaimed as "fascists" on its front page on November 28, 1944. The article was entitled "The Purging of the University from Fascist Agents Started: the first groups of professors were fired."[5] Only several of these people had participated in the country's political life. The "black list" included the names of eleven outstanding representatives of the medical profession.

History Professor Vera Mutafchieva elaborates further on the "witch hunt":

---

[4] Dertliev 1996, p. 111.

[5] *Izgrev* [*Sunrise*] daily, November 28, 1944.

> The Academy of Sciences was not spared either. The autonomy of universities and academic institutions was interpreted in a new way, and so was the tenure of professors, who very quickly became quite replaceable. Their jobs were taken by high school teachers or graduates of Soviet communist party institutes, or - in the best case - by assistant and associate professors from the University of Skopje, which had been closed. Quite often the motivation for appointing a certain individual was cited with touching frankness, "He wants to become professor in ..." Why shouldn't he want it?
>
> The changes in the "world view" of those university lecturers who had been spared by the purge would have appeared comical, if it were not so sad. Most of them rushed to join the communist party. Few of the new professors were old communists. The Fatherland Front committees in the university departments, party organizations, and Dean's offices periodically reported the course of the "ideological restructuring" of academia, assessing faculty members individually for their progress in this respect. Every academic who had managed to hold on to a position at the University signed a very detailed declaration about his professional activities, as well as about his parents' property ownership, about his public actives before and after [September 9, 1944 - *author's note*]. According to the laws of Vishinskiy [a Soviet lawmaker in Joseph Stalin's time - *author's note*], liability was not personal but rather hereditary and collective; therefore, an inherited apartment in Sofia or a mill owned by a person's parents in some village could ruin that person's university career.[6]

On July 8, 1947, the Politburo of the Central Committee of the Bulgarian Workers' Party (communists) adopted a list of regulations regarding faculty appointments at the University of Sofia:

> 1. In all elections for full- or part-time professors and lecturers at the University, our party activists in the respective department are to consult with the Personnel Department and the Cultural Commission of the Central Committee [of the BWP(c) - *author's note*].
>
> 2. In the event of a contest between anti-fascist academics only, the contest is to take place without the interference of the Party, leaving the candidates to compete with their research and academic work only.
>
> 3. In the event of the appearance of a reactionary candidate or candidates, the Party should intervene through the Fatherland Front group of professors to secure the election of the progressive candidate. If the balance of power necessitates it, the Party may convince an individual candidate who is a party

6 Mutafchieva 1995, p. 16.

> member to withdraw his application, so as not to split votes and to prevent a reactionary from entering the University.
>
> 4. In more complicated and serious cases, the matter is to be investigated by a party commission within the Central Committee, composed of representatives of the Cultural Commission and the Personnel Department, party activists in the respective department, and headed by the secretary of the party organization and one or two professors specializing in the field (party members) from the respective discipline. This commission is not a permanent body, but will be formed for each individual case."[7]

This is how the professors who were to educate several successive generations were appointed.

. . .

The Bulgarian Workers' Party (communists) thoroughly purged the student body of every Bulgarian university. Professor Mutafchieva offers the following description of this inhumane procedure:

> The question about the composition of the student body, which would become the intelligentsia of tomorrow, came up third. According to class and party criteria, the admitted students proved to be some very unevenly selected youth. Frequent purges, resulting not only in being expelled from the University, but also in suffering from permanent unemployment, deportation and concentration camps, sharply improved the party structure in the University.
>
> ...
>
> By 1950 the Dean of the Faculty of History and Languages reported the exciting achievement that the vast majority of faculty members were party members and the student body had also been purged to become "eligible for promotion".[8]

If you did not come from a "progressive family", i.e. from a communist or Fatherland Front background, if you had the misfortune of being the son or daughter of "former people" - as the communists insolently referred to educated and affluent Bulgarians - it was difficult in those turbulent times to experience any joy in your university years. The law student Emilia Staneva, daughter of a lawyer and a handicapped veteran from the First World War, describes how she felt:

---

[7] Ognyanov, Dimova, Lalkov 1992, pp. 115-116.

[8] Mutafchieva 1995, p. 16.

From my very first day [in September of 1947 - *author's note*] at the Sofia University, I could feel the sense of oppression and the post-September 9th atmosphere in the law school. We were all herded into one of the largest lecture halls of the University where they kept us for four hours. Each of the students was given a form to be returned on the next day filled out with the most detailed information about his or her family, including social origin, material status, occupation of the parents, party affiliation of the student and of the parents in the past and in the present, etc., etc.

The following day we returned the completed forms and were divided in groups of 15-20 people. Then those responsible for our groups were introduced to us as they took our fate as students into their hands. The word "fate" may seem too strong, but it is very precise.

We felt like someone was watching: whom we communicated with, how we were dressed, whether we wore make up, etc. We were always under the impression that someone was analyzing even the minutest details. Gradually the joy of youth vanished; the carefree attitude was replaced by the anxiety that you may have done something wrong, that you may have said something somewhere that might not be approved.

We were compelled to attend meetings lasting for several hours in the cold winter days of 1947/1948, when the lecture halls were not heated due to the severe economic situation. At these meetings, or "gatherings" as they preferred to call them, we were told that we must develop into "well-shod Marxists." I could never accept the word "shod," because to me it is associated with horses, not people. However, I never, not even once, dared to raise an objection, because that was the universally accepted expression, and the only consequence of such an objection would have been for me to be "black-listed." They kept explaining to us that there was no point in attending some "irrelevant" lectures, because that was a waste of time. "We don't need Heidelberg-type students who listen to all kinds of lectures for general education and culture. We need focused and concentrated cadres who will build socialism."

In the second year we experienced the most severe stress. Students were expelled *en masse* - not for "negative performance", but because of the "sins" of their parents. For example, if they had a father who was sentenced by the so-called People's Court, or who was a factory owner (that could also be someone who had a small workshop), or who had received foreign education (in a foreign language high school or in a university abroad), or simply someone of "bourgeois origin" (at that time everyone more educated, more cultured and well-mannered was treated as "bourgeois"), or if you had a nice home that had to be vacated so that some "comrades" could move in, which meant that the family had to be deported and hence the children became non-trustworthy, etc.

The meeting at which students were expelled was scheduled for the early afternoon. The commission of the "Grand Inquisition" read the name of the student who was singled out for expulsion, his or her biography, the "offences," and the conclusion. The student had to leave the auditorium immediately, not having the right to voice any objections. At first this happened in dead silence because we were all shocked and petrified, seeing how our fellow students were declared "criminal elements." However, gradually some students who supported the leaders of the meeting started shouting loudly "Out!" and "Enemy!", booing, and so on. The expelled students were young, nice and capable people, whose future was dead from that moment on.

I can't remember a more horrible day than that at the University. Shock and suffocating pain were raging in my soul. It seemed to me that something was being broken in me forever. A sense of helplessness and fear fettered thought. Fear before some invisible enemy lurking everywhere. You lose your faith in friendship, in sincerity. You don't know whether the student next to you is asking for your opinion so as to use it against you the next day.

The meeting continued until 2 a.m. This procedure was repeated two more times, after which they decided that the University had been purged of "dangerous enemies" and "enemy elements."

In the first year we had several professors who were erudite and well bred. I am happy that I had the opportunity to talk with them on legal matters. Their guidance remained invaluable. However, in the next year they were fired from the University as "enemies." The law school lost many worthy intellectuals.

With the professors who replaced them, there were awkward moments when they were hostile to you if you did well on the examinations. Their negative reaction was that you "knew more than the others", more than the "comrades who were forced to fight for our freedom in the forests", "you were able to speak with a rich vocabulary" and "you were not sufficiently involved in public work."

I hear some people say that the university years are among the best in one's life and that university memories are among the happiest. Alas, not everywhere and not for all![9]

After the university circles were thoroughly purged of "dangerous enemies", the communist party found a convenient and effective way to control the selection of the subsequently admitted students. The state leaders, the high-ranking party activists, the members of the secret services and the "active fighters against fascism and capitalism", as well as their families and their close associates, were admitted to the higher educational institutions with privileges, although they often had not completed high school.

In addition, for eighteen years - until 1962 - the youth of Bulgaria had the right to be allowed to take the entrance examinations for the universities only after receiving the "blessing" of the communist masters. This took the form of the notorious and coveted "certificate" issued by the district committees of the

[9] Emilia Staneva in a conversation with the author, Sofia, Bulgaria, August 16, 1999.

Fatherland Front or by other state and public authorities after inquiry with the services of the People's Militia. That piece of paper, which showed whether you had the right to go to the university or not, had become a document that was equivalent to an acquittal or death sentence for young people. Your whole future depended on it, not on your performance in high school or on your intellectual capacities. Just in case, in order to make sure that no "enemy element" sneaked into the universities, periodic purges were still carried out until the end of the 1950s. From the vantage point of the communist rulers, this was justified because sometimes an "enemy" managed to enter an institute of higher learning.

The life story of Ivan Emanuilov Ivanov, Professor of Cellular Biology at New York University, is an excellent illustration of these developments:

> In 1948 my family was deported to Pazardzhik. I enrolled in the high school there. I became the leader of the school's brass band and joined the basketball team. I was one of the dozen or so good players who represented the town in all possible contests. In April 1951, in a campaign that we subsequently understood to be on a national scale, my father Emanuil Georgiev Ivanov was arrested at 4 o'clock in the morning. We were not told what the charges against him were or where he was being taken. About four months later we received a postcard from him from Belene. This is how we learned that he was in a concentration camp. That meant a double stigma for me; I was deported and my father was in a concentration camp. The whole town knew.
>
> I graduated from high school in 1952, first in my class. My grade point average was 5.96 [out of 6.00 - *author's note*]. There was a tradition of handing out the diplomas for completed secondary education during a special ceremony, where the person with the highest grades received an award and delivered a speech. However, that tradition was broken for the first time in 1952, apparently because I would have had to receive the award and address the audience.
>
> We were summoned one by one to the Principal's office, where he handed us our diplomas. I was the last to receive mine. Students with much lower grades than mine came out of the office carrying awards. When I walked into the room, the Principal was slightly embarrassed. He handed me my diploma, looked aside, and said, "About your application to study in an university... forget it, it won't happen." That was my award.
>
> The Principal was correctly informed. In 1952, my right to go to university was taken away from me. I had applied to the School of Polytechnics in Sofia to study civil engineering. I did it through the Pazardzhik section of the Committee for Science, the Arts and Culture. Such was the procedure then.
>
> It was not easy to find work in Pazardzhik, so I became a porter at the railway station. I worked with the Gypsies and supported my mother, who had no means of supporting herself. We lived in utter poverty. There were days when my mother went to the church and brought us food that was offered

there during commemoration services for the dead. Some days we had boiled wheat for lunch and again for supper. On other days some kind neighbor helped...

Regulations were changed, and the next year the applications for admission to the university entrance exams were not to be submitted at the local sections of the Committee for Science, the Arts and Culture, but at its Central Office in Sofia and the higher educational institution for which you were applying. This time I wrote that I wanted to study physics or mathematics, knowing that there were never enough candidates for mathematics. I wanted to try what seemed to be the safest bet, because if that year I failed to obtain permission to study again, I had to go to the army. People like me were sent to the labor troops for conscription service.

I mailed my application and in February or March 1953, while I was still working as a railway porter, I was notified by the University of Sofia that my documents had been received and that the dates for the examinations had been fixed for the end of June. I felt like the happiest person on earth. I started studying for my physics test, leaving the preparation for the exam in Bulgarian literature for the last week.

Basketball helped me to go to Sofia precisely at the time of the entrance exams. A week before and during them, there was a national championship of the sports organization *Stroitel* [Builder]. We represented its Pazardzhik branch. This was a gift from heaven for me, because I was deported from the capital city and it was difficult for me to spend more than a day or two in Sofia due to mandatory address registration.

Halfway through my first week in Sofia, I met a friend of mine, who - like me - was not admitted to the exams the previous year. He asked me, "Did you see your name on the list of those allowed to take the tests?" His question struck me like lightning from a clear sky. "What list? We are allowed to take the exams, aren't we? I have a note to come on this and that date." He replied, "Ah, that, yes, I received the same card, but now there is a list of the people who may take the tests, in the courtyard of the University."

I went to the courtyard of the University and saw that my name was not on the list. At that moment I nearly had a heart attack, a stroke, or something like that. I was in a terrible state of mind when I returned to the hotel where my basketball team was staying. I felt mentally deranged, drained of energy. I could not feel my body. I was shell shocked.

I had nothing to hide, so I told everybody what had happened. The leader of our team, who was a gym teacher at the Agricultural High School in Pazardzhik, and whom I knew very little, came and started asking questions. His name was Georgi Aynaliev, now deceased. When I told him what happened, he burst out shouting and swearing, and finally said, "You will be OK." Then he grabbed me by the hand and took me straight to the Central Office of the Committee for Science, the Arts and Culture.

We stormed into the Personnel Department and Aynaliev immediately started banging his fists on the table and yelling at a clerk, "There must be some mistake here! And it should be corrected this minute!" He was shouting at her with so much authority and addressed her so aggressively that the woman was taken aback. Her shock grew after he took a communist party badge out of his pocket and declared that he was the party secretary of Pazardzhik. It was my turn to be afraid now because I knew he was lying. A thought even crossed my mind, "I will be sent somewhere, but I have no idea where." The gym teacher never stopped yelling and banging on the table. The frightened woman took out a thick folder. Then for the first time I saw that at the age of 18 I had a security file two inches thick! The clerk from the Personnel Department started timidly, "There are things here, which, you know..." Georgi Aynaliev interrupted her roughly, "There is absolutely nothing. These are all the writings of informers. You know what is happening in the countryside. There is so much envy. This is our best student in the school and in the whole town!" She countered, "Well, comrade, if this is so, why don't you write a statement and refute these things yourself?" Aynaliev did not hesitate for a moment, "Of course, I will write it immediately. Just give me a sheet of paper and I will write it here and now!"

We went out in the corridor and he said, "Tell me about yourself." I started giving him facts: date of birth, other dates, father, mother, sister, everything. He interpreted the facts in his own way; some sort of statement resulted, and he signed it. He pushed it into the hands of the woman from Personnel. She told him confidentially, "We'll have a committee meeting here at the end of the week to consider other cases of this kind. Let's see what will happen. Maybe it was a mistake. Check at the University at the end of the week. There will be an additional list posted then."

On Sunday night, the night before my first exam, there was a new list for all possible departments of the University, posted at the same place in the courtyard. It contained 20 or 30 names of persons additionally admitted to the entrance exams. My name was among them.

I had only twelve hours to prepare for the examination in Bulgarian literature. A friend of mine came to the rescue. We went together to the city park for about two hours, and we drafted a model essay. The essay had everything that was necessary: typical texts at the beginning and end, a typical introduction and a typical conclusion. That was all that was required during communism, clichés. We knew it too well. I refreshed my memory with some quotations from the poems of Smirnenski, Vaptzarov, Botev, Vazov and Yavorov. These were the names that were a safe bet for all exams. My "preparation" proved to be perfectly adequate. I got the maximum mark in Bulgarian!

I had studied for my physics test, and I got a 6 there, too. I was among the first to become a student of physics at the University of Sofia. During the summer, I was recruited for the basketball team of the University and started playing immediately. Basketball saved me from so many misfortunes.

I was an excellent student. My grade point average was above 5.5. I never had any problem with my studies. My poor father was the problem.

In 1954 we were informed that he had died in the Central Prison in Sofia, where he had been transferred from the Belene concentration camp. We learned later that he had passed away during protracted and painful interrogations at the State Security division in the prison, but at that time we did not know anything. No one from our family had seen him after his arrest in April 1951. We were only allowed to send him a postcard once every four months. All of a sudden they told us that he was dead. A militiaman escorted my sister and me to the outskirts of the Central Cemetery in Sofia where they had already buried my father. He pointed to a pile of earth and said, "That's your father." That was all.

What was the crime committed by Emanuil Georgiev Ivanov, for which he paid with his life and his family suffered for years? In 1935 he started working in the police as a lawyer. His last position there was Director of the Police School. I think that was until 1941, when my father handed in his resignation of his own free will. After a quarrel with the Minister of the Interior and Public Health, he decided to start his own private practice as a lawyer. Immediately after September 9, 1944, he was stripped of the right to practice his profession. Then he was deported from Sofia and subsequently sent to a concentration camp. There was no reason for him to stand trial, and no one ever charged him with a crime.

In November 1956, just after the Russians squelched the Hungarian Revolution, I went to a class at the University. Before the professor appeared, the secretary of the Dean's office came into the lecture hall and read my name and the names of two girls, fellow students of mine, before all 120-130 physics students gathered in the auditorium. Then she told us to go to the Dean's office immediately.

We got up and followed her. When we reached the Dean's office, she ordered us to "Leave the University immediately, this very minute, because you have been expelled." "Why? How is this possible? Why?" we asked in shock. "Go and ask Comrade Petrov from the Personnel Department." The girls started crying, and - together with Doncho, who was the only one among our colleagues who accompanied us - we held them up because they were about to collapse. Supporting them, we went to Petrov. We knocked on the door of his office, stepped in and said, "We were informed that we had been expelled and we were sent to you to hear why." He answered, "You know very well why. There is nothing for me to explain further."

Soon we learned that on the very same day students had been purged from all of the higher education institutions in Bulgaria. This is how the members of the Bulgarian Communist Party dealt with the fear that shook them when the Hungarians rebelled against the regime. Before the Soviet Union entered

Hungary and crushed the revolution with tanks our communists were so scared that they did not even dare to speak. However, when everything was over, in order to boost their own confidence, they started deporting families, dismissing people, and expelling students. All kinds of excuses were fabricated. For instance, one rumor they circulated was about anticommunist slogans in the men's room of the School of Physics. Supposedly I wrote them or the girls who were expelled with me.

I admit that back in the fifties I was so scared that I did not dare to do anything. I had grown up with the feeling that anyone at any time could ask me a question like a policeman and that I had to answer. I was constantly feeling some guilt, some anxiety, some responsibility although I had not done absolutely anything. Quite the contrary, I was active according to the communist norms, in sports and music.

When they sent me away from Sofia University, I went to the Dean of the School of Physics, Professor Asen Datsev, Member of the Bulgarian Academy of Sciences. He asked me, "Tell me, what is your credit?" I answered him, "Excellent student." "This is not important," he snapped back. I was so outraged that I got up and started to leave. "Where are you going?" the academician shouted after me. "I'm leaving," I said. "Why are you leaving?" "Because," I replied, "you, my Dean, have just told me that it is not important to be an excellent student in physics." "Wait, wait, you are a very interesting man." Datsev was not even angry. It seemed as if he wanted to tell me condescendingly, "Are you really so naive?" Instead he asked out loud, "Tell me, are you a member of the Young Communist League, do you take part in communist demonstrations, do you chant slogans?" "Is that what you wanted to hear from me? Of course, I can't afford not to. And I do. Because I'm afraid. However, I don't dare to stand in the first rows. I am not an activist, because everybody has put the black smear on my back. I play basketball, and I devote a lot of time to it." "Ah, yes, this is interesting," he said and added "Look, there is nothing I can do at the moment. Go to the army now, become a soldier. When you finish your conscription, call me. Things will be different then and I guarantee that you will complete your education." That was the most that the Dean could promise.

I lost one year. Then again basketball brought me back to the University. In June, 1956, I was recruited for the central team of *Academic*, the team of the best basketball players from all the universities in Sofia. That was an enormous honor for me. When I was expelled in the fall, Academic could not help me. But when the communists calmed down a little the next year, the team restored me to the School of Physics. The two girls who were expelled with me had to wait five more years until their student's rights were restored to them.

In the autumn of 1977 I paid a very belated visit to Pazardzhik, where I wanted to see Georgi Aynaliev. I was returning to that town for the first time after 1953. My friend Nanko found the address of the retired gym teacher and the two of us went to visit him. My savior from the old days was not at home.

> He was somewhere in the area, a referee of a soccer game. We waited for him to return home and spent a wonderful evening together. Aynaliev had almost forgotten my story. However, after I reminded him of the incident, he admitted that he had never been a communist party member. He lied about everything to the woman from the Personnel Department of the Committee for Science, the Arts and Culture. "But what about the party badge you showed her?" I asked him. He replied, laughing, "It was my wife's. Wherever I could, I used it to get along." "You didn't just use it for yourself," I added with deep gratitude.[10]

...

Bulgaria started fighting against Germany on October 8, 1944. The army fought the Nazi troops in Yugoslavia, Hungary and Austria until May 1945. The toll the Balkan country paid for victory over fascism amounted to 40,000 people dead, injured, or missing.

The decision of the Fatherland Front government to join the Allied Forces had been a just one. However, it also served another purpose. Sending all the troops - including the reserves - to fight outside the country allowed the new rulers to purge their countrymen with impunity. The national army, with its cultivated patriotic spirit, would have defended the people and the sovereignty of the state.

On December 4, 1944, the Central Committee of the BWP(c) published the following declaration in its daily newspaper:

> Without purging the army from fascist elements, there is not and there cannot be a real people's, democratic, national army. The Workers' Party (communists) hopes that all honest and patriotic officers will contribute to the speediest possible completion of the purge, so that the army and its people's officers can devote themselves unperturbed to their work.[11]

This text, entitled "The Workers' Party (Communists) and the Officers," was menacing both with its content and its language. Was the party suggesting that red soldiers and officers should assassinate the others during military operations? Was it not shameful that the Russian word for "purge" was used with such ease when it concerned human lives?

However immoral the purge may have been, it was conducted on the battlefield every day. Soldiers and officers who did not follow the Bolshevik doctrine were shot without a tribunal, by deputy commanders responsible for

---

[10] Prof. Ivan Emanuilov Ivanov in a conversation with the author, New York, U.S.A., March 18, 2000.

[11] *Rabotnichesko Delo* daily, December 4, 1944.

political training, i.e., former partisans or communist activists, who were attached to every military unit. Other military men whom the new regime found uncomfortable were brought back to Bulgaria under arrest, to be thrown into prisons or sent to concentration camps. Most army officers who survived the war and came home became victims of staged political trials. The least that they were subjected to was demotion, dismissal from the army, or deportation with their families.[12]

Gocho Chakalov, a liaison officer with the U.S. Allied Control Commission in Bulgaria, wrote about the time after September 9, 1944, in his memoirs:

> In the meantime, the militia had plans to arrest some officers who were coming back from the front line and who were to be handed over to the "people's court". These officers were fully aware of the fate awaiting them in Bulgaria, but none of them had even a fleeting thought of crossing over the line on the battlefield and saving their lives. The soldiers loved their officers. One of them was arrested and taken into custody in the corner building in Slaveykov Square, which was turned into one of the numerous stations of the militia. Soldiers gathered in the square, with machine guns pointed at the windows of the detention center. A lonely tank was moving from Tsar Osbovoditel Boulevard down Levski Street in the direction of the square. The situation was critical. At that moment, the officer in question appeared at a wide open window and asked the soldiers to go away. His argument was that it is not right for one Bulgarian to be saved by Bulgarians shooting at other Bulgarians.
>
> Naturally, the resolution of that particular incident did not solve the problems of the army, which had enjoyed the love and respect of the nation. The army was not a trustworthy supporter of the so-called "people's rule." If it had not been for the tacit (but not inactive) presence of the Soviet Army in the country, the developments would probably have been much like what happened in Hungary after First World War, after the two years of rule by the communists of Bela Kun.[13]

Bulgaria did not have Hungary's luck. The troops of the Third Ukrainian Front had settled smugly onto its territory. While they were resting and enjoying the free delicious food, the Bulgarian Workers' Party (communists) was active and tireless.

Professor Dinyu Sharlanov elaborates on this in his book *The Tyranny: Victims and Executioners*:

---

[12] Dyanko Markov in a conversation with the author, Sofia, Bulgaria, August 25, 1998.

[13] Chakalov 1993, p. 80.

> According to the report of the Minister of Justice [Mincho Neychev, a communist - *author's note*] of May 1945, during the "spontaneous purge" from September to the middle of October of 1944 the number of the soldiers, sergeants, majors and officers [who were killed - *author's note*], together with those sentenced to death by the so-called People's Court, totaled 1,282 people. During the same period, according to Colonel Georgi Damyanov, Head of the Military Department of the Central Committee of the BWP(c), 720 partisans and former political prisoners were given officer's ranks, although many of them had no secondary school education or any military training whatsoever. By the beginning of 1946, a general's rank had been given to 41 former political emigrants to the Soviet Union and to 8 reservists and active officers who participated in the military coup on September 9, 1944.[14]

> In the summer of 1946, 5,000 out of a total of 5,500 officers in the Bulgarian army were dismissed. In order to provide some explanation for these dismissals to the Allied Control Commission and to the Bulgarian public, trials were staged among the active officers following the instructions of Georgi Dimitrov. The official explanation was that the officers were getting organized in order to bring down the Fatherland Front rule.[15]

The political trials were assisted by special legislation. On March 17, 1945, a "Decree on the Protection of the People's Rule" was enforced. It was supported unanimously by all parties in the coalition government of the Fatherland Front. It contained sixteen repressive articles, six of which provided for capital punishment.

For several years, that piece of legislation permitted the physical elimination or imprisonment of the active opponents of communism in Bulgaria. The irony is that several of the politicians who voted for it later also became its victims.

Its Article 1 was most frequently referred to:

> Whoever forms or leads, in the country or abroad, any organization with fascist ideology, which has set for itself the aim to bring down, undermine or weaken the rule of the Fatherland Front [a regime established not through democratic means but by a military coup - *author's note*], shall be punished with life imprisonment or death. The members of such organizations shall be punished with prison sentences of no less than 5 years.[16]

---

14 Sharlanov 1997, p. 72.

15 *Ibid.*, p. 268.; Racho Stanimirov, *Memoirs or Reproduction of the Truth.*

16 Ognyanov, Dimova, Lalkov 1992, pp. 29-30.

Articles 2, 3 and 4 describe the actions of the members of the illegal combat groups and the partisans prior to September 9, 1944. Nevertheless, this did not prevent the legislators from insisting on capital punishment for others employing the same tactics:

> Article 2. Whoever destroys military materials, installations, water tanks, railway, postal, telegraph, telephone and mining equipment, water-treatment or sewage installations, state-owned or public buildings, etc., as well as whoever destroys or plunders public food reserves and other materials, shall be punished with life imprisonment, or, in severe cases, with death.
>
> Article 3. Whoever attempts to organize a *coup d'etat* or a rebellion, insurgence, terrorist act or any other similar crime posing a threat to society, pursuing the aim stipulated under Article 1, shall be punished with severe prison sentences or death, and the leaders and the organizers shall be punished with death.
>
> Article 4. Whoever leaves his permanent residence and joins or signs into a group organized and armed for the purpose of committing a crime under the present decree shall be punished with life imprisonment or death.[17]

...

In spite of the physical and administrative terror that followed immediately after September 9, 1944, the new Bulgarian masters still faced some obstacles at the beginning of their rule. Not all levels of the state apparatus were thoroughly purged. The country was a constitutional monarchy, and the Fatherland Front government was not internationally recognized. The citizens, although frightened and disturbed, had not yet been coerced into silence. Many openly opposed the oppressive regime.

Any kind of resistance could easily be crushed by the soldiers of the Soviet occupation army, threatening the people of Bulgaria. However, the international situation did not allow for aggressive intervention of that type. The U.S.S.R. was an ally of the Western democracies and it had to exercise some constraint, at least ostensibly.

The agrarian leader Nikola Petkov, the social democrat Grigor Cheshmedzhiev, and the lawyer and finance professional Petko Stoyanov tried to take advantage of that situation. In the summer of 1945 they handed in their resignations as government ministers in Kimon Georgiev's government and left the Fatherland Front together with their followers. Subsequently they founded opposition parties: the Bulgarian Agrarian People's Union - *Nikola Petkov* (BZNS

---

[17] *Ibid.*, p. 30.

- *N. Petkov*), the Bulgarian Workers' Social Democratic Party (united) (BWSDP(u)) of Kosta Lulchev, and the group of independent intellectuals led by Professor Stoyanov. The Democratic Party, which refused to join the Fatherland Front in 1943, also came out in open opposition to the government after its leader Nikola Mushanov served a one-year prison sentence from the "People's Court" as a member of Konstantin Muraviev's Government. Dimitar Gichev, who shared Mushanov's fate, supported the BZNS - *N. Petkov* by annexing to it his wing known as BZNS *Vrabcha-1*. The Radical Party (united) also declared itself in opposition to the Fatherland Front.

At the end of August 1945, Joseph Stalin sent a letter to the leaders of the BWP(c), in which he ordered them to legalize the opposition, so that the red party would be able "to have a grip on it and to force it to be loyal."[18] With his typical cynicism, the world communist leader assured his emissaries in Bulgaria of the following:

> You can even benefit from having an opposition of 50 or 60 people - you can brag to Bevin [Ernest Bevin, the British Foreign Secretary - *author's note*] that there is an opposition in your country.[19]

The Fatherland Front government followed the advice of the Soviet dictator. On September 7, 1945, it legitimized the opposition parties and gave them permission to publish newspapers. It had no choice. Elections were coming up, and the British and American observers in Bulgaria were very keen on implementing the Yalta Agreement, which stipulated that free and fair elections were to be held for a Parliament.

At that time, the Bulgarian Workers' Party (communists) was in the Fatherland Front coalition with the following parties subordinated to it: the Bulgarian Agrarian People's Union, the Bulgarian Workers' Social Democratic Party, *Zveno*, and the Bulgarian Radical Party. Still, the alliance was not large enough to win a free election. The BWP(c) had had less than 6,000 members prior to September, 1944. After a year of the Fatherland Front in office, the number of its members rose to 250,000. Still, even with its associated parties - the agrarians dubbed "orange" on account of the color of their banner, the social democrats who had remained with them, the *Zveno* people, and the 500 or so radicals - there were not enough supporters to guarantee the Fatherland Front victory.

---

[18] Sharlanov 1997, pp. 29-30.

[19] *Ibid.*, p. 30.

The only solution remaining for the communist rulers was demagogy, lies, and violence. First, the Prime Minister from *Zveno*, Kimon Georgiev, came to their rescue. In his pre-election speech on October 20, 1945, he made the following pronouncement:

> The new regime in Bulgaria is not Soviet, and private ownership will not be abolished.[20]

Although the regime was not "Soviet", it was strongly supported by the Soviet Union. "Big Brother", as the communists called the U.S.S.R., had made antidemocratic practices possible in Bulgaria. An international agreement helped.

The Allied Control Commission for Bulgaria, created on November 29, 1944, to observe the political developments in the country, was run only by five high-ranking army officers from the U.S.S.R., led by the commander of the occupation forces. The representatives of the military missions of Britain and the United States in the same commission were not given any decision-making power.[21]

This situation was the outcome of a brief controversy between the foreign ministers of Great Britain and the Soviet Union, Eden and Molotov, at their meeting in Moscow in October 1944. The dispute was settled on the basis of the fact that the Balkan Kingdom had been occupied not by Allied but by Soviet troops.[22]

It is hard to tell whether the British Foreign Minister troubled himself to ask Molotov how it was possible for the U.S.S.R. to declare war on Bulgaria and enter its territory without any coordination with the Allies. Indeed, just before its army crossed the Danube, the Soviet Union had assured the Western democracies that it perceived no role for itself in their further discussions concerning Bulgaria.[23] Real life proved the opposite.

On November 4, 1945, Joseph Stalin sent the Bulgarian-born Georgi Dimitrov back to Sofia, clearly showing that the power of the communists in the country was solidifying. At that time Dimitrov was a Soviet citizen, Member of the Supreme Council of the Soviet Union and had already served as Secretary General of the Communist International (1935-1943). His full devotion to the U.S.S.R. dictator was his most outstanding quality.

---

20 *Izgrev* daily, October 21, 1945.

21 Chakalov 1993, p. 73; Konstantinov 1997, p. 295; Sharlanov 1997, p. 19; Boll 1985.

22 Chakalov 1993, pp. 76-78.

23 *Ibid.*, pp. 32, 56, 128.

In *Dimitrov & Stalin*, a volume with letters from the Soviet archives, published by Yale University Press, the editors included the following text:

> On November 3, Dimitrov sent Stalin a letter thanking him for having given him the opportunity to work under Stalin's direct guidance for so many years; he had learned a good deal from Stalin, and he appreciated having enjoyed Stalin's confidence. "Of course I will continue to make every effort to justify your confidence. But I beg you to give me the opportunity, in the future as well, to call on your exceptionally needed valuable advice".[24]

Georgi Dimitrov had no reason to worry. Stalin would not forget him or the Balkan state that was occupied by his forces. Through his "valuable advice," delivered via his loyal agent Dimitrov and his successors, the Bolshevik leader would be the *de facto* ruler of Bulgaria until his death in 1953. After that point, the Communist Party of the U.S.S.R. would not change the course of its policies with regard to the People's Republic of Bulgaria.

. . .

In the fall of 1945, democratically minded Bulgarians were hoping for two things, the success of the opposition parties and the intervention by the victorious western democracies in defense of human rights. However, the expectation of help from abroad lacked foundation in reality. At the meeting in Moscow in October 1944, Joseph Stalin had already succeeded in convincing Winston Churchill that the U.S.S.R. should receive 80 per cent influence in Bulgaria, while Britain and the United States shared 20 per cent. The latter figure soon lost all meaning due to the presence of Soviet occupation troops.[25]

Still, the opposition parties fought against the new communist regime with vigor and courage. On November 18, 1945, they boycotted the elections for the Twenty-Sixth Ordinary National Assembly, justifying their actions with the fact that normal conditions for free and fair voting were manifestly nonexistent in Bulgaria. The U.S. political representative Maynard Barnes supported the statement of the opposition politicians. He declared that his country would not establish diplomatic relations with Bulgaria if the elections were tainted.[26]

The elections were held anyway and a Parliament made up of representatives from the parties in the Fatherland Front resumed work. With their docile behavior and total subordination to the BWP(c), these members of the

---

[24] Dallin and Firsov 2000, p. 262.

[25] The United States never agreed to this. For a full treatment of this topic, see Boll 1985.

[26] Chakalov 1993, p. 93; Konstantinov 1997, pp. 300-31.

legislative body set the tone for all National Assemblies in Bulgaria during the entire communist times. The only exception was the Sixth Grand National Assembly.

The newly-elected Parliament was headed by the lawyer Vasil Kolarov, who had just returned from Moscow after twenty-two years in emigration. He was the second most important Bulgarian in the international communist movement, a former Secretary of the Executive Committee of the Communist International and Stalin's active assistant in the political repression against Bulgarians and other foreign nationals in the Soviet Union. However, the "hero" was undoubtedly the first man in the party hierarchy, Georgi Dimitrov, the leader of the Bulgarian communists, a former worker in a printing house, who had only completed elementary school. As a Member of Parliament, he dictated the decisions of the entire legislative body.

On the Inauguration Day of the Twenty-Sixth Ordinary National Assembly, Dimitrov insisted on merging the legislative and executive powers with the political organization that he led. This entirely totalitarian proposal was declared to be a characteristic feature of democratic society:

> The third means [for the final consolidation of the new political order in Bulgaria - *author's note*] is the indissoluble cohesion between the Fatherland Front, the Fatherland Front-oriented National Assembly and the Fatherland Front-led government in their creative and practical activities for the overall consolidation of the democratic regime in the country, for the constant political education of the people in the democratic spirit, and especially for its young generations.[27]

As if to confirm his dictatorial convictions, Georgi Dimitrov urged the National Assembly "to cleanse the cities of idlers and parasitic elements, which are sponging on the money of the people and are bringing only immorality to society."[28]

In fact, this "cleansing" was already well under way without the intervention of the high institution. In those years, if a man, a woman or an entire family were declared to be "idlers" or "parasitic elements", they would be sent to concentration camps or at least deported from the place where they lived. All that was necessary for that was for some informer to have filed a "signal" about them to the special services of the Ministry of the Interior.

---

[27] Georgi Dimitrov, Traycho Kostov, Anton Yugov, *Speeches on the Response to the Coronation Speech before the Twenty-Sixth Ordinary National Assembly*, Publishing House of the Bulgarian Workers' Party (communists), Sofia, 1945, p. 15.

[28] *Ibid.*, p. 18.

The informers usually pursued personal benefits. These "honest Fatherland Front activists" freed homes in the cities for themselves and their families, after the legitimate owners were forced to leave with a few hours' notice. Quite frequently, the new settlers in such houses and apartments inherited even the clothes and personal belongings of the people they had evicted.

Dimitrov knew about this and encouraged the practice. He wanted to be promoted from party leader to leader of the whole nation, and for that purpose he needed more members in the ranks of the BWP(c). The world-famous communist was not worried that the informers may be the dregs of society. He gladly embraced them in his political organization.

Traycho Kostov, First Secretary of the BWP(c), a man who had spent seven years in Moscow in the higher circles of the Communist International, also gave vent to his anger on Inauguration Day. The scathing attacks of this fanatic were directed against the democratic opposition, which he branded in the title of his speech as a "Political Screen and Representation of the Reactionaries and the Remains of Fascism."[29]

Human destinies in totalitarian regimes are unpredictable, even to those who created them. In 1949, Kostov himself would be condemned by his comrades as an "enemy", sentenced to death and hanged for his activities against the communist party. In fact, hundreds of other communists, proclaimed to be "enemies with a party membership card", found themselves in prisons and concentration camps at the end of the 1940s, together with the members of the opposition whom they despised so much.

...

Back in 1945-1946, no representative in the National Assembly could suspect that he or she could fall from grace. Undisturbed by anyone, communists and Fatherland Front activists worked diligently side by side in the plenary hall. The builders of dictatorship passed laws daily and unanimously, disregarding the Tarnovo Constitution, which was still in place.

In April 1946, they introduced censorship over the opposition press, with the justification that its publications harmed the interests of the state, created moods and attitudes that endangered public peace and order, and disturbed Bulgaria's relations with other countries.[30]

Again in violation of the Tarnovo Constitution, on September 8, 1946, the Fatherland Front government held a national referendum on whether Bulgaria

---

[29] *Ibid.*, p. 29.

[30] Ognyanov, Dimova, Lalkov 1992, pp. 23-24.

was to be a constitutional monarchy or a people's republic. According to the official report, more than 92 per cent of the population voted against the monarchy.

How could this be possible, when a mere three years before the referendum, on August 28, 1943, the entire Bulgarian nation, including members of the BWP(c), had accepted the news of the unexpected death of Tsar Boris III as a national tragedy?

> In 1943, King Boris's death struck a nation - which though shaken and divided on many issues was nevertheless orderly and intact - with an explosion of desolation. The king's death exposed, abruptly, the hopelessness of Bulgaria's future. Boris's burial became a symbol. It was as though the entire nation attended its own funeral.
>
> How otherwise explain the extraordinary outburst of public grief, a display of unrestrained emotion such as had never been seen before in Bulgaria? During the days before the service at Alexander-Nevski Cathedral and the burial in the Rila monastery, immense crowds flowed silently toward the church's square, waiting patiently for their turn to enter and pay their last respects to the deceased king. Women made no effort to control their tears; men were not ashamed to cry; rifles shook as guards-of-honor presented arms.[31]

For decades people recalled the referendum's threats, forgeries and lawlessness. In the privacy of their homes, many of them would tell the truth to the younger members of their families, and when the free press was restored in Bulgaria after 1990, some of the witnesses spoke about that farcical referendum in their books and articles. Gocho Chakalov has the following recollection of the "secret" ballot:

> In the village of Dragalevtsi, for example, where the author of these lines exercised his voting rights as a citizen of the future People's Republic, the blankets forming the room in the polling station were placed at about two feet above the floor, which made it easy to trace accurately the voting preferences of the citizen who had walked in to cast his or her "secret" vote. One set of ballot papers were at one end of the room, the other set was at the opposite end. While no one could see which paper the person was putting into the envelope, it was clear which stack of ballot papers the person used. Besides, there were only three ballot papers "for the monarchy", with the ugliest possible black letters on them, placed like a fan on the table. After each free Bulgarian citizen exercised his or her voting right, an individual with a culpable

[31] Groueff 1987, p. 383.

look (with unspecified status in the electoral commission) walked into the room to see the configuration of the "black" ballot papers.[32]

The Bulgarian Workers' Party (communists) had "prepared" the referendum so well because it would serve an important purpose. By eliminating the royal institution, the BWP(c) removed an essential obstacle on the road to establishing its own dictatorship, as well as the total political and economic subordination of Bulgaria to the Soviet Union.

After the results of the "nationwide consultation" were made public, the body of Tsar Boris III was taken out of its grave and defiled. The 9-year-old Tsar Simeon II was exiled from the country together with his mother and his sister. His uncle, the Regent Prince Kiril, had already been shot by the communists in the night of February 1, 1945.

The referendum was followed by another crucial event. The elections for the Sixth Grand National Assembly - which had to draft and adopt the new Constitution for the just born People's Republic of Bulgaria - were scheduled for October 27, 1946. That was the climax of the post-war political struggle in the country.

[32] Chakalov 1993, pp. 97-98.

7. The Travesty of a Sequence of Trials, a Free Election and a Grand National Assembly

The pre-election rally of the united opposition occurred on October 19, 1946. Thousands of Bulgarians who had come from the countryside, as well as almost the entire population of the capital city, convened in the center of Sofia. The participants were inspired by the idea of democratically removing the pro-Soviet regime, which had seized power through a military *coup d'état.* That memorable and exciting day in October gave confidence to the parties outside the Fatherland Front. They understood that they had a strong impact on the people, who considered them their only resort for a free future. The event would also be the last voluntary gathering of thousands of Bulgarian citizens in the name of democracy for 43 years.

The communist rulers interpreted the rally of the opposition differently. To them it was a signal of warning that they had to increase the political terror. The Minister of the Interior, Anton Yugov, was at ease with that sort of task. The communist activist, with a two-year Soviet training in the "secrets of the People's Militia," turned Bulgaria into a gigantic concentration camp. Under his guidance, young communist members of the so-called Revolutionary Youth Union took an active part in "combat" units employed for beatings, while executives of the Militia continued their own repressive measures.[1]

On November 29, 1946, Peter Koev, a Member of the Sixth Grand National Assembly from the opposition agrarian party, wrote the following in a letter to his party's leader, Nikola Petkov:

> In a few words I will describe to you how interrogations are conducted at the Directorate of the Militia, so that you have an idea about the systematic, planned, and consistent policy of terror against the detainees, used to wring "confessions" out of the accused and to form the basis of charges. They crush you and bring you to a state of utter physical and moral collapse. At that point a person becomes indifferent to his fate and to his life, yearning only to come to some end, whatever it is, just to stop the unbearable suffering, which is not limited either in time or in magnitude. The collapse comes at a moment when you are defeated by the conviction that you are absolutely defenseless and that there is no legal basis, no law and no criminal liability for those in whose hands you happen to be. They themselves suggest the same to you all along.
>
> Unlike the usual criminal proceedings in court, here you are condemned first, and only then are charges and evidence sought. The lacking evidence is provided through terror, which may be physiological (starvation, sleeplessness,

[1] Dertliev 1996, p. 160; Sharlanov 1997, p. 15.

thirst), physical (beating, standing up for days and nights without rest), or psychological (hints that your relatives have been arrested, deported, etc., etc.)[2]

After describing his own torture, Koev warns Nikola Petkov:

> For someone subjected for the first time to such long-lasting terror, it is unthinkable to withstand it and not to sign anything that has been handed to him.[3]

The future would demonstrate the reliability of that letter. Several months later, having been "processed" by the State Security once again, Peter Koev became the central witness in the trial against Nikola Petkov and helped the communists put a rope around the neck of the leader of the opposition.[4]

...

The Bulgarian experts in torture had mastered the so-called "Soviet scientific method of conducting investigations" and applied it extensively against political detainees for years. In 1986, the attorney Dincho Dinchev remembered:

> In the summer of 1949, Dr. Atanas Kralevski disappeared all of a sudden. Neither his family, nor we - his friends - knew where he was. I started looking for him at the Prosecutor's Office. Then I went to look for him at the Investigation. No one knew anything about the doctor. A few days passed and only then we learned that he had been arrested and kept in the basement of a building at the end of *Oborishte* Street, opposite the Military Academy. That was where some of the services of the State Security and of the Intelligence Unit were stationed in those days.
>
> I was the first lawyer who went to see Dr. Kralevski after he was transferred to the Central Prison in Sofia. There he told me that he had been tortured during the interrogations. "How exactly," I asked him. He answered, "During the hottest days they closed me in something like a chimney, built out of bricks and about 12 ft. tall. I couldn't sit down because it was too narrow, and I could barely breathe. I don't know how long I spent there, standing in that chimney. Two or three days, it seemed to me. From a small hole in the wall they prodded me with a stick from time to time to wake me up if I had dozed off. Sometimes they would let me have a sip of water or would shove a piece of

---

2 Dertliev 1996, p. 175.

3 *Ibid.*, p. 177.

4 Sharlanov 1997, pp. 114-118, 128.

dry bread into my mouth. And someone hissed in the darkness, "Will you sign the confession?"

I asked the detainee, "What do they accuse you of?"

"I don't know exactly. I think it's for telling jokes," the doctor replied.

"And did you confess?"

"I haven't confessed, because I haven't done anything," Kralevski persisted.

I was astonished by his courage and tried to give him more strength, "Don't you ever admit anything. Don't admit before we have seen what the charges against you would be. The indictment will come and then we'll see what this is all about."

The indictment said that from 1948 until May 1949, Kralevski disseminated falsehoods in Sofia, whose nature bred mistrust in the people's government and disturbed the public, and in July 1949 he slandered the recently deceased leader Georgi Dimitrov.

Such fabrications were typical during communism. The red rulers meant to instill fear in the representatives of the medical profession by condemning and sentencing a prominent colleague of theirs in a public trial. Atanas Kralevski was perfectly suited for that purpose. He was a pulmonologist, well known in the whole country. After specializing for two years in Berlin, this excellent diagnostician was the first to introduce the *Jakobaeus* lung operation in the Balkans in 1936. At that time the surgery meant salvation for tuberculosis patients.

The unusual thing about this forged trial was that Dr. Kralevski did not plead guilty even after he saw the indictment. Theophil Stoyanov, the attorney I had recommended, refused to defend him. "Why, Theophil," I asked him. "Because he does not want to plead guilty," was the lawyer's brief answer.

After a number of difficulties, I found another lawyer with whom I defended Kralevski. His case was heard on November 11, 1949. I remember to this day that we were in Hall 22 of the Court of Cassation. A Russian colonel attended the hearings as an observer. The hearings were behind closed doors. The doctor did not plead guilty even in court. This thwarted the plans of the communists and prevented them from raising the noise they wanted in connection with the trial. However, their revenge was the sentence against the physician.[5]

The conduct of Dr. Atanas Kralevski was an exception. The "scientific method" usually yielded excellent results. Often the physical torture of the

---

[5] Dincho Dinchev, memoirs from the investigation and trial of Dr. Atanas Kralevski, 1986, personal archive.

detainees was combined with moral torment that was even harder to bear. Among the favored tricks was to stage a fake rape of their daughters.[6]

Thus, almost all prisoners submitted confessions that they personally wrote and signed, if not days later, at least within weeks. This was the way in which the notorious "confessions" of those days were secured. According to the legal expert Andrey Y. Vishinskiy - Stalin's chief Public Prosecutor and Minister of Foreign Affairs of the U.S.S.R. - the confession was the only necessary proof of guilt, on whose grounds the detainee was convicted and sentenced.[7]

During the second half of the 1940s, the officers of the State Security Service with the Directorate of the People's Militia and the Intelligence Unit of the Army General Staff were regularly sent to the Soviet Union to be trained in the craft of inquisition. In order to ensure "quality control," Moscow sent advisers with high professional qualifications to assist their colleagues working round the clock in the interrogation cells of Bulgaria.[8]

. . .

There is one known instance of a tortured Bulgarian citizen, which was covered by the international press. On February 26 and March 5, 1950, the newspaper *New York Herald Tribune* announced that an employee of the American Legation in Sofia, Michael Shipkov, was forced by the State Security Service of the People's Republic of Bulgaria to confess things about himself, his colleagues, and some of his acquaintances, which were entirely false. The unusual aspect of this otherwise typical story for those times was that on August 22, 1949, that is, the very morning after his "confession," Shipkov went to work and wrote a 8,000-word affidavit about his experience. After detailing the torture he had undergone, the translator informed the American Legation of the following:

> I wrote six lined pages, beginning with my unfortunate origin and education, my formation into a class enemy, then a description of my espionage with stress on each individual task - who had entrusted me with it, when, how I had achieved it, whom I had enrolled to help, how I had handed in my report. At the end, a plain statement of the purpose I had been pursuing - the destruction of the regime through foreign intervention. Signature after that - and although my deposition was controlled and checked paragraph by paragraph by the two lesser persons on duty, one of the superiors insisted that I

---

[6] Ivanova 1995, p. 113; Sharlanov 1997, pp. 30-32.

[7] Sharlanov 1997, p. 30.

[8] *Ibid.*, p. 31.

> add specific information as to my secret preference for the British and on my spying for them on the Americans.[9]

Michael Shipkov's affidavit was the first written testament to convey the methods with which the communists extorted confessions from their detainees to the West. In the early 1950s, when the USA and the People's Republic of Bulgaria discontinued their diplomatic relations and Michael Shipkov was detained under charges of espionage, the U.S. State Department publicized the entire text of the affidavit through the prestigious newspaper *New York Herald Tribune*. *Time* magazine also covered the case in an article entitled "How They Do It", while the National Committee for Free Europe published a brochure with the complete affidavit. It had been Mr. Shipkov's wish that the document be used against the communists if they should utilize his "confession" against the American employees of the Legation, his friends, and the acquaintances whom he had slandered.[10]

On March 5, 1950, *New York Herald Tribune* published:

> As a result of the publication, on Feb. 21, 1950, of the Bulgarian Public Prosecutor's indictment of Michael Shipkov, the American Legation learned with regret that this innocent employee has fallen once again into the hands of the Bulgarian Security Militia. Accordingly, the Department of State is honoring the request of Michael Shipkov to publish his sworn affidavit, which he concluded by writing:
>
> "I want the legation to bring to the knowledge of the militia that any attempt of theirs to make use of that statement of mine (i.e., his forced confession) will be countered by exposure of this...I furthermore request that this statement here be made public and used to justify both the good name of the Legation and my name in case the militia attempts to make use of the confession they drew out of me."
>
> ...
>
> The pattern of Mr. Shipkov's confession has become tragically familiar, whereas the method of how such confessions are extorted has remained a mysterious enigma. For the first time, however, a victim of this apparently hypnotic process has had the spiritual fortitude and courage painfully to piece together again the shattered pieces of his moral character and to reveal in detail how a man of integrity can be completely broken and forced to describe in his own words a fantastic story of imaginary crimes of espionage and treason.[11]

[9] *New York Herald Tribune,* March 5, 1950; Shipkov 1950, *passim.*

[10] *New York Herald Tribune,* February 26, March 5, 1950; *Time* magazine, March 13, 1950; Shipkov 1950, *passim.*

[11] *New York Herald Tribune,* March 5, 1950.

Michael Shipkov's affidavit was released exactly as he wrote it, untouched and without a comma or word removed. Days after this happened, in Bulgaria the former translator in the American Legation in Sofia was sentenced to 15 years in prison, charged with spying on behalf of the United States.

. . .

The autumn of 1946 paled beside the first months after September 9, 1944, in terms of the number of Bulgarians killed for their convictions. However, before, after and on the very day of the elections, the red rulers successfully applied their slogan, "We took the power with blood, and we shall relinquish it with blood." This happened at the time when observers from the Western democracies, which had just defeated Hitler's National Socialism, were still present in Bulgaria. So were the Soviet occupation troops. According to data reported in the opposition press by journalists, correspondents, and people from the towns and villages, twenty-two election advocates for the opposition were murdered, and thousands of opposition supporters were abused and taken into custody. The documented cases of violence, vote rigging, and manipulation of all kinds were stunning with their brutality.

Twelve days after the elections, the united opposition issued the following official declaration:

> The parliamentary groups of the Bulgarian Agrarian People's Union - *Nikola Petkov*, the Bulgarian Workers' Social Democratic Party (united), and the independent intellectuals feel bound by the historical moment to declare the following:
>
> - The elections for the Sixth Grand National Assembly were held under unconstitutional and fascist laws, and with unprecedented terror, including threats and forgeries before, during, and after the elections, and that today's composition of the Grand National Assembly does not represent the real will of the people.
>
> - This terror cost human lives, as well as the beating and suffering of peaceful and innocent people from the villages and towns.
>
> - The persecution continues to this day, and for thousands of urban and rural dwellers, there is no peace and security...[12]

[12] *Svoboden Narod* [Free Nation] daily, November 8, 1946.

This was how on October 27, 1946, out of about 4,250,000 voters in the country, 2,265,000 people chose to elect the Bulgarian Workers' Party (communists), guaranteeing its parliamentary majority with 270 seats in the Sixth Grand National Assembly. In January 1940, that same party had won only nine seats in the Twenty-Fifth Ordinary Assembly! In the 1946 elections, more than 600,000 votes were also cast in favor of the political organizations united with the communists, thus adding another 89 to their seats in Parliament. There is no nation that would be capable of changing its political thinking so quickly, without being subjected to violence and threats.

In his book *Liaison Officer (1941-1946),* Gocho Chakalov reveals the electoral strategies of the communists:

> There was terror everywhere and it was exercised quite openly. For instance, it was sufficient for a person to be visited by the mayor on the eve of the elections and that mayor to give him the right ballot paper and to tell him that it is marked in a special way, unknown to him, and that he expects to see that ballot paper among those taken out of the ballot box. Who would be the person who would set fire to his home for just one single vote of the millions that would decide the outcome of the elections?
>
> During these elections, in which the opposition also participated, the municipal authorities included the names of many unknown people in the voter registers. In addition, loyal party members received several voter cards each and cast their ballots in several places. I am not making any of this up. A young acquaintance of ours boasted before all members of our family that he voted eight times so as to ensure the victory of the people's party coalition.[13]

That victory was not at all certain. The two years after the communists took power were extremely difficult for the population, both in political and in economic terms. The Soviet occupation had already cost the Bulgarians nearly 24 billion levs by June 30, 1945.[14] Comfortably settled on the country's territory, the troops were in no hurry to withdraw. Stalin kept them there to guard the communist regime in the "fraternal Slavic country" to the end of 1947.

The Fatherland Front government was generous to Yugoslavia, too. It granted to its western neighbor financial assistance amounting to six billion levs and sent enormous quantities of coal, industrial raw materials, weapons, military equipment, building materials, and foods to the Federal Republic.[15]

---

[13] Chakalov 1993, p. 80.

[14] Konstantinov 1997, p. 299.

[15] *Ibid.*

The costs of Bulgaria's participation in the final phase of World War II amounted to 160 billion levs. That sum corresponded to the annual Gross Domestic Product of the country.[16] In addition, in 1945 and 1946, the Ministry of Social Policy and some public organizations offered financial assistance to BWP(c) members, amounting to one billion levs.[17] Within two years the reserve warehouses were emptied and the state treasury was almost spent.[18]

The quality of life of the population deteriorated sharply. During World War II, Bulgaria was one of the few countries in Europe whose population was not starving or suffering from real deprivation. Under the Fatherland Front government, food and essential commodities almost disappeared from the market and food stamps were becoming prevalent.

However, the insecurity and fear that most of the Bulgarians lived in were far more painful than the hardships in their everyday life. In the cities people dreaded the confiscation of their property, while men and women in the villages were scared that their land would be put into state cooperative farms, as was the case in the Soviet Union. Under the new government, which called itself the "people's power," nothing was safe. Your property, your savings, your job, and even your life could always be taken away. There was no reason for the voters to be so pleased with the new regime that they would elect 359 communists and pro-communist deputies to the 460 seat Sixth Grand National Assembly.

. . .

Although thousands of Bulgarian citizens were thrown into prisons and labor camps, where they were deprived of their voting rights, the opposition parties did well in the elections. A total of 1,205,530 Bulgarians voted for the coalition of the Bulgarian Agrarian People's Union - *Nikola Petkov*, the Bulgarian Workers' Social Democratic Party (united), and independent intellectuals, which amounted to 101 seats in the Sixth Grand National Assembly.[19] This result was "the largest opposition vote recorded in any Eastern European country in post-war elections".[20]

---

[16] *Ibid.*

[17] Mutafchieva 1995, p. 16.

[18] Konstantinov 1997, p. 299.

[19] Sharlanov 1997, p. 95; Dertliev 1996, p. 160.

[20] Dolapchiev 1971, p. 62.

On December 5, 1946, from the rostrum of the newly inaugurated Parliament, the social democrat Kosta Lulchev challenged the officially announced election results:

> It is not true that the opposition groups in Parliament have 1,200,000 votes for them. It is not true. The truth is that 2,500,000 votes were cast for the opposition groups in Parliament...And if only 1,200,000 votes came out of the ballot boxes, this is due to the ingenuousness of the administration and to those who organized the elections...The political history of Bulgaria has never registered 22 murders during elections.[21]

Just two days before Lulchev's protest, from that very same rostrum the leader of the united opposition, the lawyer Nikola Petkov, spoke about the election events:

> What can we say about the sixteen new graves in which valiant allied agrarians are resting for their courage to stand up and fight for the freedom of the Bulgarian people? Shall we speak about the vote rigging, about the torn and burnt ballot papers, about the issuing of blank electoral cards, about opposition observers expelled from the polling stations, tortured, and subsequently persecuted...
>
> Here is a curious case of moral harassment. The candidate in the parliamentary elections from Harmanli, Manol Zografov, was beaten before the elections. While he was in bed, he received a ticket for his burial issued by the Harmanli Municipality and stamped with the seal of the Bulgarian Workers' Party (communists). Here is the burial ticket that was given to him so that he can be buried![22]

According to the annals of the Sixth Grand National Assembly, once again chaired by the communist Vasil Kolarov, the Members of Parliament from the Fatherland Front met the accusations of Lulchev and Petkov with silence.

They met the following words of Kosta Lulchev with silence as well:

> The only appeal that can be sent today to the government and to the rulers is, "Enough, enough, enough blood of the Bulgarian nation spilled!"[23]

A month after the elections, on November 22, 1946, the Bulgarian communist leader Georgi Dimitrov removed the leader of *Zveno*, Kimon

---

[21] Dertliev 1996, pp. 181-182.

[22] *Ibid.*, pp. 177-178.

[23] *Ibid.*, p. 184.

Georgiev, and stood at the helm of the country as Prime Minister of the third Fatherland Front cabinet. The parties allied with the BWP(c) had fulfilled their role. Gradually, their members were dismissed from their positions in the government and replaced by communists. The Fatherland Front activists did not protest. The more active among them were rewarded for their contribution to the imposition of the red dictatorship with diplomatic appointments or well-paid sinecures in state and public institutions.

. . .

The real political struggle was waged elsewhere and between other protagonists. The battlefield was the plenary hall of the Sixth Grand National Assembly, and the warring parties were the Members of Parliament from the united opposition and those from the Fatherland Front parties, supported by the ministers of the government. Between November 1946 and September 1947, that battle was unusually vicious, including means not normally permitted in a Parliament such as insults and threats, often uttered in inappropriate and cynical language. At stake was whether Bulgaria would be a communist Soviet-type state or a parliamentary democratic republic with a free civil society and equality of rights. Here are some excerpts from the debates and some individual statements:

> Svetla Daskalova (opposition agrarian): The entire educational policy of the government so far has been a blatant refutation of the declaration made in the draft [of a newly proposed Law on Higher Education - *authors note*]. Instead of all citizens having access to the higher schools, today access is given only to those who have the blessing of the Fatherland Front.
>
> Dinyu Todorov (pro-government agrarian): Were you selected to be the victim on this topic?
>
> Svetla Daskalova (opposition agrarian): Others have been deprived of the right to study high science.
>
> Katya Avramova (communist): Prove it. Don't just claim.
>
> Svetla Daskalova (opposition agrarian): To divide the citizens into two groups, to give rights and privileges to some, and to deprive others...
>
> Petko Kunin (communist): Who are these "others"?
>
> Svetla Daskalova (opposition agrarian):...and to claim that you are democratizing higher education is already close to demagogy.
>
> ...
>
> Svetla Daskalova (opposition agrarian): No other power has given so many privileges to its party members as the Fatherland Front has done.
>
> Katya Avramova (communist): This statement does not sound convincing.

Svetla Daskalova (opposition agrarian): The higher educational institutions were filled with young people, many of whom have not even completed their secondary education. Professor's titles were granted to people whose only merit is that they are good party members.

A voice from the majority: Give us names!

Svetla Daskalova (opposition agrarian): Scholarships and grants were given and are being given to young people close to the rulers, while at the same time most of the village youths are outside the universities, only because they are good sons of their fathers.

...

Svetla Daskalova (opposition agrarian): Third, the proposed law stipulates the foundation of higher education to be ideological uniformity. According to that principle, the spirit of scientific philosophy, i.e., the spirit of dialectical and historical materialism, should prevail in all types of higher education institutions.

Dr. Kiril Dramaliev (communist): You don't understand these things.

Svetla Daskalova (opposition agrarian): All types of institutions of higher education should churn out young people with the same world outlook, with identical political convictions, a world outlook and convictions illuminated by the light of Marxism-Leninism.

Dr. Kiril Dramaliev (communist): With a scientific world outlook.

Valko Chervenkov (communist): These are your fabrications!

Svetla Daskalova (opposition agrarian): To demand that every professor develop and teach his discipline based on the precepts of dialectical and historical materialism is an encroachment upon scientific and academic creativity, academic freedom, and scientific freedom.

Valko Chervenkov (communist): Stop biting the ass of historical materialism! You don't understand anything! Sit down in your place!

...

Svetla Daskalova (opposition agrarian): Let us imagine spiritual uniformity for a moment: a multitude of university graduates who think, feel and act in the same way, a multitude in which every member is identical in his intellectual structure to everyone else, a multitude formed by one human being replicated dozens or thousands of times in other human beings, a multitude of uniform people, deprived of individuality...

Dimitar Kotev (communist): And not even one fascist among them.

One of the communists: What a terrible picture that would be!

Svetla Daskalova (opposition agrarian): ...a multitude with herd instincts and psychology.

...

Svetla Daskalova (opposition agrarian): Who gave the government the right to impose on the sons and the daughters of the Bulgarian people a philosophical view whose scientific value is still disputed? (Applause from the opposition). Who gave it the right to introduce university departments to teach the ideological views of one single party in the state-owned scientific institutions and in the universities?

Petko Stoenchev (communist): You are far too late.

Svetla Daskalova (opposition agrarian): What would happen in the institutions of higher educational, if every political party wished to have a department teaching its own political ideology in every institution of higher education?

Dimitar Kotev (communist): Do you have such an ideology?

Dinyu Todorov (pro-government agrarian): Ghosts and vampires [the surname of Svetla Daskalova's husband is Vampirski - *author's note*] cannot be tolerated.

Svetla Daskalova (opposition agrarian): Is there no danger in that case that the universities would be turned into the political parties' clubs for indoctrination? No! This path is uncertain and dangerous! It reveals the lack of even the least concern for a real higher education of the people.

...

Svetla Daskalova (opposition agrarian): A professor or a candidate for professor cannot hold a university position, or if he has taken it, he cannot keep it, if he has been branded as a fascist or an anti-people's scholar.

Katya Avramova (communist): The branding has not been in vain.

Svetla Daskalova (opposition agrarian): Do you know, ladies and gentlemen, how easy it is for a good Bulgarian to be qualified as a fascist or as an individual involved in activities against the people?

Petko Kunin (communist): Who is that good Bulgarian?

Katya Avramova (communist): Professor Petko Stoyanov.

Dinyu Todorov (pro-government agrarian): Have you been authorized by Petko Stoyanov to defend him?

Svetla Daskalova (opposition agrarian): Do you know how many honest scholars, good Bulgarians, devoted to cultural advancement, would remain out of the universities only because ill-intentioned party activists may accuse them of fascist or anti-national activities, out of envy or for personal gains?

...

Svetla Daskalova (opposition agrarian): In the proposed law the concept "fascist" and "activity against the people" should be strictly specified, so as to avoid abuse. Otherwise, the way it has been presented to us, it is neither more nor less than a political means for the annihilation of a political adversary (applause from the opposition and shouts "true!") and moral harassment of the youth already struggling in academia.[24]

Anton Yugov (communist): Respected Members of Parliament, we assert that the opposition of Nikola Petkov, Pastuhov, Lulchev and Girginov is the

[24] Mutafchieva 1995, pp. 173-179.

center of reactionary fascist elements. There is no conspiratorial, anti-national and criminal activity, which has been revealed, whose origin cannot be traced back to the opposition headquarters of these gentlemen.

Nikola Petkov (opposition agrarian): That is so only if you beat them [the detainees under investigation - *authors' note*] so that they can tell you what you want to hear! When you beat them, when you terrorize them, they will tell you what you want to know!

Dobri Terpeshev (communist): But nevertheless they tell the truth. Whether we beat them or not, they tell the truth.[25]

Rayko Damyanov (communist): You are instigators! ...Sit down, you scum! ...Traitor! ...A fascist can't say anything other than that! [to Dimitar Stoyanov, opposition agrarian - *author's note*] ...Provocateur!...You are a saboteur!...Here is the biggest bandit! ...Fascist!...Go away, you scoundrel! ...Bandit! ...Provocateur, provocateur! ...You, scoundrel, where were you? ...Spy, rotten spy! ...Sit there, bandit! ...Scoundrel, robber!...Listen, why don't you go for a treatment![26]

Georgi Dimitrov (communist): These parasites [i.e., the Members of Parliament from the opposition - *author's note*] will pay for this!

Nikola Petkov (opposition agrarian): You are parasites. You all live like parasites. Your language is highly inappropriate for a Prime Minister. No one lives like you, as the biggest millionaire on earth.[27]

Georgi Dimitrov (communist): I propose that every Member of Parliament from the opposition, who causes obstructions to the planned activities, be expelled. I also suggest the parliamentary whips take their places and everyone who has been expelled to be thrown out of the National Assembly like a dirty rag... Remember and write down the following: "the Grand National Assembly is running out of patience! There is very little patience left!"[28]

Todor Zhivkov (communist): This whole apparatus of black marketeers and profiteers, of social butterflies and degenerates, gave their entire support and all their forces to the opposition during the elections on October 27... International spy services are the ones actually in charge at the central offices of Nikola Petkov and Kosta Lulchev.[29]

Dr. Peter Dertliev (opposition social democrat): I need to ask you which one of you killed Zamfir Filipov. I want to ask you, you, who are claiming this

---

[25] Dertliev 1996, p. 192.

[26] *Ibid.*, p. 217.

[27] *Ibid.*, pp. 196-197.

[28] *Ibid.*, p. 213.

[29] *Ibid.*, pp. 232-233.

and that, "Aren't you accomplices?" When someone is dead and you defend the assassins, you are accomplices.

When Peter Kalev was taken into custody in Lyaskovets and was then dumped dead in front of his home, I'd like to ask you, who are paid by the Bulgarian people to defend law and order, "What are you?" I will say it in your face, "You are murderers!"

Valko Chervenkov (communist): Boy, you will pay for this statement with your head.[30]

Georgi Dimitrov (communist): Maybe you don't know Petkov's secrets... He will tell them to you!

Nikola Petkov (opposition agrarian): Tell them to us so that I can come up with an explanation. I will tell you who is a foreign agent. I have never been a citizen of a foreign country!

Georgi Dimitrov: It is an honor to be a citizen of great Russia!

Nikola Petkov: You became a Bulgarian citizen two days before the elections.

Georgi Dimitrov: Soon you will receive your documents with your signatures. I will show you!

Nikola Petkov: You have been a foreign citizen for twenty years. You have no right to speak like that.[31]

Peko Takov (communist): Can you imagine what a serious fact was reported by Kocho the Barrel [Kocho Bonev - Member of Parliament from BZNS - *N. Petkov - author's note*]? He said that a parliamentary candidate from his party was pinched during the elections, and because she was pinched, he insists that we declare the elections in Nova Zagora invalid.

Kocho Bonev (opposition agrarian): Her arm was broken and she was raped.

Georgi Dimitrov (communist): Maybe she was pleased to be pinched.[32]

Georgi Dimitrov (communist): Such things can happen in Greece, not in Bulgaria.

Nikola Petkov (opposition agrarian): Greece and Bulgaria have nothing in common. There is a civil war in Greece, whereas in Bulgaria there is only a defenseless and persecuted opposition.

Georgi Dimitrov: You are an opposition that is working to bring civil war to Bulgaria.

---

30 *Ibid.*, pp. 211-212.

31 *Ibid.*, p. 222.

32 *Ibid.*, p. 240.

Nikola Petkov: You are doing damage to Bulgaria by talking like this, Mr. Prime Minister.

Georgi Dimitrov: In your newspapers you openly appeal for resistance and for the toppling of the present regime. Openly! And you will answer for it!

Nikola Petkov: This is not true. If you provide conditions for work, we will come and cooperate with you as of tomorrow. Allow for freedom and you will see whether this is true.[33]

Georgi Dimitrov (communist): Your Koev should be hanged!

Nikola Petkov (opposition agrarian): You are Prime Minister! You have no right to talk like that! Are you a master who can pass sentences? You are assuming the role of a judge! Don't forget yourself! Don't threaten! You have no right to threaten like that in a Grand National Assembly and to assume the role of a judge! Who are you and what are you?

The Fatherland Front majority (booing): Spy! Conspirator! Out!

Nikola Petkov: He is not God here. He has no right to threaten.

Georgi Dimitrov: You must be grateful for our common sense and patience, because if we decide, none of you will remain here... In a month, not later, we shall speak with you. Your company is bankrupt.[34]

The threats of the Prime Minister of the People's Republic of Bulgaria, Georgi Dimitrov, who had merged the three branches of state power into his own persona, came true. Nikola Petkov's "company" was indeed bankrupt. Soon the fates of the leader of the democratic opposition and its representatives would be directed by events taking place on the international arena.

---

33 *Ibid.*

34 *Ibid.*, pp. 220-221.

8. Last Bricks in the Construction of a Communist State

Between July 29 and October 15, 1946, there was a meeting in Paris of the Council of Foreign Ministers of Great Britain, the United States, the Soviet Union, France, and China, with representatives of sixteen states that had fought against the Axis forces in World War II. The task of the Paris Peace Conference, as the meeting is best known today, was to draft peace treaties with Italy, Bulgaria, Finland, Romania and Hungary. At the end, the participants reached an agreement and the five peace treaties were endorsed.

The one with Bulgaria was signed on February 10, 1947. Days after this, Great Britain recognized the government of the People's Republic of Bulgaria; it ratified the peace treaty in April.[1] On June 5, 1947, the U.S. Senate also ratified the Peace Treaty with Bulgaria.[2]

What was happening at the same time in the People's Republic?

On October 21, 1946, Nikola Mushanov's opposition Democratic Party published a draft of a Constitution of Bulgaria in its newspaper *Zname* [Flag]. It was based on the Tarnovo Constitution, and it opposed the official version of the Constitution that was proposed by the Fatherland Front.[3] At the end of 1946, the government banned *Zname*. In May 1947, it did the same to the newspaper of the Bulgarian Agrarian People's Union - *Nikola Petkov*, *Narodno zemedesko zname* [Agrarian People's Flag], and the newspaper of the Bulgarian Workers' Social Democratic Party (united), *Svoboden narod* [Free Nation]. In short, the opposition press in Bulgaria was liquidated.

On the very day when the United States Senate ratified the peace treaty with Bulgaria, the Sixth National Assembly was debating the draft of a new Constitution:

> Vladimir Poptomov (communist): Was it not Nikola Petkov, the so-called Fuehrer of the opposition, who wrote an article in their newspaper *Zemedelsko zname* of November 27, 1945, under the insolent title "Hands Off the Sacred Values of the Bulgarian Nation, the Tarnovo Constitution"?
>
> Nikola Petkov (opposition agrarian): It is sacred because it reflects the liberties of the Bulgarian nation.
>
> Vladimir Poptomov (communist): In that article Nikola Petkov even declares himself against any amendments to the Tarnovo Constitution whatsoever.
>
> Nikola Petkov (opposition agrarian): This is a lie!
>
> ...

[1] Chakalov 1993, p. 103; Konstantinov 1997, p. 308.

[2] Sharlanov 1997, p. 107.

[3] Ognyanov, Dimova, Lalkov 1992, pp. 82-88.

Prime Minister Georgi Dimitrov: Read it yourself before the Grand National Assembly!

Nikola Petkov (opposition agrarian): If that had been true, you would not have written a letter to me from Moscow, asking me to remain in the Fatherland Front. If I was such a reactionary, why did you write that letter to me?

Prime Minister Georgi Dimitrov: This is why you will go to prison now! (Applause from the majority.)

Nikola Petkov (opposition agrarian): You can take your revenge now, because you are a vindictive person, but you will not achieve anything. Taking revenge is not governing. You will understand this best.

Prime Minister Georgi Dimitrov: There is no revenge here. There is justice and fair retribution. (Shouts of "that's right" and applause from the majority.)

...

Prime Minister Georgi Dimitrov: You are relying on foreign assistance. Nobody will save you. Remember this! (Applause from the majority and shouts, "True!")

Nikola Petkov (opposition agrarian): I am surprised that you are afraid of one man and one newspaper. You, who were the hero of Leipzig, you are a coward now, and you fear a man and a newspaper. This is a fact. There is no need for you to be concerned about this.

Dimitar Kotev (communist): You are a traitor.

Nikola Petkov (opposition agrarian): Only cowards resort to violence. And it is a pity that you have fallen prey to fear. You can't even make twenty steps without agents.

Prime Minister Georgi Dimitrov: You are a great hero, but nothing will save you. I am telling you! I will tell you that you are political scum. (Exclamations of "that's right" and prolonged applause from the majority.)

Nikola Petkov (opposition agrarian): You don't even take twenty steps without agents around you. There are no conspirators. This is the strongest evidence that you are a dictator and that you are afraid.

Prime Minister Georgi Dimitrov: You are being used [by the Western powers - *author's note*] and you will be discarded like a squeezed lemon. (Applause from the majority.) This should serve as a lesson for all our colleagues, including Lulchev.

Nikola Petkov (opposition agrarian): Don't forget that you will not dissuade them (pointing to the opposition). You will see that you will not dissuade them because it is not about one person, it is about a way of thought.

...

Prime Minister Georgi Dimitrov (to Nikola Petkov): This is your last chance to be talkative. This is your last word here; hence, you are loquacious. (Applause from the majority.)

> Nikola Petkov (opposition agrarian): And my last words as a man will be "long live freedom!"[4]

Late in the evening on June 5, 1947, the Sixth Grand National Assembly, dominated by communists and members of the Fatherland Front, stripped Nikola Petkov of his immunity as Member of Parliament. The leader of the democratic opposition in Bulgaria was accused by the District Prosecutor of Sofia of having created "military and fascist clandestine organizations deliberately and in a premeditated fashion" with the aim of "preparing a *coup d'état* with armed forces against the people's power."[5] Nikola Petkov was taken from the Parliament building with armed guards and was handed over to the investigators of the Directorate of the People's Militia.

Several days later, the newspaper of the French Socialist Party, *Le Peuple*, declared:

> In view of the fact that Bulgaria is occupied by the Soviet Army and that the government entirely relies on it, the accusation [against Nikola Petkov - *author's note*] is simply impossible and ridiculous.[6]

What was the evidence for the clandestine preparation "of a *coup d'état*" by the opposition leader? It consisted only of the confessions extorted from Peter Koev, Colonel Marko Ivanov, and Colonel Boris Gergov, all crushed with torture, and the articles of Nikola Petkov himself, published in the *Narodno Zemedelsko Zname* newspaper.[7]

Professor Dinyu Sharlanov reveals some interesting moments in the attempts of the U.S.A. and Britain to save the agrarian Nikola Petkov. The following is based on excerpts from the minutes of meetings and government statements:

> One day after the arrest, American and British political representatives in Sofia insisted on an urgent meeting with the Bulgarian Prime Minister. At 11 a.m. on June 7, 1947, the U.S. political representative John Forner was received by Georgi Dimitrov. Forner stated that he had come to receive information "on the issue of Mr. Nikola Petkov's arrest" and that this event would not only attract the attention of the U.S. government, but "would (also) make it very

[4] *Ibid.*, pp. 107-109.

[5] Sharlanov 1997, p. 107.

[6] *Ibid.*, p. 98.

[7] *Ibid.*, pp. 98-99.

bitter." The ironic response of Georgi Dimitrov was, "I hope America will not declare war on us."

The Bulgarian Prime Minister informed Forner that the authorities had been watching the activities of Nikola Petkov and his followers for a long time and had found actions on their part aiming to "prepare for a *coup d'état.*" He warned the American political representative that "no interference can help either Petkov or the others... However, if he is your agent, an American agent, go ahead and defend him. But you deny all that."

At that point John Forner took a more direct approach. He told Georgi Dimitrov, "This is a very unfortunate coincidence. The very moment the U.S. Senate ratified the peace treaty, Nikola Petkov was stripped of his immunity. I assume that my government will consider this act, namely, the arrest of Petkov, to be an act of violence, which is in contradiction with the spirit of the peace treaty... In the past day or two I have been thinking about Petkov's detention and I came to the conclusion that the Bulgarian government is preparing for the liquidation of the opposition before the peace treaty is fully ratified."

At 12:30 p.m. the same day, the Bulgarian Prime Minister was also visited by Britain's political representative in Sofia, J. S. Sterndane Bennett. The conversation between the two of them proceeded in much the same way as the one with the American representative. Above all, Bennett pointed to the fact that the eradication of the opposition press, the mobilization of idlers [sending jobless people to labor camps - *author's note*], and the arrest of Nikola Petkov suggested "a very precisely worked out plan for eliminating the opposition and establishing a totalitarian state."

After John Forner informed his government in Washington about the outcome of his conversation with Georgi Dimitrov, the U.S. State Department came out with an official statement on July 11, 1947. It reminded the Bulgarian government of the requirements under Article 2 of the Peace Treaty: "Although the Yalta Agreement, the terms of the cease-fire agreement, and the provisions of the peace treaty guarantee human rights in Bulgaria, the chief leader of the Bulgarian opposition is being accused of treason. He will certainly be tried and sentenced in Bulgaria, "not in Washington or London," but it is equally certain that when he is brought to trial and indicted in his own country, the same indictment will be valid for the present-day Bulgarian regime in the minds of many Bulgarians, and certainly in the opinion of all nations outside Bulgaria, who support freedom."[8]

Georgi Dimitrov was right again. America did not declare war on Bulgaria. On August 14, 1947, the U.S. President Harry Truman signed the Peace Treaty with the People's Republic of Bulgaria.

---

[8] *Ibid.*, pp. 111-113.

Two days later, on August 16, in the grand hall for ceremonial occasions in the Palace of Justice in Sofia, the communist court indicted the defendant Nikola Petkov for organizing a military conspiratorial organization, "which had set for itself the aim to overthrow, undermine, or weaken the established power in the state by means of armed force - with a *coup d'état* - for which, according to Article 1, paragraph 1 of the decree on the Protection of the People's Power and Article 51, paragraph 2 and Article 60 of the Penal Code, he is sentenced to death by hanging and will pay a fine of five hundred thousand (500,000) levs to the State Treasury."[9]

On August 26, 1947, the Minister of Justice, Radi Naydenov, member of the Bulgarian Agrarian People's Union subordinated to the communist party, proposed legislation to the Sixth Grand National Assembly for the dissolution of the Agrarian Union of Nikola Petkov. All Members of Parliament from the Fatherland Front voted in favor of the Minister's suggestion. It became a law with the following content:

> Article 1. The Bulgarian Agrarian People's Union - Nikola Petkov, the Agrarian Youth Union belonging to it, and all their subdivisions and sections shall be banned and dissolved.
>
> The parliamentary group of the BZNS - N. Petkov shall also be dissolved. The mandate of its members will be revoked and their replacement by the next candidates in the representation lists from which they have been elected will not be allowed.
>
> Article 2. All property of the Bulgarian Agrarian People's Union - Nikola Petkov, of the Agrarian Youth Union belonging to it, and of all their subdivisions shall be transferred to the state.[10]

In August 1947, the Soviet Union was the last of the Allied Forces to ratify the peace treaty with Bulgaria, which officially became effective on September 15. Consequently, the Allied Control Commission in Sofia had to discontinue its work, and within 90 days the Soviet occupation troops had to leave the country. On September 19, John Forner informed the Foreign Ministry of the People's Republic of Bulgaria on behalf of the U.S. State Department that his government was ready to establish diplomatic relations with Bulgaria.[11]

Four days later, at 1 a.m. on September 23, the leader of the democratic opposition, Nikola Petkov, was hanged at the Central Prison in Sofia. In the history of Bulgaria, the gallows of the member of the first Fatherland Front

---

[9] *Ibid.*, p. 138.

[10] Ognyanov, Dimova, Lalkov 1992, pp. 116-117.

[11] Sharlanov 1997, p. 238 (Annexes).

government after the bloody September 9, 1944, became a symbol of the bitter truth that no fair alliance can exist with the communists. As a result of the physical liquidation of Nikola Petkov and of the banning of his party and its subdivisions, the beheaded Bulgarian opposition and the democratically inclined portion of the Bulgarian nation were totally disempowered.

. . .

At the end of September 1947, Moscow called an international meeting of representatives of nine communist and workers' parties in Poland. The meeting condemned global imperialism and prescribed the strategy of the international communist movement against it. It was decided to begin the determined ideological fight against the West and create a Communist Information Bureau (Cominformburo) with its seat in Belgrade.

On October 20, 1947, the United States renewed its diplomatic relations with Bulgaria.

Several days later, the Central Committee of the Bulgarian Workers' Party (communists) convened at an extraordinary assembly. Its task was to coordinate the party's political line with the decisions reached in Poland. In practice this meant a renewed attack on the anticommunist population and any political organizations that still existed outside the Fatherland Front. Thus, the Democratic Party was banned in 1947.

Finally, in December 1947, the Soviet occupation troops withdrew from the territory of Bulgaria, leaving behind a politically crushed nation, deprived of its rights, and a totalitarian communist government, recognized and legitimized by the democratic West. If it was deemed necessary, the Soviet troops could always come back - as was the case in Hungary in 1956 and in Czechoslovakia in 1968 - to suppress any aspirations towards freedom and democracy with brute force.

. . .

On December 4, 1947, in a "calm" work environment - which meant that the opposition Members of Parliament were indicted, involved in political trials, deported, sent to labor camps, or seeking ways to affiliate themselves with the Fatherland Front parties - the Sixth Grand National Assembly adopted the Constitution of the People's Republic of Bulgaria. It was called Dimitrov's Constitution, and it imposed a Soviet-type regime in Bulgaria.

The Constitution legitimized procedures that had become daily occurrences immediately after September 9, 1944, such as the merger of the legislative, executive and judiciary branches of government and the total subordination of all institutions to the red party. In addition, the new Constitution also gave some long-awaited advantages to the Bulgarian Bolsheviks. It allowed Georgi Dimitrov and his clique to usurp economic power. Immediately after the Constitution was adopted, a series of steps in that direction were taken:

> On the morning of December 23, 1947, the Council of Ministers adopted the Bill on the Nationalization of the Private Industrial and Mining Enterprises, and gave orders that the nationalized enterprises included in the list be seized immediately.
>
> The takeover of the enterprises started at 11 a.m. and it took their owners completely by surprise. The newly appointed directors, the commandants and the representatives of the militia took part in the campaign. Then, meetings and rallies of the workers were organized in the nationalized enterprises.
>
> Radio Sofia announced the adoption of the Bill on the Nationalization of the Private Industrial and Mining Enterprises by the Council of Ministers at 2 p.m. In the afternoon, before the start of the session of the Grand National Assembly, the above-mentioned bill was distributed to the deputies. It was adopted the next day, on December 24, and enforced immediately after its adoption. At 7 p.m. in the evening Radio Sofia announced its final adoption.[12]

All bank capital was also nationalized that day. The nationalization of the foreign and domestic trade enterprises followed in the early months of 1948. On April 15, 1948, the *State Gazette* published the Law on the Expropriation of Large Urban Real Estate.

The concept of "large urban real estate" proved to be very flexible. The local committees of the Bulgarian Workers' Party (communists) and the special commissions set up for the purpose decided whether any relatively attractive piece of property qualified as "large urban real estate" or not, as well as who its new owner would be. Article 13 of the law contained the following provisions in its last paragraph:

> Residential buildings may be made available for other purposes as well, subject to decision by the Council of Ministers.[13]

"Other purposes" meant the distribution of luxurious apartments and villas to leading communist figures, who did not pay a cent for them. Most of that valuable property was subsequently "purchased" at ridiculously low prices by the people who had moved in. Many of the so-called "active fighters against fascism

---

[12] Ognyanov, Dimova, Lalkov 1992, p. 129.

[13] *Ibid.*, p. 132.

and capitalism" or their progeny still live comfortably in the "large urban real estate" previously owned by their class enemies.

However, the expropriation of factories, mines, banks, companies, apartments, and villas was not the worst that befell their owners. For decades they and their children and grandchildren had to answer the questions "has property of your family been nationalized" and "have you been affected by the measures taken by the people's power" when submitting their job or school applications or requesting permission to travel abroad. If the answer to any of these questions was "yes," the request was almost invariably rejected.

"Special deliveries" of luxury goods and numerous other privileges for the higher ranks of the BWP(c) became a daily occurrence as soon as the "people's power" was fully instituted. The practice was broadened to a much larger circle of red party members up until 1991. After that point they no longer needed it. With time many of the leaders of the communist party and its secret agents became millionaires on a global scale. Eventually, the system of "special deliveries", legitimized on May 6, 1948, with a decision of the Politburo of the BWP(c) Central Committee, became much too modest for their appetites and enterprises.

...

The Second Congress of the Fatherland Front was held in February 1948. On that occasion it adopted as its primary goal the establishment of a socialist system in the People's Republic of Bulgaria. Consequently, the organization was restructured and acquired a mass character, which meant that all citizens of the country were pressured to become its members. Local Fatherland Front clubs were established in villages and urban areas, and the FF changed its name to Unified Social-Political Organization. These clubs worked until late at night and were really busy. Their activists controlled the population by writing references and by issuing various documents according to the instructions of the BWP(c).

It appeared that after September 9, 1944, social life in Bulgaria had either regressed to the Middle Ages, or that the country had somehow been transposed thousands of miles northeast into the confines of Soviet Union. Ordinary Bulgarians needed the blessing of the new feudal lords - the communists - for any action that they wished to undertake. The red regime closed the state borders and introduced an entirely new measure - new at least for Bulgaria, not for Czarist Russia and the U.S.S.R. - a permanent residence permit, needed in order to live in the capital or any other city.

In 1948, the Bulgarian Workers' Social Democratic Party, which was a member of the Fatherland Front, officially adopted the political program of the

BWP(c) and joined its ranks. In this way, the "docile" social democrats were painlessly transformed into privileged communists.

Their "disobedient" colleagues from the Bulgarian Workers Social Democratic Party (united) had the opposite fate. The time had come to take the punishment that Georgi Dimitrov had been promising them for a long while. In November 1948, nine members of the leading body of the opposition BWSDP(u) and Members of Parliament from the Sixth Grand National Assembly, headed by Kosta Lulchev, were brought to trial and received severe sentences. Simultaneously, hundreds of other social democrats in opposition were deported and sent to concentration camps. By the end of 1948, the "people's democratic" communist government had entirely liquidated the democratic opposition in Bulgaria.

Pleased with what had been achieved, the Bulgarian Workers' Party (communists) held its Fifth Congress in December 1948. The members of that meeting concluded the process of Sovietization and officially imposed the Moscow model on the ideological, political, social and economic life of the People's Republic of Bulgaria. At that Congress the BWP(c) restored its original name - Bulgarian Communist Party — which it was to bear proudly until it changed it once again in April 1990.

In the beginning of 1949, two other political groups in the Fatherland Front - *Zveno* and the Radical Party - discontinued their independent existence and announced their merger with the Unified Social-Political Organization. From that moment on, the BCP ruled over Bulgaria for four decades with the full support of only one other party, which it had formally preserved, namely the Bulgarian Agrarian People's Union.

Before it turned into an obedient puppet of the communists, BZNS had a rich and dramatic history. The organization was established by a group of intellectuals in 1899 under the name of Bulgarian Agrarian Union. Its goals were educational. Later it became a political party, defending the interests of the rural population. In 1901, its members numbered 35,000, and it had 23 seats in the Eleventh Ordinary National Assembly. During the same year, the organization changed its name to Bulgarian Agrarian People's Union and increased its influence substantially.

To this day, BZNS remains the only peasant party that has run a European state. Between May 21, 1920, and June 9, 1923, its leader Alexander Stamboliyski was Prime Minister of Bulgaria, with an autonomous agrarian government.

In the past, the union of the peasants had opposed the actions of the communists often. However, some BZNS representatives, the so-called "orange agrarians," who participated in the Fatherland Front, subordinated the agrarian union to the interests of the red party and deprived it of its independent identity. That happened in the following way:

> At its Twenty-Seventh Congress (December 28-29, 1947) the Bulgarian Agrarian People's Union hailed the agenda of the communist party, aiming to "establish a socialist society" in Bulgaria. Unlike the other Fatherland Front parties, it preserved its autonomous existence, for which it paid by relinquishing its own political agenda. At the meeting of the Supreme Council of the union, held in October and November of 1948, the organization's founding principle to serve all social strata of agrarians was rejected, and the union was proclaimed to be the class organization only of some of the poor and middle-class peasants. The Agrarian Union declared that it would work to achieve the re-education of the allied agrarians in the spirit and principles of the "people's democracy" and the "construction of socialism" and that it recognized the "leading role of the working class" and of its communist party.[14]

The sessions of the Supreme Council of BZNS in the autumn of 1948 were chaired by Georgi Traykov, who was awarded with the position of Deputy Chairman of the Council of Ministers for betraying the original union's ideas.

However, the biggest humiliation for the Bulgarian Agrarian People's Union remains the sad fact that it greatly assisted the BCP in the coercive assimilation of the Bulgarian villagers' land into cooperative farms, following the Soviet model. Instead of defending the interests of the agrarians and farmers, who had organized in cooperatives and guilds of their own free will well before September 9, 1944, BZNS took an active part in the disgraceful collectivization process. Cooperative land ownership was imposed on the population through physical and moral abuse, including the forced resettlement of entire villages and isolated rural neighborhoods.

The collectivization of the agricultural lands, which was executed against the will of the people, was one of the cruelest crimes of the totalitarian regime. It is no accident that the peasants rebelled in several regions of the country. Dinyu Sharlanov discussed the matter in a book:

> Collectivization in agriculture on a mass scale, but through coercion, started in 1949-1950. It clashed acutely with the age-old attachment of Bulgarian peasants to the land. This explains why the collectivization turned into their real drama. The peasants resisted with all possible peaceful means. Riots and open discontent of the peasants with the cooperative farms broke out in the spring of 1950 in more than 80 villages (in the areas around Teteven, Kula, Pleven, Plovdiv, Asenovgrad, etc.). The government response amounted

[14] *Ibid.*, p. 138.

> to threats, arrests and concentration camps. Information released by the Militia Directorate to the Politburo [of the BCP - *author's note*] in April 1951 indicates that the number of arrested peasants exceeded 25,000. The report informs the Politburo members that 2,418 middle-class peasant families were "resettled," together with 710 families of rich peasants, the so-called "kulaks." The cited figures do not include the thousands of peasants detained for a day or two in the municipal barns, where they were beaten to secure their "voluntary" signing of applications to become members of the cooperative farms. About a dozen court trials followed for the so-called "instigators" of "unrest" and the "plundering" of the property of the cooperative farms by the peasants. Other measures were also taken to force the peasants into cooperative farms. Their sons and daughters were not allowed to study at universities or to occupy positions as civil servants unless their families joined the cooperative farms.[15]

The coercive methods of the communists proved to be productive once again. By 1957, all peasants in Bulgaria were deprived of their land. The countryside was gradually transformed from a veritable Garden of Eden into a desert.

...

In the late 1940s and the early 1950s, in part through laws, in part without, the private pension savings and health insurance of the Bulgarian population were nationalized. The money went into the state budget, which was actually equivalent to the funds of the red party.

In order to obliterate the remains of the pre-communist Bulgarian state completely, in 1951 the First National Assembly [the Dimitrov Constitution provided for a new numbering of the National Assemblies - *author's note*] unanimously adopted the bill proposed by the Minister of Justice, the agrarian-communist Radi Naydenov. It consisted of the following sole article:

> All laws and the entire secondary legislation adopted prior to September 9, 1944, shall be revoked on the grounds that they contravene the Dimitrov Constitution and the socialist legislation of Bulgaria, adopted after September 9, 1944, and shall henceforth be considered invalid.[16]

However, there was still some resistance to the communist dictatorship. Professor Nicola Dolapchiev offered the following testimonial:

---

[15] Sharlanov 1997, pp. 188-189.

[16] Shorthand transcripts, First National Assembly, 4th vol., 33, Nov. 9, 1951.

It must be pointed out, that the hatred of the Bulgarian people for the Communist regime and the widespread resistance against the Soviet tyranny found another impressive expression. In May, 1953, the tobacco workers in the towns of Khaskovo and Plovdiv rose against the Communist authorities and raised their voice of protest with slogans like 'bread and freedom.' The riots were so serious that the Communist Minister Yugov, a former tobacco worker himself, was sent to suppress those disturbances. As usual, the Communists tried to minimize the importance of those riots and to explain them as a repercussion of the revolt in East Germany and a result of malicious instigations by Western capitalists. But the mere fact that the mutiny among the Bulgarian workers took place one month before the events of June in Germany best repudiates the untruthfulness of the Communist contention.[17]

[17] Dolapchiev 1971, p. 79.

9. Persecution of Religious Institutions

In order to make sure the rule of the Bulgarian Communist Party would endure completely unimpeded, the totalitarian regime had to cope with yet another influential, traditional establishment, namely the national Orthodox Church. For centuries, the church had been the second most important institution after the state administration. The Bulgarian national identity was preserved largely because of Christianity.

In 865 AD, the Bulgarian ruler Khan Boris I accepted Orthodox Christianity, from the Byzantine Empire, as the official religion of his state. He converted the entire population, regardless of ethnicity, to Christianity in order to consolidate the Bulgarian nation. In 870 AD, the Khan succeeded in obtaining relative independence for the Bulgarian Church from Constantinople. After defeating the Byzantine troops near the Aheloy River in 917 AD, his son Simeon I proclaimed himself Tsar of the Bulgarians and Byzantines. He also proclaimed the Bulgarian Church autocephalous. Ten years later the Patriarch in Constantinople recognized the Bulgarian Patriarchate, which became the spiritual center of the Orthodox Slavic East during the Middle Ages.

In the 9th century, Bulgaria not only adopted Christianity, but it also welcomed the disciples of the brothers Constantine Cyril, the Philosopher, and Methodius, who created the Glagolitic alphabet in 855 AD. Khan Boris I secured favorable conditions for all of them in the Bulgarian capital, Pliska. Soon after their arrival, a new alphabet - to be used by the Slavs, was created and dubbed Cyrillic in honor of Constantine Cyril. Thereafter, two literary schools flourished in Pliska and Ochrid, both of which were on Bulgarian territory.

The Ochrid School, under the guidance of the disciple of Cyril and Methodius, Kliment of Ochrid, was one of the earliest institution of higher education in Europe. In the late 9th and early 10th centuries, 3,500 priests and deacons graduated from it and devoted themselves to teaching and other literary activities. Thanks to the clergymen educated in Ochrid, Pliska and Preslav, Bulgaria was the only country on the continent creating literature in its own vernacular at the time. Its monks were the first to translate the Holy Scriptures into a Slavic language, thus breaking the trilingual dogma of Hebrew, Greek, and Latin. Soon thereafter the Bulgarian alphabet and literature spread to the Russians, Serbs and other Slavic peoples.

In 988 AD, Kievan Russia officially adopted Christianity and imported the liturgical books for its holy services from the Bulgarians. The newly converted Russians made transcripts of the works written during the rule of Khan Boris I and the Golden Age of Tsar Simeon I. The Old Bulgarian language became the basis of Church Slavonic, which is used in Orthodox Church services all around the world to this day.

For centuries the prestige of the Bulgarian Orthodox Church was enormous. In times of peace it was the center of education, literature, arts, and culture. During the five centuries of Ottoman dominion, it preserved Bulgarian identity. Bulgarians revered the names of patriarchs, bishops, monks, clergymen, and deacons together with the names of the Christian saints. Their Vitae and worthy deeds were well-known and remembered, because they had contributed to the moral uplifting of the lay population. They also inspired the struggles for national independence and for political freedom. It was precisely that tradition that threatened the communist dictatorship, and the BCP took measures to squash it.

. . .

In spite of its hatred for the Bulgarian Church, it was not possible for the Bulgarian Communist Party to ban or liquidate it. Eighty-five percent of the country's population belonged to the Christian Orthodox religion, and that would have been too much of an outrage. Once again, the problem was tackled in a roundabout and surreptitious manner, as Lenin had taught the Bolsheviks. The institution of the Orthodox Church was to be preserved formally, stripped of its identity, and transformed into an obedient servant to the red party.

The first step was to purge or corrupt the clergy itself. Under the pretext of "disagreement with the Fatherland Front" and "hostile attitude to the U.S.S.R.", those clergymen and monks who believed in God and had a clean, independent and incorruptible conscience were subjected to terror and extermination. For this the BCP used the familiar means of murders without due process, staged trials, and concentration camps. In 1997, Peter Semerdzhiev - a man who held a number of high positions in the totalitarian apparatus after September 9, 1944 - wrote the following in a book:

> There were 46 people who suffered from repressions in the district of Vratsa alone. In and around Sofia, 36 priests were subjected to repressions, 16 of whom were killed, whereby 12 of them, led by Archimandrite Dr. Ireney, were pronounced "missing without a trace", and two Archimandrites, Stefan Yaov and Yoan, were sent to concentration camps. The priests who became victims of repressions in and around Plovdiv were 21 in number. Even in such a remote and isolated area as the town of Gotse Delchev (Nevrokop) there were 12 victims of the measures enforced. The People's Court inflicted irreparable damage on the Orthodox clergy in all administrative districts of Bulgaria. The charges brought against them were strikingly unfounded. Most of the clergymen were arrested for making pronouncements against communists or partisans and for criticizing the Soviet Union. Such instances seriously

undermine the superficial impression that the Bulgarian Orthodox Church had remained unscathed when the decree on the People's Court was enforced.[1]

According to another source in which the names of the victims of the purges are given, four priests were assassinated in the Sofia region, 12 Orthodox clergymen were pronounced missing, and 34 were sentenced to life imprisonment, solitary confinement in prison, or sent to concentration camps.[2]

The reprisals against the "disobedient" priests gradually frightened the clergy. Some chose to perform the various religious rites perfunctorily. Others joined the Bulgarian Communist Party, and some were recruited as agents of the secret services.

...

The report submitted by the informer-priest Georgi Bogdanov to the Central Committee of the Bulgarian Workers Party (communists) on April 18, 1947, reads:

> Comrades,
>
> On the 4th of this month the Metropolitan Bishop of the Sliven Diocese Evlogiy suddenly passed away. Not only the Church but the entire public is faced with the question who the next Metropolitan Bishop should be. This issue is of great interest to our Party [BWP(c) - *author's note*] as well, for which it is not at all the same whether a metropolitan diocese is headed by a more progressive and democratic bishop, who would contribute to the democratization of the Church, or by a bishop with a reactionary mentality, who would do everything he can to preserve the Church in its present form and state. For this reason we, the priests who are members of the Party from the dioceses of Sofia and Sliven, after discussing the issue of the choice of the future Metropolitan Bishop of Sliven, and bearing in mind the qualities of all bishops applying for that vacancy, hereby decided to make a recommendation to the Party's Central Committee.[3]

That particular "servant of God" proceeded to list the names of eight bishops applying for the diocese of the Metropolitan Bishop of Sliven. Three of

---

1 Semerdzhiev 1995, pp. 411-412.

2 *Pravoslaven Pastir* [Orthodox Pastor] newspaper, *Martyrs from the Time of Communism,* No. 2, May 1992.

3 Report by the priest Georgi Georgiev Bogdanov from the Board of the Bulgarian Union of Priests to the Central Committee of the BWP(c), Sofia, April 18, 1947, Archives of the Directorate on Religious Denominations with the Council of Ministers.

them were characterized as "enemy of the Fatherland Front", "reactionary and fascist" and "most adamant reactionary." His letter ends as follows:

> Comrades, having critically examined the merits and the shortcomings of the listed eight bishops, who are candidates for the Sliven diocese, we, the party-member priests Georgi G. Bogdanov, Boris Popov, Nikola Demirevski and Dimitar Hadzhiyski, unanimously agreed to recommend that the Party support the candidate Bishop Nikodim Stobiyski, Rector of the Theological Seminary in Plovdiv, who would be supported by us and by the entire progressive community. He was a member of the Church delegation that visited the Soviet Union, and both there and after his return to Bulgaria, his conduct has been good and he has made favorable comments about the Russian Orthodox Church and about the great Soviet Union.
>
> In the report that we received from the Sliven diocese there are indications that the progressive clergymen there, and especially the priests who are party members and the entire progressive Fatherland Front community, are inclined to support his candidacy.
>
> Comrades, should the Party's Central Committee decide to support the candidacy of Bishop Nikodim, it would have to do what is needed through Fatherland Front channels and especially with the help of the clergymen in the Party to launch and support his election.[4]

The informers served the communist party faithfully. The Politburo of the Central Committee of the BCP later even felt empowered to select the Patriarch of the "autonomous" Bulgarian Church:

> Decision 'A' No. 145 of the Politburo of the BCP Central Committee of March 8, 1971:
>
> To launch and support the candidacy of the Metropolitan Bishop of Lovech, Maxim, for Head of the Bulgarian Orthodox Church.
>
> To assign the necessary preparatory work for securing the election of Metropolitan Bishop Maxim for Patriarch of the Bulgarian Orthodox Church to the Chairman of the Committee on Church Matters at the Ministry of Foreign Affairs, Comrade Mihail Kyuchukov.[5]

At the end of this document the signature of the dictator Todor Zhivkov is followed by those of six leading members of the Bulgarian Communist Party. At the beginning of 2010 the Patriarch of the Bulgarian Orthodox Church still remains that same Maxim.

---

[4] *Ibid.*

[5] Decision 'A' No. 145 of the Politburo of the BCP's Central Committee of March 8, 1971, Sofia, Archives of the Directorate on Religious Denominations with the Council of Ministers.

...

The old metropolitan bishops, ordinary bishops, monks, and priests died one by one, or were killed, sentenced, deported, sent to concentration camps, or merely fired and replaced by persons obedient to the regime. In addition, the atheistic rulers adopted legislative measures aimed at reducing the influence of the Orthodox faith on the population.

At first the Church bravely struggled to maintain its independence. On November 1, 1946, the Holy Council, led by the honorable Exarches Stefan - who had had a decisive role in the rescue of the Bulgarian Jews in World War II - officially declared:

> The announced draft of a new Constitution, which is to be debated by the Grand National Assembly, contains provisions that radically change the centuries-old relations between the Bulgarian State and the Bulgarian Orthodox Church from a legal and moral perspective.
>
> ...
>
> Article 64 of the proposed Constitution stipulates that "education shall be secular and in a democratic and progressive spirit." The Bulgarian Orthodox Church is also in favor of democratic and secular education, being the first institution to have created and supported such education, starting with its first teacher, St. Kliment of Ochrid, then Neophyte of Rila, until today. However, the word "secular" in the cited text cannot fail to evoke dismay, because such a characterization of people's education is not only rather vague and fluid, but also because it can serve as the basis of a distinctly anti-Church and anti-religious tendency in education. Therefore, in this case the Church cannot fail to raise its voice in warning.
>
> To this day our Church maintains its firm conviction that religious education should be taught to the predominantly Christian Orthodox Bulgarian nation as an elective subject, i.e., according to the wishes of the students and of their parents.
>
> However, if "secular" education is understood to mean instilling of anti-religious or anti-Christian ideas among the students of the Bulgarian nation, this would violate the freedom both of conscience and of religion, irrespective of the form that this abuse may acquire. Therefore, one should not even allow the thought to cross one's mind that the Bulgarian school would provide anti-religious moral instruction and education, or that it would serve as an instrument for undermining the foundations of Christian morality...

> For this reason the Holy Council of the Bulgarian Orthodox Church insists that this Article be complemented with the words "but neutral in terms of world outlook".[6]

The leadership of the country was not in the least moved by the objections of the highest body of the Orthodox Church and ignored its suggestions concerning the Constitution. In December 1947, the Dimitrov Constitution was adopted with all provisions contained in the officially publicized draft. On July 4, 1948, the *Izgrev* newspaper published the position of the National Council of the Fatherland Front regarding the work of the Church:

> Following the provisions in the Constitution on the separation of the Church from the State and the existence of complete freedom of conscience and religion in the People's Republic of Bulgaria, and bearing in mind the recent increase in the frequency of anti-Fatherland Front acts committed by individual clergymen who are using the Church pulpit, the name and the means of the Church for campaigning and propaganda against the people's power, the National Council of the Fatherland Front considers that:
>
> 1. The task of the Church is to make sure to satisfy the religious needs of the believers; the Church pulpit is to be used only for religious service, but under no circumstances should it be used as a tribune for anti-Fatherland Front campaigning and propaganda; the Fatherland Front cannot tolerate clergymen who encourage hostile moods and actions against the people's rule, or anti-Soviet moods and actions for that matter.
>
> 2. The Church should make sure that its clergymen are exemplary citizens of the Republic. It should ensure their good conduct and should take the necessary steps against any manifestations of degradation. It should concern itself with the good state of its property and with its upkeep.
>
> 3. The Church does not conduct any special religious propaganda among children. The education of children is secular and is entrusted exclusively to the state and democratic public organizations. No children's religious organizations are permitted.
>
> 4. The publications of the Holy Council and the Union of the Clergy should consistently follow the political line of complete collaboration with the people's power, so as to prevent blatant fabrications and falsifications, numerous instances of which have been noted recently.
>
> 5. The Holy Council should revoke its ban on the participation of priests and other Church staff in the Fatherland Front and in the structures of the people's power because this ban breaches the Constitution of the People's

---

[6] From the Statement of the Holy Council of the Bulgarian Orthodox Church on the main principles in the new Constitutions regarding the Church, November 1, 1946; Ognyanov, Dimova, Lalkov 1992, pp. 90-91.

> Republic of Bulgaria, which guarantees equal civil and political rights to the clergy.
>
> 6. The mass pilgrimages to the Rila Monastery have acquired the character of something of a demonstration against the people's power and should henceforth be discontinued.
>
> This decision was adopted by the Executive Committee of the Fatherland Front on June 8 of this year with the participation of two representatives of the Holy Council, who expressed for the record some reservations on item 3.[7]

On September 8, 1948, two months after that decision of the Fatherland Front was published, the communist rulers forced Exarches Stefan, the Head of the Bulgarian Orthodox Church, to leave office.

. . .

At the Fifth Congress of the Bulgarian Workers' Party (communists) in December 1948, Beltcho Nikolov delivered the following fiery speech:

> The time has come for a final break with religion, something that has poisoned for centuries and continues to poison the soul of our people. Religion is nothing else but the cradle of the black fascist past, a cover for a new enslavement of the Bulgarian people. It is a shame and a disgrace that there are some among us, communists, who have taken Communism to heart, but at the some time are weak on the subject of religion.
>
> I propose that everyone who attends church services or protects the church should be punished at once by being expelled from the Party and persecuted more intensely than any other fascist.
>
> For the time being, while the road is lighted by the brilliant and great doctrine of Marxism-Leninism and Georgi Dimitrov's regime, religious people are abnormal. The fight against these enemies must be persistent and merciless.
>
> There has not been, there is not, and there will not be a greater and more sacred religion than Marxism. Every communist is an enemy of religion; religion is in the last days of its existence. Therefore, I appeal to all to fight religion to the point of its destruction. Onward without a god or church! Onward with our glorious Communist Party under the wise leadership of comrade Dimitrov![8]

At the beginning of 1949, the Sixth Grand National Assembly of the People's Republic of Bulgaria adopted the Religious Denominations Act. It

---

[7] *Izgrev* daily, Beltcho Nikolov, *The National Council of the Fatherland Front on the issue of the work of the Church*, June 8, 1948, July 4, 1948.

[8] *Rabotnichesko Delo* daily, December 1948.

required that the clergy and officials in the various religious denominations be only Bulgarian citizens, honest and trustworthy (Article 10); authorized the Directorate on Religious Denominations to suspend or dismiss clergymen (Article 12); gave orders when and how the state power was to be mentioned during the religious services (Article 18); subordinated the establishment of organizations pursuing religious goals and the publishing of printed materials for religious education to the laws and administrative regulations of the BCP (Article 20); banned the education and organizing of children by the religious denominations (Article 20); prohibited the opening of hospitals and orphanages (Article 21); prohibited contacts with foreign organizations without the specific permission of the Directorate on Religious Denominations (Article 22); prohibited religious denominations functioning abroad to open their subdivisions in the country (Article 23).[9]

The restrictions and bans listed above affected not only the Orthodox Church, but also the Catholic, Protestant and Armenian Churches, as well as the Judaic and Moslem religious institutions in Bulgaria, whose lands and property had been almost entirely nationalized. Deprived of their own financial resources, the Christian churches and the other religious institutions were forced to depend on state subsidies and to cooperate with the communist government.

...

In 1971, Nicola Dolapchiev wrote in his book *Bulgaria - The Making of a Satellite - Analysis of the historical developments 1944-1953* the following:

> Soon after the Orthodox Church was in this way subjugated by the Communist Government, a ruthless blow was struck against the Bulgarian Protestant Church by the sinister trial of the Fifteen Evangelical Pastors in February, 1949.
>
> The trial had been carefully planned and the procedure followed the familiar pattern. The 15 Pastors were members of the Supreme Council of the United Evangelical Church, which incorporated the Methodist, Adventist, Baptist and Congregational Churches. Their following in Bulgaria is over 20 thousand. The Pastors were arrested six months before the trial opened. For two weeks before the trial the alleged voluntary confessions of all the accused were published verbatim in the Government-controlled newspapers. An official bulletin issued a week before the trial stated that the preliminary judicial investigation was carried out in accordance with the laws of the country and had established their guilt. The case for the prosecution was based on the

[9] Asenov 1998, pp. 7-8.

alleged voluntary confessions of the accused. Each Pastor in turn pleaded guilty to charges of espionage, treason and illicit currency dealings. Under the then existing law a conviction on one of these charges was punishable by a sentence of death. In nearly all the confessions the Pastors went out of their way to incriminate themselves in pre-war espionage activities, which had nothing to do with the charges against them. The prosecutor demanded maximum sentence for four of the accused. On March 8, the sentence was pronounced. Four accused, including the chief defendant, Pastor V. Zyapkov, were sentenced to life imprisonment. The remaining were sentenced to terms of imprisonment ranging from 1 to 15 years.

The issue about the persecutions of the Bulgarian Protestant Pastors and about the trial against Cardinal Mindzenti in Hungary were submitted to the General Assembly of the United Nations in April 1949. The Soviet Bloc's delegations had denied that persecutions or anti-religious trials had taken place in Bulgaria and Hungary and had insisted that the trials of the Church leaders involved crimes punishable under the penal codes of the countries concerned, namely, high treason and espionage. In their opinion, the trials had not been motivated by the position of the accused as Church dignitaries. In this way the Communists tried to contest the competence of the United Nations.

...

The Soviet delegate Mr. Gromyko likewise held that the accused had been convicted not on any religious grounds but because they had been proved guilty of political offenses, and in particular of conspiracy to overthrow the democratic regimes in their countries. The judgement passed on the accused was not inconsistent with the peace treaties, but, on the contrary, was in complete conformity with the obligations set forth in those treaties.

...

The United States delegate, Mr. Cohen, rightly pointed out that in both countries a clear pattern was discernible; a minority group had seized power through force and intimidation and it had maintained itself in power by methodically eliminating the leaders of political parties or religious groups who had refused to bow to the dictates of the Communist Party and support the totalitarian regime it had imposed. Those leaders had been brought to trial on the pretext that they had violated national laws.

...

The Australian delegation had quoted articles from the Bulgarian penal code, which created new and vague crimes. It had cited provisions of the law for the Attorneys-at-Law, which prevented the proper defense of the accused, and of the militia law under which the police agencies in Bulgaria could enter private houses and conduct searches without previous warrants. It had drawn attention to the Bulgarian Press law limiting freedom of expression and the law for cults giving the Ministry of Foreign Affairs full control over religious activities. It had described the unfair way in which the Bulgarian Government, in its official publications, had joined with the Press to assert the guilt of the

> Protestant Pastors before they were brought to trial. None of those official enactments and administrative acts had been denied; apparently they could not be denied.
>
> ...
>
> Turning to the question of the confessions on which the Government case was based, Sir Alexander Cadogan [the United Kingdom delegate - *author's note*] said that they had been obtained in conditions of complete secrecy, while the defendant had been held prisoner. In the case of the Bulgarian pastors one of the principal charges against the accused had been that they had given what is known as secret information to foreign agents. One of the accused was represented as having confessed that he had given such information to a named member of the British Legation in Sofia. It so happened, that the individual named had not even been in Bulgaria at the time when the defendant was alleged to have given him the information. Documentary proof at his whereabouts during the whole period in question could be produced. Thus that confession had been false.[10]

...

In his talk *The Repressions Against the Catholic Church and Against Catholics in Bulgaria (1944-1989),* given in the Bulgarian town Koprivshtitsa in September 2004, the History Professor Svetlozar Eldarov reports:

> Catholics in Bulgaria are a minority religious community that does not exceed one per cent of the country's population. In the mid-20th century they numbered about 50,000.
>
> ...
>
> Until the communist regime was established, they enjoyed all constitutional rights and freely professed their religion.
>
> After the *coup d'état* in September 1944, the Catholics in Bulgaria were confronted with the all-subordinating power and militant atheism of the totalitarian state. Unlike the Bulgarian Orthodox Church, which suffered the most from the anticlerical moods of the new regime and gave many victims on account of its status as the predominant religious denomination, the Catholic Church initially enjoyed relative peace. This atypical reserve on the part of the communists was due mainly to the Paris Peace Conference, which had to resolve the post-War situation in the country. For this reason the Catholics were spared during the first wave of the political repressions.
>
> ...
>
> The years 1946-1948 were a brief transitional period from ostensible tolerance to creeping discrimination. During that period a number of legislative

[10] Dolapchiev 1971, pp. 207-210.

measures were adopted and enforced, which increasingly restricted the activities of the Catholic Church especially in the educational and social spheres, as was the case for the other religious denominations in the country. The expropriation of Catholic property took place on a larger scale; the interference in the internal structure and activities of the colleges, orphanages and charity organizations intensified; censorship and control over the printing and publishing activities tightened.

...

The final transition from creeping discrimination to open repression was made with the adoption of the Religious Denominations Act on 24 February 1949, which banned all activities of the Church outside the church building. Relations with the Vatican were severed, Mons. Francesco Galloni was not allowed to return to Bulgaria after a trip abroad, and the Apostolic Delegation in Sofia was closed down. Under the Religious Denominations Act, all foreign nationals who were members of religious orders and congregations, were forced to leave the country. The State confiscated all Catholic hospitals, orphanages and other similar institutions in exchange for minimal compensation, far below the real value of the property. The buildings of the already closed schools, boarding schools and colleges were also expropriated. The publication of the *Istina* newspaper and the other printed editions of the Catholic Church was stopped. Atheist propaganda became particularly brutal, and the bishops in the three dioceses were forced to send out messages to the believers on various domestic and international events in the spirit of the official political rhetoric.

...

The Prime Minister Valko Chervenkov personally insisted on dealing with the Catholic clergy in an uncompromising manner. On June 26, 1952, he placed the following resolution on top of the report of the Minister of the Interior: "It is necessary to act with determination with respect to the Catholic bandits, which includes arresting the Catholic Exarch, if there is evidence to support this. You must stop before nothing. Keep me informed on the issue. It is necessary to prepare well a trial on the basis of the disclosures made and to raze to the ground the nests of the Catholic bandits in Bulgaria. In addition, we shall consult our Soviet friends. When the investigation is basically completed, make a concise presentation on what has been discovered, which we shall send to our friends with a request for advice, and we shall destroy the Catholic bandits. We are destroying the bandit contacts of the Catholic Church with the Vatican; the Vatican is organizing nests of criminals here. A trail against the bandits in Bulgaria will have an anti-Vatican and anti-Papal spearhead."

The "big hunt" for Catholic clergyman was followed by retributions against them in the courtroom. Asen Chonkov, parish priest in the village of Bardarski Geran, Nikopol Diocese, became sadly famous for being the first defendant in a series of trials.

...

A trial was organized in Plovdiv on June 6, 1952, "behind closed doors" to the public, at which the case against the Capuchin Father Yosif Tonchev was heard. The charge against him was also espionage, but his sentence was most severe. Yosif Tonchev was sentenced to death and executed on January 23, 1953.

The first four trials lasted only one day. They were not made public and did not have a strong response in the Bulgarian community, except in the circles of the Catholic Church. In contrast, the mass arrests in 1952, conducted with deliberate ostentatiousness, clearly showed that the authorities had changed their tactics and were preparing for a public trail.

The 40 people arrested in July 1952, among whom there was one Bishop, 25 priests and one nun, were accused of spying and subversive activities against the people's democratic rule. "Confessions" were wrung from them by subjecting them to physical and psychological torture. The most frequently used method was the so-called "merry-go-round" - 24-hour interrogation for days, whereby the investigators rotated, while the detainees were kept on the verge of total physical and mental exhaustion, when they were no longer capable of making a difference between reality and fantasy. The "merry-go-round" was usually diversified with beatings.

...

In less than three months, the investigation on case No. 859/1952 concerning the "spying and conspiratorial Catholic organization in Bulgaria" was ready. That was the charge in the courtroom farce enacted in Sofia from 29 September to 3 October 1952, which was extensively covered by the media. The case was heard by a panel of the Supreme Court, and a display was set up in the courtroom for part of the "evidence" planted by the secret services during the arrests and searches, including machine guns, guns, bombs, pistols, radios, and gold coins. From the indictment and from the minutes of the court sessions, extensively covered in the newspapers, it appeared that the defendants participated in a large espionage organization that had been created and headed by the Vatican.

On October 3, the court pronounced the sentences, which had a petrifying effect on account of their severity. Four people were sentenced to death by firing squad, namely Bishop Evgeniy Bosilkov from the Nikopol Diocese, a Passionist, and the Assumptionists Kamen Vichev, Pavel Dzhidzhov, and Yosafat Shishkov. The other sentences varied from 3 to 20 years of imprisonment.

...

The death sentences were executed at 11:30 p.m. on November 11, 1952, at the Central Prison in Sofia. The executions of Evgeniy Bosilkov, Kamen Vichev, Pavel Dzhidzhov and Yosafat Shishkov were not publicly declared until the end of the communist regime in Bulgaria.

On October 29, 1952, the Sofia Regional Court heard the case of Bishop Ivan Romanov, Vicar of the Sofia-Plovdiv Diocese. The charge had already become traditional; it was espionage. The sentence was relatively light - 12 years in prison - but for the 74-year-old bishop it was tantamount to execution. Bishop Ivan Romanov died in prison just two months later, on January 8, 1953.

Between December 2 and 4, 1952, the Sofia Regional Court heard another case of Catholic priests and civilians accused of espionage. In that trial ten people were brought before the court, one of whom was sentenced to death, one received a sentence of 20 years in prison, two were sentenced to 15 years of imprisonment, two received 10 years in prison and two were to spend 6 years in prison.

With this the series of trials against Catholic bishops, priests and laymen ended. At the same time, however, two dozen Catholic priests, monks and nuns were sent without trial or sentence to labor-correctional communities, a euphemism used in the past for the communist concentration camps.

...

Instead of organizing trails and executions, the State Security changed its tactics and started recruiting agents among the circles of the Catholic clergy and believers. In the 1950s there were about 1,000 Bulgarian Catholics whose names were kept on record at the Clergy and Sects Department, and more than 100 individual and group investigations and recruitment operations were organized. The apparatus of agents steadily grew from 68 informers and agents in 1953 to 339 in 1958. The activities of the State Security against the Catholics in Bulgaria were accompanied by serious administrative restrictions for the priests who remained free, coupled with fierce atheist propaganda among all social strata.[11]

. . .

The severe repression against all religious groups did not keep the Bulgarian Communist Party from declaring that the population of the People's Republic enjoyed religious freedom. At the same time, people were urged to desecrate Christian Orthodox monuments. In the late 1940s and the 1950s public organizations and school boards encouraged citizens and students to write graffiti on the walls of churches and monasteries, and destroy icons, Bibles, and religious literature. Furthermore, the red rulers substantially reduced the number of monks in the monasteries, thus causing their depopulation and in many cases even demolition. In the 1970s, Ruse was proclaimed an atheist city and its citizens were not even allowed religious funeral services. Throughout Bulgaria the government was watching who was attending Church and made lists of individuals who went to the traditional liturgy on the night before Easter. For

[11] Eldarov 2004, pp. 86-96.

the sake of "tradition", eggs were dyed for May Day, the International Labor Day - instead of Easter - in the homes of the communists.

Lyubomir Mladenov, Head of the Directorate on Religious Denominations at the Council of Ministers from 1997 to 2002, explains the condition of the Bulgarian Orthodox Church as follows:

> During communism students with bad grades enrolled in the Theological Seminary and the Theological Academy. Students with good grades who applied for these institutions were persuaded that they would have no future after graduating, that they would be persecuted, that education there is obsolete, retrograde and reactionary. As a result, the graduates both of the Academy and the Seminary were mostly mediocre young men. This affected what the communists referred to as the "cadres of the Church". The Church did not need educated people with outstanding intellectual potential. It needed impersonal individuals. In other words, the government was relying on the gradual decline of the institution of the Orthodox church, in the hopes that it would stop functioning all by itself.
>
> When the changes in Bulgaria at the end of 1989 took place rather suddenly, the Church employed mainly people of mediocre abilities. A large number of them also worked for the State Security. No dissident movement existed in the Church. There were no outstanding personalities who could start its revival.
>
> None of the Church leaders succeeded in riding the wave of democracy, figuratively speaking. Had there been such a person, under certain circumstances he could have become a popular political leader. In my opinion, people would have accepted him with great enthusiasm. However, this did not happen. The Church elders shut themselves up in their cocoons. They did not take part in any demonstration or rally of the Union of Democratic Forces. In 1992, during the term of Philip Dimitrov's government, they never said that the new democratic regime allowed for the development of an autonomous and strong Bulgarian Church. Conversely, they maintained their old contacts with the Bulgarian Communist/Socialist Party, which still had power over them. None of the Orthodox bishops demonstrated a real commitment to the democratic changes in Bulgaria. This is very indicative of their true stance and no less sad.[12]

[12] Lyubomir Mladenov in a conversation with the author, Sofia, Bulgaria, July 20, 1998.

10. Terror and High Treason

By the mid-1950s Bulgaria had plunged into the darkness of totalitarianism. The fate of its citizens fell into the hands of the Bulgarian Communist Party and depended solely on their membership in it and their support for it.

The individual destinies of the political figures with democratic convictions, outlined below, reflect the choices Bulgarians faced at the time. Some took the road to the gallows, the prison cells, the swamps of the concentration camps and the solitude and misery of life in deportation, while others preferred high government positions or sinecures. The difference between the two was so enormous that some could not resist the temptation, and bent. The best did not.

Konstantin Muraviev (1893-1965) - Agrarian, graduate of Robert College in Istanbul and the Military Academy in Sofia., diplomat, Member of Parliament, former government minister, member of the opposition from 1939 until 1944, Prime Minister of Bulgaria (September 2-9, 1944).

Sentenced to life imprisonment in 1945 by the so-called "People's Court". Released from prison in 1955. Arrested again in 1956 and sent to the concentration camp on the island of Belene in the Danube River for five years.

Krastyu Pastuhov (1874-1949) - Social Democrat, held a degree in law from the University of Sofia and had specialized in Germany, attorney, Member of Parliament, former government minister, member of the leadership of the Bulgarian Workers' Social Democratic Party, participant in the opposition between 1939 and 1944, opponent of the Fatherland Front.

Since June 1945 member of the Central Committee of the BWSDP (u), which was in opposition to the communist rule.

Sentenced to five years in a maximum security prison in 1946. Strangled in his cell at the age of 74.

Tsveti Ivanov (1914-1950) - Social Democrat, Editor-in-Chief of the *Svoboden Narod* newspaper of the opposition Bulgarian Workers' Social Democratic Party (united).

Sentenced to one year, 7 months, and 15 days in a maximum security prison in 1946. Arrested again in 1950 and sent to the concentration camp in Belene. After pricking himself on a rusty nail, he was denied a tetanus shot and died of tetanus at the age of 35.

Nikola Mushanov (1872-1951) - Democrat, held a French law degree, judge, prosecutor, attorney, Member of Parliament, Leader of the Democratic Party from 1938 until it was banned in 1947, former government minister, Prime

Minister of Bulgaria and Minister of Foreign Affairs and Religious Denominations (1931-1934), one of the leaders of the opposition from 1939 until 1944, opponent of the Fatherland Front, Minister without Portfolio in Kostantin Muraviev's government.

Sentenced to one year in prison by the "People's Court" in 1945. In 1947, deported and forced to take permanent residence in Tarnovo, and in 1949 banished further away from Sofia to the village of Zagrad near Tutrakan. Arrested by the communists in April 1951, at the age of 79. Died in a torture cell in the detention facilities of the State Security.

Stoycho Mushanov (1892-1975) - Democrat, law degree obtained in France, Member of Parliament, Labor Director, Permanent Representative of Bulgaria at the International Labor Committee with a seat in Geneva, former government minister, Speaker of the Twenty-Fourth Ordinary National Assembly, member of the legal opposition between 1939 and 1944. In August 1944, special envoy of the Prime Minister Ivan Bagryanov to Cairo to conduct peace negotiations with Great Britain and the United States.

Active member of the Democratic Party, which was opposed to the Fatherland Front.

Deported to Targovishte in October 1947. In 1949 sent to the concentration camp in Belene and subsequently sentenced to twenty years in prison.

Alexander Girginov (1879-1953) - Democrat, doctor's degree in Law from the University of Leipzig, attorney, Member of Parliament, former government minister, member of the opposition from 1939 to 1944, Minister of Finance in Konstantin Muraviev's government.

Member of the managing body of the Democratic Party, which was opposed to the communists, and director of its newspaper *Zname*.

Sentenced to one year in prison by the "People's Court". Deported to Razgrad and subsequently to Dulovo in October 1947. Sent to the Belene concentration camp. Died while incarcerated on the island of Persin in the Danube at the age of 74.

Atanas Burov (1875-1954) - Member of the Bulgarian Conservative Party, received a degree in political science and finance in Paris, banker, shareholder, Member of Parliament, Deputy Speaker of the Fifteenth Ordinary National Assembly, former Minister of Foreign Affairs who succeeded in minimizing the reparations and compensations that Bulgaria was obliged to pay to Greece after the First World War. Member of the opposition from 1939 to 1944, Minister without Portfolio in Konstantin Muraviev's coalition government.

Member of the anticommunist legal opposition.

Sentenced to one year in prison by the "People's Court" in 1945. In 1947, deported to Dryanovo. Sent to a labor camp near Dulovo in 1949. Arrested in April 1950 and held in detention by the investigation until November 1952. Sentenced to 20 years in a maximum security prison, stripped of all civil rights for 23 years and sentenced to confiscation of all his property. Died in the Pazardzhik prison at the age of 79, deprived of medical care.

Dimitar Gichev (1893-1964) - Agrarian, graduate of the Theological Seminary in Sofia, Member of Parliament, former government minister, one of the co-founders of the Bulgarian Agrarian People's Union *Vrabcha*-1 and its leader for many years, member of the opposition from 1939 to 1944. Refused to join the Fatherland Front, Minister without Portfolio in Konstantin Muraviev's government.

In 1945 he merged the BZNS *Vrabcha*-1 with the opposition Bulgarian Agrarian People's Union - *Nikola Petkov.*

Sentenced to one year in prison by the "People's Court" in 1945. In April 1948, sentenced to life imprisonment in a maximum security prison, in addition to a fine of 500,000 levs, permanently stripped of civil rights for "spreading false rumors, for sabotaging the people's power and for instigating the formation of clandestine armed groups."

Nikola Petkov (1893-1947) – Agrarian, son of the famous politician Dimitar Petkov, held a degree in Law from Paris, diplomat, journalist, Member of Parliament, founder of several wings of the Bulgarian Agrarian People's Union, one of the co-founders of the pro-Soviet clandestine Fatherland Front and member of its National Committee, participant in the political preparation of the military coup on September 9, 1944.

Minister without Portfolio in the first Fatherland Front government of Kimon Georgiev, Secretary General of the BZNS Standing Committee. Left the Fatherland Front government on July 30, 1945, and founded the opposition party BZNS - *N. Petkov.* Leader of the united opposition in the Sixth Grand National Assembly.

In 1947, accused of counter-revolutionary activities, sentenced to death and hanged.

Kosta Lulchev (1882-1965) - Social Democrat, leader of the opposition Bulgarian Workers' Social Democratic Party (united) since 1945 and Director of its newspaper *Svoboden Narod*, Member of Parliament in the Sixth Grand National Assembly.

Arrested in July 1948. On November 15 of the same year sentenced to fifteen years in a maximum security prison for "breeding distrust in the government" and for "undermining the prestige of the Bulgarian State."

Petko Stoyanov (1879-1973) - Radical Democrat and subsequently Democrat, later "independent intellectual", held a degree in Law from St. Petersburg, specialized in financial and economic studies in Munich. Finance Professor at the University of Sofia, Dean of its Law School, Deputy Director of the Free University, Member of Parliament, Member of the Academy of Sciences since 1935, member of the opposition from 1939 to 1944, joined the Fatherland Front at the end of August 1944.

Minister of Finance in Kimon Georgiev's first government.

Resigned from the government in August 1945 and joined the opposition, boycotted the elections for the Twenty-Sixth Ordinary National Assembly and associated his activities in the Sixth Grand National Assembly with the opposition Bulgarian Agrarian People's Union - *Nikola Petkov*.

Stripped of his rights as Member of Parliament in June 1947. In 1949, sent to the Belene concentration camp and expelled from the Bulgarian Academy of Sciences.

Vergil Dimov (1901-1979) - Agrarian, graduate of the Higher Cooperative School in Czechoslovakia, degree in Law from the University of Sofia, attorney, Member of Parliament, former government minister, one of the founders of the BZNS *Vrabcha*-1 and member of its leadership, member of the opposition from 1939 to 1944, opponent of the creation of the Fatherland Front, Minister of the Interior and of Public Health in Konstantin Muraviev's government.

Sentenced to life imprisonment by the "People's Court" in 1945. Pardoned in October 1955.

Since 1957, included in the composition of the Supreme Council of the pro-communist Bulgarian Agrarian People's Union.

Svetla Daskalova (1921 - 2008) – Agrarian, daughter of the eminent Agrarian Rayko Daskalov, degree in Law from the University of Sofia.

Member of Parliament from the opposition BZNS - *N. Petkov* in the Sixth Grand National Assembly.

In 1951, arrested and send to Belene.

Between 1958 and 1990, Member of Parliament in seven successive National Assemblies of the People's Republic of Bulgaria. From 1962 to 1966, Deputy Chairperson of the Bureau of the Fourth National Assembly. From 1966 until 1990, Minister of Justice in totalitarian Bulgaria and member of the Standing

Committee of the Bulgarian Agrarian People's Union. Member of the National Council of the Fatherland Front, the Committee of the Movement of Bulgarian Women, and the Board of the Lawyers' Union. Received the title of "Lawyer of Merit" during the communist regime.

...

The biographies of the five prominent communists listed below, four of whom were Prime Ministers of the People's Republic of Bulgaria in succession from 1946 until 1962, eloquently suggest how non-Bulgarian the Bulgarian version of communism actually was.

Traycho Kostov (1897-1949) - completed the Reserve Officers' School in Sofia and studied Law at the University of Sofia.

In September 1923, Kostov participated in the preparation for the insurgency in Bulgaria following the orders of the Communist International. In 1929, he was sent to Moscow by the party of the Bulgarian communists. In 1930, he was admitted as member of the Union Wide Communist Party (bolsheviks). He worked in the Foreign Bureau of the Central Committee of the BWP(c) and in the Executive Committee of the Communist International. He was ordered to go back to Bulgaria in 1931 and was included in the Central Committee of the BWP(c). In 1932, he emigrated again to the Soviet Union and worked at the Communist International. In 1935, he was sent back to Bulgaria to implement the decision of the Seventh Congress of the Communist International to build a united front. In 1936, he became a member of the Politburo of the BWP(c) Central Committee. Between 1936 and 1938 he worked for the Communist International again.

In 1945, Traycho Kostov was re-elected as Politburo member and First Secretary of the Central Committee of the BWP(c). He became Member of Parliament in the Twenty-Sixth Ordinary National Assembly and in the Sixth Grand National Assembly. From March 1946 until March 1949, he was Deputy Chairman of the Council of Ministers and a minister in four governments. In April 1949, Kostov was relieved of all these positions and was appointed Director of the National Library.

As the head of the political operations of the Central Committee of the BWP(c), Traycho Kostov was the first assistant to Georgi Dimitrov and Vasil Kolarov in the forceful communization and Sovietization of Bulgaria. Following the orders of Joseph Stalin, he was accused in 1949 of anti-Party and anti-Soviet activities. He was expelled from the communist party and brought to court, where he was sentenced to death and hanged at the age of 52.

Georgi Dimitrov (1882-1949) - completed primary school, worked in a printing house, Member of Parliament, prominent figure of the international communist and trade union movement, Secretary General of the Executive Committee of the Communist International from 1935 until its dissolution in 1943.

In September 1923, following the orders of the Chairman of the Communist International, Grigoriy Zinovyev, Georgi Dimitrov instigated and led popular unrest in several regions of Bulgaria. After the uprisings were crushed, he fled abroad. For a while he settled in Vienna and worked at the Communist International Bureau there, in addition to organizing a Foreign Bureau of the BWP(c) Central Committee. In March 1933, he was arrested in Berlin and accused of setting the Reichstag on fire. At the trial in Leipzig he bravely defended the ideas of the international communist movement and aggressively attacked Hermann Goering in his capacity of President of the German Parliament. The Court acquitted him.

The Leipzig trial brought world fame to Dimitrov. After he was released from prison, he received Soviet citizenship and settled in Moscow. From 1937 until 1945, the "hero from Leipzig" was deputy in the Supreme Counsel of the U.S.S.R. in addition to his leading position in the Communist International.

Georgi Dimitrov initiated and created the clandestine pro-Soviet Fatherland Front in Bulgaria. Following Stalin's instructions meticulously, he masterminded the terrorist acts of the Bulgarian Workers' Party (communists) from abroad.

Dimitrov returned to Bulgaria in November 1945. He became Secretary General of the BWP(c), Member of Parliament in the Twenty-Sixth Ordinary National Assembly and in the Sixth Grand National Assembly. From 1946 until July 2, 1949, he was Prime Minister of the People's Republic of Bulgaria. On that date he died in the *Barvikha* Sanatorium near Moscow after years of alcohol abuse. His body was embalmed, sent back to Bulgaria, and exhibited in a mausoleum in the centre of Sofia, specifically built for the purpose. In the summer of 1990, it was taken out of the mausoleum through underground tunnels and buried in the Central Cemetery of Sofia. The mausoleum building was demolished in 1999.

Vasil Kolarov (1877-1950) - obtained a degree in Law from Geneva and completed the Reserve Officers' School in Sofia, attorney, Member of Parliament, from 1921 until 1943 member of the Executive Committee of the Communist International and its Secretary in 1922 and 1923.

Along with Georgi Dimitrov, Kolarov organized and led the riots in September 1923 and directed the Foreign Committee of the Central Committee of the BWP(c) in Vienna. At the end of 1923, he settled in Moscow. In addition to his leading position in the Communist International, Vasil Kolarov was Professor at the Institute of History of the Academy of Sciences of the U.S.S.R., the Higher Party School of the Central Committee of the Union Wide Communist Party (bolsheviks) and the *V. I. Lenin* Military and Political Academy. Along with Georgi Dimitrov, he directed the clandestine armed struggle of the communists to usurp power in Bulgaria from Moscow. He participated in the drafting of the Fatherland Front Program in 1942.

On September 9, 1945, Kolarov returned to Bulgaria. He became Speaker of the Twenty-Sixth Ordinary National Assembly and subsequently of the Sixth Grand National Assembly. From December 1947 until July 1949, he was Deputy Chairman of the Council of Ministers of the People's Republic of Bulgaria. After the demise of the leader Georgi Dimitrov, until his own death in January 1950, Kolarov led the country in the capacity of Prime Minister. He was buried near the back entrance to Georgi Dimitrov's mausoleum. His remains were transferred and buried in the Central Cemetery in Sofia in 1990.

Valko Chervenkov (1900-1980) - completed the International Leninist School in Moscow.

Following the orders of the Communist International, Chervenkov participated actively in the preparations for the armed unrest in Sofia in September 1923. In 1925, he emigrated to the U.S.S.R., where he became Desk Officer in the Balkan Secretariat of the Communist International and Director of the International Leninist School. He was also in charge of a sector of the Propaganda Department in the Executive Committee of the Communist International and became Director of its schools from 1939 until 1945. Between 1941 and 1944, Valko Chervenkov was member of the Foreign Bureau of the Central Committee of the BWP(c) and Editor-in-Chief of the *Hristo Botev* clandestine radio station, which broadcast from Moscow.

In September 1944, Chervenkov returned to Bulgaria and was elected member of the Politburo and Secretary of the BWP(c) Central Committee. Between 1950 and 1954 he was Secretary General of the CC of the Bulgarian Communist Party. Between 1950 and 1956 he was Prime Minister of the People's Republic of Bulgaria.

In 1962 Valko Chervenkov was expelled from the Bulgarian Communist Party, for organizing trials against its leading figures in 1949 and 1950.

His communist party membership was restored in 1969.

In September 2000, the Bulgarian Socialist Party demonstrated its communist heritage by honoring him with a celebration and a monument in his birth place, Zlatitsa, for the one hundred years anniversary of his birth.

Anton Yugov (1904-1991) - completed junior high school, worker in a tobacco factory.

Following a decision of the Central Committee of the BWP(c), in 1934 Yugov went to the Soviet Union, where he studied in the International Leninist School in Moscow. He was sent back to Bulgaria in 1937 and became a member of the Politburo of the Central Committee of the BWP(c). From 1941 until 1944 he headed the Military Commission of the CC of the BWP(c) and was member of the General Staff of the so-called "People's Liberation Insurgent Army". From October 1941 until September 1944 he was Secretary of the CC of the BWP(c).

Anton Yugov took an active part in the military coup on September 9, 1944. On that date he became Minister of the Interior, a position he held in the years of darkest terror and lawlessness. For his contribution to the "consolidation of the people's rule" he was appointed Deputy Chairman of the Council of Ministers between 1950 and 1956 and was Prime Minister of the People's Republic of Bulgaria from 1956 until 1962.

In 1972 Yugov was expelled from the communist party on charges of "fractious anti-Party activities".

Eighteen years later, in January of 1990, the "reformed" communists of Bulgaria took him back in their party, and he died as a member of the Bulgarian Socialist Party.

To this day the followers of communism in Bulgaria have a lot for which to be grateful to these five bolsheviks, all of whom became devoted emissaries of Soviet Russia in their own homeland. Without the enormous efforts of Dimitrov, Kolarov, Kostov, Yugov and Chervenkov to please Joseph Stalin, it would have been impossible for Bulgaria to turn into a totalitarian communist state, ready to betray its own interests following the orders of its "Big Brother".

...

The anti-Bulgarian policy pursued by the Bulgarian government in Pirin Macedonia remains a characteristic example of treason in the country's history:

> The instructions to that effect [i.e., that the region of Gorna Dzhumaya, or Pirin Macedonia in geographic terms, be separated from Bulgaria and annexed to the Macedonian People's Republic within the confines of the Federal Republic of Yugoslavia - *author's note*] were given to Georgi Dimitrov by Stalin during one of Dimitrov's visits to the Kremlin on June 7, 1946. In the course

of their conversation, the dictator from the Kremlin declared with utter cynicism, "The fact that there is no developed Macedonian consciousness among the population does not mean a thing..."[1]

Having subordinated its own people to the empire of communism, the BWP(c) immediately executed the orders of the Soviet dictator. The Tenth Party Assembly in August 1946 proclaimed the "cultural and national autonomy of the Pirin region to be the first step towards its incorporation in the Macedonian federal unit, which is a part of Federal Yugoslavia."[2]

The decisions of that meeting led to the "denationaliziation of an ethnic community by its own state".[3] On November 16, 1946, the official newspaper of the BWP(c) *Rabotnichesko Delo* impressed the following upon its readers:

> After the People's Republic of Macedonia was established, it is clear for every person with sound thinking that the unification of the remaining parts of the Macedonian people can be done only on the basis of that republic, which is within the confines of the Federal People's Republic of Yugoslavia. And this corresponds to the vital interests and the future peaceful development of Bulgaria in closest cooperation with fraternal Yugoslavia.[4]

In fact, the brutal attempts of the rulers to instill a Macedonian national self-identity among the population of the Gorna Dzhumaya region had started immediately after September 9, 1944, following the orders of Moscow. The regime punished all local resistance with murder, imprisonment, concentration camps or at least deportation.

The supreme trial for the people in this beautiful part of Bulgaria came during the "census" of its population in the last days of December 1946. The officials conducting the census, accompanied by officers of the militia and communist activists, tirelessly went from home to home and, with violence and threats, succeeded in coercing 70 per cent of the population to register as Macedonians.[5]

After the "census", hundreds of Bulgarian families, proclaimed to be Macedonians, were forcefully and urgently deported not only to Macedonia, but to distant Voyvodina in Yugoslavia as well.[6]

---

[1] Konstantinov 1997, p. 314.

[2] Ognyanov, Dimova, Lalkov 1992, p. 191.

[3] Konstantinov 1997, p. 314.

[4] *Rabotnichesko Delo* daily, November 16, 1946.

[5] Konstantinov 1997, p. 315.

[6] *Chronicle of a National Treason*, documentary film of Milena Milotinova, 42 minutes.

At the end of May 1948, however, the development of events took an unexpected turn: Moscow officially announced the rift between the Yugoslav Communist Party and the Cominformbureau. Actually the split was between the party of the Yugoslav communists and the Union Wide Communist Party (bolsheviks) of the Soviet Union, or, in other words, between Joseph Stalin and Josip Broz Tito.

The "fraternal" relations between Dimitrov's Bulgaria and Tito's Yugoslavia were suddenly severed. On July 12 and 13, the Bulgarian Workers' Party (communists) held its Fifteenth Assembly. It announced an end of a policy it had pursued with brute force during the previous four years.

On December 19, 1948, Georgi Dimitrov declared the following in his report to the Fifth Congress of the BWP(c):

> Our Party agreed to the introduction of the official Macedonian language as a mandatory subject in all schools in the Pirin region, and allowed a large number of Macedonian teachers from Skopje to go and teach there, and Macedonian book-sellers to open shop, so that literature in the Macedonian language could be disseminated. This was proof that our Party treats the unification of the Macedonian people with the greatest sympathy.
>
> However, our Party was betrayed in its good will by the leaders in Belgrade and Skopje. Most of the teachers and booksellers sent by Skopje, apparently following the directives of their Yugoslav masters, turned into agents of a Great Yugoslavia and their work amounted to anti-Bulgarian chauvinist propaganda. Later - after the betrayal of the Soviet Union by Tito's group - they became an overt anti-Soviet ring of agents.[7]

Then Dimitrov went on to contradict the official policy of the BWP(c) prior to the summer of 1948:

> The population of the Pirin region, however, did not succumb to that malicious anti-Bulgarian and secessionist propaganda. It has a negative attitude to the annexation of these lands to Yugoslavia, before the federation between Yugoslavia and Bulgaria has been put in place, because from times immemorial it has been economically, politically, and culturally linked to the Bulgarian people and does not wish to be separated from them.[8]

Such was the example of the "leader" of the nation, Georgi Dimitrov, in his capacity as Secretary General of the Central Committee of the Bulgarian Communist Party and Prime Minister of Bulgaria.

---

[7] Ognyanov, Dimova, Lalkov 1992, p. 181.

[8] *Ibid.*, pp. 182-183.

His disciples followed that model.

...

The culmination of high treason was that of the last communist dictator, Todor Zhivkov, who ruled the People's Republic of Bulgaria from 1954 until 1989 as a leader of the Bulgarian Communist Party. Twice - in 1963 and again in 1973 - he offered the Bulgarian state, founded in 681 AD, on a platter to Nikita Khrushchev and Leonid Brezhnev, and proposed that Bulgaria become the sixteenth republic of the Soviet Union.[9]

The book *1963 - The Negation of Bulgaria* contains the report of the assembly of the Bulgarian Communist Party's Central Committee held on November 1963, where the issue of the accession of Bulgaria to the U.S.S.R. was discussed:

> Academician Todor Pavlov, Member of the BCP's Central Committee and of its Politburo: "There is no point in holding a referendum on this issue, but we must organize a campaign, to clarify the whole issue, so that there will be no hesitation among the masses and the decision will be accepted unanimously."
>
> Dimo Dichev, Head of the Foreign Policy and International Relations Department of the Central Committee of the BCP: "Our communists have never been brought up in any other way except to think that the Soviet Union is our fatherland."
>
> Tsola Dragoycheva, Member of the BCP's Central Committee and Chairperson of the National Committee for Bulgarian-Soviet Friendship: "I share the enthusiasm and the joy to be working as a communist where the Party sends me, for the transition of our country into the big family of the Soviet Union, so that we can become one of the republics of the Soviet Union."
>
> Radenko Vidinski, Member of the BCP's Central Committee: "There can hardly be a greater joy for me than to see my people in the great family of the Soviet people. Therefore, I would support the proposal to join the great family of the Soviet people this moment not with one hand, not with two, I would support it with five raised hands, if I had them!"
>
> Lachezar Avramov, Candidate-Member of the BCP's Central Committee: "All generations of Bulgarian communists, both our fathers and grandfathers, and we ourselves have cherished in our hearts the dream of turning our country into a part of the great Soviet Union."
>
> Dimitar Dimov, Candidate-Member of the BCP's Central Committee: "During a conversation with Georgi Dimitrov in Varna, Georgi Dimitrov said to me that his ideal was for Bulgaria to become a member of the family of the

[9] Zhivkov 1991, pp. 37-48; Melone 1998, p. 71.

> Great Soviet Union. With the proposal of the Politburo, presented by Comrade Todor Zhivkov, we are actually beginning to make this dream come true."
>
> Todor Zhivkov, First Secretary of the BCP's Central Committee and Chairman of the Council of Ministers: "The Political Bureau believes that after this assembly there should be no talking in any form to anyone anywhere. Let us not forget that the great Bulgarian chauvinism is very deeply rooted in some circles and among some people in our country. I am not talking about the former people [term used by the communist to refer to noncommunists and anticommunists - *author's note*]. I have members of the Party in mind, especially ones among the intelligentsia and among some youth circles. We must bear that in mind. We shall not make a short-lived merger overnight; we shall do it once and for all and thus set an example for all countries."[10]

A similar meeting of national traitors took place in July 1973. It is impossible to tell how far this initiative would have gone if the Soviet leaders Nikita Khrushchev and Leonid Brezhnev had not refused the deal because of foreign policy considerations of their own.[11] It is good that they did so, after all. Otherwise, one fine day there would have been an announcement on Bulgarian national television, proclaiming that the People's Republic of Bulgaria had been bestowed the high honor of being included in the great Soviet Union.

What would the Bulgarians have done had that become a fact? Who could they have complained to? After all, the request for the annexation of their country to the U.S.S.R. would have been written and formally signed on behalf of the Bulgarian people themselves.

As it was mentioned previously, the building of communist Bulgaria was finally completed in the mid-1950s. This left an imprint on the mentality of the entire nation. Almost no one believed that things could be reversed and that the communist dictatorship could collapse. How could anyone think otherwise when the all-powerful Soviet Union was behind the BCP? And if someone hoped that it was possible not to die as a slave in his or hers own homeland, the relatives and friends proclaimed that person a "wild day-dreamer."[12]

. . .

The writer and journalist Vasil Stanilov published a small book in 2000 with the title *A Brief Inquiry*. It presents the life stories of three Bulgarian young men who were tortured by the communist militia in the late 1950s. Soon after that they

---

[10] Anakiev 1994, *passim*.

[11] Zhivkov 1991, pp. 37-48.

[12] From the diaries of Dr. Atanasa Donkova-Kralevska, kept at the time of the communist regime, private archive.

were sent to the most severe concentration camps of the "socialist" state - Belene and Lovech - without trial or verdict. In the early 1960s - already "in freedom" - they were deported for life from their hometown of Sofia to remote parts of the country. The names of the first two are Bozhidar Petrov and Boris Gikov. The "crimes" which they commited were playing guitar, listening and dancing to American music, and wearing western style clothes. The life of the third - Nikola Dafinov, was ruined because he studied English, French and Italian and dared to speak with some western tourist.

In his book Stanilov lets the victims of the red terror describe their cruel suffering and wretched lives in their own words.

Bozhidar Petrov:

> From 1959 to 1960 [at this time he was 16-17 years old - *author's note*] I was detained at the *Moskovska* Street office of the Ministry of the Interior seven times. The reasons were that I had been wearing tight pants, listened to western music, danced American dances, etc. One Saturday evening we were dancing in the club at *Gocho Gopin* Street. At about 8 p.m. a number of men from the Ministry of the Interior entered the club in plain clothes and uniforms. They made most of us (the boys) take our pants off with our shoes still on. A few of us, myself included, refused. Then they took us away in a car with covered windows, which was parked in front of the club and dropped us off at 5 *Moskovska* Street a few minutes later. We entered the waiting room and they began calling us in one by one. When my turn came I entered a furnished room in which there were two officers in uniform. "Take off your pants right away, motherfucker," yelled one of them. He came close to me and hit me in the face. "Wait! Don't beat me. I haven't done anything," I screamed. "The pants are new and they are mine." "Take him downstairs," said the other officer. They took me outside and called a sergeant-major who took me down the stairs towards *Dondukov* Boulevard.
>
> ...
>
> I lay down and lifted up my feet as I had been told to do. A man in a blue shirt and tie, with his sleeves rolled up, was standing above me. "Count to 50 out loud and if you don't scream loudly, you'll be spared and we'll let you go." He started the punishment. Next to me they were beating another victim. A long rubber hose was swishing through the air and hitting the soles of my feet. I alone know the pain. I counted to 50 and moaned softly. "Stand up," said my executioner, bathed in perspiration, "Give me your hands." I propped myself up by the wall, but when I tried to stand up, a pang made me collapse to my knees. I could not stand up and I stretched out my hands while kneeling. "Count to 20," he ordered and began. He would hit me and I would count. That hurt too, but it was nothing compared to the pain in my soles. "Now go to the bathroom. In an hour there will be an examination and whoever has any

marks from the beating will be beaten again." I dragged myself on my stomach in the direction he had indicated.[13]

In January, 1961, Bozhidar Petrov was sent to the concentration camp of Belene, known also as "the camp of death". Here are some of his painful memories:

The monster Gazdov [he, Goranov and Gogov ran the camp - *author's note*] appeared once again during the morning inspection. He took two men out of the formation. They were father and son, the Grigorovs from Sofia. They were particularly cultured and pleasant people. They were taciturn and were always together. Gazdov ordered them to grab a hand-barrow [a long piece of wood with two handles on each side, shaped like a stretcher - *author's note*] each and, sneering, cynically explained that they would be brought back in those very barrows in the evening. Then he took out his pocket mirror, in which he had the habit of observing himself and smoothing his bangs, and said, "Look at yourselves for the last time!"

I did not see to which quarry the condemned went to work that day. Yet, in the evening, before we headed back, two bags were loaded onto the hand-barrows, exactly as Gazdov had promised.[14]

Ivan Barzakov from the Plovdiv area was taken out of the prisoners' formation. After Goranov and Gazdov thrashed him, Yovo, the sergeant-major, tied him on the pole under the search light. It was 20 degrees below zero. We were all watching this new inquisition technique. Gazdov ordered a hose brought in, which was attached to the faucet at the sink. They started pouring water on the wretch, who was turning into a block of ice before our eyes. To our surprise, he was still alive in the morning. It was not until the following evening that we saw the bag [with his dead body - *author's note*] next to the toilet. The struggle with death would bear miracles.[15]

One of my friends from Sofia, Emil Parvanov, arrived one day in March. He had also been detained for a "brief inquiry." He was sixteen years old. In a very short time the camp was filled with innocent people without any stain on their lives. They were simply scapegoats of the establishment, sacrificed for the wellbeing of the totalitarian regime. In the beginning of the summer the prisoners numbered 1500. We could not even get to know each other. No one could keep track of who had arrived, why, and when he was murdered. The number of bags by the toilet was increasing. They were more than ten a day,

---

13 Stanilov 2000, pp. 8-10.

14 *Ibid.*, pp. 65-66.

15 *Ibid.*, pp. 63-64.

rotting in the heat, but the "morning-truck" could not keep up. The guards would break two or three bludgeons a day. There was a designated person responsible for supplying new ones, which were made out of dogwood.[16]

A youngster of about 25, whose name I cannot remember, jumped on the tracks at the Large Quarry while the train was maneuvering. The wheels severed both his legs but he survived. The sergeant-major guard asked the group leader Levordashki what was happening. Levordashki took a military hammer. They dragged the youngster off the tracks and Levordashki hit him in the chest with the hammer. The victim died and the sergeant-major nodded to the murderer approvingly. At the evening inspection Gazdov and Goranov delivered threatening speeches, saying that no one should dare commit suicide. They did not want to be deprived of the joy of taking our lives personally. They were both judges and executioners.[17]

There were very few of us, young boys between 17 and 20. Nikola Milkov Dafinov had been detained because he knew "capitalist" languages and had been speaking with imperialists. We used to sleep side by side on the second plank bed. Emo the Piccolo had also spoken with capitalists. He knew fascist languages as well and so did Boyko and a couple other people from Sofia.[18]

At the end of 1961 the management suddenly changed. Gogov, Goranov, and Gazdov suddenly disappeared. So did some of the sergeant executioners, including Krastev, Yovo, and Vutov.

...

General Mircho Spasov [Deputy Minister of the Interior - *author's note*] could tell that the entire affair was becoming unveiled and had decided to act early in order to avoid surprises.[19]

The joy [being released from the concentration camp - *author's note*] I felt was beyond description or comparison. That lasted very briefly, however, only until I discovered that my entire family had been deported to a village over 400 kilometers away from Sofia. A colonel from the People's Militia Directorate had moved into our home. We remained homeless for ten years. At the time Colonel Chakarov was responsible for the deported. The same man used to come and inspect the camp with General Mircho Spasov.

Chakarov had power, a lot of power. We would petition for appeal before the Minister of the Interior and the government, and he would show us our petitions when we would go see him. He would laugh and say, "Don't you

---

16 *Ibid.*, pp. 67-68.

17 *Ibid.*, p. 77.

18 *Ibid.*, p. 78.

19 *Ibid.* pp. 82-83.

understand that I am the one deciding everything?!" There were many of us, ill-fated wretches, gathered from all over the country in his waiting room by the *Lavov* Bridge. He would limp while passing us by and send half of us away with the words "Do you have a permit? Go then, before I've made you follow the standard procedure!" People left crying.

...

In 1963 a number of public figures stood up for us, including the actor Vladimir Trendafilov, the writer Dimitar Simidov, and the singer Magda Pushkarova, among others. The Minister annulled the deportation order and allowed us to resettle. However, Chakarov was the one who presented the Minister's printed order to us not to be deported. He read it out to us and showed us an additional warrant with which he demanded that we drop any claims to retrieve our home. "If you agree, sign individually." My father said not to sign anything, and I heeded his advice, of course. Chakarov placed the Minister's order before us and crossed out my brother's and my name from the list. Colonel Chakarov was in charge of our fates.

...

It was not until 10 years later that the Colonel deigned to return our dwelling to us and we came home. At last the entire family came together. I was already married and had a son.

...

Thousands of people, deported throughout the country according to the notorious Article 14, depended solely on Colonel Chakarov. Our passports had stamps "Deported" and new addresses in them. One could only work in the village spelled out in one's passport. We were paid for our work days at the end of the year. The compensation for raising crops and other agricultural work was 80 stotinki [one stotinka equals one hundredth of a lev - *author's note*] per work day. The locals were able to survive because they had their own livestock and small plots of land. There were abandoned houses in the villages, which were rented out to us, so we would have a place to live. We had to sign in with the mayor of the village every day. People were suspicious of us initially, but that changed gradually, and they taught us how to do farm work and helped us. There was no work during the winter. Those who had resources were well off, but those who relied solely on their wages had nothing to eat and could not pay their rent. The locals came at our rescue in such difficult moments.

...

Militiamen and their families had moved into our own homes. They paid the nominal rent of 5-10 lev a month, and we had no way of protesting or pursuing legal action.[20]

---

[20] *Ibid.*, pp. 88-91.

Boris Gikov remembers the following about Belene and Lovech, where he spent two and a half years:

> After a thorough search we were divided into brigades. Nasko and I ended up in the same brigade and shack. Nevertheless, we were still in a sorry plight. We had been completely stripped of our clothing during the search. They had shaved our heads and made us change into old prison and military attire. They had also taken away our personal belongings, which I never saw again.
>
> If I say "shacks," maybe someone will imagine structures resembling bungalows. In fact, we were accommodated in dug-outs. One would come down a set of stairs and directly enter a room on both sides of which there were double plank beds with battered and moldy straw mattresses and torn military blankets. About 100 people were packed into each of these dug-outs. They were built out of mud and interwoven sticks.
>
> There was no hygiene to speak of. Thousands of bed bugs were constantly falling off the sticks and keeping us from sleeping. In addition to the bed bugs, there were mosquitoes.
>
> There were two to three thousand prisoners in our section of the camp alone. The heads of the camp were Colonel Trichkov, Major Gogov, Captain Atanasov, Major Neshev (whose wife, Totka Nesheva, was responsible for the women in the concentration camp), Major Goranov, and others, whose names I no longer remember.
>
> The older prisoners told us that last year the move to work site number 2 took place in the form of a race with the horses of the guards and their German Shepherd dogs, bred specifically for the purpose. Of course, the bludgeons of the guards were also used to club the helpless running prisoners for allegedly trampling "the young poplar trees." Not only were there no poplar trees to speak of, there was nothing planted in the ground at all. In order to avoid the blows, the prisoners would hurry along, ignoring any belongings and articles of clothing that fell off them.
>
> ...
>
> The entire camp was surrounded by a fence whose poles were bent inwards at a right angle, just like the fences in the Nazi camps we had seen in the movies. Along the fence, at 40-50 meter intervals, there were wooden towers with armed guards who would shoot any trespassers.
>
> ...
>
> Accompanied by the guards, who were armed with sub-machine guns, and a prisoner foreman, we went to the work site. We were divided into couples and given a work quota we were supposed to fulfill. We had to dig, load and transport 10 cubic meters of soil and sand, while the women had to put out 8 cubic meters, or so we were told.
>
> Only those who have had to move sand with a hand-barrow know how hard that is to do since part of the load falls off with every step. If we could not

fulfill our daily quota - as was the case with Nasko and myself on several occasions - we would be called back to work after dinner. We would chop wood or grind food for the farm animals in the camp until late at night. The older prisoners called the additional work shift "a dance party" because of the electric lights.

Among us there were political prisoners, criminals, convicts, and people with no verdicts. It was impossible to tell how these thousands of people had ended up there, so Nasko and I tried not to stray from each other.[21]

The initial quota was 3 trolleys of stones per person. Later the number increased to 10. As work was done in groups, 50 trolleys were expected from 5 people. Any group that had not fulfilled the quota stayed back at the gate. Then, they were taken into the room for those on duty one by one and beaten with a hose.

Festering wounds eventually developed on the bodies of the beaten prisoners. There were no dressing materials for the wounds, medication, or a proper medical professional. There was a sham doctor, Gosho from Varna, who carried a canvas bag around with him, in which there was a little cotton and some antiseptic.

Given the increase in the beatings, there were a number of deaths. First died Hristo from Varna, after him Ariko the Jew, who refused to work because he was sick.

From the middle of 1960 onward the number of murders increased by the day. There were times during the morning inspection when Gazdov would tell some of the prisoners to take the hand-barrow. That meant that a person would be killed during the day and carried back in the barrow in the evening.

...

Representatives of various ministries and institutions visited the camps, among whom we recognized Mircho Spasov and Chakarov. After their departure the conditions invariably worsened and the frequency of the beatings increased.

The villa for the staff of the Ministry of the Interior in Lovech was under construction. Every evening each of us would carry a large stone for the completion of the villa. Whoever picked a smaller stone was beaten.

...

Gazdov and Goranov had thick dogwood canes made by Zhelyu Dinev from Stara Zagora. The canes were heated over a fire for greater sturdiness. God help whoever experienced the sturdiness of those canes! I personally knew the sturdiness of Goranov's cane. Someone had discredited me before the officer and said that I had spoken out against Goranov, so the latter called me over by the smithy of the quarry one evening. Goranov told me to lie on my stomach and started hitting me. I couldn't stand the pain and I got up, so he

---

[21] *Ibid.*, pp. 21-25.

clubbed me on the head. I fainted. I don't recall how I was carried over to the so-called infirmary, which had nothing to do with the way in which it was referred to, except that there was a doctor there. Doctor Mirinski, who was also a prisoner. He dressed my wounds. In the morning I regained consciousness. I would also like to note that Doctor Mirinski himself had been severely beaten upon his arrival in the camp.

...

The bodies of the deceased were undressed and placed in sackcloth bags, which were tied. We loaded the bags onto a truck and they were driven over to Magaretza, a small island on the territory of the former camp at Belene. The bodies were buried in very shallow holes and the pigs raised on the island would dig them out.[22]

One morning, on my birthday [already "in freedom"- *author's note*], two men in plain clothes and one militiaman came to our house and searched it without presenting any sort of warrant. Then, they invited me to the headquarters for another "brief inquiry." They took me to the office of the manager, where there were several men in plain clothes. One of them asked me how I had survived the camp. I replied that despite the torture, despite the enormous amount of work...Another man in plain clothes told me that I may have worked a lot, but I also talked a lot. As a result there was a warrant for my permanent deportation from Sofia. They requested that I sign the warrant. I refused. I explained that I was employed, my wife was pregnant, and there was no reason for which I should be deported. They responded that nothing could be done since there already was a printed order from the Ministry of the Interior, specifically from Colonel Chakarov, who was in charge of these matters. As I continued refusing to sign the warrant, they said that validating the document was not a problem. It could also be signed by two witnesses; even their own staff could do that...

They took me to the basement and locked me up in a cell, which I recalled from before. There were another fifteen candidates for deportation there.

...

In the beginning of 1965 I was summoned to Botunetz as a laborer. I was clearly being watched there as well. Even though I had the right to receive correspondence, the telegram announcing the death of my young son was not given to me. I found out about it much later and was unable to attend his funeral. I think that was done so I could not take advantage of the leave of absence that was due in such cases...

...

I was in Nozharevo once again. The population was Turkish. They were kind and affectionate people...Thanks to their empathy, I was able to lead a bearable life until 1970, except for the 8 months I spent in prison for having

[22] *Ibid.*, pp. 33-37.

left the village. I had gone to Sofia without permission because my father was seriously ill.[23]

Nikola Dafinov - the seventeen year old language lover, who was sent to Lovech concentration camp in December 1960, recalls:

I was told the story of the founding of the camp. About a hundred people went on strike in the Belene camp and were taken here as punishment. That was the beginning. That happened at the end of 1959. The prisoners built their shacks themselves, and then went on to work in the two quarries nearby. The original head of the camp was Colonel Trichkov from Belene, who retired in 1960 and was replaced by Major Gogov, a vicious shrimp, who also had a thick cane. First Lieutenant N. Gazdov from the State Security services was unanimously acknowledged as a humanly inconceivable kind of monster.[24]

It was December 19, at 5:30 a.m.. Searchlights were illuminating the endless road to "the Quarry of Death." I was seventeen and could not yet grasp where I was, let alone why. I was among the last few in line. In the very back two prisoners were carrying a wooden hand-barrow, which resembled a stretcher. That was a stretcher for the murdered as I would find out on my first day in the camp, December 19, 1960.[25]

I noticed that one of us was lying still on the ground. I came closer and noticed that he was still breathing. He was a very pleasant old Jew from Sofia. He used to have a contractor's office in the building above the *Crystal* café. I cannot remember his name any more and even at the time I had barely met him earlier. He was also new to the camp; he had been there only for several days. I pulled him by the side, propped him up and rushed back to set a full trolley in motion. It had been sitting there for a little while and I knew that every delay meant a blow with a bludgeon. When I ran down to the ramp, following the accelerating trolley, I was unable to flip the container properly. The trolley got stuck; my hands hurt so badly that I could not complete the task on my own. Zlatko, an elderly lawyer from Sofia who would record the number of trolleys in his notebook, came to my rescue. A gypsy working on the quarry also came over. Together, the three of us managed to loosen up the trolley and flip it, so I could unload it. On my way back up with the trolley, tears of pain were running down my cheeks. Then, I saw the Jew, who was still

---

23 *Ibid.*, pp. 92-95.

24 *Ibid.*, p. 45

25 *Ibid.*, p. 49.

lying there, this time barefoot. Someone had stolen his sandals. If we all had good comfortable shoes, I doubt anyone would have stolen his torn sandals.[26]

During a morning inspection in the end of 1962, Ivan Panteleev read out the names of Little Kole [Nikola Dafinov - *author's note*], Emil Parvanov, and Traycho Srabcheto. We had to stay in the camp at their disposal. My heart skipped. After everyone else went to work, they called us into Gazdov's office one by one in order to inform us that we were free to go. They made us sign a written statement that we would never speak about where we had been and what we had seen with anybody and under any circumstances.

...

By the end of March all prisoners who had been condemned to their deaths in the absence of any crime or verdict, following State Security decree 0789, were liberated. About 100 to 150 people remained, including all the murderous foremen.

In my opinion many more than 1,500 people passed through the labor camp, and hundreds were murdered. There is no way that the killed were only 140 people.[27]

I heard that many of the survivors of the labor camp in Lovech were immediately deported to distant villages.

At the same time I found out that Mircho Spasov had already become a Socialist Hero [highest honor title in communist Bulgaria - *author's note*]. Delcho Chakarov, untouched by anyone, had become the Head of the Department of Investigation. There were several generals in that department, but he was above all of them. In the same department were employed Colonel Kovachev and his subordinates: A. Uzunov, Vuchkov, Lukanov, and the old Peshev.

...

The good thing in my misfortune was that I lived among Turks. They understood me, helped me, and I think they loved me. There were tens of people from Sofia in the nearby villages, tens of broken families thanks to the deportation and resettlement services.

...

I was allowed to return to Sofia in the beginning of 1969.

...

Article 14 was still enforced. There were more cases of compulsory resettlement without any trial for the victims or a verdict. Delcho Chakarov was still Chairman of the Compulsory Resettlement Commission.[28]

---

[26] *Ibid.*, p. 52.

[27] *Ibid.*, p. 85.

[28] *Ibid.*, pp. 98-101.

> After the Helsinki Accords of 1976, Article 14 was dropped. I returned to Sofia. Actually, my broken body and my muddied semi-living soul returned to Sofia...[29]

According to inconclusive data, from the year 1944 to the year 1962, 285,000 people from all stocks of life were sent to the concentration camps of communist Bulgaria. That means one person of 28 from the total population.

. . .

With this kind of massive terror inflicted on every age group, little by little, the citizens of the People's Republic of Bulgaria adapted to the requirements of the totalitarian society. When the U.S.S.R.-led troops of the Warsaw Pact trampled the Prague Spring with their tanks in 1968, even the tiniest of hopes for change was squashed. A large number of people, who had shirked the Bulgarian Communist Party until then, joined it for a safer life and a more successful career. In this way communism not only changed the state system, it affected the conduct of ordinary human beings.

Fortunately, as November 1989 demonstrated, it failed to affect the souls of a large fraction of the Bulgarian nation.

The others were to live with its poison forever.

---

[29] *Ibid.*, p. 104.

PART THREE

OPPOSITION AND COLLABORATION

11. The New Opposition

The Union of Democratic Forces was founded on December 7, 1989, in Sofia, in the building of the Sociology Institute of the Bulgarian Academy of Sciences. The name was coined by the union's first Chairman, the philosopher Dr. Zhelyu Zhelev. Expelled from the ranks of the communist party in 1965, Zhelev was one of the constituters of the Club in Support of *Glasnost* and *Perestroika* in Bulgaria.

The Founding Declaration of the UDF was signed by the Club for *Glasnost* and Democracy, the *Ecoglasnost* Independent Society, the Independent Society for the Protection of Human Rights, the *Podkrepa* Independent Labor Federation, the Committee for the Protection of Religious Rights, Freedom of Conscience and Spiritual Values, the Club of Individuals Subjected to Repressions after 1945, the Independent Students' Society, the Civic Initiative Movement, the Bulgarian Workers' Social Democratic Party (united), which restored its official status on November 26, 1989, and the *Nikola Petkov* Bulgarian Agrarian People's Union, which renewed its existence during the first days of December. The Union of Democratic Forces indicated in its Founding Declaration:

> The new political situation in Bulgaria calls for the unification of the efforts and the potential of the independent associations in order to further the development of the democratic process. Founded solely on the coordination of the independent associations' actions in the common struggle for democracy, the UDF still preserves their autonomy, specific profile and subject of activity, prestige and place won in the country's public life; in that sense, the UDF unites the efforts of the associations of which it is composed, not the associations themselves.[1]

The UDF platform contained general requirements concerning a civil society, political pluralism, a multi-party system, the rule of law, a market economy, as well as some more concrete aims, including the following:

---

[1] Express edition *New Political and Public Forces*, BTA *Paralleli*, *Courier* Press Service, Sofia, the work on the material was editorially finished on February 21, 1990, p. 4.

> Establishing an equal status of all forms of ownership before the law; drafting new labor and social legislation providing for the right of workers to unionize and the right to strike; drafting a new democratic Constitution; bringing the Bulgarian legislation into accord with the Universal Declaration on Human Rights and other legal agreements related to the Helsinki process; depoliticizing the army and the militia; organizing democratic parliamentary elections; rehabilitating all individuals subjected to unlawful repression by the totalitarian system; establishing complete freedom of speech, press, meeting and association; establishing the legal and financial independence of the mass media and of the publishing houses.[2]

The program of the Union of Democratic Forces did not include the aspiration to participate in the government of the state. Its Founding Declaration specifically emphasized that the UDF was not a party, but a coalition of independent associations.

...

As early as 1983 and 1985, the ideological brain trust of the Bulgarian Communist Party's Central Committee - the Academy of Social Sciences and Social Management, later renamed to Institute of Contemporary Social Theories - held two meetings: one in Varna and one in Rudartsi, near Sofia. The participants in these meetings were not well known BCP members. They included Zahari Zahariev, Dragomir Draganov and Nora Ananieva, all of whom later acquired broad notoriety in the renamed communist party. More importantly, however, a number of non-party members were also present at the meetings, some of whom later joined the leaderships of political organizations opposing the red party. In Varna and in Rudartsi communists and noncommunist discussed the state of European social democracy and the modern left-wing parties abroad. They considered creating a Social Democratic Party in Bulgaria, as well as a political environmental organization of the type of the green parties in Europe. Thus, the BCP was planning on founding the nucleus of a future opposition, much like Iliescu had done in neighboring Romania.[3]

One could ask whether the communist leaders had remembered the advice that Joseph Stalin had given to the Bulgarian Workers' Party (communists) in August, 1945, when he suggested that it is sometimes useful that groups with noncommunist sentiments be legalized so they can be controlled and eventually

---

[2] *Ibid.*

[3] Ivan Kurtev in a conversation with the author, Sofia, Bulgaria, August 18, 1998.

forced into loyalty. Indeed, the Bulgarian Communist Party benefited from the establishment of more than fifty political and public organizations officially registered between mid-November 1989 and February 1990. Later they multiplied, forked, split and united, and thus distracted the public. At the end of 1989, the BCP also encouraged the revival of some of the "enemy" and "fascist" formations, banned in the second half of the 1940s. Several former members of the old political organizations, who had survived the persecutions, restored two parties from the left of the political spectrum, namely the Social Democratic and the Radical Democratic parties, as well as the centrist-right Democratic Party.

Most Bulgarians associated little with these parties. Nevertheless, many people joined one of them simply because its name sounded attractive. Others remembered a grandfather who had belonged to this or that party in the past, and hastened to follow his example. Some tried to quickly become involved in the country's dynamic political life and take a prominent place in it, while others were actually horrified by the very idea of party membership because even the thought had a "communist" ring to it. The latter often preferred the independent trade union *Podkrepa*. Finally, many men and women joined one or even several of the associations in the Union of Democratic Forces in order to support and strengthen what the population considered to be the only anticommunist organization in the country.

People lived in a real fever. The political novelties of the day were discussed with excitement in many homes. And at the end of 1989, something new happened every week, if not every day, something that no one had even dreamed of on New Year's Eve eleven or twelve months earlier. In December the Democratic Party's official status was restored and, for the first time in the country's history, a Green Party was created. In January 1990, these two organizations joined the Union of Democratic Forces.

...

The news that the Green Party had been founded was announced by its leader Alexander Karakachanov. All Bulgaria knew that he had been dragged in the street and arrested by the militia during the "incident" in front of the *Crystal* Café two weeks before the Berlin Wall fell.

Karakachanov was pleasant-looking and quite young. He was born in Sofia in 1960 in the family of a communist general in the militia, rumored to be ruthless with his political adversaries. Alexander went to high school in Moscow, where his father served as a military attaché of the People's Republic of Bulgaria in the 1970s. Then he earned a degree in philosophy from the *Kliment Ohridski*

University of Sofia. Since 1988 Karakachanov had been working for a program of the Medical Academy devoted to the study of the human brain.

The dissident activity of Alexander Karakachanov consisted of his participation in the founding of the Committee for the Ecological Salvation of Ruse and the Club in Support of *Glasnost* and *Perestroika* in Bulgaria. After *Ecoglasnost* was created, he was one of the ten coordinators of the independent movement and its sole Secretary. Alongside his dissident activities, in 1988 he became an elected member of the communist Sofia City People's Council. Some observant Bulgarians viewed this discrepancy in Alexander's political record with suspicion. Still, Karakachanov's name was among the first to be associated with the dissident organizations and with the well-known protest actions of the ecological society. This is probably why most people liked him, and, touched by his youth, they were willing to overlook his participation in the governing body of the totalitarian mayoralty of Sofia and for his father's political background. Too many Bulgarians had suffered because of blacklisted family members and had had to spend their lives as "second class" people. They did not want to resemble the communists and persecute their children. They were trying to forgive and forget.

The Green Party is an excellent illustration of the misnomers adopted by the new political organizations. The party's Agenda was primarily focused on economic problems considered from a free market perspective, rather than environmental issues. At the time its Political Declaration was the only one claiming the right to participation in the government of Bulgaria. There was even an appeal for the rejection of the communist system:

> The main proposition of the party, expressed in its Political Declaration, focuses on the individual and the quality of his or her life. Political democracy, a sensibly structured economy, and environmental sustainability are indissolubly linked elements of the overall complex of prerequisites allowing the individual to lead a satisfactory life.
>
> According to the party, the results of the past 45 years in Bulgaria are as followed: an economy ruined by the absurd economic concepts of the ruling BCP; democratic institutions destroyed or stripped of any significance - not accidentally but systematically - in accordance with the political doctrine of the party concealing its aspirations to absolute and indivisible power behind hollow philanthropic phraseology; an ethnic problem artificially created through chauvinist propaganda, trumped up accusations, and frenzied propaganda aiming to mislead and oppose the Bulgarians to the Bulgarian Turks; a complete lack of international prestige; and all this amidst poisoned air, land, rivers and sea, resulting from an aggressive attitude to Nature, from its irresponsible torture and megalomaniac fantasies of riverbed alterations and the

> correction of Nature. In the long run the country proved to be on the brink of a national catastrophe. Therefore, an overall change of the system of governance is needed and the party is striving towards representation in government and considers all independent organizations in the Union of Democratic Forces to be its allies. Radical change is needed, not *perestroika*![4]

The Agenda and the Political Declaration were drafted by two people outside Karakachanov's closest circle. Both authors later headed the Union of Democratic Forces and became Prime Ministers of the Republic of Bulgaria. The main part of the Agenda of the Green Party was drafted by an Assistant Professor of Economics at the Higher Institute of Mechanical and Electrical Engineering in Sofia. Five months later that man ran in the parliamentary elections on the UDF ballot and was elected deputy in the Grand National Assembly. In the spring of 1997, the economist and mathematician Ivan Kostov became the second Prime Minister of Bulgaria from the blue coalition.

The Political Declaration was written by the first democratically elected Prime Minister of Bulgaria after World War II, the lawyer Philip Dimitrov. At the constituent assembly of the Green Party he was elected its Deputy Chairman. Dimitrov declared that his main interest did not lie in the betterment of the environment. As a member of the Committee for the Protection of Religious Rights, Freedom of Conscience and Spiritual Values, he was opposed to the complacent and criminal jeopardizing of the health and life of the population. However, for Philip communism was the prime cause for the pollution of both the environment and moral values.

Karakachanov did not object to the election of the 34-year-old lawyer as his deputy. Dimitrov did not appear particularly competitive. He had the face of an intellectual, glasses, thick black hair and beard, and was always polite. Except for the unusual resolve he manifested occasionally, Philip looked more like the scholar and writer - which he actually was, than a politician. Karakachanov thought that the declaration Dimitrov had drafted was extremely sharp. Indeed, he had tried to stop Philip from reading the statement "We do not distance ourselves" [from the slogan "Down with the BCP!" shouted at a rally - *author's note*] on television in January of 1990. However, the documents drafted by Philip Dimitrov attracted people with strong convictions to the Green Party and contributed to its popularity. Alexander Karakachanov needed just that.

...

[4] Express edition *New Political and Public Forces*, p. 8.

The governing body of the Union of Democratic Forces, known as the Coordinating Council, consisted of three representatives from each member organization. At first it held its meetings in a lecture hall at the Sociology Institute of the Bulgarian Academy of Sciences. Later the communist government ceded a building to the opposition and the meetings were held at 134 *Rakovski* Street. In either location, however, the halls were never big enough. Everyone wished to participate in these historic assemblies. People joked that some leaders brought their entire parties. After mid-January 1990, the principle of one vote per organization was adopted.

Voting was too formal at first. The parties, the associations and the *Podkrepa* trade union easily reached agreement. The shared sense of inexperience and the fear that everything could end with some kind of catastrophe, possibly a personal one, created cohesion in the Coordinating Council.

The Chairman, Dr. Zhelyu Zhelev, born in 1935 in the village of Veselinovo, Shumen district, was a short man, with a spry figure for his age. His hair was already grey and he combed it forward. His eyebrows were black and attributed a specific expression to his face. His smile vaguely suggested a good nature, but everything else about him spoke of stubbornness and willfulness.

Zhelev had proven that he possessed these qualities. As a child and adolescent he had grown up deprived of information and was educated in the dogmas of communism. At 18, he cried when he learned about Joseph Stalin's death. Later, when he was a student of philosophy at the University of Sofia – at a time when the communist cult of personality was under criticism - his admiration for the Soviet dictator waned and his criticism of the totalitarian system emerged.

In 1961, Zhelyu Zhelev applied for and was admitted in the ranks of the Bulgarian Communist Party. He was appointed to the Philosophy Institute of the Bulgarian Academy of Sciences and to the Philosophy Department of the University of Sofia. He was preparing a dissertation on the philosophical definition of matter, in which he disputed the views of Vladimir Ilich Lenin. This was when Zhelev's troubles with the communist party started. The situation was exacerbated after the young scholar succeeded in publishing an article whose content was similar to that of his dissertation in a journal in the German Democratic Republic. In 1965, he was expelled from the BCP and soon after that he was deprived of the right to live in Sofia.

Zhelev spent seven years in his wife's native village of Grozden, near Burgas. There he wrote his book *Fascism*, hinting at similarities between the communist and fascist totalitarian regimes. He also completed a new dissertation. In 1974, back in Sofia, Zhelyu Zhelev defended his dissertation in philosophy. Four years later, he submitted a new academic work on the relational theory of personality and obtained the academic degree of Doctor of Philosophical Sciences. After 1975, he was Senior Research Associate and head of a section at the Research Institute of Culture. *Fascism* was published in 1982 but was soon removed from the market. In 1988, Dr. Zhelev participated in the creation of two dissident formations: the Committee for the Ecological Salvation of Ruse and the Club in Support of *Glasnost* and *Perestroika* in Bulgaria.[5]

In spite of his brave criticism of communist theories and dogmas aggressively imposed for decades, and in spite of his rejection of the totalitarian system, Zhelyu Zhelev - as he has explained himself - remained a Marxist. This fact disturbed many Bulgarians, who believed that his attachment to the theories of Marx and Engels contradicted his position as chairman of a democratic union.

Suspicious by nature, Zhelev trusted only his old friends and colleagues, most of whom came from communist circles. One of them was Petko Simeonov who even busy founding dissident organizations, maintained his membership in the Bulgarian Communist Party. There was an explanation for this. Petko was born in the present-day town of Montana in 1942 in the family of people enjoying the privileges of "active fighters against fascism and capitalism." He earned a Ph.D. in philosophy from the University of Sofia, and in his youth joined the red party. It was only later that Simeonov began to doubt some of its dogmas and to demonstrate disagreement with certain decisions of the BCP. A Senior Research Associate at the Sociology Institute of the Bulgarian Academy of Sciences and its Scientific Secretary, he was relieved of the latter post because of his participation in the protests of the Committee for the Ecological Salvation of Ruse.

Petko Simeonov's connections with influential communists were close and long-standing. As Dr. Zhelev's most trusted assistant in the UDF Coordinating Council, he was always perfectly informed about the intentions and wishes of the new leaders of the Bulgarian Communist Party. This gave him confidence, and for a long time he dominated the meetings of the UDF's leading body - in his role of mediator between the UDF and the BCP - together with Chairman Zhelev.

The Secretary of the UDF Coordinating Council, Peter Beron, a 49-year-old well-read man with diverse interests, was very much unlike Zhelev and Simeonov. He was born in the capital city and held a degree in zoology and biology from the University of Sofia. He had spent his life as a non-party member, but somehow succeeded in his academic career. Beron was a Senior

[5] *Demokratsiya* daily, Dr. Zhelyu Zhelev in a conversation with Adam Michnik, *The time has come to say everything*, August 11, 1990.

Research Associate with a Ph. D. in biology, head of the Zoology Section at the National Natural History Museum of the Bulgarian Academy of Sciences, and Professor of Zoogeography at the Department of Biology of the University of Sofia. He had specialized in France and in Czechoslovakia, where he participated in various research projects. His first book appeared in France while he was still a student. He worked in Nigeria for three years as the manager of a nature reserve and organizer of the fight against poachers, and took part in a British cave exploration expedition to New Guinea. He was Chairman of the Bulgarian Federation of Cave Exploration. In 1988, Beron joined the Committee for the Ecological Salvation of Ruse. He participated in the establishment of *Ecoglasnost* in April 1989 and was elected Secretary of the association.

The supporters of the UDF took an immediate liking to Peter Beron. This was due to his emotional nature, his talent as a public speaker and, last but not least, the fact that his name was identical to that of a famous figure from the days of the Bulgarian National Revival. The historical Peter Beron - who lived in the nineteenth century, was a philosopher, medical doctor, encyclopedist, and scholar well-known in Europe who also had done great services to his native land. In the tumultuous and exciting days at the end of 1989, this coincidence seemed to confirm the political rebirth of Bulgaria.

. . .

The general agreement among the members of the Coordinating Council was sometimes compromised by four people. The first two were the leader of *Podkrepa*, Dr. Konstantin Trenchev, and the Chairman of the Committee for the Protection of Religious Rights, Freedom of Conscience, and Spiritual Values, the monk Christophor Sabev.

Trenchev was born in Stara Zagora in 1955. He graduated from the French Language School and received a degree in medicine in Sofia. After 1987 he was working as Assistant Professor in the Department of General and Clinical Pathology of the Higher Medical Institute in his birthplace. In 1988 Konstantin Trenchev joined the dissident Independent Society for the Protection of Human Rights. The following year in Plovdiv, he founded the *Podkrepa* Independent Trade Union. After that he acquired national fame.

Christophor Sabev, born in Gabrovo in 1946, had two university degrees and a specialization at the Physics Institute of the Academy of Sciences of the U.S.S.R.. He obtained his degree in atomic physics from the University of Sofia in 1972 and a second degree in theology from the Theological Academy in 1985. In October 1988, Sabev founded the Committee for the Protection of Religious Rights, Freedom of Conscience, and Spiritual Values in Veliko Tarnovo, for which the Holy Synod of the Bulgarian Orthodox Church excommunicated him. Later his liturgies and candle lit vigils in the squares of Sofia brought him recognition among the residents of the capital city.

Both Trenchev and Sabev were rather unbalanced and unstable. While the clergyman was to make all his future blunders with good intentions, driven by vanity and lack of political instinct, the doctor was a much more complicated phenomenon. His strange wish to play the role of a military commander and to appear on television in camouflage military uniforms was combined with a penchant for populism, which he used well to maintain his high approval rating until 1992. Only then did persistent rumors about his connections with the Bulgarian mafia and his aggressive attacks against the democratic government of Philip Dimitrov finally discredit the leader of *Podkrepa.*

However, initially the UDF supporters were prepared to overlook the personal shortcomings of Dr. Trenchev and the Reverend Sabev as well as the rumors that the two of them had grown up in the families of "active fighters against fascism and capitalism". What they liked about the men was that they spoke like convinced anticommunists. The fact that both Konstantin Trenchev and Christophor Sabev were arrested by the communist authorities in 1989 made them look like heroes.

The other source of dissent in the Coordinating Council were two Bulgarian politicians of an older generation, who competed fiercely.

Milan Drenchev, Secretary of the restored *Nikola Petkov* Bulgarian Agrarian People's Union, had a rich biography as an opposition figure. He was born in the village of Vinishte in northwestern Bulgaria in 1917. While he was still studying in the Economics Department of the Law School of the University of Sofia, he had established contacts with BZNS *Pladne.* The adventure-seeking and ambitious agrarian leader Dr. Georgi M. Dimitrov, known as Gemeto - who served the Communist International at times, Yugoslavia at times, and Britain at times - involved Drenchev in a conspiracy regarding the transportation of explosives, sabotage, preparations for terrorist assaults, and the dissemination of clandestine literature. Milen Drenchev was arrested by the police in 1941 and sentenced to life imprisonment. He was freed by Konstantin Muraviev's government on September 8, 1944.

After the imposition of communist rule in Bulgaria, Drenchev's sufferings continued, without having participated in any anticommunist conspiracy. Between 1945 and 1953 he was arrested several times, tortured, deported and sent to the concentration camps: Kutsiyan, Bogdanov Dol and Belene. In 1955 Milan Drenchev was given a 10-year prison sentence. He was finally released in 1962. For political reasons he was never allowed to work either as an economist or a lawyer.

Dr. Peter Dertliev, the leader of the resurrected Bulgarian Workers' Social Democratic Party (united), descendant of Bulgarians from Macedonia and Aegean Thrace, was born to a family of teachers in the village of Pisarevo near Lovech a year before Drenchev. He became involved with the social democratic movement while he was still in high school. As a medical student in Sofia he was elected Secretary of the Social democratic Youth Division of the Medical School. In 1943 he was appointed Assistant Professor of Anatomy in the Medical School in Sofia, where the events of September 9, 1944, caught up with him.

In 1946, the doctor became Secretary of the Youth Union for Social Democracy. At the end of the same year he was elected deputy in the Sixth Grand National Assembly on the ballot of the opposition Bulgarian Workers' Social Democratic Party (united). When the communists undertook the final liquidation of the opposition, the persecutions against Dertliev started. He was arrested in 1948 and sentenced to ten years in prison. He was sent to labor camp at Rositsa and Belene. From 1958 until his retirement, Peter Dertliev worked as a physician specialized in lung diseases.

People spoke a lot about Dr. Peter Dertliev and Milan Drenchev and their parties. At the end of 1989, few had noticed the democrats led by the 80-year-old lawyer Boris Kyurkchiev, or the radical democrats of Dr. Elka Konstantinova, Bulgarian literature professor. Little was known about her two ambitious deputies, Alexander Yordanov and Mihail Nedelchev, who were soon to play roles of their own in the life of the blue union.

. . .

"Change" was the major goal of the Union of Democratic Forces. Gradually a dispute arose in its Coordinating Council about whether to define "the change" in negative or positive terms. Those who claimed to be in favor of a positive approach rejected the mention of anticommunism. They were unable to grasp that in this particular case, however paradoxical it might sound, the prefix "anti" had the positive meaning they were striving for. It simply meant freedom.

Due to internal strife the opposition alliance often appeared indecisive. But the Bulgarians who wanted political improvements understood that "change" signified toppling the communist regime. Yet, they liked radical politicians and often took their words for deeds and their shouting for the expression of principles. It would not be too long until they understood their mistake.

12. The Hot December

In the months after the appearance of the Union of Democratic Forces, no one was interested in the exact number of former members of the communist party in the Coordinating Council of the coalition or in the leaderships of the associations and political parties of which it was composed. Likewise no attention was paid to the fact that the UDF united the efforts of the groups making it up and not the actual organizations themselves. For the democratically minded Bulgarians what mattered was that, as they believed, the union was anticommunist. It was their party and the only political force to their liking.

This was understandable. Those who did not agree with the regime needed a legal organization that matched their views, and they idealized it. The UDF gave them support and strength. They treated as communist everyone who did not like the blue union. In contrast, all those in the UDF were their brothers and sisters.

Two days after the UDF was founded, about five thousand people from Sofia rallied in its support. With banners and slogans, they demanded a multi-party system and the resignation of Georgi Atanasov's government, which had been in power since 1986. Its spokesman, Philip Bokov, responded to the spontaneous civilian protest, with the claim that the actions of the "extremist elements" could "set the development of the country back decades."[1] Did this man mean that the Bulgarian Communist Party was ready to resort to its repressive methods of the earlier decades? Or maybe Bokov was unable to understand that the wish for a multi-party system did not mean extremism.

On December 10, the Union of Democratic Forces held the first rally for which it had official permission from the authorities. More than 70,000 excited people streamed to the square in front of the *St. Alexander Nevski* Cathedral to welcome the new opposition leaders.

A Western diplomat expressed his surprise at the powerful wave of popular anger against the totalitarian rulers as follows: "It looked as if the sun had risen in the middle of the night."[2] The foreigner was right. The sun had risen over Bulgaria.

The participation in protests gave people a new sense of confidence. It made them believe that they could have an impact. It gave them faith in their own strength. For the first time in decades, Bulgarians were not dragged to the squares against their will, as flocks of sheep, to support some decision of the leadership of the communist party. They gathered as socially conscious human beings to openly oppose the existing state system, which they hated and dreaded.

---

[1] *The New York Times*, December 11, 1989.

[2] *Christian Science Monitor*, December 20, 1989.

They had years of experience reminding them that any action in the name of freedom was to be punished. Thus the citizens who filled the streets, squares and parks of Sofia in a show of disagreement with the official regime were fighting against the most awe-inspiring enemy possible, namely their own fear.

In that historical moment, the Bulgarian Communist Party did not plan to use force against the public. However, the population was well aware that the government could change its mind. Despite that knowledge, people gathered in rallies and demonstrations, enchanted and staggered by the unfamiliar taste of freedom, with the firm belief that they were ready to oppose everyone who tried to take it away from them. The communist rulers chose to follow the wise advice of Vladimir Ilich Lenin, "one step back, two steps forward."

. . .

On December 11, the Central Committee of the Bulgarian Communist Party began a three-day meeting "On the State of the Country, the Party and the Immediate Tasks". Peter Mladenov, the new Secretary General of BCP's CC and Chairman of the State Council, reported the following alarming facts:

> We should start the objective assessment of the socio-economic state of the country with the observation that the previous leadership left us a legacy of progressive economic decline.
>
> ...
>
> The headlong increase in our foreign debt in convertible currency is extremely alarming. The gross foreign debt of the country in convertible currency exceeds 10 billion U.S. dollars. Our gold currency reserve is estimated at about 1.3 billion U.S. dollars.
>
> ...
>
> At present, our gross debt exceeds the annual revenues in free convertible currency several times. Merely the interest on the debt that we would have to pay in the next six years amounts to 44.5 billion dollars. If we fail to change things, more than half of our annual revenues in convertible currency would have to be spent on repayment of the debt. The repayment would also absorb a substantial part of the increase of the national income.
>
> ...
>
> By and large, we can speak about a relative - in some cases also of an absolute - decrease in the efficiency and competitiveness of the Bulgarian economy. The key factors underlying this menacing tendency are the grave investment errors of the past two decades. At the same time, it should be pointed out that we are lagging behind seriously in the sphere of technology and in the quality of our commodities.

All of the above support the conclusion that the national economy is in a period of progressive economic decline.

...

The factories and plants, which yield no profit and bring no currency, are weighing the national economy down. These are industrial facilities that live off the entire society. The heavy machine-building plant in Radomir alone, which is highly inefficient, has cost the budget more than BGN 1.2 billion. There are serious negative consequences from the construction of some plants in Ruse, the operation of the foundries in the town of Rakovski, and even the widely publicized upgrade of the chemical plants in Devnya.

...

Millions of hectares of land became unusable and were thus destroyed. The depopulation of entire regions in the country and the rigid attachment of the agro-industrial and industrial-agrarian complexes to their respective types of production narrowed the scope of agricultural production. From a traditional exporter of agricultural produce, Bulgaria has turned into an importer of potatoes, beans, cabbage, onions, animal feed and other agricultural products worth hundreds of millions of dollars. The intensive migration from the rural to the urban areas created serious social problems and - what is most important - increased the gap between the Bulgarian economy and the climate and environment of the country, thus destroying agricultural traditions built over centuries.

...

Social, professional, hierarchic and class privileges were created. The arbitrariness of the distribution of wealth and goods resulted in confrontations and the deliberate flaring of antagonism between various groups, notably between workers and peasants, workers and intellectuals. These distortions killed the faith of many people, generating disillusionment and cynicism in them. The hard-working nature and sense of duty of the Bulgarian people gave way to a consumerist attitude to life. Conditions were created for corruption, the flourishing of a "shadow economy" and diverse mafia-like organizations.

...

Our fertile lands are soaked with chemicals; our clear waters are poisoned and blackened as a result of pollution; the air in a number of cities is virtually hazardous for the population's health.

...

The socio-economic situation in Bulgaria at the end of the eighties, can be described figuratively as a pre-apoplectic state.[3]

These facts were completely forgotten by the communists during their election campaigns in subsequent months and years. While visiting places with

[3] *On the State of the Country, the Party and the Immediate Tasks*, Partizdat, Sofia, 1989, pp. 27-30, 32-35.

no means of subsistence due to the destruction of arable land and the inefficiency of the industrial enterprises, the red demagogues blamed the poverty of the people on the democrats and their governments. But in mid-December 1989, the Bulgarian Communist Party was pursuing something else: through partial criticism of the party's former policies its Secretary General was trying to create the impression that the BCP had changed and that it was capable of taking the country out of the "state of crisis." That was the time of revelations:

> We do not intend to reassure the Bulgarian public that the transformations that we intend to undertake will be painless. Clashes and collisions could be possible both in the public and in the economic spheres. However, we have no alternative other than the cardinal political transformation to a system of democratic socialism for the well-being of the people, despite the difficulties we would have to overcome along our way as a party and political leadership.
>
> ...
>
> We should pursue the line of progressive reduction of the state subsidies, we should oppose the policy of resuscitating enterprises and activities that are in a state of actual insolvency. Only in this way can we expect to reduce taxes and ensure the necessary conditions for the prevalent majority of economic entities to become self-supporting.[4]

From Mladenov's words it was crystal clear that it never even occurred to him that another political party could take over the government of Bulgaria. His report was permeated with communist ideology, including the phrases: "Party and state", "the Party as the political vanguard of the people", "Leninist norms of Party life," "worthy of the legacy of our teachers Blagoev and Dimitrov", "on the sound grounds of living Marxism, free of deformations", "close links with the U.S.S.R., the Warsaw Treaty and the Council for Mutual Economic Assistance", "the Party has an invaluable heritage and traditions", etc.

In his speech about the future of the People's Republic, the Head of State envisioned a "socialist civil society", "socialist market economy", "socialist people's rule", "socialist state of law and order", "a real socialist parliament", "a struggle to reform for the future of socialism", and a "new socialist Bulgaria.".

Still, he also raised issues discussed in the agenda of the Union of Democratic Forces, including developing of all forms of ownership on the basis of their equality before the law, conducting free and democratic parliamentary elections, and drafting a new democratic Constitution. Mladenov even set deadlines for the resolution of these matters. The elections were to be held no later than the second quarter of 1990. The draft of the Constitution would be

---

[4] *Ibid.*, pp. 40-41.

ready the same year and would be debated freely and democratically by the entire Bulgarian nation.

Peter Mladenov went further and proposed an amendment to the then current Constitution. The conclusive remarks of the meeting read as follows:

> The Central Committee assigns to the Members of Parliament from the Bulgarian Communist Party the submission of a proposal for the rescinding of paragraphs 2 and 3 of Article 1 of the Constitution during the forthcoming session of the National Assembly.[5]

Here is the text of the paragraphs in question:

> (2) The Bulgarian Communist Party is the leading agent in society and in the State.
>
> (3) The Bulgarian Communist Party leads the building of a developed socialist society in the People's Republic of Bulgaria, in close fraternal cooperation with the Bulgarian Agrarian People's Union.[6]

Lavish promises followed:

> In the coming months and over the entire next year the government will secure additional quantities of staple foods and non-alimentary commodities. In 1990, opportunities are to be provided for a substantial increase in the number of apartments built through re-allocation of resources and through the closing down of non-priority and ineffective production entities.
>
> ...
>
> The plan for the next year is to increase substantially the share of capital investment in new agricultural equipment and technologies. It is also necessary to speed up the modernization and technological upgrades of a number of production entities in the food and light industries.
>
> ...
>
> Further socio-political development in Bulgaria is possible only on the basis of the democratization of socialism, including the endorsement of the principle of pluralism. This will also be the basis for the legislative reform in our country, which will be introduced in the near future.[7]

---

[5] *Ibid.*, p. 13.

[6] Constitution of the People's Republic of Bulgaria, proclaimed on May 19, 1971, by the Fifth National Assembly.

[7] *On the State of the Country, the Party and the Immediate Tasks*, pp. 42-43, 45-46, 50.

The leader of the Party and State, Peter Mladenov, subtly reminded the population that the "principle of pluralism" has its limitations because there are "good" and "bad" agents of opposition:

> It is an indisputable fact that a new policy of the Party and State vis-à-vis the groups and trends in society is needed. It cannot be based on our earlier experience, because such experience does not exist. A new global approach is needed to take into account the growing significance of the human factor and of public consciousness. These are phenomena with an enormous potential for accelerated development, which society must utilize. We value highly the patriotic and civil orientation of these public factors.
>
> Alongside these factors, there are forces with other goals and ambitions which would push society into anarchy and tragedy if they are given the "freedom" they demand. We believe that Bulgarian society and the Bulgarian people possess sufficient political maturity and would prevent the plunging of our fatherland into such a cataclysm.[8]

Mladenov stressed that the problems of the nation, irrespective of the amendments to Article 1 of the Constitution, would be resolved by the supreme bodies of the Bulgarian Communist Party:

> The leadership of the Party is aware of the existence of a difficult problem, which is connected with the tension created among a part of our population, some of whom left the country this year [the Bulgarian Turks - *author's note*]. We all understand that the problem is complicated. Therefore, the Politburo believes that the Party's Central Committee would do well to subject this problem to a deep and comprehensive analysis, and consequently propose ways of solving it.[9]

Peter Mladenov warned his comrades that the Bulgarian Communist Party had no time to waste:

> Our Party has no right to delay the timely analysis and solution of the newly-emerging problems and situations. It cannot afford to lag behind the development of events. Every delay can prove to be fatal for the fate of the socialist society in Bulgaria. Similar lessons have also been drawn from the development of events in some fraternal countries.[10]

---

[8] *Ibid.*, pp. 49-50.

[9] *Ibid.*, p. 50.

[10] *Ibid.*, pp. 57-58.

Envisioning the future of the People's Republic of Bulgaria as a "democratic socialist state with the rule of law" and a "socialist market economy", the CC of the BCP concluded that it had "completed its mission successfully," much like it had done at the end of each of its previous meetings. However, one of the pronouncements at this one is worth considering at greater length:

> The Central Committee proposes the adoption of resolute measures for the stabilization of the state of the internal market. The plan for 1990 ackowledges that it is necessary to secure more food, non-alimentary commodities of prime necessity, and services for the population. By restructuring the production process, the import, and export, the Central Committee means to provide additional quantities of consumer goods and raw materials.[11]

For the entire duration of the meeting of the leading body of the BCP - three days and three evenings - the people of Sofia surrounded the big grey-stone building of the communist party headquarters. They held often fading candles in their frozen fingers under the glowing red light of the five-pointed star. The party decisions had no value for them. It was as if they anticipated the horror, misery, hunger, electrical shortages, ice-cold homes, empty shops, food lines that started to form in the middle of the night, food rationing coupons and total hopelessness to come during the communist governments in 1990 under Prime Minister Andrey Lukanov.

Furthermore, on December 13, the very day when Mladenov's vision of a new socialist republic of law and order was adopted by the Central Committee, the Bulgarian Communist Party did not fail to pay tribute to its repressive past. It posthumously rehabilitated one of its most ardent supporters, and one of the most active instigators of political terror in Bulgaria, Traycho Kostov. Soon thereafter the party re-opened its ranks and embraced the 85-year-old Anton Yugov as well, a man who had the blood of thousands of innocent Bulgarians on his hands. It was obvious that the BCP was not prepared to part with its Bolshevik past.

...

December 14, 1989, was a turning point in the peaceful revolution in Sofia. People often recalled that date in the following years, discussed it, reproached and reassured one another about it. Something was irretrievably lost that day,

[11] *Ibid.*, p. 4.

which gave the communists the opportunity to push things in the direction of their choice despite the aspirations of anticommunist Bulgarians. For years men and women wondered whether their country would have become a much happier and more advanced state if the leaders of the Union of Democratic Forces had been at the right place that evening, if they had listened to the wishes of their supporters, and if they had tried to negotiate with the communists from a position of strength.

The questions were numerous and painful. Why did so many of the demonstrators obey the UDF speakers on the balcony of the Students' Club and go home as advised? Was there really any danger of bloodshed if people continued to press for their demands? Would it not have been better, they asked themselves, if a few of them had died on that night, thus showing to their own nation and the world the real face of the Bulgarian communists? Why did they continue to support the UDF leaders after that disappointment? Should they have forgiven them at all? These questions were meaningless. The historic opportunity of that December night had been irretrievably lost.

On December 14, the Union of Democratic Forces had not organized a rally in front of the National Assembly. The plan was for a chain of people holding hands to be formed around the Parliament building as a symbolic demand that Article 1 of the Constitution be revoked. The university students independently decided to remind the totalitarian National Assembly that they insisted on the elimination of the so-called "ideological disciplines" from their curricula. Several hundred students appeared before Parliament at the time fixed for their protest.

Quite unexpectedly, in the early hours of that winter evening, the square in front of Bulgaria's legislative body was filled to capacity with about 50,000 citizens of Sofia who had come on their own initiative, after having heard on the radio about the protests. Fully convinced that the BCP was making desperate attempts to retain Article 1 of the Constitution by procrastinating on the issue of its rescinding, people loudly expressed their indignation at the eternal lies of the communists and warned the rulers that they would no longer allow them to continue with their deceit.

Ten years later, the *Nedelnik* weekly wrote:

> December 14, 1989, can be considered to be a key date in the evolution of democracy in Bulgaria. On that day, Sofia witnessed something it had not seen for 45 years. At 3:00 p.m., the Speaker of the Bulgarian National Assembly Stanko Todorov announced in the plenary hall that the demand for revoking Article 1 of the Constitution (on the leading role of the Bulgarian Communist Party) had to wait for one month. Then several thousand protesters surrounded the Parliament building and demanded its immediate revoction. The first

slogans of the discontent were born then: "Down with the BCP!" and "Both before and now the BCP is a Mafia!".

The Coordinating Council of the UDF was faced with a delicate situation and did not know what to do. Long discussions were held over three positions. The first option was to lead the masses, to enter the National Assembly and to take power.

The second option was for the UDF to stand at the head of the demonstrators, but with the aim of protecting them against rash and maybe even provoked actions. The third option - the UDF to distance itself from the protesters - was rejected from the very beginning.

The newly-elected UDF leaders chose the second option. However, the rally did not disperse, in spite of Dr. Zhelev's appeals. Todor Zhivkov's successor Peter Mladenov was forced to come out in front of the National Assembly and to appeal for order and calm so as to prevent bloodshed. Angered that the multitude was drowning out his speech with their shouts, he went back into the building, uttering the phrase that was to cost him his career later: "It would be best if the tanks came!"[12]

It was sheer luck that the video camera in the hands of Evgeniy Mihaylov captured that moment of communist sincerity.

Ivan Kurtev, Deputy Speaker of the Thirty-Seventh and Thirty-Eighth National Assembly and Member of Parliament from the Union of Democratic Forces, examines the date in question and its consequences:

For me, December 14 remains the key moment. Just a week after the UDF was established, the streets and the squares started to participate in the country's political life for the first time. This proved that people could not be guided or manipulated by the UDF leaders because by far not all obeyed their appeal to disperse and go to their homes to see whether we would be covered on the evening TV news. I think the latter suggestion was made by Ivaylo Trifonov from the balcony of the Students' Club.

The rally on December 14 was spontaneous. It had nothing to do with the human chain around the National Assembly that had been organized by either *Podkrepa* or *Ecoglasnost*.

Around 5:30 p.m. there were quite a few people in the square, but it was only towards 7:30 p.m. that their number reached about 50,000. After the UDF leadership urged us to go home, which happened before 8:00 p.m., some citizens left indeed, but most remained in the square. Then came the promise that Article 1 of the Constitution would be abolished in a month, after which came Peter Mladenov's blunder about the tanks.

---

[12] *Nedelnik*, November 10, 1999.

> The most important thing about December 14 was that most of the demonstrators refused to obey their leadership, elected only a week earlier. I personally felt some doubts about whether these leaders were taking us along the best road and whether what they wanted was the best and most appropriate.
>
> The supporters of the claim that the conduct of the UDF leaders was justified insist that if the people had not left the square, bloodshed would may have occured. I am convinced that precisely at that moment the communists were so frightened that there was not only going to be no bloodshed, but the situation would have taken a similar course to that of the events of January 10, 1997. Only this would have been much earlier and the timing would have been better. Events would have developed much more quickly, and the Round Table discussions, the elections and everything else would have taken a different course.
>
> The second very important thing that night was that on December 14 the street was shouting "Down with the BCP!" and that flags of the European Union were being waved. Some people voiced their indignation with questions like "What is this? Don't we have our own Bulgarian flags? What does that European flag mean?" Most probably they were agitators.
>
> December 14 was the first purely anticommunist rally. On November 18 and December 10, the people who had gathered in the square in front of the *St. Alexander Nevski* Cathedral were anticommunists, but from the rostrum all was spoken indirectly, cautiously, beating about the bush. After December 14, people were no longer afraid to bring their anticommunism out into the open. After that date, the UDF supporters were no longer uncritical of the conduct and statements of the leaders of the union. Grassroots UDF structures were already being created in the first days of 1990.[13]

The Bulgarian Communist Party was indeed helpless on the evening of December 14, 1989. The desire of the Head of State Peter Mladenov to bring in the tanks was a habit from the past and a retrospective dream. Just over a month after the fall of the Berlin Wall, when the attention of the entire democratic world was riveted to the events in Eastern Europe, it was too unrealistic to imagine that tanks' muzzles could be aimed at protesting citizens. This would have been undesirable for the BCP, whose party money was already earning interest in Western banks.

With the help of the leaders of the Union of Democratic Forces, the communist party quickly coped with its impasse and restored its control over the situation after December 14. The memories of that evening left mixed feelings of doubt, shame and guilt in the minds of thousands of Bulgarians. Later that

---

[13] Ivan Kurtev in a conversation with the author, Sofia, Bulgaria, August 18, 1998.

prompted them to make several clumsy and unsuccessful attempts to recreate the situation. For more than seven years the notion of a Bastille that was never stormed tormented the noncommunist population of the capital city. It was only on January 10, 1997, that catharsis was finally achieved and the act of powerlessness was obliterated.

...

One of the protesters immediately reacted to the events that took place in front of the highest legislative body of the People's Republic of Bulgaria on December 14. That was the writer and journalist Vasil Stanilov, who declared a hunger strike the next morning. The text of his declaration suggested resolve and civic integrity:

> I hereby declare that I participated in the rally on December 14, 1989, in front of the National Assembly. I am not a member of any political party or group. I take as a personal insult the qualification of our conduct as uncivilized. I have not heard any appeals containing the word "death". If there were, they were made by agitators.
>
> The way in which the Bulgarian National Television reported the events infringes upon my dignity as a journalist. It is strange that for decades it showed not without sympathy really extremist actions of students and citizens in France, Chile, Korea, the U.S.A., and in many other places. This time we saw only one single frame on its screen: the close-up of a woman with an ugly expression on her face while she was trying to whistle. She was selected as a symbol for all of us who had gathered there in that square.
>
> The spontaneous rally, not organized by anyone, gave vent to the discontent against the decision of a Parliament that had awakened for the first time in 40 years and realized that it is possible to cast a "no" vote as well.
>
> Protesting against the lawyers who did not find legal grounds for abolishing Article 1 of the Constitution for fear or through incompetence, I appeal to Mr. Peter Mladenov as the Head of State and insist that this Article be suspended. Precedents exist in Bulgarian history. I appeal to him and ask that he act as a real statesman and place Bulgaria among the civilized nations.
>
> For me personally, every minute under totalitarian rule is unbearable.
>
> I hereby declare that I am starting a hunger strike until Article 1 is suspended or revoked.
>
> My strike is individual. It is an expression of agreement with all who fear the next maneuver of the Bulgarian Communist Party, and who have doubts that the National Assembly will revoke that article within a month.

> I hereby swear to the sincerity and integrity of my intentions. December 15, 1989, Sofia, Vasil Stanilov.[14]

Stanilov's hunger strike lasted seventeen days. After receiving official assurance from the authorities that his demand would be met, he discontinued his protest. Following his example, twenty other Bulgarians declared hunger strikes until Article 1 of the Constitution was abolished.

. . .

On Friday, December 15, at 9:00 a.m., the second sitting of the twelfth session of the Ninth National Assembly began. The people's deputies behaved as if nothing special had happened the previous night. They all rose to their feet unanimously to pay tribute with one minute's silence to the memory of "one of the brightest names in our modern history", a name that lives "in the Pantheon of the nation's memory", the name of the "outstanding and remarkable builder of new Bulgaria", the "eminent activist of the Bulgarian Communist Party", "the remarkable political figure and martyr of the Fatherland," none other than Traycho Kostov, hanged 40 years previously by his fellow communists.[15]

After the ceremony, the Speaker of the National Assembly, Stanko Todorov, read the following text:

> The National Assembly approves the proposals submitted by the parliamentary groups of the Bulgarian Communist Party and by the Bulgarian Agrarian People's Union regarding the revoking of paragraphs 2 and 3 of Article 1 of the Constitution of the People's Republic of Bulgaria. This is an important step along the road to the promotion and consolidation of political pluralism and the building of a democratic state with a rule of law.
>
> Pursuant to §2 of Article 142 of the Constitution, which sets a minimum period of one month for debates and discussions on a bill for its amendment, the National Assembly decided to adopt these amendments conclusively at its next session scheduled for January 1990.[16]

It is unlikely that the people comfortably seated in the spacious plenary hall were pleased with what they had heard, but nothing could be done about it. The multitude outside was losing patience and was becoming menacing. In step with the times the partisan-general Slavcho Transki proclaimed over-zealously, "It

[14] Declaration of Vasil Stanilov, December 15, 1989, personal archive.

[15] Annals of the Second Session of the Twelfth Session of the Ninth National Assembly, December 15, 1989, p. 120.

[16] *Ibid.*, pp. 120-121.

should be said that the Members of Parliament are fully convinced that these paragraphs should be revoked."[17] Then, all voted unanimously for the resolution that in January 1990 the leading role of the BCP in society and in the State would be revoked.

In fact, even sanctions against those responsible for the overwhelming poverty in Bulgaria were considered. Stanko Todorov opened the debate about the "Proposal for the election of a Parliamentary Committee to examine and resolve some urgent issues connected with deformations and violations of the law in the state, public, and economic life." Fourteen people were nominated as members of that Committee, whose Chairman was to be Andrey Lukanov, Minister of Foreign Economic Relations only a month previously. When the nomination was put to the vote, one out of the 400 Members of Parliament voted "against," while another one abstained.

The vote "against" came from the notorious communist Ognyan Doynov:

> Comrades Members of Parliament! I wished to speak on item 10 yesterday, because, as you know, I was accused of being one of the three principal culprits for the grave state of the economy, on the basis of the decision of the committee established within the Party's Central Committee.
>
> Since I categorically object to this, I have prepared a statement that I can read, or - if the Speaker of the National Assembly deems it more appropriate - I can also deposit it with the National Assembly.[18]

The Speaker deemed it more sensible that the document be deposited. Who knew what the criticized Deputy might say? G*lasnost* in Bulgaria had not yet progressed so much as to permit views on economic matters to be read in public, before the BCP had had a chance to decide how to handle them. In fact, there was an established procedure. The sins of the leading figures in the economy were usually known and they were duly noted in their personal files. However, that information was used only if the need arose, i.e., if the perpetrators committed offenses before their bosses.[19]

Pressed against the wall, Doynov "spilled the beans":

> In this regard I object to the proposal that Comrade Andrey Lukanov chair the Committee because I believe that many of the accusations against me concern him.[20]

---

[17] *Ibid.*, p. 21.

[18] *Ibid.*, p. 122.

[19] Luchnikov 2000, p. 39.

[20] Annals of the Second Session, p. 123.

The majority of the Bulgarian population would agree with Ognyan Doynov's latter statement. Lukanov and Doynov were precisely those who the nation held directly responsible for the unbearable foreign debt of the People's Republic of Bulgaria. People were convinced that these two high-ranking economic leaders illegally stashed away substantial sums abroad and that both of them were connected with money laundering. The matter was discussed in the foreign press. The newspaper *Nova Makedoniya* wrote the following:

> Concerning the organization [the financial giant *Multigroup*, created in 1988, and its numerous daughter companies in Bulgaria and abroad - *author's note*], two former high-ranking Bulgarian officials from Zhivkov's regime are indicated as its founders and leaders. The first one, Ognyan Doynov, has emigrated to the UK and, later, to Austria. The second one, Andrey Lukanov, became the first Prime Minister of Bulgaria after the fall of communism. According to some sources, Lukanov and Doynov had opposing interests, but their common economic interest generated a cooperation between them.[21]

Ognyan Doynov, engineer by training, was a member of the Politburo of the BCP's Central Committee for eleven years, a member of the State Council, Deputy Prime Minister from 1974 until 1976, Minister of Machine Building from 1984 until 1986, and Deputy Prime Minister and Chairman of the Economic Council from 1986 until 1987. Between 1980 and 1984, he headed the Bulgarian Chamber of Commence and Industry. A part of his career was spent with the Bulgarian trade and diplomatic missions abroad.

In 1990, Doynov was expelled from the party of the socialists/ communists on the grounds that he was to blame for the "deformations" in the management of the economy of Bulgaria. That was the only sanction imposed on him. Everything else that happened to the former *nomenklatura* cadre seemed more like a reward for good service to the bank accounts of some of his high-ranking colleagues in the state apparatus. During the some year - at the time of Andrey Lukanov's government - Ognyan Doynov settled with his family in Vienna, where he spent the last ten years of his life in luxury. In 1992, he refused to return to Bulgaria and face charges under the famous Court Case No. 3 on the "economic catastrophe" in his homeland. Doynov demonstrated his "patriotism" much later. In February 2000, he was buried in the Central Cemetery of Sofia, in accord with his wishes.

Andrey Lukanov was First Deputy Prime Minister of the People's Republic of Bulgaria from 1986 until 1987 and Minister of Foreign Economic Relations

[21] *Nova Makedoniya*, *Bulgarian International Octopus*, November 2, 1995.

from August 1987 until November 1989. Precisely from 1986 to 1989 Bulgaria's foreign debt to the West increased by 6,551,000,000 U.S. dollars, i.e., from 4,119,000,000 it reached 10,650,000,000 U.S. dollars.[22]

The Bulgarian Communist Party never looked into these figures closely. It did not humiliate Lukanov by throwing him out of its ranks. On the contrary, after November 10, 1989, he was promoted to leading positions in the party and placed at the top of the state hierarchy.

Still, other unpleasant things happened to Andrey Lukanov. Following the orders of the Prosecutor General of the Republic of Bulgaria, Ivan Tatarchev, on July 7, 1992, he was stripped of his legal immunity as Member of Parliament in the Thirty-Sixth National Assembly. Lukanov was arrested and detained for investigation. He was accused of contributing to the economic ruin of Bulgaria by granting credits and non-refundable aid amounting to millions of dollars to communist parties in developing countries to support their terrorist activity. At the end of 1992, Andrey Lukanov managed to escape the wrath of Themis with the help of secret and open communist collaborators. He could not escape the bullet of his assassin, who took his life on October 2, 1996, most likely due to hostile economic interests.

On a brighter day in the life of Andrey Lukanov - December 15, 1989 - he became Chairman of the Parliamentary Committee and was charged with the responsibility of investigating "deformations and violations of the law in the state, public and economic life" of the People's Republic of Bulgaria. From the very beginning of its "reformation," the Bulgarian Communist Party relied on him. He was needed. The *Atlantic Monthly* published the following commentary linking Lukanov's name to the appearance of organized crime in Bulgaria:

> It began in the late 1980s, before the fall of the Berlin Wall, when a middle-aged Bulgarian apparatchik, Andrei Lukanov, who was born in the Soviet Union and had spent many years there, realized that the Communist system was dying. He began developing a plan to turn local Party leaders into economic leaders. The aging Todor Zhivkov, who had been the Communist party boss of Bulgaria since 1954, hated Lukanov, seeing him as a radical reformer. But Lukanov understood the future. Just as another middle-aged apparatchik, Slobodan Milosevic, realized that ethnic nationalism was the only way for his generation of Communists in Serbia to preserve their villas and hunting lodges, Lukanov understood that just through an economic reform the Communists could keep the power in Bulgaria. In 1990s Lukanov twice served as Prime Minister of Bulgarian governments composed of ex-Communists; he

[22] Nedev 1999, p. 41.

> used privatization as a mechanism to help found the most powerful of the oligarchical groupings, Multigroup, by transferring state assets to his friends.[23]

After Andrey Lukanov was appointed Chairman of the Parliamentary Committee called upon to put the "socialist legal state" in order, the Ninth National Assembly proceeded to approve the other fourteen members *en bloc*. It turned out that all deputies supported their nominations. Only after the unanimous vote, one of them, Yanko Markov, complained:

> Comrade Todorov, I didn't hear who the other members in the Committee are.
>
> Speaker Stanko Todorov: We will give their names to you later, Comrade Markov.[24]

. . .

Christmas of 1989 was celebrated in Sofia with vigils and prayers organized by the Reverend Christophor Sabev where the force of religion was opposed to communist atheism and the perverse moral values of a totalitarian society. On the day after Christmas, another vitally important issue came to the fore and eclipsed all other events. That had to do with the names of the Bulgarian Moslems.

The removal of Todor Zhivkov from power caught the Bulgarian Turks and Bulgarian-speaking Moslems not with their Islamic names, but with Slavic ones imposed on them in the 1980s. The "renaming" process was remembered for its violence, resistance, and propaganda lies.

It is to the credit of the Bulgarian nation that just a few people actively supported the repressive actions of the rulers, and the relations between ethnic Turks, Bulgarian-speaking Moslems and Bulgarians did not change substantially. Nevertheless, the suffering, the horror and sense of helplessness among the Moslems in Bulgaria were not forgotten after the changes in the communist party and state apparatus. These people continued to live in uncertainty and fear, with the names forced upon them against their will.

Some leaders of the Union of Democratic Forces, like Rumen Vodenicharov and Konstantin Trenchev, with their frenzied statements and actions, incited nationalist passions among some strata of the population. Thus, they actually assisted the plans of the Bulgarian Communist Party to generate ethnic conflict.

---

[23] *Atlantic Monthly,* Robert D. Kaplan, *Hoods against Democrats*, December 1998.

[24] Annals of the Second Session, p. 127.

After December 26, Bulgarian ethnic Turks and Bulgarian Moslems congregated in front of the Parliament building, demanding the restoration of the names they had been given at birth. With unexpected speed, on December 29, the communist authorities granted their right to their original names.

From January 3 to 10, 1990, the very same authorities organized rallies and protest actions through their party units and servile trade union organizations all over the country. The participants in these events categorically objected to having names restored according to the religious denomination.[25] The ruling party also encouraged the establishment of the National Committee for the Defence of the National Interests, which later split into several new satellites of the communist organization.[26]

The BCP did not forget its most loyal *nomenklatura.* It gave orders to the directors of the industrial enterprises in the countryside to transport their subordinates to Sofia immediately in buses provided by the official trade union. These workers were to voice the protest of the Bulgarian nation against the decision of the leaders of the State to restore the names of the Moslems. Yet, attendance was poor at the nationalist rallies. When the buses with the "protesters" arrived, they failed to make an impression on the citizens.

On December 20 the political changes in Romania started with mass murders in Timisoara and Bucharest, culminating on Christmas with the executions of Nicolae Ceausescu and his wife Elena, broadcast on TV all over the world.

The population of Bulgaria was shocked and taken aback. The opponents of the communist regime were alert. Still they knew that there was no way back. The fight for a free, independent and democratic Bulgaria had to continue at all cost.

...

More turmoil was in store for the Bulgarians in the last days of the last month of that unusual year. On the day before Christmas Eve, the *Podkrepa* Independent Labor Federation announced its decision to hold a general strike on December 26, demanding that a caretaker government be appointed and a date set for parliamentary elections. Representatives of other UDF member organizations also took part in the meeting with the trade union leadership to discuss what needed to be done.

---

25 Dimitrov 1995(a).

26 *Ibid.*

It was a failed debate. Philip Dimitrov, who attended the meeting as a representative of the Committee for the Protection of Religious Rights, Freedom of Conscience and Spiritual Values, disapproved of the idea because it did not correspond to the real situation in the country.[27] Dr. Trenchev, the leader of *Podkrepa,* was an hour and a half late for that meeting. When he finally appeared, he declared that there was nothing more to be discussed. The strike would take place in the way that he had planned it anyway.[28]

It proved impossible to organize a general political strike in Bulgaria at that time. People had not yet overcome their fear to that extent. And nobody explained to them what exactly they would gain if *Podkrepa*'s demands were met. In order to cover up the failure, on December 27, Konstantin Trenchev declared irritably before the UDF Coordinating Council, "Block the strike as symbolic. I shall make a statement on TV."[29] Even in that symbolic strike, the turnout was unsatisfactory.

The anticommunists were disappointed, but that was for the better. The failure of the protest deprived Andrey Lukanov of one of the most propitious opportunities to propose himself to the Union of Democratic Forces as Prime Minister in the caretaker government. After all, who else if not he, the "opponent" of the dictator Zhivkov, the "soul" of the inner-party coup, and the man whose advice was sought after and listened to by at least half of the UDF leaders, could be placed at the head of the executive power at that moment? Lukanov became Prime Minister of Bulgaria six weeks later anyway. However, he received his new post from the communist Head of State Peter Mladenov and the communist National Assembly. The danger of Andrey Lukanov becoming Prime Minister with the support of the democrats, thus allowing the BCP to acquire full control over their movement, was averted.

The scenario of the general strike was a flop. The protests of a small part of the population against the decision to give the Moslems their names back also failed to incite an ethnic crisis in Bulgaria. The Bulgarian Communist Party had no choice but to delay the course of events in some other way. It deemed that safest and most beneficial option was to convene a National Round Table discussion.

---

[27] *Ibid.*

[28] *Ibid.*

[29] Minutes No. 2 of the meeting of the Coordinating Council of the Union of Democratic Forces, held in Sofia at 12:40 on December 29, 1989, p. 4.

13. Demagogy in Action

For some the National Round Table was "the shortest, most successful and fruitful period of the Bulgarian transition to democracy."[1] For others it was "yet another plot against the interests of the people of Bulgaria; it marked the start of the long, slow, difficult and painful road to democracy, dominated in the first decade by five communist governments or governments supported by the communists."[2] For yet another group of people the "Round Table" was a "cruel betrayal of the aspirations of the prevalent majority of the nation to free themselves from the communists." The supporters of the latter view were convinced that "the Union of Democratic Forces should not have agreed under any circumstances to start building a law-governed and free Bulgaria together with the communists or - to be more precise - with them in the lead."[3] Others believed that the National Round Table was "an attempt by the communists to convince the leaders of the opposition of the need for a Bulgarian *perestroika* - reform - rather then genuine change" and thought that the "failure at the first elections in June 1990 was due to the hesitant and collaborative stand that the UDF took at the Round Table."[4] For a different set of people, foreigners in this case, the negotiations held at the "Round Table" were a "key factor in securing agreement among the competing political forces on the ground rules for creating national unity."[5] In theory, the National Round Table was useful to both sides participating in it. In practice, only the more dexterous and better prepared side benefited from it in the end.

On December 27, 1989, the Central Committee of the Bulgarian Communist Party officially announced that an agreement had been reached with the Union of Democratic Forces regarding an open discussion in the form of a "Round Table." The same day, the UDF leadership had the following debate:

> Peter Beron: There are serious things ahead of us. Andrey Lukanov called and said that they were ready to accept any option. He wanted to specify some details, namely the venue, topics, whether the "Round Table" would be general, or whether it would be divided by topic of discussion, etc.. It has been proposed that we hold the "Round Table" in the first half of January. We have to give our opinion on where the meeting will be held, what issues will be discussed and who will participate in it. No firmly fixed framework has been

---

[1] *Nedelnik* weekly, November 10, 1999.

[2] Dyanko Markov in a conversation with the author, Sofia, Bulgaria, September 1, 2000.

[3] Professor Dr. Georgi Markov in a conversation with the author, Sofia, Bulgaria, August 25, 1998.

[4] Melone 1998, p. 53.

[5] *Ibid.*, p. 6.

proposed so far. This is an opportunity from which we can benefit. I suggest that we form a group for preliminary contacts with the BCP.

Zhelyu Zhelev: We have decided to hold a public exchange of opinions. Today's *Rabotnichesko Delo* demonstrates readiness for political dialogue, but mentions only three points. No answer is given to our declaration of December 19, 1989, which has not been considered or been published.

Deyan Kyuranov: I propose that the committee for preliminary contacts consist of four people and that decisions be made by no fewer than two people. The meeting should not be at the National Assembly, but on neutral grounds.

Peter Beron: The place where the meeting will be held does not matter: Wherever it is, it will be on state grounds. I propose one of the decision-makers to be myself or Zhelyu Zhelev. I have reservations about the proposition that the talks be held with the government. It is not a political organization, whereas we are. We have to talk with the authorities.

...

Hristo Marinov: Let us discuss whether we should consider giving up the government as our interlocutor in the negotiations and appealing to public forces instead. The UDF is a public force, and so are the Bulgarian Communist Party and the Agrarian Union. The government is not a public force.

Zhelyu Zhelev: We want to talk with the authorities. Before we start the negotiations, we have to demand that the declaration of December 19 be published. I propose to amend that declaration to the effect that we want a dialogue not with the government but with the authorities.[6]

The talks continued on December 28 and 29 as well:

Plamen Darakchiev: Has our agenda been established?

Dr. Peter Beron: The specific agenda is unclear.

Dr. Konstantin Trenchev: I suggest that we meet tomorrow at 10 a.m. to discuss the details.

Dr. Zhelyu Zhelev: The agenda should address only political issues, without the economic problems.

Dr. Peter Beron: The "Round Table" will be about the governance of the country.

Dr. Zhelyu Zhelev: I suggest that we make a list of issues to be raised at the first meeting, that is, what we are going to demand at that meeting.

Georgi Avramov: Above all, printing facilities.

Dr. Peter Beron: We would like to propose that *Otechestven Front* [pro-communist daily newspaper of the Fatherland Front - *author's note*] become the newspaper of the opposition.

---

[6] Minutes of the meeting of the Coordinating Council of the Union of Democratic Forces, held in Sofia at 12.40 p.m., December 27, 1989, p. 2.

Dr. Zhelyu Zhelev: The issue of whether *Otechestven Front* can become the newspaper of the UDF has been discussed. I welcome this idea. Let the name of the newspaper remain *Otechestven Front* for the time being.

Georgi Avramov: Our newspaper should have a name of its own."[7]

Georgi Avramov: Should the "Round Table" be permanent or temporary? I suggest that it should be permanent, with working groups that will research the issues and submit them for resolution.

Peter Beron: I don't subscribe to that proposal.

Georgi Avramov: The resolution of the issues on which no agreement can be reached would be left out and the next issues on the agenda would be taken up.

Yanko Yankov: The unresolved issues would be discussed a second time and, if no solution can be found still, we would decide whether to stop the "Round Table" and undertake joint action.

Prof. Dr. Chavdar Kyuranov: There will be issues for which we may not be able to reach a final solution. It is not necessary to declare a permanent "Round Table".

Ivan Nevrokopski: It would be incorrect to accept a permanent "Round Table." That is dangerous. We need to demand that certain deadlines for resolving the issues be fixed, so that there would be no procrastination and so that we could put pressure on our opponents. We can agree to hold a "Round Table" within certain limits, with a concrete agenda and depending on the outcome, we may prolong it. We should not create the impression that the "Round Table" could be endless.

...

Dr. Konstantin Trenchev: I suggest that we start the essential negotiations on January 20. We need time to inform the members of the formations within the UDF and take care of some organizational matters.

Georgi Avramov: It is necessary to consult with the masses. We should not only hold consultations among ourselves, but also to hold conversations with the members of the coalition.

Prof. Dr. Chavdar Kyuranov: I support Dr. Trenchev's view. We shall be opposing experienced people, we need to be united against them. New situations will also emerge in the country. We need to have time to adapt to the newly-emerging situations.[8]

After heated discussions about what is to be done and how it is to be done, the UDF Coordinating Council appointed a 14-member delegation, chaired by Dr. Zhelyu Zhelev, to hold talks on matters of procedure. A group of five

---

[7] *Ibid.*, 12.30 and 2:15 p.m., December 28, 1989, pp. 1-2.

[8] *Ibid.*, 11.30 a.m., December 29, 1989, p. 2.

experts headed by Professor Dr. Chavdar Kyuranov was also formed to assist in the process of future negotiations.

The first preliminary meetings between the communist government and the Union of Democratic Forces were held on January 3 and 4, 1990, in the building of the National Assembly. Several political and public organizations from the time of the totalitarian regime insisted on being included as independent partners in the discussions. The UDF refused to sit at the "Round Table" together with the Fatherland Front, the Bulgarian Trade Unions and the *Dimitrov* Young Communist League, recalling their close connection with the red party.

It was decided that the debates would be held between the Union of Democratic Forces and the Bulgarian Communist Party, with the same number of representatives from either side. The communist party and the opposition democratic alliance reserved the right to include persons from other organizations in their quotas. The National Round Table was due to open on January 16, 1990, in the afternoon.

Several hours before the scheduled event, the leaders of the opposition had another meeting:

> Peter Beron: On the issue of our conduct at the "Round Table", we have agreed that our delegation will have 37 members. The leaders of the organizations that are members of the UDF will be seated at the table, with two persons behind each of them. This number includes the representatives of the Green Party. Later we have to let the Democrats and the Union of Private Producers be part of the delegation as well. We must try to have a more solid presence at the "Round Table".
>
> ...
>
> Petko Simeonov: We don't have designated committees and people in charge on all issues. No such committees and responsible figures have been appointed to handle the issues of legislation and matters in the socio-economic sphere. We wasted a lot of time due to the organizational problems of the Coordinating Council. It is necessary to create an organizational mechanism. We need to appoint people responsible for drafting our propositions regarding each item on the agenda of the "Round Table". Every association that is a member of the UDF may have its own stand, which should be taken into account.
>
> ...
>
> Hristo Peev: It seems that we are not ready for the "Round Table". We have not agreed upon our stand regarding some of the issues. It is necessary for us to take a firm stand, which will differentiate us from the authorities.
>
> Peter Beron: Let us not forget that the first stage of the "Round Table" negotiations starts today. This stage will end on January 24, but this does not

mean that the negotiations will not continue after that date as well. At today's meeting we shall agree upon the frequency of the next meetings.

...

Peter Beron: I suggest that we vote upon the following regarding today's "Round Table" meeting:

The "Round Table" meetings may start only provided the following conditions have been met:

1. We are formally allowed to publish newspapers and everything necessary for them has been secured, including paper, a printing house, and distribution mechanisms.

2. A specific building is assigned for us to move into within five days or less.

3. Radio and TV broadcasting time is made available for us within 2-3 days. If necessary, we will demand the presence of Stoyan Mihaylov [high ranking communist official, responsible for culture issues - *author's note*] in order to arrange for the details.

In the event that all or some of these conditions are not met, the meeting will be interrupted for consultations and we will announce that we cannot continue with the Round Table discussions.

The proposal was accepted with 12 votes in favor and one against.

Georgi Spasov: We proceed now to a discussion of the topic of today's meeting, namely the issue of the political system.

Peter Beron: We must discuss our conduct, if we don't withdraw from the meeting. What shall we do if they give in on the issue of the political system? Let us not claim authorship of the proposal on this issue. Instead, we must start with the liquidation of the power monopoly of the Bulgarian Communist Party and with its separation from the state in terms of structures, financing and personnel. It will be necessary for us to introduce the essential issues, and I suggest that this be done by Zhelyu Zhelev. We have left it to them to determine the frequency of the meetings.[9]

On January 17, the discussion in the Coordinating Council of the Union of Democratic Forces was tense:

Peter Beron: Blagovest Sendov is worried that the Komsomol [the youth communist organization - *author's note*] and the Trade Unions will not be admitted to take part in the "Round Table". I told him that we are not against their participation, but that they would have to choose which side of the table they wish to be on.

Dr. Konstantin Trenchev: We must demand that the government formally declare it will not persecute the representatives of the opposition. The

[9] *Ibid.*, 9 a.m., January 16, 1989, pp. 1-4.

agreement to make a building available to the UDF and let the opposition publish a newspaper was signed by Dr. Zhelyu Zhelev and Svetla Daskalova, but not by Andrey Lukanov, who declared that these issues had been solved.

Dr. Lyubomir Pavlov: Kasmetski told me that Philip Bokov did not allow outsiders to be present during the editing of the TV footage.

Georgi Spasov: As far as the newspaper goes, first we spoke about a circulation of 75 thousand, but later we agreed upon 100 thousand. Regarding the building, we asked for 75-80 rooms in one building or more, but no more than three buildings, ready to be used. They should be equipped with desks, chairs, telephones, etc. They were not ready with their answer about the building. We agreed to discuss the options tomorrow, January 18, at 6 p.m.

Milan Drenchev: I suggest that we ask for a document certifying that the building has been made available and for another one regarding access to radio and TV. I would like to draw your attention to the fact that nothing was said about us, the members of the UDF delegation, neither our names, nor our capacity or who we are. We must insist at all cost on live TV coverage of at least a part of the Round Table discussions.

Dr. Zhelyu Zhelev: Our demands have not been met and we must decide whether we would walk out until our demands are met. How are we to proceed if they give us a building tomorrow and secure the publishing of a newspaper, while denying us access to the radio and TV?

Peter Beron: We already walked out yesterday. If we do it again, the effect will be greatly diminished. If tomorrow morning we receive assurances that our demands will be met by the evening, we must remain at the meeting.[10]

The Union of Democratic Forces participated in the National Round Table until May 15, 1990, when its final minutes were signed by the participants in the discussion. Four days afterwards, and three weeks before the fateful elections for the Grand National Assembly, the UDF opened its First National Conference to discuss the practical issues of the election campaign.

...

Philip Dimitrov drafted some proposals on his own to be discussed at the "Round Table" and waited for the UDF leadership to invite the union's members to offer their assistance in the preparation for the national debate. When this had not happened three days before the start of the negotiations, Philip asked for a meeting with Petko Simeonov. The lawyer's wish was to be allowed to present three of his proposals before a working group or before some other body of the democratic alliance.

---

[10] *Ibid.*, 4 p.m., January 17, 1989, pp. 3-4.

Dimitrov entitled his first proposal "Urgent Measures." In it he insisted on immediate changes in some criminal and civil laws. These measures were identical to the ones he had posted on the notice board of the attorneys' café on November 11, 1989. The second proposal concerned amendments to the Constitution. Dimitrov recommended amendments only to the provisions hampering the democratization process. He also suggested a brief new text that would change the type of political system in the country. The lawyer entitled his third proposal "Creating a Constitutional Court." He anticipated that his last idea would not be understood and accepted, and he was ready to give it up.[11]

At the arranged meeting Philip told Simeonov, "Petko, I'm sure that you have done most of the work. However, here is another little thing that I have come up with. Let's sit down and discuss it." To the lawyer's utter surprise, the Chairman of the Club for *Glasnost* and Democracy responded, "Come on, give your proposals, boy!" Simeonov admitted to Dimitrov that the UDF had not formed a working group to prepare for the "Round Table". Their entire preparations consisted in specifying matters of procedure and coming up with about a dozen demands that Petko Simeonov had jotted down in his notebook. These demands included closing down the communist party structures at people's work places, placing the local communist radio stations in subordination to the mayors, making several buildings available to the UDF, allocating the paper and printing facilities needed for an independent press, and several more.

Simeonov agreed to present Dimitrov's proposals before the Coordinating Council. Parts of the "Urgent Measures" were incorporated in his own speech at the "Round Table", which followed the introductory statement of UDF Chairman Dr. Zhelev. Dimitrov's idea for a Constitutional Court was rejected. After a heated debate, Philip Dimitrov was given the floor on the third day of the negotiations to personally introduce his proposed amendments to the Constitution.[12]

The Bulgarian Communist Party had somehow already been informed about Dimitrov's proposed changes. It introduced similar amendments to the Constitution to be debated in Parliament, in addition to a text about the creation of a presidency. The enthusiasm with which the communists agreed to the proposals deprived Philip Dimitrov of his small victory and made the hitherto unknown Assistant Professor at the Sofia University Law School Stoyan Ganev famous a month later because of his recommendation that reforms in Bulgaria

---

[11] Philip Dimitrov in a conversation with the author, New York, U.S.A., April 14, 1998.

[12] *Ibid.*

should start with elections for a Grand National Assembly that would draft and vote for a "radically new democratic Constitution."

The leadership of the Union of Democratic Forces, and above all Dr. Zhelyu Zhelev, accepted Ganev's initiative with delight. In contrast, Philip Dimitrov was skeptical. As he expected, the convening of a Grand National Assembly in 1990 delayed the adoption of legislative changes with immediate practical results. All this played into the hands of the communists-turned-socialists. While meaningless debates were held in Parliament on matters of principle for a year, they succeeded in rallying and regrouping their ranks, and taking care of their money. What's more, the 1991 Constitution was the product of a legislative body in which the communists had the majority. It is no secret that some of its provisions are hampering the country's democratic development to this day.[13]

...

From the very first days of the debates at the National Round Table, two different approaches for attaining the desired changes emerged in opposition circles. Unfortunately, the approach of the UDF leaders prevailed. Their tactics were to announce a demand and wait for the ruling party to satisfy it. For a long time, the Chairman, Zhelyu Zhelev, did not allow anyone to even mention that the Union of Democratic Forces was fighting for power. He stubbornly denied all "accusations" of that nature.

When the date for the elections for the Grand National Assembly was fixed, and Dr. Zhelev finally announced this perfectly natural political goal for the union, there were still opposition leaders who did not accept it.

The other political agenda, which Philip Dimitrov called "operational", was based on the conviction that no one was capable of forcing the communist party to draft a decree against its own domination in government. Yet, a certain kind of pressure could force it to say "yes" to a well-drafted law, "especially if it did not include too many words."

It was probably sheer delusion to expect that the BCP would be prepared to take such pressure regularly. But there is no doubt that "operationality," i.e., the development of a plan of action for attaining a specific goal, was lacking in the conduct of the Coordinating Council of the Union of Democratic Forces.

...

---

[13] Ivan Kurtev in a conversation with the author, Sofia, Bulgaria, August 24, 1998.

In the beginning, Andrey Lukanov headed the red delegation at the National Round Table debate. Soon he was succeeded by Georgi Pirinski - one of his most trusted followers - and by Alexander Lilov, a former member of the Politburo and of the BCP's Central Committee. The two of them continued to maneuver the disputes skillfully to the end and close the "Round Table" with success for the communists.

Thus, the leaders of the BCP created the impression, both in the country and abroad, that they were sharing the responsibility of reforming the Bulgarian political system with the democrats. They retained complete control over the country's governance, the process of political change, and the financial resources of their party and its satellites. They presented their party before the West as a moderate, sensible and trustworthy partner. They ostensibly accepted the platform of the democrats, which allowed them later to accuse their opponents of reluctance to cooperate, and of extremism. While continuing to rule and pillage the country, the communists established a Grand National Assembly with a task of secondary importance for the moment, namely the drafting of a new Constitution. They scheduled the parliamentary elections in June, thus leaving the Union of Democratic Forces insufficient time to prepare for them.

From that moment on, the "reformed" communists did everything they could to brainwash the population into thinking that the alternative to the National Round Table was nothing but civil war. The possibility of an armed conflict provoked by their political adversaries was as unlikely as it was ridiculous. By conviction, the democrats ruled out the use of violence as a means of attaining power. Moreover, for decades the BCP had control over the entire state and military apparatus: 90% of the army officers and almost the entire staff of the militia were its members.[14] Thus, the communists knew what they were doing. By spreading rumors about impending acts of violence on the part of the opposition, they skillfully conducted their election campaign. They deliberately tried to present the UDF as a destructive force threatening social peace and stability.

In some respects, the "Round Table" was a success for the democrats as well. It brought official recognition to the Union of Democratic Forces. People became acquainted with the opposition leaders. Their names became well-known. Indeed, the radio and TV broadcasts did not help the population fully grasp the values, significance, nature and principles of democracy. However, the presence of the UDF in the media convinced the nation that at least in Sofia one had the liberty of speaking about freedom without being punished or persecuted, as had been common practice during the "dictatorship of the

---

[14] Melone 1998, p. 49.

proletariat." It might sound unbelievable, but people continued to be deported or forcefully resettled for political reasons even in the 1980s of the 20th century, without the right to a day in court and without appeal. For this reason speeches against totalitarian rule in the Bulgarian media were a real miracle. In the beginning, men and women could hardly believe their ears, and they never got enough.

Toward the end of the negotiations, anxious questions began to surge one after another in the minds of a considerable part of the Bulgarian nation: What was actually achieved by the discussion that dragged on for four months? Didn't two sides participate in it, two sides with radically opposed views on the political system? Then, why was it necessary for the UDF leaders to force the communist to accept democratic principles that were totally alien to their party? By authorizing political change, the Bulgarian Communist Party - monstrous in the eyes of the noncommunist population by its repressive past and economic crimes - was becoming something of a "founding father" of democracy in Bulgaria! What was the meaning of a "political agreement" between the dictators and the democrats who had to defend their opposing views before the entire nation in the election struggle? Why was it necessary for the UDF to run to the rescue of the communists, who had plunged into an ideological crisis, and help their party disguise itself as a democratic political force? Could it be that the differences between the two political factions were becoming blurry?

The National Round Table reminded the people with a democratic consciousness that, sadly, many of the leaders of the Union of Democratic Forces had been BCP members until very recently and their reasoning was far from anticommunist. This prompted many of them to ask themselves whether there were persons linked to the totalitarian secret services - and obliged to obey their instructions - on the side of the democrats at the "Round Table".

Even if we put aside all emotion, the reckoning is clear and simple. The National Round Table and the preparations for it took nearly five months out of the six months during which the Union of Democratic Forces had been in existence. They deflected the attention of its Coordinating Council from the task of building a solid organizational network in the country. Preparations for the elections for a Grand National Assembly in June, 1990, were left on the back burner, especially in the countryside. The winner in the game - the Bulgarian Communist Party - made perfect use of those same months.

. . .

It must not have been easy for the Secretary General of BCP's Central Committee Peter Mladenov and his associates to draft the report to be delivered at the Fourteenth Extraordinary Congress of their party. They would have been totally lost without their communist insolence and demagogy. Mladenov opened the Congress on January 30, 1990, with the following reassuring statement:

> Comrades, our party awoke from its lethargic sleep. Never before have its members been so frank with one another, so open in terms of thought and conduct.[15]

The report of the leader of the red party sounded new, but the abundant contradictions and lies in it were old enough. The communist-reformist, who had declared himself resolutely in favor of the revival of the BCP in the spirit of pluralism and democracy referred to the cruel political terror of his party until 1947 as "development of the country following a people's democracy model."[16] He spoke about "complete and final 'de-Stalinization' of the party ranks" and at the same time praised the ideas and the deeds of Stalin's faithful servant and disciple Georgi Dimitrov. And more, and more...[17] After forty-six years of dictatorship of the Bulgarian Communist Party, undisturbed by anything and anybody, its Secretary General had the impudence to declare:

> We are the bearers of the brightest ideals of the people. It is true that we have been unable to attain them so far. But this is precisely why we wish to be renovated, so that we can at long last carry our original mission to the end.[18]

The Fourteenth Extraordinary Congress was closed on February 2, 1990. It adopted a Manifesto for Democratic Socialism in Bulgaria and a new Statutes of the Party. The former Politburo and Central Committee were replaced by a new leading body, namely the Supreme Party Council. It was headed by the seasoned communist strategist Alexander Lilov.

The time was ripe for the renaming of the Bulgarian Communist Party. The numerous proposals for new names included: Party for Democratic Socialism in Bulgaria (Communists), Communist Party for Democratic Socialism, Bulgarian Socialist Party, Renovated Bulgarian Communist Party, Bulgarian Democratic

---

[15] Fourteenth Extraordinary Congress of the Bulgarian Communist Party, January 30 - February 2, 1990, Publishing House of the BCP, Sofia, 1990, p. 13.

[16] *Ibid.*, p. 7.

[17] *Ibid.*, pp. 17, 20, 80.

[18] *Ibid.*, p. 47.

Communist Party, etc.[19] Clearly, the word "communist" was dear to the hearts of the BCP members, since it participated in ridiculous phrases like "Democratic Communist Party". However, the historic moment demanded sacrifices. In order to preserve the organization undivided, and bring the old leaders, the younger recent recruits, and the "active fighters against fascism and capitalism" together, the party needed an umbrella name. Obviously, according to the logic of the communists, it was sufficient for a criminal to change his name to have his evil deeds pardoned.

In the first days of April 1990, the communists in Bulgaria ceased to exist. Nearly a million socialists appeared in their place as members of the Bulgarian Socialist Party (BSP). Given the composition of the organization, its new name meant a strong reluctance to change rather than a desire for reform.

At the some time there were some changes in the state apparatus. The Ninth National Assembly, elected during the totalitarian regime, appointed Andrey Lukanov Prime Minister on February 8. On March 29 he imposed a moratorium on the repayment of Bulgaria's foreign debt, which had increased to 12 billion U.S. dollars in the meantime. With that act he declared before the world the bankruptcy of the state.

Peter Mladenov retained his post as Head of State, albeit under a different title. On April 3, 1990, he became President of the People's Republic of Bulgaria and Supreme Commander of its Armed Forces.

Thus, before the elections for Grand National Assembly, the Bulgarian Communist Party did everything that it had to do and anything that it could do to hold on to power. It started its existence under a new name with the old conviction that the political events in the country would not take a radical turn and that the communists could continue governing the Bulgarians.

---

[19] *Ibid.*, p. 68.

PART FOUR

CIVILIAN EMOTION

14. "The Inebriation of a Nation"

In the winter and spring of 1990, the Bulgarian people experienced enough events to fill an entire lifetime. Such a stirring of the spirits had not been seen for decades. The communist world seemed to be crumbling. A big part of the nation was suddenly awakening from its nightmarish slumber and was attempting to regain its democratic thinking. Concessions that were common until very recently seemed no longer comprehensible. The bitterness of many people at their own conformism made them bold, brave, and resolute - much to their own surprise. Parents for the first time told their grown up and even middle-aged children that their ancestors had been victims of the red terror. Mothers and grandmothers ordered commemoration services in churches for their long-missing husbands. Spouses on the brink of divorce were reunited by a common political outlook and a sense of inspiration. Other families split as husbands and wives made their individual moral choices. Squabbles between parents and children started in the homes of some communists. However, most of the households of BCP members were even more united by their attachment to the privileges that the totalitarian system had secured for them. Friends for many years stopped seeing each other on account of previously unnoticed differences in their political views. Others shared with friends for the first time the truth about the death of their fathers. New relationships were created at the rallies, vigils, and processions.

The first issue of *Svoboden Narod* - the newspaper of the Social Democrats, which had been banned by the red rulers of the country in 1947 - came out on February 1, 1990. It was followed by *Demokratsiya,* the daily newspaper of the Union of Democratic Forces, and several other periodical publications, collections of political poems, memoirs, and documentary books. They had small circulations, and people queued from the early hours of the morning to buy them. They read and discussed them avidly.

There was a lot to learn from these books and periodicals, especially for the younger generations. Those who had lived in pre-communist Bulgaria, on the other hand, could hardly believe their eyes. For decades they had lost all hope of seeing the day when the crimes of the "people's rule" would be discussed openly by the media. That moment had come.

The news about the official unveiling of the secret about the political labor and concentration camps of totalitarian Bulgaria spread with lightning speed all over the country. Many people in cities and villages had heard about them or had experienced their horror first-hand or through the fate of their relatives. However, for years those who had miraculously survived the inferno of the Bolshevik "labor correction communities" did not dare to speak about their experiences in public. This may be due to the fact that they were forced to sign an oath of silence before being released. In 1990, some people for the first time broke it.

The disclosure of the extremely severe working regime and the beastly conditions in which the camp inmates lived shocked democratically minded Bulgarians. The inhumanity of the heads of the concentration camps and their subordinates, all of whom were communists, became public knowledge. Their cruelty was manifested not only against the living inmates, but also against the corpses of men and women, barely recognizable after mutilation, severe beating, and torture.

The number of the death camps in the People's Republic of Bulgaria proved to be much larger than most people suspected. A map of their locations, printed in 1990, showed that they were fairly evenly distributed all over the country: from the Sveti Vrach railway station in the southwest, near the town of Sandanski, all the way to the village of Nozharevo in the northeast, near the town of Silistra. From the Belene islands in the Danube to the village of Nikolaevo near Kazanlak in Central Bulgaria. The government had opened the first concentration camp promptly after September 9, 1944. The last two - the camp for men near the stone quarries in the vicinity of Lovech and for women in the village of Skravena near Botevgrad - were finally closed in 1962. For 18 years, the red dictators locked any individual unwelcome to the regime into the hell of torture. A hint from the militia sufficed for the authorities, who rarely waited for a prosecutor's order to detain people.

In 1990 the Bulgarians repeated with hatred and disgust the names of the former Deputy Minister of the Interior, General Mircho Spasov, appointed by the BCP's Central Committee to control the concentration camps; the head of the camp near Lovech, Major Peter Gogov; the State Security agent Nikolay Gazdov, and the labor boss Tsvetko Goranov. The latter two had been active at several concentration camps. Revulsion and vitriol accompanied any mention of Juliana Ruzhgeva - a sadist inquisitor and murderer of countless helpless women sent to the camp in Skravena. The cited individuals were still alive and proud members of the Bulgarian Communist Party.

The new democratic press began discussing prominent Bulgarians, who had been fated to slander, lies, defamation and oblivion for 46 years. Articles appeared about their work, listing their merits to their homeland and contributions to science and culture. Their works were published. Their photographs were shown, and readers saw noble and intelligent faces, in stark contrast to the gorilla-like communist dignitaries, whose images had filled newspapers, books and magazines for decades.

People remembered or learned for the first time about the prominent journalists, publishers, and editors like Danail Krapchev, Rayko Alexiev, Todor Kozhuharov, Stefan Tanev, Matey Bonchev-Brashlyan, and many more. These individuals had used their professional competence and foresight to warn their readers about what the Stalinist regime meant and what was in store for Bulgaria if it fell into the bloody and deadly embrace of Bolshevism. Each of these talented men was murdered or incarcerated after September 9, 1944, for his incorruptible civic dignity, willingness to speak up, profound love for Bulgaria and concern for its future.

Love for the country of their birth also brought to trial the writers Zmey Goryanin, Trifon Kunev, Dimitar Talev, and Fani Popova-Mutafova, the father of Bulgarian caricature and cartoons, Alexander Bozhinov, the philologist-historian Academician Mihail Arnaudov, the historian Academician Ivan Doychev, the lawyers Encho Mateev and Svetoslav Nelchinov, the biologist Professor Dr. Stefan Konsulov, and hundreds of other outstanding academics, public figures and journalists, many of whom were totally unknown to the Bulgarians born during the decades of communism.

The name of Professor Dr. Alexander Stanishev, a brilliant surgeon and an outstanding scholar, executed by the "People's Court", became known to a number of physicians for the first time. The same was true of Professor Boris Yotsov, a famous expert in Slavonic studies, who also met his death at the hands of the quasi-court. The democratic press discussed the achievements of Professor Dr. Slavcho Zagorov, awarded in absentia for his contribution to Bulgarian statistical science and practice with a death sentence by the pseudo "People's Court". In his communist homeland, Zagorov was proclaimed to be a "fascist", "traitor" and "an epitome of mediocrity." In the West he was among the most educated and influential statisticians. The methods devised by Slavcho Zagorov, who in exile became a Professor at the University of Vienna, were crucial for the building of the scientific base of the European Union.

Through articles about their life or through their own books and works, Bulgarians learned about dozens of scientists, lawyers, diplomats, journalists and businessmen, who were banished from Bulgaria after September 9, 1944, and resettled all over the world. They had made their contributions to the development of foreign science, economy and culture, unable to impact their own country in any way. Most prominent among them, to name just a few, were Stefan Popov, Stefan Groueff, Dr. Panayot Panayotov, Hristo Boyadzhiev, and Dr. Hristo Ognyanov.

It pained people to realize how much talent and energy had been drained from their homeland after the establishment of the totalitarian rule. At the same time, the citizens were riveted on the present time of turmoil. The course of events at that point seemed unpredictable.

Between January and May, the population followed the debates of the National Round Table and discussed them excitedly. Many Bulgarians also participated in dozens of demonstrations organized by the Union of Democratic Forces. With hitherto unknown zeal and attention, they watched TV programs that sometimes showed incredible sights. For example, on Easter, the most celebrated holiday for the Christian Orthodox world, the leaders of the recently renamed communist party, headed by Peter Mladenov, Andrey Lukanov and Dobri Dzhurov, were standing piously and holding burning candles in front of the altar of the *St. Alexander Nevski* Cathedral. It apparently did not matter to the communist leaders that Easter was almost forbidden the previous year and that they - considering themselves atheists, had not even entered a church for the funeral services of their closest relatives.

...

It should be noted that not the entire population shared that feverish excitement. Many people remained without any opinion during the winter and spring months of heated discussions, conversations, debates and confessions. They did not take part in the events; they did not read about them, and they remained unperturbed. Instead, they were deeply worried that their peace and calm were being disturbed, and the existence that they were used to was being threatened. They either claimed not to be interested in politics, or they repeated that all politicians were similar and that it was all the same to them who ruled the country.

Some other citizens were more sincere. They openly regretted the demise of Todor Zhivkov's regime. They claimed that under his rule everything was peaceful and there was calm in the streets and order in everything. Freedom of the spirit apparently had no value for these people. They were brainwashed with communist clichés and false promises.

There were also persons who had not yet overcome their cowardice and were refraining from expressing any views. Among them there were people who had suffered under communism: the fear of what they had experienced made them timid and mistrustful. They had serious reasons for that. Thousands of agents and collaborators of the secret services, as well as voluntary informers, existed in the People's Republic of Bulgaria. Just in the first two years after

September 9, 1944, the State Security system succeeded in building a network of 100,000 agents and informers. That figure increased substantially throughout the next decades. The recruiting of agents and informers continued until the last day of the communist regime. If we add to their numbers the members of the BCP, who were obliged under the statutes of their organization to spy and report on non-party members, the apprehensions and suspicions of the scared Bulgarians become more than understandable.

The agents coming from outside the communist circles were divided into three main groups: people who were recruited by the State Security through violence and against their will, individuals who voluntarily agreed to act as informers for personal benefits such as a better job, career, travels abroad, material incentives, fees, etc., and others who offered their services to the repressive apparatus out of misanthropy, envy and malice. The individuals from the latter two categories often served the authorities with a greater zeal than even the communists themselves. This explains why the unexpected turn of political events after November 1989 scared them to death.

There was not much that stirred in the Bulgarian villages. The commotion in the cities seemed not to affect them. People in the rural areas watched events on television and were frightened, rather than exhilarated. They kept repeating that they were peasants and had enough problems of their own.

The intensity of the moment permeated only Sofia and the big cities. There it was apparent in people's homes, at their workplaces, in the streets and on the public transportation vehicles. The confrontation between the two principal groups of Bulgarians - communists and anticommunists - was unconditional. The citizens were divided into "blue," a label that the Union of Democratic Forces supporters had chosen for themselves on account of the color of the UDF flag, and "red," which indicated members and followers of the Bulgarian Communist Party. People went so far as to avoid clothing in the color of their political adversary.

It is to the credit of the victims of communism and of their successors that not a single one of them resorted to a personal vendetta and not a single drop of blood was shed. What the opponents of the BCP dictatorship wanted was for the communist party to admit its guilt, to apologize to its victims, and to allow the still living henchmen and the principal persons responsible for the national catastrophe to be brought to trial. That affected the initiators, commandants, and staff of the sinister concentration camps, notably Anton Yugov, Mircho Spasov, Peter Gogov, Nikolay Gazdov, Tsvetko Goranov, Juliana Ruzhgeva. The assassins and aggressors responsible for the disappearance of the so-called "missing persons" were also expected to be brought to justice, because in the smaller towns and in the villages their identities were known. People also hoped that the most eminent figures of the communist party, especially Todor Zhivkov and his close associates for so many years, should be held responsible for their political and economical crimes.

Once again, the democrats proved that they were of a different mindset than the communists. They felt a deep hatred towards terrorism and personal revenge. Thousands of them had spent their lives as orphans, in misery and persecution, because they had fathers - and sometimes also mothers - who had been killed without trial or sentence, or by the macabre mockery that communist courts represented. These people were hoping for the triumph of justice in a legitimate judiciary system and in fair trials. They patiently waited for the hour of just retribution with the ardent wish that they, the "blue" voters, would win the first free elections in decades. In the spring of 1990, the election radio show of the Union of Democratic Forces confidently counted the minutes until the end of communism in Bulgaria.

...

The conduct of the members of the ruling communist party and their relatives and supporters is worth considering at greater length. For forty-six years they were used being at the helm of political, state and economic power in the country. Until January 1990, Article 1 of the Constitution of the People's Republic stipulated that the Bulgarian Communist Party had the leading role in society and in the governance of the state. In other words, everybody knew that welfare, a myriad of privileges and fringe benefits came with the red party membership card. Eventually, the members of the communist party in the late 1980s numbered almost a million – one ninth of the population of the country.

Some of the party members were communist hard-liners. Others were career-seekers. A third category consisted of politically ignorant individuals, fed distorted teachings of history, politics and moral values for decades. A fourth category - mainly young professionals - joined the BCP with a slight feeling of shame, justifying their act before friends and colleagues with the lame excuse that they were doing it so as "to conquer the party from within" or "to prevent others from trampling them." The first option never materialized, while the second statement was rather insolent to begin with, because it implied that they wished to trample others.

However, irrespective of the way they had joined the BCP, the rank-and-file members of the communist party acted in almost perfect accord during the first tense months of 1990. Just few of them were indignant at what they read, saw or heard in the media. Those people were predominantly young persons from whom the crimes of totalitarianism had been kept secret until that time. They joined the rallies and demonstrations of the UDF supporters with tears in their eyes and faces betraying the shame they felt.

There were also communists who immediately joined the ranks of the democrats, not driven by any moral considerations, but for the same reasons for which they had joined the BCP earlier. They anticipated that power would soon be on the side of the UDF. In order to prove to the people around them that they had indeed changed their credo, they often behaved in a more heated and aggressive fashion than most convinced anticommunists. The rather controversial subsequent political developments in Bulgaria put these "turncoats" to a real test. For two decades they had to yo-yo between the principal political forces in an attempt to find the winning one.

Still, the solid mass of communist hard-liners did not even wish to open the new democratic newspapers or to read the new books of memoirs. When information was presented on television about the historical crimes of the BCP, they turned off their TV sets. These people continued to use the word "fascists" when referring to their political adversaries, just as they had done in the past decades. Due to their distorted notions of heroism, those who had persecuted and destroyed "enemies of the people" and "former people" felt even prouder and worthier of respect than before. Knowing all too well their own methods of aggression and violence, the hard-liners were trying to persuade their more naive fellow-communists that a "witch hunt" was in store for them. They spread rumors that the UDF would kill them, and deport them, taking away their apartments, houses, villas and cars, and persecuting their children for life. All together the red mass felt perplexed, frightened, and ready to fight to preserve the power of the BCP. Even people who until recently had been critical of their party started stubbornly repeating that they themselves had done nothing wrong, that they personally had not done anyone any harm, that it would be wrong to believe that their life had passed in vain while working for the totalitarian system, that their partisan fathers were heroes, and other similar claims.

Typical of the mentality of the communist party members was that they measured everything through the prism of their own interest and the interest of their families. Not one single demagogical phrase of theoretical communism was in circulation. Those upon whom special privileges had been bestowed, namely the "active fighters against fascism and capitalism", actually showed leniency toward the economic system of their enemies. Some of them already big businessmen, they dropped the last noun from their title and diminished their merits to mere "fighters against fascism." The striking similarities between the communist and the fascist regimes never crossed their minds.

Fossilized in their thinking, most of the members of the BCP did not pay attention to the shocking revelations about the economic collapse of the country made public by their own Secretary General, Peter Mladenov, at the December 1989 meeting. They blamed their low living standards solely on the democratically minded people and their rallies, demonstrations, and vigils. For them it did not matter that at that time the Union of Democratic Forces still did not have any participation in the government of the country.

. . .

The culmination of that eventful winter and spring, of all that seething emotion and incredible excitement - a phenomenon referred to in the classical Bulgarian literature as "the inebriation of a nation" - came on June 7, 1990, the day of the pre-election rally organized by the Union of Democratic Forces.

The rally was just three days before the elections that were so crucial for the awakened part of the Bulgarian people. Having demonstrated patience for decades, they could no longer wait even several days. Having recovered from the stupor in which they lived, and felt the shame of their inaction, many citizens believed that their adversaries would prove to be few in number and that there would be no hesitation about the future path of Bulgaria. Thousands streamed to the boulevard leading up to the airport for the last rally before the big VICTORY. They went there on a beautiful and sunny day, wearing their best clothes, happy and smiling. For these people there was no way back. They were all singing the new hit by Vasko the Patch, "Communism is going away!," and the joy beaming from their faces was surreal.

On that same day the communists also held their pre-election rally. Nervously, they gathered in the square in front of the mausoleum where the mummified carcass of their leader Georgi Dimitrov had been lying since 1949. Their faces were twisted with malice and indignation. Someone was trying to wring the power from their hands, deprive them of the privileges they had enjoyed for forty-six years, take away their possessions, their higher salaries and pensions, make them equal to everyone else, and turn them into ordinary citizens.

On that day, two different worlds crossed paths in the streets of Sofia. One carried hope; the other horror. Bulgaria was split in two. However, there were no clashes.

15. The Elections of 1990 – Free or Manipulated?

The Union of Democratic Forces lost the elections on June 10, 1990. The communists were jubilant. They had been skulking in their homes for a while, but in the evening of that day they were congratulating each other publicly and opening bottles of scotch and champagne. They could not hide their joy about a victory that had seemed uncertain. The only disappointment for the red party members and supporters was its overwhelming loss in Sofia and most big cities. Still, the Bulgarian Socialist Party won 53% of the seats in the Seventh Grand National Assembly, which gave it an absolute majority.

As a result of that election, the communists would draft once again the Constitution of Bulgaria. In the process they would make sure they would never be held accountable for their crimes. In addition, the high-ranking *nomenklatura* would benefit financially. The victory of the BSP gave them the time they needed to accumulate illicit capital for their companies and expropriate state assets.

The votes of the smaller towns and villages provided the principal support of the communists-turned-socialists. Paradoxically, the villages had suffered severely as a result of communism through coercive collectivization. In the 1940s and 1950s, it was hard for the Bulgarian farmers to relinquish the land that they had inherited or acquired with hard labor. Government agents forced them out of their houses by night, beat them, and kept them under arrest until they wrote a "request" to join the cooperative farms. Those who refused often disappeared without a trace. Many others were sent to concentration camps.

By the mid 1950s, the villages in Bulgaria were entirely dominated by Soviet-type farms, and in many regions of the country they were depopulated. Fertile, arable land gradually became barren. Orchards with rare fruit disappeared. Faultlessly cultivated vines wilted. Having assumed the role of feudal lords, the bosses of the cooperative farms and local party leaders stole from the communal property and managed the estates irresponsibly. Meanwhile, the peasants worked without motivation. The authorities sent high school and university students to harvest the crops during the summer vacation and in the autumn, but the results were not good. Bulgaria started importing potatoes and onions from Poland. Beans, a common ingredient in the national cuisine, became a luxury. Meat was increasingly expensive. Turkey and lamb were a rare sight.

In fact, by 1990, the farmers who had experienced the forced collectivization were either dead or old and helpless. While the Union of Democratic Forces still did not have structures of its own in most places in the countryside, the Bulgarian Socialist Party made every possible effort to preserve its influence over the rural areas.

. . .

Unfortunately, the BSP's manipulations were invisible to the official observers of the elections, especially to the foreign teams. Few could guess that during the spring of 1990 many small towns and villages were visited by people who had been born in them, but had left them to take communist party positions in the capital city. Stopping by various houses, they reminded their fellow townsmen or villagers how they had helped a son or a daughter of theirs to find a job in Sofia. They threatened that their children would be fired if the family voted with the blue ballot. They claimed that if the UDF won the elections, it would take away their pensions, reducing them to poverty. They instigated the people in the countryside against the "blue cities." They deceived the uneducated by charging that democracy meant misery, chaos, disorder, and depravity. One of the red propaganda leaflets read as follows:

THE BULGARIAN SOCIALIST PARTY says:

NO!	YES!
- to complete Negation	- to Realism
- to Pessimism	- to Optimism
- to the "shock therapy" for emerging from the economic crisis	- to the gradual transition to a stable market economy
- to mass unemployment and inflation	- to the social security of the population
- to the domination of Private Capital that will enslave thousands of working people	- to equality between the different forms of ownership
- to the high fees for tuition for kindergartens and medication	- to free education, health care, privileges for the elderly, the sick, the mothers, and the children
- to economic dependence on foreign countries	- to equitable cooperation with all countries
- to demagogy and violence	- to sound reason, pluralism, and consensus
- to a new totalitarian regime under the banner of the UDF	- to democracy and to the changes that have been started and continued by the BSP.

FELLOW COUNTRYMEN!
We believe in your political realism, civic wisdom and valor.
We believe that you will make the right choice on June 10th.[1]

---

[1] Election propaganda leaflet of the BSP during the elections for Grand National Assembly in June 1990.

The rally at the *St. Alexander Nevski* Square on November 18, 1989, Sofia

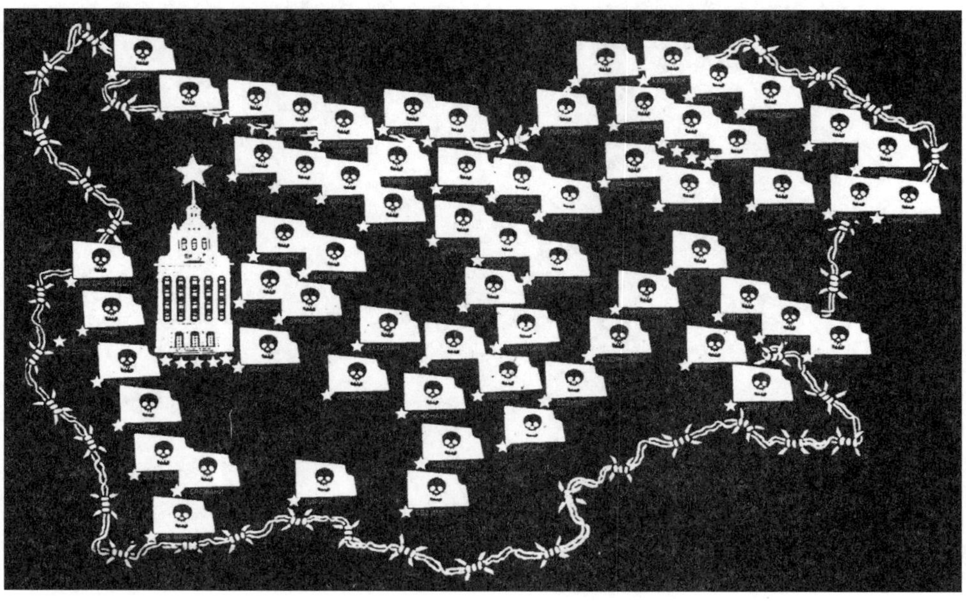

Map of the concentration camps of the People's Republic of Bulgaria

The writer and journalist Vasil Stanilov on a hunger strike,
December 1989 – January 1990, Sofia

The last day of Vasil Stanilov's hunger strike, January 1990, Sofia

Pre-election rally of the UDF, June 7, 1990, Sofia

The actor Yossif Sarchadzhiev at a rally in support of the students' strike, June 1990, Sofia

Sit-in strike in front of the President's Office, July 5, 1990, Sofia

The City of Truth in front of the Headquarters of the Bulgarian Communist Party, July 5 – August 27, 1990 Sofia

The tent of the physicians and pharmacists at the City of Truth

The residents of the City of Truth in front of the National Assembly, July 27, 1990

The Headquarters of the Bulgarian Communist Party on fire, August 26-27, 1990, Sofia

Procession in Sofia against the government of Andrey Lukanov, November 1990

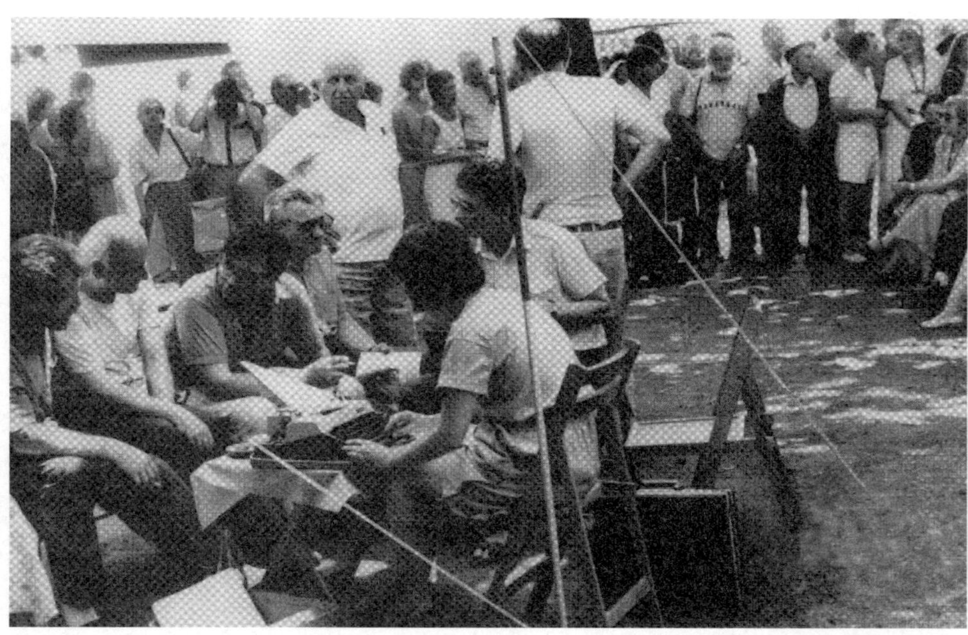

The camp of the 23 Members of Parliament from the UDF who went on hunger strike, July 1991, Sofia

In front of *St. Kliment Ohridski* University of Sofia on the day the Constitution was signed, July 1991

Students on the roof of *St. Kliment Ohridski* University of Sofia in protest against the new Constitution, July 1991

Pre-election dispute at Radio *Sofia* between the leader of the UDF Philip Dimitrov and the leader of the BSP Alexander Lilov, October 1991

Philip Dimitrov with supporters of the UDF, October 13, 1991, Sofia

The leader of the UDF Philip Dimitrov celebrates the election victory of the blue alliance on October 13, 1991, Sofia

Philip Dimitrov leads the rally of the election victory of the UDF, October 14, 1991, Sofia

The president of the Republic of Bulgaria Dr. Zhelyu Zhelev signs a decree for Philip Dimitrov to form a government, October 1991, Sofia

First meeting of the UDF government, Nikolay Vasilev, Philip Dimitrov and Svetoslav Luchnikov, November 9, 1991, Sofia

The Prime Minister Philip Dimitrov in his office, January 1992

Philip Dimitrov and Stefan Savov in the National Assembly, 1992

The President of the U.S.A. George Bush Senior and the Prime Minister of Bulgaria Philip Dimitrov in the White House, March 1992, Washington D.C.

Ivan Tatarchev, Prosecutor General of the Republic of Bulgaria (1992-1997) in a conversation with the author, September 2000, Sofia

Ivan Kurtev, Deputy Speaker of the Thirty-Eight National Assembly, in his office, August 1998, Sofia

Philip Dimitrov leads a rally against the government of Lyuben Berov, 1993, Sofia

Procession in Sofia against the government of Zhan Videnov headed by the leaders of the UDF, December 1996, Sofia

In front of the National Assembly, January 10, 1997, Sofia

The president of the Parliamentary Assembly of the Council of Europe Rene van der Linden hands the medal „Pro Merito" to Latchesar Toshev in recognition of services rendered to the European cause, January 23, 2006 (photo: Council of Europe)

Prof. Ivan Emanuilov Ivanov, January 2008, New York

Yosif Sarchadzhiev with his wife Rayna Tomova in their summer house, July 2000, Sinemorets, Bulgaria

Anna Sarchadzhieva with her father Yosif, April 2009, Sofia

Rosen Donkov
celebrates his birthday in 2002, Sofia

The psychiatrist Dr. Krum Savov during his visit in the U.S.A., May 2003

Philip Dimitrov during a visit to Philadelphia, April 2009

In this leaflet the left-hand side alludes to the disaster that would be brought about by a UDF victory. In contrast, the right-hand side was meant to evoke the merits of the BSP, the party that had led the country to economic and moral collapse after forty-six years in government. Clearly, the authors relied on the lack of political memory of the people and on their susceptibility to demagogy, rather than "political realism, civic wisdom and valor." Later these inconsistencies were confirmed during the socialist governments of Andrey Lukanov (1990) and Zhan Videnov (1995-1997), when Bulgaria reached rock bottom, and the economy collapsed.

In addition to propaganda and personal manipulation, the "renovated" party resorted to various enticements and subtle threats. The mayors of the smaller towns and villages distributed money in blank envelopes and promised various favors and benefits in order to induce people to cast the red ballot. On Election Day, in many places in the countryside, there were calm and well-dressed communist party activists and militiamen in civilian clothes in front of the polling stations. Their smiling faces were a reminder of the fear instilled in the population for decades, of earlier threats, promises and bribery. Just a look at them was sufficient to influence votes.

The Bulgarian Roma community in Pazardzhik was openly urged to vote for the BSP in the polling stations, with the cue given to them: *kirmiz*, meaning "red". The previous night, the militia had made rounds in the Roma neighborhood, entering one house after another, and threatening retribution if people failed to vote for the Bulgarian Socialist Party.[2]

Similar campaigns were organized during the spring of 1990 in many regions of the country, in order to confuse and frighten the population. Years later a UDF parliamentary candidate related the story of a tragicomic occurrence during his campaign before the elections in northeastern Bulgaria. A middle-aged man had stood briefly at the door of the Club of the Union of Democratic Forces, looked furtively around and said quickly, "I want you to know that I am with you." Then he had thrust his hand into his pocket, taken out a UDF button, showed it to the blue candidate and immediately put it back into his pocket."[3]

...

Things were different in the country's capital. People there had lost their fear. The rallies, demonstrations, vigils, and processions had taken it away. For most

[2] Sarchadzhiev, *Diary*, Sofia, 2 a.m., June 12, 1990.

[3] Philip Dimitrov in a conversation with the author, Philadelphia, U.S.A., April 2, 1998.

of the citizens of Sofia, communism belonged to the past. Hence, when the election results were announced, they stared at their TVs, dumbfounded. As if someone had issued a call, the UDF supporters rushed out into the streets. Around dawn on June 11, the city center was filled with men and women, startled, crying, numb with sorrow. Some were in their pajamas and night gowns, but no one wanted to go back home to dress. People felt that they had to stick together in their disappointment, terrified that they would continue to be governed by the old rulers. They streamed to the huge open space in front of the Palace of Culture, inside which the heads of the Union of Democratic Forces were. Soon the square was filled to capacity. The citizens of the capital city waited to hear what their leaders had to say. Yet, the latter were in no hurry to appear before the crowds.

A television studio had been set up in the building of the Palace of Culture where high-ranking figures from the renamed Bulgarian Communist Party were being interviewed. Professor Chavdar Kyuranov, who had officially returned to the red side, Philip Bokov, and Georgi Pirinski spoke. Complacent, they celebrated their victory and claimed that the elections in Bulgaria had passed in a calm and normal atmosphere. They even boasted that the nation had once again entrusted the power to them.[4]

Something unexpected happened around 3 a.m., disrupting the TV coverage. The actor Yosif Sarchadzhiev burst into the improvised studio, uninvited. He tried to give information about a number of violations of the Electoral Law, which he had seen as a UDF observer in the town of Pazardzhik and the villages around it. He had a videotape containing evidence to support his claims. The communist politicians met Sarchadzhiev's words with ridicule and haughty irony. This was too much for Yosko, as his fans call him. He shouted accusations at them and burst into tears. The television studio interrupted the broadcast, refusing to publicize the manipulation of the elections, particularly in the countryside.

Twenty-four hours after his appearance on national television, Yosif Sarchadzhiev wrote in his diary:

> Yes, we lost the elections. People were crying in front of the building of the Union of Democratic Forces in Pazardzhik. Thousands and thousand of young people were crying that night. I am shocked by the fear in these people, who did not even dare cry in public and hid. I am horrified by the conservatism of the parents who voted against their children.
>
> I returned to Sofia nearly dead with fatigue around 2 a.m. [on June 11 - *author's note*]. I saw in the streets crowds of people crushed by the loss of the

4 Sarchadzhiev, *Diary*, 2 a.m., June 12, 1990.

elections. Some were crying here, too. At home I saw on television that there was an election broadcast led by Kevork. I went to express everything that was welling up in me. Luckily, other witnesses from Pazardzhik had come and brought the videotape that we had succeeded in shooting. I tried to be calm and to stick to the facts, but Kyuranov and Pirinski made me lose my temper. I burst out and shouted to them: "Shame on you! The whole population is watching us on their TV sets. How dare you manipulate the people even now?!" And then I started crying. No, I didn't act then. I was sincere, although I was aware that I was creating a national controvercy.

Outside, in front of the Palace of Culture, the enormous multitude was roaring. That gave me the energy and confidence to stop pretending to be polite. From that moment on everything was like a dream. They interrupted the TV program. Everybody started shouting. It looked as if they were ready to lynch the communists. I was screaming and drinking some cold coffee. An emergency press conference with foreign journalists was called in one of the halls. In the meantime I spoke with a loudspeaker from the balcony of the Palace to the agitated people gathered below. I don't remember what I said. I only know that Rumyana Uzunova [from the Bulgarian service of *Radio Free Europe - author's note*] was standing next to me, holding my hand. She was crying. I could barely hold back my tears. The people below were shouting in desperation. Communism had made them mad. I made an extra effort and tried to breathe courage into the crowd below. I thought I would faint from exhaustion any minute. Then, as if in a dream, I gave interviews here and there together with these young people from the Gypsy neighborhood in Pazardzhik, who had dared to come to Sofia.

Petko Simeonov and Zhelyu Zhelev started to retreat slightly. It became boring and inaccurate. The people underneath were frustrated. Zhelyu tried to calm them down but then the real flames erupted. Peter Beron and Emil Koshlukov were speaking passionately and provocatively. Petko Simeonov shouted: "What shall I do with my conscience?" Everybody was shouting without restraint and with utter excitement. They were hurling abuse at Bokov and Pirinski, who grinned sheepishly as if they had shit their pants. Especially the women were so furious, it seemed to me that they were ready to tear Bokov to bits. Then the Coordinating Council of the UDF decided to hold a meeting to formulate its response to the government today. We started towards the exit. People lifted me and carried me on their shoulders. I gave another speech. It sounds ridiculous, but it was a fact. Imagine that: me - a politician!?

...

That was the exhilaration of desperate people. And I am no longer like that. Something in their desperation gives me hope that everything has shifted and that a little effort is needed to break out of that rottenness that is threatening to suffocate us.[5]

---

[5] *Ibid.*

The televised outburst of Bulgaria's most popular actor added to the emotions and excitement that were running high. The dam of discontent opened its floodgates. People started shouting at the top of their voices that the elections should not be recognized. Illuminated by searchlights, they were waiting tensely for the UDF leadership to finish their meeting. Their waiting seemed endless. At long last, the leaders emerged with stony faces. At first no one understood what their decision was.

All eyes were riveted on Dr. Zhelev. He urged the citizens of Sofia to calm down and to go back to their homes. He told them that the elections would be recognized. The square froze in grave silence. Then there was a rising murmur of indignation. Zhelev sensed the changing mood and started to explain. He said that it would not be a good idea to provoke an international scandal, that the elections had proceeded tolerantly on the whole, and that according to the observers the violations were insignificant. "We are all exhausted, let's disperse,"[6] he insisted.

Zhelyu Zhelev himself started walking toward the office of the Union of Democratic Forces. An enormous crowd followed him. However, when they reached the UDF building, dozens of people sat or lay on the pavement of *Rakovski* Street, thus expressing their disagreement with the recognition of the elections. This was the beginning of a massive student and civilian protest. In the summer of 1990, the "street" became the center of political events in Bulgaria.

. . .

In the evening of June 11, UDF Chairman Dr. Zhelyu Zhelev spoke before hundreds of thousands of people gathered around the Palace of Culture in Sofia, and characterized the preliminary results of the elections as a "fraud" and the actual elections as "entirely discredited and manipulated."[7] Three days later, at the press conference of the political leaders of the country, Zhelev declared that the elections were "legitimate" and "democratic", and accepted the results. Only the United States observers were ready to dispute that "legitimacy", but the UDF Chairman dissuaded them. He recognized the elections with a document sent to the Central Election Commission that only he himself signed.[8]

---

[6] Rayna Tomova in a conversation with the author, Sinemorets, Bulgaria, July 10, 1998.

[7] *Demokratsiya* daily, Mihail Konstantinov, Nikolay Valchanov, Angel Zhivkov, *The election Results Separated Us from Europe by a Year and a Half*, June 27, 1991; Sugarev 1993, p. 8.

[8] *Ibid.*

Six weeks later, the Seventh Grand National Assembly elected Dr. Zhelyu Zhelev as President of the Republic of Bulgaria with the support of the Bulgarian Socialist Party. After half a year, the Secretary of the Central Election Commission, Dimitar Popov, was appointed Prime Minister of Bulgaria by that same communist-dominated Grand National Assembly.

The Chairman of the Central Election Club of the UDF, Petko Simeonov, never made public the abundant record documenting violations of the Election Law that Yosif Sarchadzhiev and other observers had given him. The materials contained evidence of noncompliance with the full set of election documents, forging and substitution of voter registers and election results, voting with transparent envelopes and other violations of the confidentiality of the vote, irregularities in the procedure for submitting the protocols, etc.[9] Yet, the Coordinating Council of the Union of Democratic Forces did not discuss these materials publicly. Nor did it publish anything about the evidence of fraud in its daily newspaper *Demokratsiya.*

Only a year later - under new UDF leadership - did *Demokratsiya* and some other media release studies by scientists, mathematicians, and statisticians. Using precise data, the authors proved that the voter registers included about 500,000 phantom voters. While Dimitar Popov claimed on June 14, 1990, in the *Vecherni Novini* [Evening News] daily, that the number of voters in the city of Sofia were 999,556, the Statistical Yearbook of Bulgaria for the same year indicated their number as 915,000. At 76% of the polling stations in the small town of Troyan there were more votes cast than there were registered voters. Nearly 100 of the 400 seats in the Parliament were won as a result of gross violations of the Election Law.[10]

The publication of these findings convinced the majority of Bulgarians that the results of the election for deputies to the Seventh Grand National Assembly were fraudulent. At that point, however, it was already too late. For pro-democratic citizens June 1990 remained the month of an enormous disappointment. Many of them lost their faith in the future of their homeland. About 150,000 people, mostly young specialists, emigrated abroad soon after Election Day.

In that sultry emotional summer only a few opponents of the totalitarian system wondered what would have happened if the Union of Democratic Forces had not recognized the election results. Would the UDF have been isolated from political life, thus causing social unrest and violent confrontation

---

[9] *Ibid.*; Yosif Sarchadzhiev in a conversation with the author, Sinemorets, Bulgaria, July 10, 1998.

[10] *Demokratsiya* daily, Mikhail Konstantinov, Nikolay Valchanov, Angel Zhivkov, *The election Results Separated Us from Europe by a Year and a Half*, June 19 and 27, 1991.

between the supporters of the two opposing parties? Wasn't such confrontation precisely what the Bulgarian Socialist Party wanted?

The Bulgarian anticommunists did not want bloodshed. Alone, without their leaders, they sought their own unique ways to vent their anger against the crimes and lies of the long-term dictators and to express their deep, immutable thirst for truth and freedom.

16. The Truth of Students and Civilians

On June 11, 1990, the global television news networks announced that the first democratic elections held in Bulgaria in almost half a century were won by the Bulgarian Communist Party, which had recently renamed itself socialist. From all of Eastern Europe, the Balkan Republic was only the second state - after Romania - with such election results.

The next day, the same TV channels reported another story. The students from the *St. Kliment Ohridski* University of Sofia had declared a strike. They demanded an audit of the election results and the resignation of the Chairman of the Committee on Television, Pavel Pisarev, for broadcasting lies. Young, good-looking people appeared on TV, indignant about the manipulations of the ruling Bulgarian Socialist Party. The students were not alone. Thousands of Bulgarians expressed their rage at the antidemocratic acts of the red party, clearly and categorically.

How did the students' strike and the civilian protest start, and what did they accomplish for the modern history of Bulgaria?

. . .

In the early hours of June 11, hundreds of people in Sofia had not returned home. Disappointed and shocked by the outcome of the elections, they left the square in front of the Palace of Culture and started walking towards the building of the UDF and the *St. Kliment Ohridski* University. They shared the belief Yosif Sarchadzhiev expressed in his diary: "Today you cannot, you should not, it would be criminal to lie low, to be silent and to wait."[1] Ten years later his daughter Anna recounts:

> We were convinced that the election results were rigged. In the early morning hours of June 11 when my father broke into tears on the TV screen, trying desperately to prove that, the TV management interrupted the broadcast. The people from Sofia who had gathered in front of the Palace of Culture went wild. Zhelyu Zhelev urged us to go home. I personally did. At that time I was 20, a first-year student of Spanish language and literature.
>
> On the morning of June 11, a colleague from the French department, Tatyana Vaksberg, called me and told me that a group of students had occupied the University of Sofia during the night. At first they were about a dozen people, namely the organizers from the Federation of Independent Students' Societies. I called other fellow students and immediately went to the courtyard of the University. It was about 11 a.m. I learned that the strikers had already

[1] Sarchadzhiev, *Diary*, June 9, 1990.

selected leaders who were guiding our protest. We barred the doors of the University. No one could go in, except us. The security guards were students. It was just before the summer examination session.

In the beginning of the strike we blocked the crossroads in front of the University. Then the boys went on "hanging strike," that is to say that they climbed on the windows and hung holding themselves on their sills for about two hours. We organized various processions, one of which was a funeral for the Bulgarian Communist Party. Everything just happened spontaneously. We relied on ourselves and on our own forces. Emil Koshlukov, the student in charge, definitely had leadership qualities. We liked him.

At first we had two demands, namely that the information about violations of the Electoral Law, deposited with the Central Election Commission, be made public by the mass media, and that the National Television's boss Pavel Pisarev resign. A group of students had collected a lot of signatures in support of his resignation during rallies even before the elections. During the time of the "Round Table" and throughout the election campaign Pisarev was conducting outright communist propaganda. This also continued after the elections. I remember how, a day or two after my father's appearance on national TV on the night of the elections, there was fragmentary "coverage" of the event that was cut in such a way as to give the impression that he was mentally deranged.

I was constantly in touch with my parents: Rayna [Rayna Tomova - screenwriter and director - *author's note*] and Yosso. My mother remembered the footage filmed by Evgeniy Mihaylov on December 14, 1989, when Peter Mladenov had blurted, "It would be best if the tanks came!" She persuaded us that we, the students, should also demand an expert investigation into the authenticity of that documentary footage and a public announcement of whether the Bulgarian Head of State had uttered that phrase or not. On June 20, we added the new demand to the Declaration of the Students' Strike Committee.

The strike gradually spread to other universities in Sofia. A students' hunger strike started in Veliko Tarnovo. Father Christophor organized night vigils with candles. University lecturers, parents of the striking students, and other citizens organized sit-ins and hunger strikes. Dr. Trenchev sent us food and blankets.

The committee of experts announced the result of its inquiry. Peter Mladenov had indeed uttered his notorious phrase! However, on the evening of July 5, he personally rejected the conclusion of the specialists. The version of the communists was that the president had said, "It would be best if Stanko [Stanko Todorov, then Speaker of the National Assembly - *author's note*] came!" Outraged, together with our lecturers, actors, prominent figures in Bulgaria's cultural scene, and other protesters, we wrote a declaration demanding Mladenov's resignation.

Then the UDF Spokesman Georgi Spasov and the Union's Secretary Peter Beron came to the University. At that time we still believed them to be with us, and we were happy to let them into the University courtyard, never imagining what the truth about this men would prove to be later. (Lord, how painful it was in the first months and years, when you didn't know who was who! Someone talks to you like an anticommunist, and when you look at his deeds you find out he is just the opposite.) So those two told us to stop the strike because - according to them - it was tragic for the country since there could be bad consequences. They also said that there was already a Grand National Assembly that would solve our problems, and so on, and so forth. We became furious and demanded the resignation of the entire government.

The Prime Minister Andrey Lukanov urgently returned from Romania and invited our leaders to a meeting. That night was particularly exciting. We were all in a frenzy. We awaited the return of our leaders in the University courtyard. They appeared, deeply worried, after which they immediately set off for the square in front of the President's Office to seek advice on what to do from the university teachers and intellectuals, who had declared a sit-in strike around the building. Rumors circulated that Lukanov was extremely nice to them and had almost convinced them to put an end to the strike. That communist was such a cunning skunk!

On July 6, Peter Mladenov handed in his resignation as President. We had already sensed that this might happen, and that's why together with the participants in the sit-in strike in front of the President's Office we had drafted a declaration containing new demands. We read it on TV. That gave rise to the civil protest known as The City of Truth, which included citizens of Sofia and university students as well.

Only a few children of communists participated in the students' strike. In contrast, we - the others - were convinced that what we were doing was absolutely fair and justified. We were firmly determined to force the rulers to give in to our demands. We were happy to learn about the resignation of TV boss Pavel Pisarev. However, when Peter Mladenov resigned, our joy sparkled like fireworks! On the next day we merged with the City of Truth, although we also held the University courtyard. Only after the headquarters of the Bulgarian Communist Party were set on fire and the police dispersed the people who had put up their tents in the City of Truth, things changed. I believe to this day that the BSP itself set fire to the building on account of the archives and also to create a situation that would disrupt the movement of noncommunists against communism, which was gaining momentum.

My motives for participation in the strike were purely civic. The correct situation was created. I couldn't remain indifferent. I had to run and join in. A young person at that age is easily fired up. Moreover, I have always hated communism because it created a dead society without freedom, absolutely dead.

> Through our strike we, the students, were fighting precisely for individual freedom. We wanted to make sure that young people remained in Bulgaria and did not emigrate. Our principal aim was for our country to become a state in which we could have a career and job satisfaction.
>
> In the summer of 1990, the students on strike were beside themselves with excitement. Nevertheless, it never even crossed our minds to resort to violence. The older people sharing our views were also non-violent. Looking back, I am even amazed that although we had lived for so long in a closed society that was not free, we conducted all our actions absolutely democratically. At that time we didn't even have any democratic culture, there was simply nowhere that such culture could have come from. We had existed only in a totalitarian society. And yet we drafted declarations and slogans, we went on hunger strikes, organized processions, vigils, sitting strikes. Those who set fire to buildings and incited the public were the communists who had started calling themselves socialists. And they are doing it to this day: just three days ago, on September 9, 2000, that is 56 years after their blood-drenched coup, they burned the flag of the European Union right in the centre of the capital of Bulgaria. What does this mean? Doesn't it prove that they have not changed?! They are just the same!
>
> Like Jesus Christ, in 1990 we responded to their actions in a different way. Because we wanted to be different. We had demonstrated civilized behavior in response to their atrocities for so many years, with the murders and what not. This is the truth. We are simply different from them![2]

The latter statement can be supported with the example of Radka Nalbantova, the Chairwoman of the Union of Cooperative Farms, headquartered in Plovdiv. In a letter read on Bulgarian Television on June 29, 1990, the communist threatened that she would block Sofia with 5,500 harvesters, 3,700 tractors and 3,400 transport vehicles, if the students did not call their strike off. The red fanatic never fulfilled her menacing promise. However, it might be interesting to check into whose hands the impressive number of farm machinery and vehicles went in the months and years to follow.

. . .

Most parents supported the strike of their children. Some organized parallel hunger strikes, others brought them food and gave them encouragement.

On July 1, Yosif Sarchadzhiev wrote in his diary:

---

[2] Anna Sarchadzhieva in a conversation with the author, Sofia, Bulgaria, September 12, 2000.

> The students' strike has lasted twenty days already all over the country. The students have occupied the universities. Rolling hunger strikes are gaining momentum. I just came back from a rally at *Democracy* Square, the unofficial name of the *September Ninth* Square, but a name that is becoming popular and was even mentioned on television. I was again close to tears. I spoke at the rally and appealed for the start of a national strike. I see no other way out. The cynicism and the sadism of the rulers had reached its culmination. A female student from the University of Tarnovo has been on hunger strike for two weeks already and is said to be very ill. In Sofia, every night we visit the parents and university lecturers in the little park near the National Assembly, who are on hunger strike in support of the students. We go with colleagues to meetings with students in the universities to give them courage and hope. We give concerts and we try to suggest to them how important they are to the Bulgarian nation at the moment. We went to the Higher Institute of Architecture and Civil Engineering, to the Higher Institute of Mechanical and Electrical Engineering, to the College of Communications, to the Higher Institute of Theatre, to the Higher Institute of Physical Culture and Sports, and several times to Sofia University. Tomorrow I am going to the Department of Agronomy. On the 18th I held a wonderful evening at the *St. Kliment Ohridski* University. Afterwards Father Christophor Sabev organized a vigil.[3]

Sarchadzhiev's diary is a truthful mirror of the events of the summer months of 1990. He kept it for himself, never intending to publish it. Most of its entries are written either on the very day of the event or immediately afterwards, and therefore it is difficult to suspect any errors due to faulty memory. The July 1 entry continues as follows:

> On the second day of the strike, when the Higher Institute of Theatre had not yet made up its mind whether to join or not, Rayna and I got hold of Krum, who is on the Strike Committee, and several other activists from the University of Sofia. We persuaded them that it was very important to demand the truth about Peter Mladenov's words "It would be best if the tanks came," documented by the camera of Evgeniy Mihaylov on December 14, 1989, during the big rally in front of the National Assembly. That was shown in the UDF campaign on television after the first round of the elections. When Emil Koshlukov was charged with being a fascist in the communist's studio and I was proclaimed to be stage-managed by Zhelyu Zhelev on that fateful night, in the early hours of the morning on June 11, when the television pulled that dirty trick, it was necessary to respond just as sharply.
>
> Therefore, we agreed to demand on behalf of the Movement of Actors for Democracy that a committee be established to prove the authenticity of

[3] Sarchadzhiev, *Diary*, July 1, 1990.

Evgeniy Mihaylov's footage discrediting Peter Mladenov. With the help of film director Rangel Valchanov we drafted a list of competent people from the cinema and from the television to be included in the jury and to prove the authenticity of the document together with the militia and with the people from the Prosecutor's Office.

We delivered letters to the Prosecution, to the newspapers *Demokratsiya* and *Duma* [Word, the daily newspaper of the BSP - *author's note*], to Kevork at the television station, and to the radio, and things started moving forward. Hristo Piskov from the Union of Film Artists helped me complete that action. The expert opinion is ready but they are still silent about it. Those above are cooking something up, but they are cornered.

If Peter Mladenov looses the presidency, Rayna and I will have contributed substantially to that. The showing of the filmed material in our TV election studio was my idea. I persuaded Jacky Stoev, a director in that studio. Rayna, on her part, wrote an appeal for the inquiry on behalf of the Initiative Club of the Bulgarian Social Democratic Party, which was printed in the newspapers. Together with Zhoro Georgiev, we also organized a demonstration in front of the Theatre Institute, a happening of sorts. It was frenzied. People stopped traffic. Some laid down in the street.

...

Rayna suggested that the students put together an official response to the writings in the *Mladezh* [Youth] daily announcing that the regular conscript soldiers would not be discharged on account of the strike, and a lot of nonsense of that kind, with the aim of setting the soldiers against the students. She spoke very eloquently at all meetings and inspired confidence. I sent a letter entitled "Courage to all students" to the *Literaturen Front* weekly. By and large, I let myself be interviewed from everywhere and anywhere about these hot days, and I offer for "voluntary exploitation" everything that they can squeeze out of me in support of the cause of the students.

In fact, this is the cause of us all. It's just that they are braver and more adamant. Nevertheless, I am proud that we, the actors' guild, became involved in the events in these days and behaved like real men. The students from the Theatre Institute, who were the last to join the strike, are now more resolved than all others.[4]

The chronicle continues on July 5 and 6:

On the afternoon of July 3, I received a call to go to the park near the National Assembly, where the university lecturers on hunger strike were stationed. Kolyo Semov and a young lady assistant professor informed me of their decision to transform their strike into a sit in front of the President's

[4] *Ibid.*

Office, if the expert opinion on the video-tape about Peter Mladenov was not released within 24 hours, i.e., until 6 p.m. on the 4th. They requested the support of our Movement of Actors for Democracy.

Zhoro Georgiev and I immediately wrote an appeal to the actors and took it to the Palace of Culture, to be read in front of 4,000 people gathered in the big hall there to mark the Independence Day of America. I took another copy to *Demokratsiya* and we started making telephone calls. In the evening Zhoro and Rayna drafted a statement to the President and his gang with various warnings about sit in strikes and handed it to the President's Office.

On July 5, I wrote an emotional appeal for help to all international theatrical institutes, and I climbed on a truck to read it in front of the President's Office. The actors were few, but the square was partly filled with about 3,000 people: writers, artists, workers, teachers, physicians. There were even seven people from the Ministry of the Interior. There were also students on hunger strike from the Theatre Institute and from the Academy of Fine Arts, all of them driven mad by communism.

That marked one of the most critical moments in that last week, possibly even since November 10. I realize that now, even without looking back from the distance of time passed. We read our declarations and sat down. A fabulous gypsy camp of inspired and desperate people.

At 8 p.m. Peter Mladenov spoke on television. Instead of admitting even a slip of the tongue and apologizing to the Bulgarian people, he lied again and went on the offensive. The square seemed to explode. I can't describe the frenzy and fury with which we wrote a cruel declaration in which we swore to stay there, in the square, until he handed in his resignation, how we ran to the University of Sofia and back, and how much brilliant human energy was squandered in despair. I read the handwritten declaration under the light of candles, perched on the rim of a fountain. The declaration was met with stormy applause and dozens of suggestions for stronger words. It was difficult for me to take the slip of paper from the hands of people who wanted to add more, pulling at the declaration and demanding stronger words.

I went to the Strike Committee in the University of Sofia to inform them about our decision. They were very confused. They did not know what to do about the strike, and our decision gave them great strength. But just at that time Georgi Spasov walked in and started persuading them to stop the occupation of the University building, because their demands were largely met, [Pavel Pisarev resigned on July 4 - *author's note*], because parliamentary struggle was needed now, because the Grand National Assembly would take care of everything else, and other conciliatory talk of the type that the UDF has been using recently in its Balkan interpretation of political tactics.

That drove the students mad, and they wrote a fierce ultimatum in which they demanded the resignation of the entire government and investigation of the corruption of all who were in power at the moment. Lord, investigation by whom?! All the investigating magistrates were theirs! Anyway, they demanded a lower circulation of the communist daily newspaper *Duma*, and added on a number of other equally unrealistic claims of that sort. I read our creation, our declaration, from a radio car. A little later the students read theirs. It was as though there was a storm of emotions on the air, over the telephones and in the streets.

At 2 a.m. the Strike Committee of the students was summoned by Andrey Lukanov. He had just come back from Romania, where he had participated in official talks about the situation in Ruse. At about 3:30 a.m. they came to us, in the square. I had wrapped myself in an old blanket and was drinking cold coffee. The students behaved bravely, but seemed confused. First of all, they were aware that many departments did not accept their extremism. Then, they had sensed that they were creating negative sentiments among people who were on their side until very recently because too many people feared the prospect of a civil war.

The night passed in anxious expectation. I was told that an order of the Prosecution had been issued for my arrest on charges of having organized civil unrest.

Today, July 6, rumors were heard that Peter Mladenov was to resign. About a dozen of us gathered and proclaimed ourselves to be a Strike Committee, and around lunchtime we drafted a declaration in which we added more stipulations to the requirement of the President's resignation. There was a demand for a public trial against Todor Zhivkov, and for stripping persons responsible for the sending of troops to Czechoslovakia in 1968 of their parliamentary immunity. Another demand concerned the persons guilty of the so-called "revival process" [the coercive renaming of the Bulgarian Moslems - *author's note*], one for bringing to justice the persons who had withheld information about the Chernobyl disaster and its tragic effect on Bulgaria, one for the trial of the individuals responsible for the economic crisis, as well as a demand for the former Bulgarian Communist - now Socialist - Party to declare its financial assets and property and that its members personal fortunes be audited. We insisted on guarantees in writing from the three major political forces that they would address these issues in the Grand National Assembly.

The declaration did not boast good legal arguments, but it was absolutely fair. It was crucial to us. Anticipating the possible resignation of the President, we had to have justification to remain in the square longer. It was important not to miss the moment of that national political inspiration, as had been the case on December 14.

At 8 p.m. the President's resignation was announced on television.

What happened in the square is hard to describe: tears of joy, people rolling on the ground, embracing, kissing as if we had won a war. With the help of a loudspeaker, we immediately announced that this was merely the beginning of the struggle. We appealed to all to remain there, in the square, until all our demands were met. The first tents began to be put up. That night it rained. I'm writing on my knee in the underground pedestrian passage.[5]

On July 12, Yosif Sarchadzhiev, who was elected spokesman of the City of Truth, listed the events of the previous week:

> Ah, Goodness, what days! When did I ever think that I would feel at home in front of the headquarters of the Bulgarian Communist Party! We received the assurance [that the Seventh Grand National Assembly would address their demands - *author's note*] of the UDF and of the Bulgarian Agrarian Union. After a lot of running around and enormous efforts we managed to wring out such an assurance from the socialists as well. However, their assurance was simply an insult and we rejected it. We are remaining in the square!
>
> ...
>
> During the day it is like a square in ancient Greece here. Too many provocateurs creep in. We welcome them and then we quickly send them home with applause. *Duma* published a lousy appeal against us. We are expecting to be attacked with physical aggression. We organized security guards and a silent sitting vigil with candles for two hours. They did not come. That crowd of antiquated communists and misguided youngsters, almost children, rushed to the Television to bring down Kevork and to defend Pisarev. The old men from the BSP are consolidating. Every evening they annoy us and stand in front of the Television building. Yesterday their procession passed along our camp. We barely prevented a scuffle.
>
> ...
>
> I forgot to mention that on July 6, after I read our declaration on the radio, I stayed to take telephone calls during the program. I had to swallow such dirt that I still wonder how I resisted spitting up on that bestialized nation and giving up everything I was doing in its name. These people don't want freedom, they really don't!
>
> No, what really keeps me here is the vast majority of the people of Sofia, who are passing all day through out City of Truth. Some of them weep in sympathy. They give us money, food, coffee, advice, or simply grab our hands and hold them with a frenzied look in their eyes. They have been brought to distraction by despair and hope, faith and doubt, guilt feelings about their past and attempts not to identify themselves with it, a willingness to fight and the awareness of their already shattered capacities.
>
> So far we have collected about 65,000 signatures of support.
>
> ...

[5] *Ibid.*, July 5-6, 1990.

> Today there was a bomb scare. We emptied the square in ten minutes and made a thorough search of the seventy-five tents with anti-terrorist squads. By the way, the militia behaved brilliantly and very correctly.
>
> ...
>
> Today we went to the Mayoralty to ask for a water cistern, telephone connection, electricity, and fire extinguishers. Let us organize a real city, what else? We have computers in the square, a printer, a typewriter, and TV sets.
>
> Incredibly witty posters and caricatures are hanging on many of the tents! This is creativity born of the impasse. I will collect the posters for an exhibition one day, a display of that pure popular humor, which has probably always saved the Bulgarians. But now, now it is not funny.
>
> Last night Civil Insubordination occupied the space in front of the Mausoleum and today Andrey Lukanov hastened to reassure the nation that the mummy [Georgi Dimitrov's - *author's note*] would soon be taken out. I noticed that only strong and drastic pressure can force this mean clique to retreat. This is something that the youngsters have understood.
>
> Oh, so many things happened during these days, but I got tired of writing![6]

The actor again took to the pen on July 17:

> I'm beginning to lose track of events. I have no time to register them. There is so much running around in order to organize the life and political actions of the City of Truth. This City is growing like a mushroom. Today it already has 102 tents. We had a problem with provocateurs and with drunks. Sincho is coping brilliantly as the commandant. A piano was brought to the square. Good musicians are playing. We sing. It started raining and we carried the piano into the underground passage. We substituted the security guards with students. Last night we had a one-hour vigil, in silence, seated and holding candles. About 10,000 people came. We find it very hard to keep quiet even for 5-6 minutes. People wish to scream. The slogans are familiar. Once again they are those of the UDF. People have no other support.
>
> It seems to me that this opposition - the Union of Democratic Forces - is not the worthiest and the strongest. We need to have new slogans, to have new ideas. It seems to me that the ideas of the street are fairer. It seems to me that the UDF leaders are thinking primarily about themselves now, about some personal benefits.
>
> Maybe I'm wrong. Maybe I'm simply not a politician and therefore I fail to understand the hidden meaning of their actions. However, I trust my intuition tremendously. There is something that I don't like about this opposition. The street, the truth is in the street. That is what can turn things around. I only hope that it will not happen irresponsibly. I don't want irresponsibility.

---

[6] *Ibid.*, July 12, 1990.

We have a church in the City of Truth already, a mobile chapel with Father Ambarev in charge. A liturgy was sung during that vigil, while at the same time the other priest, Father Christophor Sabev, was reading the Lord's Prayer at the other end of the square and was hurling one anathema after another against the communists. There was something desperate in the highest degree. This is how hope is born. Only when we touch the bottom, we can hope to show our heads above the water.

We argue a lot during our council meetings. We have an enormous tent that we borrowed from the film studios, in which the Strike Council holds its meetings. Two people can no longer understand each other, and we are thirty-five on that Council. Bulgarians are always like that. This is not the way to build democracy! But what can we do? This is the country in which we were born. And we have to make the best of it.

We are preparing a meeting with our supporters for tomorrow and we shall announce to them the new form of struggle, related to our wish to hold a hearing of Todor Zhivkov in the National Assembly. Maybe we'll lie down in the street and give up food for 24 hours. This should stir the government. It should stir the Grand National Assembly as well.

We already have two Russians, political emigrants, in our tents. Political emigrants in Bulgaria! What a paradox!

The National Assembly disappointed us terribly today. The fact that the UDF bent its head, that it retreated, frightened the people who had high hopes. Only the street can do something decent.

...

There is an incursion of aged and enraged communists in front of the television building. They are shouting things that someone put into their heads, without being able to understand anything. Yes, alas, they decided the fate of their children.[7]

On the next day, July 18, Yosif Sarchadzhiev wrote:

What a hard day! Today, actually starting yesterday, we organized an enormous rally and we drafted a petition together with the actress Eli Skorcheva and a student. At 4 p.m. we took it to the National Assembly. We had arranged for Stoyan Ganev and two other Members of Parliament to meet us in front of the militia cordon. Then we developed a plan about how the evening was to pass and what our actions would be. We decided to make a pile of useless old objects at 6 p.m. in front of the Mausoleum, and announced this on the radio. We wanted to sit along the entire *Ruski* Boulevard for four hours as a silent presence, but in the meantime Georgi Dimitrov's mummy was

[7] *Ibid.*, July 17, 1990.

> secretly taken out of the Mausoleum and cremated. Since 10 p.m. there have been no guards in front of the Mausoleum. Victory!
>
> The vote in the Grand National Assembly on whether to read our petition was 178 for and 178 against. How funny! We are a factor in their decisions.
>
> Today the first issue of the newspaper of our City of Truth came out. Its name is *Gradat - Ploshtad Demokratsiya* [*The City - Democracy Square*].
>
> There is an outbreak of some intestinal disease and that worries us. We brought a large tent for the City's commissariat and another one for a hospital. There is always someone on duty with us from the *Pirogov* Emergency Hospital. There is a group of physicians who are on permanent strike, who have brought quite a lot of medicines and equipment with them. We are all subjected to medical examinations. Generally speaking, the city leads a normal life. A city of tents. There is no such thing anywhere else in the world. At least not to my knowledge.[8]

It is curious to know that on that very same day, July 18, 1990, the deposed communist dictator of the People's Republic of Bulgaria Todor Zhivkov, who was responsible for numerous crimes and who kept death camps in his state until 1962, sent an appeal to the Seventh Grand National Assembly with the following content:

> Distinguished Members of Parliament,
>
> I am appealing to you with regard to the arbitrariness that the Prosecutor General has been committing against me during the last months and those who are standing behind him and are stage-managing the investigation with the following two requests:
>
> First, I ask that the Grand National Assembly put an end to the arbitrariness against Todor Zhivkov and his family.
>
> Second, I ask, that a personal bodyguard to be made available to me, if possible, until the birth of my great-grandson in October 1990. After I see my great-grandson, I shall give up all claims for security and other forms of care-taking, which are a standard practice in the civilized countries vis-à-vis people who have been in my official position.
>
> I am ready to come before the Grand National Assembly and the entire Bulgarian nation, of which I am an integral part, and tell the truth about my tenure in office and my activities during that time.
>
> Sincerely, Todor Zhivkov[9]

---

[8] *Ibid.*, July 18, 1990.

[9] Appeal by Todor Zhivkov to the Seventh Grand National Assembly, Sofia, July 18, 1990, Library of the National Assembly.

Apparently, Zhivkov had his own personal and family complaints and sentimentalities. In contrast, the City of Truth had taken upon itself a number of tasks that concerned the entire nation. Yosko has preserved the following record of the emotionally charged events of July 20:

> Yesterday was a horribly hectic day. We had to prepare for today's meeting when we would adopt a Charter of the City of Truth and inaugurate the National Movement *In the Name of Truth*. We held a meeting of the entire City of Truth, which already numbered more than 150 tents and about 800 inhabitants. It lasted four hours. It turned out that there were such differences between us that it was sheer luck that we didn't split up last night. With a lot of effort, I succeeded in gaining control over the passions of the crowd and postponed the debates on the Charter for today. We nominated a committee to contribute to the Charter and propose several drafts. Instead, a radically new version of the document appeared, and this triggered new heated debates until noon.
>
> We have an architectural office in the City of Truth. The architects made a splendid plan last night and tomorrow we are going to urbanize our settlement. We shall introduce some functional order, in compliance with the laws of a real city. Late into the night I walked along the *Svoboda* [Freedom] Avenue - the name we have given to the little central street formed between the two main groups of tents - and listened to the arguments of excited, tormented, and humiliated people.
>
> We have to speak to the people every evening. We have to make use of that seething passion and to channel it. The communists are good at this. They are terrible scoundrels!
>
> ...
>
> Yesterday we organized a campaign for blood donation in the City of Truth. We collected 80 liters of blood from 60 people. The medical people said that they had never achieved that in one day at the Blood Donation Center. Just a short while ago I climbed on the tribune of the Mausoleum, where young people are singing and dancing. We organized an enormous Evening Freedom Party.
>
> The Civil Insubordination Movement has blocked the main entrance to the communist party headquarters with benches and some witty slogans. I must copy all the slogans and graffiti in the City of Truth. I never believed that there were so many people with such a keen political sense of humor.
>
> I was interviewed by a Russian journalist today. He asked me whether I thought that there was too much anticommunism in this City of Truth. "Yes," I answered him. "And how can it be otherwise when only they have ruled over us so far and they created the entire lie?"[10]

---

[10] Sarchadzhiev, *Diary*, July 21, 1990.

Suffering from a slipped disk and unable to move much, Sarchadzhiev resumes his chronicle about the City of Truth of July 28:

On the 23rd, in the morning, we had a visit from Elen Petrov, the Deputy Mayor of Sofia, and officers from the Sofia City Directorate of the Ministry of the Interior. In the tent of our headquarters we exchanged information and assurances of our best mutual feelings. Ha-ha! They insisted that we distance ourselves from the people of Civil Insubordination, who have barred the main entrance of the communist party headquarters and have surrounded themselves with many humorous and appealing posters. Their demand, after scoring a victory in taking Dimitrov's mummy out of the Mausoleum, is to remove the five-pointed star from the Communist Party Headquarters and the emblem with the communist symbols from the national flag. We tried to explain to our visitors that these people are outside the City, but that their demands are just.

I got a cassette from an officer in the State Security Committee containing his recordings. They are nothing special. We knew it all. A stagehand from the National Theatre offered me his services as my bodyguard. I am receiving more and more threats from communists recently.

A Decree of the Council of Ministers was issued, with ill-disguised threats against all forms of protest. It was inspired by a declaration in the Grand National Assembly concerning the unrest in Kardzhali and Haskovo against the ethnic Turks there. However, the Decree introduced a reference to equality between all forms of protest, and this got us worried. We understood that it was directed basically against us. Immediately we expressed our indignation on the radio.

A bus with a red flag crossed the square and created a surge of excitement and indignation among the people, whose nerves were on edge anyway. There are all kinds of rumors about a raid against the settlement.

In the early evening, there was a meeting at which satiric writers read their works. It was a tremendous success. We came out with a declaration regarding the 12-day hunger strike of Trayko Etov and demanded an apology from Elena Poptodorova, who had said in the National Assembly that she didn't know whether to call our city a City of Truth or a City of Lies. If she refused, we would block the entrances to the Supreme Party Council on Wednesday, July 23, at 6 p.m.

Georgi Dimitrov was buried. There was an enormous procession of mourners. People were weeping. What horror!

...

On the 24th we had a meeting with Members of Parliament from the Union of Democratic Forces. They seem a little confused by our presence in the square. They cannot express open support for us; some of them even think that we are harming them. We all attacked them for their indecision in

Parliament, although I personally believe that they are in a difficult predicament and not everything depends on their goodwill. Generally speaking, we made it clear to them that we would not leave the square easily, while also assuring them that we would not undertake actions that would create a lot of tension.

That tension was created by the communists, who could have brought peace a long time ago if they had met our demands. But that meant that they had to take off their masks and reveal their criminal faces, which would have deposed them as a political force. Power was salvation for them at that moment. They had to hide their money. They had to salvage what they had plundered. No, they are simply sick people.

Just after dawn we came under attack. There were about 1,000 militant old men from the Bulgarian Socialist Party who were mobilized by our ultimatum that we would guard the entrances to the BSP building. They had been rallying all night in their clubs. They stepped out of two buses, led by organizers with walkie-talkies. They started tearing down the posters and slogans of Civil Insubordination and tried to push the protesters away from the benches in front of the Supreme Party Council. We sounded the loud siren. The citizens of the City of Truth rushed to defend the six men from Civil Insubordination. Several blows were exchanged. Then the militia finally appeared, having miraculously hidden precisely during the attack on the protesters. Our telephones were disconnected. We organized a double human chain.

I was sent to talk to the Civil Insubordination people and to try to persuade them to get up and avoid bloodshed in the confrontation. They adamantly refused. One of the boys was crying. I felt like a traitor to their lonely and proud struggle. So when the communists demanded to speak to me and to Spartak, we strongly defended the Insubordination people. Although we made it clear that they were not representing the City of Truth. The militia offered us metal fences and ropes, and now our boundaries are strictly defined.

...

On July 25 we received an invitation from Andrey Lukanov for talks over coffee. What insolence! We held long discussions on whether to accept, and if we did, in what form. That was just after the eventful night with the attack, and our nerves were on edge. But we were proud. We refused. We also refused because we had a scheduled meeting for that day with representatives of the UDF, BSP and the Agrarians. I didn't go. I didn't feel like engaging in dumb conversations. Rayna went, and she was naturally very adamant.

We received food from the Catholic community, as well as 500 levs in cash, donated by Konyovo and some other villages. From a man producing plastic bags we got 1,500 levs. Vegetables came from a greengrocer.

On the 27th in the morning we found a dead drug addict behind the tent of our hospital. We managed to convince the media that he was not from the City of Truth, which was indeed true. That was important because the previous day there had been a pitiable demonstration organized by the socialist youth at which one of their leaders claimed that our City was full of drug addicts and prostitutes. They are trying to discredit us in every way possible. It is true that the City's intellectual image is becoming more and more blurred. We already have 160 tents and more than 1,200 permanent residents. But there is nothing we can do about it. This is the miniature model of the big city with all its weaknesses. However, we are united by one idea, namely to save ourselves from communism.

...

We organized a big rally-concert with Lili Ivanova. My speech was quite inspired. Thank God, I didn't speak like an actor. By this time I have learned to speak like a normal human being, which does not mean that I speak without emotion.

At one point Rayna, that crucial figure in our Movement, though not very visible, interrupted the concert. She informed the enormous multitude gathered in the square that the Grand National Assembly was debating at that very moment whether or not to broadcast live on the radio and television the questioning of Todor Zhivkov. The most likely decision would be for him to be heard secretly. We invited the people in a civilized but firm fashion to march down the *Tsar Osvoboditel* Boulevard to the National Assembly and demand that Todor Zhivkov be heard openly and by all.

So far, so good. We invited them. But the crowd rushed. We barely managed to get to the lead of the procession and halt the masses determined not only to reach the National Assembly building, but to storm it. We were in front of the barriers placed around the National Assembly by the militiamen. There were more and more people behind us who were pressing us against the iron fences. Zhoro Georgiev and I ran out to contact a group of Members of Parliament to calm down the demonstrators. When we came back, the people could no longer be held back and they swept the barriers away. The militia made way for us. We surrounded the National Assembly. The shouts and the booing were deafening. Attempts were made to enter the building. There were more than 20,000 of us. That happened around 8:30 p.m.

I didn't know what to do. I asked the people to sit down. Just at that time a torrential rain started. Many left, frightened. So much for their revolutionary enthusiasm. We found out about what was happening inside the National Assembly through transistor radios pressed against loudspeakers. There was a storm inside. Minister Semerdzhiev [Minister of the Interior in Andrey Lukanov's government - *author's note*] had a nervous breakdown and handed in his resignation, theatrically seeking a gun to kill himself. The rain continued to pour over us. We took off our clothes down to the waist. A car from the Civilian Initiative arrived. We started to draft a declaration. Stoyan Ganev came out of the National Assembly and started to calm the people down from the top of a car. Some left.

Those of us who remained - at first 2,000-3,000 that later dwindled to 1,000-1,500 - were like Tarzans, half-naked and soaking wet, singing and screaming, swearing and crying. We were waiting for the debates in the

National Assembly to end and for the Members of Parliament to come out, so we could bar their way with a human chain. There was a clash with the militiamen who were around. I saw attempts to grab at the throat of Andrey Lukanov. All Members of Parliament were booed, even those from the Union of Democratic Forces. People were shouting "Resign" and "Traitors!"

Spite broke out from the rain and the taut nerves. Anarchy erupted. The crowd was showing its teeth. Now it was a mob. At that time I was powerless. I did not succumb to emotions, but there was nothing I could do to restore any semblance of order. I got terrible cramps in by back. The pain was virtually unbearable. It took me great efforts to drag myself home. I felt sick. Nevertheless, around 2 a.m. I went to the City of Truth to discuss the action. We stayed there until 3:30. Was what we did necessary?

Today, July 28, I only went to the meeting at lunchtime. Actually, we had a meeting with Zhelyu Zhelev in his office just before that. He is undecided about extreme actions and he is probably right. Maybe we are imagining that the majority of the people would support us if we declared a strike. We were kidding ourselves, maybe because we were eager to give each other courage.

For tomorrow, Sunday, the Green Party and I have organized a cleaning and digging of the yard of the Archaeological Museum around which the tents have been put up. I don't want us to look like vandals. I hope I shall have enough strength to go.[11]

The entry in the diary of the actor on July 30 reads:

I cannot analyze and generalize. I have one comment, though. We are all sick, poisoned and inadequate. Even in the Movement *In the Name of Truth* we are already polarized into extreme revolutionaries, moderates and chickens. I am wandering from one group to the other, trying to bring fire and water together.

Yesterday we cleaned the little garden of the Archaeological Museum. The most important event was the meeting of representatives of all Cities of Truth in Bulgaria, our first national conference. We spent four hours in debates, exchanges of experience, doubts and emotions in order to make our position clear and come out with a declaration that is pretty much toothless. My prediction is that unless at this moment the bigger and better part of the Bulgarian intellectuals come out to support us actively, the Movement is faced with the risk of losing its identity, of turning into the scum of society and losing the trust of the people.[12]

---

[11] *Ibid.*, July 28, 1990.

[12] *Ibid.*, July 30, 1990.

The diary of Yosif Sarchadzhiev contains the following information about the last day of July, Monday:

> I spent the whole day on the premises of the National Television. Then in the City we listened to the live broadcast from the Grand National Assembly. There were a lot of people gathered. They wanted us to go and to surround the National Assembly building again. However, we did not make up our minds to go after the outcome of the last occasion in the pouring rain. Besides - in my opinion - we did not have sufficient reason. According to the revolutionaries in the Movement, that was when we missed a considerable chance and allegedly repulsed a large mass of people with our indecisiveness. The game with Kyuranov as a cover-up for Valkov [regarding the election of a new President - *author's note*] is transparent, but how can you react to this! They are playing cat and mouse with us. The demand to adopt a declaration - and they will adopt it tomorrow at the National Assembly - that would condemn us for the human chain in front of Parliament on Friday during the big rain will be yet another blow that the UDF will not be able to stand up against.
>
> Resistance, in our opinion, means that they should leave the National Assembly, and after leaving it they should declare a parliamentary crisis with all its consequences. The latter could be grave, but there is no other way out with that communist majority in the National Assembly.[13]

On August 6 Yosko continues his confession as follows:

> I have skipped a whole week. This is a whole epoch. I seem to be unable to follow events. What is the point of registering facts when they become meaningless only several hours later? It is likewise stupid to draw conclusions, because today's conclusions will be proved wrong tomorrow. Nevertheless, I owe it to myself, I owe it to my weak memory to make a small "survey" of events. But what should I start with?
>
> I was ill. I am still coughing and I feel languid, maybe due to mental fatigue.
>
> Parliament chose Zhelyu Zhelev to become President. Dertliev frightened the communists and they did not vote for him. They voted for Zhelev, for Zhelyu, as a compromise, fearing a total parliamentary crisis. I am aware that this crisis can be provoked with a strong participation on our part. We are the foundation for everything. The street is the only thing that frightens them.
>
> The City of Truth grew and spread all the way to the Mausoleum. It is almost unmanageable. The centrifugal forces in it will blow it to pieces. Yesterday five men stripped naked in front of the Mausoleum. The militiamen came running to me, shouting: "Yosko, what should we do with them?" "Arrest

---

13 *Ibid.*, July 31, 1990.

them," I said. They moaned and groaned. This is what our state is like. No one assumes responsibility for anything.

I refused to participate in Angel Wagenstein's film. I felt relieved.

We had a meeting of the entire City of Truth and we nearly fought to the death with the extremists. They refuse to leave its confines, while we believe that they are responsible for discrediting it. We, i.e. the Initiative Committee, which they do not recognize as the legitimate leadership, believe that this is perfect timing from a political point of view for us to leave the square and organize ourselves into a powerful national movement, which would be able to bring at least 300,000 people out into the streets. That is where the real power is.[14]

The political events that followed confirmed Sarchadzhiev's views, shared by many other Bulgarians. If back in the summer of 1990, the inhabitants of the City of Truth had accepted the proposal of the Initiative Committee, an active, popular, antitotalitarian opposition would have been formed and legitimized. People would not have had to count on a semi-communist opposition, as the Union of Democratic Forces proved to be, since most of its first leaders were connected in one way or other to the red party.

Again on August 6, Sarchadzhiev noted in his diary:

I learned last night that some of the people who joined the Movement sought political asylum in the U.S. Embassy behind our backs at a time when we already have our own President. This is a big blunder. These people are political loafers! They are blowing the very idea of the Movement to pieces.

Rayna has a brilliant idea about the organization, but how can we realize it with these people for whom the Movement is merely a cover for their personal ambitions? The other day the guards of the City of Truth decided on someone's instigation to arrest the leadership. I was not there. A boom of dissent followed. I barely managed to bring the situation back to normal. However, my buffer function will not lead to anything good. This simply postpones the bursting of the boil. It does not heal. I was never cast for the role of leader, although I'm the only one that both sides trust. This is because I'm able to hide my real feelings. This occupational disease of mine is useful in this case. I believe that what I'm doing is driven by what is good for the Movement. But is it really good?

Yesterday, after yet another stormy meeting, we barely succeeded in drafting a joint declaration between the two groups - those who are remaining and those who are leaving the City. I read the declaration on TV last night, announcing that we were going to dissolve the City in its current form and

---

[14] *Ibid.*, August 6, 1990.

> transform it into a symbolic presence, leaving only the church, the hospital, the Mayor's office and the press center.
>
> ...
>
> The days are flying. When did August come! I did not feel anything this summer, besides maybe infinite fatigue. Shall I be able to return to my routine at the theatre or will I be lost to what I have thought all my life I was born to do?
>
> I am leaving out many important things from our activities, but who can tell whether they are still important?[15]

The entry in the actor's diary at 0:30 a.m. on August 27, 1990, is very dramatic, much like the events described in it:

> I'm just coming back from the square. The building of the Bulgarian Communist Party has been in flames for three hours. There is something horrifying. Most of the several thousand people gathered there - 3,000 to 5,000 - behave as if they have come to watch a show. The militiamen are also sitting, as if they are in a theater. The fire-fighters are making feeble attempts to extinguish the fire. I personally stood in the periphery, in the shadow, wearing a hat that almost covered my eyes. Why? Because I don't want to be associated with forces that I don't like. Well, yes, they are doing something that so many people wanted to do, but didn't dare to express their feelings, let alone act upon them.
>
> We lived to see this defeat of the BCP. But what if it is actually their celebration? Could this be a prelude to martial law? Could it be that everything has been instigated by the communists themselves? Then all our efforts are going down the drain. Maybe this is an ordeal that we have to surmount: we have to pass through the fire of that hell.
>
> Some people from the original Initiative Committee and I started meeting again in order to find a form for the Movement, which would make sense and would bring together as many people as possible. We want to create a popular front, which - although it pursues moral goals - at some point, when the time is ripe, could perform our "velvet revolution." What a joke! That is, if time does not run ahead of us, resulting in a crude revolution because hunger is knocking on our door and the situation in the Persian Gulf can lead to an enormous war. Then all the plans and calculations that we have been making may prove to be nothing but wishful thinking.
>
> ...
>
> Now, going back in my thoughts, I wonder whether everything we did - demonstrations, processions, hunger strikes, vigils with candles, campaigns in

---

15 *Ibid.*

different enterprises, petitions, declarations on the radio and TV, memoranda, the Charter and all the rest - had any meaning whatsoever.

It did, of course it did. Dozens, no, thousands, even hundreds of thousands of people declared every day that they are ready to follow us. How many people stop me in the streets, hug me, kiss me and tell me, "Lead us! Lead us!" Where to lead them? This City of Truth generated many illusions. It gave rise to hopes and expectations that I will not be able to meet, at least not at the present moment. I don't believe that I will ever be able to do it.

After all, something enormous was achieved. I shouldn't spit on what we have done, because its importance will be judged in the future. It has left a deeper imprint in the minds of people than any other party, any other power struggle or dispute in the National Assembly. We created that street spirit, that City. It was more of a City of Hope, because it cannot be said to have been a City of Truth. Truth has many faces. Yes, that was a City of Hope. Its tents gave shelter to tortured people. It gave that impetus that even the greatest leader would hardly have been in a position to give.

For the time being everything is uncertain. Every instant bears surprise. And at this very moment, when I am waiting for my family to come back from the square, I realize how frail and defenseless we are before laws that are not susceptible to human willpower. Thank the Lord that at least that man, Plamen, and the others, did not set fire to themselves. They had sworn that if the hated five-pointed red star did not disappear, the star that the communists did not dismantle from the top of their headquarters, they were going to burn like torches. Still, something did go up in flames.

Yes, but what if the whole thing was a provocation? I think that is what it was. There are examples of that in history, the most recent one of which was the Reichstag in Berlin. What would it cost the communists to do it?![16]

. . .

In August 1998, eight years after the special security forces crushed the city of tents in the morning after the fire and chased away the remaining protesters, the actor Georgi "Zhoro" Georgiev, the first and only Mayor of the City of Truth, shared the following:

I totally devoted myself to that City of Truth, with the absolute conviction that during that July, in the center of Sofia, we, the citizens of the City of Truth, were demolishing the 45-year-old fortress of the tyrannical Bulgarian Communist Party. Right under the windows of its stronghold - its Central Committee - we were making obscene gestures at it. It was great. I felt secure in the awareness that I was standing side by side with Yosko Sarchadzhiev, Encho

---

[16] *Ibid.*, 0:30 a.m., August 27, 1990.

Mutafov, Eli Skorcheva, Sasho Kazandzhiev, and dozens of writers, artists, physicians, actors and other people. I was moved to tears by its thousands of inhabitants, lying on the yellow pavement and in the tents put up around the fountain in front of the Presidential building.

At that time I took pride in the City of Truth. It was a phenomenon of anticommunist resistance, the only one of its kind in Eastern Europe. After us, the Russian anticommunists put up their tents in the *Kremlin* Square. With the City of Truth in Sofia and with the dozens of other similar demonstrations in other cities of Bulgaria, we were one step ahead of the others. With the City of Truth we gave an example to the world. Cameras from all the electronic media were shooting day and night. We gave interviews in all languages, and the most important message was "Communism in Bulgaria is going away, so children, sleep peacefully tonight." [Refrain of one of the popular songs of the Bulgarian democrats - *author's note*].

The City of Truth fell into oblivion. This is natural. It played its central or supporting role in its time. The dynamic events connected with the country's economic and political reform took over our everyday lives. Nevertheless, it is unnatural that with the passage of time the assessment of the City of Truth is becoming deformed and some people pretend that no such thing ever happened. Or if it did happen, so what? They hint that there were communists in the City of Truth, and - even worse - secret service agents. This is highly probable: they were everywhere. The whole of Bulgaria was a totalitarian police state. However, the City of Truth was run not by the communists and not by the secret services. The active presence of several anticommunist friends was the guarantee of its anticommunist nature. I would like to ask all those who are speaking against the City of Truth, or prefer to ignore it in silence, to explain where they were hiding in the summer of 1990, especially in July. Who was stopping them from coming to us and reducing the relative number of communists and secret service agents with their own presence?!

Now they are sitting on the benches of the National Assembly.

I have no idea whether this attitude to the City of Truth is official or not, but whatever it is, I am certain of two things. First, the people denying its importance today were not with us. And second, the typical Bulgarian syndrome - the mentality of downplaying everything in the creation of which you have not taken part - came to the foreground.

I also suffer for all the men and women who lived in the City of Truth, as well as for all who came to us every day, bringing food, giving us courage, with tears of hope in their eyes. I shall be grateful until I die to all who still remember our anticommunist city. It was sheer coincidence that I was chosen to be the Mayor of the City of Truth, among the dozen or so intelligent people - I refrain from calling them intellectuals, they were writers, actors, physicians, etc. - who had gathered spontaneously around the fountain near the Presidential building to find a way to legitimize the tent city. Yosko Sarchadzhiev proposed me as the first Mayor to be elected on the principle of rotation. I gave the City its name also by chance. That gives me pride. On the second or third day of the city's existence, a reporter from the newsroom of the Bulgarian National Television asked me, "What is the name of your city?" Without having thought about it or asked anyone's permission, I replied, "The City of Truth." The tents welcomed and applauded this improvised baptism. And my godchild - the City of Truth - started its tour around the world with the name I had given it.

For personal and family reasons I was both citizen and Mayor of the City. From the very beginning I had dedicated my presence and participation in it to the memory of my parents, Nadya and Georgi Mekicharski, as well as to my uncle. My emotions, my hurling myself into events, was the result of hereditary anticommunism and the fact that my parents had suffered during the communist regime. I wished to take upon myself a small part of their suffering by doing something at last, after the long silence.

There was plenty of work.

We succeeded in providing water and electricity to the City of Truth. It was then that I understood that the Bulgarian Communist Party was, if not scared, at least strongly perturbed, because the authorities instantaneously sent people who brought electricity to the City. We drafted the best layout in which to put up the tents so as to leave passages between them. We were asked by the Ministry of the Interior to register the inhabitants of the City. All kinds of people, totally unknown to us, started coming. They brought us a typewriter and ribbons for it. We had nothing at first, because we had gone to the square empty-handed.

Our press center started functioning. Journalists from all over the world started coming, from Bulgaria as well. We organized press conferences and gave interviews. We put TV sets in some of the tents and watched the news in the evenings. The news were often about us. We released a daily newsletter. We were doing this all by ourselves - we, the untrained politicians.

Our job would have been infinitely more difficult without the computer brought by one of the City's most ardent and most devoted citizens, Mihail Peychev. He was an engineer who passed away in 1992, a splendid man.

The boys and girls calling themselves "Civil Insubordination" camped a little further away from the City of Truth. They provoked certain confusion and insisted on more drastic methods in the struggle. People started saying that they were secret service agents and provocateurs. I personally did not think that was so, but we did not allow them into the City of Truth. We decided that our protest against communism should be with peaceful means only.

One afternoon the U.S. Ambassador, Mr. Sol Polansky, came to visit us, walking the very short distance from the American Embassy, located around the corner from the camp. He was very kind and showed keen interest.

Politicians and Members of Parliament also came. For example, Peter Dertliev kept asking us, "What next? What do you want? And what is it that you don't want?" Some communists also came, some of them writers, who said that what we were doing is being filmed from a window of the BCP's Central Committee building across the square and that all our "outrages" were being seen from there.

I shall never forget how all of a sudden the notorious terrorist Mitka Grabcheva turned up in the square on one of the hottest days in July. In her youth she had assassinated peaceful citizens "in the name of the people" and her victims were quite numerous. At first glance, she was a skinny old woman in trousers, but that was only at a first glance. Quite unexpectedly, that seasoned communist took a pistol out of her hip pocket. She was ready to shoot at people! Provoked by the gun pointed at them, they threw themselves against her. I can claim with certainty that I saved her from being lynched. I quickly summoned several people to guard the raving Grabcheva and we led her to the Central Committee of the Bulgarian Communist Party.

On another day the film director Hristo Ganev came. He was holding a machine gun in his hands, one of those children's toys with springs. He came straight from the Central Committee building, and started playing around, shooting. The people around him realized immediately that he was a communist. He pretended he was playing, but all the time he was hissing, "I'll kill you all."

Numerous provocations like this happened.

The citizens of the City of Truth were expressing not only their personal protest against communism and against the manipulations of the red rulers. We were expressing the protest of many other people as well, because while we were about 3,000 residents, tens of thousands of people passed by the tents every day. They brought us food, mineral water, toilet paper and anything else they could think of. They stayed with us for a whole day sometimes. This is how they expressed their shock with the election results and their support for the students' strike and the City of Truth.

During these tumultuous years I can say that a lot was happening without the involvement of political organizations. I personally can vouch that this was the case with the City of Truth. The Union of Democratic Forces did not organize us. There was nothing of the sort. No one called me; no one asked me to do anything; no one instigated me. Neither did anyone instigate Yosko or any of the others around us. No one told us what tasks to undertake. We were doing everything alone, in support of the Union of Democratic Forces.[17]

---

[17] Georgi Georgiev in a conversation with the author, Sofia, Bulgaria, August 20, 1998.

17. Power Management at the Top

While the country was seething in the summer of 1990 with passions and protest actions against the communists were common, the political party leaders and new Members of Parliament were also quite busy.

On June 29, the Supreme Council of the Bulgarian Socialist Party nominated Andrey Lukanov for the position of Prime Minister for the second time. On July 6, the day when President Peter Mladenov officially handed in his resignation, the Coordinating Council of the Union of Democratic Forces re-elected Dr. Zhelyu Zhelev as its Chairperson. Milan Drenchev, Philip Dimitrov, and Christophor Sabev became his deputies and Stoyan Ganev and Mihail Nedelchev took the position of UDF spokespersons.

The next day the UDF's managing body discussed the status of the Parliamentary Alliance of the Democratic Forces (PADF) with the UDF Members of Parliament. The following parties participated in the blue alliance: the *Nikola Petkov* Bulgarian Agrarian People's Union, the Bulgarian Social Democratic Party, the United Democratic Center, the Democratic Party, the Bulgarian Radical Democratic Party, the Green Party, the *Ecoglasnost* Independent Society, and the Federation of the Clubs for *Glasnost* and Democracy. Zhelyu Zhelev was elected Chairman of the Parliamentary Alliance, and Peter Kornazhev and Stoyan Ganev became his deputies.

The Seventh Grand National Assembly, with 400 Members of Parliament - 366 men and 34 women - was inaugurated with an official ceremony on July 10. The distribution of seats by party was as follows: Bulgarian Socialist Party - 211, Union of Democratic Forces - 144, Movement for Rights and Freedoms - 23, Bulgarian Agrarian People's Union - 16, Fatherland Alliance - 2, Fatherland Labor Party - 1, Social Democratic Party (non-Marxists) - 1 and two independents.[1]

The left side of Parliament, i.e., the side reserved for the "socialists", was populated by a number of wealthy individuals. Surprisingly, several of the organizers of the first anticommunist mass rally in Sofia were also sitting on the left, unperturbed. Some of the more notable persons among them were the journalist Stefan Prodev, Editor-in-Chief of the bright-red daily newspaper *Duma*, the painter Svetlin Rusev, the screenplay writer and film director Angel Wagenstein, and Professor Chavdar Kyuranov, ever-present at the meetings of the UDF Coordinating Council during the first months after it was established. In fact, Professor Kyuranov was subsequently promoted to member of the Presidency of the Supreme Council of the Bulgarian Socialist Party.

---

[1] Seventh Grand National Assembly 1990-1991, October 30, 1991, Sofia, Library of the National Assembly.

Over the next months and years, more persons connected with that memorable date, November 18, 1989, chose to be seated among the ex-communists, and so did prominent members of the leadership of the Union of Democratic Forces. Some did not go that far, but still regularly voted in unison with their red adversaries, an act of political "transfiguration" which will be discussed at greater length.

The Parliamentary Group of the Bulgarian Socialist Party was headed by the Chairman of that party's Supreme Council, Professor Alexander Lilov, a former member of the Politburo and Secretary of the Central Committee of the Bulgarian Communist Party. In fact, most of the BSP Members of Parliament were known to the general public as prominent members of the renamed political organization.

Quite a few persons who had made their mark in politics only recently also took their place in the newly elected Assembly. The leader of the Movement for Rights and Freedoms (MRF) Ahmed Dogan particularly attracted public attention. He and his party, which consisted almost exclusively of representatives of the Turkish ethnic minority, acquired notoriety at the time of the National Round Table. In view of the fact that the BCP had very recently subjected nearly one million Bulgarian Moslems to forced assimilation, it would have been logical for the MRF - established in March 1990 - to join the Union of Democratic Forces. However, that did not happen. Dogan declared that he did not want to include the Movement for Rights and Freedoms in the opposition coalition, and the UDF itself showed hesitation on the issue. Surprisingly, Rumen Vodenicharov, the defender of Moslems in Bulgaria in his capacity of Chairperson of the Independent Society for Human Rights Protection, opposed the establishment of the MRF in the first place and its participation in the delegation of UDF at the "Round Table". As a Member of Parliament in the Seventh Grand National Assembly, he proceeded to vehemently attack his colleagues with Turkish identities.[2]

The controversy about the Movement for Rights and Freedoms was further exacerbated in 1991 when the matter was brought to the courts of justice. The Bulgarian Socialist Party disputed the right of the MRF to exist, citing Article 11 (4) of the Constitution of the Republic of Bulgaria, which explicitly bans the establishment of political parties on ethnic, racial or religious grounds. After debates in the Supreme Court and in the Constitutional Court, the Movement was officially granted the right to participate in the country's political life. Years later it became known that the MRF had been created with the assistance of the

---

[2] 140th plenary session of the Seventh Grand National Assembly, Sofia, Wednesday, May 29, 1991, Library of the National Assembly.

high circles of the communist party, especially Andrey Lukanov. No wonder that the Movement for Rights and Freedom plays a major part in Bulgarian politics in favor of the ex-communists to this day.

In 1990-1991 these circumstances were still unknown, although Ahmed Dogan appeared strangely mysterious. He rarely came to the sessions in the plenary hall of Parliament. His biography was full of controversy, and his acts as a politician were unpredictable, extreme, and inconsistent. It wasn't until October 22, 1997, that the mystery was unraveled by than Minister of the Interior, Bogomil Bonev.

During a televised plenary session of the Thirty-Eighth National Assembly, Minister Bonev announced - albeit in an incomplete and fragmentary fashion[3] - the results of the check for possible affiliation of the Members of Parliament and persons in the government with the former State Security services. He read the following text concerning the leader of the Movement for Rights and Freedoms:

> Ahmed Demir Dogan, Parliamentary Group of the National Salvation Alliance, part-time collaborator of the Military Counter-Intelligence Department of the District Directorate in the city of Varna and of the First General Directorate between 1974 and 1988. There is a declaration of willingness to collaborate, signed by him personally. There is written evidence of and receipts for sums received from the State Security. Notified with a letter. Failed to appear before the Commission. No objection has been deposited.[4]

Thus, Minister Bonev confirmed that Dogan had been a paid informer of the communist secret services. The data presented in 1997 did not match the image of the Turkish leader popularized in 1990. At that time other things were known about him.

Ahmed was born in 1954 in a village in the Varna district. He obtained his degree in philosophy from the University of Sofia, then earned a Ph.D., and became Research Associate at the Institute of Philosophy of the Bulgarian Academy of Sciences. He had allegedly been persecuted by the totalitarian authorities for his political convictions and actions. In June 1989 he was arrested

---

[3] *Demokratsiya* daily, Todor Yanakiev, *Was the Law on the Secret Service Files Enforced Fully in 1997?*, March 5 and 6, 2001.

[4] Report and discussions on the investigations concerning persons who have been found to belong to the former State Security – Article 4 of the Law on the Access to the Documents of the Former State Security, Thirty-Eighth National Assembly, 58th plenary session, Sofia, Wednesday, October 22, 1997; Fact-Finding Protocol on the work of the Commission for Access to the Documents of the Former State Security, adopted by the Thirty-Eighth National Assembly on July 30, 1997, and promulgated in the *State Gazette* with Decree No. 306 of August 4, 1997, of the President of the Republic of Bulgaria, Sofia, Library of the National Assembly.

and accused of organizing and leading an anti-government organization. He was sentenced to ten years in prison. The changes after November 10, 1989, brought him amnesty. In other words, Ahmed Dogan was known as a hero who fought against the Bulgarian Communist Party and the atrocities to which his fellow ethnic Turks had been subjected. However, the truth was very different: since the age of 20 - and throughout the entire process of coercively changing the names of the Turkish population in Bulgaria - he had been acting as an informer for the highest and most secret subdivisions of the State Security apparatus.

In his report, Minister Bogomil Bonev also named several leaders of the Movement for Rights and Freedoms who had worked for the secret services of dictatorial Bulgaria for many years. Among them were Yunal Said Lyutfi - part-time collaborator to the Second General Directorate on Turkish issues from 1965 until 1990, expelled from the State Security apparatus in 1992, and Kadir Djalil Kadir - part-time collaborator to three State Security directorates between 1957 and 1965. These two former agents started their official political careers with seats in the Seventh Grand National Assembly and were subsequently promoted to higher positions in the country's administration. Before becoming a boss in the National Audit Office, Kadir was elected Deputy Speaker of the Thirty-Sixth National Assembly. In turn, Yunal Lyutfi was appointed to the same prestigious position in the Thirty-Seventh National Assembly.

In 1997, the seven-member commission headed by the Minister of the Interior made public the covert activities of another couple of prominent MRF figures and active Members of Parliament:

> Kemal Eyup Adyl, Parliamentary Group of the National Salvation Alliance, part-time collaborator to the District Directorate of the State Security in the town of Silistra on Turkish issues between 1978 and 1989. His file contains a declaration of willingness to cooperate, signed by him personally. Notified with a letter. Failed to appear before the Commission. No objection has been deposited.
>
> Osman Ahmed Oktay, Parliamentary Group of the National Salvation Alliance, part-time collaborator to the District Directorate of the State Security in the town of Silistra on issues connected with the Sixth Directorate of the State Security between 1975 and 1983. His file contains a declaration of willingness to cooperate, signed by him personally. Notified with a letter. Failed to appear before the Commission. No objection has been deposited.[5]

. . .

[5] *Ibid.*

Unlike Ahmed Dogan and his associates, Academician Nikolay Todorov, who was elected Speaker of the newly constituted Seventh Grand National Assembly on July 17, 1990, aroused no public interest whatsoever. In both his appearance and conduct, the former Vice President of the Bulgarian Academy of Sciences evoked the utter boredom of the totalitarian days during which he had built his career.

The atmosphere in the plenary hall of the Parliament became visibly tense only when it was time to hold elections for President of the People's Republic of Bulgaria after Peter Mladenov's resignation.

The formal procedure began on Friday, July 20. Alexander Lilov nominated Professor Chavdar Kyuranov for President and Professor Velko Valkanov for Vice President on behalf of the Bulgarian Socialist Party. Then Zhelyu Zhelev announced the decision of the Union of Democratic Forces to elect Dr. Peter Dertliev for President and Dr. Peter Beron for Vice President. The Parliamentary Group of the Bulgarian Agrarian People's Union also nominated a presidential candidate, namely the Chairman of the organization Victor Valkov.

Four days later the Grand National Assembly voted twice. None of the candidates for the position Head of State succeeded in receiving the required two-thirds of the 400 votes. The same thing happened on July 26. On July 30, the BSP suddenly withdrew the candidacy of Chavdar Kyuranov. A fifth vote followed, resulting in 257 votes for the agrarian Victor Valkov and 130 votes for the social democrat Peter Dertliev.

The next day brought a new surprise. The leading candidate Valkov withdrew from the elections. Dertliev followed suit. On behalf of the Parliamentary Alliance of the Democratic Forces, Stoyan Ganev proposed another UDF candidate, the Union's Chairman Dr. Zhelyu Zhelev.

Later most Bulgarians perceived the actions described above as a comedy meant to fool the public. It gradually became evident that the choice of Head of State in the summer of 1990 was made not by the Grand National Assembly, but by some important people from the Bulgarian Socialist Party. What other explanation could there be for the fact that the leader of the opposition alliance obtained the votes of most of his political adversaries? Furthermore, the future noncommunist President often played directly into the hands of the BSP during his term.

Professor Dragomir Draganov, Deputy Chairman of the BSP Parliamentary Group in the Seventh Grand National Assembly, claims that Dr. Zhelev's candidacy for President had been discussed by his red party even before Peter Mladenov handed in his resignation. According to him, some of the hard-liners in the organization, led by Lilov, opposed that option. The deal was sealed through behind-the-scenes maneuvering between Andrey Lukanov and a part of the UDF leadership. The promise given to Zhelyu Zhelev was that he would receive the votes needed for the position in exchange for his word that he would propose General Atanas Semerdzhiev as Vice President, in addition to some other conditions. The historian Draganov accused the first UDF leader of lacking the courage to admit the compromise he made.[6]

Dragomir Draganov's claims are supported by the minutes of the session of the Grand National Assembly when the voting for President took place. Prime Minister Lukanov declared the readiness of the Parliamentary Group of the Bulgarian Socialist Party to support the candidacy of the opposition leader.

The transcripts of the parliamentary debates on that same date reveal another curious detail. The Deputy Chairman of the Parliamentary Alliance of the Democratic Forces Stoyan Ganev requested the floor to say the following a few minutes before the actual voting:

> The President of the Republic has the constitutional right to nominate his deputy. We believe that he can also be representative of another political force, as a demonstration of political compromise.[7]

Obviously Ganev was aware of the agreement, and this was a hint to the communists that Zhelev would not forget his commitment. With this statement he also set the stage for the UDF Chairman's next move.

Two hundred eighty four of 389 Members of Parliament voted for Zhelyu Zhelev to become the President of Bulgaria. Dr. Zhelev pronounced the oath of the Head of State. He signed the written oath as well and thanked the Seventh Grand National Assembly for the high confidence vested in him. Immediately afterwards, although this was not on the agenda, the leader of the opposition declared the following:

> I would like to nominate General Atanas Semerdzhiev for Vice President of the Republic, without electing him right now.[8]

Still, upon the wish expressed by the majority of Members of Parliament, the voting took place immediately. The Minister of the Interior in the communist governments of Georgi Atanasov and of Andrey Lukanov was sworn in as Vice President.

---

[6] *Nedelnik* weekly, November 10, 1999.

[7] 13th plenary session of the Seventh Grand National Assembly, Sofia, Wednesday, August 1, 1990, Library of the National Assembly.

[8] *Ibid.*

Most of the elder communists could envy Atanas Semerdzhiev's biography. Born in 1924, he was already a partisan at the age of 18. At 19, he was in command of a partisan group and a member of the communist party. At 20, he headed a partisan detachment that grew to become a brigade. After September 9, 1944, Semerdzhiev graduated from high school, completed a military training course at the Military School in Sofia, and earned degrees from the *M. V. Frunze* Military Academy and the *K. E. Voroshilov* Military Academy of the General Staff of the Armed Forces of the Soviet Union. From that time on he occupied various positions of command in the General Staff of the Bulgarian People's Army and leading positions in the state apparatus.

At the time of his election for Vice President, the General had been Member of Parliament for many years and had written several books. He was member of the Bulgarian Communist Party's Central Committee, which automatically promoted him to membership in the Bulgarian Socialist Party's Supreme Party Council. Thus, Zhelev had proposed one of the most merited and loyal cadres of the red party, with a solid Bolshevik training, to act as his right hand. However, in the general joy and excitement over the fact that the UDF Chairman had become President of the Republic, most noncommunists naively thought that the blue President had made a wise tactical move.

It was only years later that certain details came to light and the name of General Semerdzhiev was associated with the illegal burning of nearly 150,000 secret files and other archives of the secret services.[9] The issue of the *Nedelnik* weekly devoted to the topic "*10 Years after November 10*" reports the following:

> One day in January 1990, a proposal was submitted to the office of General Semerdzhiev, at that time Minister of the Interior in Georgi Atanasov's communist government. The then Deputy Minister of the Interior General Stoyan Savov suggested the destruction of the secret archives of the State Security. The Minister did not hesitate even for a moment, he was the product of the Soviet school and everything had been coordinated in advance. The destruction of the operational reports and archives began. By December 31, 1990, the number of documents destroyed was 132,581 out a total of 279,704 registered documents. The most valuable ones were wiped out. This was done to protect a large number of "particularly valuable collaborators" of the State Security, some of whom had infiltrated the leading structures of the Union of Democratic Forces.[10]

...

[9] Prof. Dr. Georgi Markov in a conversation with the author, August 1998, Sofia, Bulgaria.

[10] *Nedelnik* weekly, November 10, 1999.

The change in the state apparatus of Bulgaria entailed alternations in the leadership of the Union of Democratic Forces as well. On August 3, Peter Beron was elected Chairman of its Coordinating Council. Stefan Gaytandzhiev became its Secretary and Petko Simeonov and Christophor Sabev were elected Deputy Chairmen. Three days later, the managing body of the UDF voted in two more Deputy Chairmen, Milan Drenchev and Philip Dimitrov. On August 9, Beron headed the Parliamentary Alliance of the Democratic Forces, adding yet another Deputy Chairman, the former secretary of the communist youth organization - the Komsomol - Dimitar Ludzhev.

Then the next round of political maneuvers began. Prime Minister Andrey Lukanov invited the Union of Democratic Forces to participate in a coalition cabinet under his leadership. He found supporters among the people around Zhelev and Ludzhev. However, most of the UDF Members of Parliament were emphatically against that proposal.[11]

On August 22, the Seventh Grand National Assembly accepted the resignation of Andrey Lukanov's first government, which had taken power in February. On the next day, President Zhelev started consultations with the political parties in Parliament in order to put together a new governing body. Then things slowed down. At one point the Union of Democratic Forces presented conditions for its participation in the coalition cabinet, then they declared firmly that they would not join in. Zhelev launched the idea of a program government. The Bulgarian Socialist Party backed that idea and appealed to all political groups in the Assembly to develop a plan together and approve it with parliamentary consensus. The BSP Supreme Party Council declared that if that did not happen, Andrey Lukanov would propose a cabinet without the participation of the UDF. On September 17, the Union of Democratic Forces announced that it would support the government only if its agenda was based on the UDF's election platform. The following day the consultations held in the President's office came to an end. Both the Union of Democratic Forces and the Bulgarian Agrarian People's Union refused to participate in the cabinet. Then, on September 20, the Seventh Grand National Assembly reelected Andrey Lukanov as Prime Minister. Two days later the Members of Parliament endorsed the composition of his one-party government of ex-communists.

...

[11] Dimitrov 1995(a).

All Bulgarians who remember the autumn during Lukanov's second government can attest to the economic catastrophe that took place at that time. Had the Union of Democratic Forces participated in a coalition government with the former communists, it would have shared the blame for the disaster. Accepting the offer of a coalition would have meant interlinking the two major political parties in Bulgaria, whose supporters had diametrically opposite political credos. That would have robbed the UDF, created only nine months prior, of its identity. The renamed communists, who had remained without any clear political identity or economic platform after they gave up the one-party dictatorship and violence, would have gotten a free ride. The "street" and especially the City of Truth were the principal reason for which that misstep was averted. One of the few politicians who was aware of that reality and discussed it openly was Philip Dimitrov:

> I went to the City of Truth all the time. I believe that it contributed favorably to the development of political events. It is true that this type of political protests are risky and that they can easily be brought to failure. Nevertheless, they raise the spirits of the people and are useful from that point of view. The students' strikes and the City of Truth actually brought about the resignation of Peter Mladenov and the election of Zhelyu Zhelev as President.
>
> The City of Truth was a spontaneous manifestation of the anger and frustration of the people, a natural reaction to the catastrophic result of the elections in June. This unique civilian protest consolidated the Union of Democratic Forces to a great extent because - let's be honest - the UDF was actually created after 1990.
>
> Zhelev was basically afraid of a revolutionary wave. The truth is that we all shared similar apprehensions. Myself included, I admit. Still, I supported the students' strikes and the City of Truth with the clear awareness that if the nation was heading in that direction, its leaders had to be with the people. However, I repeat that I was scared. I was against Zhelyu's urging us to withdraw ignominiously. I have always believed that civilian protests should be concluded with at least a semblance of victory. You may not have attained all that much, but there should still be something to be claimed as a victory as a result of the protests. Otherwise people will lose faith, and despair.
>
> It was no secret even then that the *Podkrepa* Labor Federation was involved in the arson of the communist party headquarters. Today, when we can look back and have a better insight into the facts of that time, it is easy to understand that with that action Konstantin Trenchev played into the hands of the communist party.
>
> Setting fire to the communist party headquarters was a provocation on the part of the BCP, aimed at exacerbating the tension and trying to strike at the Union of Democratic Forces. If you read issues of the *Duma* communist daily

of August 12-26, 1990, you will see the idea of fire persisting almost fanatically on the pages of that newspaper. From August 12 onward there is talk of forest fires, all kinds of fires. This is very intriguing from a psychodynamic point of view, because it is an attempt to suggest the idea of fire and arson.

The result of the blaze was quite unlike the expectations. The communists underestimated two things. First, it never crossed their minds that the people would not hurl themselves into all that commotion. They expected that crowds of UDF supporters would fiercely storm the communist stronghold and create mass unrest. Then they would have justification to crush them. But the citizens did not do that. They stood about thirty feet from the building and watched. I won't pretend that there was no joy in the hearts of the anticommunists. But nevertheless they did not start aggressive actions. The second thing that the BCP failed to foresee was that, while Trenchev was incition the protesters, the other UDF leaders acted sensibly.

I went into the communist party building to take people out. About a dozen persons had rushed in. Twenty at the most, all of them had no presence in the UDF. There were several boys and girls who I personally led out. They stood there as if they were watching a theatre performance and generally they did not know what they were doing in there. I never learned how they had found themselves in. The others were aggressive guys, apparently inspired by Trenchev's appeals. He himself was walking around, instigating. A day or two previously, and especially on the day of the fire, he kept repeating, "We'll set fire to that monster, if they don't remove the five-pointed star, we really will." There was more talk like that.

After the fire the communists started some sort of investigation, but it had lost its meaning. Their first game had failed. Their second game, however, was highly successful. That was their plan to destroy archives and files. I saw it with my own eyes. There were files upon files with documents in the garages of the communist party building and incendiary materials right next to them. Indeed these were strange sights.

In 1990 the communists were the strongest party, and they were trying to force us to take part in a coalition government. They still believed that they had control over the Union of Democratic Forces. Although the possibility of a compromise crossed Zhelyu's mind at some point, the City of Truth - and this is one of its biggest merits - made it absolutely impossible to even talk about such things. The people vehemently rejected the mere idea of a coalition with the reds.[12]

---

[12] Philip Dimitrov in a conversation with the author, Philadelphia, U.S.A., April 2, 1999.

PART FIVE

PHILIP DIMITROV AND HIS TIME

18. In the Darkness of a Sinister Autumn

To this day the memory of the autumn of 1990 sends shivers down the spine of every one who lived through it. Even the most orthodox communist, who has not made a profit from the collapse of the totalitarian system, would admit that the second government of Andrey Lukanov brought about one of the most sinister periods in Bulgaria's history. During "Lukanov's autumn" - as that time is commonly referred to - Sofia and all other cities looked like they had been hit by the plague or a plunderer's army of thousands.

The grocery stores were in shambles, with no regular illumination or heating. Their walls were dirty and their shelves were empty. If lucky, one could spot only some old cans. Vegetables and fruit were virtually nonexistent on the market. Bread was scarce. It was a heroic feat to purchase a bluish-looking chicken or a bottle of grape brandy. Pharmacies had become altogether superfluous because they lacked even the most basic medicines and first aid supplies. It was a real horror if one had to go to the hospital, where medication, X-ray plaques, food, toilet paper, and electricity were either lacking or extremely scarce. Only schoolchildren could find some joy in those days. They were often given unexpected holidays when there was no heating or electricity in their schools.

The capital city of Bulgaria looked grey and deserted and its population was frightened. The payphones in the streets were all broken, while the telephones in the people's homes functioned erratically. There were power cuts all times of the day and night, and it required great courage to enter an elevator because of the likelihood of getting stuck in it for hours. People slowly climbed the stairs to their dark and cold apartments in which often there were neither candles nor matches.

The situation was particularly ominous in the later autumn days, when there was no electricity in many districts of the cities. On a rare occasion the headlights of a car would pierce the complete darkness of the dirty streets and boulevards. Virtually nobody could afford the luxury of driving. The price of gas skyrocketed. Besides, fuel could hardly be obtained. In the absolute darkness people rarely dared to leave their homes.

Except at 4-5 a.m. Then some brave family member would sneak out of his cold bed, often not even brushing his teeth for lack of toothpaste or washing his face for lack of soap. He would rush breathless to some shop rumored to have a few liters of milk or yoghurt, twenty or so kilograms of cheese, or two or three dozens bottles of vegetable oil for sale. If one wished to acquire any of these scarce commodities, especially if he had small children, sick or old people at home, one had to make sure to get in line as early as possible.

It should be stressed that the miserable living conditions at the time of Andrey Lukanov's government took place while the servicing of the 12-billion-dollar foreign debt was suspended, market reform had not started, the material losses resulting from the crisis in Yugoslavia did not exist, and the additional plundering of Bulgaria and of its population, which was done between 1993 and 1997, had not yet had its impact. Another process was in full swing under the aegis of the Prime Minister. Before the eyes of the hungry and exasperated Bulgarians, the ex-communist dictators and their close associates were becoming economic dictators *en masse.* Former and present high-ranking state officials, sportsmen, State Security agents, and people working in the sphere of foreign trade opened private banks, insurance and body-guard companies, and business ventures. They formed powerful financial groups, privatized enterprises, bought hotels, buildings, luxury cars, erected palace-like residences, or emigrated abroad as millionaires.

What was the origin of these enormous resources of hard currency in the hands of these people? During communism, they had received their wages in Bulgarian levs. Even though their salaries were much higher than those of ordinary Bulgarians, they could not have obtained such money by legal means. Evidently the open transformation of the red elite into a class of millionaires in 1990 had been planned, prepared and triggered well in advance. The working people in Bulgaria could only worry about making ends meet. For decades to come that concern would paralyze their thoughts and actions.

The so-called "red grannies" were extremely active during "Lukanov's autumn". These exalted communist women, often wearing expensive fur coats and hats, and not looking undernourished at all, marched in the streets of Sofia beating spoons on empty pots and pans and protesting against the hunger brought upon them. Ignoring the facts that their party had won the parliamentary elections and that it had a majority in the Grand National Assembly and ran the government, the red women blamed the crisis on the Union of Democratic Forces, which had never been in power!

Only the new President came from the UDF, but he was not in charge of the executive power. He had some legislative rights, but his functions were mostly ceremonial. So during the autumn of 1990, Dr. Zhelev toured Europe and the United States, evoking spontaneous applause among fellow Bulgarians abroad and the approval of foreigners with the claim that there was no longer communism in Bulgaria. In his optimism, the Head of State ignored the fact that the renamed party of the communists was at the helm of the nation. Zhelyu Zhelev also forgot the promises he gave the Bulgarian nation in August 1990:

> I intend to use most actively the power, given to me according to the Constitution, to revoke all drafts of legislation submitted by the government and by other institutions that run counter to the Constitution and the laws. Above all, I will veto any proposals that violate the fundamental human rights of the citizens.
>
> ...
>
> At the same time, I shall use my right to propose drafts of laws given to me by the Constitution, in order to launch legislation aimed at defending socially disadvantaged individuals, people with small pensions and low wages, the unemployed, etc.[1]

President Zhelev, having planned to "clean up all that secondary legislation characterizing totalitarian rule,"[2] including decrees, ordinances and the like, actually revoked only the Ordinance Temporarily Restricting the Right to Permanent Residence in Sofia and the Larger Cities of Bulgaria, from which he had suffered himself. In this way he demolished one of the fortification walls of feudal communist Bulgaria. Unfortunately, much to the disappointment of UDF supporters, that admirable act was his first and last in the implementation of his ambitious plans. Two lawyers from the Union of Democratic Forces, Philip Dimitrov and Yordan Sokolov, urged him in vain to fulfill his promises of a "regulatory revolution."[3]

. . .

What was the top figure in the executive branch, Prime Minister Andrey Lukanov, doing in 1990? How did he manage to reduce the population to systematic undernourishment in only six months, while the state was being led to total economic collapse? Lukanov's name had been bandied about in the slogans of the Bulgarian Socialist Party before the elections that year. The BSP had insisted that he was the most experienced economist in the country, endowed with rare intellectual capacities, and the only one who could pull Bulgaria out of its economic crisis.

---

[1] *Demokratsiya* daily, *Rapid democratization – appeal by the President of the Republic Dr. Zhelyu Zhelev to the Bulgarian Nation*, August 6, 1990.

[2] *Demokratsiya* daily, Dr. Zhelyu Zhelev in a conversation with Adam Mihnik: *It Is Time to Say Everything*, August 11, 1990.

[3] Dimitrov 1995(a).

As the *Nedelnik* weekly reminded us in November 1999, the consequences of his government were just the opposite:

> Instead of reforming the economy, Lukanov's second one-party government outlined a policy that led to unprecedented deficit, generated by the removal of price control. Commodities started to disappear; wages grew. All this led to incredible, soaring inflation. Bulgaria was on the verge of introducing food rationing. The Bulgarian National Bank, which was subordinated to the Cabinet, was feverishly printing money without control. New banks and bank branches sprang up like mushrooms. The future private banks (First Private Bank and Bank for Agricultural Credit), into which billions disappeared, were supported by open and clandestine government decisions. The amendment to Decree 56 of the Council of Ministers legitimized the uncontrolled sale of state property at dirt cheap prices.
>
> However, Lukanov's greatest sin was the moratorium imposed by his government on the foreign debt. The State refused to pay. Lukanov had declared the moratorium back in March 1990, thus predetermining the country's economic blockade for years to come.[4]

What were the plans of that hereditary communist, born and raised in Moscow, and placed at the top of the government pyramid by the Bulgarian Socialist Party? Where did the stopped payments to the country's foreign creditors go? Was it into his own pockets or those of his close associates? Who purchased the Bulgarian securities at the international stock markets, after their prices had plummeted as a result of the moratorium? With which economic groups was the Prime Minister connected? What shares did he have in the private financial empire *Multigroup*, which had already accumulated enormous capital before the official fall of communism with his direct assistance? Where did he invest his money? What business operations was he masterminding? What were his links with Robert Maxwell? Why did the mysterious Western magnate visit Lukanov immediately after he announced Bulgaria's bankruptcy? How did it work out that some enterprises went bankrupt and were subsequently privatized? How did the newly-opened private banks acquire their capital? What about the numerous powerful companies with semi-legal activities and the dozens of publishing houses that flooded the market with pro-communist or yellow literature? Who gave permissions to Russians, Ukrainians and other foreign nationals to buy real estate along the Bulgarian Black Sea coast in gross violation of the laws?

---

[4] *Nedelnik* weekly, November 10, 1999.

All these questions were never answered, but one thing is certain. Andrey Lukanov was shot and killed in front of his home in the morning of October 2, 1996. That mob-style hit justified the suspicions of many Bulgarians that the communist "reformer" had been connected with the global criminal economic under world.

...

On October 25, 1990, the new UDF Chairman, Peter Beron, and the leadership of the organization authorized the Member of Parliament Alexander Yordanov to read a political declaration in the Grand National Assembly. With his sonorous voice the opposition deputy announced the position of the Parliamentary Alliance of the Democratic Forces:

> The conduct of the parliamentary majority is being stage-managed by persons bearing responsibility for the catastrophic plight of Bulgaria. Their aim is clear: to gradually transfer the blame from the guilty to the innocent, to imitate willingness for reform, but essentially to drag out the process of democratization in order to give an opportunity to some circles in the Bulgarian Socialist Party to transform the political power monopoly that they had until very recently into an economic power monopoly.
>
> We assess this behavior of theirs as anti-national, immoral and detrimental to the people.[5]

Further on the document read that "only the prompt and resolute rejection of the bankrupt political and economic system of socialism could guarantee tomorrow's free, fair and prosperous life of the nation."[6] It insisted that the Bulgarian Socialist Party, as the successor of the Bulgarian Communist Party, should publicly take the blame for the country's disastrous economic situation and its bad international reputation, and reveal the political and economic responsibility of certain individuals and groups for the national catastrophe. The declaration specifically insisted on the following measures:

> The government should make a firm commitment in its legislative initiative and practical actions to ensuring that the market reform does not legitimize and augment the material wealth of the individuals who profited from the totalitarian rule. In more specific terms, the government should do the following:

---

5 49th plenary session of the Seventh Grand National Assembly, Sofia, Thursday, October 25, 1990, Library of the National Assembly.

6 *Ibid.*

> 1. Propose special legislation for the confiscation of such property.
>
> 2. Publish a report on the sources and amounts of property acquired as a result of holding leading positions in the totalitarian system. The report should include information about the staff housing program of the Security Directorate, the conditions under which they built houses, the way Security Directorate resources were spent for the personal needs of high-ranking leaders and their families, and the amount of foreign currency made available to them for free or at lowered exchange rates.
>
> 3. The government should undertake specific actions to bring back to the country the money and property that has been exported by such individuals, or declare that it has revealed certain violations.
>
> The same is to be done vis-à-vis companies with shares owned by Bulgarian citizens living abroad.
>
> The government should also submit detailed information on the decisions and persons responsible for the accumulation of the foreign debt, as well as who made the decisions to stop payments on it and how.
>
> Taking into account the catastrophic economic situation in the country and the numerous attempts to transform state property into property of individual parties and private companies, the Parliamentary Alliance of the Democratic Forces insists that the Bulgarian Socialist Party, as a legal, logical and moral successor of the Bulgarian Communist Party, should return to the state and to the people freely and unconditionally all its movable assets and real estate within a specified period of time, with the exception of what has been acquired from the proceeds of membership dues. The reason being that the BCP has robbed the Bulgarian people for decades through its totalitarian economic and social policies favoring solely the Party.[7]

The assessment of the program of Andrey Lukanov's second cabinet, given by the opposition parliamentary alliance, was:

> At the same time, we define the intentions proclaimed in the program of the government of the Bulgarian Socialist Party as vague in terms of time and pace, mutually contradictory, mutually destructive even and - above all - as totally divergent from the logic of the historical process today, particularly from the political context in which the reform of the economic system is to take place.[8]

This was followed by a warning:

---

[7] *Ibid.*

[8] *Ibid.*

> We appeal with this Declaration to the entire Bulgarian nation and we are fully aware of the exceptional responsibility we must take for all our words and actions. We declare that the future of the one-party governments is directly dependent on the readiness of the parliamentary majority of the Bulgarian Socialist Party to undertake rapid and categorical legislative measures and conduct constructive dialogue and share thoughts and ideas on all issues, problems and requirements formulated in the present Declaration.[9]

After Alexander Yordanov read the declaration and the Members of Parliament from the UDF bloc welcomed it with standing ovation, the floor was given to Alexander Tomov, Deputy Chairman of the Supreme Party Council and Coordinating Secretary of the Bulgarian Socialist Party.

The expert adviser on economic matters in the Council of Ministers at the time of the communist governments of Grisha Filipov and Georgi Atanasov made an attempt to remain polite in the beginning of his speech. But soon the insolence of the reds gained momentum. Tomov accused the Union of Democratic Forces not reporting exact facts and specific names connected with the plundered state property. Yet, it was impossible for the opposition to get hold of such data, having had no access to the archives, or participation in the affairs of the executive, judiciary and political powers of totalitarian Bulgaria. Tomov spoke as though the UDF had not just insisted in its declaration on receiving that type of information precisely from the party that had ruled the country for the past 46 years. At last, the future leader of the Euro-Left and prominent capitalist committed himself to the following statement before the Grand National Assembly and before the Bulgarian nation:

> In addition, although I have been in the party leadership for only about ten days, I would like to declare before you that after the inspection made, we have no evidence of transformation, transfer or any other procedures involving the movement of party property and assets into private hands.[10]

Alexander Tomov - who would later own a major soccer team - used a well-tried and successful trick: to shed any responsibility by "passing the ball back." Instead of providing specific evidence of economic abuses by his party, or promising to do so, the politician/tightrope-dancer stubbornly insisted on receiving it from his powerless opponents.

---

[9] *Ibid.*

[10] *Ibid.*

The discussion transformed October 25 into a typical day in the work of the Seventh Grand National Assembly. Over the years the renamed communists went on to polish their cynical tactics even further.

...

November brought neither warmth to the homes of the Bulgarians, nor food to their shops. Instead, there were hot political events and endless disputes and turmoil.

At the end of October Peter Beron had already announced that the UDF would not support the program of Andrey Lukanov's Council of Ministers. The Chairman of the democratic coalition proposed that the socialist government should either shoulder the responsibility for the implementation of its own plan or step down.

On November 5, the Union of Democratic Forces declared its readiness to assume power. It would accept the participation of representatives of the Bulgarian Socialist Party in the cabinet.

That same day, another strike was announced at the *St. Kliment Ohridski* University of Sofia with specific social, academic and political demands, such as: nationalization of the property of the Bulgarian Socialist Party, criminal liability for the people responsible for the catastrophic position of Bulgaria, and making public the findings of the Credentials Committee of the Grand National Assembly.

The next day, President Zhelev appealed to the student groups to stop their actions. He argued that civilian peace had to be preserved to allow the political forces to hold talks among themselves. Regardless of the President's opinion, the strike spread to other universities both in Sofia and in the countryside. By November 19, their number on a national scale reached fifty universities and colleges.

Not only the number, but also the resolve of the students taking part in the protests was impressive. On November 10, the strike committee of the University of Sofia announced that the strike would continue, even if a change of government took place, until the students received guarantees from the cabinet that their demands would be met.

The older generation stood side by side with the young people again. University lecturers, scholars, scientists and journalists established a public council in defense of the students on strike at the *St. Kliment Ohridski* University.

The Union of Democratic Forces continued to ardently discuss the idea of forming a government dominated by its members. On November 12, at a meeting of its Coordinating Council, fifteen organizations supported the proposal, but only four expressed readiness to participate in the Cabinet. These were the Green Party, the Bulgarian Radical Democratic Party, the United Democratic Center and the Federation of the Clubs for *Glasnost* and Democracy.

The Bulgarian nation's patience with the horrible living conditions was gradually running out. Toward the middle of the grim November, the UDF urged its supporters to stage mass protest rallies and demonstrations against Andrey Lukanov's government. Opinion polls indicated that the support for the Union of Democratic Forces had risen lately from 37 to 44 per cent.

On November 18, 1990, just as had happened the previous year, tens of thousands of citizens of Sofia streamed in front of the *St. Alexander Nevski* Cathedral to express their indignation with the leadership of the communists/socialists. The next day the students on strike appealed for a national strike with political demands. The *Podkrepa* Federation of Labor declared readiness for a strike. It issued an official warning that if the Cabinet did not resign, it would declare an effective general political strike on November 26. On November 20, the UDF supported *Podkrepa*'s decision. As an expression of solidarity with the students, the Academic Council suspended all classes at the University of Sofia. Dressed in mourning, members and supporters of the Movement of Actors for Democracy lined *Rakovski* Street in silence on November 21 and 22, insisting that Andrey Lukanov should step down. The following day a chain of protesters formed around the National Assembly building.

Encouraged by the rising wave of civilian unrest, the Parliamentary Alliance of the Democratic Forces demanded a vote of no confidence for the Prime Minister and his government on November 22. The same day Parliament held an undisclosed vote and adopted the budget proposed by Andrey Lukanov. The Members of Parliament from the Union of Democratic Forces, the Bulgarian Agrarian People's Union, and the Movement for Rights and Freedoms boycotted the vote. There was one exception: Rumen Vodenicharov. He officially declared his support for the red budget and announced that he was leaving the UDF parliamentary group.

Vodenicharov's act stirred the UDF electorate. He became the first among the founders and leaders of the Union of Democratic Forces who not only split from that organization but turned into one of its most vocal enemies. The anticommunists from his constituency in Sofia, who had voted for him, collected signatures demanding his withdrawal from the Grand National Assembly. They had voted for him to be their Member of Parliament and to defend their interests, not the interests of their political opponents.

The indignation of the voters with Rumen Vodenicharov's departure contrasted with the malicious joy of the communists. The latter were openly jubilant with the renegade behavior of the former spokesman of the Union of Democratic Forces. The *Duma* daily was pleased to publish laudatory articles about its former opponent.[11] From that moment on Vodenicharov himself contributed regularly to the publications of the socialist/communist party and its supporters as a preferred interviewee and author.[12]

His views as an "independent Member of Parliament" in the Seventh Grand National Assembly constantly coincided with those of the Bulgarian Socialist Party. In fact, on May 29, 1991, the former Chairman of the Independent Society for Human Rights Protection voiced his nostalgic feelings for the totalitarian era from the rostrum of the Parliament:

> The majority of the citizens are progressively sobering up and are beginning to realize that in order to restore equilibrium in our society, we should not attach absolute importance to the rights of the citizens. Instead, we should seek to constantly change through legislation the balance between the rights and the restrictions of these rights.[13]

The renamed Bulgarian Communist Party rewarded Rumen Vodenicharov for that conduct. At the elections for President of the Republic of Bulgaria in January 1992, he was the BCP candidate for Vice President.

Several years later, in August 1998, at the funeral of the communist dictator Todor Zhivkov - who died just months after he had been admitted as a member of the Bulgarian Socialist Party - Vodenicharov, then Chairman of the International organization Helsinki Watch in Bulgaria, of all things, an organization bound to watch out for the human rights and dignity of each

---

[11] *Duma* daily, *Cruel, bitter and power-thirsty Katanovs*, November 24, 1990; *Duma* daily, *The collecting of signatures for the withdrawal of Roumen Vodenicharov from Parliament is illegal*, November 26, 1990.

[12] *Duma* daily, *Show prudence*, March 9, 1991; *Duma* daily, *The violation of the Election Law may raise doubts about Parliament,* March 15, 1991; *Duma* daily, *Talks with a political corpse*, May 14, 1991; *Zora*, *The Bulgarian nation is in danger*, June 4, 1991; *Zemya* daily, *Language as the bone of content*, June 10, 1991; *Zora*, *Magistrates of censorship and of the wet rope*, July 16, 1991; *Zemya* daily, *The opposition – a look from within*, July 16, 1991; *Duma* daily, *The Bulgarian nation is in danger*, September 13, 1991; *Duma* daily, *Trio in retro style*, November 18, 1991; *Duma* daily, *Is there a chance for the survival of "Fascism", or rather of its author?*, January 7, 1992; *Duma* daily, *Semi-Himalayan interview with Roumen Vodenicharov*, January 10, 1992; *Duma* daily, *The Constitution has been suspended, Roumen Vodenicharov claims*, March 14, 1992; *Duma* daily, *Shame on the leaders of the UDF(d)*, March 23, 1993; *Duma* daily, *Encroachment upon the immunity of the Members of Parliament, Roumen Vodenicharov assumes*, June 29, 1992; *Duma* daily, *July 12, 1991 – a date that binds us by obligation*, July 11, 1992; *Duma* daily, *The pendulum swings back*, January 25, 1994; *Duma* daily, *Freedom of choice: Ahmed or Mehmed*, June 13, 1994;

[13] 140th plenary session of the Seventh Grand National Assembly, Sofia, Wednesday, May 29, 1991, Library of the National Assembly.

member of the nation, unashamedly shared his hatred of minorities with the mourners:

> Has Bulgaria run out of capable people to leave the entire government and its entire property in the hands of Gypsies and Jews, while the President has been elected for the second time with the decisive help of an ethnic and religious party banned by the Constitution?[14]

He concluded, with tears in his eyes, by assuring the dead leader:

> Rest in peace, dear Todor, a part of your political opponents have become your followers already.[15]

In his emotional speech over the coffin of the deceased dictator, Rumen Vodenicharov declared that Bulgaria had become an industrial and social state precisely under his rule, that Zhivkov had created the strategic gold and foreign currency reserve of the country, as well as an affluent middle class. The speaker referred to the political adversaries of the former communist ruler as "ungrateful compatriots" and the date of his demise - August 5 - as "tragic" for Bulgaria. In order to support this last statement, the nearly 60-year-old man cried before the microphone.[16]

It seemed that this was not the very same man who on November 18, 1989, gave the following description of Todor Zhivkov's legacy before the many thousands of people who had gathered in front of the *St. Alexander Nevski* Cathedral:

> The treasury is empty. There is an enormous state debt. There is an excessive, unproductive and repressive state apparatus. There are ethnic tensions and a consequent shortage in work force. Lawlessness is prevalent, in the sense that the law does not apply equally to all. The decades of moral ambivalence caused a deep decline of the nation's values. A number of national virtues were lost, and this - in our opinion - is a more disturbing heritage than the economic decline and the pollution of the environment.[17]

...

---

[14] *Demokratsiya* daily, Ekaterina Nikolova, *BSP turned Zhivkov's funeral into a political rally*, August 10, 1998.

[15] *Ibid.*

[16] *Ibid.*

[17] Tape-recording of the rally on November 18, 1989, at the *St. Alexander Nevski* Square, Sofia, Bulgaria.

In all fairness, it should be admitted that Rumen Vodenicharov was at least open about his crossing over to the reds in the autumn of 1990. In contrast, at the some time several individuals in the UDF leadership, whose loyalties secretly lay with the BCP, were evoking dismay with their advice and actions and creating confusion among the blue coalition supporters. It is a good thing that the people did not always follow the advice and guidance of those leaders.

For instance, when the first plenary session of the Seventh Grand National Assembly was opened, Stefan Gaytandzhiev - than Secretary of the Union of Democratic Forces and later Deputy Chairman of the Parliamentary Group of the Bulgarian Socialist Party - insisted that the UDF structures in Sofia should secure access to the National Assembly building for the Members of Parliament from the Movement for Rights and Freedoms, in the event that anti-Turkish groups tried to prevent them from entering. This strange suggestion was not accepted because the problem was supposed to be resolved by the state power personified by the Prime Minister Andrey Lukanov and the former partisans, the Minister of the Interior Atanas Semerdzhiev and Defense Minister Dobri Dzhurov. This refusal prevented the confrontation that Gaytandzhiev apparently wished to occur between the local UDF organizations, the police and the army.[18]

There is another example. On August 31, 1990, the Grand National Assembly adopted the Law on the Amendments to the Law on People's Councils, and decided to establish provisional regional and municipal executive committees until local elections were held. The municipalities were to be run by representatives of the different political forces in accordance with the outcome of the June elections.

In the beginning of September, futile negotiations regarding the formation of the provisional local governments started. On October 8, Zhelev appealed to the Members of Parliament in the Grand National Assembly to set a date for the local elections. This did not happen. The negotiations on the exact individuals to be appointed at the mayoralties continued throughout the entire month.[19]

Much to the surprise of the local UDF structures, Petko Simeonov gave them instructions not to run for mayors but for secretaries of the municipalities. The argument of the Deputy Chairman of the Union of Democratic Forces was that the secretaries would be the people who actually organized the elections and that for the UDF this was more important than being in government.[20]

---

[18] Ivan Kurtev in a conversation with the author, Sofia, Bulgaria, August 18, 1998.

[19] *Nedelnik* weekly, November 10, 1999.

[20] Ivan Kurtev in a conversation with the author, Sofia, Bulgaria, August 18, 1998.

In practice it was the opposite. The mayor's position proved more useful in the preparations for the parliamentary elections on October 13, 1991. Unfortunately, in four Sofia municipalities, the UDF organizations obeyed Simeonov's orders and traded the mayor's post for a secretarial one. Thankfully, the remaining twenty municipalities disobeyed the instructions of their leader, and their representatives became mayors.[21]

Another curious opinion was prevalent among the UDF leaders. It was claimed that the people to be sent to these provisional local governments should be expendable, assuming *a priori* that they would be a failure due to lack of experience. The key figures in the coalition stayed away from the municipalities, to be ready for future actions on a bigger scale.[22] This theory, too, proved to be illogical. Most of the persons who were "sacrificed" did not do badly at all. Instead, the people in their constituencies bore more easily the hardships of "Lukanov's autumn" than in the red municipalities. The blue mayors organized neighborhood "soup kitchens" and arranged the distribution of clothing and food to the homes of the poor, invalids, and sick. Moreover, in the course of their work in the mayoralties, these UDF politicians became among the first activists of the coalition with management experience.

Unfortunately, the first UDF mayors were surrounded by communist *nomenklatura* and their hands were almost completely tied.[23] Furthermore, their so-called UDF leaders did not always assist them even when they were in a position to do so. For instance, on October 17, 1990, the Chairman of the Green Party Alexander Karakachanov became Mayor of Sofia. At that time he was still a member of the UDF leadership, but his actions seldom suggested loyalty to the "blue idea." The young man soon came into conflict with the UDF mayors of the Sofia municipalities. He tried to give them orders, but they resisted him. Many of the documents regarding violations of the law that the anticommunist mayors gave Karakachanov vanished in his office.[24]

...

Understandably, there were many disappointments and doubts in the souls of the Union of Democratic Forces supporters during the icy and hopeless days and nights of Andrey Lukanov's second government. The wish to depose the communist who had been declared a reformist became paramount.

---

[21] *Ibid.*

[22] *Ibid.*

[23] *Ibid.*

[24] *Ibid.;* 49th plenary session of the Seventh Grand National Assembly, Sofia, Thursday, October 25, 1990, Library of the National Assembly.

Yet, this proved to be impossible through parliamentary procedures. With a secret vote - a procedure on which the socialist majority always insisted - the Seventh Grand National Assembly attested its confidence in the Prime Minister. There was nothing left for the Parliamentary Alliance of the Democratic Forces but to suspend its participation in the plenary sessions of Parliament on November 23, 1990.

The legal heir to the property and assets of the Bulgarian trade unions loyal to the Bulgarian Communist Party, the Confederation of Independent Trade Unions in Bulgaria, declared a "special boycott" of the government on that same day. Parallel with this, the organization announced that it would not issue strike appeals.

On the other hand, *Podkrepa*, supported by the noncommunists, launched an active campaign. On November 25, it announced the start of a general political strike throughout the country at 6 a.m. the next day. In protest against the red government people all over Bulgaria stopped work in the morning of November 26. In the evening of that same day, the UDF rally in Sofia, organized in support of the strikers, lasted for hours. It was followed by a wave of demonstrations and processions. The anger and the indignation of the people seemed endless. The strike, with the demand for the immediate resignation of the Prime Minister and his government, lasted through November 27 and 28. All citizens discontented with communism were united.

However, differences of opinion appeared in the Union of Democratic Forces on a crucial issue. On November 28 and 29 the democratic coalition was embroiled in a heated debate on whether the UDF parliamentary group should return to Parliament after a resignation of Andrey Lukanov. Several members of the UDF leadership insisted that it would be much more sensible for the opposition alliance to continue its boycott, thus provoking a parliamentary crisis to be followed by general elections. The timing seemed right. According to opinion polls, the UDF approval rating was higher than ever, already about 20 per cent higher than that of the BSP.

The idea of early parliamentary elections was supported by Philip Dimitrov, Edwin Sugarev and Yordan Vasilev. Their opponents, led by Petko Simeonov, Dr. Peter Dertliev and Dimitar Ludzhev, defeated them in the debate. Thus, the Parliamentary Alliance of the Democratic Forces gave up its initial intentions and decided to return to Parliament after Prime Minister Andrey Lukanov resigned. President Zhelyu Zhelev supported the position of forming a cabinet without new elections and his protégé Ludzhev immediately started consultations with the political forces.[25] The UDF Coordinating Council

[25] Dimitrov 1995(a), *passim.*

endorsed the candidacy of Peter Beron, Chairman of the coalition and of the PADF, for Prime Minister.

On November 29, 1990, Andrey Lukanov submitted the resignation of his government. Some Bulgarians still believe that after plunging the country into economic chaos, dooming it to financial isolation for years and setting up the conditions necessary to continue draining the national treasury, the Bulgarian Socialist Party deliberately abdicated.[26]

The day that Andrey Lukanov resigned, *Podkrepa's* President Dr. Konstantin Trenchev terminated the general strike. For many people that action seemed somewhat premature. They thought it would have been better for the mass protest to continue throughout the negotiations with the communist/socialist party for the formation of the new government.

Feverish discussions were going on in the last days and nights of November on the possibility of signing an agreement among the political organizations. Something else was also brewing in the President's office and in the high strata of the Bulgarian Socialist Party. The time bomb exploded in the first days of December, the most appropriate time for the renamed communists.

...

At the end of October 1990, Peter Beron subjected the draft-budget submitted in the Grand National Assembly by Lukanov's government to devastating criticism. In response, the red Prime Minister threatened to destroy the UDF leader politically. The very next day the communist daily *Duma* mentioned the alias "agent Boncho" without citing any further details. Beron had opposed the BCP/BSP, and he had to take his punishment like every informer who tries to step out of the control of his former bosses.

The blow against the Union of Democratic Forces came suddenly. It deeply disturbed the nation and considerably diminished its confidence in the opposition coalition. All the more, it was dealt by the blue President of the Republic, who was the only person to see the secret service file of his successor Beron, who at that time was very popular with the people. There was something obscure and rather alarming about the whole story, taken up by the communists and finalized by Dr. Zhelyu Zhelev and Dr. Konstantin Trenchev.

In October, the Bulgarian Socialist Party started dropping hints about the secret files of voluntary informers of the communist State Security machine. In this way it exercised psychological pressure on its former collaborators in an attempt to bring them back to their senses and persuade them to act in its

---

[26] *Nedelnik* weekly, November 10, 1999.

interests. Many may have been scared, but that was not the case for the UDF Chairman. Peter Beron's confidence came from the fact that his organization was in a position of strength, firmly demanding to have majority in the next government. The communist-cum-socialist cabinet had brought the country to an unprecedented economic crisis, and Bulgarians were ready for nationwide protests.

That was precisely when the scandal blew up. On December 3, just after Peter Beron flew to Italy to take part in a scientific conference, it was announced at a briefing of the Union of Democratic Forces that he would probably withdraw from the posts of Chairman of the Coordinating Council and of the Parliamentary Alliance of the Democratic Forces. The next day, at the meeting of the UDF leadership, Petko Simeonov stated that there was evidence that Beron had been a State Security agent, that he had admitted it himself and had asked to be relieved of his positions of leadership before him and Zhelyu Zhelev. The Deputy Chairman of the coalition, Philip Dimitrov, failed in his attempt to postpone the decision on that issue until after the biologist came back from his trip so the latter could present his side of the story. The UDF management body voted for the dismissal of its Chairman in his absence.[27]

On December 4, while speaking to the Bulgarian News Agency, *Podkrepa's* President Dr. Trenchev confirmed the *Reuter's* report that the leader of the democratic opposition had links with the State Security services. On December 6, Peter Beron resigned from both chairmanships. His resignation was accepted immediately. The Union of Democratic Forces demanded from *Podkrepa* documentary evidence and an explanation regarding the source of its information on the so-called "Beron case." Trenchev gave only a vague answer. He claimed that the information about the UDF leader was not from the special services but from an "absolutely official source" at a level guaranteeing its reliability.

At a rushed press conference held on December 7, Konstantin Trenchev denied allegations that in the past he had signed a declaration expressing his willingness to collaborate with the bodies of the Ministry of the Interior of totalitarian Bulgaria. Three days later at a UDF briefing, Peter Beron declared that he had never been on the staff of the Sixth Department of the State Security, and that he had not admitted such a thing to anybody. Regarding his links with the State Security, the scholar explained that he had deliberately written reports to that institution, because he preferred, in his words, "the

[27] Philip Dimitrov in a conversation with the author, Washington, D.C., U.S.A., February 12, 2000; Dimitrov 1995(a).

respective services to receive my interpretation of the things happening in our institute, and not the interpretation of the communists or of someone else."

On December 14, Dr. Zhelyu Zhelev announced in a radio interview that he had familiarized himself with Beron's file in his presence, and that the Chairman of the UDF Coordinating Council had handed in his resignation at Zhelev's insistence. Peter Beron immediately responded by saying that he had neither seen his file, nor that Zhelev had familiarized himself with it in his presence. The former UDF Chairman qualified as "strange" the President's statement that he had demanded his resignation. The dispute about the actual nature and sequence of events continues to this day between the second UDF leader and those who discredited him. Regardless of that, Beron had already lost his importance as a capable democratic leader.

The results of the political scandal brought grave consequences for Bulgaria. The Union of Democratic Forces failed to take the position at the helm of the nation and lead the country along the path of reform. The Bulgarian Socialist Party fulfilled both its wishes: the next government had a broad coalition base, and the Seventh Grand National Assembly continued its work.

An additional after-effect of discrediting Peter Beron was the substantial drop in the approval rating of the UDF, while the prestige of the BSP - and hence its self-confidence - grew considerably. The first phenomenon was understandable, while the second one provoked dismay. Could it be that the primitive tricks of the communists-turned-socialists - assisted in this case by two of the blue leaders - had succeeded again in manipulating public opinion? If one thought even for a moment, he would see clearly that the unmasking of "agent Boncho" discredited not only the Union of Democratic Forces, but also the Bulgarian Socialist Party. In its capacity of legal successor to the communists, that political organization had encouraged and continued to encourage the infiltration and maintenance of informers in all strata of Bulgarian society, including dissident circles.

...

A year after its creation, the Union of Democratic Forces plunged into a deep crisis. It happened just days after the fiasco of Andrey Lukanov's government, when the blue alliance had had a good chance of assuming power. However, the ghost of the secret communist services turned the unavoidable into the impossible. From that moment on it invariably hovered over political events in Bulgaria. Every time the socialist party needed it, it took the trump card out of the "secret files" either on its own or through stooges.

Still, it was necessary for the Union of Democratic Forces to act. The time had come to think about a new coalition leader. A National Conference of the UDF was held in Plovdiv on December 8-9. It proclaimed the inevitability of forming a government and discussed the rules for electing the Chairman of the organization. On December 10, at a UDF briefing it was announced that Dr. Peter Dertliev, Petko Simeonov, Stefan Gaytandzhiev, Stoyan Ganev, Alexander Yordanov, and Philip Dimitrov were the candidates nominated to chair the Coordinating Council of the Union of Democratic Forces. The first three were presented as "moderate", while the next two were described as "radical." The final choice was the least famous among the six candidates. Here is the course of events:

The voting took place on December 11, with the participation of the 15 organizations that were members of the UDF. Just before the start of the voting procedure, Dertliev requested to be struck from the list of candidates. This act of the ambitious 74-year-old politician surprised many. It took several months before it became clear that Dr. Dertliev had actually planned to take the Bulgarian Social Democratic Party out of the coalition at the worst possible moment for the UDF and forget his anticommunist convictions.

At the first round Dimitrov received 4 votes. Yordanov had 3. Simeonov received 2 votes, and so did Gaytandzhiev and Ganev. There was also one blank ballot and one abstention. At that time Petko Simeonov withdrew from the race and appealed to those who had voted for him to vote for Philip Dimitrov. The results of the second tour were as follows: Dimitrov - 7 votes, Yordanov - 4, Gaytandzhiev - 2, Ganev - 1, and one invalid ballot. The third tour ended with 8 votes for Dimitrov, 5 for Yordanov, 1 for Ganev, and one invalid ballot. According to the established procedure, it was necessary for the elected candidate to win by qualified majority. Alexander Yordanov ceded in favor of Philip Dimitrov, so a fourth round was not necessary.

...

Today Bulgarians with noncommunist thinking can easily imagine what would have become of the Union of Democratic Forces if, in December 1990, one of the other candidates had been elected Chairman of its Coordinating Council instead of Philip Dimitrov. The roads that Dertliev, Simeonov, Gaytandzhiev, and Ganev chose leave no room for doubt that under their leadership the opponents of the red regime in the country would have been left without a political organization.

Regardless of whether this was his own decision, or as many people believe - Peter Dertliev acted under duress from the communists - the Marxist-Social democrat did everything within his power to ruin the UDF at the next parliamentary elections in October 1991. And that was not all. After that year, on a number of important occasions he lent a "fraternal shoulder" in support of his former adversaries and inquisitors - the renamed communists. Following his conduct, and recalling various moments in the life of the politician-physician, some Bulgarians suspect that he had also been recruited in the past by the State Security services.[28]

The subsequent actions of the Deputy Chairman of the Union of Democratic Forces, Petko Simeonov, did not surprise people as much. He had provoked mistrust in many of them for a long time. In the capacity of Editor-in-Chief of the *Demokratsiya* daily and member of the Committee for verification of the parliamentary elections in June 1990, he failed to make public the evidence of vote-rigging and manipulation on the part of the Bulgarian Socialist Party. Simeonov simply remained a *perestroika* man. When the blue coalition started strengthening its structure and its anticommunist character in 1991, he and his followers from the Federation of the Clubs for Democracy split off and became its opponents. Petko Simeonov went on to chair a succession of small formations outside of Parliament, and his fame gradually faded away. Incidentally, his name came up once again in an embezzlement scandal at the Foreign Aid Agency whose Director he had been for a year and a half.

As a leader, Stefan Gaytandzhiev would have been even more ruinous to the future of the Union of Democratic Forces. The philosopher, who was UDF Secretary and member of the *Ecoglasnost* leadership, left the opposition coalition with a part of his organization in 1991. However, that did not end his political career. In the Thirty-Seventh National Assembly, Gaytandzhiev was given the high-power position of Deputy Chairman of the Parliamentary Group of the Bulgarian Socialist Party. He held that position in the Thirty-Eighth National Assembly as well, this time as the only deputy to the Chairman of the already doubly diminished socialist parliamentary group. Stefan Gaytandzhiev fulfilled his obligation to the BSP diligently and turned into one of the most malicious and active enemies of the UDF.

Within just a year or two the next claimant for UDF leadership, Stoyan Ganev, succeeded in utterly outraging even his most ardent supporters with a series of unprincipled actions. In hindsight his 1990 proposal that Bulgaria should start the processes of democratization and transition to a market economy not by adopting the appropriate laws but through parliamentary

---

[28] Maria Govedarova in a conversation with the author, Sofia, Bulgaria, August 23, 1998.

elections for a Grand National Assembly, which would draft a new Constitution, appears suspicious. Stoyan Ganev rapidly rose in the hierarchy of the opposition coalition. He became UDF spokesman and Deputy Chairman of the Parliamentary Alliance of the Democratic Forces in the Seventh Grand National Assembly. As Minister of Foreign Affairs in Philip Dimitrov's government, he stood out as one of the most stubborn critics of every cabinet initiative. After a series of schemes and plots against the executive body of which he himself was a member, against the Prime Minister, and against the interests of the UDF, the lawyer Ganev ended his political career ignominiously in 1993. In 2001, he tried to start it again, but it did not work.

The last unelected candidate for head of the UDF Coordinating Council, Alexander Yordanov, Deputy Chairman of the Bulgarian Radical Democratic Party and subsequently its Chairman, remains a leading member of the UDF until today. Intelligent and emotional, he was among the favorites of the UDF supporters at first. He earned their affection with his rich and flowery speeches, in which he coined memorable phrases, colorful metaphors and comparisons, as well as his sonorous voice and imposing presence. The anticommunists in Bulgaria also loved the *Vek 21* [*21st Century*] weekly newspaper where he was Editor-in-Chief. Yordanov was well liked while he was Spokesman of the Parliamentary Alliance of the Democratic Forces in the Grand National Assembly and Chairman of the UDF Parliamentary Group in the Thirty-Sixth National Assembly. However, when he became Speaker of the Bulgarian Parliament for two years in 1992, Alexander Yordanov disappointed his admirers to some extent.

Obviously a lot happened later. But in December 1990, all five politicians listed above enjoyed popularity and influence to a greater or lesser degree. The choice of Philip Dimitrov as the opposition leader of Bulgaria surprised the citizens of the country, who knew very little about him. The daily *Demokratsiya* did not add much to their knowledge. It only published the following brief report:

> Philip Dimitrov, 35 years old, is the new Chairman of the UDF Coordinating Council. He was elected at the third round of the secret voting this afternoon.
>
> He completed his secondary education at the English Language High School in Sofia and holds a degree in Law from the University of Sofia *St. Kliment Ohridski*. He is a member of the Green Party, married, and not a member of any "informal" organizations before November 10. He has never been a member of the Bulgarian Communist Party. He is not a Member of Parliament.
>
> ...

> "We are not a conspiratorial organization, and the more that is known about us, the better," Mr. Dimitrov said shortly after he was elected Chairman of the UDF Coordinating Council. "The Chairman of the Coordinating Council is actually a moderator. He does not even have voting and decision-making rights," Mr. Dimitrov explained. He hopes that with the help of all organization members of the UDF, big and small, work can continue in the best way possible.[29]

And that was that. The third leader of the democratic opposition remained largely unknown to the broader public. Maybe the politicians who elected him thought that this would not change. The only thing that mattered to them was that the new leader of the coalition would not be one of them. They needed a Chairman with no reputation or authority, so that the Union of Democratic Forces would be weakened. Some of the leaders of the political parties and federations were openly striving towards such an outcome for their own personal reasons or on the orders of the communist/socialist party.

Philip Dimitrov, the UDF Deputy Chairman for International Relations, seemed suitable for their purposes. He was quiet, polite, peaceful and ready for compromise, without influential friends and without any real enemies. He also was the only one among the candidates for the high office who was not Member of Parliament, which gave them additional certainty that they would be able to manipulate him.

Indeed, who could assume then that from that moment on the "UDF stack of cards" - about which Andrey Lukanov in an interview confessed that the Bulgarian Communist Party had put together and meant to control[30] - would be shuffled? Who would suppose that this young lawyer would succeed in laying the foundation of a united party of the noncommunists in Bulgaria, in place of the loosely bound coalition with most diverse interests? On December 11, 1990, hardly anyone could have guessed that Philip Dimitrov would lead the Union of Democratic Forces four years and prove himself worthy of the position.

---

[29] *Demokratsija* daily, *The new Leader of the UDF,* December 12, 1990.

[30] Melone 1998, p. 70.

19. An Attempt at a Portrait of Philip Dimitrov

Back in 1992, someone wrote that it was high time for the Bulgarian people to give up the character traits acquired in imitation of the communist dictator Todor Zhivkov - a stubborn know-it-all attitude, vulgar cunning, and crude pragmatism - and to acquire those of their Prime Minister, Philip Dimitrov. Indeed, the leader of the Union of Democratic Forces from 1990 to 1994 possesses qualities that many Bulgarians lost during the communist era: straightforwardness, incorruptibility, tolerance, consideration for others, idealism, faith in God, and a lack of malice, jealousy, and avarice. Maybe this is why, for many people he was an old-fashioned politician, while others viewed him as a leader of the future. Dimitrov, however, proved to be useful precisely in the present, with his intelligence, perspicacity and consistency. He fulfilled his crucial mission during some of the most critical years in the political life of post-communist Bulgaria. Then he loyally continued to be of service to his successors in the name of democracy and integrity.

Philip Dimitrov largely remains a mystery, especially if one only hears and reads the contradictory reports about him. Some accuse him of vanity, dictatorial style, haughtiness, and extremism in his views and actions. Others blame him for his excessive tolerance, extreme adherence to principles, and superfluous gentlemanliness. Some would add that he is the mastermind of the UDF, a moral model in politics, or even that he is secretive and has a definite passion for behind-the-scenes games. Others believe that he is cordial, warm and selfless as a person, or that he is inaccessible, cold, and reclusive. Some say he has done a lot for Bulgaria, while others assert that he has not done anything the way he should have. Hardly any contemporary Bulgarian politician has evoked more conflicting feelings of love and admiration and of hatred to the extent of total negation and contempt. There is nothing half-way about him.

. . .

A lot could be understood about Philip Dimitrov, his character and inner spiritual self, by reading two of his books. *For They Lived, Oh Lord* is probably one of the wisest and most beautifully written works of historical fiction in Bulgarian. What is even more amazing is that it was written when the author was just over 30 years old. He deftly takes on the role of the narrator, an "uneducated and not very literate" old man called Todor who lived on the turbulent Balkan Peninsula in the early 14th century, and creates dozens of flesh and blood images of men, women, children, and youth of different nationalities and faiths.

Dimitrov does not idealize his characters. They are never staunchly black and white. Instead, they are real people, torn by passions, ambitions, contradictions, righteousness, and sin. Their personal fates, love affairs, feelings, eroticism, aspirations, and yearnings have been rendered with psychological insight and enviable knowledge of the depths of the human soul. Philip does not glorify historical events in his book either. They have been rendered truthfully and accurately, without any outbursts of patriotism. He is primarily interested in their impact on the lives and fates of the ordinary people to whom he has given all his love.

The author's gift for languages is apparent in his apt use of Old Church Slavonic, which matches the frequently metaphysical content of the text. Nevertheless, *For They Lived, Oh Lord* sounds very contemporary at times, if not in style and in the choice of lexical means, at least in content. When Dimitrov interprets public and political events dating back to the Middle Ages, he alludes to the faults and crimes of the totalitarian society in which he wrote the novel. Today it is easy to read between the lines of the book and recognize the future fate of Philip Dimitrov himself as a politician and statesman:

> How difficult it is, oh Lord, for people to face something that is new and different from their crushing daily lives with an open heart. How difficult it is for them to make their own what someone else has already been lucky to meet and find beautiful. When he offers it to them, they seem to feel that he has gone one step ahead of them, which makes them feel inferior and makes them embittered about him in vain.[1]

It is also possible to understand Philip's attitude towards violence through his writing:

> Through him they would have proven that war is not a great deed before which to stand in awe, but an ordinary brigandage, even when its aim is claimed to be just. That is so because even the oppressed and the tortured - I witnessed that with real horror, Lord, in the rebellions of the zealots in Thessaloniki - slaughter their oppressors in the name of justice. They massacre the tormentor's children out of pain, claiming they wished to eradicate oppression in this way as well as the possibility of revenge in the future. They also please their flesh with their women and daughters, and they cannot justify this with anything else but their own malice, selfish needs, and desires. Moreover, simple folk often see war as a means to put some money aside, to get something for themselves and have women with impunity.[2]

---

[1] Dimitrov 1997, p. 25.

[2] *Ibid.*, p. 84.

The passage below shows why Dimitrov did not try to have his book published immediately after he completed it in the spring of 1989, but offered it to print after the collapse of the communist regime:

> In an empire like the Byzantine one even the Patriarch is subordinated to the Emperor, meaning that even the spiritual leaders of the people have to serve and invariably obey the ruler. Thus, the spiritual leadership is tied to the tyrant's carriage and has the sole purpose of supporting his rule. Nothing can improve in such a reign. In contrast, I have heard that in the Anjou Kingdom, the severe Dominican monks, the kind Franciscans and the wise silent Benedictines aspire to God's words in different ways, each calling the people to the Kingdom of the Lord in his own way. If practice is not different in its essence, it is bound to turn into a narrow cell and those who remain in it are unfortunate. At the same time those who can still serve God with their hearts would be following their own way, eventually finding themselves left out of the cell and proclaimed to be its enemies. Such a kingdom is essentially incorrigible and it is no wonder that Byzantium is doomed to die.[3]

The religious tolerance of the old man Todor permeates the entire novel and suggests that the person who created his character detested all dictatorial principles restricting speech, faith and thought:

> Can wisdom be locked into a single faith? Could it not be that people of a different faith have among them men worthy and wise, so that we mistakenly brush away lightly what they have achieved? And even I who knew least and had read least of them all, even I did not exclude myself from their deliberations, and they accepted me as their equal. They were not trying to impose their learnedness upon me because they thought that the more diverse the knowledge and thoughts of the people were, the easier it would be through their communion to come together to the truth.[4]

Philip Dimitrov, the man accused by the members and supporters of the renamed Bulgarian Communist Party of "blue fascism" and "witch hunts" wrote the following:

> Punishment, Lord, has something to do not with the transgression, but with power. And so those who "dispense punishment" are fighting not against transgressions, they are fighting for power and power alone. Hence it is easy for

---

[3] *Ibid.*, p. 87.

[4] *Ibid.*, p. 119.

> them to punish people for being Jews, for being rich, for being poor or for having experienced violence, for having put up a fight or for not caring, or for something their ancestors had done once upon a time. Everything can be a pretext for the man aspiring to power to wield punishment.[5]
>
> It is true that King Mihail took several cities from the Byzantines, but I see no merit in chronicles that measure the greatness of a state by the lands conquered and forget about the life of the people in these lands and in their former confines. A powerful state is not one that has the broadest borders, not even one that has the most numerous troops, but rather one in which people think calmly about tomorrow, in which the peasants are not hungry, the city dwellers are respected and profit from their work, and the dynasts serve their master not because they are afraid or with hatred, but because they are enlightened and they see that his wishes and aspirations are much like their own.[6]

If the word "zealots" is substituted with "communists", it becomes evident what Dimitrov had in mind when he wrote his book and where he got his in-depth understanding about the crimes of the poor citizens of Thessaloniki, who rebelled against the feudal system:

> The zealots had proclaimed themselves to be the defenders of the faith, but the first thing they had forgotten was God's highest command to love and respect one's neighbor. They had come to respect only themselves. They had proclaimed that they were rising against the excessive wealth of the minority in the name of the well-being of the majority. However, instead of something good, they had given the majority only fear, trying to instill base feelings among them. They made everyone watch everyone else and count the other's jewels and the morsels on his plate, so that by betraying the other to the merciless power he would be able to enjoy not so much what had been taken away, but the very fact that something is being taken away from someone else.[7]

Here is the opinion of the future Prime Minister of Bulgaria on the natural reaction of the population to economic reforms. The text reads as if it has been written for our days and demonstrates the author's skill in depicting the characters of people accurately:

> He viewed his power with a becoming seriousness and was watchful. Heeding Dimitar's opinions above all, trying through moderate easing of the

[5] *Ibid.,* p. 154.

[6] *Ibid.,* p. 214.

[7] *Ibid.,* pp. 301-302.

> life of the ordinary people and through equally moderate restrictions on the wealthier ones to make the life of his people easier, while preserving and even augmenting the power of the state and of the troops. However, as it often happens, these sensible measures, being indeed moderate, barely made those who benefited from them happy. Thus, the beneficiaries often turned into even greater opponents to the changes than the ones who had been deprived of some of their wealth. Because those who have riches, however sensitive they may be to any encroachment upon their wealth, have more strength to look to the future. They only have to be convinced that what they are being deprived of today could come back to them in one way or another tomorrow. In contrast, those who have become shortsighted under the burden of their poverty, are hardly tempted by anything that is in the distant future. They wish to get everything here and now, except if the future is flooded with an incredibly bright light, or when they are promised rivers of milk and honey that have never flowed in this world, nor - apparently - ever will.[8]

The last lines of *For They Lived, Oh Lord* indisputably express the credo of the author himself, for whom "there is no wisdom without a heart":

> And even if every word of the Holy Scripture was mistaken, these two still remain: Love and Freedom. And what other words can be the pillars of God's testament but Freedom and Love.[9]

With his second work *The True Story of the Knights of the Round Table,* Philip Dimitrov turns to the young readers, retelling for them in an accessible and beautiful way the legend of King Arthur and his knights. Written in a very short time, this tale is a reminder of the somewhat forgotten moral virtues of valor, loyalty, courage, honor and duty. The book is also a rejection of treachery, treason and cunning.

However, for the adult reader the same text can be interpreted in an entirely different way. Through its allegories and the wisdom of experience, it imperceptibly leads us to our times, bringing to mind Dimitrov's own acts as a politician and statesman, as well as those of his supporters and of his enemies.

Many were misled by the title *The True Story of the Knights of the Round Table.* When rumors spread about the book back in 1997, quite a few Bulgarians expected that it would provoke a political rather than a literary sensation. Initially they thought that Dimitrov had decided to expose the secret negotiations around the National Round Table in 1990 and the subsequent political games. In fact, the tale was written in the spring of 1986. The only

---

[8] *Ibid.,* pp. 305-306.

[9] *Ibid.,* p. 319.

reason that the acts of the former UDF leader and Prime Minister of Bulgaria could be discerned in this work was that Philip Dimitrov never betrayed his principles. What he believed in the mid-1980s, remained valid in the mid-1990s, and later too.

...

There was a great disconnect between the moral values advocated in the fiction written by a humanist who became a politician and the Bulgarian post-communist reality. This was clearly demonstrated by the socialist, pro-socialist and tabloid press that spewed indiscriminate propaganda against the third UDF leader. Obviously, the shuffling of the "stack of cards" was not to their liking. They accused him of everything and anything, attributing all kinds of vices and shortcomings to him. When Philip Dimitrov became Prime Minister of Bulgaria, there was no limit to the distortions, outright lies and scheming against him.

The trouble was that the slander against him was spread not only by the reds. There were quite a number of noncommunists who repeated the media clichés without thinking of the real political situation in the country and without realizing who Dimitrov was fighting against and what his aspirations were. On the other hand, those who thought more rationally and more independently, and evaluated the motives behind his actions in the context of current events, discovered different traits in his character. Here are the opinions of the actor Yosif Sarchadzhiev, the screenplay writer and director Rayna Tomova, and the linguist and actress Anna Sarchadzhieva:

> Yosif: Philip Dimitrov turned into the epitome of the incomprehensible man. He remained enigmatic to the majority of people. He passed as a bright star, but nevertheless some lack of clarity remained in his presence. Why? Because his very character did not make it possible for him to stoop and go lower than he would be prepared to go. His enigmatic nature did not come from his hiding something, but simply because he does not explain what he means to the end. He believes that his interlocutor would be able to understand him immediately. This is why he is not a leader for the square and for the street.
>
> Rayna: He is a politician. Philip is a great politician. And it is not true that he remained incomprehensible and undeciphered. Something very strange happened with him. A part of the UDF supporters almost rejected him and would not accept him as Prime Minister. They said, "Yes, it is true that he is very devoted to the cause. But he is much too intelligent, he speaks much too vaguely and his very presence is much too ambiguous for him to be the head of state at this moment." The rest of the people, with whom I identify, watched

him with admiration, even bordering on deification. This is how I personally considered Philip Dimitrov when he was Prime Minister. He evoked only admiration in me when he appeared on the TV screen and when he spoke in Parliament so intelligently and always so accurately. Therefore, my impression is that he did not remain incomprehensible, but that he was accepted absolutely controversially.

Yosif: Philip evolved very much. During the brief period when he was in charge of the government of Bulgaria, it was possible to see how his speeches and statements became more and more accessible and clearer. There was another thing: he had a very clear logic when he spoke, and he knew what he was achieving with it. He was not an elementary populist. He did not speak about elementary issues. He would not rally the masses in an elementary way. He did not provoke superficial sentiments.

Rayna: He possesses intelligence of the highest kind.

Yosif: Yes, he does. And this is why the communists were so dead set against him. Philip Dimitrov was a very strong adversary. With his analytical mind, he thwarted their scheming and games.

Rayna: And he remained absolutely unyielding to pressure. One of the very few politicians during that time who was absolutely unsusceptible to unacceptable compromise. He did not show even an ounce of collaborationism with the communists. He simply said, "I swear I shall never call that party socialist, only communist." Philip kept his word, for which he was repeatedly accused by the communists in Parliament - with some justification - that it was unconstitutional for him to dare, as Prime Minister, to refer to that party in this way, that this party had a name and that it is a socialist party, the Bulgarian Socialist Party, etc., etc. I have listened to him hundreds of times. I wanted to see whether he would yield to the pressure in the long run, as a statesman, not as a political figure, but as a leader of the state. But this never happened.

Yosif: Philip was like an ice-breaker. The times required of him to be that way. It was not possible to maneuver. That is precisely his big merit in Bulgarian history. If he had succumbed to the treacheries that started then, like those of Zhelyu Zhelev, instead of doing what he did, instead of opposing them, we would not have today's UDF. With his conduct Philip Dimitrov laid the foundations of the organization. Thanks to him it did not implode. Philip kept the worthy people and threw out the secret agents, the traitors and the informers that had infiltrated the democratic union. A lot of courage is required to do this, and he found that courage.

Rayna: Dimitrov did the dirty work. He preserved the whole but had to perish politically in the process. I would like to say something about his exceptionally dignified and consistent conduct after 1994, when he was no longer so popular. Then he was neither Prime Minister, nor UDF leader. I made a point of watching his statements, his reactions, his evaluations about Ivan Kostov and the others who came to power. Such dignified behavior!

There was not a single note of bitterness in Philip, or one of self-admiration, not even once.

Yosif: Ivan Kostov is the political child of Philip Dimitrov. Philip launched him, made way for him and pushed him forward. What is more, he created the right atmosphere for him. This is very important and very rare. This is what I call a true politician of the highest rank, one who thinks about the future. Philip saw that Kostov was the man for the times ahead and that at that moment Ivan appeared to be the most promising figure in the eyes of the voters. If Dimitrov possessed any natural meanness, he could have worked maliciously against Kostov, but he did just the opposite. Generally speaking, Philip created many of the leading politicians today.

Ivan Kostov is the other side of Philip Dimitrov. If these two men could blend to form one person, that would have been the perfect politician, but then everything would have been somewhat blander. It is good that both of them exist. Their personal qualities are developed to the extreme and Bulgaria needs both of them.

As a matter of fact, I know very little about Philip as a person, because we have not been in close contact. Nevertheless, I sense a tremendous poetic charge in his soul. That is evident in his books and it also transpires in his relationships beyond the strictly official contacts. Externally he demonstrates a stony and even iron appearance, but to me this is a kind of mask that hides an extremely tender soul. A fragile soul, if you wish. After one of the rallies I asked him if he was deeply religious. He answered, 'No, I am not religious, I have faith.' There is nothing strange in this. Philip is not dogmatic. Religion can be a dogma. Faith is something else.

Philip Dimitrov had premonitions. When UDF politicians came to us in the City of Truth or when we met with them outside the tent city, all of them were displeased with our presence in the square, especially those who were Members of Parliament in the Grand National Assembly like Stoyan Ganev, Grandpa Stefan Savov, Beron, and Alexander Yordanov. Zhelyu was not with us either. He summoned us to dissuade us. Apparently we were a thorn in their side, because we were preventing them from cooking up their own little games. Philip, who was then Deputy Chairman of the UDF, was among the few people who stood firmly behind us. He was aware that a street movement, a mass presence in the street was keeping the communists in check and that only the events taking place in the streets and squares gave the UDF confidence and a strong position. Philip sensed this and he supported us.

Rayna: This man is capable of incredible perseverance.

Anna: He is not a person that thinks one thing and says something else, and this can be sensed.

Yosif: His frequent appearance among the people in the City of Truth was very refreshing. You could acquire real self-confidence by communicating with him, although he is never intimate. Philip does not wear the mask of hatred on his face. However, you can sense his hatred for communism without any outward expression, without his demonstrating it. It is the opposite with me. Simply my profession and my emotionality are such that I show it. He does not have to show it; his actions prove it, and they were supported by his logic, by his managerial logic. At the public rallies Philip Dimitrov spoke in a calm voice, and this had a very strong effect. He did not show off his rhetoric, like the informer of the secret services Georgi Markov did.

Anna: He inspired confidence. His speeches from the rostrum were the speeches of a man who is true to his thoughts. That had a very strong impact on me. It inspired tremendous security in me and in many of the people listening to him in the squares. One could sense depth in what he was saying in terms of tone, conduct, and content. He was able to communicate his deep confidence to us. Psychologically that was the impact that Philip Dimitrov had on me.

Yosif: Exactly! In terms of tone, in terms of conduct, in terms of content, he is a psychoanalyst of the masses. The other speakers were much more emotional and hot-tempered, while Philip calmed down the emotions and brought in reason. He is definitely a rational person and that was very much needed at a time of excessive outbursts of pathos, leading nowhere. Dimitrov was putting things where they belonged and was channeling the flood into the riverbed. This is extremely important for a politician, and he was good at it. Politics in this country was initially a lot of shouting and street enthusiasm. Philip transformed these rampant emotions into a weapon by channeling them. He is a very interesting person, multi-faceted, I think. He has many layers. When we are talking now, it appears that he is a man who only thinks and acts rationally and with a cool head, without feelings, but that is not the case. It seems to me that just because he is so strongly emotional he needs his strong will to...

Anna: Self-control, Philip Dimitrov has self-control. He analyzes. But nevertheless his emotion is felt and this is why his words have such a strong impact.

Yosif: He manages to control the excessive emotions and to choose the most suitable thing that needs to be said, and say it. This is why he was so good in the TV debates with the communists. He finds the hyperbole, he finds the image that can best explain the facts. Therefore, I say that he is an emotionally rich personality.

There was a horrifying truth in his statement that Bulgarians would be going in circles in the desert for forty years like the Jews did before they reached the Promised Land. He said it on television when he was Prime Minister. For me this was the most open and sincere thing I have ever heard from a politician, but the people did not like that. They did not like the bitter truth of the message "Bulgarians, have no illusions, know what is in store for you after communism."

Rayna: One of his last speeches in Parliament as Prime Minister was also remarkable. I don't remember the words exactly, but I do remember the impression I still have after that speech so full of insight. It was a look into Bulgaria's tomorrow. That really struck me. Almost as a prophet Philip foretold what came next, namely the mafia gaining ground, the corruption...I personally have a very high regard for his work as Prime Minister of Bulgaria in an extremely difficult situation.

Yosif: If only he was not forced to appoint several people in his cabinet on the insistence of Trenchev and of some other people, who betrayed him, who led him to slip on a banana peel, I think he would have done much more in spite of the resistance of Parliament. His team betrayed him. In spite of the hurdles, an improvement in the life of people was clearly felt during Dimitrov's rule. The trouble is his enemies didn't leave him alone. I think they organized 41 strikes against him. Then, to manipulate public opinion, they accused him of being against everything and everybody.

Philip did an enormous amount of work in his last two years as the UDF leader. That was when he finished the big cleaning of the Augean stables. Thanks to him, Ivan Kostov took over a strengthened organization. However, not everyone understood that. And many of the UDF supporters started hating Philip.

Rayna: What about the invitation that he extended to the communist leader Zhan Videnov for a meeting in the beginning of 1994, which provoked the elections in December? That was yet another big sacrifice on Philip's part. Some of the UDF supporters accused him of that, too. People started saying, "Look, Dimitrov made sure to bring the communists back to power with an absolute majority," and they started hating him. However, Philip Dimitrov actually shortened the period of "timelessness" during Berov's government, when the country was being destroyed and plundered, without the crimes being blamed on the communists. In the long run, Philip sped up the processes that brought the Union of Democratic Forces back to power in 1997.

Yosif: Obviously, Dimitrov's arguments then were that if the communists won the elections and took the power, they would ripen, rot and fall off the political stage. He foresaw all that! Philip's passion for psychiatry and psychotherapy is something that should not be ignored. This lawyer is interested in the innermost and invisible layers of the human soul. That is very rare.

The conduct of Philip Dimitrov as UDF leader and as Prime Minister of Bulgaria was firm and consistent. He managed to create the impression of being tolerant and open to suggestions, but above all he firmly defended the anticommunist cause. Some people accused him of being dictatorial. Such reproaches appear ridiculous to me. There was no other option then.[10]

---

[10] Yosif Sarchadzhiev, Rayna Tomova and Anna Surchadzhieva in a conversation with the author, Sinemorets, Bulgaria, July 10 and 11, 1998.

Dr. Krum Savov, a psychiatrist, holds the following view of the first democratically elected Prime Minister of Bulgaria after World War II:

> Philip Dimitrov won me over right from the start by being reasonable. The least that can be said about him is that he is a wise man.[11]

Maria Govedarova, a retired accountant, shares the opinion:

> Philip Dimitrov is an accomplished democrat. He is a very honest man, extremely honest, to my mind. He is also ambitious, very ambitious. He wanted people to believe him. Highly intelligent, he argued very well with the communists, with restraint and wisely. He did everything within his power to put Bulgaria back on the road to democracy.[12]

Ivan Kurtev, Member of Parliament from the UDF, Deputy Speaker of the Thirty-Seventh and Thirty-Eighths National Assemblies, also thinks highly of Philip Dimitrov:

> Philip is the martyr of our revolution, a highly intelligent man who did a great job in those days. He left behind a Union of Democratic Forces without the problems it had earlier, a normal UDF. Maybe career-seekers or dishonest people could sneak in in the future. Perhaps even the odd former informer or secret service agent could do that. However, the practice of sitting in meetings for 7-8 hours and being unable to reach a decision on things that are so important both for the UDF and the nation, would hardly ever happen again.
>
> As the leader of the blue union, Philip Dimitrov was trying all the time to play down the conflicts in order to avoid splits in the organization. He was very patient and very tolerant. Yet, he never gave in on essential matters - matters of principle, never.[13]

This is how the actor and then Director of the *Vazrazhdane* Theater in Sofia Georgi Georgiev (Zhoro) evaluated the role of Philip Dimitrov:

> After all the disappointments, Philip Dimitrov's presence at the head of the Union of Democratic Forces bred trust in the organization among many UDF supporters. He was the first leader of the opposition who always used the word "communists", not "socialists." And he is doing it to this day. People liked this tremendously. They had the feeling that many UDF leaders were flirting with

---

[11] Dr. Krum Savov in a conversation with the author, Plovdiv, Bulgaria, August 23, 1998.

[12] Maria Govedarova in a conversation with the author, Sofia, Bulgaria, August 23, 1998.

[13] Ivan Kurtev in a conversation with the author, Sofia, Bulgaria, August 18, 1998.

the renamed party. Whether it was flirting, agreement, or reconciliation does not matter; the idea was that it would be something like the soviet *perestroika*. Since he was the only persistent anticommunist, Dimitrov acquired many enemies. For a certain period of time he seemed to remain rather lonely.

In my opinion, Philip Dimitrov's weakness consists of the fact that he is an isolated person. Probably over years of re-evaluation he would come to the conclusion that this can be the conduct of a writer, of an intellectual, but not of a public figure. I think that this peculiarity of his was to his detriment. He has to build better communication skills and overcome his coolness, his aloofness, his restraint and possibly also some inner complexes. He should improve the communication, not with the people he knows, but with the rest. However, when he says something, he does not go back on his word, and this is good.

In his televised debates with the communist leaders Dimitrov crushed them like a tank. Ivan Kostov, for example, is different. He expresses his view, but allows for an answer. He is ready for dialogue, while Philip Dimitrov does not want an answer from them. He simply crushed them intelligently.

For this reason from the very beginning he had the strongest anticommunist presence in my eyes. Everybody else was ready for a compromise, for closeness. Only he was not. Many people are trying to belittle his merits. However, for an enormous majority of the UDF supporters in Bulgaria, he remained the first politician who started speaking in the language of the anticommunists. That position of his was very important in those revolutionary years.

When he spoke, he often started with introductory words, which were sometimes a bit too much, but at the end came something that provoked a burst of applause. After the vulgarity in Bulgarian public life - I am referring to Tano Tsolov, Peko Takov and the rest of the communist dignitaries - at long last an intelligent miracle came, a miracle that spoke with the words of a sage. We had all been plunged in vulgarity, the whole nation, and we were unable to gain an insight into everything that he was telling us. We expected Philip to be one of us, shouting at the public rallies, but he was not that. He was for that part of the people who understood him. For example, my wife Keva was crazy about him, and not only she, while I sometimes had the impression that he was wasting my time. I would have preferred his speech to be more direct.

The strong personality of Philip Dimitrov, albeit controversial and with all the criticism that could be addressed to him, precisely his strong personality put all cards openly on the table. That divided people into those who were with him and those who were against him. Everyone found an argument in support of his/her own attitude. Some said that he spoke unintelligibly because he was weak. Others claimed that he was the firmest of all democratic leaders.

In front of the UDF Central Office in Sofia, at 134 *Rakovski* Street, some of the people fought in support of Philip, while other fought against him. Many politicians would have envied him for such a polarized scene, because there are many whose names we don't even know - unknown Members of Parliament and cabinet ministers that no one has heard about.

Philip Dimitrov proved to be someone who played successfully his role in a difficult stage in Bulgarian history. He was extremely useful to democratic Bulgaria, but not to himself personally. The time of his leadership was unfavorable. He had nothing to back him, neither Parliament, nor a unified party, nor a mature nation. He was a lonely intellectual who did not wish to betray himself, not that he was able to do it anyway. He would not have turned into a populist to win more votes.

Before our eyes Dimitrov created politicians who had the needed qualities. He discovered Nadezhda Mihaylova, who became Minister of Foreign Affairs in 1997. He appointed her to become the spokesperson of the UDF and head of the Press Center of his government, and sent her to be trained at the Harvard School of Government. Our President Peter Stoyanov was Deputy Minister of Justice in his government. The present Prime Minister Ivan Kostov was his Finance Minister. The Speaker of the Bulgarian National Assembly Yordan Sokolov was his Minister of the Interior. The Mayor of Sofia Stefan Sofiyanski became during his time Deputy Chairman of the UDF National Coordinating Council. Today I trust all these people who grew up around Philip. They attained a lot in politics and a lot for Bulgaria.

The time while Philip Dimitrov was in the center of the political scene proved to be inadequate to himself personally. It did not support him. It is very different now. There will probably be no more UDF rallies at which we would be shouting "Down with ...!" Yet, Philip would sound much more comprehensible to the people today. He would win them over with his sense of perspective, with his culture, with ideas about the future and with social policy. There would still be two poles in public opinion. Some Bulgarians would surely grumble, "Is that one back again?" Others would be pleased, "Good, we are ready for him now![14]

. . .

Indeed, Philip Dimitrov's personality proved to be in opposition to a part of the Bulgarian nation. He possessed patience, sound judgment and foresight. He knew that the road to affluence was long and that in order to reach its end, it was necessary to make persistent constructive efforts accompanied by deprivations. Readiness for action was required as well. Through his policies Dimitrov succeeded in improving perceptibly the quality of life in the country during his short term in office. Bulgarians wanted more. They were not prepared to wait. They were yearning to live better, like people in the West did. Few were

[14] Georgi G. Georgiev in a conversation with the author, Sofia, Bulgaria, August 20, 1998.

aware that the wish of the people to have instant prosperity was unrealistic after decades of communist dictatorship.

With his experienced eye, Dr. Heinz Brahm, for many years Research Director of the Federal Institute of Eastern European and International Studies in Cologne, Germany, and one of the best known analysts of communist and post-communist societies, observed the following:

> Dimitrov's moral irreproachability tended to increase the aggressiveness of his critics. Maybe Philip Dimitrov was more suited to the Western world than to Bulgarian reality.[15]

Who is this man with such an atypical nature for present-day Bulgarians? How did he spend his childhood, his adolescence and his youth, before he wrote his name in the most recent history of his nation?

...

Philip Dimitrov was born in a cohesive patriarchal family, affected by communism, but not eroded by its poison. His father was a theologian. His mother could not complete her university education for political reasons and was compelled to work in the industrial sector. Philip grew up predominantly around his mother, grandmother, sister, and aunt. His grandmother, who was an educated woman, a mathematician, looked after him during the day. She taught him to read before he went to school, giving him not only children's books but more serious literature as well. It was precisely his grandmother who first taught him concepts like "honor" and "duty" that later became so deeply ingrained in his character. Having been formed as an individual mostly by women, they remained for Philip the object of permanent admiration and understanding.[16]

Years later, he would tell the journalist Eleonora Vladimirova:

> First of all, I don't agree with you that our society is feminized. It is feminized only to the extent to which a large portion of the slaves are female slaves. Women bear the burden of obligations and responsibilities approximately double to those of the men, and they have been given every opportunity to suffer as much as we do. Women continue to be underestimated. Men have been hit in terms of their full potential as the chief provider for the family. However, women, who also have the dubious "pleasure" of being the pillar in their families, acquire the feeling of a double

[15] Brahm 1998, pp. 28-29.

[16] Vladimirova 1991, pp. 21-23.

> inferiority, failing to cope with those specific things that give the inner atmosphere of a family. Women lack the time for sufficient care for her children, and as a result fall out of touch with them. They can feel worn out in their relationships because they are usually not treated with sufficient respect, and I mean the respect that is due to a lady. Man has his ways out, after all, for which he receives a pat on the back in the long run. Women could have them too, but there are sanctions and branding for that in this country.
>
> Everything that we are talking about eventually comes to: the role that men and women should have in the family structure. They both have a bad status in the Bulgarian family hit by communism because their reciprocal functions can neither be defined, nor exercised.[17]

Ever since he was a young child, Philip Dimitrov has known that the communist system is not good for people. Nevertheless, in his adolescence he read Karl Marx and Friedrich Engels "like mad" with the profound conviction that their works are mandatory reading. He devoted special attention to Marx and studied almost all his works. Later he recalled:

> Much to the horror of my father, my mother and their friends, I must have been about 17 when, reading Marx and Engels, I announced to them that it could not be denied, after all, that the socialist idea is more progressive than the capitalist one. I remember that one of the friends of my parents exclaimed, "Could it be that Philip has a communist girlfriend?"[18]

At the age of 21, Philip drew his conclusions and told the people around him about the absurdities, errors, contradictions and logical inconsistencies in dialectical and historical materialism.[19] The young man had reached these conclusions after "the hard toil of thought".

Completely modern in terms of conduct and habits, Philip Dimitrov has a marked passion for the past. He is interested in Antiquity, the Bible, the religions of the world, as well as the history of the nations, philosophy, classical music and literature, the art of the Middle Ages and that of the Renaissance. It is public knowledge that, parallel with his law studies, he devoted a lot of time to psychiatry and to individual and group psychotherapy. This is how he came to that:

> Everything started from the moment when a classmate and girlfriend of mine told me one day: 'You are a great psychasthenic!' At that time I was 18. I

[17] *Ibid.*, pp. 21-22.

[18] Philip Dimitrov in a conversation with the author, New York, U.S.A., March 20, 1998.

[19] *Ibid.*

> immediately started reading psychiatrists, the translations of Freud and other specialists. I was greatly intrigued, to the extent that I seriously considered studying psychology. However, law was something I had always known that I would study, so I chose it instead. When I was admitted to the Law School in Sofia, parallel with the lectures in law I started attending various lectures and seminars at the Medical Academy. Initially I went there with friends of mine who were medical students.[20]

Philip gradually attracted the attention of the faculty members. One day, the head of a department called him and suggested that they work together. The student admitted that he was not studying medicine but law. That Associate Professor had a choice of throwing him out of class or ignoreing the regulations of the university. He chose the latter. Dimitrov started work in the First Clinic of the Medical Academy, and there he met the psychiatrist Dr. Zhoro Kamenov, who taught him psychoanalysis. Philip treated patients between 1976 and 1985, applying various methods. He considers 1984 to have been his culmination in psychotherapy, when he used the psychodynamic method with which the therapist is maximally involved, and does not adhere merely to the role of a "white screen" as in pure analytical therapy.[21]

Philip Dimitrov has always supported the theory that the problem of communism lies in the nature of its regime, not in the personal shortcomings of Todor Zhivkov. In other words, Zhivkov was not to blame for the state of affairs - as most members of the Bulgarian Communist Party claimed, but the actual political system, which periodically reported one error after another, decade after decade. Is this not the best proof that communism is actually inapplicable?

When asked what is most abhorrent about communism, Dimitrov speaks of the brutality and the vulgar ambition to impose power. He goes on to explain that the other horrifying thing about the red totalitarian system is the prospect it offers the individual for a place in the world, without choice and free will.

Philip also thinks it is ridiculous to compare Christianity with Marxism merely because both teachings demonstrate concern about the poor. For him, in the Christian variant this is the result of the moral efforts of the individual, whereas in the communist one it is the work of impersonal commissars allocating rations in the different drawers of bureaucracy. In the first case those who have more are invited to give a share of what they possess, whereas in the second case an institution resembling a zoo is created. In theory, the warden of the zoo distributes the meat equally among the lions caged there, but actually he

---

20 *Ibid.*

21 *Ibid.*; Vladimirova 1991, pp. 19-20.

is giving much more to the lions he likes better. According to the lawyer, the inhumanness of the approach toward the individual makes existence in the communist society hopeless.[22]

. . .

Philip Dimitrov has been asked repeatedly what he thinks about himself and his character. He replies to such questions frankly, conscientiously, without posing and with humility.

Before Eleonora Vladimirova, he says that he is a poor actor and hence he prefers to improvise. He adds that he admits his own mistakes so that people would not talk about them behind his back, and that his self-control is a trait cultivated during his upbringing at home and a result of his practice as a psychotherapist.[23] In his conversation with Vladimirova in 1991, the Chairman of the Union of Democratic Forces declares:

> This is what I like as a personal position in politics: not to sit and build abstractions, but to take up things that have a bearing in practice.
>
> ...
>
> We need pragmatism in everything. However, not any pragmatism, but the intellectual kind.[24]

In another interview Dimitrov shares[25] that both politicians and statesmen need to think about things in terms of tasks to be completed. For him, assuming responsibility in government means knowing what one wants, how to do it and how to make things happen. Philip does not hide his pride with his consistent conduct and with the fact that he can subscribe to what he said in January 1990 and at any subsequent moment. He claims that he never felt an enormous need to be in power or to lead events. He was in the spotlight only when it was necessary and then he fought for the first prize.

The former UDF leader and Prime Minister of the Republic of Bulgaria sees himself as a man of compromise rather than someone plunging into situations and conflicts "head first." He apparently regrets some features in his character:

> If something, albeit right, is said to the wrong people at the wrong time, it is no longer right. I have had this problem all my life. I personally can swallow

---

[22] Philip Dimitrov in a conversation with the author, New York, U.S.A., March 20, 1998.

[23] Vladimirova 1991, pp. 9, 15. 25.

[24] *Ibid.*, pp. 24-25.

[25] Philip Dimitrov in a conversation with the author, New York, U.S.A., March 20, 1998.

humiliation and trouble relatively easily when I know in the name of what I am doing it. However, apparently this is not true of everybody. I am fully aware that some people from among our supporters, who did not like me, could have been won over with a slightly more flattering and flexible attitude toward them, which I - so help me God, not out of disrespect, but just like that, from all that confusion, and because of my deep conviction that they were all thinking like me - did not do. They thought that I was predetermining things.[26]

When asked how he managed to achieve the visible improvement in the standard of living of the Bulgarians while he was at the helm of the executive branch, Dimitrov answered with enviable modesty:

> This was not my merit. This was the merit of the actual process. I simply acted as a statesman who was not impeding the process.[27]

When reminded of the views of some authors that precisely he, while he was at the head of the country, did a lot in a very short time, Philip replied with a sigh, "Yes, but it remained unfinished."[28]

Having come to power after parliamentary elections in which the Union of Democratic Forces won by just 1 per cent over the Bulgarian Socialist Party, Philip Dimitrov never forgot that his government was hanging by a thread. To this day, his strongest feeling when he thinks about the thirteen months spent as Prime Minister of Bulgaria is his sense of racing against time.

---

[26] *Ibid.*

[27] *Ibid.*

[28] *Ibid.*

20. Agreement Honored "in the Communist Fashion"

On December 7, 1990, Dr. Zhelyu Zhelev nominated the 63-year-old judge Dimitar Popov for Chairman of the Council of Ministers. Popov had been Secretary of the Central Election Commission for the elections for Seventh Grand National Assembly in June. That very same National Assembly, in which the communists/socialists had an absolute majority, approved the President's proposal and asked the lawyer Popov to form a cabinet.

In order to sign a power-sharing agreement, the political movements with parliamentary representation began negotiating in late November and continued in December as well. The students on strike were indignant. On December 7, they declared that for them the negotiations meant that problems of vital importance for the future of the nation were going to be solved behind their backs. Four days later, the National Students' Strike Committee announced the end of the strike that had continued for over a month. Classes resumed.

The public exposure of the Chairman of the UDF Coordinating Council, Peter Beron, as collaborator of the secret security services had had its impact. On December 11, the opposition organization already had a new leader - Philip Dimitrov, but its prestige was substantially diminished. The Bulgarian Socialist Party gloated and demonstrated its usual attitude of superiority.

It was in this atmosphere that the final talks on forming a coalition "government of national consensus," as it was called, took place. They started on the day after Philip Dimitrov was elected leader of the opposition alliance. At first, the Union of Democratic Forces insisted that the Ministry of the Interior and the economic teams in the cabinet be headed by its representatives. The Bulgarian Socialist Party was opposed to that. Then the opposition proposed that the Minister of the Interior should be from the UDF with a Deputy Prime Minister from the BSP to monitor his work. Once again, the party of the socialists disagreed. It wanted the Minister of the Interior to be from the BSP with a Deputy Prime Minister from the UDF. After a meeting of the Coordinating Council, the UDF emphatically reiterated its claim for the Ministry of the Interior.

In the end, the realities of the day won. The Bulgarian Socialist Party had the majority in Parliament and the final word. As a result of the negotiations, the UDF received the Ministry of Finance with Minister Ivan Kostov, the Ministry of Industry, Trade and Services with Minister Ivan Pushkarov and the Ministry of Education with Minister Georgi Fotev. The Deputy Prime Ministers were representatives of the three most numerous parties in the Grand National Assembly: Alexander Tomov from the Bulgarian Socialist Party, Dimitar Ludzhev from the Union of Democratic Forces, and Victor Valkov from the Bulgarian Agrarian People's Union. The Prime Minister Dimitar Popov and the

Minister of the Interior Hristo Danov proclaimed themselves to be pro-democratic independents. With the exception of one or two agrarians, the remaining members of the Council of Ministers were from the BSP. Some of them had just completed their term in Andrey Lukanov's government. On December 20, 1990, the Grand National Assembly voted in the 78th government of Bulgaria.

...

On the third day of 1991, the political movements represented in the Seventh Grand National Assembly signed an agreement for a peaceful transition to a democratic society. Concerning the obligations of the Assembly, the document contained the following text:

> The legislative work of the Grand National Assembly should focus on the drafting and adoption of the following priority laws: the Constitution, the laws on farmland, local self-government, administrative and territorial division, election of local government bodies (Election Act) and privatization.[1]

The deadlines for this were fixed. The draft of the Constitution of the Republic of Bulgaria had to be submitted in February 1991 and adopted in March, along with the Election Act. The elections for local governments were due to be held in March, while those for an Ordinary National Assembly would be held by the end of May. The term of office of the new cabinet would end with the election of the following Parliament.

The parliamentary groups reached agreement on two other important issues. It was decided that the Bulgarian Socialist Party, as the successor of the Bulgarian Communist Party, carried the responsibility for the rule of Bulgaria in the past decades. The parties, the coalitions, public, political and trade union organizations and their companies, also agreed to account for their property and the way in which it had been acquired.

On January 28 at a briefing of the Union of Democratic Forces, its Chairman Philip Dimitrov drew attention to the fact that the political agreement of January 3 had been breached. The Bulgarian Socialist Party had not declared the nature of its property and was trying to delay the elections. It turned out that the lawyer was right.

---

[1] Agreement between the Political Forces of the Republic of Bulgaria, Sofia, January 1991, Library of the National Assembly.

On the next day, representatives of the BSP parliamentary group made the statement that the agreement between the political movements represented in the National Assembly cannot be considered binding. They also proposed that the local elections be postponed for the summer and the parliamentary elections for the end of 1991.

Indeed, there was no need for the former communists to rush things. On February 3, 2000, one of the leaders of the UDF, Alexander Yordanov - then Ambassador of the Republic of Bulgaria to Poland, Latvia, Lithuania and Estonia - wrote:

> The Grand National Assembly was elected for the purpose of drafting a new Constitution. Instead, the communist majority was bogged down in pseudo-legislative activities aimed at guaranteeing the dominating role of the communist *nomenklatura* in the country's public and economic life. The period of the Grand National Assembly coincided with the most widespread plundering and destruction of state property by means of exporting state capital to foreign banks through private companies. Later the propaganda machine of the communist party would blame the 'opposition and democracy' for all this. A part of the opposition served as political cover. The fact that the opposition remained in Parliament, and the manipulation of the possible disclosure of the secret files of activists of the UDF and agrarians who had collaborated with the State Security, practically legitimized the unimpeded plundering of the state and the transformation of the political power of the former communists into economic power.
>
> The agreements signed by the leaders of the opposition with the parliamentary majority of the Bulgarian Socialist Party called for the adoption of the Constitution by the end of March and new elections for an Ordinary National Assembly in May or June. Instead, the actual work on the Constitution started only in the beginning of March, and everything was done to prolong the life of the Grand National Assembly throughout 1991. At the same time, all over the country people who had supported the UDF at the parliamentary elections insisted that the Grand National Assembly should be resolved and new elections organized.[2]

...

In February and March 1991 a difference of opinion emerged in the leadership of the Union of Democratic Forces. The reason was the attitude of the organization towards the Seventh Grand National Assembly. Philip Dimitrov, Yordan Vasilev, Edwin Sugarev, Alexander Yordanov, Georgi Markov, Stoyan

---

[2] Ribareva and Nikolova 2000, pp. 314-318.

Ganev and Stefan Savov defended the idea of the need to provoke the dissolution of Parliament. Their arguments were that under the guise of reforms conducted by the government, the Bulgarian Socialist Party was taking charge of all economic power with impunity while redistributing state property among various party-owned private companies.

The idea of preserving the *status quo* at the Grand National Assembly was defended by the Federation of the Clubs for Democracy led by Petko Simeonov, the Green Party through Alexander Karakachanov, Peter Dertliev's Bulgarian Social Democratic Party, the *Nikola Petkov* Bulgarian Agrarian People's Union of Milan Drenchev, and the *Ecoglasnost* Independent Society through Georgi Avramov and Peter Slabakov. The latter two politicians would subsequently become Members of Parliament from the renamed communist party. The President of the Republic Zhelyu Zhelev hesitated in his allegiance but finally leaned in favor of the *perestroika*-type dissidents.[3]

Uninformed about the disputes in the UDF leadership, blue Sofia fully shared the views of the "rebels" led by Philip Dimitrov. On March 17, 1991, a mass rally of the opposition coalition was organized to insist on parliamentary elections no later than June. The protest by thousands of people was organized by the Sofia City Consultative Council (SCCC) of the UDF, which was established in June 1990. Its members, representative of the municipalities in Sofia, were displeased not only with the work of the Grand National Assembly, but also with the conduct of some of the UDF leaders. They were particularly outraged by UDF Secretary Stefan Gaytandzhiev, who assured them that demonstrations are no longer necessary, that the revolutionary period is over, and that the road to democracy is open, while Bulgaria was stripped to the bone by the plundering activities of the untouched *nomenklatura*.[4]

In order to protest against such opinions, the SCCC resumed its weekly public rallies and invited politicians who were not in the collaborationist circle. The speeches of Philip Dimitrov, Yordan Vasilev, Stefan Savov, Elka Konstantinova and the provisional blue UDF mayors of the Sofia municipalities diverged from the views of those who insisted on a "middle course." Instead, the opinions of the speakers were close to the sentiments and aspirations of the people filling the square. The blue leaders insisted that the Seventh Grand National Assembly be dissolved, that a Constitution drafted by a Parliament with a communist majority should not be adopted and that parliamentary elections should be held. The sooner all this was done, the better.[5] The

---

3 Dimitrov 1995(a).

4 Ivan Kurtev in a conversation with the author, Sofia, Bulgaria, August 18, 1998.

5 *Ibid.*

expectation was that these elections would certainly be won by the UDF because the popularity of the organization had increased substantially once again.

In March the lawyer Svetoslav Luchnikov submitted a draft of the Constitution of Bulgaria on behalf of the Bulgarian Radical-Democratic Party. This was an updated republican [as contrast of monarchical - *author's note*] version of the Tarnovo Constitution. It was professionally put together and demonstrated deep thinking and common sense. In spite of the indisputable merits of the text, it was rejected with scorn by the red party, which had its own views on the fundamental law of the country.[6]

In the middle of that same month, the UDF National Coordinating Council (NCC) chose Chairman Philip Dimitrov to be the one conducting negotiations for the unification of the entire democratic opposition in Bulgaria. Soon after that the UDF resolutely opposed the official stance of the Ministry of Foreign Affairs of the Soviet Union that the trials of former communist and state leaders in the former socialist countries would be considered equivalent to the persecution of dissidents.

On March 30, the UDF National Coordinating Council called a meeting of the representatives of the Coordinating Councils of all municipalities in the country as well as the UDF Members of Parliament. The participants in the forum concluded that it was unreasonable to expect that a legislative body with the composition of the Seventh Grand National Assembly would adopt a Constitution and laws promoting the overall dismantling of the totalitarian system. The vast majority expressed the wish to hold new parliamentary elections by mid-June.

With the typical spring storms in March, the winds brought new hope to the UDF leadership. After a series of disappointments and doubts, little by little faith grew stronger in the hearts of the democrats that their union was consolidating its anticommunist position and winning over broader sectors of the population. Still, some UDF leaders opposed the policies of Philip Dimitrov and his supporters. So did some Members of Parliament from the parties and organizations united in the opposition parliamentary alliance. The opponents of the UDF leader were displeased with his efforts to coordinate the conduct of different groups - members of the blue coalition - in Parliament, to build a stronger link between UDF structures outside Sofia and the organization's center and to transform the heterogeneous alliance into a nationwide political organization. Back in February 1991, in his lecture before the *Konrad Adenauer* Foundation in the Federal Republic of Germany, Philip Dimitrov had declared that the Union of Democratic Forces was a coalition in form, but that it should

---

[6] Dimitrov 1995(a).

become a party in essence.[7] Very soon his enemies in the UDF consolidated against him and his plan.

...

On April 4, the Grand National Assembly discussed an addendum to the political agreement of January 3, 1991, entitled *Decisions in Connection with the Work of the Grand National Assembly*. Its first provision read as follows:

> The work on drafting the new Constitution should be organized so that the debates about the draft in Parliament will start no later than the beginning of May 1991. In addition to the Constitution, it is necessary to adopt the Election Act for the general parliamentary elections. After the new Constitution is adopted, Parliament should make an official decision to dissolve in time for the elections for an Ordinary National Assembly.[8]

The dissolution of Parliament was to take place "in time" for the elections, but no deadlines were actually specified. A majority vote ratified the document.

Then Yordan Vasilev read a declaration drafted at the end of March and signed by 44 UDF Members of Parliament, in which they stated that the January agreement between the political forces had been breached by the Bulgarian Socialist Party. The schedule agreed upon had not been followed. The necessary laws for a change in the political system had not been drafted. The draft of the Constitution had not been submitted for discussion. Finally, two of the standing committees in Parliament did not function at all.[9] The protesting Members of Parliament proposed that precise dates be set for the adoption of the Constitution and the dissolution of the Grand National Assembly, followed by elections for an Ordinary National Assembly. If their demands were not met, they would leave the supreme legislative body at the end of April, letting their remaining colleagues to bear the burden of the "unpredictable consequences of such inaction".[10] The very same day Philip Dimitrov announced at a press conference that the leadership of the opposition alliance supported the statements of its Members of Parliament.

---

[7] Philip Dimitrov in a conversation with the author, New York, U.S.A., March 20, 1998.

[8] *Decisions in Connection with the Work of the Grand National Assembly*, Sofia, April 4, 1991, Library of the National Assembly.

[9] 116th Session of the Grand National Assembly, Sofia, Thursday, April 4, 1991, Library ofthe National Assembly.

[10] *Ibid.*

The rallies organized every Monday by the UDF National Coordinating Council and the Sofia City Consultative Council brought thousands of citizens to the *Prince Alexander Battenberg* Square. With their slogans and loud exclamations, they insisted on putting an end to the unnatural situation of parliamentary domination by a party that had lost the confidence of the voters. With shouts "Everybody!", "Everybody!" the citizens of Sofia enthusiastically welcomed the suggestion of the speakers that the entire Parliamentary Alliance of the Union of Democratic Forces should leave the Grand National Assembly and provoke new elections. The excitement of the population grew every day.

Unexpectedly a scandal - best known as "the hyphens" - exploded again. Its aim was to destroy the Union of Democratic Forces "from within". That happened just days after information from the former German Democratic Republic was leaked and it became known that the removal from power of the communist dictatorships in each of the countries of the former socialist camp was accompanied by a special plan devised by the totalitarian secret services.

21. Differences in Tactics or Something More?

The Political Declaration of the Bulgarian Social Democratic Party and of the *Nikola Petkov* Bulgarian Agrarian People's Union of April 10, 1991, published in the *Svoboden Narod* daily, read:

> Today, when the decisive phase of the struggle for democracy is beginning, the unity of the democratic movements is in jeopardy. Fragments of the old organizations and newly-created factions and movements from the former communist party joined the UDF ranks. Their extremist actions deflected the sympathies of many well-intentioned Bulgarians and allowed the former and present rulers of the state to preserve their organizations, plunder the wealth of the nation, and continue exercising their power.
>
> Initiatives have been undertaken recently to transform the UDF into some kind of impersonal movement that will give an opportunity to a group of aggressive people to manipulate the organization. Structures and citizens' committees are being created locally, which threatens the unity of the UDF. This is a Bolshevik strategic move to conquer the organization from within, with which we are already familiar.
>
> In our concern about the democratic process in the country, we declare the establishment of "UDF-Center." UDF-Center is open to all truly democratic organizations in the UDF.[1]

The UDF supporters were puzzled by the description of the establishment of local UDF structures and citizens' committees as a "Bolshevik strategic move." They considered that to be something that the opposition coalition should have done at its very inception. On the other hand, what was this talk about "the unity of the democratic movements is in jeopardy" when at the same moment the two most numerous and influential parties in the UDF were leaving the coalition and founding a new formation hostile to the other groups in the union, namely "UDF-Center"? In addition, the very name "center" revealed beyond any doubt the political orientation of the new alliance - closer to the renamed communist party of the country. Was the moment - before the second parliamentary elections and the first local elections after decades of totalitarian rule - the right time to seriously shake the foundations of the Union of Democratic Forces? Why did the social democrat Dr. Peter Dertliev and the agrarian Milan Drenchev attempt to attract "all proven democratic organizations in the UDF" to the UDF-Center established by them? Could it be that the two elderly men who had suffered the repressions of the Bulgarian Communist Party were trying to transform the anticommunist opposition into a political center in

[1] *Svoboden Narod* daily, April 11, 1991.

this way? Why was this happening? Had anyone else suggested the idea? What was this leading to?

The anxiety of the UDF supporters grew after a number of publications announced that, in all probability, Alexander Karakachanov's Green Party and the *Ecoglasnost* Independent Society of Peter Slabakov, Stefan Gaytandzhiev and Georgi Avramov were going to follow the Bulgarian Social Democratic Party and the *Nikola Petkov* Bulgarian Agrarian People's Union and split from the UDF. If these internal divisions continued, what would remain of the Union of Democratic Forces - the only real opposition to the Bulgarian Socialist Party?

The political crisis called for tact and sensibility on the part of the UDF leadership. The Chairman of the National Coordinating Council stepped up to the task with his typical self-control. Philip Dimitrov succeeded in retaining balance in the coalition, insisting on compromise and unity. Here is how the daily newspaper of the social democrats assessed the first meeting of the UDF leadership after UDF-Center was formed:

> After several appeals on the part of the Chairman of the National Coordinating Council Mr. Philip Dimitrov for a constructive and efficient approach in the discussions, it was proposed that all UDF member-organizations vote whether they wish to continue to abide by the union's statutes. Without hesitation and with full unanimity they all declared their loyalty to the blue opposition.
>
> A change in the statute of the local UDF organizations was also approved and they will be subsequently referred to as UDF clubs or committees. It was also decided that all the departments of the Coordinating Council be subordinated to the Central Election Club of the UDF in order to help prepare for the approaching elections.[2]

That same day, the daily newspaper *Demokratsiya* published an interview with the UDF leader. It contained certain details on the agreement that had been reached, which would later prove to have been only a temporary truce:

> It is also important to stress that the emergence of divergent ideological trends in the UDF does not mean that the unity of action has been violated. Today's decision of the Coordinating Council supports this. It can be summarized in the following few points:
>
> In compliance with the resolution of the national meeting of the representatives of the coordinating councils in the municipalities of the country, the National Coordinating Council decided that the UDF candidates should run at the next parliamentary and local elections as candidates of the

[2] *Ibid.,* April 12, 1991.

Union of Democratic Forces, rather than candidates of its constituent parties and organizations. It was also decided that during their terms in office they would act as representatives of the UDF.

A second decision that was also voted upon with unanimity was a confirmation that all parties and organizations in the UDF would abide by the one party, one vote principle.

The third decision of the Coordinating Council was to amend the UDF Statutes - specifically Article 21 - in order to encourage the establishment of clubs in towns or villages in which there were no UDF member-organizations, or coordinating councils. That amendment allowed for the establishment of such clubs or committees in every populated area, where they would, of course, be under the political guidance and control of the municipal coordinating councils.[3]

Only hours after all members of the National Coordinating Council of the Union of Democratic Forces voted on unity of action among its political organizations, one of them, Dr. Peter Dertliev, announced at a press conference that "the Bulgarian Social Democratic Party and the *Nikola Petkov* Bulgarian Agrarian People's Union would run in the coming elections with a preferential proportional representation ballot, i.e., that the people would vote not only for the UDF as a whole, but also for its individual formations."[4]

. . .

The Bulgarian Social Democratic Party (BSDP), which was the successor of the noncommunist Bulgarian Workers' Social Democratic Party (united), attracted hundreds of Bulgarians immediately after it was restored - first under its old name - at the end of 1989. In the summer of 1990, its members numbered 50,000, half of whom lived in Sofia. In another eighteen months the BSDP doubled its membership.

The Thirty-Eighth Congress of the Bulgarian Social Democratic Party was held in March 1991. It adopted Statutes according to which the party could form political alliances only subject to decision by its Congress, or at the initiative of its National Committee, endorsed by a Congress decision. The very next month that regulation was breached by the leader of the organization. On April 10, 1991, Dr. Dertliev surprised his fellow-party members not less than he surprised the rest of the Bulgarian citizens by announcing that he had created UDF-Center together with the agrarian Milan Drenchev.

---

[3] *Demokratsiya* daily, April 12, 1991.

[4] *Ibid.*

Naturally, the elderly doctor made steps to legalize his actions in violation of the party's Statutes. With a *fait accompli*, he convened the BSDP National Committee and received approval for his act. Still, the meeting did not go smoothly. Five social democrats abstained during the vote. Ivan Kurtev, provisional UDF Mayor of the *Lozenets* Municipality of Sofia, and Dimitar Kumanov, UDF Member of Parliament in the Grand National Assembly, resolutely opposed the formation of UDF-Center. The two men began to explore the views of the rank-and-file social democrats and discovered that the founding of UDF-Center had met the strong disapproval of the local organizations in Sofia. It was evident that most people who had joined the BSDP were UDF supporters first and only then social democrats.[5]

Seven years later, Ivan Kurtev gave the following account of that period:

> Dertliev tried to gain control over the situation in Sofia with a conference at the *Aura* Club at the end of May. At that time there were about 30,000 social democrats in Sofia. However, the BSDP members at the meeting discredited him and categorically opposed UDF-Center.
>
> After the conference 15-20 of us gathered and decided to form an Initiative Committee that would organize an extraordinary congress to change the BSDP leadership. The party had virtually left the original UDF. It is true that the BSDP still participated in the meetings of the UDF National Coordinating Council, but it did that as UDF-Center, a structure within the lager political structure.
>
> During the hunger strike in July [of 39 UDF Parliament Members - *author's note*], the UDF National Coordinating Council allowed the Initiative Committee to organize an extraordinary congress of the BSDP and to attend UDF meetings as an observer. Two weeks later, the same decision was made with regard to the Initiative Committee organizing an extraordinary congress of the Green Party, the *Ecoglasnost* Independent Society and the Federation of the Clubs for Democracy, which were united in a new organization called UDF-Liberals in May.
>
> The congress of the social democrats took place on August 18-19, 1991, in full compliance with the law. It had the necessary quorum. It elected the new leadership of the organization and laid the foundations of the Social Democratic Party (SDP) that did not leave the Union of Democratic Forces. Shortly thereafter, a similar Extraordinary Congress of the Green Party and the National Forum of the Federation of the Clubs for Democracy took place. At that point the UDF National Coordinating Council accepted the organizers of the latter congress as regular representatives in the union. Peter Dertliev, Alexander Karakachanov and Petko Simeonov left the opposition coalition.

---

[5] Ivan Kurtev in a conversation with the author, Sofia, Bulgaria, August 18, 1998.

As a result the sections of the Bulgarian Social Democratic Party, the Green Party and the Federation of the Clubs for Democracy which remained in the democratic alliance under new names rid themselves of communist collaborators. These were the first manifestations of a larger process of political disassociation, dubbed "the flaking off" by Father Christophor Sabev. The trend continued in almost all member organizations in the UDF, including the agrarians, *Ecoglasnost*, and the democrats. Virtually every member organization split into two formations: one in the Union of Democratic Forces and the other one outside it.

The conduct of many of the first blue leaders makes me believe that the leadership of the opposition parties was initially put together by the communists. There is every reason to presume that the people appointed to these positions were expected to pursue a definite agenda. However, after the rally on December 14, 1989, things changed. People from the streets started joining the political organizations in Bulgaria. Some of them reached the top of the UDF, thwarted the plans of the communists, and build the foundations of a democratic state.

Those were turbulent times. One could even say that they were revolutionary times. Progress was made in politics for a short time that takes decades under normal circumstances. Especially if you are loyal to the political force to which you belong.

The split of the BSDP in the summer of 1991 was very useful because the structures of the social democrats were the only UDF structures in many cities and towns. Those of them that remained in the opposition coalition contributed substantially to the victory of the Union of Democratic Forces in the October elections that year.[6]

. . .

On April 15, 1991, Philip Dimitrov declared the following before tens of thousands of citizens of Sofia gathered at the *Prince Alexander Battenberg* Square:

> The immediate change of the system cannot happen without a change in the parliamentary majority. This is our position and we are going to defend it![7]

From the same rostrum Stefan Savov, the newly-elected Chairman of the Democratic Party and Member of the Seventh Grand National Assembly, insisted:

---

[6] *Ibid.*

[7] *Demokratsiya* daily, April 16, 1991.

> In order to have elections in June, we, the Members of Parliament, should leave the Grand National Assembly by the end of April. I appeal to you to ask the people you have voted for to leave the Grand National Assembly because the hour of truth has come, because we cannot change the regime with these people in Parliament![8]

Indeed, Savov left the plenary hall of the Grand National Assembly on April 23, together with Georgi Markov, Yordan Vasilev and Zlatka Ruseva. Just a couple days later it became apparent that their act had been justified and that a legislative body with a communist-socialist majority would not do anything useful for the nation. This transpired on April 25, 1991, when the PADF of the UDF proposed that the agenda of the Grand National Assembly include a decision on the report submitted by the Minister of Finance Ivan Kostov. In response, 157 Members of Parliament from the Bulgarian Socialist Party voted against any debate on this extremely important document, and no discussion took place.

There was nothing surprising in the fact that the renamed communists ignored Kostov's report. Addressed to the Prime Minister of the Republic of Bulgaria, Dimitar Popov, it concerned their material interests:

> Mr. Prime Minister,
>
> In implementation of the Agreement of the Political Movements of January 3, 1991, please find enclosed a report on the finances allocated from the state budget to the political parties, socio-political, trade union and other public organizations in the period from February 1, 1949, until December 31, 1990.
>
> The receipt of the sums was unjustified, because:
>
> No normative act - a law, decree, ordinance or decision of a state body - has been found to stipulate the annual allocation of funds from the state budget for the Central Committee of the Bulgarian Communist Party, the Central Committee of Dimitrov's Young Communist League (DYCL), the Standing Committee of the Bulgarian Agrarian People's Union and the National Council of the Fatherland Front.
>
> The National Assembly had not planned, approved or adopted a report on these sums in the State Budget Acts for these years.
>
> The legitimate way for the State to treat these financial resources is as "unfounded enrichment" according to Article 55 of the Obligations and Contracts Act.
>
> My obligations as Minister of Finance of the Republic of Bulgaria require of me to insist on the following:

---

[8] *Ibid.*

The Supreme Council of the Bulgarian Socialist Party, as the legal successor to the property of the Bulgarian Communist Party, should reimburse the sum of BGN 1,772,300,000 taken from the state budget, of which there is written evidence. Together with the interest accrued until March 31, 1991, the total due is BGN 2,700,400,000.

The National Executive Council of the Bulgarian Democratic Youth, in its capacity of legal successor to the property of the DYCL, should reimburse the sum of BGN 353,000,000, taken from the state budget, of which there is written evidence. Together with the interest accrued until March 31, 1991, the total due is BGN 570,500,000.

The Standing Committee of Bulgarian Agrarian People's Union should reimburse the sum of BGN 164,300,000 taken from the state budget, of which there is written evidence. Together with the interest accrued until March 31, 1991, the total due is BGN 291,900,000.

The National Council of the Fatherland Front should reimburse the sum of BGN 127,800,000 taken from the state budget, of which there is written evidence. Together with the interest accrued until March 31, 1991, the total due is BGN 205,200,000.

The present document is to be considered as an invitation to the respective organizations to reimburse the sums within thirty days. If they fail to do so, the interest under the law for overdue state receivables will start to accrue.

With the present document I hereby inform the Council of Ministers that in view of the extremely difficult conditions connected with the implementation of the 1991 state budget of the Republic of Bulgaria, the amounts due will be included as a source of revenue in the planned update of the budget necessary in order to meet urgent social costs.

Sofia, 25 April 1991.[9]

The leader of the Union of Democratic Forces Philip Dimitrov expressed public support for the demand of the UDF minister. Dimitrov's speech before the rally at *Battenberg* Square on the following Monday provoked people's indignation with the BCP/BSP and triggered their angry shouts "Give back the money!" Hundreds of citizens went to the party headquarters of the recent communists to protest against their disrespect for the law.[10]

Obviously, no one there heard them. Instead of urging his party to reimburse the money stolen from the people, the Member of Parliament from the Bulgarian Socialist Party Ivan Ivanov, better known as Ivan the Stalinist, earned the applause of his fellow party members with sarcastic comments like, "I hear that Ivan Kostov is unable to draft the budget of Bulgaria."[11]

---

[9] *Demokratsiya* daily, April 26, 1991.

[10] *Ibid.*, April 30, 1991.

[11] *Ibid.*, May 8, 1991.

...

On 26 April, 36 Members of the Grand National Assembly from the parliamentary group of the Union of Democratic Forces came out with a declaration, part of which read as follows:

> The Republic of Bulgaria is in a state of economic and moral catastrophe. It is hard and painful to endorse the new democratic values in practice. The aggressiveness and backwardness of the communist *nomenklatura* increases. We are witnessing the total sabotage of the economic reform by the state-owned companies.
>
> In the Grand National Assembly the parliamentary group of the Bulgarian Socialist Party only votes for laws supporting the idea of a prolonged, gradual and essentially slow reconstruction of the country's economic and political life. The repeated violations of the Political Agreement and the mutual agreements reached by the political movements have resulted in crises in the work of Parliament.
>
> ...
>
> With increasing alarm, we are also watching the attempts of certain revenge-seeking fractions of the BSP to turn back Bulgaria's political clock. We also qualify the wish of some Members of Parliament to place the interests of their party above the interests of the people and the country as morally corrupt. All proposals to return the property of the BSP and of the other parties and organizations connected with the totalitarian regime to the people are invariably rejected.
>
> There is a real danger that the Grand National Assembly would adopt undemocratic laws and an undemocratic Constitution. The status of the Privatization Bill is particularly alarming. After being repeatedly postponed, today it is openly blocked by the BSP parliamentarians. There is obvious reluctance to resolve the issue of restitution or denationalization of property, without which the socially just privatization of the economy is unthinkable.
>
> ...
>
> In order to adopt a really democratic Constitution, we propose to vote for the dissolution of the Grand National Assembly on May 15th and to set July 14th as the date for parliamentary elections. Prior to that the Grand National Assembly should accept the proposal submitted by the Parliamentary Alliance of the Democratic Forces that the finances deflected from the budget for the BCP and DYCL in the 1949-1990 period should be considered as revenue in the 1991 updated state budget.
>
> ...

> If the Grand National Assembly fails to vote on this demand of ours, we hereby declare that we shall discontinue our participation in the sessions of Parliament.[12]

The document was read by the Co-Chairman of the PADF Stoyan Ganev. However, the other Co-Chairman of the group, Peter Dertliev, opposed him immediately. On behalf of the *Nikola Petkov* Agrarian Union, the Bulgarian Social Democratic Party, *Ecoglasnost*, the Green Party and the Federation of the Clubs for Democracy, the elderly social democrat accused the 36 Members of Parliament of brinksmanship and declared that their act was a threat to "our fragile democracy."[13]

. . .

On April 29 the UDF National Coordinating Council had a stormy meeting. At the regular press conference after it, Philip Dimitrov gave a diplomatic answer to the question concerning the debates on the two essentially opposed declarations by the leaders of the Parliamentary Alliance of the Democratic Forces:

> We found that there are priorities in our immediate political work on which all organizations in the UDF are united. They are the immediate return to the state of the property of the BCP/BSP and its subsequent use to ease the plight of the people, parliamentary elections prior to the local elections necessary to keep the reforms on track, tolerant relations among the groups with divergent ideas in the UDF - a natural occurrence which actually demonstrates different tactics for the attaining of a common goal - and the loss of the elections for the BSP, which is inevitable and which will allow for a coalition government by the UDF and some of the other opposition movements.[14]

During these hectic months the task of the UDF Chairman was not easy. He had to find ways to highlight the common aspects of the individuals and groups in the UDF and unite them. Essentially, he had to coordinate the political strategy of an organization torn by conflicts and clarify the ideology of an unstable coalition. At the same time Philip Dimitrov had the equally important obligation to keep the faith of the people in the UDF alive.

---

[12] *Ibid.*, April 27, 1991.

[13] *Ibid.*

[14] *Ibid.,* April 30, 1991.

The situation in the UDF in 1991 was much more complicated than it appears at first glance. The internal clashes were not always due to profound differences in the convictions of the parties. Very often they were prompted by discrepant values, mutual suspicions, superfluous emotions, ruthless ambitions and inadequate conduct. A deeper understanding of human nature was needed in order to grasp precisely what was taking place. Philip Dimitrov possessed that and had his own theory:

> Since we all know the methods of the communist party, I would not be surprised if their people are deliberately scattered across the political spectrum. It is perfectly possible that there may be agents infiltrated into the UDF, whose task is to spoil our good work, so to say. However, you probably guess from my tone that I don't consider this possibility seriously. I treat the problems within the UDF as more solemn because they involve human choice. At every moment it is necessary that each individual questions who he is, where he is and what he is doing there. The other scenario tends to oversimplify things. I repeat that I am not rejecting the possibility of sabotage and spying, but that is not sufficient to explain the great complexity of the situation. Actual experience holds a lot more surprises than orchestrated scheming does.[15]

The UDF leader offered a way out of the situation that had emerged:

> In the UDF we must find the diagonal in which, while preserving individual preferences for one tactical approach or another, we will be able to act together. In other words, the unifying factor will not be a formula or a magic act. The unifying factor will be common sense.[16]

Philip Dimitrov insisted on a united opposition that would be the "moral complement to the election result."[17] His wish did not come true. The two trends in the Union of Democratic Forces were irreconcilable and their split was inevitable.

. . .

On May 8, 1991, a coup of sorts took place in the Parliamentary Alliance of the Democratic Forces. After a meeting of only 70 of its members that lasted four hours, the Co-Chairman Stoyan Ganev from the United Democratic Center and the Spokesman Alexander Yordanov from the Bulgarian Radical Democratic

---

[15] Vladimirova 1991, p. 8.

[16] *Ibid.*, p. 6.

[17] *Ibid.*, p. 7.

Party were dismissed in a secret vote. There were 48 votes "for", 20 votes "against" and two "invalid" votes. Two spokesmen were elected to replace Yordanov, namely Vladimir Sotirov from the Green Party and Georgi Mishev from the Federation of the Clubs for Democracy. The Deputy Chairman Peter Kornazhev from the Bulgarian Social Democratic Party retained his position, but another three Deputy Chairmen were also voted in. They were from the *Ecoglasnost* Independent Society, from the Federation of the Clubs for Democracy, and from the *Nikola Petkov* Bulgarian Agrarian People's Union. Last but not least, the Parliamentary Alliance of the Democratic Forces was left with just one Chairman, namely the leader of the Bulgarian Social Democratic Party Dr. Peter Dertliev. Thus, as of May 9, the UDF-Center and the "*perestroika*-supporters" and "liberals" in Parliament had ousted the remaining member organizations of the UDF from power and assumed the role of docile opponents to the former communist party. It was no surprise that when the Speaker of the Grand National Assembly Nikolay Todorov announced the changes in the leadership of the Parliamentary Alliance of the Democratic Forces, a burst of applause came from the left in the plenary hall, i.e., from the side of the Bulgarian Socialist Party.[18]

The National Coordinating Council of the Union of Democratic Forces responded to these events. On May 10, *Demokratsiya* published "The NCC Position on the Declaration of the 36 UDF Members of Parliament:"

> The NCC of the UDF notes that the actions and the declaration of the 36 Members of Parliament who stated that they would discontinue their participation in the work of Parliament after May 15, if the BCP/BSP and its satellites fail to return their property and no decision for the dissolution of the Grand National Assembly is made (so that the President would be in a position to appoint new parliamentary elections), do not constitute a violation of the parliamentary rules. They are in compliance with the official position of the UDF, the decisions of the NCC of the UDF as of March 21 and April 8 this year, as well as those of the national conferences of the UDF representatives in the entire country and the National Consulting Committee. The protest actions also comply with the political agreement of January 3, 1991, and help the UDF attain its goals.[19]

From that moment on, the leadership of the Union of Democratic Forces encouraged its Members of Parliament to leave even more vigorously. Its efforts were supported by dozens of leaders of UDF parties and local organizations in

---

[18] *Demokratsiya* daily, May 10, 1991.

[19] *Ibid.*

Sofia and throughout the country. If the remaining members of the opposition did not leave Parliament, people would "legitimately express their vote of no confidence for the Members of Parliament elected on the UDF ballot."[20]

At a plenary session on May 9, an UDF Member of Parliament urged the Seventh Grand National Assembly to discuss an ordinance for its dissolution. The matter was put to the vote. There were 231 votes "against", 43 "for" and 6 abstentions. Forty-nine members of the Parliamentary Alliance of the Democratic Forces, together with 159 former communists, were against the discussion on the dissolution of the Grand National Assembly. Only 38 UDF Members of Parliament voted for it. Almost all representatives of the Bulgarian Agrarian People's Union and the Movement for Rights and Freedoms gave their negative vote.[21]

On that day, another extremely important issue failed to be resolved. Once again, the supreme legislative body of Bulgaria brazenly diverted the proposal of an UDF Member of Parliament, that a decision take place regarding the reimbursement of the billions acquired unlawfully by the Bulgarian Communist Party and its satellites.[22] The poverty of the people and the urgent social needs of the State did not evoke concern in the Bulgarian Socialist Party. After all, it did not anticipate elections in the near future and it felt no need to appease the masses with false propaganda. Still, the red party was in charge of the executive, judicial and legislative branches of government.

---

[20] *Ibid.*, May 9, 1991.

[21] *Ibid.*, May 10, 1991.

[22] *Ibid.*

22. Five Revolutionary Months

On May 14, 1991, Tuesday, 39 Members of Parliament from the Union of Democratic Forces left the Seventh Grand National Assembly. Their reasons for doing this were stated in a declaration:

> On April 26, a group of Members of Parliament appealed to all parliamentarians to make a decision in the Grand National Assembly regarding the reimbursement of the money illegally obtained by the Bulgarian Communist Party (Bulgarian Socialist Party) and the dissolution of Parliament by 15 May, so that the President would be in a position to set the date for parliamentary elections in mid-July.
>
> Even our attempts to include this appeal in the agenda proved to be futile.
>
> If today we, the undersigned Members of Parliament from the UDF, are leaving the plenary hall of Parliament, that is not out of disrespect for parliamentary democracy. It is simply that this Parliament has proven itself to be unable to fulfill the high mission assigned to it by the voters. The low degree of public trust in the Grand General Assembly makes the artificial prolongation of its agony dangerous for the nation's future.
>
> ...
>
> The Grand National Assembly adopts compromise-ridden, controversial and inadequate laws. It suffices to point out the Land Act or the Foreign Investments Act. Now a similarly imperfect Constitution draft is being proposed, guaranteeing the impunity of the main agents responsible for the national catastrophe, and the inviolability of their ownership of property stolen from the people. Society is wasting invaluable time while this "parliamentary theater production," following the script of the BSP and stage-managed by that party, continues.
>
> ...
>
> Remaining true to our word of April 26, implementing the decisions of the UDF, and above all taking into consideration the wishes of the hundreds of thousands of people committed to the idea of immediate and radical change in the political system, we are ending our participation in the sessions of the Grand National Assembly. We are anticipating the decisions of the National Conference of the UDF and appeal to our parliamentary colleagues to follow us and to give a chance to the President to set the date for parliamentary elections.
>
> The nation has the last word.[1]

The document was signed by 39 people. With three or four exceptions, these were the same persons who placed their signatures below the declaration of April 26, 1991.

---

[1] *Demokratsiya* daily, May 15, 1991.

The UDF supporters were in rapture with this act of the 39. The Members of Parliament who were elected on the UDF ballot, but chose not to leave, received a *Open Letter from 159 Intellectuals*:

> ...Friends, freedom is not a fact. Bulgaria is still entangled in the net of communism, which we need to tear. The "stigma on our forehead" remains. The BSP is preparing a new and very dangerous Bulgarian-Soviet Union treaty behind your backs, which will regulate our eternal isolation from Europe. The BSP is secretly exporting the last riches of Bulgaria. The BSP is not giving back the stolen billions and it is not repenting. The BSP is preparing for new manipulations of public opinion and provocations against the opposition. It is preparing its economic domination under new circumstances. The BSP maintains the ethnic tensions in Bulgaria and banishes the cream of the Bulgarian intellectuals and of our youth. The blood of Bulgaria is being drained!
>
> Friends, they are cunning, cynical and unscrupulous. You will be duped again, you are just a convenient cover. Bulgaria needs elections quickly, as well as new air, new people, new ideas and a new image before the world. "Do not pour new wine into old wineskins," the Savior advises us. We do not believe that the wine of democracy poured into a communist wineskin would be real.
>
> If you remain in Parliament today, the generations to come and history will judge you! It may be too late tomorrow. Shall we wait for fatigue and apathy to break the spirit of the people, so that they can lose faith in the great alliance of the opposition? Is this not precisely the aim that the communists are pursuing? Yet, they are mistaken in their belief that only we would be ruined. Communist rule would spell doom for all.
>
> It is not normal for you to be supported with declarations from the BSP organizations. It is not normal for you to receive indignant letters in Parliament from the people who had voted for you...[2]

...

The Second National Conference of the Union of Democratic Forces on May 19 was organized out of a sense of responsibility for the future of democratic Bulgaria. Its delegates were called upon to decide what the strategy and tactics of the opposition would be in preparing the future elections.

The UDF National Coordinating Council dispatched well devised questionnaires to the coordinating councils in the country, which had to be filled out and returned before the start of the Conference. The questions asked for the opinions of the UDF structures concerning the work of the Grand National Assembly, the conduct of the Members of Parliament who left it and those who

---

[2] *Ibid.*, May 17, 1991.

remained in it, the dissolution of Parliament, the date for the elections and other current issues. In addition, the questionnaire required that the respondents indicate with what majority the decisions had been reached, as well as what organizations had voted "for" or "against" it.[3]

It was planned for the local coordinating councils from each of the 273 municipalities to participate in the conference with two delegates. Another meeting was scheduled at 9 a.m. on May 20 for the regional and district coordinators. The leadership of UDF member parties and organizations, UDF representatives in the government, the leadership of the Parliamentary Alliance of the Democratic Forces, and prominent emigrants were also invited.[4]

As could be expected from the events preceding it, the National Conference of the UDF "was a stormy event, where occasional comments threatened to make the hall explode."[5] The delegates welcomed Dr. Peter Dertliev with shouts "BCP!", "BCP!" Unperturbed, the leader of the social democrats declared that the appropriate representatives of the Bulgarian Social Democratic Party were its legitimately elected leaders and that their opponents would be considered proxies of the UDF rather than the BSDP. The physician insisted that "the BSDP aims for a specific kind of unity of action, unity of action among diverse agents" and rejected the idea of building a "unified blue party in opposition to the red."[6]

The Chairperson of the Bulgarian Radical Democratic Party Elka Konstantinova expressed a different opinion. On behalf of her political organization she stated that the Grand National Assembly should be dissolved immediately so that elections could be held in July. Professor Konstantinova reminded the Members of Parliament that they had been elected on the UDF ballot and not as representatives of their respective parties. The radical democrat proposed that no one should talk about his own party before the next parliamentary elections. Whoever disagreed with her idea was free to leave the opposition alliance.[7]

For Alexander Karakachanov, the leader of the Green Party and interim mayor of Sofia, the UDF being organized as a party was absolutely not an option.[8] Likewise, the Deputy Leader of the UDF National Coordinating

---

[3] *Ibid.*, May 8, 1991.

[4] *Ibid.*, May 17, 1991.

[5] *Ibid.*, May 20, 1991.

[6] *Ibid.*, May 22, 1991.

[7] *Ibid.*

[8] *Ibid.*

Council Petko Simeonov vigorously appealed to the National Conference not to give in to manipulations and turn the coalition into a party.[9]

After a nine-hour debate and the public announcement of the results of the inquiry conducted in the regional organizations, the forum adopted the following resolutions:

> The National Conference of the UDF accepts that preserving the unity of the parties and organizations in it is mandatory in order to win the coming elections. Only the UDF as an open movement [term used as forerunner of a political party - *author's note*] for democracy, as a political agent unified in its actions and free from party bias, could guarantee real change of the political and economic system in Bulgaria.
>
> Given that the delegates to this National Conference are the legitimately elected representatives of 230 UDF organizations, the Conference is the supreme body expressing the Union's political will. The resolutions made at the Conference are binding for all operational bodies of the UDF. The outcome of the Conference also reflects the results of the inquiry conducted, which shows that 87% of the municipal UDF coordinating councils are in favor of abiding by the political agreement of January 3, 1991, and of immediate parliamentary elections by the end of July 1991.
>
> At the National Conference of the UDF the following was decided:
>
> 1. The resolutions of this National Conference shall be binding to all member parties, organizations and movements in the UDF. The Parliamentary Alliance of the UDF shall be obliged to comply with these resolutions. A National Conference shall be convened by the UDF National Coordinating Council or by 1/5 of the municipal organizations of the UDF.
>
> 2. The attendees of the Conference support the Members of Parliament who discontinued their participation in the plenary sessions of the Grand National Assembly on May 14, 1991.
>
> 3. The attendees of the Conference demand that the UDF Members of Parliament who did not leave should present a motion on May 21 or May 22, 1991, for the immediate dissolution of the Grand National Assembly. If the parliamentary majority fails to accept this sensible solution, for which there is awareness and understanding in the nation, the attendees of the Conference insist that the remaining UDF Members of Parliament leave the Grand National Assembly. As soon as parliamentary elections have been scheduled for July, we oblige all Members of Parliament to return to the plenary hall and pass a new election law along with the necessary economic laws.
>
> 4. The National Coordinating Council has until May 30, 1991, to draft a new agreement between the political organizations in the UDF. The agreement should call for renouncing any party bias and all quotas in the nomination of

[9] *Svoboden Narod* daily, May 21, 1991.

the UDF candidates in the elections. That should happen in the name of the unification of all democratic movements aiming to change the political system into a single open UDF movement.

5. The attendees at the National Conference of the UDF support the efforts of the President and the government to allow the country to emerge from the national catastrophe resulting from the communist rule.[10]

Only three delegates voted against the cited text. It should be noted that the most numerous among the 434 delegates attending the meeting were the members of the two parties in UDF-Center. The *Nikola Petkov* Bulgarian Agrarian People's Union had 82 representatives at the Conference, while the Bulgarian Social Democratic Party had 72.[11]

The results of the voting showed that the members of the Union of Democratic Forces and some of its leaders had conflicting positions on vitally important and topical issues. People insisted on early elections in which the opposition should run as a cohesive organization. They insisted that any attachment to the individual parties should give way to the interests of the nation. In contrast, their leaders, Peter Dertliev, Petko Simeonov, Alexander Karakachanov and several others, continued supporting the Grand National Assembly with a BSP majority. They rejected the proposal that the UDF become a "blue" party with the excuse that such an initiative "had a taste of Bolshevism".[12]

Then, the cited individuals and three of their adherents set off to revoke the legitimately voted decisions of the mass UDF forum. In the early hours of May 20, they prepared a coup in the UDF leading body, allegedly "in the name of democracy." After a clandestine gathering, the six politicians met the dawn with a press release signed only by Petko Simeonov on behalf of the NCC of the UDF. At 6:30 a.m. the "defenders of democracy" took the document to the Bulgarian News Agency and the Bulgarian National Radio and proclaimed that the resolutions of the conference that had just ended were illegitimate. At 7:00 a.m. their declaration was broadcast on the radio.[13] Behind the scenes, the conspirators had requested President Zhelev's cooperation. He offered them his assistance.

. . .

---

[10] *Demokratsiya* daily, May 20, 1991.

[11] *Ibid.*

[12] *Ibid.*

[13] *Ibid.*, May 21, 1991.

The morning after the Second National Conference of the UDF, Philip Dimitrov was busy preparing to leave his home to go to the meeting of the UDF National Coordinating Council, scheduled for 9 a.m. At 7:50 his telephone rang and he recognized the voice of the secretary of the President of the Republic. Politely but firmly, the woman invited him to appear immediately in the office of the Head of State. The UDF leader judged that there was time until the start of the meeting and accepted the invitation. He assumed that Zhelyu Zhelev wanted to tell him something urgent.

However, when he took a seat in the President's office, Dimitrov could tell right away that he was wrong. Zhelev appeared calm, benevolent, at ease and politely offered him coffee. Everything suggested that he had nothing to tell him and the dialogue between the first and third in command at the Union of Democratic Forces started slowly and clumsily. The coffee cups were refilled a number of times. Philip kept looking at his watch. The President assured him that there was no need to hurry because the NCC meetings always started late. The entire conversation amounted to such small talk and vague assurances. At first the lawyer complied, but when the time for the start of the meeting came very close, he got up impatiently and declared that he could not stay any longer.

Upon his arrival at the UDF headquarters, Philip Dimitrov was surprised to see that some of the NCC members, most of whom shared his ideas, were talking excitedly in front of the building. He was even more surprised when he saw that the entrance to the UDF office building on 134 *Rakovski* Street was cordoned off and guards were letting some people in while asking others to stay out. When Dimitrov himself approached the entrance, he did not fail to notice the disappointment in the glances that the guards exchanged.

A revelation awaited him in the conference hall where the National Coordinating Council usually held its meetings. The meeting had started and Petko Simeonov was seated comfortably at the center of the long table, that is, in the usual place of the head of the organization. Simeonov was startled and visibly irritated upon Philip Dimitrov's entrance. However, he quickly regained his composure and indicated one of the vacant chairs at the end of the room to Philip. The hall was filled by representatives of the formations opposed to the idea of leaving Parliament and to the vision of UDF as a national movement.

Dimitrov had experience dealing with crises from his practice in psychotherapy. He picked up the chair that had been pointed to him and carried it to the chairman's table. Simeonov did not budge. Philip was not perturbed in the least. He sat close to him and from time to time pulled his chair a little closer to the center.

Viewed from a distance, the scene must have been very funny. However, Philip's maneuver had a serious and intended effect. Petko Simeonov was losing his poise, and Philip Dimitrov took advantage of his confusion. He took over chairing the meeting and gave the floor to the President of the *Nikola Petkov* Bulgarian Agrarian People's Party, Milan Drenchev, notorious for his slow and fragmented manner of speaking. While the elderly agrarian kept talking and talking, the NCC members who had not been allowed to enter the meeting earlier started coming into the room one by one.[14]

The plot failed. The late night press release was not legitimized through a manipulated vote. The meeting of the NCC of the UDF took place with all the regular members in attendance. Thus, on May 20, 1991, the National Coordinating Council officially endorsed the decisions of the Second National Conference of the Union of Democratic Forces.

. . .

The attack of the schemers and their supporters continued in different ways. On May 22, the representatives of the Parliamentary Alliance of the Democratic Forces who had still remained in the Grand National Assembly came out with an official statement in which they declared themselves against the resolutions of the national forum and the resolutions that the UDF leadership had voted on three days earlier.[15] The following day, a rumor spread that the Green Party, the *Ecoglasnost* Independent Society and the Federation of the Clubs for Democracy were about to establish a new political formation called UDF-Liberals.[16]

The Member of Parliament from the UDF Edwin Sugarev, who had left the Grand National Assembly together with 38 colleagues, gave his opinion of the situation to a journalist:

> ...At the National Conference the UDF hard-liners proved that they cannot be lied to and fooled, and that they would not neglect the UDF cause in the name of someone's narrow political or personal interests. Therefore, the UDF will not remain spineless if some conceited leaders leave it in the form of political bare bones. The trouble is elsewhere: all victories of the opposition so far resulted from moral superiority over the ruling party. The "last supper" of the Bulgarian opposition [the plotters within the UDF - *author's note*] gave birth to a new political demagogy on top of the big treachery. Their maneuvers are already fatal for all who are hesitant and are waiting to see whether we are indeed the same scum as all the rest. The superlatives with which some UDF members praised Parliament, the vulgar over-enthusiastic back-slapping, the

---

[14] Philip Dimitrov in a conversation with the author, Newark, U.S.A., June 1, 2001.

[15] *Demokratsiya* daily, May 23, 1991.

[16] *Ibid.*, May 24, 1991.

> insolence with which they balanced between small truths and big lies remind me of a time I do not want to remember, but which I fear will come again.[17]

In the very same issue of *Demokratsiya* daily the Group of the 39 wrote the following:

> ...The development of the political and economic situation in the country indisputably demonstrates the correctness of our understanding that a radical change of the system is needed. We are convinced that this is what we have been elected on the blue ballot for, not for a Soviet-type *perestroika*.
>
> We express our disappointment with the position of Members of Parliament elected on the same ballot, who ignored the demands of the UDF National Conference, of the vast majority of coordinating councils, as well as of the majority of local organizations and movements which are UDF members.
>
> We reiterate that the UDF is a national movement of millions of people united by an indivisible idea. Therefore, we consider any manifestation of party bias or personal ambition as harmful and absurd. We declare our firm position against the nomination of candidates for Members of Parliament on a party basis...[18]

The day when the *Demokratsiya* newspaper published these two articles, the Seventh Grand National Assembly decided, with an enormous majority, to dissolve only after it had adopted the country's new Constitution. The Bulgarians following the development of political events were not surprised by the results of that vote. The past weeks had assured them that after the 39 Members of Parliament left the legislative body, those who chose to stay did not have any particular differences of opinion with the representatives of the renamed communist party.

...

On May 30, the UDF National Coordinating Council, whose meetings were conducted by two authorized representatives of each UDF member organization, convened. The NCC adopted a resolution stating that the Members of Parliament elected on the UDF ballot, who had not left Parliament, no longer represented the opposition. Then, the Third National Conference of the UDF followed suit on June 22. Its decisions angered the leaders of the

---

[17] *Ibid.*, Edwin Sougarev, *The Last Supper*, May 28, 1991.

[18] *Ibid.*

Bulgarian Social Democratic Party. On June 30, the BSDP National Committee held a meeting about which the press reported the following:

> At the meeting it was voted to reject the resolutions of the Third National Conference of the UDF for "contravening both the BSDP Statutes and the principles enshrined in the UDF Articles of Association." The opinion of the leaders of the social democrats is that with the "establishment of civilian committees having the right to make nominations for elected positions in central and local government bodies, and with the endorsement of the National Conference as the supreme body of the UDF, a decisive step was made towards the transformation of the UDF into a 'blue' party, thus actually putting an end to the democratic coalition of the Union of Democratic Forces." According to the social democrats, "the newly-established UDF National Movement is neither identical to the UDF coalition nor is it its legal successor." Hence, the BSDP will not participate in the former organization.[19]

On July 1, the BSDP still voted at the meeting of the supreme body of the UDF. The only difference was that the authorized representatives of the BSDP opposed each decision made, irrespective of the fact that the latter were based on resolutions adopted democratically by a representative part of the nation. The text discussed and voted on at the meeting read as follows:

> I. During the period preceding the elections the National Coordinating Council adopts the following political principles, previously endorsed by the National Conference of June 22, 1991:
>
> - The UDF is a national movement of parties, other organizations and citizens aiming for a rapid transition to a market economy, the removal of the Bulgarian Socialist Party from political power through elections and the restitution of the property plundered by the BCP/BSP to the people (12 people voted in favor; the BSDP was entirely against the proposition; the *Nikola Petkov* Bulgarian Agrarian People's Party members all abstained from the vote).
>
> - Within the framework of a general political and election platform, the parties in the UDF preserve their organizational and ideological autonomy and participate in the political leadership of the movement through their representatives in the coordinating councils (13 people voted in favor; the BSDP was entirely against the proposition).
>
> - During the pre-election period, the coordinating councils will be assisted by citizens' committees composed of UDF supporters, including non-party members, members of parties in the UDF, as well as members of parties and other organizations outside the UDF, who accept the overall goal of the movement and wish to joint UDF's campaign (12 people voted in favor; the

[19] *Ibid.*, July 1, 1991.

> BSDP was entirely against the proposition; the *Nikola Petkov* Bulgarian Agrarian People's Party members all abstained from the vote).
>
> - The UDF platform is founded on the Agenda of the UDF adopted with millions of votes a year ago which has been developed and rendered more concrete in accordance with the socio-economic and political situation as well as the real hopes of the voters (13 people voted in favor; the BSDP was entirely against the proposition).
>
> - The nominations for UDF candidates will be made in compliance with a most democratic procedure, which rules out the party quotas; the candidates will be proposed by the parties, by other organizations in the UDF, by citizens' committees and coordinating councils, as well as UDF supporters; the candidates will be discussed at open public fora, after which the final candidates will be determined by the municipal coordinating councils (11 people voted in favor; the BSDP and the *Nikola Petkov* Bulgarian Agrarian People's Party were entirely against the proposition; the Green Party members all abstained from the vote).
>
> II. The National Coordinating Council believes that it is the moral and political duty of the UDF before the millions of supporters of the union's cause to run in the elections with a single blue ballot and one list of candidates (if the proportional representation system is chosen). This would rule out any competition between candidates who share the same goal in the election campaign, namely to remove the BSP from power through elections (11 people voted in favor; the BSDP and the Green Party were entirely against the proposition; the *Nikola Petkov* Bulgarian Agrarian People's Party members all abstained from the vote).
>
> III. The National Coordinating Council believes that there is a real danger that the adoption of a Constitution which is not approved by the general public and a number of political parties and movements, would turn into a destabilizing factor for the democratic process in Bulgaria (12 people voted in favor; the BSDP was entirely against the proposition; the Green Party members all abstained from the vote).[20]

Seven successive votes "against" on the part of the BSDP were sufficiently convincing proof that the attempts at reconciliation were futile. From that moment on the leading body of the Union of Democratic Forces had no choice but to react unequivocally:

> At its regular meeting, the NCC of the UDF familiarized itself with the views and decisions of the BSDP National Committee. These views and decisions contravene and essentially reject the fundamental principles of the UDF, adopted at the National Conference and voted again by the NCC.

---

[20] *Ibid.*, July 2, 1991.

The destructive position of the BSDP leadership is ill-timed. It introduces unnecessary tension and conflicts within the UDF. While respecting every political position and ideological diversity in general, the NCC of the UDF recognizes the fact that the union is in a pre-election period, when unity of action, consensus and a constructive attitude are of greater significance than the separatism of any given political formation.

We appeal to the BSDP members and supporters to continue to work in support of the UDF cause.[21]

. . .

In the hot summer days of 1991, Philip Dimitrov did violate the Statutes of the Union of Democratic Forces. On July 6 and 7 he called a meeting of the National Coordinating Council at which he invited members of the opposition from all over the country rather than the authorized representatives of political organizations. The official goal of the meeting was to exchange views on the divisions in the UDF. However, the deeper purpose was to consolidate the noncommunist movement into a national structure and thus take the first step in transforming the blue coalition into a party.[22]

On July 8, the NCC announced its decision that the Union of Democratic Forces would not participate in the adoption and signing of the Constitution drafted by the Seventh Grand National Assembly, and that membership in the opposition was incompatible with voting to approve the fundamental law. This resolution was adopted with the support of nine UDF formations. It was opposed by the Bulgarian Social Democratic Party, the Federation of the Clubs for Democracy and the Green Party. The *Nikola Petkov* Bulgarian Agrarian People's Party abstained from taking any stand on the issue.[23] The same day Peter Dertliev, Petko Simeonov and Alexander Karakachanov left the NCC of the UDF.

On July 9, the new Constitution was adopted by the Grand National Assembly. The leadership of the legislative body, dominated by the communist-socialists, came out with a proposal for the Members of Parliament, cabinet ministers, the President, the Vice President, the Prosecutor General and the Chairman of the Supreme Court to take a second oath [the first one was taken at the opening of the Assembly - *authors' note*] of allegiance to the Constitution. The

[21] *Ibid.*

[22] Philip Dimitrov in a conversation with the author, New York, U.S.A., March 20, 1998.

[23] *Demokratsiya* daily, July 9, 1991.

proposal was accepted with 252 votes "for", five votes "against" and three Members of Parliament abstaining from the vote.[24]

The requirement for a "second oath" was not accidental. In accordance with Article 7, Paragraph 4 of the Regulations of the Work of the Grand National Assembly, the Members of Parliament who had not signed the Constitution were stripped of their mandate.[25] Thus, the pro-communist majority in the Grand National Assembly could act as it pleased for as long as it wonted.

The UDF National Coordinating Council immediately countered the blow:

> ...The decision to take an oath of allegiance before the new Constitution by Members of Parliament who have already taken an oath is against the law and illogical. Its aim is only to humiliate the Members of Parliament who had opposed its adoption, or to revoke their election. It is also an exertion of pressure upon those who remained in Parliament to adopt the Constitution before which they would subsequently be made to take an oath. The aim is to create a parliament composed only of people who think alike. This is strongly reminiscent of the brutal measures against the opposition back in 1947. At any rate, the Members of Parliament representing the UDF will no longer be in Parliament. The foremost political movement in Bulgaria will be deprived of parliamentary representation and will not be able to participate in the discussions on the Election Law, the budget and important economic laws, such as those concerning the privatization and restitution of property. Such parliamentary activity has nothing in common with democracy and is a disgrace for Bulgaria.
>
> In this situation, we can only resort to peaceful, legal extra-parliamentary modes of action. We insist on a referendum that would approve the Constitution with a two-thirds majority.[26]

In the presence of Philip Dimitrov, on July 10, the Parliamentary Group of the UDF National Movement, the successor of the *Group of the 39*, discussed the idea of declaring a hunger strike. Shortly thereafter, the newspaper of the former communists, *Duma*, published Stefan Gaytandzhiev's reaction to the idea of a hunger strike. The man who had competed for the position of Chairman of the Union of Democratic Forces seven months prior declared the following:

> Things are acquiring a hysterical character. There is mass hysteria in the Coordinating Council. Emergency psychiatric care is urgently needed.[27]

---

24 *Ibid.*, July 10, 1991.

25 *Ibid.*

26 *Ibid*, July 11, 1991.

27 *Duma* daily, July 11, 1991.

On the same day, *Demokratsiya*, informed its readers that during the night of July 10/11, the opposition Members of Parliament who had left the Grand National Assembly had started a hunger strike in the little park near the *St. Sophia* Church, to last until the date for the referendum was set.[28] The National movement *In the Name of Truth* - founded after the City of Truth was abolished in the summer of 1990 - appealed to the citizens to start peaceful protests in support of the strikers.

...

Once again, Bulgaria exploded with conflicting passions, rapture and indignation; the defense of communism and its total negation. Twenty-three men and women of different ages, went on hunger strike in the centre of Sofia. With this act they insisted on the dissolution of the Grand National Assembly, the revoking of the second oath and a nationwide referendum on the Constitution. Hundreds of people throughout the country who backed them declared consecutive and permanent hunger strikes. Others booed them and ridiculed their act.

The square in the center of Sofia filled up with the familiar faces of the residents of the City of Truth. The staff of the *Pirogov* Emergency Hospital was there once again, ready to offer medical care. Eighteen UDF mayors from the Sofia City municipalities joined the hunger strike every evening after work. Conversely, their boss, Sofia Mayor Alexander Karakachanov, sent a letter to the UDF in which he banned the participation of citizens in the protest. The students started a sitting strike on the roof of the *St. Kliment Ohridski* University of Sofia.

Unmoved by the general excitement, the Seventh Grand National Assembly retained its equanimity and continued to work in full harmony and understanding among the parliamentary groups that had remained in it. On July 12, 309 Members of Parliament, including the second Chairman of the Union of Democratic Forces, Peter Beron, officially signed the new Constitution of the Republic of Bulgaria. That happened with a standing ovation, embraces and even kisses exchanged among representatives of the former communist party and the so-called opposition parties.

None of the signatories of the fundamental law of Bulgaria appeared troubled in the least by the fact that this most important state document exonerated the countless crimes of the communist regime. It lifted entirely the

---

[28] *Demokratsiya* daily, July 11, 1991; *Ibid.*, July 12, 1991.

responsibility from the perpetrators and failed to guarantee a radical change of the political and economic system. Its legal imperfections forced the Constitutional Court to interpret and clarify its hastily drafted provisions with difficulty for years.

Without any remorse, the day Parliament legalized the new Constitution, it announced that a second oath of allegiance would be given and that there would be no referendum. A bitter truth for Bulgaria was confirmed by a statement by Angel Wagenstein, a former dissident who subsequently became Member of Parliament from the Bulgarian Socialist Party. When asked by a journalist whether he would run in the next parliamentary elections, the screenplay writer and film director produced the following uncensored sentence: "No, I won't, but I'm happy that we managed to f... those bastards! [Meaning the opposition to the former communist party - *author's note*]"[29]

That was not all. At the solemn moment of the signing of the Constitution, followed by champagne being poured into the glasses of the Members of Parliament, a group of citizens and some members of the Grand National Assembly who had refused to sign the fundamental law were beaten by officers of the Ministry of Interior not far from the Parliament building.

That day in Bulgarian history, sinister for some, joyous for others, ended with a grand protest rally and concert of the Union of Democratic Forces at *Prince Alexander Battenberg* Square. The politicians on hunger strike were standing next to the UDF Chairman at the rostrum. After the end of the event, attended by many thousands, they went back to their sleeping bags and inflatable rubber mattresses under the open sky. They were accompanied by the refrain of very popular song at that time, "How long are we going to continue in the same way? Please, God, show the way and give light and freedom to Bulgaria!"

The following day, July 13, the strikers, who already numbered 27, added another demand to their list. On the insistence of Philip Dimitrov, Edwin Sugarev and Spas Dimitrov, they requested that a date for early parliamentary elections be set.

The students, full of energy and fresh and original ideas, expressed their demands while singing the following verse at a procession: "We want a referendum, not a DertLilov-type constitution!"[30] [A pun out of the names of the leaders of the social democrats and of the renamed communists, Peter Dertliev and Alexander Lilov - *author's note.*]

On July 15, *Demokratsiya* daily wrote the following under the title *The Health of the Members of Parliament on Strike Is Deteriorating*:

[29] *Ibid.*, July 13, 1991.

[30] *Ibid.*, July 15, 1991.

Here is the statement of the medical consulting team from the *Pirogov* Institute: "After the paraclinical tests on the third day of the hunger strike, all without exception were diagnosed with hypoglycemia. This is a clear consequence of total fasting," Dr. Milan Milanov declared. "It already leads to physiological damage...On top of everything else, this extreme situation triggers some old, hidden diseases as well, which additionally complicates their condition."[31]

In spite of the painful deprivations and health risks, the hunger strike of the UDF parliamentarians lasted for nine days until July 19.

. . .

On the fifth day of the protest, the National Coordinating Council discussed the issue of the UDF Members of Parliament who had signed the new Constitution. It was voted that the UDF member parties and organizations would propose representatives of their own choice to the leading body of the UDF whose signatures did not appear below the Constitution. The representative of the Bulgarian Social Democratic Party left the meeting in protest, whereas the Green Party and the Federation of the Clubs for Democracy voted against.

There was tension with the *Podkrepa* Federation of Labor as well. Its President Dr. Konstantin Trenchev declared that the referendum on the adoption of the Constitution should be held before the parliamentary elections, evidently meaning to delay the latter. Philip Dimitrov thwarted the attempt of the trade union to impose its demand by threatening to resign. Then, in the late afternoon on July 15, President Zhelyu Zhelev visited the camp of the strikers and talked to them for about an hour. The following day, the Head of State issued a decree setting the date for the parliamentary and local elections on September 29, 1991.

On the eighth day of the hunger strike, the representatives of the newly established Parliamentary Group of the UDF National Movement Alexander Yordanov, Alexander Yanchulev, Stoyan Ganev and Ilko Eskenazi entered the plenary hall of the Grand National Assembly for the first time in two months. Their aim was to defend personally the proposal of their fraction and the demand of the strikers for a referendum on the Constitution.[32] They were supported by the Movement for Rights and Freedoms, which came out with a declaration of its own, stating that the provisions of the Constitution did not

[31] *Ibid.*

[32] *Ibid.*, July 19, 1991.

guarantee the application of the principle of political pluralism and the liberty of ethnic self-identification in Bulgaria.[33]

No discussion of the referendum on the Constitution was included in the agenda of the legislative body. There were 201 votes "against", 30 "for" and 15 abstentions. At that point the Members of Parliament from the UDF National Movement left the plenary hall.[34]

The day before the hunger strike ended - Thursday, July 18 - the blue Member of Parliament Yordan Vasilev described the protest in the following way:

> The hunger strike was successful. Above all, this is a moral victory. This is actually the second stage in our struggle, which is yet to be assessed. The plan of the communists for *perestroika* and for postponing the elections collapsed when the group left Parliament. The hunger strike revealed the true face of everyone and it became clear who is opposition and who is not.[35]

Not everybody wanted his face to be revealed. For example, the Member of Parliament Vladimir Sotirov, who was elected with the UDF ballot but remained in Parliament and signed the disputed fundamental law, had the following complaint to share:

> We accuse the BSP for assisting our being discredited as collaborationists. Nora Ananieva could have kissed Dertliev in some corner, without announcing it loudly on the microphones.[36]

Evidently, the spokesman of the Parliamentary Alliance of the Democratic Forces Sotirov had no remorse for his own actions and for the actions of his colleagues. The only thing that he would have preferred was everything to have been done in hiding, behind the scenes, so that the names of the opposition parliamentarians whose conduct was equal to that of the communists would remain untarred and luminous in history.

In contrast, Philip Dimitrov was dealing with a different set of issues. He focused on the preparations of the parliamentary elections and the physical condition of the hunger strikers. With a letter dated July 18, 1991, he appealed to them to stop their protest:

---

33 *Ibid.*

34 *Ibid.*

35 *Ibid.*

36 *Ibid.*

Dear friends,

I am appealing to you as Chairman of the National Coordinating Council of the Union of Democratic Forces, of which you are a part. You must go on living in good health.

Your efforts and your suffering during these days have yielded results for the cause of democracy, which are obvious to all.

The BSP is afraid of elections. There will be elections: they have been scheduled for September 29. Thus, the first of your demands was met.

The Grand National Assembly dissolved itself.

The attempt to remove you from the plenary sessions proves that the Bulgarian Communist Party is afraid of your words.

As a result of your strike, you received the support of the cabinet ministers and the President. Now you can go back to the plenary hall to defend your principles, as you had declared on May 14.

The issue of requesting the opinion of the nation on the new Constitution has already been raised. From now on you will have the opportunity to defend your democratic wish in the present and in the future parliament. The communists are obviously afraid to hear the voice of the people and you helped make this known to everybody.

The hunger strike is not an instrument of violence. It is a means of creating a forum to be heard.

Your voice has been heard.

The election campaign is starting and the UDF needs you. The supporters of democracy want you to be in good health and with enough stamina to work for the victory of the democratic forces.

For these reasons I appeal to you to put an end to your hunger strike and begin making active efforts towards the election victory.

We need you now. Immediately![37]

...

On July 22, the Parliamentary Group of the UDF National Movement was renamed into Parliamentary Group of the Union of Democratic Forces. Two people were elected as its co-chairmen, namely Stefan Savov and Stoyan Ganev. Yordan Vasilev and Alexander Yordanov became its spokesmen. A day later 38 Members of Parliament, who had left the legislative body in May, returned to Parliament. They were ready to participate in the work of the regular National Assembly into which the Seventh Grand National Assembly had transformed itself after the signing of the Constitution.

At the end of the month, the National Coordinating Council appealed to the organizations within the UDF to run in the election with a single blue ballot and

[37] *Ibid.*

one list of candidates. All noncommunist formations were invited to sign a declaration of intent not to participate in a coalition with the BSP during the election campaign and thereafter.

In mid-August, the leading body of the UDF faced serious difficulties with the leaders of the *Podkrepa* Federation of Labor, who launched a fierce campaign against the UDF government ministers, Ivan Kostov and Ivan Pushkarov. The situation was complicated further by the fact that the date for the parliamentary and local elections had been set and preparations for them were in full swing.

At that very moment *Podkrepa* started organizing a general strike. The UDF Chairman-immediately told Dr. Trenchev that the opposition union would not support the protest.[38] The trade union leader limited the scope of his plans, but did not give them up altogether.

The strike of the miners was announced on August 18, 1991. It coincided with the coup attempt against Mikhail Gorbachev, which could have become a splendid excuse for the former communists of Bulgaria to follow the example of the anti-democratic forces in the Soviet Union.

At the end of the first day of the protest, Philip Dimitrov gave a televised speech in which he appealed for an end to the strike and officially announced that the UDF would not support it. The blue leader shared his apprehensions that the strike may be used to postpone the elections scheduled for September 29. The lawyer went on to say that the strike currently served the interests of forces striving to destabilize the country and alluded to a "coup."

It became clear to everybody that the leadership of *Podkrepa* and that of the UDF had clashed. However disappointing that may have been to some, there was no other way out. On August 19, the world witnessed a *coup d'etat* in the Soviet Union, followed by a six-month martial law in the vast multinational state.

The President of the Republic of Bulgaria, Dr. Zhelyu Zhelev, the UDF National Coordinating Council, a number of parties and organizations immediately came out with declarations in which they expressed their concern with the news coming from the U.S.S.R.. Only the Bulgarian Socialist Party, which claimed to be reformed, plunged into not so mysterious silence. It completely failed to declare any position on the coup against Mikhail Gorbachev, the father of the *perestroika*, whom it was supposed to admire profoundly.

Without taking into account the risky situation, the chairman of the miners' strike committee, Zhelyazko Atanasov, declared that the second stage of the miners' protest would start. On August 20 all strikers would go underground. In

---

[38] Philip Dimitrov in a conversation with the author, Philadelphia, U.S.A., April 2, 1999.

response, Dimitar Popov's government issued a declaration stating that the strike committee had changed its demands and that it was misinforming the miners and society about the agreements reached. The document also pointed out that the demands of the organizers of the strike concealed their true political goals and ambitions. Then, the attempted coup in the Soviet Union failed on August 21. *Podkrepa* expressed its readiness to negotiate with the government right away. The following day Konstantin Trenchev finally called off the miners' strike.

On August 26, the leading body of the blue organization pointed out that the conduct of the BSP during the coup had demonstrated solidarity with its organizers. The same day Philip Dimitrov also sent a letter to the President of the State Security Committee of the U.S.S.R., Vladimir Bakatin. In it he asked that if any collaboration was discovered between the Soviet organizers of the coup and the Bulgarian Socialist Party, that fact should be made public. No answer followed.

...

President Zhelyu Zhelev rescheduled the parliamentary and local elections for October 13, 1991. On September 9, eighteen parties and organizations in the Union of Democratic Forces signed a political agreement. Several of them had new leaders. Just weeks after being included on the UDF ballot, the *Nikola Petkov* Bulgarian Agrarian People's Union decided to run on its own.

On October 11, 1991, Philip Dimitrov made a televised pre-election speech before the Bulgarian nation:

> The Union of Democratic Forces does not need to advertise itself in this election. During these months we all understood that our demands for rapid change were justified. It is clear that slow changes are equivalent to prolonged agony, enduring suffering and wasted efforts.
>
> We stand for the revival of Bulgaria. This simply means a normal life for each and every one of us, including members of the communist party. It means guaranteed tranquility and comfort in our families and a chance to raise our children and take care of our parents in their old age.
>
> Every person who does not vote at these elections is actually helping the agony go on. Every person whose vote has been lost because he voted for a small party or formation that failed to cross the threshold, will have protracted the agony as well.
>
> The road ahead of us is not easy. We have to cope with the entire heritage of communism, and the measures should be resolute and efficient. Naturally, we shall cooperate with other noncommunist formations in Parliament.

> However, if we wish to build a decent home, it is not possible to use the plans of many architects. There should be an organizing principle, a single organizing force, so that the result can be a decent home. Today only the Union of Democratic Forces can be that force because it is the biggest political formation that will run in these elections and will enter Parliament.
>
> You have one day for thought. Use it to think. You have the right to prefer one ballot over another. This is the voice of the heart. However, if you wish Bulgaria to rise to its feet and to be revived, the voice of reason says that the road is through the blue ballot, or rather through the three blue ballots: for Members of Parliament, for municipal councilors and for mayors.
>
> I hope you will hear the voice of reason.[39]

At the end of September opinion polls predicted that the Union of Democratic Forces would get 25 per cent of the votes of the Bulgarian citizens. The Bulgarian Socialist Party was expected to receive 23 per cent of the votes. The Thirty-Sixth National Assembly was also anticipated to have representatives of the Movement for Rights and Freedoms, the *Nikola Petkov* Bulgarian Agrarian People's Union, UDF-Center, UDF-Liberals and Bulgarian Agrarian People's Union-United.

---

[39] *Demokratsiya* daily, October 12, 1991.

23. Semi-victory for the Democrats

The predictions about the October 1991 elections did not prove accurate. The Central Electoral Commission allowed 63 parties and coalitions to run in the competition. It registered 6,790,006 eligible voters, 86.9 percent of whom appeared at the polling stations. In the end, however, only three organizations were represented in the Thirty-Sixth National Assembly: the Union of Democratic Forces, which received 34.36 percent of the votes and 110 seats, the Bulgarian Socialist Party for which 33.14 percent of the population voted and it got 106 seats, and the Movement for Rights and Freedoms with 7.55 percent of the votes and 24 seats in Parliament. The remaining sixty organizations failed to cross the 4 percent threshold and were not included in the national legislative body, in accordance with the new Election Act.

Much to the surprise and bitter disappointment of their leaders, UDF-Center, UDF-Liberals and the *Nikola Petkov* Bulgarian Agrarian People's Union failed to get sufficient votes to enter the Parliament. These ambitious men had had different plans and expectations when they led their parties and coalitions out of the Union of Democratic Forces. They had hoped to attract most of the UDF electorate to their formations and thus dominate the political life in Bulgaria. It had not even occurred to Dertliev, Karakachanov, Simeonov and the other opponents of the UDF that they could remain outside of the National Assembly. They had envisioned themselves as founders of "the country's future political structure."[1] What kind of Parliament could there be without them?

At the same time, the noncommunist voters wondered why these politicians had chosen to stay outside of the UDF. The separation of their parties and groups and their differentiation into autonomous electoral units reduced the advantage of the blue union over the party of the former communists by at least 10 percent and left the UDF with a precarious majority of only one percent over its political adversaries.

As the German daily newspaper *Frankfurter Allgemeine Zeitung* explained to its readers, the result from the parliamentary elections in Bulgaria was a semi-victory for the democrats.[2] The UDF did not have a sufficient parliamentary majority to form its own government. Thus, it was bound to confront many difficulties and be forced to make concessions.

Nevertheless, on October 14, 1991, during the rally celebrating the first election victory of democrats after the communists usurped power in 1944, Philip Dimitrov spoke with an air of optimism. He declared with conviction that

---

[1] *Demokratsiya* daily, April 12, 1991.

[2] *Frankfurter Allgemeine Zeitung, Ein halber Sieg,* October 15, 1991.

there were "two types of elections, won and lost ones. We won." Then he added, "The era of communism in Bulgaria is over."[3]

The local and foreign press suggested that the role of the third organization represented in the National Assembly would complicate the situation further. It was evident that the party of the Turkish ethnic minority would be "a decisive factor for Bulgaria in a Parliament blocked by two equally strong polar opposites."[4] The Bulgarian Moslem had experienced the aggression of the red dictatorship until very recently. As an opponent to the former communist party, the Union of Democratic Forces was a natural coalition partner for the Movement for Rights and Freedoms. Yet, such a coalition would play directly into the hands of the Bulgarian Socialist Party. In that case, the communists/socialists were certain to claim that the country was run from Ankara rather than Sofia. The issue was sensitive given the country's history of five centuries under Ottoman domination.

On the day following the elections, the Chairman of the UDF National Coordinating Council, soon to be the country's Prime Minister, resolutely rejected any possibility of a coalition with the former communists. With respect to the MRF, Philip Dimitrov said he supposed the Movement would not wish to form an official coalition with the UDF. Nevertheless, he stressed that he would rely on the "support of the ethnic Turks in Parliament."[5]

. . .

Work in the Bulgarian legislative body started without further ado. Nothing suggested that the Thirty-Sixth National Assembly was to turn into an arena of countless intrigues and treachery.

On November 4, 1991, the day of the official opening of the newly-elected Parliament, Philip Dimitrov was the first to speak from the rostrum. The leader of the UDF declared that "Today we can say that the cycle of totalitarianism in Bulgaria is finally over." He was vigorously applauded by the UDF, MRF and the cabinet ministers, but not by the members of the renamed communist party.[6] In contrast, Professor Alexander Lilov, the former ideological strategist of

---

[3] *Ibid.*, *Bisherige Opposition – Wahlsieg in Bulgarien*, October 15, 1991; *The Philadelphia Inquirer*, *Bulgaria Communists likely out*, October 15, 1991.

[4] *Demokratsiya* daily, Petko Bocharov, *The Guilty*, October 19, 1991; *Frankfurter Allgemeine Zeitung*, October 15, 1991; *The Philadelphia Inquirer*, October 15, 1991; *The Washington Post*, October 14, 1991; *Chicago Tribune*, October 29, 1991.

[5] *The Philadelphia Inquirer*, October 15, 1991.

[6] First plenary session of the Thirty-Sixth National Assembly, Sofia, Monday, November 4, 1991, Library of the National Assembly.

Todor Zhivkov's regime and current leader of the Bulgarian Socialist Party, drew the applause of his fellow-party members when he said that the parties in power will continue to alternate.

Then, without wasting another minute, the red politician started manipulating his listeners. He alluded to an imminent dictatorship and announced that his party stood for the "protection of the interests of the working people." He went on to declare, "We say a firm 'No!' to speculation and to the re-establishment of wild capitalism in Bulgaria."[7] It should be noted that this statement was uttered before the communist party had made any sort of attempt to return the billions of dollars and levs stolen from the population and account for the dozens of communist-owned enterprises in the country and abroad.

Yet, Lilov was already cunningly coaxing the UDF:

> Let us put an end to the political repressions and the thirst for revenge. Let us stop the persecution and elimination of political opponents through coercive rather than democratic means. Let this sinister cyclical trend of violence in our political reality stop at long last. We all know that it took away a large part of the fertile minds of our nation. In addition to costing us our blood, violence is shortsighted policy. Those who are victims of violence today, gentlemen, will start dispensing violence tomorrow.[8]

Just and sensible words ostensibly. Yet, they sounded more than insolent as they were pronounced by a top-ranking communist functionary and ideologue, considering the fact that the BCP-BSP had not apologized for the tens of thousands of lives taken and the hundreds of thousands of lives ruined during its dictatorship. In addition, not one of the living concentration camp managers and inquisitors or politicians responsible for the countless crimes of the regime had been sent behind bars. All this didn't stop Alexander Lilov from preaching about morality!

That day Ahmed Dogan responded well to the reds. His speech included the following:

> We would be inexcusable idealists and simpletons if we assumed that communism would step down from the political scene on its own. Yes, communism is inevitably going away and should pass into oblivion. Still, while departing from the political scene, the derivatives of the communist party are

---

[7] *Ibid.*

[8] *Ibid.*

> constantly reorganizing and making use of the entire range of social, political and economic acts of mimicry.
>
> That is precisely why we have to help them find their real place in Bulgarian political life and make sure that there will be no relapses of totalitarian regimes and ideologies. That can only happen when justice is brought to bear not only upon individual puppets of history, but upon their party as a whole. In this case the issue at hand is the proven crime of a political organization responsible for the current national catastrophe in the Republic of Bulgaria. Any other approach would only prolong the agony of the preceding stage and multiply the labor pains of the democratic processes in our homeland.
>
> Making the right choice is necessary even more on account of the fact that communism is making its last attempt to divert the focus of political tension by generating interethnic conflicts in certain regions of the country. The communists' attempts to allude to questions of national security evoke not only smiles and pity, but also signal that they will not stop short of anything to save themselves from the Golgotha of history.[9]

The Chairman of the Movement for Rights and Freedoms also promised the support of his parliamentary group to the Union of Democratic Forces:

> A parliamentary center may have been needed last year. This year the idea of a parliamentary center no longer signifies a middle ground facilitating dialogue in Parliament. That idea may even prove to be harmful at some point. Instead, it should be understood well that accelerated democratization presupposes a bipolar structure of Parliament with the clear domination of the democratic forces in it.[10]

That was what Ahmed Dogan declared the day of the opening of the National Assembly. Only several months later, instead of fighting against the former totalitarian and criminal party through legal means, he did everything within his power to make sure that the UDF cabinet would stop governing the country. For years, the MRF parliamentary group would vote in unison with the communists-socialists and form coalition governments with them. Today the statement made by the MRF leader on November 4, 1991, is believed by many to have been stage-managed by none other but the BSP.

Soon Dogan amazed people further. He openly manifested his personal sympathy for two of the most despised communists in Bulgaria, Todor Zhivkov

---

[9] *Ibid.*

[10] *Ibid.*

and Andrey Lukanov. In that regard Dr. Heinz Brahm wrote the following in his study entitled *The "Blue" Government of Philip Dimitrov*:

> On December 30 [1992 - *author's note*], the former communist Prime Minister Lukanov was released from preliminary custody. The BSP and the MRF, under the chairmanship of the Deputy Speaker of the National Assembly Kadir Kadir (MRF), had dropped the charges against him. Dogan, who had acted as a fierce anticommunist and anti-socialist earlier, no longer tried to disguise his political U turn. Even before Lukanov was set free, Dogan had attempted to visit him and failed for lack of permission by the General Prosecution. In 1993, Dogan even met with Todor Zhivkov, who was known for his hostile attitude to the Turks.[11]

It seemed an incredible lack of decency for the leader of the party of the Turkish minority in Bulgaria to go see Zhivkov. In this way Dogan provided moral support and showed respect for the dictator who had masterminded the so-called "revival process", in which the names of the Turks and Moslems in Bulgaria were changed coercively. Today the reasons for his strange act are no longer secret.

...

The Thirty-Sixth National Assembly elected its leaders on November 4, 1991. Stefan Savov, Member of Parliament from the Union of Democratic Forces and Chairman of the Democratic Party, became Speaker. The two elected Deputy Speakers were Snezhana Botusharova from the UDF and Kadir Kadir from the MRF. The Bulgarian Socialist Party initially refused to have a Deputy Speaker of its own, but later nominated Yordan Shkolagerski. The Parliamentary Group of the Union of the Democratic Forces was headed by Alexander Yordanov, with two deputies, Edwin Sugarev and Zlatka Ruseva.

At that point preliminary work on the formation of the government had already begun. Ivan Kurtev, the first leader of the Social Democratic Party who had broken out of Dr. Dertliev's BSDP in order to remain in the UDF, made the following entry in his notebook on October 28, 1991:

> Negotiations with the MRF. Delegation of Ahmed Dogan, Osman Oktay, Yunal Lyutfi and one more member of the MRF leadership. From the UDF: Philip Dimitrov, Stefan Savov, Stoyan Ganev, Alexander Yordanov, Nikolay Vasilev and myself. Mihail Nedelchev and Edwin Sugarev joined us later.

[11] Brahm 1998, pp. 30-31.

> The Turks seem like sensible and realistic people to me. They are convinced of the need for coordinated efforts in the National Assembly. They are not insisting on having ministerial offices and prefer to participate in the government at secondary positions. They propose that we appoint ethnically Bulgarian deputy ministers whom they trust and who have been suggested by them. They will also have one Deputy Speaker of the National Assembly and chairpersons of some parliamentary committees. Absolutely no other demands.[12]

In the autumn of 1991 there was no way for Ivan Kurtev to tell that absolutely all of the cited MRF leaders were collaborators of the communist State Security system.[13] His diary continues as follows:

> November 6, 1991. After the session of the National Assembly, we gathered to discuss the new government in the restaurant of the ASP [Alternative Socialist Party founded in February 1990 by former members of the Bulgarian Communist Party, which joined the UDF after the elections for a Grand National Assembly in June 1990 - *author's note*] on *Uzundzhovska* Street. Our meeting was attended by Philip Dimitrov, Stefan Savov, Yordan Vasilev, Mihail Nedelchev, Ventsislav Dimitrov, Stoyan Ganev, Elka Konstantinova, Ivan Kostov, Georgi Markov, Edwin Sugarev, Ivan Pushkarov, Oleg Chulev, Ilko Eskenazi, Asen Michkovski, Nikolay Vasilev, Boyko Proychev, Radoslav Nenov, Dr. Vasil Mihaylov, Hristo Velev, Plamen Darakchiev and myself. Dogan, Oktay and Lyutfi were invited as representatives of the MRF. The talks continued until 3 a.m. without reaching a final decision.
>
> Our work was further complicated by the fact that the alcohol got to some of the people quickly after a long and hard day and their garrulousness went beyond all limits. The frivolous conduct of Asen Michkovski from the ASP was the most irresponsible. That man was not sober even while we were making the election lists, and he was disruptive. It is clear that he does not hold his liquor well. He is a good economist and he will probably participate in the country's government, but falling asleep at the table when the nation's fate is being decided is something that I shall never be able to understand. Asen Michkovski fell asleep at the table while we were forming the first democratic government of Bulgaria after 50 years!
>
> I am increasingly alarmed by the ambitions of *Podkrepa* to dictate political life in Bulgaria. The Alternative Socialist Party is apparently one of the means by which *Podkrepa* wishes to influence the UDF.

---

[12] Kurtev, *Diary*, October 28, 1991.

[13] Fifty-eighth session of the Thirty-Eighth National Assembly, Sofia, Wednesday, October 22, 1997, Library of the National Assembly.

Some of the leaders of the UDF and *Podkrepa* think they have already attained "Olympic heights" in politics and seem to forget the fate of others like Dertliev, Simeonov and Karakachanov. Most probably we, the people who had gathered last night, are neither the best politicians, nor the most capable persons in this country, and possibly others could have formed a better government and could have governed better. However, since we are called upon to effect the change of the system, we have to approach our obligations with maximum seriousness and responsibility.

The main problem is associated with the office of the Foreign Minister. Philip Dimitrov and Stoyan Ganev are willing to take that position. Philip has reservations regarding Stoyan Ganev's qualifications. However, if Dimitrov does not propose a third option, he will probably be forced to entrust foreign policy to Stoyan. Most of us, myself included, agreed that a person with a strong presence is needed in the Foreign Ministry. As a Prime Minister, Philip will not be able to manage those affairs at all on his own.

There still was much uncertainty about the Defense Minister's position. We discussed Ivan Glushkov, Angel Dimitrov, Vladislav Daskalov and even Dimitar Ludzhev, but none of these people had broad support.

There appear to be no problems with the choices of Minister of Transportation (Alexander Alexandrov), Minister of Science and Education (Nikolay Vasilev), Minister of Environmental Protection (Valentin Vasilev), Minister of Finance (Ivan Kostov), Minister of Industry (Ivan Pushkarov), Minister of Health Care (Nikola Vasilev), Minister of Internal Affairs (Yordan Sokolov), Minister of Justice (Svetoslav Luchnikov), Minister of Construction (Nikola Karadimov), and Minister of Communications (Stefan Sofiyanski).

Tomorrow night we shall continue the discussions because Philip will have to propose his cabinet to the National Assembly on Friday.

November 7. This time we were more efficient. We decided that there would be no ministries of foreign economic relations and communications. In addition to the ministers endorsed yesterday, the new nominations are as follows: Stoyan Ganev for Minister of Foreign Affairs, Vekil Vanov for Minister of Labor and Social Policy, Dimitar Ludzhev for Minister of Defense, and Stanislav Dimitrov for Minister of Agriculture. The office of the Minister of Culture remained vacant because Ivan Radoev refused to take it.

In the absence of the Prime Minister, his deputies would be Stoyan Ganev and Nikolay Vasilev. Philip Dimitrov proposed that Sofia Mayor Yanchulev be Minister for the Capital, but that idea was not approved.

Professor Nikolay Vasilev reacted in a very caustic way to the fact that Shotlekov's nomination for Minister of Labor and Social Policy was dropped; Vasilev threatened to leave the cabinet. He also left the meeting, which was held on the top floor of the UDF building on *Rakovski* Street. They chased him down the stairs, persuaded him to stay, etc., etc. Then he calmed down, but I am not quite sure of his intentions.

> November 8. Today was the happiest day in my life. For the first time after 47 years Bulgaria has a government without communists. After two years of labor pains, at long last the road to democracy is open.[14]

. . .

Back on October 15, 1991, the National Coordinating Council of the UDF had already reached the decision to propose Philip Dimitrov for Prime Minister. Professor Elka Konstantinova was nominated for the office of Minister of Culture just one hour before the members of the new cabinet were put to the vote in the plenary hall.[15] Stoyan Ganev remained a disputed candidate for the position of Foreign Minister until 3 a.m. on November 7, while Dimitar Ludzhev's nomination for Minister of Defense was discussed only in passing. Still, later that same day these men took two of the positions with the most responsibility in the government proposed to the National Assembly for endorsement. How did all that happen?

Philip Dimitrov has an answer to this question:

> Ahmed Dogan had said that he did not want any positions in the government for the MRF. I admit I was relieved when I heard that because I was among the very few who supported the idea that Turks should join the cabinet. Stefan Savov was against this but his opinions were not extreme. In contrast, Stoyan Ganev made a sharp turn in his views and embraced an anti-Turkish attitude in the summer of 1991. Until that time, he was considered to be a great friend of the MRF; yet, during an official meeting he made a scene and said that he would not sit at the same table with Dogan, who was a representative of an ethnic party banned under the Constitution.
>
> Naturally, I was extremely surprised that the day before the voting of the government in office, Ahmed Dogan announced that Stoyan Ganev was his nomination for Foreign Minister. Dogan insisted that Ganev should be given that position. I, on the other hand, was keen on Ganev not being Foreign Minister.
>
> Dogan told Ivan Kostov, who was sent as an emissary to the MRF, that Stoyan Ganev and Dimitar Ludzhev were the two nominations that he supported. The MRF leader refused to participate in the government, but insisted that these two individuals be proposed as ministers.
>
> Our relations with the MRF were very complicated. The movement avoided the signing of an official agreement with the UDF at least twice, with the pretext that that would intensify the nationalist propaganda against the

---

14 Kurtev, *Diary*, November 6-8, 1991.

15 *Ibid.*

Turks. During the 1991 elections, the MRF sharply differentiated themselves from the UDF. Then, when the MRF entered Parliament, they started showing interest in us again.

At that point I could not afford to quarrel with Ahmed Dogan, so I accepted his demand. I gave in on Ganev, who had the support of Georgi Markov as well. Dimitar Ludzhev also became a member of the cabinet. At the time he did not seem that unsuitable to be Defense Minister. Dimitar was a man of enormous energy who had the habit of taking up one hundred eighty-six things a day. It is quite a different matter that he never managed to finish them all. Anyway, his bubbling energy was noticeable and impressed people. Besides, he had contacts in the United States and had a pro-NATO orientation.

Forming a Council of Ministers always implies compromise and bargaining. Yet, there were also tricks we had to deal with, such as Georgi Markov's strategy for obtaining the office of Minister of the Interior. I proposed that that ministry be headed by Yordan Sokolov. Markov definitely supported this nomination, transforming it virtually into his own idea. He himself swore that he was not interested in the ministerial post, while he was actually very keen on the Interior Ministry. It was just as he had done months previously when he swore that he did not want to go to Parliament but still ran in the elections.

Georgi Markov liked the idea of inviting Sokolov for that ministry because he thought the latter would not accept the office. I spoke to Sokolov personally and he agreed. Later I learned that after I announced that officially, Markov called Sokolov and tried to dissuade him from taking the ministry. If Sokolov had listened to him, Georgi Markov would have attained his goal: on the very last day we would have remained without a Minister of the Interior and he would have pretended to make a concession by taking over the sector. Thank God that Yordan did not refuse. Otherwise, it would have been a big mess. I managed to put that whole puzzle together piece by piece years later.

Podkrepa also took an active part in the selection of the cabinet ministers. It supported the nominations of Nikola Vasilev for Minister of Health and Nikolay Vasilev, the Chairman of the Alternative Socialist Party, for Minister of Science and Education, among others. The remaining government ministers were negotiated among the parties.[16]

. . .

On November 8, 1991, the Thirty-Sixth National Assembly voted in the 79th Council of Ministers of Bulgaria. From the Union of Democratic Forces and from the Movement for Rights and Freedoms 128 Members of Parliament gave their vote in support of the proposed government, while 90 voted against it.

---

[16] Philip Dimitrov in a conversation with the author, Philadelphia, U.S.A., April 2, 1999.

Through a vote behind closed doors, Philip Dimitrov received the confidence of a total of 131 Members of Parliament for the post of Prime Minister. The opponents to his nomination were 94.

Afterwards, each of the three parliamentary groups represented in the legislative body made a brief statement. Alexander Yordanov from the UDF pointed out that "the team consists of professionals who have proven that they are real democrats and that this will be a government of action." He added that the UDF "will preserve its oppositionary attitude and carefully watch the actions of the ministers, so that it may be known that in Bulgaria there is separation of power once and for all."[17] Then, in his congratulatory address to the new cabinet, Yunal Lyutfi assured the government on behalf of the MRF that "the movement will firmly support its actions."[18] At last, the Bulgarian Socialist Party also expressed its best wishes for the UDF government after having tried to discredit it in every possible way prior to the vote.[19]

That day the plenary session lasted twelve hours. In the very beginning Philip Dimitrov made the following announcement:

> The country is going through its most difficult period since World War II. This is a period of economic collapse, unemployment and a three-digit inflation rate. We also find ourselves in foreign trade isolation; we are losing shares in traditional markets in the Soviet Union, Eastern Europe and the Middle East. There are unjustifiably optimistic expectations for rapid and easy success, economic growth and an improvement in the living standard of the people. Naturally, there were certain achievements in that regard in 1991 already. Nevertheless, the shortage of consumer goods on the market has not been overcome and the foreign currency market is fluctuating and boding the serious threat of speculations. The country's economy is far from stable. It is exposed to severe blows in the energy sector, specifically in the supply of fuels, as well as trade and finance. Negotiations with our creditors are stagnant. The demands for the servicing of our foreign debt are firm, while those who are indebted to us are not servicing their Bulgarian creditors. The threat of unemployment and the already existing unemployment are burdening every Bulgarian family. Currently, there is no drive for improvement in the effectiveness and quality of production.[20]

---

[17] *Demokratsiya* daily, November 9, 1991.

[18] *Ibid.*

[19] *Ibid.*; Ivan Kurtev in a conversation with the author, Sofia, Bulgaria, August 28, 1998.

[20] Fourth plenary session of the Thirty-Sixth National Assembly, Sofia, Friday, November 8, 1991, Library of the National Assembly.

In his speech the UDF Chairman declared that the program of his government is of a long-term pragmatic nature, and that the main prerequisites for its success were social calm and civil peace. He defined the country's economic stabilization and the fight to curb inflation as the first short-term economic objectives of the Council of Ministers. Their next objective would be to put an end to the decline in production and control the growing unemployment rate. Dimitrov specifically stressed the egalitarian economic approach of his government:

> The government refuses to implement a selective economic policy and redistribute the funds in the state budget for different sectors and producers. The financial resources for such a policy are lacking. It will very quickly turn into a mere campaign for assisting hopeless companies and activities, and it will prolong the agony of the economic crisis, without giving great hopes for the future.[21]

The Prime Minister to be went on to explain that the cabinet's other priority concerning the economy would be achieving rational employment and control over unemployment. This goal was followed by plans to encourage private business and family entrepreneurship. The next task the government had set for its economic policy was to strengthen the foreign currency market and stimulate foreign investment in order to revitalize the national economy.

In the same speech Philip Dimitrov addressed the government's planned legislative initiatives. After being endorsed by the National Assembly, this legal framework would let the ministers work efficiently:

> Priority will be given to legislation necessary for the change in the regime of foreign investments. As I said already, our task will be to attract a maximum of investments, establish an adequate banking system, regulate the state enterprises, and manage the complex privatization and re-privatization processes. That includes making amendments to the legislation in order to facilitate the speedier return of land to its rightful owners, and - of course - drafting legislation for the creation of a modern social security and medical insurance system. In addition, there will be bills aimed at an overall tax reform.[22]

Dimitrov announced that the foreign policy of his government would be to seek out European solutions to Balkan problems. In other words, the

---

[21] *Ibid.*

[22] *Ibid.*

government would work to build good neighborly relations with the countries in the Balkan Peninsula, without making any territorial claims against them. The cabinet would also foster friendly relations with Europe, the USA and all democratic states. Bulgaria would seek to join European structures and institutions and would undertake the necessary steps for participation in the European Union. At the same time, the foreign policy of the country would be to maintain amicable and mutually beneficial relations with the Soviet Union and its republics.

At the end of his speech, Philip Dimitrov said the following:

> Today we are aware that we cannot promise complete happiness to anyone or ensure the instantaneous resolution of the enormous problems facing the state. There are difficult winter months ahead of us, pent up dissatisfaction, and - as I mentioned already - expectations for quick fixes, while the real problems are numerous.
>
> We are looking forward to receiving the support of the Bulgarian Parliament and of the Bulgarian people because we are ready to work for the resolution of these problems. We are not promising any magical results; we are promising exertions and difficulties and we are taking on the responsibility of doing everything within our power to overcome them.[23]

Unfortunately, the Prime Minister was heard only by a part of the nation. The rest were used to communist lies and deception and were either outraged by Philip Dimitrov's honest words or did not bother to remember them. People wanted "magical results" overnight.

---

[23] *Ibid.*

24. On the Thorny Path to Democracy

To this day some people recall the government of Philip Dimitrov with nostalgia. Given that its achievements were not so numerous, such feelings may be a bit of a surprise. As the former Prime Minister himself put it, one third of his ministers were deliberately causing harm, another third had no idea why they were in the team, and only a few strong individuals with outstanding qualities, like Ivan Kostov and Svetoslav Luchnikov, made their mark on Bulgarian history. In fact, Kostov went on to be Prime Minister for longer and attained more than Dimitrov. Hence, there can be only one explanation for people's preference for the first cabinet of the Union of Democratic Forces - it tried to revive forgotten moral values in the Bulgarian State, bringing them to the forefront of the political arena.

Philip Dimitrov had no chance of being either particularly effective, or particularly successful as the leader with executive power. He did not have the support of the National Assembly or the President of the Republic. In addition, he was forced to work with a government fractured by divergent interests and agendas. Often there was a note of fatalism in his speeches, and the perceptive observer could easily tell that Dimitrov did not believe he would hold on to his position for long. The accelerated pace of his governing suggested a race against time.

Prime Minister Dimitrov's first televised address to the nation was filled with imagery from the Old Testament, specifically from Exodus. In it, he suggested that the Bulgarians could wander in the desert for forty years before they freed themselves from communism. For the less educated Bulgarians, the story sounded abstract and vague, while the others found it convincing and wise. Several months later, the press attacked Philip Dimitrov with the criticism that he had imagined himself to be Moses.

Dimitrov did not seek to aggrandize himself. He was thinking about responsibility rather than power, about efforts rather than rewards, about tenacity rather than triumph. He did not expect that he would be the one to reach the Promised Land of a functioning democracy and market economy. Yet, he was convinced that he was called upon to blaze the path leading to it. And he was firmly resolved to fulfill that onerous duty.

It is said that the democratic functioning of state institutions was restored by the UDF government in 1992. Unfortunately, this claim is exaggerated. It is unrealistic to think that this could have been achieved in a few months. The impact of communism on the minds of the people was still strong, and the mafia of the secret services had taken over the economy already. Moreover, Philip Dimitrov was aware that it was unlikely for him to make great strides in the fight against organized crime: his cabinet's proposals for effective measures against the mafia were rejected by the National Assembly, lost in the numerous parliamentary committees, or implemented only partially.

However, the blue Prime Minister sensed that he was capable of making a significant contribution in a different way. The legacy that Dimitrov wished to leave to the nation was one of moral principles of conduct. He did his best to show Bulgarians that it was important to follow the principles of democracy. He knew that his success as a politician and statesman would be contingent on the extent to which he himself could meet the standard he had set. Hence, with unshaken persistence the lawyer refused to adopt a "more conciliatory and mainstream line of behavior."

Another difficult task of Philip Dimitrov's government was to stress the significance of the rule of law for a functioning democracy. That cabinet's efforts were a complete reversal from one of the fundamental policies of communist rule - the utter disregard for the law.

The Communist Party Headquarters in the second largest city of Bulgaria - Plovdiv - were a typical example of that policy. In 1968, a permit from the municipality was necessary for the BCP to begin construction on publicly owned land. However, the land was simply seized by the red party, which never became the legal owner of the plot. During communist dictatorship it would have taken only a few minutes for the BCP to obtain the document from the municipality. Still, the authorities felt offended by the thought that any law could restrict their power. "The Party has so decided" was a sufficient justification for any deed. Abiding by the law was considered a humiliation. After almost fifty years of lawless communist behaviour, the Bulgarian population needed to witness respect for the law on the part of the government once again.[1]

Philip Dimitrov was the first - and for a certain period of time the only politician - to call the mafia by its real name. He made sure to let it be known that the economic formations of the State Security services were breaking the laws. Dimitrov resolutely opposed the dangerous tendency for these formations to present themselves as legitimate companies and promote their managers as national heroes of sorts. Furthermore, the Prime Minister was trying in every way possible to encourage in people realistic expectations about their standard of living. On several occasions he deliberately started his addresses in Parliament with the sentence "Ladies and Gentlemen, as I have told you recently, there is no such thing as a free lunch." In his public speaches, Dimitrov also used common Turkish words accepted in the Bulgarian language, without worrying that this irritated some stylists. He was trying to demonstrate that the ethnic

---

[1] Philip Dimitrov in a conversation with the author, Philadelphia, U.S.A., September 18, 2008.

Bulgarians had strong ties with their Turkish fellow-countrymen. It was characteristic of the Premier to fight for the separation of powers and to show respect for all state institutions, regardless of their willingness to cooperate with the UDF government or not.

At the end of 1992, when the renamed communists took control in the next government of Bulgaria, they stopped the implementation of most of the reforms that the UDF cabinet had introduced during its brief time in office. However, Philip Dimitrov and a few of his ministers had already succeeded in giving wings to freedom of thought and expression and allowing private business initiative to thrive. Dimitrov was always convinced that this process was irreversible and that the brutality and complete lawlessness of the communist regime were no longer possible.[2]

. . .

In November 1991, when they first entered their offices, some of the ministers in the government of the Union of Democratic Forces found all drawers, cabinets and files emptied. Others were welcomed warmly by their subordinates, which actually did not amount to much. Subsequently, behind their backs, the mid-level *nomenklatura*, trained and recruited during the totalitarian rule, impeded the implementation of the new ministers' orders and instructions.

For half a century, the entire administrative apparatus of the country had been largely communist. Hence, most members of the bureaucracy were neither capable nor willing to change the existing system and lay the foundations for radical transformation. It was imperative that most of the public administration staff be replaced. Unfortunately, the pool of competent and well-meaning specialists from whom to pick was not large at the time.

The German political scientist Heinz Brahm elaborated:

> If the goal was indeed to achieve a sharp change in the course of the country, it was necessary to replace the more or less corrupt high-ranking representatives of the former regime in the state banks, the media and at least in the major educational institutions. The decision reached [by Philip Dimitrov's government - *author's note*] was to remove all of the highest ranking representatives of the communist *nomenklatura* from their offices. For lack of time and due to considerations of efficiency, it was not possible to check each case individually. Communism was not a small-scale harmless event. The crimes perpetrated in the period from Georgi Dimitrov's to Todor Zhivkov's time could not simply be forgotten, just like that, with a wave of the hand.

[2] *Ibid.*, February 12, 2000.

> After 1944, the communists sent thousands of people they considered inconvenient to the firing squad and concentration and labor camps. The UDF abided by the laws when it dismissed high-ranking representatives of the communist regime from their positions.[3]

A good example for such a law was the Banking and Credit Act. It banned high-ranking communist party members from managerial positions in the banking sector for a period of five years.[4] The document aimed at the decommunization of Bulgaria and alleviation of the material losses and moral suffering of its people. In the form in which it was originally proposed by Dimitrov's cabinet, the act could have been a significant contribution to the financial stability of the state and its population.

In November, the Thirty-Sixth National Assembly adopted the original Banking and Credit Act. The Bulgarian Socialist Party could not live with this decision. It took the issue to the Constitutional Court, which proclaimed the document as unconstitutional. Given the heavily pro-communist composition of the Constitutional Court at the time, that ruling was not surprising. Hence, the Banking and Credit Act was revised substantially before it was implemented, and it did not prevent senior activists of the Bulgarian Communist Party from continuing with their illegal monetary transactions. The results of which were felt most tangibly in 1996, when these "bankers" succeeded in transferring practically all the public funds to private bank accounts.

In December 1991, UDF Member of Parliament Georgi Panev proposed another decommunization legislation in the National Assembly, which triggered great excitement and many debates among the intellectuals. The "Panev Act" infuriated the reds because it restricted their influence in the educational and research sector by eliminating their privileges. In fact, there were also many alleged noncommunists who stood against the document and branded it as superfluous and anti-humane. They either could not grasp its meaning fully or had personal reasons for fearing some of its provisions. The proposed legislation not only prohibited the upper crust of the former dictatorial party from senior positions in universities and research institutions for a period of five years, but it also required that candidates for higher academic office sign a declaration that they had never been informers of the State Security services. Tragically, many Bulgarian scientists and scholars could not place their signature on such a document.[5]

---

[3] Brahm 1998, p. 13.

[4] *Ibid.*

[5] *Ibid.*, pp. 13-14.

In contrast to those who rejected the "Panev Act," most democratically minded citizens found it much too mild. They had forgotten neither the selection criteria for the communist academic and research staff nor the ways in which those academics had brainwashed their students and society. Most noncommunists thought that these people deserved a more serious punishment for their deeds. Still they were happy when the "Panev act" was adopted.

Clearly, it was difficult to please everybody and at the same time to act effectively. Some cabinet ministers, irrespective of the complaints of the communists-socialists, set out to change the staff of their institutions. At the Council of Ministers, headed by Philip Dimitrov, 260 people were fired immediately, leaving only half of the staff intact. Between November 1991 and May 1992, the Ministry of Foreign Affairs also dismissed 215 diplomats and 105 technical staff members. More than a dozen generals and over a thousand army officers were retired from the Ministry of Defense. About 2,000 out of about 8,000 managers of state-owned companies were changed, and 968 people from National Television were dismissed. The Ministry of Finance of Ivan Kostov refrained from firing staff with the explanation that the UDF did not have enough economic experts of its own.[6]

. . .

The blue government had prepared its legislative policy well, but the so-called "Sokolov" and "Luchnikov" projects were not lucky. During the winter of 1992 they were lost in the archives of the parliamentary committees and were never brought to the plenary hall of the National Assembly. That was hardly accidental.

The first piece of legislation provided for amendments to the Law on the Ministry of the Interior allowing for personnel changes. The second bill proposed amendments to the Law on the Property of Citizens, facilitating the confiscation of property acquired illegally by individuals and companies. The "Luchnikov" document would have helped stop financial crime in the country in 1992. That would have turned Bulgaria into a state governed by the law, which was what it needed above all.

The supporters of the former totalitarian regime continued complaining about the UDF government's measures and accused Dimitrov's cabinet of a "witch hunt." Additionally, the "red", "pink" and "yellow" press never stopped telling the readers that the authorities were acting just as the communists had after September 9, 1944.

---

[6] *Ibid.*, pp. 12,14.

Naturally, the pro-communist media never mentioned that in the 1940s and 1950s people were not just asked to retire or were dismissed from managerial positions for five years. Instead, they were killed without a trail, tried by pseudo-courts that passed thousands of death and life imprisonment sentences. Those media never discussed the dozens of concentration and labor camps, the prisons filled to capacity with innocent people, the deportations, the seizing and nationalization of property, the annulling of diplomas, academic degrees, professional, educational and civil rights, the closed state borders. The communist propaganda machine brainwashed the uneducated and they often said that everything was "just as it was then." This claim sounded absurd coming from former communists who would freely go abroad carrying substantial sums in foreign currency with them, or send their children and grandchildren to expensive schools, colleges, and universities in the West.

In February 1992, the Bulgarian Socialist Party was livid when twenty-three UDF Members of Parliament submitted the draft of the Law on Decommunization in the Public Sphere for approval in the National Assembly. On this occasion Georgi Panev wrote the following:

> First of all, I would like to point out that the demagogic claims of the socialist propaganda in connection with the submitted legislation are actually unfounded and they are yet another trick of the so-called "constructive" opposition. The official publication of the Bulgarian Socialist Party [the daily newspaper *Duma - author's note*] "sounded the alarm" that more than 120 thousand people and their families would lose their jobs if the law was passed. It is obvious that the "comrades" cannot imagine their life if they are not bosses because the proposed legislation provides for certain restrictions only for certain leading positions in the public sphere. It does not in any way constitute a ban of professions, and in that sense, it is not repressive. There is nothing shameful and undignified in working for one's own good and for the good of society, without being necessarily in a leadership position.
>
> The important fact is that the bill does not refer to any office elected directly by the population. The right to elect and be elected is an inalienable right guaranteed by the Constitution.
>
> The time frame for the enforcement of that law is five years. Its aim is above all to break the bonds between the communist party and the mafia, which is the legacy left behind by the union of party and state. The elimination of the influence of the mafia over the public sector would be to a great extent a measure against the illegal penetration of speculative capital into the emerging market economy. It would prevent the spread of corruption and do away with the privileges stemming from affiliations with the former communist party. It is also necessary to give up the established standards of thought and conduct,

> which are in opposition to the new approach and type of behavior required of civil servants in the course of the country's democratization.
>
> The secretaries of the grass-root communist organizations and all higher-ranking communist party activists are among the people who would be affected by that five-year "quarantine." The deep reason for this is that they were in charge of the symbiosis between the Bulgarian Communist Party and the State, which led the country to a national catastrophe. People feel they were civilian agents of the communist police sate. Naturally, there were exceptions to this rule, but it should be borne in mind that no law is absolutely fair.[7]

Today it is regrettable that the so-called "Sokolov," "Luchnikov," and "Panev" acts were either enforced solely for the duration of Philip Dimitrov's government or not approved by Parliament at all. If these bills had been fully implemented in their original form at the end of 1991 and 1992 and had been preserved by the following governments, Bulgaria would certainly not be considered currently as the most legally dysfunctional member of the European Union.

...

On the fourth day after the opening of the Thirty-Sixth National Assembly, the Union of Democratic Forces Parliamentary Group proposed a law for the return to the people of the state property stolen by the totalitarian political organizations. The event was covered by the daily paper of the UDF:

> ...The document on the restitution of expropriated public property consists of eight articles, four pages of support for the proposed legislation, eight pages listing the real estate that the Bulgarian Socialist Party (BSP)–acquired during 1990, one page listing the companies managing BSP assets (as of December 31, 1990), as well as one page listing the municipal BSP councils on the territory of Sofia.
>
> For over 45 years the Bulgarian Communist Party (subsequently BSP), the Fatherland Front (subsequently Fatherland Union), Dimitrov's Young Communist League (subsequently Bulgarian Democratic Youth) and the Union of Active Fighters Against Fascism and Capitalism (subsequently Union of Active Fighters Against Fascism) ran the entire country and thus brought Bulgaria to the most severe economic crisis in its long history. That was specified in the section elaborating the need for such legislation. As the Bulgarian State and the Bulgarian people were systematically growing poorer, Bulgaria's living standard ranking dropped from number 10 (ahead of countries

[7] *Demokratsiya* daily, February 26, 1992.

like Sweden, Norway and Denmark at the time when Greece was in 28th place, according to data of the League of Nations for 1939) to the unenviable second to last place in Europe. At the same time, the Bulgarian Communist Party and its satellite organizations were amassing enormous wealth. Suffice it to say that in 1991 the BSP declared property worth more than BGN 640 million, after having established private companies with a capital total of BGN 299 million in 1990. Just two days before the Dimitrov's Young Communist League renamed itself to Bulgarian Democratic Youth, it established companies worth more than BGN 80 million. Although not all data are available for the 1945-1990 period, it has been found that the Bulgarian Communist Party has taken more than BGN 2,200 million out of the national budget. Moreover, the transfer of funds was done illegally, not in the form of subsidies to the party, but on grounds completely unrelated to the activities of any political party, such as "technological development", "education", etc. Even the actual bank transfers were made in a conspiratorial way, indicating only the secret bank account of the Bulgarian Communist Party's Central Committee. The documents in the State Archives reveal a deliberate lie, namely that the BCP Central Committee building had been erected with voluntary donations by Bulgarian communists. The truth is that the money for its construction was also taken from the national budget and the construction was supervised by the Council of Ministers.

...

Hence, the section supporting the proposed legislation includes the claim that it would be fair for all assets accumulated by the Bulgarian Socialist Party and the remaining organizations to be returned to their legitimate owner, namely the Bulgarian State and the Bulgarian people. The said legislation provides for the return of property in the simplest and most expedient way. Therefore, a list of the property found to belong to or to be kept by the BSP and the remaining organizations was annexed to the bill. The BSP's Supreme Council had already provided the National Assembly with a list of the real estate that the BSP had transferred in 1990, the property rights, as well as the 172 pieces of real estate acquired in 1990 (the same property that the BSP acquired in exchange for the 45 that it "relinquished"). However, the real estate owned prior to 1990 was omitted from the list. Yet, such information will not be difficult to obtain. All companies whose founding documents show BSP participation will be considered subject to expropriation from their owners and will be returned to the State. In all remaining cases the participation of the BSP and of the other related organizations in the ownership will be ascertained using all means for evidence collection permitted under the Code of Civil Procedure.

The BSP and its related organizations (the Fatherland Front, Dimitrov's Young Communist League and the Union of Active Fighters Against Fascism and Capitalism), the companies, trade corporations, non-profit associations and other legal entities, including persons, managing and using assets of the BSP

> and the cited organizations, are obliged to file a declaration detailing the assets they own. Failure to comply with that obligation or filing declarations with a false contents will be punished with prison sentences of five to ten years. A similar sanction applies for those who obstruct the enforcement of the legislation.
>
> The Minister of Finance has the right to demand declarations from all persons and legal entities and add to the list real estate and companies subject to restitution to the State. He can also examine the receivables of local and foreign persons and legal entities, as well as deposits in local and foreign banks and savings accounts.
>
> ...
>
> Within one month after the legislation is enforced, the BSP and its satellite organizations are obliged to file declarations on all assets owned by them. Such declarations also need to be filed by the companies, trade corporations and non-profit associations, and all legal entities with a seat in the country, the grace period being two months for those abroad (if assets of the BSP and its satellite organizations have been invested in them).[8]

The lawyer Velko Valkanov, one of the leaders of the socialist parliamentary group which called itself Parliamentary Alliance for Social Democracy, responded to the UDF bill in a somewhat surprising way. The alleged social democrat neglected the fact that the proposed legislation was intended to facilitate the restitution of unlawfully seized assets to the Bulgarian State, which was in such a tragic condition at that moment. For Velko Valkanov the said document was only a "weapon of political repression" aimed at "very specific political organizations."[9]

Valkanov was well aware that the parliamentary majority did not support the Bulgarian Socialist Party at the time. The bill was passed regardless of his protest. Nevertheless, the reasons for his efforts to please the leadership of the BSP were soon to be revealed. Under the new Constitution, the Bulgarian President would be elected through a direct vote. The party of the former communist nominated Velko Valkanov - ostensibly not one of its members - for President in the elections scheduled for January 12, 1992.

...

The decision to nominate Dr. Zhelyu Zhelev as the presidential candidate of the Union of Democratic Forces in the forthcoming elections was not easily taken.

---

[8] *Demokratsiya* daily, Neven Kopandanova, *The Illegally Plundered Property Will Be Returned by Law – This Is What the Renamed Communists Call Fascism and Repressions*, November 14, 1991.

[9] *Ibid.*

The philosopher still believed that he was the worthiest candidate for the office and that it was only natural for the blue union to back him.[10] However, his conviction was not shared by all UDF members and supporters. During the past tense months, Zhelev had demonstrated that his views were closer to the centrist coalition of Petko Simeonov, Alexander Karakachanov, Peter Dertliev and other political figures who broke away from the democratic coalition than those of the UDF proper.

Still, Simeonov was the only one who categorically supported his friend's nomination for President of the Republic. The Coalition of the Bulgarian Democratic Center, in which both the Liberal and the Social democratic Bloc participated, was hesitant about the nomination.[11]

The *Podkrepa* Labor Federation nominated Stefan Savov, the Speaker of the Thirty-Sixth National Assembly, as an alternative candidate for the high office. However, this nomination was risky. The 67-year-old democrat was not broadly popular. He was inclined to aggrandize himself, which hurt his image. Thus, it was unlikely that he would obtain a majority of votes as the UDF candidate.

Eventually, Dr. Zhelev became the presidential candidate nominated by the UDF due to the decisive intervention of Philip Dimitrov. At that point, the Chairman of the Democratic Party Stefan Savov, which had the highest number of representatives in the UDF Parliamentary Group, underwent a change of heart. Having been a supporter of Dimitrov's so far, he now opposed the Prime Minister. It came out that Savov wished to become Head of State more than anything. Philip Dimitrov's attempt to reason with him and explain that if he ran, the communist candidate would become the next President of Bulgaria, did not diminish the ambitions of the vain democrat, nor did it help him understand why this would have happened.

It was very simple. Zhelyu Zhelev had declared publicly that if the Union of Democratic Forces failed to nominate him as the next President, he would run as an independent candidate. In practice this meant that the UDF would compete against its first Chairman, which would have discredited the coalition in the eyes of the voters. Moreover, Zhelev hinted that if the coalition did not support him, he would wage an aggressive campaign against it. Thus, Dimitrov was convinced that not supporting Zhelev would have hurt the UDF.

Later Philip Dimitrov questioned his decision to intervene in the candidate selection and back Zhelev. He asked himself whether that was a fatal mistake. Dimitrov's doubts may be justified. At the end of 1991, however, the Prime

---

[10] *Ibid.*, November 19, 1991.

[11] *Ibid.*

Minister believed that one could work with Zhelyu Zhelev, even considering his temper:

> Stefan Savov, Georgi Markov, Stoyan Ganev and the people around them treated Zhelev badly and were rude to him. This cooled down our personal relations with Zhelyu Zhelev and caused his bitterness and malice. The President simply became inaccessible, and unable to use common sense. His opponents not only incited him against themselves, but also caused serious tension within the UDF Parliamentary Group. There were Members of Parliament in the group who were amazed by such conduct. When the group began breaking up, many of its members joined the government's opposition without thinking and out of good feelings for Zhelyu.
>
> What was even worse, Zhelev's critics at that time provoked his scheming. Zhelyu would not have thought to scheme if he had not been pestered and were left alone to exercise his presidential power unperturbed. His power was rather restricted anyway.
>
> To my mind, Zhelev was provoked to a large extent. Now, the fact that he allowed himself to be provoked and preferred the course that he chose, i.e., to do the things that he did and not something else, is entirely his own responsibility before history.
>
> Zhelyu Zhelev is probably the person who inflicted the greatest damage to Bulgaria at that time, without ever having been a member of the communist secret services. He is just a person with limited capabilities, a suspicious and excessively ambitious man. As such, he was manipulated in a very cruel way by the communists.
>
> He felt very comfortable with them. He felt good having his coffee with some of them, not with me. His memories from his youth were with them. His values were shaped by those circles, and so were his fantasies, personal contacts and friendships. It should be admitted that the circles outside the communists often appeared to him in a repulsive light. These people must have seemed haughty, snobbish and provocative to him.
>
> I repeat, many people may not agree with my interpretation of the events, including my friend Edwin Sugarev. They firmly believe that Zhelev intended from the very beginning to do what he did. However, I personally believe that if we had taken his mentality and his temper into account, we could have preserved our good relations with him.
>
> A considerable part of my term in office as Prime Minister was spent in attempts to play down the wild hatred between Zhelev and Savov. That was a waste of time, given the subsequent course of events.[12]

---

[12] Philip Dimitrov in a conversation with the author, Philadelphia, U.S.A., February 12, 2000.

On January 12, 1992, Dr. Zhelyu Zhelev and his running mate for the office of the Vice President, the poet Blaga Dimitrova, did not get the majority vote in the first round of the presidential elections. A total of 5,139,884 Bulgarian citizens voted. The candidates of the Union of Democratic Forces received the support of 2,273,468 individuals. The presidential candidates supported by the Bulgarian Socialist Party, Velko Valkanov and Rumen Vodenicharov, claimed to be running as independents. They received the votes of 1,549,754 pro-communist individuals. George Ganchev and the second UDF leader, Peter Beron, were nominated by the Bulgarian Business Bloc and obtained the votes of 854,020 Bulgarians.[13] Thus, none of the candidates managed to earn the majority of valid votes.

A second round of elections was due according to the Constitution. It had to be held between the first two candidate slates within seven days of the first round. In that period the pair nominated by the UDF campaigned with the slogan, "Democracy or Communism." On January 19, 1992, they got 53 percent of the votes. On January 22, the President of the Republic Dr. Zhelyu Zhelev and his Vice President Blaga Dimitrova, pronounced their oath of office before the National Assembly in the presence of Philip Dimitrov's government. They pledged that they would abide by the Constitution and the laws of the country and that they would be guided by the interests of Bulgaria in all their actions.

In January 1992, the UDF supporters were jubilant with the outcome of the presidential elections. It gave them yet another reason to hope that communism in their country was about to end for good. At the time the UDF had a parliamentary majority in the Thirty-Sixth National Assembly, albeit a slim one. The Movement for Rights and Freedoms supported the UDF Members of Parliament. The first UDF leader was President of the Republic and its third in command was Prime Minister. What more could be expected?

Unfortunately, there were many surprises and disappointments in store for democratically minded Bulgarians. As far as Dr. Zhelev goes, to this day many are convinced that he failed to fulfill his pledge of allegiance to Bulgaria.

...

According to Heinz Brahm, on January 15, 1992, Bulgaria acted the way Europe should have, whereas Europe's conduct for months was of the type that could be expected from a Balkan state. The statement of the German specialist in political sciences was prompted by the fact that Philip Dimitrov's government recognized the sovereignty of four republics on that day - Macedonia, Slovenia,

---

[13] *Demokratsiya* daily, January 15, 1992.

Croatia, and Bosnia and Herzegovina. With that act of valor, Bulgaria was first in the world to legitimize the status of the four nations, which had broken off from Yugoslavia and declared their independence. The small country set an example to the European Union and to the other democratic states. The latter responded slowly and irresolutely to the new realities in the Western Balkans and eventually followed suit.

Philip Dimitrov's cabinet made this diplomatic move in order to improve Bulgaria and Macedonia's bilateral relations. Furthermore, the Bulgarian government demonstrated respect for the newly differentiated state and also protected it against a potential Serbian invasion.

Even before January, the renamed Bulgarian Communist Party clearly demonstrated that it was against recognizing Macedonia. For various reasons, the idea did not have the support of the Speaker of Bulgarian Parliament, Stefan Savov, and the Minister of Foreign Affairs, Stoyan Ganev, either. These two men believed that it would have been better for Bulgaria to follow the line of conduct of the European Union. Conversely, "many Bulgarians were regretful that the West was extremely condescending vis-à-vis Belgrade, but remained deaf to comments and advice from Sofia."[14]

The UDF government's decision-making process was also rather convoluted. On January 15, 1992, the ministers convened for a meeting that lasted from 9 a.m. to 7 p.m. At the end of it, they voted in favor of recognizing the former Yugoslav republics of Slovenia, Macedonia, Croatia, and Bosnia and Herzegovina. Before going home, the ministers reviewed the issue one more time over a cup of coffee. Indecision gained the upper hand and the government chose not to announce the result of its internal vote before the return of Stefan Savov from Spain and Stoyan Ganev from Germany. The latter had even called the cabinet and advised them not to hurry.

However, shortly after most of the ministers left, Philip Dimitrov suddenly changed the course of events. He realized that the possibility for the government to reverse the decision reached would be fatal both for the prestige of Bulgaria and for the cabinet itself. Dimitrov made the casual remark "Gentlemen, why don't I immediately recognize Macedonia" to the people who happened to be still in his office, including his adviser Konstantin Mishev and Interior Minister Yordan Sokolov. The Prime Minister shared his intend to rush to Parliament and announce that the Council of Ministers had recognized the former Yugoslav republics. Mishev advised him, "Hurry so as not to miss the 8 o'clock news!" Then, Philip Dimitrov telephoned President Zhelev to inform him of his decision to take the responsibility for recognizing Macedonia.

---

[14] Brahm 1998, p. 22.

The journalist Valeria Kalcheva provided the following account of the events:

People who were present during that telephone conversation claim that the Prime Minister told them that the President had said to him that Dimitrov would "make history" with that decision.

The Prime Minister went to Parliament. The plenary session was chaired by Snezhana Botusharova. Alexander Yordanov had formally proposed to extend the meeting by thirty minutes until 8:30 p.m. so as to give an opportunity to the Prime Minister to be heard. Philip Dimitrov announced the following: "After familiarizing itself with all available data and discussing the information coming through various diplomatic channels, including the information provided by the foreign minister Stoyan Ganev, who is flying to Bulgaria at this moment (the latter comment provoked animation and laughter among the BSP members), the Bulgarian government decided to recognize the former Yugoslav republics of Slovenia, Macedonia, Croatia, and Bosnia and Herzegovina. The decision was reached at a meeting to which the chairpersons of the Parliamentary Committee on National Security and on Foreign Policy were invited." His words were met with booing from the left, while the UDF Members of Parliament gave him a standing ovation. The Prime Minister continued, "This decision is an expression of the final position of the Bulgarian government and of the Bulgarian State, which is subordinate to definite principles the most important among them being the right to self-determination of the population of each of these republics. This act is a manifestation of our wish to establish peace and cooperation in the Balkans, in Europe and throughout the world where our voice can be heard."

Snezhana Botusharova thanked Philip Dimitrov with the comment that it was good that "the government found the time to inform the Members of Parliament about its decision." Alexander Yordanov rushed to the rostrum and qualified the event as a "memorable and great moment." On behalf of the Movement for Rights and Freedoms, Ivan Palchev congratulated the Council of Ministers with the words "At long last we have a government of action that is assuming its responsibilities before the nation and before the world." Philip Bokov [from the BSP - *author's note*] countered, "there is a significant discrepancy between the Prime Minister's statement that the foreign minister has been consulted and the actual facts. Both last night and earlier today the Minister of Foreign Affairs appealed to the government to wait before making that decision..."

Mr. Bokov was basing this claim on several visits he had made to the Ministry of Foreign Affairs together with Asparuh Panov from the UDF. The two had traced Minister Stoyan Ganev's telephone calls in which he attempted to convince his colleagues to wait for a more definite decision on the part of the European Union. However, Ganev's first Deputy Minister, Stefan Tafrov, was trying to persuade Bokov and Panev of the opposite. He even spoke in their presence with the cabinets of President Havel and of President Mitterrand.

The Foreign Minister heard the news at the Sofia airport from Alexander Yordanov, the Chairman of the Foreign Policy Parliamentary Committee. Stoyan Ganev also learned that Stefan Tafrov had already explained the government's decision in a live televised interview. President Zhelev had given his support for the decision in a special TV appearance after the evening news.

The rest of the cabinet ministers also learned about the change in tactics from television. The scandal went out of control. Shocked, Stoyan Ganev made a dramatic statement before the media.

Around 10:30 p.m., the cabinet [according to Philip Dimitrov, in the presence of Stoyan Ganev, Stefan Savov, Alexander Yordanov and Stefan Tafrov - *author's note*] met again at the Council of Ministers. Thus started one of the longest nights for the UDF government. The most recent actions of the Prime Minister were discussed.

The Prime Minister's secretary responded to his wife's telephone calls with the words, "I don't know what is happening. I can only hear that they are quarrelling." According to people who were present, most of the accusations were hurled at the present Ambassador to the UK, Stefan Tafrov, and his supervisor at that time, Stoyan Ganev, even wanted to hit him...

According to some, the hasty act of recognizing Macedonia was meant to serve solely as a trump card in the election campaign of the UDF candidates for President and Vice President - Zhelyu Zhelev and Blaga Dimitrova - just before the runoff in the presidential elections. The supporters of that move justified it with the argument that every delay could provide an opportunity for obstruction on the part of the BSP. What is more, they claimed that if that anticipatory move had not been made, Macedonia would hardly have been recognized later.

The supporters of the decision also claimed that the recognizing of Macedonia served as a guarantee that the country would not become the target of a Serbian invasion. They also viewed it as a deterrent to the flourishing of nationalist tendencies, and a way of preventing the unfavorable consequences for Bulgaria of an ambiguous position with regard to Macedonia...[15]

. . .

In an article published sixteen years after the historic act, Philip Dimitrov explained his motives for recognizing the former Yugoslav republics of Slovenia, Macedonia, Croatia, and Bosnia and Herzegovina:

---

[15] *Standart* daily, Valeria Kalcheva, *Philip Dimitrov: "Gentlemen, Why Don't I Recognize...",* June 20, 1995.

Out of all the countries in the region, Bulgaria was affected the most by the events in the former Yugoslavia because of its proximity to Macedonia. For the rest of world, Macedonia's case offered no solution to Yugoslavia's problem. Still, it did resolve the issue of containing the problem within the "Western Balkans" rather than affecting "the Balkans" in their entirety.

If the war were to spread to Macedonia, the flow of refugees was bound to awaken all nationalistic passions from the first half of the century, even with the most restrained behavior on behalf of the Bulgarian government. The further spread of the conflict on an international scale could hardly have been avoided. Bulgaria would have been an additional source of tension and the entire region would have reverted to its history of decades earlier. Bulgaria could not have withstood a flare-up of nationalist sentiment like the one in neighboring Greece. Bulgaria was fighting for its future and the future of the region. Greece could afford to delve into the past.

The Bulgarian government was familiar with the mores in the region and Milosevic's propaganda. The recent multi-million demonstrations in Greece under the motto "Macedonia is Greek" (whatever that meant) were no source of comfort either. The cabinet believed in the effective involvement of the international community, and the official recognition of the independent states seemed like the most reasonable way to accomplish this. Otherwise, the events in Yugoslavia could easily have turned into an "internal" problem, i.e. an incessant source of self-destruction. The alternative - no recognition in the absence of a clear guarantee for dialogue - was an invitation for partitioning, i.e. new conflicts. Kosovo's recognition today is in many ways an expression of the understanding that subjects of international law can more easily be influenced in a positive direction, i.e. to act peacefully and respect human rights.

For Bulgaria, the recognition was also a lesson in laying the foundations of a country which seeks to redefine its place in the world. The UK Ambassador at the time, Richard Thomas, phrased it best. His answer to the question how the UK would react to a possible recognition of the independent states by Bulgaria, was "If you recognize them, we will certainly not support you; if you do not, we will simply fail to understand you." Bulgaria was to decide on its future on its own.

In Bulgaria things were dramatic in their own way. The Parliament was divided. The government was a little less so. The president did not want to help out in the decision: he was between two election rounds. In the end, the Prime Minister managed to impose his will and declare an immediate and unconditional recognition of the four former Yugoslav republics.[16]

...

[16] *Foreign Policy* magazine, Bulgarian Edition, Philip Dimitrov, *The Bulgarian Recognition of the Parts of Yugoslavia*, July-August 2008.

From the very beginning, the Ministry of Foreign Affairs under Stoyan Ganev started leading a life of its own. Ganev simply did what he wanted, irrespective of the government's foreign policy. He was guided either by narcissism or - as some people believed - orders given to him by circles opposed to the Prime Minister. In the last days of 1991, Minister Ganev surprised Philip Dimitrov with a tour of the Arab world, which implied that he was serving Russian interests. In a number of cases he totally disregarded the recommendations of the Prime Minister or presented him with a *fait accompli.* Taking off in a plane to somewhere, Ganev would request his formal approval for the trip from the air.

There were two options for Philip Dimitrov, namely, to dismiss his foreign minister or to swallow the insults. The second option was more sensible because Stoyan Ganev had the support of the *Podkrepa* Trade Union Federation and the Movement for Rights and Freedoms. Ganev was also backed by some members of the UDF parliamentary group, including Georgi Markov, Ventsislav Dimitrov [both later unveiled as an agents of the secret services - *author's note*] and other influential parliamentary figures. After the presidential elections and the recognizing of Macedonia, the Foreign Minister also received the support of the head of the legislative body, Stefan Savov.

Having picked the second option, Philip Dimitrov handled much of the foreign policy of his government himself. He focused on the integration of Bulgaria into the European Union and its institutions, improvement of the relationship with the USA, accession of the country to the defense structures of the West, and on establishing friendly relations with the neighboring countries and with all democratic states in the world.

Even before he became Prime Minister, while he was Chairman of the Union of Democratic Forces, Dimitrov had attracted the attention of the political elite of Western Europe. After his meetings with its representatives, German, French, Italian and other newspapers wrote that communism in Bulgaria was indeed going away. The invitation of Pope John-Paul II for a private audience with a delegation headed by the UDF leader was recognition of the new image that Bulgaria was beginning to have abroad. The meeting with the Head of the Roman Catholic Church, which took place on October 30, 1991, lasted three times longer than the Vatican protocol assumed.[17]

In the beginning of March, 1992, Philip Dimitrov made a tour of the U.S.A. with a part of his team. He had dozens of talks with high-ranking politicians, as well as with financial and broker's institutions. After meeting the Bulgarian Premier, the Secretary of State Lawrence Eagleburger at the time of George

---

[17] *Demokratsiya* daily, October 31, 1991.

Bush Senior qualified Bulgaria as the "hidden pearl of the Balkans" and promised to defend its interests before the International Monetary Fund and the World Bank.

The American press gave a very positive assessment to the governmental visit:

> "The visit of the Bulgarian Prime Minister was a feast" - this was the title in today's [March 10 - *author's note*] *Washington Times* by Celeste McCaul.
>
> ...
>
> The visit to Chicago that just ended was commented upon in the extensive article by Richard Longworth in the Business Section of the *Chicago Tribune*, entitled *Bulgaria Is Striving to Turn into a Bridge for Business.* The article explains that "Prime Minister Philip Dimitrov, who flew from coast to coast to raise US interest in Bulgaria - one of the most stable post-communist states - stressed the opportunities for US business circles to invest in the country's development into a commercial bridge between Europe, the Middle East and the former Soviet Union."
>
> ...
>
> The newspaper also cited the Prime Minister's explanation to the business elite in Chicago that "Bulgaria is not a Balkan state, in the sense that it does not resolve its problems in the traditional Balkan way. Instead of unrest and clashes, the Bulgarian nation has found the way of living in peace." Furthermore, the author of the article pointed out that the US government had allocated funds in order to encourage privatization and investments in Bulgaria, as it had done for Hungary, Poland and the Czech Republic prior to that...[18]

Almost immediately after his return from the United States, Philip Dimitrov paid an official visit to Israel. One of the aims of that trip was to neutralize the impression left by Stoyan Ganev's tour of the Arab states and to demonstrate the changed orientation of Bulgaria's foreign policy.

Two months later, Philip Dimitrov visited Turkey and signed a cooperation treaty with its government. That act normalized the relationship between the two countries, which had been strained by the assimilation policy of the Bulgarian Communist Party towards the Moslem minority in Bulgaria. The Prime Minister did not neglect Greece either, and succeeded in warming to some extent the relationship between the two countries which had cooled after Bulgaria recognized Macedonia.

On May 7, 1992, the Republic of Bulgaria attained yet another token of recognition. It joined the Council of Europe as a full member. Thereafter, the

---

[18] *Ibid.*, March 11, 1992.

road to membership in the European Union was open and the country started association negotiations in 1992.

. . .

One of the most important prerequisites for reorienting Bulgaria's foreign policy towards the West was to clarify its relations with its former "Big Brother." The Russian Federation emerged after the disintegration of the Soviet Union in December 1991. At that time the Bulgarian break-away was especially painful for Russia for a number of reasons. This is how Philip Dimitrov summarized the situation:

> Bulgaria had become the fourth among the former communist countries [Poland, the Czech Republic and Hungary were the first three - *author's note*] claiming to be doing quick and successful reforms. For Russia this was unacceptable. The three were already lost (since the late 80s), but could Yeltsin permit another one to break radically out of the Russian sphere of influence? The battle for Bulgaria was also crucial for Russia's foreign policy on the Balkans. An old Russian saying from the period of Russian expansion efforts on the Balkans during the 19th century was put back in use. A transcription of it would be "As the hen is not a bird, Bulgaria is not abroad" [meaning Bulgaria was considered Russian territory - *author's note*]. The aim was to fit Bulgaria into the Russian concept of "near abroad", i.e. a group of countries "legitimately" treated as a zone of Russian influence.[19]

In his effort to see the problems of Bulgaria in a broader regional perspective, Dimitrov wrote:

> In early 1993, Russian foreign minister Kozyrev first promoted the idea of the so called Orthodox Arch and then the notion of a Byzantino-Slavic Cultural Space that was meant to include Romania, Bulgaria, Serbia and even Greece into the Russian orb (together with Belarus and Ukraine). This was accepted by many European countries as a legitimate reaction of the former Empire. (To the French it probably seemed innocently similar to the concept of *francophonie.*) They hardly noticed that such constructs were going a bit further than trying to preserve some influence over the former captive countries. (The idea of including Greece - a devoted EU member though at times a somewhat reluctant NATO ally - was of course highly unrealistic, but it bespoke a certain ambition cherished in Moscow.)

---

[19] Dimitrov 2004, p. 42.

> To the East Europeans this initiative as well as Russia's categorical stand on the Baltic countries' future was a clear attempt to block what had been the desired development for them for decades and for which people had made great sacrifices (including their own lives). It was evident that the imperial claims of Russia for a sphere of influence were not gone. Here was an attempt to divide Europe and distance it from the US (in other words to oppose NATO to the EU and thus damage the Trans-Atlantic relationship). That was becoming one of the most prominent characteristics of the foreign policy of New Russia.
>
> The last of these perceptions proved to be completely legitimate in the long run.[20]

By the end of 1991, Dimitrov's government was faced with a bitter revelation. The "huge Soviet market" - a term coined by the communist leaders to explain the economic need for their subservience to Soviet Union and Russia - proved to be a burden for Bulgaria. The Russian side was sending no payments for the contracted goods already shipped to Russia. Four hundred million dollars of debt might sound like a small problem for big countries, but for Bulgaria, which had inherited a currency reserve of only a few tens of millions of dollars from its totalitarian governments, this was a real sore spot. The leadership of the Russian Federation, which ran the Russian trade companies at the time, was demonstrating an imperial approach. Their negligence seemed to say, "No matter what the contract says, the Bulgarians can wait". Philip Dimitrov responded in a very clear way, "If Russia does not pay its bills, Bulgaria will simply not send its goods." This was not the tone that Russia was accustomed to hearing from Bulgaria.

The former Prime Minister also explained:

> While trying to reestablish control at least over some former members of the Soviet Union (namely Ukraine, Belarus and Moldova) and keep the Baltic states from fully tying themselves to the West, Russian foreign policy also aimed at creating a stronghold on the Balkans. The behavior of the Bulgarian government was completely unacceptable to Russia. The independence of Poland, Hungary and Czechoslovakia was a painful but well-known fact. The West would not give them up and these states had done what was necessary to guarantee that their split with Russia was final. Bulgaria was the fourth country actually trying to achieve the same level of independence. A potential success for Dimitrov's policy would set a very bad example for all the other countries in the former Easter Block. Bulgaria had to be stopped.
>
> ...

---

[20] *Ibid.*, p. 41.

> President Yeltsin announced a visit to Bulgaria and other neighboring countries in early August of 1992. However, the Bulgarian Prime Minister contacted the Federal Yugoslav one - the recently elected reformist Milan Panic - and urged him to tour the Balkan capitals just a couple of days before the Russian President. A bold agenda to achieve independence and recognition along with human rights protection was announced during the four-hour visit of Prime Minister Panic to Sofia. (Unfortunately, soon after that Milosevic prevailed in the internal struggle, Panic was ousted and his five-point agenda was never implemented.)[21]

By no means would Philip Dimitrov permit the Russians to take - or pretend to be taking - the initiative of solving the Balkan problems. This betrays another trait of his policies: he tended to think that his country and he were capable of outmaneuvering Russia.

When President Boris Yeltsin arrived in Bulgaria the day after Milan Panic left, he was yelling at the members of his delegation in a manner which one of the witnesses described as follows: "This should have been the way Peter the Great was shouting at his boyars. If they had had beards Yeltsin might have been pulling them by the beards too." In one of his dramatic outbursts he even claimed not to know that Russia had not yet recognized Macedonia and shouted at his Deputy Foreign Minister, "How many times have I told you to recognize this Macedonia!"

During an official lunch Yeltsin talked mainly to President Zhelyu Zhelev. In fact, there was no particular agenda of the visit to be discussed at the executive level. When the lunch was over, however, the Russian President turned to Philip Dimitrov and uttered the only phrase he addressed directly to him during the entire visit, "Mr. Dimitrov, I am following what you are doing very, very attentively." As Dimitrov shares, it sounded pretty ominous.[22]

The President of the Russian Federation followed up on his threatening words. A month later the former Soviet Ambassador to Bulgaria, the KGB offices Victor Sharapov, came to visit Sofia. His "vacation" did not end until the government of Philip Dimitrov was voted out of power.

...

As Peter Mladenov had announced in his report to the Plenum of the Bulgarian Communist Party's Central Committee in December 1989, the economic situation in Bulgaria towards the end of the communist regime was more than

---

[21] *Ibid.*, pp. 42-43.

[22] Philip Dimitrov in a conversation with the author, Philadelphia, U.S.A., February 1, 2009.

tragic. There was no way in which it could have become any better by the beginning of 1992. In fact, in March 1990, Prime Minister Andrey Lukanov declared a moratorium on servicing the foreign debt. As a result, Bulgaria lost the confidence of the global financial markets. It became impossible to obtain new credit. Potential investors withdrew. At the same time, a substantial part of the state-owned assets were transformed into private assets owned by former communist figures.

On top of everything else, there were external factors which rendered the material situation of the country even more difficult. During the red dictatorship, the Bulgarian economy was tied almost exclusively to the U.S.S.R. and to the Council for Mutual Economic Assistance, popularly known as COMECON. However, COMECON ceased to exist in 1991, and the U.S.S.R. disintegrated prior to paying its debts to Bulgaria. As a result of these changes, the Balkan country lost its markets from communist times. In addition, on account of the embargo, Iraq still had a debt to Bulgaria amounting to USD 1.2 billion.

The crisis in former Yugoslavia also brought misfortune to its eastern neighbor. Although some firms violated the embargo imposed upon Serbia and Montenegro and made millions in illegal profits, the Bulgarian government strictly abided by the sanctions. That alone resulted in enormous economic losses, not to mention that foreign companies were afraid of investing their capital in the turbulent Balkan Peninsula. The armed conflicts in some of the former Yugoslav republics separated Bulgaria from Europe even geographically.

At that extremely tense and difficult moment, several men, who had set for themselves the goal of improving the living standards of the Bulgarian population, stood at the head of the state. A lot was expected from them. Many people forgot that the blue political leaders had come to the helm of a bankrupt state, without international prestige and established trade relations.

...

During its election campaign, the Union of Democratic Forces had proclaimed privatization as its primary task. According to the cabinet's agenda, the laws needed for the implementation of the economic reform had to be passed as soon as possible. However, there were serious obstacles. In January 1992, the Chairman of the Economic Committee of the National Assembly and Member of Parliament from the UDF, Asen Michkovski, submitted a bill opposing the privatization legislation proposed by the government. That economist - member of the Alternative Socialist Party of ex-communists which joined the UDF - insisted on the adoption of only one law under which state ownership was to be transformed into private. He claimed that secondary legislation could be added to it subsequently, if necessary.

The Minister of Finance Ivan Kostov and the Minister of Industry Ivan Pushkarov, who already had some experience from their involvement in Dimitar Popov's cabinet, disagreed with Michkovski. They preferred a gradual transition to a market economy and proposed starting with the restitution of smaller private property and ending with the privatization of big enterprises. According to them, several different laws were needed for the purpose.[23]

It was common knowledge that Asen Michkovski represented the interests of *Podkrepa* in the UDF Parliamentary Group. However, the leadership of the trade union had long stopped making demands solely with regard to its members. In fact, in the beginning of 1992, Konstantin Trenchev renewed his insistence that ministers Kostov and Pushkarov be removed from executive power.

Ivan Kurtev's diary and his personal memoirs complete the picture:

> On January 21, 1992, there was a joint meeting of the cabinet ministers and the UDF Parliamentary Group that lasted four hours. Major differences of opinion emerged between the government and the economists around Michkovski with regards to privatization legislation. The government recommended step-by-step privatization, which would start immediately in the spheres of trade and services. Philip Dimitrov proposed that the Commerce Act be amended so that the so-called "small-scale privatization" could be implemented without further delay. The economists from the Alternative Socialist Party insisted upon a universal law, which meant delaying the onset of privatization. At that time Michkovski claimed, "I shall be in a position to submit this draft in February." The truth is that the draft of the universal law on privatization was delayed by a whole year.
>
> January 28, 1992, was a difficult and tense day. *Podkrepa* demanded the resignation of Pushkarov and Kostov. We had elected them on November 8, and on January 28 they already demanded their resignation! In turn, the former pro-communist union, currently called the Confederation of the Independent Trade Unions in Bulgaria, insisted on the resignations of Stanislav Dimitrov and Alexander Alexandrov. At the meeting of the UDF National Coordinating Council, Philip Dimitrov expressed his conviction that this amounted to a large-scale campaign against the government with the ultimate aim of attaining its resignation.
>
> The communists, Valentin Mollov from the *168 Hours* Press Group, and the two trade unions were the cause of all that. As usual, the Alternative Socialist Party sided with Trenchev's wishes. They were threatening to organize

---

[23] Brahm 1998, p. 16.

strikes and internal opposition within the UDF if the demands of *Podkrepa* were not met.

I snapped back and made my strongest statement before the Coordinating Council so far, "We will certainly have a hard time with the guys from *Podkrepa*, but to my mind there is only one explanation for the attempt to provoke a cabinet crisis. This is an attempt to restore the so-called by the communists 'democratic socialism' with the assistance of the breakaway factions [of the UDF - *author's note*] outside Parliament. All this is caused by fear of privatization and restrictions on the communist mafia." I declared that I fully supported the government and was ruling out the possibility for concessions. Mihail Nedelchev supported me. The resolution adopted was to this end even though Yordan Vasilev had suggested various concessions. Vasilev had had a meeting with Trenchev that afternoon and was advocating for the reorganization of the Ministry of Industry and Trade in a heated manner. At the end of the day, the Parliamentary Group supported all the members of the government with only one abstention. I was not convinced that the end of the crisis had come.

February 4, 1992. The attack against Pushkarov and Kostov lasted a whole week. *Podkrepa*, Valentin Mollov, the communists, Dertliev's men and all other UDF opponents proved to be in the same camp. The culmination came during today's meetings of the National Coordinating Council and the Parliamentary Group. Once again, there were only displays of verbosity and speeches without arguments. Essentially there were no decisions made or any results. The session of the Parliamentary Group lasted five hours in the presence of Zhelyu Zhelev and almost all cabinet ministers. Trenchev came too, listened to several speeches and presented his conditions, or rather, his ultimatum, with his characteristic gentle, haughty and indifferent tone. Then he left. The discussion lost its focus and drifted on to minor and personal matters. I was very disappointed by Zhelev, who plunged into explanations about his own rights and incompetent speculations on the return of the land to its rightful owners. Then Savov explained to him how limited his rights are by the Constitution. Stefan Savov was constantly bickering with Zhelev. Savov was essentially telling him that we are a parliamentary republic and he will do as we say, which was not right either.[24]

. . .

According to Philip Dimitrov, the blow *Podkrepa* dealt on Ivan Kostov and Ivan Pushkarov was calculated well and meant as an attempt to wrest the economic levers out of the hands of the executive power. Apparently, the union leadership was attempting to acquire control over the industrial enterprises and banks. For

[24] Ivan Kurtev, *Diary*, January 21 – February 4, 1992.

the purpose it needed to run the Ministry of Industry and Trade and the Ministry of Finance.[25]

From the day it had stepped into office, the government of Philip Dimitrov was continuously threatened with strikes by the two major trade unions. That was not surprising given that the Confederation of Independent Trade Unions was the successor of the totalitarian trade unions. However, such actions clashed with the officially proclaimed anticommunist position of *Podkrepa*. Yet, the blue trade union had arranged for the biggest protests against the cabinet, most notably the miners' strike in March 1992.

Faced with the enormous difficulties posed by union protests, the Prime Minister was aware that certain concessions were necessary. The Small-Scale Privatization Act was withdrawn in the name of the unity of the UDF Parliamentary Group.[26]

Still, several documents of major importance for the consolidation of the national economy were voted upon and adopted in the first months of 1992. Ivan Kostov and Ivan Pushkarov hastened to draft the Investments Act, whose goal was to increase the influx of foreign capital into the country. The National Assembly adopted that act on January 16, 1992, but it did not provide for preferences for the foreign investment funds, which was a major omission according to some political scientists.[27]

The lawyers Vasil Gotsev and Alexander Dzherov drafted the bill on restitution which was submitted for debate by the UDF Parliamentary Group and was adopted at the end of February by Parliament. That document restored part of people's property by returning to them the apartments, houses, cottages, shops, workshops, warehouses, etc. nationalized by the communists.

It would not be an exaggeration to say that after the Restitution Act was enforced, the image of Bulgaria started changing radically. The grey urban scenes from totalitarian times gradually gave way to sights more typical of the Western world. Neat and even pretty grocery stores, boutiques, cafés and restaurants replaced the ugly empty shops and unattractive restaurants. Many buildings that had been left unkempt in the past were painted and refurbished. The most significant change was that more than 800,000 Bulgarians found jobs in the private sector in 1992. That figure was twice the number of people who had been laid off after some loss-making enterprises were closed.[28]

---

[25] Philip Dimitrov in a conversation with the author, Philadelphia, U.S.A., March 20, 1998 and April 2, 1999.

[26] Dimitrov 1995(a).

[27] Brahm 1998, p. 18.

[28] *Ibid.*, p. 16-17.

The restitution of the expropriated farmland to its former owners proved to be a much more difficult process. Vasil Gotsev, a team from the Ministry of Agriculture, and the UDF Parliamentary Group drafted amendments to the Land Act. The latter had been adopted by the Grand National Assembly but was inapplicable in practice. Parliament approved the amendments in the spring of 1992. Irrespective of the improved text of the document, Philip Dimitrov's government encountered innumerable obstacles when trying to enforce it. The situation was complicated even further by the fact that, unlike the capital and the bigger cities, most of the villages and small towns in Bulgaria had elected former communists for mayors during the elections for local government in October 1991.

In addition to personal and political problems, there were also technical issues. The ownership maps for many places had been destroyed. Another problem was that industrial enterprises had been built over a part of the farmland. Also, former cornfields, vegetable gardens and orchards had been incorporated in the towns and villages that had grown in the past half century. In other cases the terrain existed but had turned into a wasteland over the years.

During the communist regime the agricultural production of Bulgaria, isolated from global technological progress, had not developed as the Bulgarian Communist Party claimed. In fact, its condition had deteriorated. In 1944 the production volume was 91.9 percent of its value in 1939, but dropped to 60 percent in 1945 and 1946. The situation was not "rosier" at the end of the communist regime. In 1988, a total loss of 491 million BGN was registered in agriculture and livestock-breeding. By the end of that same year, the agricultural organizations accumulated BGN 2.76 billion debt.[29]

Starting a private farm in the 1990s was more than difficult. The farming machinery of the communists was either obsolete or stolen by the former managers. People had almost no equipment with which to work the farmland that had been restored to them. Even the basic machinery for transporting one's scanty produce was often lacking. It is worth repeating that this was happening in a country where most of the population had owned land prior to being forced into Soviet-style farm cooperatives.[30]

Naturally, in 1992 people in the villages had thousands of reasons to be discontent and in despair. The trouble was that they often directed their anger not against those who had deprived them of their lands for decades, but against those who were trying to restore their ownership.

---

[29] *Demokratsiya* daily, Svetoslav Luchnikov, *The Facts*, February 22, 2001.

[30] An interview with Dr. Panayot Panayotov by the author, *I Regret that Soviet Bolshevism was not Defeated along with Fascism and Nazism*, *Pro&Anti* weekly, September 30, 2005; Panayotov 2002, pp. 66-68.

In spite of the difficulties, there was much enthusiasm about the restoration of private ownership of farmland. Evidently, the popular notion that the Bulgarian people had been a nation of land owners before the communists came to power was justified. A total of 1.7 million land restitution applications were filed by August 4, 1992, which covered 94 percent of the farm land in the country.[31]

On April 23, 1992, the Thirty-Sixth National Assembly passed a law regulating large-scale privatization. The smaller enterprises would be sold while the larger ones would become shareholding companies. The military industry and the energy industry remained state-owned. A Privatization Agency was established with the aim of launching and controlling the large-scale privatization process.[32] Philip Dimitrov's government never had the chance to go so far as to implement these plans.

...

At the Fourth National Conference of the Union of Democratic Forces in April, the Prime Minister committed to making structural and personal changes in the Council of Ministers. He made that decision under pressure from *Podkrepa*, Stefan Savov, Georgi Markov and Stoyan Ganev. However, Philip Dimitrov had had such intentions for some time. He had consulted President Zhelev, the Speaker of Parliament Stefan Savov, cabinet ministers and Members of Parliament about the issue. After all the meetings, it was leaked that Dimitrov had demanded the resignation of Dimitar Ludzhev.

The rumor turned out to be true. After the strike of the miners in March organized by *Podkrepa*, the Minister of Defense Ludzhev turned from an enemy of Konstantin Trenchev into a person who shared his ideas. These two men caused strife in the Council of Ministers and the Parliamentary Group. In addition, Dimitar Ludzhev had become involved in "shady arms deals."[33] He had authorized a delivery of weapons for the Bolivian army to a nonexistent person. Regardless of whether he had signed the document as a result of criminal intent or through gross negligence, it was obviously too risky for a person like him to be at the head of such an important ministry.[34]

Once again, the Movement for Rights and Freedoms chose the country's defense minister. This time it was the lawyer Alexander Staliyski. Philip Dimitrov

---

[31] Brahm 1998, p. 17.

[32] *Ibid.*, pp. 17-18.

[33] *Ibid.*, p. 24.

[34] Philip Dimitrov in a conversation with the author, Philadelphia, U.S.A., April 2, 1999.

had in mind for the position Peter Stoyanov - the future President of Bulgaria. Nevertheless, the Prime Minister again gave in to the MRF in order to keep their support in Parliament.

Dimitrov insisted on keeping the two economists, Kostov and Pushkarov, but he could no longer retain them in the cabinet. The *Podkrepa* trade union adamantly demanded that both should go. The attack against the Minister of Industry and Trade was particularly strong. Every day the Premier received calls from the UDF Parliamentary Group with demands to replace Pushkarov. Stefan Savov also pressed and urged. The Head of State Zhelyu Zhelev mentioned that he would give documents to the Prime Minister against Pushkarov. Yet, they never arrived in the Council of Ministers.[35]

Eventually, Ivan Pushkarov was dismissed. The Movement for Rights and Freedoms replaced him with Rumen Bikov, a chemical engineer. In 1995, Bikov abandoned politics and went into private business.

Philip Dimitrov did everything possible to keep Ivan Kostov as a member of his cabinet. For the Premier, Kostov was the strongest and the most useful economist in the government. Dimitrov considered him to be the actual driver of reform in the entire economic sector. Kostov and the Prime Minister shared mostly similar views on the principal issues. Their differences of opinion were on the way privatization was to be effected, on fiscal matters and the restitution. Initially Ivan Kostov viewed the restoration of property to its former owners with "moderate skepticism". For him this was more a way of seeking out fairness than carrying out effective privatization. He believed that the economic decisions were more important than rehabilitating the victims of communism, whose loses - in Philip Dimitrov's words - "could never be fully restored." Over time, Ivan Kostov changed his views on the restitution of private property, while Philip Dimitrov broadened his understanding of economics.[36]

On May 20, 1992, two new ministers joined the government. Stanislav Dimitrov, who handed in his resignation upon the insistence of Stefan Savov and Georgi Markov, was replaced by Georgi Stoyanov at the Ministry of Agriculture. The latter institution was also renamed and reconstructed as the Ministry of Agricultural Development, Land Use and Land Restitution. Alexander Pramatarski was appointed as the head of the newly established Ministry of Trade.

Philip Dimitrov also dismissed one of his deputies. Stoyan Ganev lost his position while Svetoslav Luchnikov, Ilko Eskenazi and Nikolay Vasilev were promoted to Deputy Prime Ministers. Although it had been necessary to make

---

[35] *Ibid.*

[36] *Ibid.*

concessions, the Prime Minister was generally pleased with the changes in the cabinet's structure and composition. Besides, removing Ludzhev from the executive branch had divided - albeit temporarily - the opponents of the UDF government. Zhelev, Dogan and Trenchev expressed their dissatisfaction with Dimitrov's move, while others supported him. The UDF Parliamentary Group felt that Dimitrov was in control of the situation and the government.

The Prime Minister dealt a blow to Dimitar Ludzhev and in that way waged war on criminal practices in the government. He also succeeded in making his colleagues understand that the games of "our boys" and "your boys" would have to stop.[37] The trouble was that these actions evoked deep fear in some politicians. In a state of panic, they focused all their efforts on preventing them.

...

On July 7, Andrey Lukanov was stripped of his parliamentary immunity and taken into custody on the orders of the new Prosecutor General, Ivan Tatarchev, appointed in February 1992. During that same month, trials started against the dictator Todor Zhivkov, his close associate Milko Balev, and the former Prime Minister of totalitarian Bulgaria, Georgi Atanasov.

However, the indictments and the trials were not about the biggest offences of the recent communist politicians but for other infringements of the law that they had committed. That irritated the democratically minded citizens and provoked deep dissatisfaction among them. The trouble was that the Constitution adopted by the Seventh Grand National Assembly in 1991 served to protect the criminals from the proper punishment for their deeds. After having completed his term in office as Prosecutor General, in September 2000, Ivan Tatarchev explained why the main atrocities of the said representatives of the communist regime were not the reason for which he put them in the dock:

> One of the big trials was against Todor Zhivkov. There were an indictment, a verdict and a sentence. However, the General Assembly of the Supreme Court of that time ruled that he had been Head of the Bulgarian State and hence could not be held responsible for his actions. For me that position is wrong because Bulgaria did not have a Head of State before the changes which took place after November 10, 1989. It had the Presidium of the National Assembly, which is a collective body. If it is a collective body, it cannot be assumed that the President of the Presidium is the Head of State. Anyway, that was the ruling of the Supreme Court and he was acquitted, unfortunately.

---

[37] *Ibid.*

Zhivkov had worked for the People's Militia. At the *Slavyanska Beseda* Hotel, he committed criminal offences after September 9, 1944. However, according to the new Constitution it is no longer possible to prosecute after so many years. Besides, there are not many survivors who could establish the link.

I wanted to institute criminal proceedings for national treason as well. However, it transpired that the leadership of the BCP had only reached the preparatory stage. The annexation of Bulgaria to the Soviet Union did not happen because the U.S.S.R. did not want it to happen. The rest was merely wishful thinking. I have read the transcripts of the BCP Central Committee and Politburo, but the Russians did not agree, so nothing was done about it.

The communists were national traitors. Most of them are not among the living. The first act of national treason was committed during the population census of 1946. They beat people to death to force them to identify themselves as Macedonians, not as Bulgarians. Then they transferred the bones of Gotse Delchev, one of the saints of the Macedonian revolution, to the Serbian communists in Skopje. There were emissaries of theirs all over Bulgaria, as well as teachers and men of letters, and if Tito had not broken up with the Comminformbureau, the region around Pirin would have been long gone into the hands of the Serbians. It was a great fluke for Bulgaria that this rupture occurred and that relations were severed.

This is why Todor Zhivkov was sentenced in 1992 to seven years of imprisonment for abuse of power and embezzlement, and not for his other crimes. Nevertheless, he was the first of the dictators in Eastern Europe to be brought to court.

When in 1992 in my capacity as Prosecutor General I issued an order that Andrey Lukanov was not to leave the country, because there was an open case against him, and when he was stopped at the Sofia Airport, he engaged in a fistfight with a female security officer there. He hit her and she hit him back. It was unthinkable for him that someone could take the liberty of impeding his travels abroad.

Lukanov most certainly had money in the West, but this could not be proven. He would never have betrayed his secrets. Therefore, no one knew in which banks he had deposited his funds, and they must have been moved from one bank to another. The foreign banks were furthermore not interested in money being drained from them.

The high-ranking communists were hoping to remain in power through the so-called "bloodless revolution" while changing their name. They turned into capitalists, or rather, into big capitalists. They were never in favor of a restoration of the regime because that was not in their interest.

Andrey Lukanov was charged with providing money and ammunition to terrorist regimes. For me these are serious crimes. He managed to sneak away. Even the International Tribunal in The Hague considered this to be aid. Obviously, there are people with a different kind of thinking even there.

One trial - there are ten or twelve trials that are still pending - which is a source of deep concern for me is the one about the communist concentration and labor camps near Lovech. It is still pending. Most of the defendants died in the meantime. When I started my work in the prosecuting magistracy, I found out that the case had been stopped. I reopened it. I even personally wrote one of the indictments, which was not my job. I would even have insisted on the death penalty, which still existed then. The case sits in the Supreme Court, in the Supreme Court of Appeal, that is. It has been there for years. It was decided first that generals needed to be present on the jury, and there were no generals. Then Mircho Spasov died and there were no longer generals on trial. Then they decided that the case should be heard in Pleven. I told them, "Bring the case here." Yet, they insisted that the case had to be heard in Pleven and then be sent back to us from there. They sent it back. I think that the people from the death camps - the torturers and the murderers - may be tried irrespective of the statute of limitations on account of the passage of time established by the Constitution of 1991. The argument is that at the time of the communist camps there was a provision in the law that banned officers and officials from the Ministry of Interior from being tried without the permission of their Minister. If they could not have been tried then, they could be tried now.

Evidence and materials against General Atanas Semerdzhiev regarding the destruction of secret service files were collected a long time ago, but the investigating authorities prevented the case from being heard by the Supreme Court with priority. The case still waits. Even my own personal file has been destroyed on the General's orders.

It seems to me that the cases that I brought into the courts will also be terminated. The period in which legal action can be pursued will end, and they will be terminated.

Another thing that I shall not forgive those in power is that they failed to resolve the issue of the ordinance about the so-called People's Court, under which 2,730 Bulgarians were executed, and which also allowed for the instituting of bogus trials against deceased individuals. I have drafted nearly two hundred proposals to be reviewed by the Supreme Court. Most of them were taken into consideration. I also sent a letter to the National Assembly with which I asked for legislation to be adopted that would do away with the consequences for the heirs. I explained to them that it was not possible to rectify the injustice in any other way. The matter had been brought to the attention of the Constitutional Court, which was asked to decide whether the so-called Ordinance-Law was to be proclaimed anti-constitutional. The judges decided that it was not their concern. However, it is a shame that now - in the year 2000 - when the UDF has had a majority in the National Assembly for three years, nothing has been done. This is a strange phenomenon. I have been reproached too, but I have submitted proposals. Two hundred cases have been heard at the Supreme Court.

> At the time of Philip Dimitrov's government work went well. People were inspired by their emotions, and although many inexperienced politicians participated in the cabinet, they acted normally. They did not try to interfere with judicial power. That government was in office for only one year, but it is the government that I liked best after November 10, 1989. Philip Dimitrov is an honest politician. He did not take advantage of his position for personal enrichment and he was doing his best.[38]

. . .

The government of the Union of Democratic Forces worked hard during the summer months of 1992 and was able to achieve much. The involvement of *Podkrepa* with the First Private Bank was investigated and evidence of illegal deals was collected. Surprise inspections were organized in the *Chimimport* and *Neftoimpex* foreign trade companies. The Credit Bank was audited. The factory for CDs and disc devices in Stara Zagora was put under investigation for breach of international law. More exigent control was exercised over the customs and the arms trade. In addition, the transactions endorsed by Dimitar Ludzhev, with a nonexistent partner in Bolivia and in the Philippines, were made public.

The Pensions Act was amended to provide for an increase of the value of the minimum pension and assist socially disadvantaged citizens. The members and supporters of the communist party, who had occupied high-ranking lucrative positions in the past, opposed that sort of social "leveling." Thus, the Bulgarian Socialist Party demonstrated its opposition to social services once again.

The Minister of Justice Svetoslav Luchnikov submitted four bills on the restitution of private property for the approval of the government. The documents' purpose was to facilitate the economic revival of old enterprises and shareholding companies. After detailed discussions and many disputes, the bills were submitted for adoption by the National Assembly.

In mid-July *Podkrepa* succeeded in organizing a five-day strike of transportation service employees in Sofia. However, the residents of the capital expressed through rallies their full support to Philip Dimitrov's cabinet. From that moment on *Podkrepa* lost many of its union members and supporters.

The Council of Ministers proposed a number of amendments to the Penal Code and the Code of Criminal Procedure, needed in order to fight organized crime efficiently. However, on July 18, the Thirty-Sixth National Assembly adopted the said legislation only partially. The former communist party was against shortening grace periods and streamlining the official procedures. Thus,

---

[38] Ivan Tatarchev in a conversation with the author, Sofia, Bulgaria, September 16, 2000.

the measures taken against organized crime were not as effective as they could have been.

. . .

On July 24, 1992, Parliament held the first vote of no confidence for the government of the Union of Democratic Forces. The Movement for Rights and Freedoms gave its support to the cabinet but its Chairman Ahmed Dogan did not. The first demand for the resignation of the Speaker of Parliament Stefan Savov had been put to the vote and rejected the previous day. It was becoming clear that the cabinet would not have the support of Parliament to run the country for much longer and the ministers were increasingly working in haste.

On July 22, the Prime Minister's adviser Konstantin Mishev went to Macedonia to arrange a meeting between Philip Dimitrov and the Macedonian President Kiro Gligorov during the visit of the two statesmen to Turkey. After returning from Turkey, Philip Dimitrov spoke with President Zhelev and some of the ambassadors about the visit of his adviser to Macedonia and about his meeting with Gligorov in Turkey. At a conference in London on July 27, he insisted on Western diplomatic support for the lifting of the arms embargo against Macedonia.

A scandal became public that same day. President Zhelev's adviser Zdravko Popov was dismissed after it was disclosed that he had visited Lebanon to negotiate with an arms dealer to supply embargoed states, probably Libya or Iraq.

By mid-summer, the government was enjoying its first economic success. At last, there was hope for the country's financial recovery. The International Monetary Fund offered a preliminary agreement for one billion US dollars to Bulgaria, which was expected to boost the bankrupt economy significantly. In addition, a delegation led by Ivan Kostov received a counter-proposal from the London Club of creditor banks, concerning the settlement of Bulgaria's foreign debt and options for a future agreement. That was a real breakthrough in the creditor banks' position. The black clouds over the first cabinet of the Union of Democratic Forces were beginning to disperse. The imminent resolution of the debt issue would limit the illegal activities of the communist economic interest groups and also stimulate the country's economy. Thus, there was no doubt that Bulgaria was beginning to rise to its feet, albeit painfully and gradually. In spite of constant abuse in the media, owned mostly by ex-communists, the government of the Union of Democratic Forces had the support of the majority of the population.

Philip Dimitrov was firmly resolved to do away with the legacy of communism as quickly as possible. He had repeatedly proposed that legislation for the declassifying of the files of the secret police be submitted to the National Assembly. As nothing had come of that, in August the Prime Minister himself ordered the files open.

Many politicians felt threatened by that. Clearly, they felt it was too early for Bulgaria to be rebuilt as a democratic state of independent and free citizens governed by the law. It was high time for the adversaries of Dimitrov and his proactive ministers to rally together and bring the cabinet down. In fact, attempts of that nature had been made since the day the Council of Ministers of the UDF stepped into office. "Insiders" were involved in the plot. The Bulgarian Socialist Party could never topple the blue government alone.

25. Bringing Down Philip Dimitrov's Government: Plots and Maneuvers

In 1992, the phrases "shady deal" and "discrediting information" were used frequently both appropriately and inappropriately. Yet, the aim was always the same, namely to weaken, discredit and eventually overthrow the country's first democratically elected government after decades of communist rule.

A scandal regarding the "shady deal" with "that list" exploded on February 9. The newspapers covered the event immediately in vague and contradictory terms. It was claimed that there was an audio-cassette tape containing the names of intelligence agents working in the Bulgarian diplomatic missions abroad, which the Minister of Foreign Affairs, Stoyan Ganev, allegedly made available to the leader of the MRF, Ahmed Dogan, who in turn allegedly passed it to a foreign diplomatic mission. Pressured by the Minister of Defense Dimitar Ludzhev and the heads of the National Security Service and the National Intelligence Service, President Zhelev demanded that the Prime Minister punish Stoyan Ganev and Ahmed Dogan. Philip Dimitrov and Yordan Sokolov tried to manage the crisis by demonstrating the absurdity of the discrediting material. The scandal gradually subsided, but Dogan displayed a spiteful attitude towards Sokolov and Dimitrov rather than Ludzhev.[1]

That whole story was characteristic of the inadequate and inconsistent conduct of some politicians during those times. Still, it prompted the UDF's National Coordinating Council, the Parliamentary Group of the UDF and the cabinet to consider the role of the special services in the state and whether it was at all appropriate for them to report to the President alone.[2] Ivan Kurtev recorded his impressions of the official UDF meeting following the scandal:

> After the UDF Parliamentary Group decided to propose that the National Intelligence Service be placed in subordination to the Ministry of Interior last Tuesday, the President waited for four days and then made a formal declaration through his spokesman. He openly confronted the parliamentary majority without having discussed the issue with them previously. At the end of the declaration, Zhelyu Zhelev stated that he would seek the support of the people. He did not explain how this could happen without violating the Constitution. Televised declarations from the *G. S. Rakovski* Legion and from Solomon Passy followed on Sunday. They supported the President and offered recommendations that sounded much like ultimatums.
>
> Apparently, that attack had been thought out in advance. This led the National Coordinating Council to conclude that a conversation needed to be

---

[1] Dimitrov 1995(a); Brahm 1998, pp. 23-24.

[2] *Demokratsiya* daily, February 26, 1992.

held between Zhelyu Zhelev and the leaderships of the UDF and its Parliamentary Group.

The meeting with Zhelev was held at the President's Office on March 6. Zhelyu kept us waiting for 20 minutes. When he appeared, he was very formal and started talking immediately without sitting down. He said that he had invited us to clear up the misunderstandings between us. He had always been with the UDF. He was keen on staying on good terms with all and stressed that the presidential institution was open for dialogue with the UDF. Members of Parliament would have precedence in meetings with him. 90 per cent of the UDF electorate was his. He was the founder of the UDF, but his tolerance had been considered a weakness. That transpired from the way we had interpreted his presidential powers. He cited statements to that effect made by Stefan Savov, Stoyan Ganev and Ventsislav Dimitrov. The claim was that Parliament was a supreme power in the country, but it was merely the supreme legislative body. The UDF Parliamentary Group had made attempts to curb the President's powers. Stoyan Ganev had filed requests for appointing diplomats abroad without discussing the nominations with the President first. "The ambassadors are the envoys of the Head of State," he said. And then he cited the number of votes with which each Member of Parliament was elected and the millions of votes cast for him. Then he derived further arguments from these figures to support his claims for greater control over the military sphere, national security and foreign policy. He appealed for constructive cooperation and complete openness between the braches of power. The legislative branch was not to be turned into another executive one, according to him. He also claimed that reforms should be conducted through democratic means and with broad popular support.

Stefan Savov pointed out the lack of substance in the mathematical argument about the President's powers, the Members of Parliament and the National Assembly as a whole. According to him, there was no presidential power under the Constitution, and the President's prerogatives were much more limited than they had been under the old Constitution. He added that the ambassadors were envoys not of the President, but of the Bulgarian State. There was a separation of powers in a parliamentary republic and parliamentary control over the executive. The President was a part of the executive branch.

In this case Savov went too far as well. He also said, "Zhelev is presiding over the country, but is not governing it because Bulgaria is a parliamentary republic." He claimed that there was a gigantic provocation meant to discredit Stoyan Ganev and Ahmed Dogan and deal a blow to the UDF and the MRF. However, that attempt had been foiled by the anticipatory actions of the UDF. At the end he added, "The lack of control over the special services and their role in the recent events necessitates their placement under parliamentary supervision."

Alexander Yordanov said that the issues under consideration had been discussed by the UDF National Coordinating Council and that the UDF no longer was what it had been when it was created in 1989. Since then a lot had happened. The UDF government was a coalition government, but it was not engaged in *perestroika* because it was changing the system. There were organized actions on the part of the BSP and parties outside Parliament, which were not successful in the elections, whose purpose was to impede the work of the cabinet. The President did not openly state his support for the UDF government. He had also failed to respond to the "prophesies" of leaders of parties outside Parliament about imminent elections allegedly scheduled for March 15 although it was his duty to do so. Zhelev had to be aware that the UDF was to effect the change of the system, not Petko Simeonov, who had a different sort of thinking and different intentions. Yordanov asked, "What would have happened if the attempt to discredit the government had succeeded and what was the President's role in that plot?" He insisted on complete openness on that issue and added, "The special services cannot remain outside of parliamentary control. The leading figures in them, who bear the responsibility for the case, ought to go." However, it so happened that they remained unchanged under the next two governments of both Lyuben Berov and Zhan Videnov!

Zhelyu Zhelev made a commitment to transparency. He said, "I am not disputing the need for parliamentary control and the results of the investigation of the last scandal will be made public." They never were.

Georgi Markov pointed out that there were obviously misunderstandings between the institutions of the Presidency and the government. The shortcomings of the new Constitution affected the presidential powers. Moreover, there was a discrepancy between his prerogatives and his actions. The President had demonstrated a distrust of the UDF, which was caused by his advisors. He often met with failed politicians who had "flaked off" from the UDF, but could it be that he never paid any attention to what they wrote and spoke? The aim of the plot had been to intensify the distrust between the institutions. The President ought to be careful not to provoke mistrust in the UDF electorate because then he would be lost. He should not be deluded that 90 percent of the UDF electorate was his. That was support for the UDF, not any single individual.

Ventsislav Dimitrov insisted on drastic cuts in the budget of both the President's office and the government apparatus. Both budgets were unjustifiably bloated while the budget of the National Assembly was the most scanty.

Mihail Nedelchev spoke about the necessity of regular discussions in the future and the need to specify the prerogatives of each of the branches of power.

Edwin Sugarev claimed that it was an illusion that 90 per cent of the UDF electorate belonged to the President. He urged Zhelyu Zhelev to tell Dimitar Ludzhev that the script for a minor internal coup that would make him Prime

Minister had failed. Then he added that the President's friends should be blamed for the current limits of the presidential powers because they had not left the Grand National Assembly and had signed the Constitution. Edwin was direct as usual and told things the way he saw them.

Zhelyu Zhelev announced something he had never mentioned earlier, namely that when the 39 Members of Parliament had left the Grand National Assembly, he had urged Dertliev to leave Parliament with his people twice before the Constitution was signed. Dertliev had refused.

Nikolay Kolev-Bosiya insisted that a way should be sought to proclaim the former Soviet Ambassador to Bulgaria, Victor Sharapov, *persona non grata*.

Stoyan Ganev addressed the issue of the discreditation plot very emotionally. He complained that Dr. Zhelev plainly did not trust him. In his conversation with Stefan Savov and with Philip Dimitrov the President had said "Whether it is true or not, Stoyan and Dogan ought to go!"

Explanations from Savov and Zhelev followed, but it did not become clear precisely what Zhelev had said. There were several other comments that basically repeated things that had already been said.

I drew everyone's attention to the curious way in which the invitations for the reception at the *Boyana* Residence on the occasion of the National Day of Bulgaria, March 3, had been handled. Zhelev had sent invitations for the reception only to a few people from the UDF. I personally was among these few. Edwin Sugarev, however, was not, although he was a prominent figure in the UDF and Vice-Chairman of its Parliamentary Group. Other important Members of Parliament had not been invited either. At the same time, invitations were extended to the close associates of Peter Dertliev and Petko Simeonov, as well as the entire leaderships of certain organizations outside Parliament.

Finally, I insisted that the meeting should end with some sort of clear conclusion and that it would be inappropriate for us to leave the hall and say conflicting things to the journalists. I recommended that we should say that an agreement had been reached regarding the need to reorganize the special services and have them under parliamentary control. In addition, we would tell the media that we had agreed to hold similar conversations regularly.

There were certain final touches to the wording, and Valentin Stoyanov and Mihail Nedelchev were chosen to inform the journalists about the meeting.

On March 6, at the beginning of the meeting, Zhelev was rather curt and inclined to argue. He gradually calmed down later and would express his agreement with brief phrases and single words more and more frequently. He tried to change the words "parliamentary control" with regard to the special services, but then he said, "OK, go ahead."

In spite of the decision to hold regular meetings, there were only two subsequent meetings between President Zhelev and the UDF, both of which took place some time in the early summer. Later Zhelyu Zhelev refused all contact with us. And then there was the press conference known as the "*Boyana* meadows".[3]

. . .

After this meeting, there were several unforeseen and incomprehensible developments on the political scene. Unexpectedly, Stoyan Ganev and Mihail Nedelchev became very close with Dr. Zhelyu Zhelev. The President included the two politicians in his delegation during his tour of Latin America in the summer of 1992. Upon their return to Bulgaria, the three men appeared to have completely forgotten the earlier animosity among them as well as their differences of opinion.

The sharp change in the relations between Georgi Markov and the President was an even greater surprise. In 1992 Markov was a very vocal opponent of Zhelyu Zhelev's and referred to him as a traitor and a fiend. In 1994, the fact that Markov was the former "agent Nikolay" of the State Security services had already been made public. Still, the Bulgarian Head of State appointed him Member of the Constitutional Court from his own quota.[4]

During the same year, the longstanding adversaries and competitors Zhelyu Zhelev and Stefan Savov also became surprisingly close. They often met and most probably discussed Savov's attacks on the Union of Democratic Forces and the Democratic Party's leaving the blue coalition before the parliamentary elections in December 1994. As a result, the democratic development of Bulgaria would be delayed for years.

. . .

In April 1992, the Movement for Rights and Freedoms pleasantly surprised the UDF with their readiness to sign a political agreement with the coalition in power. The document was meant to secure closer cooperation between the leaderships of the two organizations and their parliamentary groups. It would also regulate the two organizations' interactions on matters related to the executive power. The agreement would be valid during the term of the Thirty-Sixth National Assembly. Both sides chose a group of representatives to prepare it. The MRF group included Osman Oktay, Yunal Lyutfi and Sherife Mustafa,

[3] Kurtev, *Dairy*, March 1992.

[4] *Nedelnik* weekly, November 10, 1999.

while the UDF was represented by Ivan Kurtev, Edwin Sugarev and Yordan Vasilev.

However, the negotiations did not progress at all. The MRF kept presenting new requests. It was a real feat for the members of the two groups to meet, as if they lived in different countries rather than the same city. Only one meeting was held and the draft of the agreement was approved by both sides. It remained to set the date for its formal signing. This did not happen. The Movement for Rights and Freedoms kept finding excuses to postpone the second meeting. In October, the negotiations between the UDF and the MRF were resumed and the document draft was updated. Nevertheless, the agreement again remained unsigned.[5]

During the summer of 1992, Bulgarians found it difficult to keep track of the scads of political developments because many of them went on holidays. Most people listened to the final speeches in Parliament before its recess in August on transistor radios on the beach or watched TV in their summer cottages. That was how they heard about the unsuccessful vote of no confidence for the government, the demand to remove Stefan Savov from the office of the Speaker of Parliament, the threats of Members of Parliament from the MRF that they would settle their scores in the autumn. It was not clear what scores and with whom.

After September 1 things became easier to follow. When the National Assembly resumed its work, attacks on the cabinet coming from the *Podkrepa* Federation of Labor, the Movement for Rights and Freedoms, the Head of State, the National Intelligence Service and a part of the UDF Parliamentary Group intensified and became more frequent. The democratically elected blue government had ostensibly become the "No. 1 enemy" of those organizations, institutions and individuals.

It should be noted that the attacks took place at a time when Philip Dimitrov's Council of Ministers had already succeeded in implementing the small-scale privatization plan, and assisted the establishment of a middle class to oppose the post-communist new rich. The cabinet had also launched the agrarian reform and attempted to stop the plundering of agricultural cooperatives. The Bulgarian currency had been stabilized and the inflation rate dropped from approximately 400 per cent in 1991 to 60 per cent in 1992. In addition, the UDF government was on the verge of signing extended financial agreements with the World Bank and the International Monetary Fund. Philip Dimitrov had received guarantees for the settling of the foreign debt. His

[5] Text of the Political Agreement between the UDF and the MRF, October 22, 1992, Library of the National Assembly; Ivan Kurtev in a conversation with the author, Sofia, Bulgaria, August 18, 1998.

cabinet had earned international respect and started the procedures for the country's entry into the European Union. Bulgaria had almost caught up with the reforms in Poland, the Czech Republic and Hungary. Contacts with potential foreign investors had been established and a lot of useful work was done to put post-totalitarian Bulgaria on the right track.[6]

In the middle of all these activities, the government of the Union of Democratic Forces was stabbed in the back. It was the President, Dr. Zhelyu Zhelev, who opened the attack. His first act was public, after which the Head of State, elected eight months previously on the UDF ticket, continued his behind-the-scenes maneuvers to bring down the cabinet. Apparently, the successes of the Council of Ministers and its increasing authority provoked envy, irritation, and jealousy in the ambitious philosopher, instead pleasing him.

...

On August 30, 1992, Zhelyu Zhelev called a televised press conference in front of his *Boyana* residence. The event was dubbed the "*Boyana* meadows" event and went down as one of the most cunning tricks in the history of Bulgaria's democratic transition. On that occasion the President frivolously distorted reality. Without saying even one good word about the blue government, and without mentioning any of its successes, Dr. Zhelev addressed the Bulgarian public with a tone of deep concern:

> ...We find ourselves facing a fundamentally wrong policy. We have confrontation instead of unification. We are faced with the incredible fact of the government having declared war on everybody. It is in fighting with the trade unions. It has waged war on the press, the entire extraparliamentary democratic opposition, which - on top of everything else - supports the UDF platform, and the Bulgarian Orthodox Church. (I am aware that there is a new development and let's hope that something comes out of this, but if the government is trying to resolve the issues with the Church in an unprincipled way, I doubt the outcome will be success.) There have been attempts to provoke a war between the principal institutions of the state, namely the Parliament, the President's Office and the government, by usurping another institution's constitutional powers.[7]

---

[6] Brahm 1998, pp. 34-35, p. 37.

[7] *Trud* [Labour] daily, August 31, 1992.

In fact, for every person with common sense it was clear that "it was precisely the trade unions, the opposition outside Parliament, and the media that had thrown down the gauntlet, not the government."[8]

The "*Boyana* meadows" press conference was announced as an analysis of current events. However, the President, who was elected by the Bulgarian noncommunists, did not utter even one sentence - either in his speech or in his answers to questions posed by journalists - reproaching the Bulgarian Socialist Party for the way it was trying to stop the country's democratization by every possible means. According to everything that Zhelev said, all the misfortunes of the country and all the bad luck of the nation were caused by UDF policy. None of the enormous difficulties that the cabinet had had in the implementation of its policy were addressed in the President's comments.

Was it possible that Zhelyu Zhelev was that inattentive or did he have ulterior motives? When asked by a journalist from the Bulgarian News Agency about his plans for the near future specifically concerning the internal political life of the country, the Head of State replied laconically, "My program for the future? Allow me to have my own secrets."[9]

Indeed, he had his secrets. After August 30 Dr. Zhelev contributed to the toppling of Philip Dimitrov's democratic government through subversive planning and scheming.

Zhelyu Zhelev never realized the extent to which he disappointed his former political supporters. He never admitted his responsibility for halting the reforms in Bulgaria for five years and for letting the mafia take control of a grey market, which affects his fellow countrymen to this day. Perhaps the former President still perceived himself as the victim of injustice. That seemed to be the case at the UDF meeting on September 18, 1992, in the *Vitosha New Otani* Hotel, when a member of the Independent Society for Human Rights Protection accused him of betraying democracy and characterized his conduct as pro-communist. Then Zhelev left the meeting in a huff and finally severed his ties with the blue coalition. Many people felt that he had been waiting for that moment for a long time.

After that incident, the National Coordinating Council of the UDF - in spite of Dr. Zhelev's faults with respect to the cause of democracy - formed a group to iron out the differences with the first UDF Chairman, and to explain to him that the lady's statement in the hotel did not express the organization's official position. The persons entrusted with this delicate task were Yordan Vasilev, Svetoslav Luchnikov, and Ivan Kurtev, who was elected UDF Secretary General

---

8 Brahm 1998, p. 28.

9 *Troud* daily, August 31, 1992.

at the meeting on September 18. In 1998, Kurtev commented on the negotiations in the following way:

> I started looking for ways to get in touch with Zhelev immediately after the group was formed because we already had precedents and we knew how difficult it was to arrange meetings with him. This time I made use of the circumstance that I had lived in the same building with his close associate, Julia Gurkovska, for some time and I knew her quite well. I managed to find her, but it turned out that Zhelyu Zhelev was resting on Sundays and was not to be disturbed.
>
> Between Monday and Wednesday of the following week, I called several more times and attempted to organize the meeting. At first, Zhelev asked for a recording of the meeting. I sent him audio-cassettes. Then he asked for a video-recording. I replied that we did not have a video-recording, but that the National TV had broadcast the event and that he could get the recording from there. Actually, I did not communicate with him personally, but through Julia Gurkovska. Then even the telephone conversations ceased and we started communicating through letters. Here is what happened. I sent a letter. The first answer was signed by him, the second one by the head of the President's Office, and the third one by his secretary. What complete disregard! Who are you to bother me? Anyway, the conversation with Zhelyu Zhelev never took place. We kept trying for four days, but he never accepted the offer to meet.
>
> From that moment on, events developed with catastrophic speed. Stefan Savov was removed from the office of the Speaker of Parliament. Then there was the so-called "Macedonian arms affair." Finally, Philip Dimitrov and his cabinet were deposed.
>
> The outcome of all this was that the President's adviser Lyuben Berov became Prime Minister of Bulgaria.[10]

The people reacted to Zhelyu Zhelev's betrayal of the cause of the Union of Democratic Forces. In the summer of 1993, noncommunist citizens of Sofia set up another tent camp in front of the President's Office in support of Edwin Sugarev, who had started a hunger strike, demanding the President's resignation. Most of these protesters were former participants in the City of Truth. They were the people who had brought Dr. Zhelyu Zhelev to the presidency in the summer of 1990.

...

[10] Ivan Kurtev in a conversation with the author, Sofia, Bulgaria, August 18, 1998.

The "*Boyana* meadows" press conference triggered a domino effect of events. On September 3, 1992, *Podkrepa* officially accused Philip Dimitrov's government of preparing a military coup. According to the trade union, the cabinet had tapped telephones and created secret police units.

The tabloids avidly spread the sensational intrigue. That was welcome news for the supporters of the renamed communist party who were ardent opponents of the UDF government. In addition, in the summer of 1992, the leadership of the MRF completely switched its political allegiance. In the beginning of the year - when Ahmed Dogan still appeared to support the UDF - he declared that he was about to propose legislation banning the Bulgarian Socialist Party. Just a few months later he and his close associates took a resolute stand against any criminal investigation of former communist leaders.[11] After Andrey Lukanov was stripped of his parliamentary immunity and a criminal investigation against him was instituted, the Turkish leaders did everything they could to discredit the UDF government with the Moslem minority and to bring it down. Most likely they were under pressure from the former communist State Security system, with which most of them had collaborated. The Counsel of Ministers headed by Philip Dimitrov was about to open the files of the secret services and the leadership of the Movement for Rights and Freedoms was in no position to support that.

...

The gravity of the political situation was openly discussed at the meeting of the Union of Democratic Forces at the *Vitosha New Otani* Hotel on September 18 and 19, 1992. So was the likelihood that Philip Dimitrov's government could be overthrown. It was decided that the current Premier would still be the nominee for Prime Minister of a new cabinet. Then, the UDF adopted a course leading to early elections on the grounds of apprehensions that the MRF was going to vote against the UDF in Parliament in the future. It was evident that Philip Dimitrov's government would no longer be able to work in that case.

On the first day of the UDF forum, a truly absurd event took place. The leading figures in the special services of the Republic of Bulgaria, led by the Head of the National Intelligence Service, General Brigo Asparuhov, held a press conference. The general, who reported directly to President Zhelyu Zhelev, announced that the executive power of his country had violated the embargo against Macedonia and was involved in a clandestine arrangement with the former Yugoslav republic. Asparuhov claimed that Prime Minister Philip

[11] Brahm 1998, p. 19.

Dimitrov had sent his adviser Konstantin Mishev to Skopje to negotiate an arm supplies deal, in violation of agreements signed by Bulgaria.[12]

The truth was that Macedonia had asked the Bulgarian government to supply it with arms, and that Philip Dimitrov had firmly refused. In order to manage the delicate situation in a diplomatic fashion, he had sent his adviser to the Macedonian President Kiro Gligorov. Mishev personally explained to Gligorov that Bulgaria intended to comply strictly with the arms embargo. Moreover, Dimitrov had the prudence to inform the ambassadors of the Western countries in Sofia about Mishev's mission ahead of time, in order to dispel any suspicions. That was what thwarted the plan of the special services - namely, the National Security Service and the National Intelligence Service - to provoke a global scandal with their improvised press conference.[13]

It should be pointed out that General Asparouhov had not reported to the Prime Minister about that case, as was required by standard government procedure. He called a press conference personally with the intention of announcing to the world that his own country was not complying with its international commitments and was violating international law. In his blind hatred of Philip Dimitrov, Brigo Asparuhov was putting down the state he had sworn to serve. There is hardly a scheme, in recent Bulgarian history concocted by a high-ranking official that was more dangerous to the interests of the nation. Yet, that was of no concern either to the Head of the National Intelligence Service, or to the politicians with whom he had masterminded this plan. What mattered to them was triggering the fall of the noncommunist government as quickly as possible.

Following General's inadmissible conduct, the Prime Minister demanded that Zhelyu Zhelev dismiss him. The President refused to do so. Then, the two statesmen reached a compromise solution: Brigo Asparouhov would apologize publicly. Yet, events took an entirely different course, and the slander campaign against Philip Dimitrov and Konstantin Mishev was soon renewed and intensified.

...

At the same time, the relationships among political parties and individual members of the Thirty-Sixth National Assembly were becoming increasingly

---

[12] *Ibid.*, p. 29.

[13] *Ibid.*; Philip Dimitrov in a conversation with the author, New York, U.S.A., March 14, 1998.

strained. Ahmed Dogan accused Philip Dimitrov of "blue fascism" and officially stripped him of his confidence. He proceeded to engage in negotiations with the leaders of the renamed Bulgarian Communist Party, Nora Ananieva and Chavdar Kyuranov. The Movement for Rights and Freedoms adamantly insisted on the resignation of Stefan Savov as well.

After several votes of no confidence in the Speaker, which came very close to succeeding, Stefan Savov handed in his resignation on September 24, 1992. At that point, according to Ivan Kurtev, the UDF missed an opportunity, which could have spared the country a lot of trouble:

> When Stefan Savov's resignation was put to the vote, he left his presiding position highly excited and announced an interruption of the session, without assigning the function of Chairman to anyone. At that time the Deputy Speakers of Parliament were Snezhana Botusharova from the UDF and Kadir Kadir from the MRF. The Bulgarian Socialist party continuously refused to propose its representative for the office.
>
> The members of the UDF Parliamentary Group gathered in one of the conference halls of the National Assembly to decide what to do. The day before I had shared with Philip Dimitrov the idea that early elections should not be ruled out. Philip tried to explain the fantastic opportunity we had to the Members of Parliament. However, he did not speak plainly but in a slightly veiled fashion, because all the information from our meetings was already being leaked.
>
> Here is what the actual situation was. Stefan Savov had not indicated who should substitute for him. Snezhana Botusharova did not convene a plenary session. Kadir Kadir would not have had the audacity at that time to do it. That was 1992. It would have provoked all who shared Rumen Vodenicharov's views to jump and to shout, 'This is where all this has led us! The Turks are ruling the country!'
>
> In other words, the absence of a chairperson would trigger a parliamentary crisis that could lead to new elections. At that time the UDF approval rating was about 44 per cent and we could rely on having our own majority in the next parliament.
>
> For me, personally, that was the second chance for Bulgaria to take a more favorable and faster course of development, after the missed opportunity of December 14, 1989. In my opinion, September 24, 1992, was the second wasted chance for the democrats.
>
> Philip Dimitrov did everything possible to explain to the parliamentarians how things stood, but the choice was theirs. He said something to the effect of "Everyone should decide for himself whether to vote for a new Speaker or not." I cannot recall the exact words but they were perfectly sufficient for people to know what to do if they wanted to comply.

Very few Members of Parliament - 15 or 17 - voted against the election of a new Speaker. The majority voted in favor of a new Speaker.[14]

. . .

A day after Stefan Savov's resignation, several members of the UDF Parliamentary Group - specifically Dimitar Ludzhev and the members of the Alternative Socialist Party - demanded the resignation of Asen Agov, the UDF-appointed Director of the Bulgarian National Television. About a week later two of Philip Dimitrov's cabinet ministers - the science and education minister Nikolay Vasilev, leader of the alternative socialists, and the health minister Nikola Vasilev - declared themselves against the government's policy.

On October 7, Victor Sharapov, KGB officer and former Soviet Ambassador to Bulgaria, unexpectedly arrived in Sofia for a visit. He went directly to the *Moskva* Hotel and stayed there until the end of the month. The day of his arrival, Philip Dimitrov had dinner with Ahmed Dogan at the *Krim* restaurant and had a serious talk with him. Dogan assured the Prime Minister that an agreement between the UDF and the MRF was possible, but that certain details needed to be specified. As soon as Dogan reached an agreement with Dimitrov on a certain point, he immediately raised new claims and pushed the set deadlines back further.[15]

In those days there was another paradox in Bulgarian political life. At a meeting of the National Security Committee of the National Assembly, General Brigo Asparouhov was commended rather than criticized for the press conference that he had organized. Outraged, the Prime Minister Dimitrov filed a demand for a parliamentary debate behind closed doors on the conduct of the Head of the National Intelligence Service. The following day, Asparouhov apologized to Philip Dimitrov in President Zhelev's office. At that very same moment Ahmed Dogan declared that the MRF's confidence in the UDF coalition government had not been restored.

On October 15, the National Assembly rejected the Premier's wish for a debate regarding General Asparouhov. The following day Parliament voted to hold a plenary session behind closed doors regarding a proposal submitted by Members of Parliament from the Bulgarian Socialist Party and the Movement for Rights and Freedoms against the Prime Minister. The MRF Spokesman Ivan Palchev announced in advance that the outcome of the parliamentary debate would be negative for Dimitrov.

---

[14] Ivan Kurtev in a conversation with the author, Sofia, Bulgaria, August 18, 1998.

[15] Brahm 1998, pp. 28-29.

The session of the Thirty-Sixth National Assembly on October 20, 1992, was yet another absurdity with regards to both process and decision making. No proof of the existence of any "arms deal" whatsoever was furnished; yet, the Prime Minister was condemned for allegedly having marred the country's prestige and for having jeopardized its national interests and security. That resolution, which defied any logic, was passed with the votes of 123 Members of Parliament from the Bulgarian Socialist Party and the Movement for Rights and Freedoms, two political organizations which until very recently had spoken of banning each other. The parliamentary representatives of the Union of Democratic Forces boycotted that session.

Ivan Kurtev comments on that disgraceful day for the Bulgarian Parliament as follows:

> All of us from the UDF left the debate behind closed doors on the so-called "Macedonian shady deal," and we watched and listened to what was going on in the plenary hall from the balcony. It was late in the evening, after 8 p.m. Brigo Asparouhov came into the parliamentary building. The BSP and MRF Members of Parliament sneaked out of the plenary hall individually, received instructions from him on what to say, and then blurted out incredible nonsense, accusations, and insults to the government from the rostrum.
>
> Kadir Kadir was chairing the plenary session in an outrageous fashion. He kept interrupting the Prime Minister and keeping him from expressing his position. The resolution adopted at the end condemned the government and the Premier for some alleged illegal arms deal that neither he nor the government had conducted.
>
> They failed to prove the existence of any shady deal. Incidentally, if there had been anything of that kind, it would have become public a thousand times by then, causing an enormous international scandal or even a trial in court. Both Philip Dimitrov and the UDF had enough enemies and it would have been impossible for something like that to be swept under the carpet. Anyway, there was no "Macedonian deal."
>
> Given that we had not won even a single political vote in Parliament after Andrei Lukanov had been stripped of his parliamentary immunity on July 7, because the MRF was already voting with the reds, it was absolutely pointless to keep a cabinet in office. It was unable to pass the laws it needed for the reforms planned. Therefore, in the autumn of 1992, it was necessary to understand clearly whether that government had the confidence of the National Assembly or not. It came out that there was no confidence in the cabinet.
>
> By toppling our first government its enemies obtained a timeout of four years during which organized crime flourished. Industrial enterprises were plundered and massive amounts of capital illegally exported from Bulgaria. The

former communists stabilized their positions in the judiciary and a number of other spheres.[16]

...

Philip Dimitrov had one last chance to prevent the imminent chaos and the plundering of Bulgaria. He could ask the legislative body for a vote of confidence for his government. There was a gleam of hope in that, albeit weak. Maybe, after all, the MRF Members of Parliament would not muster up the courage to unite with the former communists – who so recently suppressed their minority rights - and topple the first Bulgarian noncommunist cabinet. Or maybe a lost vote could trigger a parliamentary crisis, leading to new elections, which the UDF was very likely to win. Public support for the government exceeded 42 per cent nationwide and there was a real boost of private business initiatives. With a resolution of the 79th Council of Ministers of the Republic of Bulgaria in hand and the approval of the UDF National Coordinating Council, on October 21, Dimitrov submitted to the Thirty-Sixth National Assembly a request for a vote of confidence in his cabinet.

Three days later, Ahmed Dogan met with President Zhelev. After their conversation, Dogan declared on national television that a "turn to the left" was needed and that an "MRF kick" was to be expected. The anticommunist population was appalled by the statement of the MRF head. Fortunately, however, there was no backlash against the Moslem minority, only against their leaders.

On October 28, 1992, the National Assembly gave a vote of no confidence to the first democratic government of Bulgaria after World War II. By secret voting 120 Members of Parliament declared themselves against Philip Dimitrov's cabinet, while 111 supported it.

Years after that blow had been dealt, Philip Dimitrov offered the following comments:

> The figures show that even if all members of the Parliamentary Group of the UDF (a total of 110 people) had supported the government in that vote - and it is clear that between 10 and 15 did not - it would still be obvious that the MRF did not vote against the cabinet unanimously. It is unlikely that Dogan simply let each member of his parliamentary group vote according to his or her own conscience. Given his intense desire to control his people, that seems improbable. Instead, he seems to have made a last test of the UDF's ability to

[16] Ivan Kurtev in a conversation with the author, Sofia, Bulgaria, August 18 and 24, 1998.

> solve its internal problems on its own by giving the coalition as many votes as it would need if still united. In case of success, he could proclaim that he had saved the government.
>
> Often accused that his party had toppled the government, Dogan kept silent. He seems to have preferred being considered totally disloyal but strong over the risk of being considered a loser. From that point on he felt no need to seek a solution to UDF-MRF relations and only faked negotiations. His task became solely avoiding elections, which could put his party in a less advantageous position after the fall of the first UDF cabinet.[17]

The result of the vote of confidence in Philip Dimitrov's Council of Ministers confirmed the suspicion that the parliamentary balance in the Thirty-Sixth National Assembly of Bulgaria had been reorganized. Some parliamentarians of the MRF and individual members of the UDF helped the former dictator's party attain its goal. The democratization and decommunization of the country have been stopped.

That was a green light for the Bulgarian Socialist Party. Many of its members would be served best at that time if the country had an inert and corrupt government of no particular political orientation. With the help of the pro-communist media and the tabloids, that cabinet would be labeled blue regardless of the fact that the loyal UDF Members of Parliament would refuse to vote for it through the end of their term in office.

---

[17] Philip Dimitrov in a conversation with the author, Philadelphia, U.S.A., March 29, 2009.

26. Lawlessness Outside of Time

The national media made tremendous efforts to distort the fateful political events that took place in Bulgaria in the fall of 1992. With respect to Philip Dimitrov, they hammered two *clichés*, namely that he had "handed off the government on a platter" and "proposed himself for a second term in office." There was no logical connection between the two assertions. On the one hand, Dimitrov had allegedly given up the government, which meant that he did not wish to be in power, and at the same time he had nominated himself as the next Prime Minister, which implied that he was eager to remain at the head of the executive.

Few people paid attention to that controversy. However, the "independent" media, sponsored mostly with red money, never stopped fabricating slanderous theories about the first UDF government. Instead of giving an objective assessment of the situation, journalists claimed that the former Prime Minister had forced his wish to lead the next government upon the coalition, driven by personal ambitions and lust for power. Had he refrained, they wrote, the UDF would have continued to lead the country through another of its representatives. This false version of the events was repeated so many times that it gradually entered public discourse and was taken seriously by the confused population.

In contrast, the version disseminated by the foreign media was far more analytical and precise. It explained that the National Assembly of the Republic of Bulgaria had toppled the UDF government and did not see fault with his Prime Minister having asked for a vote of confidence. Thus, the foreign journalists accounted for the fact that changing the political system was an endeavor that could not be carried out without parliamentary support.

...

On November 4, 1992, the Chairman of the Union of Democratic Forces was nominated for a second term as Premier at a meeting of the political organization. Initially even Ahmed Dogan did not object. Not only had Philip Dimitrov not proposed himself to be the next Prime Minister, he was actually being used as a scapegoat. That fact was corroborated by Rayna Tomova, who attended the meeting as a guest:

> Philip complied with a decision, adopted by a vast majority of the leaders of the UDF member organizations. He could not tell them, "No, I cannot agree to be nominated again because this would negatively affect my political future." I remember that Elka Konstantinova said something to the effect of, "Of course, Philip ought to be nominated again. If we don't put forward Philip's name, that would mean that we admit the existence of a "Macedonian

> deal" and that he had something to do with it." As was to be expected, the National Assembly of Bulgaria rejected Philip Dimitrov as the next Prime Minister with its new majority, composed by the "ants" [UDF members of Parliament from Zhelyu Zhelev's circle who started voting with the BSP - *author's note*], MRF and the renamed communist party.
>
> The other accusation that the enemies of the UDF government were trying to instill in the minds of public was that Philip Dimitrov had "handed the government on a platter over to the opposition" by asking for a vote of confidence in Parliament. In my opinion, that act saved the UDF and was good for the future of Bulgaria. If he had not done it, the communists would have managed to destroy the democratic union.
>
> Through the vote of confidence, Philip Dimitrov protected the UDF from further slander. Others, too, in addition to Zhelev and Asparouhov, had launched an active campaign against the cabinet and were fabricating scandals like the alleged "Macedonian deal." They would continue to organize such campaigns until they destroyed the Union of Democratic Forces. Therefore, the vote was not only a sensible act, it was also an act of sacrifice. Philip preserved the whole; he preserved the UDF, but he himself burned out politically.[1]

The Secretary General of the UDF from September 1992 until December 1994, Ivan Kurtev, recalled six years later:

> Indeed, the vote of confidence was the Prime Minister's idea, but its execution was not a one-man act. It was discussed by the UDF Parliamentary Group, the Council of Ministers, and the UDF National Coordinating Council. Therefore, no less than 150 people were directly involved with the decision. Philip Dimitrov's proposal had the approval of the entire leadership of the Union of Democratic Forces.[2]

The UDF cabinet under Philip Dimitrov had already shown with its deeds that it was fully determined to carry out the necessary reforms and overcome the consequences of communism. It had not been reluctant to govern Bulgaria. It had been treacherously toppled.

...

In contrast, there was another party that was reluctant to become involved with introducing order in the state, because it had its own affairs - primarily financial -

---

[1] Rayna Tomova in a conversation with the author, Sinemorets, Bulgaria, July 10, 1998.

[2] Ivan Kurtev in a conversation with the author, Sofia, Bulgaria, August 18, 1998.

that it needed to take care of. When the Bulgarian Socialist Party, as the second largest presence in Parliament, received from the President the mandate to form a government, it gave it to a man by the name of Peter Boyadzhiev. No one had heard anything about him because he had spent many years living in France. It is hardly possible that the former communists were unaware of the fact that Boyadzhiev had dual citizenship, which prevented him from heading the executive branch. According to the Constitution, this was the chance for the third largest political organization with parliamentary representation - the Movement for Rights and Freedoms - to form a cabinet.

Ivan Kurtev gave the following account of the negotiations between the UDF and the MRF at the end of the year:

> When in December 1992, the MRF received the mandate to form the government, we renewed our talks with its leadership. Following the decision of the UDF National Coordinating Council, we proposed to nominate Svetoslav Luchnikov for Prime Minister, although he had no wish whatsoever to take that position. The MRF declared that Luchnikov was unacceptable to them.
>
> Then, something interesting happened. Philip Dimitrov was uncomfortable informing Svetoslav Luchnikov that the MRF did not want him. That meant telling him, "Look, we nominated you, the entire country learned about it, and now we are to replace you with someone else." However, when he broke the news to the elderly lawyer, his response was "I don't care whether I am Prime Minister of Bulgaria or doorman at the UDF central office in *Rakovski* Street. It is important for me to be of service to the UDF."
>
> Our next nomination was Yordan Sokolov. The MRF leaders insisted that the two parliamentary groups get together and choose the next Prime Minister. This seemed illogical at first, because we had 110 Members of Parliament, while they had only 24. That would have meant that whoever we nominated would be chosen. However, the MRF relied on the so-called "ants" to help them discredit the nomination of the UDF National Coordinating Council. Then they would nominate someone either from the *Podkrepa* union, or from the Alternative Socialist Party, or God knows from where. At the time this already meant that their nominee would be someone who would certainly be an enemy of the Union of Democratic Forces and of the Bulgarians with noncommunist convictions.
>
> Yunal Lyutfi and other representatives of the MRF told a heap of lies to the two parliamentary groups. They said that the UDF leadership did not accept to sign the agreement, that it was dragging its feet, and that it had refused to give the MRF the positions in government that it demanded.
>
> This time the MRF wanted the Ministry of Justice and had proposed for minister a lawyer from the Central Cooperative Council, an ethnic Bulgarian. We proposed that they should have a Deputy Prime Minister who would

oversee the Ministries of Defense, Interior, and Justice. We recommended that that person be Emil Buchkov, a lawyer and member of their parliamentary group. They refused, demanding instead of the Ministry of Justice, several deputy ministers and the office of Secretary General of the Ministry of Interior.

The worst thing was that as soon as we satisfied a wish of theirs, they made another claim the very next moment or gave up their first claim and insisted on something totally different. It was more than clear that they wanted the whole thing to fail and that the Prime Minister had already been chosen.

Our suspicions were correct. Indeed, we found out later that Zhelyu Zhelev's adviser Lyuben Berov had already been invited for the Prime Minister's office back in November.

The MRF raised all kinds of demands and conditions before the UDF. However, in Lyuben Berov's cabinet, for which Parliament voted with their mandate, they had only one cabinet minister. That was Evgeniy Martinchev, a former member of the communist *nomenklatura.* That was all. They waged fierce battles with us for the office of Secretary General of the Ministry of Interior. Later, in Berov's government, they did not take that office.

At the morning meeting when Yunal Lyutfi presented a biased view of the situation to the UDF Members of Parliament, it became clear that they wished to discuss Yordan Sokolov's candidacy among themselves first. Sokolov was asked to appear before them. They made him wait for hours in the corridors of the National Assembly before they finally met with him. Towards the evening, around 6 p.m., the meeting of Yordan Sokolov with the MRF parliamentary group finally took place. There he was subjected to a humiliating interrogation. Osman Oktay then came to me and told me that they would tell us the outcome of the meeting in a little while. That "little while" took 4-5 hours and after 11:30 p.m. Ahmed Dogan came to me and told me, "I don't accept Sokolov. Sokolov doesn't accept me and I don't accept him. This won't work." For a whole day, for more than twelve hours they strung us along and scorned us.

This was not happening for the first time. Throughout all the negociations we kept arranging meetings with them that never took place because they never came.[3]

Ivan Kurtev also shared a "happier" memory:

While Lyuben Berov's election was talking place, I was sitting on the stairs leading to the library, just opposite the hall where the voting was happening. I was watching the people who entered the hall because those who entered, would vote in his favor.

---

[3] *Ibid.*

A journalist walked past me and asked me, "What are you doing here, are you controlling the members of the UDF Parliamentary Group?" My answer to her was, "Of course, but I think that it is pointless." I blurted it out just like that, for fun. Then, I added, "What I am doing is indeed pointless because the voting did not work out." The woman was startled, "It didn't? What do you mean?" Then I jokingly explained to her that they only had 118 people in the hall and that they needed 121 for the vote to be legitimate.

The journalist lost all interest in me and rushed down the stairs. Just at that moment, Asen Michkovski appeared. She went to him and started explaining something to him, short of breath. I was amused because I knew that the voting had already taken place and that 121 Members of Parliament had cast their vote.

A moment later, three parliamentarians from the UDF who had not yet openly sided with the breakaway faction supporting Berov's government, dubbed "the ants", rushed in. These were Ivan Pushkarov, Svilyana Zaharieva, a teacher from Montana, and I can't remember the third one. It was perfectly obvious that they had rushed in so that the coveted number 121 could be attained. Just three more Members of Parliament had stepped in, the minimum number needed for a majority.

That made me think that the traitors in the UDF Parliamentary Group were not only these 23 UDF Members of Parliament who voted for Lyuben Berov and his government, and that there existed a second layer that appeared whenever it was needed. Unfortunately, my suspicious were confirmed. In September 1994, only 35 of the 110 members of the UDF Parliamentary Group remained with us. All the others had regrouped. Over fifty people had joined the group of the first 23. Among those who broke away were Dimitar Ludzhev and the people around him, who were also close to the President, the Alternative Socialist Party, the parliamentarians connected with *Podkrepa*, and - finally - the Democratic Party of Stefan Savov. That's how it was.[4]

On December 30, 1992, 124 Members of the Thirty-Sixth National Assembly, out of 149 who attended the vote, elected Professor Lyuben Berov for Prime Minister of the Republic. His cabinet was endorsed with 127 votes. Dark days for the population of Bulgaria ensued.

...

In his last speech before Parliament as Prime Minister, Philip Dimitrov predicted the onset of an era of corruption and criminal activities. In 1995, he summarized the two-year term of the government of the economist Lyuben Berov in a study:

---

[4] *Ibid.*, August 24, 1998.

...The important events during that period were few. The developments in society were mostly of an underground nature. “Facts” very often proved to be mere rumors. Alleged events turned out to be ordinary intrigues.

Instead of legislation, there were empty debates pushed forward by the parliamentary majority. Instead of administrative measures, the government produced only words and always procrastinated. Instead of any development of reforms, there was only slow and gradual crumbling of what had already been achieved. Instead of events, there were periodically stage-managed campaigns in the media.

Berov's government declared that it would implement the program of the Union of Democratic Forces. Of the 44 pieces of legislation submitted to Parliament by Philip Dimitrov's government, it allowed only four to be considered, two of which had been substantially modified.

...

Hence, the first basic characteristic of that period was the government's impeding the development of a middle class, accompanied by a cruel impoverishment of the population, especially the elderly retired people. In spite of his pledge to implement the UDF program, Berov refused to complete the new Pension Act, which the UDF had promised to have ready in 1993, and failed to submit it to Parliament.

The second closely related characteristic was the green light given to vulgar and organized crime through the complete loss of interest in law enforcement on the part of the administration. Each action of the government against organized crime was clearly marked by reluctance. In many cases the administration openly stimulated the activities of dubious groups.

The third characteristic was the discrediting of the democratic state institutions, the Bulgarian National Assembly in particular. Its rating in the eyes of the general public dropped to unprecedentedly low levels, especially after several well masterminded campaigns in the media to suggest that Parliament was useless. The media also suggested that the Members of Parliament were thinking about their own affluence only (which, unfortunately, was quite plausible, given the crooks that became emblematic examples of parliamentary disgrace). In the first half of 1993, the theme of the need for a "firm hand" featured very prominently in the media, and sociological surveys devoted considerable attention to it. Claques like Dimitar Ludzhev exclaimed in public "Incidentally, who is the Bulgarian De Gaulle?" They were discreetly pointing in the direction of Mr. Zhelev, who blinked timidly and later (e.g., in his speech before Parliament on June 3, 1993) modestly offered his services in overcoming the situation in which "the state cannot guarantee the life and the rights of its citizens."

The fourth principal characteristic of that period was the attempt to instill a skeptical attitude in the population regarding integration with European and especially with Atlantic institutions. The same people who had prevented

Bulgaria from making use of the exceptional U.S.A. and European offers of support through the International Monetary Fund and the World Bank - the institutions had prepared a preliminary extended financial agreement for one billion dollars to the Bulgarian government – all of a sudden started complaining that the West was not helping Bulgaria. Their secret aim soon became very obvious. They meant to keep Bulgaria from actively pursuing European and Atlantic integration and directed its foreign policy towards dependence on Russia by advocating "Orthodox arcs", "Pan-Slavic spaces", etc.

Nevertheless, the most noticeable and unambiguous characteristic of politics during the period of timelessness was the common aim of discrediting and destroying the Union of Democratic Forces. The persons who had gained control over the principal state institutions, the communist party, the "independent" and dependent media, and the pseudo-democrats, all of them, probably guided by different motives, had a common enemy, namely "change". Change was hateful to those who had nostalgic feelings for the time of Todor Zhivkov. It was repulsive for those who neither understood it, nor could imagine themselves out of the communist sheep-fold. It was also menacing for many who had already got what they wanted. They had had enough of the transition and wished it to stop. The aim was to try to force those who were still expecting something from the political change to give up on it. The opponents of change were too many, because in 1991-1992 the reforms were only able to affect parts of the bigger cities and very small parts of the smaller towns. Many people in the cities and practically everybody in the villages remained untouched by the changes and hence could not benefit from them. A series of expensive campaigns were necessary to lead them to become tired of and repulsed by the UDF, i.e. to make them turn away from the driver of change. The need to put a face to all the evils, sins, and crimes attributed to the UDF, turned the UDF Chairman and Prime Minister into the principal target for the calumnies that were really discrediting the transition.

This tendency was clearly manifested as early as 1992 and it did not happen only in Bulgaria. The leaders of the democratic transition in the Czech Republic, Poland, and Hungary were similarly accused of homosexual preferences, mental disorders or associations with the communist secret services. Accusations of corruption were also quite frequent, especially given that the impoverished and injured people were particularly sensitive. Unfortunately, a considerable number of prominent figures in the democratic transition succumbed to the temptation of bribery entirely or partially, which lent credibility to all kinds of fabricated stories.

The period of timelessness proved to be a strategically ingenious creation of the communist party and its deliberate and unwitting accomplices. It added a nasty overtone to many of the normal aspirations of the Union of Democratic Forces and its supporters. They had wanted to put their own house in order, get rid of a certain crook or some political vandal, and identify the moral aspect of their goals. Bulgarian voters felt powerless at first. Later they also became

> tired. It was only too natural for them to become angry and even disgusted. The deft use of timelessness prompted them to associate their disgust with the betrayal of the changes with the changes themselves. Moreover, they were told repeatedly that the UDF was in power and that Berov's two repulsive years were part of UDF's time in office. Many believed that. They looked at the President of the Republic, several cabinet ministers and those who most furiously resisted the change, remembering that they had seen them in the UDF and had even identified them with the UDF. How could they help believing that the UDF was indeed in power? How could they resist associating the failure and their betrayed hopes with the UDF? All this lasted two whole years ...[5]

When President Zhelev's adviser, Professor Lyuben Berov, handed in the resignation of his cabinet in September 1994, he left Bulgaria in a much more pitiable state than when he took over. The living standards were in total decline. Inflation was soaring. The legislative branch was in complete stagnation. Organized crime flourished. The state-owned enterprises were surrounded by private companies that robbed the country. Powerlessness, timelessness, lack of action and lack of moral principles were the salient features of Berov's government.

...

The Union of Democratic Forces neither wished nor could afford timelessness. The blows it received from all sides continued to be sudden, dangerous, and threatening to its survival. The accusations of its enemies exceeded all kinds of imaginable insolence.

Philip Dimitrov did not despair. Having devoted himself to the task of "putting the UDF house in order", he followed his initial plan with the support of his close associates. That is to say that he worked to preserve and consolidate the Union of Democratic Forces and to prepare its transition to a party. Capable and promising political figures like Ivan Kostov, Ivan Kurtev, Nadezhda Mihaylova, Latchezar Toshev, Peter Stoyanov, Yordan Sokolov, and several others were promoted and encouraged, while others who were harmful to the UDF were dismissed. Incidentally, with the exception of the Alternative Socialist Party, all other groups and factions broke away from the Union of Democratic Forces in the vain hope of being able to complete with it.

The trouble was that the slander and accusations against the "dark blue" democrats [those who remained in the UDF - *author's note*] were influencing

---

[5] Dimitrov 1995(b).

public opinion. The popularity of the UDF among the masses had diminished. The organization had been slandered by the propaganda against it and the fact that Berov was still perceived by many as an UDF Prime Minister.

In order to end the confusion and the period of timelessness brought about by the government of Lyubomir Berov, Philip Dimitrov took action. To the surprise of his supporters and enemies alike, the leader of the Union of Democratic Forces invited his Bulgarian Socialist Party counterpart, Zhan Videnov, to his office on 134 *Rakovski* Street. Dimitrov proposed parliamentary elections. Videnov agreed. Then, each of the two political opponents publicly declared that his party would win the elections.

. . .

The Bulgarian Socialist Party got an absolute majority of votes in the parliamentary elections for the Thirty-Seventh National Assembly on December 18, 1994. Its turn to run the country openly with its own government had come. In January 1995, Zhan Videnov, Chairman of the Supreme Council of the Bulgarian Socialist Party, stood at the head of the executive branch. This 35-year-old man, who held a degree in foreign trade from Moscow, gave a firm promise to the nation to cope with the country's problems and bring Bulgaria out of the crisis. Then, he proceeded to subsidize bankrupt companies, thus actually subsidizing the mafia and accelerating the plundering of the country.

At the end of 1996, the international press dubbed Bulgaria the most corrupt state in the former socialist camp and claimed that five billion US dollars had been drained from the country's budget during the tenure of the cabinets of Lyuben Berov and Zhan Videnov.[6] No one was disputing the sad truth that in two years the red Premier and his ministers had reduced the Republic of Bulgaria to total ruin and brought it to the state of a Third World country.

In the last days of December 1994, Philip Dimitrov resigned from the office of Chairman of the Union of Democratic Forces. When some of its members tried to stop him, he calmly replied that after losing elections, the only dignified act of a leader is to step down and take the negative repercussions upon himself. He reminded them of the ancient legends that after a drought or other natural disaster, or after an unsuccessful war, the chief impaled himself on spears driven into the ground, so that his tribe could survive.

Philip Dimitrov was not simply telling stories. He never missed the opportunity to define the future development of the blue organization. The

---

[6] *New York Times*, October 29, 1996.

lawyer's last demand addressed to the next Chairman of the UDF, Ivan Kostov, and his other close associates was that the coalition be transformed into a party.

Thus, the leader of noncommunist Bulgaria for four turbulent years fulfilled his duty. After him, a group of active and gifted politicians headed by Ivan Kostov succeeded in rebuilding the democratic organization. Soon the Union of Democratic Forces would prove to be the only political power whose capacity to help the country get back on the right course was indisputable.

Epilogue

It would be unfortunate if Bulgarians forget 1996 and the beginning of 1997. During the former year, the nation was in pain and horror. In the latter, people could hold their heads up with pride after a nationwide rebellion against the former communist party, born out of hunger and despair.

After two years, the government of the Bulgarian Socialist Party had swindled every last penny from the population and exhausted its proverbial patience. The situation was already hopeless during the summer of 1996. Prices soared by the hour. Commodities disappeared from the market every day. Salaries and pensions were not paid regularly. The banks stole the money of the people. The cabinet was printing cash for which there was no coverage. Many industrial enterprises were totally plundered and ruined. Criminals, disguised as traffic policemen, regularly stopped cars and robed the passengers. Shootings in cafés and in the streets were a daily occurrence. Gangsters engaged in an open war with each other, while exporting millions of dollars from the country with impunity. Western media reported that Bulgaria seemed to be the most corrupt and the least financially stable state among the former communist countries.

Then came the uprising, bloodless, peaceful, civilized.

. . .

Rosen Donkov, an engineer, has a clear memory of the night just before his twenty-sixth birthday:

> The winter of 1996-1997 was incredibly difficult for the entire nation, not just certain individuals. Everyone had to deal with the empty stores, the soaring prices, the shortages of fuel and gas, the intermitent central heating in the cities, the hyperinflation and incredible drop of the exchange rate of the lev. On top of everything, people had lost absolutely all their savings in the bankrupt banks. Those were artificially created and artificially ruined banks. Bulgarians both in the rural and the urban areas have always put something aside for a "rainy day." Some put aside a sack of wheat, others some money. Suddenly, they had nothing. They were robbed clean.
>
> Both in Sofia and in the countryside people were furious with the government of Comrade Zhan Videnov. If one listened to him, everything was running smoothly and beautifully. That was typical communist talk about the "bright present" and the even "brighter future". That talk went on at a moment when every lucid individual was perfectly aware that Bulgaria was in total poverty and absolutely isolated from the world. That cabinet took every possible step to isolate Bulgaria. It seemed to be doing everything contrary to what could logically make things work.

Our only joy was that we elected the UDF candidate Peter Stoyanov President in November 1996. That man united a large part of the population. It is no accident that his popularity rating is among the highest to this day. Somehow Stoyanov succeeded in captivating the Bulgarian people, possibly with his unfamiliar face and new type of conduct. He won people over with truths stated directly, straight into the eyes of the people, and with appeals to close down the factories billowing illusions.

On January 10, 1997, there was a protest rally in Sofia organized by the Union of Democratic Forces. It started from the Palace of Culture in the morning and ended at the Parliament. There were several additional branches of the procession, coming from other parts of the city. Still, all of them gathered in front of the building of the National Assembly. Around 2 p.m., it seemed as if the entire population of the capital had come in front of Parliament, which had been cordoned off and surrounded by iron fences. People started throwing snowballs and breaking windows. It was about 10 C degrees below zero and there was lot of snow.

Later, when the minutes of the meeting of Videnov's cabinet that day became public, it transpired that there had been about 100 government agents among the protesters. That fact confirmed the suspicions that they had been the ones who had made the attempts to break into the Parliament. Well, not all snowballs were theirs.

I personally went to Parliament around 5 or 6 in the afternoon. I left home with the thought that the riot police may try to disperse crowds with cold water. I didn't want to get too wet, so I went out lightly dressed. When I went there, I saw my father and some neighbors, who had been there since the morning.

I had a strange feeling. For me the situation was tragic and inspiring at the same time. Although the people were frozen stiff and knew that they would be coming back to their unheated homes, there was something coming from them that gave hope, at least to me. It inspired in me an unswerving desire to fight.

A car was parked in front of the central entrance to the National Assembly, a red *Zastava. Darik* Radio was broadcasting from it with loudspeakers. That was our only connection with the rest of the world.

The square was packed. On the left side of Parliament there were people all the way to the *St. Alexander Nevski* Cathedral. There were both very young and very old protesters. I met some fellow students that I never thought I would see at a protest rally. They were generally passive and uncommunicative, but there they were. There were also many policemen, but no tension was felt between them and the citizens.

At one point the leaders of the opposition left the plenary session of the National Assembly and came out. That was almost the entire parliamentary group of the Union of Democratic Forces. Among them were Nadezhda Mihaylova, Ivan Kostov, Philip Dimitrov, Ivan Kurtev, Stefan Savov, Ekaterina Mihaylova and Yordan Sokolov. The speeches of the Mayor of Sofia Stefan

Sofiyanski and the President-elect Peter Stoyanov, who was not yet sworn into office, were among the best. They succeeded in calming us down by saying something like, "People, you are right, but please stay calm and don't provoke the authorities!"

By that time Parliament was already surrounded not only by police but also by special troops of the Ministry of Interior. However, as I said, there was no tension. In fact, from time to time the people would shout joyously, "The army is with us!" and "The police is with us!"

The whole time *Darik* Radio kept reporting that truckloads of troops and policemen were heading from the countryside to Sofia. They were due to arrive from the east, then there was a broadcast that they were coming from some other direction. We had no idea what to expect.

The stairs leading to the entrance of Parliament were free from security guards. If anyone rushed them, the citizens stopped him with shouts, "Stop! Don't do that! We are not like them." We discussed our wish to attain our goals only through peaceful and legal means. Our goal was to be able to lead a normal life, nothing else.

Hardly anyone could deny that our life in January 1997 was beyond abnormal. Hence, our slogans were desperate: "We want to live! We want bread! Allow us to exist!" Naturally, there were also the standard shouts of "Red Mafia!" and "Down with the BSP!" That day we did not carry banners or slogans.

I personally can't say that I was really hungry that winter, but I had the feeling that I shouldn't spend the coins in my pocket just like that, because I might need them for something more important than what I needed at the moment. And while I was debating with myself whether to part with the little money I had, I had no idea whether it would be worth anything at all later in the evening.

I left the square just before midnight. Frankly, I was chased away by the bitter cold. I had come out much too lightly dressed. Besides, I would turn 26 in less than an hour. I had to get back home.

Until that moment, there were no truckloads of police or army reinforcements coming either from the east, or anywhere else. Apart from the troops of the Ministry of Interior and the Sofia policemen, there were no official representatives of the authorities in front of Parliament. I estimate that there were about 20,000 people in the square when I left.

I came home and was immediately glued to the radio. Around 1-1:30 a.m., I was horrified to hear over *Darik* Radio that hundreds of policemen had indeed come off trucks in front of the National Assembly. They had come from the countryside to Sofia. With masks, helmets and batons, they attacked the defenseless peaceful protesters and beat 200-300 of them so badly that at least half of them had to be hospitalized. Among them was the former Prime Minister of Bulgaria, Philip Dimitrov, who was admitted to the *Pirogov* Emergency Hospital with head and kidney injuries. The protesters were beaten not only in front of the Parliament, but also a long way into *Tsar Shishman* Street, as they were fleeing from the brutal scene in the square.

The physical violence exercised by the authorities against the people produced the opposite effect to the one intended. The protesters were not frightened and did not hide in their homes. On the contrary, since January 11, they took part in anti-government rallies every day. In mid-January, the students also organized and contributed substantially to the victory. The mass protests continued until February 4, when Nikolay Dobrev gave up the presidential mandate of the Bulgarian Socialist Party to form a government.

I was at home on that day, studying for some exam, or rather pretending to be studying, because I was listening to *Darik* Radio. The reporter Tomislav Rusev announced, "We won! At such and such time Dobrev handed back the mandate!" My immediate thought was, "We pressed them and we defeated them!" Then enormous joy swept over me. It was simply incredible. The absolute despair I had felt turned into absolute hope.

Later, I don't remember whether it was days, weeks or months later, there were rumors that when Nikolay Dobrev handed back the mandate to President Peter Stoyanov, he was accosted by angry BSP activists who threatened to beat him on his way back to the central office of the Bulgarian Socialist Party at *Pozitano* Street. The rumors went on to say that Dobrev took out his pistol to protect himself and shouted, "What do you want? The blood of all Bulgarians on my hands!?" If this is true, that man deserves respect. That would be so only if this is true, however.

Maybe about a year ago, Zhan Videnov came out with a disgusting interview against Dobrev discussing his death, accusing him of having betrayed the party, the government, the state, and so on, and so forth. On the next day, the son of the late Dobrev published a rebuttal in the *Trud* daily, which basically corroborated the rumors about the events at *Pozitano* Street, on February 4.

From the TV coverage of the protests it seemed to me that people were not following the UDF leadership. The leaders were following the masses. Although they were at the head of the processions, it appeared as if the people were leading them. I had the feeling that Ivan Kostov and the others did not know what to do exactly after more residents of Sofia than they expected joined the protests. They were uncertain whether to openly lead them, or whether to let them to take care of things on their own. It seems to me that the people were ahead of their leaders on that occasion. The rebellion had spread to the entire nation, including the students, who also did a great job.[1]

Among the students was Andrey Radev. In the summer of 1998, the young philosophy teacher gave the following account of the protests:

[1] Rosen Donkov in a conversation with the author, Sofia, Bulgaria, September 18, 2000.

On January 14, 1997, late at night, we drafted a declaration consisting of five points that covered exactly what we, the students, demanded. Our demands included bringing to court the people responsible for the most recent national catastrophe. We were also urging all parliamentary groups in the Thirty-Seventh National Assembly to renounce their potential mandates to form a government and to schedule early parliamentary elections within four months at the most.

Immediately afterwards, we started our daily marches along the central streets of Sofia. They usually started between 1 and 2 p.m. at the central building of the University. These marches were separate from the UDF rallies. Our itinerary was usually chosen so that we would block certain central crossroads in Sofia for an hour or two with our long processions.

Things were proceeding quite smoothly before the communist party received the mandate to form a government. At that point the tension between the politicians and the population was exacerbated. A national political strike could break out any minute. In the town of Dupnitsa people blocked the E79 international road, i.e., the road leading to the Greek border. If I am not mistaken, that was the first time a road was blocked. Then we heard that police reinforcement from Kyustendil was sent to Dupnitsa. There was a long-lasting rivalry between these two towns. There was talk of half of the Dupnitsa policemen joining the barricades together with their fellow-citizens, during their time off work.

We received a call from Dupnitsa, asking us to send students from the University of Sofia to support the protesters there. How could this dispatch of students be organized? You could not simply tell your classmate, " Come, let's go to the barricades!" No one was prepared to go anywhere. I still took off with a group of students. We went to all the barricades in and around Dupnitsa and took turns standing on guard there. The suspense was high and growing. After Dupnitsa, road block were set up at a major crossroads near Sliven on the road leading to the Black Sea. At that time in Sofia there was constant talk of troops being sent to the ring road around the city by Zhan Videnov's government.

We had no idea what would happen but we were prepared for anything. When the situation was the most heated, Nikolay Dobrev handed back the mandate to President Peter Stoyanov.[2]

The psychiatrist from Plovdiv, Dr. Krum Savov, has not forgotten the exciting events, which took place in Bulgaria during the winter of 1996-1997:

At the end of 1996, things were heading south. Our life was getting worse and worse by the hour. Our chances of mere survival were questionable. There

---

[2] Andrey Radev in a conversation with the author, Sofia, Bulgaria, July 20, 1998.

was total insecurity with respect to our purchasing power. We were not sure whether we would be able to buy anything by the end of the day with the meager sums that we received as wages, pensions or salaries, not to mention that even receiving that money was not certain at all. Food disappeared from the stores within several weeks. The shelves were empty. We were all shocked and frightened. We attempted stocking up with non-perishable goods, but even that proved to be impossible, because these goods had also disappeared and could not be purchased. Everything seemed horrifying and gloomy. In the backdrop were the incredible stubbornness and resistance to stepping down of Zhan Videnov's government. There was a shortage of bread even. As a psychiatrist, I had a monthly salary of BGN 5,000-6,000, which was equivalent to two US dollars at the exchange rate in January 1997. This situation made the people grim, depressed, indignant, grumbling, and rude to each other. The suspense was rising and the population needed to react in some way.

Everything changed towards the end of December, when torch-bearing protest processions fortunately started in Plovdiv. They demonstrated that people were not asleep, that people were not silent, that people were discontented and wanted to do something to improve their lives. Every evening a flood of torches filled Plovdiv's main street, from the *Stefan Stambolov* Square in front of the Town Hall to the Mosque and even further. The people disregarded the cold weather, snow, fog and darkness. Everyone seemed to be taking part. All who could still walk participated, including very old men and women, over 80, supporting themselves on walking sticks or on the arms of younger fellow citizens. The streets were also filled with very young children, some on their parents' shoulders.

The processions were peaceful. Of course, people shouted, chanted, stopped in front of the District Committee of the Bulgarian Socialist Party and threw stones in front of the building. Soon the pile of stones became a cairn. Policemen stood in a double cordon on the sidewalk. They stood there quietly and very often it was possible to see from their expressions that they agreed with us, the protesters. We chanted, "Down with the BSP!" or "UDF!" and sometimes also "Murderers!" The citizens of Plovdiv carried buckets with holes, cans, tambourines, rattles or whistles, and made all kinds of noises, but they did not do anything else. Every day we passed peacefully along a specified route.

In the mornings, when I would open the *Demokratsiya* newspaper, I would check the map of the protests. At first they were in the bigger cities, including Sofia, Plovdiv, Varna, Burgas, and Ruse. Gradually the section of the newspaper where these events were covered grew until it finally filled a whole page. After the blood-drenched night in front of Parliament on January 11, 1997, local anti-governmental actions took place on a national scale.

People were expressing their indignation in cities, towns and villages. The protests were gradually spreading throughout Bulgaria. When I would read the news, I would pull out the map of the country and look up the places where protests were said to have taken place. I remember being impressed that the people in a village with a population of 123 people, whose average age was 65-70 years, had also organized a rally.

The processions with torches in Plovdiv were organized by the local clubs of the Union of Democratic Forces, the United Democratic Forces and the Internal Macedonian Revolutionary Organization. Unexpectedly, the students became a strong and powerful wave in the streets and squares. One evening, a procession of representatives of all universities in Plovdiv joined the civilian procession like a stream of fresh water flowing into a river. The young people came singing songs, chanting slogans and raising substantially the mood of the older protesters.

In accordance with the Constitution, the new President, Peter Stoyanov, gave Nikolay Dobrev the mandate for a government of the Bulgarian Socialist Party. We had no idea what would happen, so it was necessary to act. It was precisely then that the barricades at the railway and major roads leading into and out of Plovdiv were set up. These barricades were made of planks hammered together and covered with stones and branches. People took turns standing guard near them at all times. They allowed passenger and express trains to go through, but stopped cargo trains or loaded trucks in the roads.

All our actions were a form of protest against a potential new red government. It should be noted that these were peaceful actions. The law student Velislav Velichkov, who was later elected to the Thirty-Eighth National Assembly, was a splendid role model at these rallies. He spoke very well to the people. The same can also be said of Father Boris, the Metropolitan of Plovdiv from Patriarch Pimen's Holy Synod, an elderly man who appealed to the demonstrators to stay calm and make sure that there is not even the slightest attempt at violence on their part. That is how it was. There was not one single incident of attempted injury, beating, or even hitting a political opponent at any of the rallies. Our barricades were a symbolic protest and a means of protection.

The students had a 24-hour presence around the building of the BSP's District Committee. The citizens of Plovdiv supported them with hot drinks and some food. Everyone who was available went to help them. Younger and older people were discussing the situation together. The students explained why they were there and what their demands were. What they wanted was to prevent the formation of a new BSP government after that party had given ample proof of its inability to govern the country. We all agreed that we had already reached the bottom of the abyss, if not deeper. Nevertheless, it was fun being with the students. They had already set up two or three tents and had a fire lit in large cans, trying to keep warm. The young people were always in a good mood. They listened to music or played concertinas and guitars. Their improvised camp was across from the cairn, which was growing bigger with every passing day.

The events during the night of January 11 in Sofia made a strong impression on people in Plovdiv. Very little was shown on television, but *Demokratsiya* covered the event extensively, citing the names of victims and eyewitnesses of the violence, describing the chase of the people from the square into the smaller side streets, up the stairs of residential buildings, and the physical violence. The image of Philip Dimitrov with a bleeding gash on his head is still before my eyes. I have heard that the former Prime Minister still has a scar on his forehead from that night.

All that made a strong impression upon democratically minded Bulgarians. Increasing numbers of people joined our processions on January 11, 12 and 13. Obviously, the brutality of the authorities did not evoke fear, but produced the opposite effect. The reaction of the people was one of courage, anger, and indignation against the red government and Members of Parliament from the BSP.

Zhan Videnov's cabinet resigned, but that did not calm people down. A new term in office of the Bulgarian Socialist Party was anticipated. None of us knew what would happen when Nikolay Dobrev entered President Stoyanov's office with a folder in his hands at 3 p.m. on February 4.

On that unforgettable day, the citizens of Plovdiv began to gather in the square long before the usual time for the start of the demonstrations, 5 p.m. It was getting dark. We were all waiting anxiously. Some carried portable transistor radios so that they could listen to the news from Sofia. Dobrev and those accompanying him were still with the President. Around 5:15 or 5:30, someone - I don't remember whether it was the Mayor of Plovdiv Spas Garnevski or someone else - came out on the balcony of the Town Hall to announce that they had received information from Sofia, personally from Yordan Sokolov. Videnov's government, which had handed in its resignation but was still in office, was preparing to crush the protesters at the barricades. It was anticipated that the security forces would take the necessary steps for destroying the barricades around 11 p.m. on February 4. The UDF leaders in Plovdiv asked us for help and for more people on the barricades, in the hopes that that would stop the authorities from resorting to violence. They invited those of us who felt sufficiently strong and willing to gather in front of one of the shops in the right-hand-corner of the *Stefan Stambolov* Square. From there the people would be transported by bus to the places where the barricades were erected.

Immediately a wave of people rushed to that part of the square. I heard a young man behind me tell his two children, "I'll take you to your mother because I am going." Hundreds, maybe thousands of people rushed to the buses, thus showing their determination to defend, what they had been demonstrating for in the past month and a half. People were elated. There was a firm resolve for resistance, and a readiness to fight for the cause to the end. It was 5:45-5:50 p.m. Then all of a sudden the news came from the transistor radios! At the same moment one of our leaders came out on the balcony and announced, 'Victory! Victory! Victory!' Dobrev had refused the mandate to form a new BSP government and had left the President's office.

This was met with loud shouts of reassurance and joy. A sigh of relief came over the enormous square. The protest turned into a rock concert and a big party. The people were overjoyed.

Emotions ran very high in those days. And, as I mentioned, I was most excited when every day in January and the beginning of February I looked up and marked the cities, towns and villages on the map of Bulgaria that were protesting against the Bulgarian Socialist Party. That turned out to be an ubiquitous peaceful movement of the nation against the communists-socialists. It was very powerful and covered vast territories. It was a peaceful and civilized protest movement, of a kind unknown to Bulgarians until then, which was unique from a global perspective as well. That made me proud to have taken part in a nationwide revolution. It had been a demonstration that Bulgarians no longer wished to be ruled by communists. Virtuously all of the population was against the detestable cabinet of the BSP at that moment, a government that had again brought the country to total ruin.

Soon the smile of the Prime Minister in the caretaker government, Stefan Sofiyanski, cheered up the Bulgarian nation and helped it relax. Then came the time of Ivan Kostov.[3]

. . .

On April 19, 1997, the United Democratic Forces, made up of the Union of Democratic Forces and the People's Union, won a landslide victory in the pre-term parliamentary elections for the Thirty-Eighth National Assembly. The coalition had an absolute majority of 137 Members of Parliament. Without further ado, the government of Prime Minister Ivan Kostov set out to bring the country out of the deep economic crisis and to build up its international prestige.

The cabinet of the United Democratic Forces achieved a lot in four years. It restructured the banking sector, raised the country's credit rating, and attained lasting financial stabilization. During Kostov's time the real economic growth was 5 per cent, poised to rise sustainably. The spending for social assistance also increased from BGN 10.4 million to 319.9 million.

In addition, the government of Ivan Kostov secured international support for economic and social reforms. Bulgaria took an active part in a number of European programs for financing, and the country's application for membership in NATO was announced. The Balkan state was dropped from Europe's negative visa list and invited to start negotiations for accession to the European Union. Bulgaria attained second place, after Hungary, in terms of the extent to

[3] Dr. Krum Savov in a conversation with the author, Plovdiv, Bulgaria, August 24, 1998.

which the legislative criteria for EU accession had been met. In May, 2000, the Thirty-Eighth National Assembly voted a Law proclaiming the communist regime in Bulgaria criminal.

In March, 2004, the Republic of Bulgaria joined NATO.

On January 1, 2007, it became a member of the European Union.

...

On the initiative of its Bulgarian member from the Union of Democratic Forces, Latchezar Toshev, on January 25, 2006, the Parliamentary Assembly of the Council of Europe adopted Resolution 1481/2006 on the need for international condemnation of crimes of totalitarian communist regimes.

On November 19, 2009, the Forty-First National Assembly of Bulgaria, referring to documents of the European institutions concerning the need to make the truth about the crimes of communism known to the general public, voted to support Resolution 1481/2006; the Resolution of the European Parliament of April 2, 2009, on European conscience and totalitarianism, and the Resolution of the Parliamentary Assembly of the Organization for Security and Cooperation in Europe of July 3, 2009, on reunification of divided Europe.

On the same day the Assembly proclaimed August 23 - the day of the signing of the Nazi-Soviet Non-aggression Pact in 1939 - as the day of remembrance of the crimes of the national-socialist, communist and other totalitarian regimes, and as a day for commemorating their victims.

Democracy in Bulgaria has been restored.

Abbreviations

ASP - Alternative Socialist Party
BCP - Bulgarian Communist Party
BGN - Bulgarian Lev (national currency unit)
BSDP - Bulgarian Social Democratic Party
BSP - Bulgarian Socialist Party
BWP(c) - Bulgarian Workers' Party (communists)
BWSDP - Bulgarian Workers' Social Democratic Party
BWSDP (u) - Bulgarian Workers' Social Democratic Party (united)
BZNS - Bulgarian Agrarian People's Union
BZNS - *N. Petkov* - Bulgarian Agrarian People's Union - *Nikola Petkov*
BZNS *Pladne - Alexander Stamboliyski* Bulgarian Agrarian People's Union
BZNS *Vrabcha*-1 - Bulgarian Agrarian People's Union *Vrabcha*-1
CC - Central Committee
COMECON - Council for Mutual Economic Assistance
DYCL - Dimitrov's Young Communist League
EU - European Union
FF - Fatherland Front
MRF - Movement for Rights and Freedoms
NCC - National Coordinating Council
PADF - Parliamentary Alliance of the Democtatic Forces
PRB - People's Republic of Bulgaria
SCCC - Sofia City Consultative Council
SDP - Social Democratic Party
UDF - Union of Democratic Forces
U.S.S.R. - Union of Soviet Socialist Republics (Soviet Union)

Bibliography

Anakiev, P. 1994. *1963 - Otrichaneto ot Balgariya [1963 - The Negation of Bulgaria]*, Ogledalo Publishing House, Sofia, 1994 (in Bulgarian).

Annuaire = Annuaire Didot-Bottin Commerce-Industrie Etrangere, Paris, 1934.

Asenov, B. 1998. *Religiite i sektite v Balgariya [Religions and Sects in Bulgaria]*, Sofia (in Bulgarian).

Bar-Zohar, M. 1998. *Beyond Hitler's Grasp - The Heroic Rescue of Bulgaria's Jews*, Adams Media Corporation, Holbrook, MA.

Boll, M. 1984. *Cold War in the Balkans. American Foreign Policy and the Emergence of Communist Bulgaria, 1943-1947,* The University Press of Kentucky.

——. 1985. *The American military mission in the Allied Control Commission for Bulgaria, 1944-1947: history and transcripts*, Boulder: East European Monographs; New York: Distributed by Columbia University Press.

Brahm, H. 1998. *"Sinyoto" pravitelstvo na Filip Dimitrov - balgarskiyat opit s nasledstvoto na komunizma [The "Blue" Government of Philip Dimitrov - the Bulgarian Experience with the Heritage of Communism],* Balkanmedia, Sofia (Bulgarian translation).

Chakalov, G. 1993. *Ofitser za svrazka [Liaison Officer] (1941-1946),* Larry Publishers, Sofia (in Bulgarian).

Courtois, S., M. Kramer *et al.* 1999, *Chernata kniga na komunizma [The Black Book of Communism]*, Prozorets Publishers (Bulgarian translation).

Dallin, A. and F. I. Firsov 2000. *Dimitrov & Stalin - 1934-1943 - Letters from the Soviet Archives*, Yale University Press.

Dertliev, P. 1996. *Den parvi - den posleden [First Day - Last Day]*, Svyat, Nauka Publishers, Sofia (in Bulgarian).

Dimitrov, P. 1995(a). *Nezhnata revolyutsiya v dati i fakti [The Gentle Revolution in Dates and Facts]*, Democracy Foundation, Sofia.

——. 1995(b). *Bezvremieto [The Timelessness]*, Democracy Foundation, Sofia.

——. 1997. *Ibo zhivyaha, Gospodi [For they Lived, Oh Lord]*, Bards Publishers, Sofia, 2nd edition (in Bulgarian).

——. 2004. *Novite demokratsii i transatlanticheskata vrazka [The New Democracies and the Transatlantic Link]*, Ciela, Sofia, 2004.

Dolapchiev, N. 1971. *Bulgaria - The Making of a Satellite - Analysis of the historical developments 1944-1953*, Foyer Bulgare, Bulgarian Historical Institute, 1971.

Eldarov, S. *The Repressions against the Catholic Church and against Catholics in Bulgaria (1944-1989)*, in: *The International Condemnation of Communism: The Bulgarian Perspective*, Vasil Stanilov Literature Workshop, Sofia, 2004, pp. 86-96.

Fol, A., I. Dimitrov, M. Lalkov, *et al.* 1981. *Kratka istoriya na Balgariya* [*Brief History of Bulgaria*], Nauka I Izkustvo Publishing House, Sofia (in Bulgarian).

Godishnik = Statisticheski godishnik na Tsarstvo Balgariya [*Statistical Yearbook of the Kingdom of Bulgaria*], General Statistics Directorate, Sofia, 1942 (in Bulgarian).

Groueff, S. 1987. *Crown of Thorns*, Madison Books, Lanham, MD, 1987.

Hickmann, A. L. 1914. *Prof. A. L. Hickmanns Geographisch-statistischer Universal-Taschen Atlas,* Kartographische Anstallt G. Freytag & Berndt, Gesellschaft m. b. H., Wien und Leipzig.

Hristov, H. 2004. *The Crimes during the Communist Regime and the Attempts at their Investigation after 10 November 1989,* in: *The International Condemnation of Communism: the Bulgarian Perspective*, Vasil Stanilov Literature Workshop, Sofia.

Iliev, B. 1988. *Revolyutsionniyat naroden sad* [*The Revolutionary People's Tribunal*], Publishing House of the Fatherland Front, Sofia (in Bulgarian).

Ivanova, R. 1995. *Druzhelyubniyat Manhatan* [*The Friendly Manhattan*], St. Kliment Ohridski University Press, Sofia (in Bulgarian).

Konstantinov, P. 1997. *Istoriya na Balgariya s nyakoi premalchavani istoricheski fakti* [*History of Bulgaria with Some Hitherto Undisclosed Historical Facts*] *(681-1996)*, Karina M. Todorova Publishers, Sofia (in Bulgarian).

Kunev, T. 1946. *Sitni drebni kato kamilcheta* [*Teeny-Weeny Just Like Baby Camels*], Sofia (in Bulgarian).

Luchnikov, S. 2000. *Istinata* [*The Truth*], Ivan Vazov Publishers, Sofia (in Bulgarian).

Melone, A. P. 1998. *Creating Parliamentary Government - The Transition to Democracy in Bulgaria*, Ohio State University Press, Columbus.

Meshkova, P. and D. Sharlanov 1994. *Balgarskata gilotina: taynite mehanizmi na Narodniya sad* [*The Bulgarian Guillotine: Secret Mechanisms of the People's Tribunal*], Democracy Agency, Sofia (in Bulgarian).

Mutafchieva, V. 1995. *Sadat nad istoritsite* [*The Judgement over the Historians*], Volume I, Academic Publishing House "Prof. Marin Drinov", Sofia (in Bulgarian).

Nedev, N. 1999. *Deseti noemvri: zagovor, prevrat ili politichesko reshenie* [*November 10 - Conspiracy, Coup d'etat or Political Solution*], International Relations Publishers, Sofia (in Bulgarian).

Ognyanov, L., M. Dimova, M. Lalkov 1992. *Narodna demokratsiya ili diktatura: hristomatiya po istoriya na Balgariya, 1944-1948* [*People's Democracy or Dictatorship - Readings in Bulgarian History, 1944-1948*], Literaturen Forum Publishers, Sofia (in Bulgarian).

Panayotov, P. 1990. *Vanshnata politika na Balgariya 1919-1945. Na emigrantski temi.* [*The Foreign Policy of Bulgaria: Emigrants' topics*], Sofia, Arges Publishers (in Bulgarian).

——. 2002. *Moyat zhiteyski pat: misli za Balgariya* [*The Path of My Life: Thoughts About Bulgaria*], Gutenberg Press, Sofia (in Bulgarian).

Radev, V. 1994. *Otrovni mitove* [*Poisonous Myths*], Vele Kralevski Publishing House, Sofia (in Bulgarian).

Raychevski, S. 2009. *Tarnovskata Konstitutsiya 1879* [*The Tarnovo Constitution of 1879*], Balgarski bestseller, Sofia (in Bulgarian).

Ribareva, I. and V. Nikolova 2000. *Protestat na 39-te: dokumentalen razkaz za gladnata stachka na "Grupata na 39-te" po povod priemaneto na novata Konstitutsiya: april - yuli 1991 g.* [*The Protest of the 39: a documentary account of the hunger strike of the "Group of the 39" on the occasion of accepting the new Constitution: April - July 1991*], Konrad Adenauer Foundation, Sofia (in Bulgarian).

Semerdzhiev, P. *Narodniyat sad v Balgariya: komu i zashto e bil neobhodim?* [*The People's Tribunal in Bulgaria 1944-1945 - Who Needed It and Why?*], Macedonia Press Publishing House, 1995, pp. 411-412 (in Bulgarian).

Sharlanov, D. 1997. *Tiraniyata: zhertvi i palachi* [*The Tyranny: Victims and Henchmen*], Strelets Publishing House, Sofia (in Bulgarian).

——. *Goryanite: koi sa te?* [*The Goryani: Who are they?*], Sofia, Prostranstvo i Forma Press (in Bulgarian).

Shipkov, M. 1950. *Breakdown; telling how the communist secret police are able to pry confessions of treason out of men and women who love their country, a story courageously laid bare for the first time in March 1950.* With a profile by Maynard Bertram Barnes, Washington, DC, National Committee for Free Europe.

Spasov, M. 1998. *Imalo li e fashizam v Balgariya: izbrani publikatsii, pomesteni sled 1989 vav vestnitsi i drugi izdaniya* [*Was There Fascism in Bulgaria: selected publications printed after 1989 in newspapers and other periodicals*], Sofia (in Bulgarian).

Stanilov, V. 2000. *Za malka spravka* [*A Brief Inquiry*], Ivan Vazov Publishing House, Sofia (in Bulgarian).

Stoyanov, Z. 1983. *Sachineniya v tri toma* [*Collected Works in Three Volumes*], Volume Three, Non-Fiction, Balgarski Pisatel Publishing House, Sofia (in Bulgarian).

Sugarev, E. 1993. *V kakvo shte vyarvat detsata ni?* [*What will Our Children Believe in?*], Demokratsiya Publishing House, Sofia.

Troanski, H. 2004(a). *Ubiystveno cherveno* [*Murderously Red*], TVR Print, Sofia (in Bulgarian).

——. 2004(b). *The Communist St. Bartholomew's Massacres - The Killings without Prosecution, Court or Sentence in the Autumn of 1944 in Bulgaria*, *The International Condemnation of Communism: The Bulgarian Perspective*, Vasil Stanilov Literature Workshop, Sofia.

Vladimirova, E. 1991. *Filip Dimitrov - po diagonala* [*Philip Dimitrov - Along the Diagonal*], Aves Publishers, Sofia (in Bulgarian).

Zhechev, T. 1995. *Bolki ot tekushtoto [Pain from Current Affairs]*, Letopisi Publishers, Sofia (in Bulgarian).

Zhivkov, Zh. 1991. *Kraglata masa na Politbyuro* [*The Round Table of the Politburo*], Interpress Publishers, Sofia (in Bulgarian).

Index of Frequently Used Names